"Chosen by God"

The Archiepiscopal Office in Novgorod the Great (1165–1478)

"Chosen by God"

The Archiepiscopal Office in Novgorod the Great (1165–1478)

Michael C. Paul
Project Editor David Goldfrank

Washington, DC

Copyright © 2025 by Michael C. Paul

New Academia Publishing, 2025

All rights reserved. No part of this book may be reproduced or transmitted in any form or by any means, electronic or mechanical, including photocopying, recording, or by any information storage and retrieval system.

Printed in the United States of America

Library of Congress Control Number: 2025917149
ISBN 978-0-6154326-9-4 paperback (alk. paper)

New Academia Publishing
4401-A Connecticut Ave. NW, #236, Washington DC 20008
info@newacademia.com - www.newacademia.com

For Veronica

Contents

List of Illustrations and Maps	xi
Acknowledgements	xiii
Abbreviations	xv
Glossaries	xviii
Notes on Spelling and Terminology	xxix

Introduction   1
   Novgorod the Great and its Place in Rus' History
   The City's Geography, Administration, and Political
     Institutions
   Organization of the Study
   Methodology and Sources
   Historiographic Issues

Chapter One: The Bishop in Theory   31
   Introduction
   The Origin of Episcopal Theory
     Biblical Sources
     Apostolic Sources
     Patristic Sources
     Ecumenical Councils and Local Synods of the
       East
   The View of the Bishop in the Rus' Church and the
     Eparchy

Chapter Two: The Archbishops and the Rus'   47
   Church
   Introduction
   The Title of Archbishop in the Orthodox Church

The Archbishops and the Metropolitans
  Luka, Nifont, and the Defense of Canon Law and Tradition
  From the Disputed Archiepiscopate (1210-1229) to the Death of Vasilii Kalika
  Worsening Archiepiscopal-Metropolitan Relations after 1352
  Metropolitan Kiprian and Novgorod
Novgorod's Absence from Momentous Church Events
Novgorod within the Rus' Church
Conclusion

Chapter Three: The Archeparchy   77
  Defenders of Orthodoxy: Paganism
  Defenders of Orthodoxy: The Catholic Crusades
  Defenders of Orthodoxy: Heresy
  Episcopal Prerogatives
    Church Consecrations
    Teaching and Preaching
    The Sacraments
  Administration of the Archeparchy
    Pastoral Visits
    The Parish Structure in the Fifths
    Relations with Pskov
  The Ecclesiastical Courts
  The Monasteries
  Conclusion

Chapter Four: Election   127
  Absence of a Background
  Ecclesiastical Election
  Episcopal Election in the Orthodox Churches
  The Pool of Candidates and the Role of the Monasteries in Elections
  The Evolution of Episcopal Election and the Origin of Election by Lot

The Consecration of the Archbishop-elect
  Conclusion

Chapter Five: Politics   159
  Introduction
  The Bishop in Politics: Divergent Catholic and
    Orthodox Viewpoints
    The Western Episcopate: Princes and Warriors
    The Eastern Episcopate
  The Archbishops' Unique Position in Politics
  The Archbishop as Ambassador
  The Archbishop as Domestic Peacemaker
  The Archbishop as Civil and Military Builder
    The Detinets
    Around the City of Novgorod
    Beyond Novgorod
  The Archbishop in Novgorod's Civil Administration
  Conclusion

Chapter Six: The Economics of the House of Holy   193
  Wisdom
  Introduction: Novgorod's Importance in the
    Economic Life of Rus'
  The Archbishops' Fabled Wealth
  The Archiepiscopal Administration
    Expenses
    Personnel
  Sources of Income
    Princely Charters
    Land
    Fines and Court Fees
    Other Sources of Income
  Conclusion

Chapter Seven: The Archbishops and Rus' Culture   225
   Introduction
   Religion and Novgorodian Culture
   I. Archiepiscopal Cultural Patronage
      A. Architecture
         1. The Cathedral of Holy Wisdom
         2. Church Patronage
         3. Cross-cultural Ties
      B. Literary and Artistic Patronage
         1. The Archbishops' Scriptorium
         2. The Archbishops and the Novgorodian Chronicles
         3. Icons and the Decorative Arts
   II. The Archbishops as Cultural Subjects
      A. The Archbishops' Saintly Cults
      B. The Archbishops in Legend
   Conclusion

Conclusion	275
Appendix	282
Notes	287
Works Cited	404
Index	467

List of Illustrations and Maps

Cover: The South View of Novgorod's Cathedral of Holy Wisdom. [Photograph March 14, 1980. © William C. Brumfield]

Fig. 1. Upper register of the Mid-15th c. Novgorodian Battle with the Suzdalians icon. [Source: Novgorod State United Museum-Reserve, Architecture and Art]   1

Fig. 2. Upper register of a 16th-century Novgorodian "Wisdom Builds her House" icon. [Source: State Tretyakov Gallery, Moscow.   31

Fig. 3. Relief from the lid of the wooden casket of Il'ia/Ioann, dated 1559. [Source: https://www.icon-art.info/masterpiece.php?mst_id=4668]   47

Fig. 4. Depiction of Archbishop Vasilii Kalika on the Vasil'evskie Gates. [Source: I. Agrieyn, Wikimedia]   77

Fig. 5. Depiction of Archbishop Aleksei at Volotovo Dormition Church: 1894-95 copy by M. F. Fomin [Source: https://commons.wikimedia.org/wiki/File:Archbishop_of_Novgorod_Alexy.png]   127

Fig. 6. The Aleksiev Cross [Source: Website of the Metropolitan of Novgorod and Staraia Russa, [Source: https://ru.pinterest.com/pin/384776361891344677/]   159

Fig. 7. From the lower left of The Vision of the Ponomar' Tarasii icon, last third of the sixteenth century [Source: Novgorod State United Museum-Reserve]   182

Fig. 8. Aerial view of the Detinets. [Source: website of the Novgorod State United Museum-Reserve, https://novgorodmuseum.ru/muzei/novgorodskij-kreml]   183

Fig. 9. Partially restored Brick-Gothic exterior of the Palace of Facets ca. 2013. [Source: Novgorod State United Museum-Reserve, https://novgorodmuseum.ru/muzei/vladychnaya-granovitaya-palata]   184

Fig. 10. Interior of the Palace of Facets, ca. 1881-1886. [Photograph: Ivan F. Barshchevskii; source: Wikipedia]	184
Fig. 11. Late nineteenth century fresco of Archbishop Feoktist, Iur'ev Monastery [Photograph: Michael C. Paul]	189
Fig. 12. The Church of St. John the Forerunner at Opoki, 1127-30, 1453 [Photograph: Michael C. Paul]	193
Fig. 13. The Church of the Twelve Apostles, 1358, 1455 [Photograph: Michael C. Paul]	
Fig. 14. The Sigtuna (Magdeburg, Płock) Gates [Photograph: Michael C. Paul]	225
Fig. 15. Copy in the State Russian Museum, St. Petersburg, of a fresco depicting Archbishop Moisei as donor of the Church of the Dormition in Volotovo Field. [Source: Daniel Mortier, Wikipedia]	246
Fig. 16. Archbishop Iona as founder-donor [Source: Novgorod State Museum Reserve, Tserkov' Simeona Bogopriimtsa Zverina Monastyria]	246
Fig. 17. The Belfry, 1439 [Photograph: Michael C. Paul]	248
Fig. 18. Millennium of Russia monument prelates, 1862 Photograph: Michael C. Paul]	272
Map 1. Novgorod and its immediate environs. [Source: Michael C. Paul]	8
Map 2. Map of the Novgorodian Lands, with the Novgorodian Fifths. [Source: Michael C. Paul]	78

Acknowledgements

I am grateful to a great many people who have helped me see this work through to completion. In my doctoral studies at the University of Miami, most notably, Janet Martin taught me a great deal of Rus' and Russian history and the historian's profession, both during my doctoral work and since then. Others at Miami helped shape my understanding and approach to history and religious studies, particularly David Kling, David Lines, Hugh Thomas, and the late Edward Dreyer.

My research was made easier by the support of many librarians and staff at a number of libraries: Predrag Matejic and Pasha Johnson at the Hilandar Research Library at the Ohio State University, the librarians at the Slavic Library at the University of Illinois at Urbana-Champaign, the Dumbarton Oaks Research Library in Washington, DC, and the Library of Congress, the Otto Richter Library at the University of Miami, as well as staff at a number of other libraries, especially the interlibrary loan departments at the various colleges and universities where I have taught and researched.

I also wish to thank the archivists who assisted me in my research in Russia generously funded under a Fulbright Senior Scholar Program grant in 2006-2007 (much of that research was in a later period, but it helped in my understanding of the Novgorodian archiepiscopate before 1478): the Moscow Fulbright Office, the librarians and archivists of the St. Petersburg Institute of History of the Russian Academy of Sciences, the Manuscripts Division of the Library of the St. Petersburg branch of the Academy of Sciences, the St. Petersburg Branch of the Archive of the Academy of Sciences, the Russian National Library, the Division of Manuscripts and Early Printed Books at the State Historical Museum, the Scientific and Research Division of Manuscripts and Reading Room One of the Russian State Library, the Russian State Archive of Ancient Acts (RGADA), and the Novgorod State United Monument-Museum.

Chapter Four is a revised and extended version of the article "Episcopal Election in Novgorod, Russia 1156-1478," that appeared in *Church History* in 2003. I am grateful to the editors of that journal for permission to use the material again.

I am grateful to David Goldfrank for his comments and corrections that did much to improve the book, and to the editors at New Academia Publishing, for their work and assistance in seeing this through to completion. I would also like to thank William Brumfield for help in finding photos of architecture for the book and allowing the use of one of his photos.

I would finally like to thank family and friends whose support and encouragement over many years was invaluable: my wife, Lan, my daughter, Veronica, my sisters, Nancy and Sue, my brother, Steve, and my friend Georgi Parpulov. There are others I should thank, but for lack of space or oversight on my part, I may have carelessly omitted them. For that, I apologize.

Abbreviations

AAE	*Akty, sobrannye v bibliotekakh i arkhivakh Rossiiskoi Imperii Arkheograficheskoiu ekspeditsieiu Imperatorskoi Akademii nauk*
AfED	*Antifeodal'nye ereticheskie dvizheniia na Rusi XIV-nachala XVI veka*
AI	*Akty istoricheskie*
ANF	*Ante Nicene Fathers*
AN SSSR	Akademiia Nauk Soyuza Sovetskikh Sotsialisticheskikh Respublik
Avraamki	*Letopisnyi sbornik imnuemyi letopis'iu Avraamki*
BAN	Biblioteka [Rossiiskoi] Akademii Nauk
BLDR	*Biblioteka literatury drevnei Rusi*
CASS	*Canadian-American Slavic Studies*
CH	*Church History*
CMR	*Cahiers du monde russe.* See also CMRS.
CMRS	*Cahiers du monde russe et soviétique*
ChIONL	*Chteniia v Istoricheskom obshchestve Nestora-letopistsa*
ChOIDR	*Chteniia v (Imperatorskom) obshchestve istorii i drevnostei rossiiskikh pri Moskovskom universitete*
DAI	*Dopolneniia k Aktam istoricheskim*
DOP	*Dumbarton Oaks Papers*
DRV	*Drevniaia rossiiskaia vivliofika*
DSHRM	*Documentary Sources on the History of the Rus' Metropolitanate: The Fourteenth to the Early Sixteenth Centuries*
DSK	*Drevne-slavianskaia kormchaia*
Ermitazh.	*Nachalo Letopisi po Ermitazhnomu spisku*
Ermolin.	*Ermolinskaia letopis'*
FOG	*Forschungen zur osteuropäischen Geschichte*

GIM	Gosudarstvennyi istoricheskii muzei
GMIRiA	Gosudarstvennyi muzei istorii religii i ateizma
Gustyn.	*Gustynskaia letopis'* (The Hustyn Chronicle)
GVNP	*Gramoty Velikogo Novgoroda i Pskova*
HUS	*Harvard Ukrainian Studies*
IIMK	Institut istorii material'noi kul'tury
Ipat.	*Ipat'evskaia letopis'* (The Hypatian Chronicle)
IZ	*Istoricheskie zapiski*
JbfGO	*Jahrbücher für Geschichte Osteuropas*
L	Leningrad
Lavrent.	*Lavrent'evskaia letopis'* (The Lavrentian Chronicle)
LZAK	*Letopis' zaniatii Arkheograficheskoi kommissii*
M	Moscow
MAIRSK	Mezhdunarodnaia assotsiatsiia po izucheniiu i rasprostraneniiu slavianskikh kul'tur
MERSH	*Modern Encyclopedia of Russian and Soviet History*
MGH	*Monumenta Germaniae Historica*
MM	Franz Ritter von Miklosich and Joseph Müller, eds., *Acta et diplomata graeca medii aevi sacra et profana*
Mosk.	*Moskovskii letopisnyi svod kontsa XV veka*
N2	*Novgorodskaia vtoraia letopis'*
N3	*Novgorodskaia tret'ia letopis'*
N4	*Novgorodskaia chetvertaia letopis'*
NGM	Novgorodskii gosudarstvennyi muzei
Nikon.	*Letopisnyi sbornik, imenuemyi Patriarsheiu ili Nikonovskoi letopis'iu*
NPK	*Novgorodskie pistsovye knigi*
NPL	*Novgorodskaia pervaia letopis' starshego i mladshego izvoda*
NPNF	*Nicene and Post-Nicene Fathers*
P	Petrograd
P1	*Pskovskaia pervaia letopis'*
PL	*Patrologiae cursus completus*, Latin series
PDRTsUL	*Pamiatniki drevnerusskoi tserkovno-uchitel'noi literatury*
PG	*Patrologiae cursus completus*, Greek series (*Patrologia Graeca*)
PKOP	*Pistsovye knigi Obonezhskoi piatiny*
PskL	*Pskovskie letopisi*

PLDR	*Pamiatniki literatury Drevnei Rusi*
Prodol. Vosk.	*Prodolzhenie letopisi po Voskresenskomu spisku*
PRP	*Pamiatniki russkogo prava*
PSRL	*Polnoe sobranie russkikh letopisei*
RAN	Rossiiskaia akademiia nauk
RFA	*Russkii feodal'nyi arkhiv* (1986 or 2008) and *Russkie feodal'nye arkhivy XIV-XV vekov* (1948 or 1951)
RGADA	Rossiskii gosudarstvennyi arkhiv drevnikh aktov
RGB	Rossiskaia gosudarstvennaia biblioteka
RH	*Russian History/Histoire Russe*
RIB	*Russkaia istoricheskaia biblioteka*
RLA	*Russko-livonskie akty*
RNB	Rossiiskaia natsional'naia biblioteka
SKKDR	*Slovar' knizhnikov i knizhnosti Drevnei Rusi*
Sof. 1	*Sofiiskaia pervaia letopis'*
Sof. 2	*Sofiiskaia vtoraia letopis'*
Sok.	*Sokrashennyi letopisnyi svod 1495 g.*
SORIaS	*Sbornik Otdeleniia russkogo iazyka i slovesnosti [Imperatorskoi Akademii nauk]*
SPb	St. Petersburg
SPbII RAN	Sankt-Peterburgskii Institut istorii Rossiiskoi Akademii nauk
SR	*Slavic Review*
ST	*Summa Theologica*
TODRL	*Trudy Otdela drevnerusskoi literatury*
Vosk.	*Voskresenskaia letopis'*
VPL	*Vologodsko-Permskaia letopis'*
ZDR	*Zakonodatel'stvo Drevnei Rusi*
ZhMNP	*Zhurnal Ministerstva narodnogo prosveshcheniia*
ZhMP	*Zhurnal Moskovskoi patriarkhii*

Glossaries

Altyn	A monetary unit; a three-kopek piece used in Muscovy.
Arshin (pl. *arshiny*)	A unit of length equal to 71 centimeters or about 2.3 feet; a third of a *sazhen'*.
Bochka	"Barrel." A unit of liquid measure equal to 130 gallons.
Chelobitie	"To strike the forehead." It was originally a low bow in submission to a high secular or ecclesiastical lord. Later it was also a written request to a high official.
Chernye liudi	"Black people." Artisans or lower-class citizens in Novgorod and other Rus' cities.
Chetverik (pl. *chetverki*)	A unit of measuring grain equal to 1/8th of a *chetvert* or 15.8 pounds.
Chetvert' (pl. *chetverti*)	"Quarter." 1.) A unit of land equal to approximately 1.35 acres, though sometimes as much as 4.1 acres. The system of measuring land was not very precise, as it was based on "good land" determined by officials sent from Moscow. 2.) A unit of weight equal to 182 lbs. 3.) A unit of liquid measure equal to 1/4 *bochkas* or 32.5 gallons
Denga (pl. *dengi*)	A silver coin equal to 1/2 kopek. A Muscovite *denga* was 1/200th of a ruble. A Novgorodian *denga* was 1/216th of a ruble. Now the word *dengi* simply means "money" in Russian.
Deti boiarskie	The term literally means "boiar's sons," although in later centuries they were no longer related to the boiars. The social rank just below the boiars.

D'iak (pl. *d'iaki*)	A secretary or clerk. *D'iaki* are known to have been associated with the archbishops of Novgorod, the Novgorodian *veche*, and the grand princely court in Moscow. In the archiepiscopal and grand princely administrations, they headed departments Each parish church was also supposed to have a *d'iak* (or female *d'iachka*) who carried out important administrative functions such as picking readers and the choir.
Funt	A unit of weight equal to around one pound.
Gorodishche	(*Riurikovo Gorodishche*) The princely residence outside Novgorod, south of the Market Side. It now stands in ruins.
Gorst' (pl. *gorsti*)	"Handful." A general unit of measure for flax.
Grivna (pl. *grivny*)	A monetary unit in Rus'. The *silver grivna* was a silver rod or oblong hexagonal ingot weighing 164 grams in Kyiv and 204 grams in Novgorod during the Kyivan period. In Muscovy, 1 *grivna* equaled 20 *dengi*. In Novgorod, 1 *grivna* equaled 14 *dengi*. There was also a *grivna kuna*, four of which equaled a silver *grivna*, and also a gold *grivna* coin. Today the hryvna is the currency of Ukraine.
Iarlyk	The patent or charter of office for the grand princely throne granted by the Khan of the Golden Horde until the fifteenth century, when the office became hereditary among the Princes of Moscow. The term is also used for immunity charters that the khans granted to the Rus' Church, exempting it from taxation or levies and so forth.

Iaroslavovo Dvorishche	"Iaroslav's Courtyard." The princely residence in Novgorod, located on the west side of the Marketplace, named after Iaroslav the Wise (Grand Prince of Kyiv 1019-1054), who was made Prince of Novgorod by his father, Vladimir (r. 980-1016). While part of it is still standing (the Trading Mart towers are said to be part of the old courtyard), it was heavily modified in the early modern period.
Kliuchnik (pl. *kliuchniki*)	"Steward." The name comes from *"kliuch"* the Russian word for key. The *kliuchnik* carried out judicial tasks and affixed seals to document.
Korob	"Basket, box." A unit of weight equal to 7 *pudy* or 252 lbs.
Kormlenie	"Feeding." The system whereby a princely or other official was maintained by taking a portion of the fees (in goods and services) he gathered in a province or district for his upkeep, rather than being paid directly by his employer or lord.
Konets (pl. *kontsy*)	"End." One of the five boroughs of the city of Novgorod.
Korablik (pl. *korabliki*)	"Little ship." The Russian name given to a gold coin that bore the image of a ship, perhaps the English Noble.
Kuna (pl. *kuny*)	A monetary unit in Rus'. The name comes from *kunitsa*, marten, and *kunii*, marten-fur. A *kuna* was equivalent to a *rezata* or 1/50th of a *grivna kun*. It is now a currency in Croatia, which also had the *kuna* in the Middle Ages.
Namestnik (pl. *namestniki*)	The lieutenant or adjutant of a prince, bishop (in the latter case often translated as "vicar"), or other important official. Usually a judicial official, though they also carried out other tasks.

Nogata (pl. *nogaty*)	A monetary unit in medieval Rus' equal to 2 ½ rezaty or 1/20th of a *grivna kun*.
Obrok	Quitrent. One part of a peasant's obligations to his lord; payment in money or in kind. The other part of his obligation (called *corveé* or, in Russian, *barshchina*) comprised labor for the lord.
Obzha (pl. *obzhi*)	A unit of land in Novgorod equal to 10 *chetverti* or 13-15 acres.
Piatina (pl. *piatiny*)	"Fifth." The organized area of the Novgorod Lands, divided into five regions called "Fifths" which made up the western part of the Novgorodian Lands around the city of Novgorod. To the east, Zovoloch'e ("the Land Beyond the Portages") was largely unorganized and sparsely populated. It included the Dvina Lands (around the Northern Dvina River) and other regions, which served as the main source of Novgorod's fur.
Piatok (pl. *piatka*)	"Five" of, for example, eggs; a term similar to a half dozen. A *desiatok* or "ten" would be the Russian equivalent of a dozen.
Podvoiskii (pl. *podvoiskie*)	A Novgorodian bailiff.
Pogost (pl. *pogosty*)	The administrative center for a rural district in the Novgorodian Land.
Polotka (pl. *polot'*)	"Half." A measure of dried or smoked fish or poultry.
Pomest'e	A service estate. The system was established in 1489 by Grand Prince Ivan III when he distributed land confiscated in the Novgorodian region to servitors on condition of service to the grand prince. A servitor was known as a *pomeshchik* (pl. *pomeshchiki*).
Portishch	A quantity of cloth.

Posadnik (pl. *posadniki*)	The mayor of Novgorod, Pskov, or other Rus' cities. Originally placed (*posadi*) in the city by the grand prince of Kyiv, they came to be elected by the *veche*, the popular assembly, in Novgorod and Pskov.
Posel'skii (pl. *posel'skie*)	Also *posel'nik*, an overseer of a *pomest'e* or *votchina* estate.
Pristav (pl. *pristavy*)	Another term for a bailiff or constable in Novgorod.
Pud	A unit of weight equal to 40 *funty* or a little over 36 lbs.
Riad (pl. *riady*)	A charter between Novgorod and its prince enumerating both the city's and the price's rights, privileges, and responsibilities.
Rezata	A monetary unit in Rus' equivalent to a *kuna*.
Ruble	A monetary unit in Rus' coming into use at the end of the thirteenth century. In fifteenth century Muscovy, one ruble equaled 10 *grivny* or 200 *dengi*. In Novgorod, one ruble equaled 15 *grivny kuny* and 6 *dengi* or 216 *dengi*.
Sazhen'	A unit of length equal to three arshyna or 2.13 meters, or just under 7 feet.
Sof'iane (sing. *sof'ianin*)	"The Men of Holy Wisdom." Members of the archiepiscopal administration in Novgorod; named after the Cathedral of Holy Wisdom ("*Sviataia Sofiia*" or "*Sofiiskii sobor*" in Russian).
Sorok (pl. *soroka*)	"Forty." A term used to refer to bundles of luxury furs (sables and martens) in Novgorod, which were tied together in bundles of forty furs each. Also called a *sorochka*. Non-luxury furs, such as squirrel pelts, were bundled in groups of 1,000.
Sovet gospod	"Council of Lords." A council purportedly made up of the *posadniki, tysiatskie,* and other members of the *boiarstvo* of Novgorod and Pskov that ran these cities and oversaw

debate at the *veche*. In Novgorod it was said to be chaired by the archbishop and, after 1433, met in the Faceted Chamber in the archiepiscopal palace.

Stol'nik (pl. *stol'niki*)	A steward associated with the archiepiscopal or princely table. From *"stol"* the Russian word for table.
Storozh (pl. *storozha*)	A guard or watchman assigned to watch the churches in Novgorod and its rural districts (and counted among the parish staff). Merchandise was often kept in the lower levels of churches in Novgorod, but they also protected the sacred vessels which were of gold and silver.
Strigol'nik (pl. *Strigol'niki*)	A member of a heretical movement in fourteenth and fifteenth century Novgorod and Pskov.
Tiun (pl. *tiuny*)	A judge, usually subordinate to a *namestnik*.
Tysiatskii (pl. *tysiatskie*)	"Thousandman," or chiliarch. Originally the commander of the town militia in Novgorod and other Russian cities, but evolving into a judicial official.
Uezd	An administrative subdivision in Rus' beginning in the thirteenth century. It was originally a group of *volostei* overseen by a *namestnik*.
Veche (pl. *vecha*)	The public assembly in early Rus' cities; the phenomenon fell into disuse in most places in the twelfth century, but lasted in Novgorod until 1478, and in Pskov until 1510.
Vedro (pl. *vedra*)	"Bucket." An old Rus' liquid measure equal to about 12 liters or 3.2 US gallons.
Veksha (pl. *vekshy*)	A monetary unit in Rus'. The name comes from the word for "squirrel" used in the Novgorodian dialect. Equal to perhaps a sixth of a *kuna*.

Versta (pl. *versty*)	"Verst." A unit of length equal to 700 sazhen' or 1.49 kilometers in the seventeenth century. By the time of Peter the Great, it was equal to 500 sazhen or 1.06 kilometers, or a little more than 0.65 miles.
Voevoda	A general or other such military commander in Rus'.
Volost' (pl. *volosti*)	A rural district in the Novgorodian Lands, a subdivision of a *piatina*, administered by a *volostel'* (pl. *volosteli*), the rural equivalent of a *namestnik*.
Zhitye liudi	"Living People." Middle class citizens in Novgorod and other Rus' cities.

Glossary of Less Familiar Ecclesiastical Terms

Antimension	"Instead of a table" in Greek. Also *antiminsion, antimensium*, and *antimens*; in Russian, *antimins*. A rectangular piece of linen or silk cloth with representations of the entombment of Christ, the four Evangelists, and scriptural passages related to the Eucharist on it and holy relics sewn into it. The *antimension* must be consecrated by the head of the church (by the patriarch or autocephalous archbishop) and always lie on the altar table (in Greek, *hagia trapeza*; in Russian, *prestol*). No sacrament, especially the Divine Liturgy, can be performed without a consecrated *antimension*.
Archimandrite	"Chief of a sheepfold" in Greek. The head of an important monastery (roughly equivalent to a Western abbot although not having subordinate monasteries or priors under him). In Novgorod, there was only one up the 15th Century (at the Iur'ev Monastery beginning in 1295 – a second is noted

	at the Khutyn Monastery by 1461), who served as the ceremonial head of the monastic clergy of Novgorod, and actual clerical foreman where there is no bishop or episcopal vicar.
Eiliton	Also *iliton*; in Russian, *liton*. A plain silk, linen, or cotton cover or wrapping for the *antimension* and used in the Liturgy much as the corporal is used in the Western Church.
Hegumen	"Leader" in Greek. The head of a monastery (one less important than those headed by archimandrites). Roughly equivalent to a prior in the West, although not subordinate to an archimandrite.
Hieromonk	A monk who is an ordained priest, much less common in the Eastern churches than in the West, where almost all monks became ordained priests by the late Middle Ages. Monks that were ordained deacons were, correspondingly, hierodeacons.
Metropolitan	More fully, "Metropolitan-Archbishop". Usually, a bishop who heads a metropolis (an ecclesiastical province) and oversees suffragan bishops (in the Western church, they are simply called archbishops), though there are also titular metropolitans, and the term is used differently in the Greek church. In Rus' and Muscovy, the church was a single ecclesiastical province under the Patriarch of Constantinople, with the metropolitan see first at Kyiv, moved to Vladimir in 1299 and then to Moscow in 1325), There were also several attempts to create metropolitanates in Lithuania and Polish-ruled Halych (Galicia).

Omophorion	"Borne on the shoulders." The specific symbol of episcopal power, particularly in the Eastern churches, but also found in some places in the West (e.g., Pope Benedict XVI wore one for a time). It is a long scarf marked with crosses that is worn around the shoulders and draping down in front.
Panagia	"All-holy" in Greek. Also spelled *panhagia* or *panaghia*. (Also called an *engolpion* – "on the chest" in Greek). A medallion usually depicting the Mother of God holding Christ. Another specific symbol of episcopal power in the Eastern churches. A metropolitan, archbishop, or patriarch usually wears two *panagii* (or *engolpia*) with the pectoral cross; a bishop wears one.
Papert' (pl. *paperti*)	An enclosed courtyard or space in front of, or around, a church. It is somewhat akin to a parvise (or parvis) in Western parlance. It is often translated as "porch," "vestibule," or "gallery." The paperti of Holy Wisdom are so much a part of the cathedral that it is difficult to say where they end and the cathedral proper begins, except that the southern *papert'*, the Martirievskaia *Papert'*, is sunken and the northern one, the Predtechenskaia *Papert'*, is set off by a metal fence.
Phelonion	In Russian, *felon*. The outer vestment worn by a priest during services in the Eastern churches, equivalent to the Roman Catholic chasuble. Rus' prelates used to wear the *phelonion* as well, but it was gradually replaced by the *sakkos* in the late medieval and early modern period.
Polystaurion	"Many crosses" in Greek. In Russian, *polystavriia* or *kreshchataia riza*. A special *phelonion* covered with crosses. A symbol of special favor granted to bishops by the metropolitan or patriarch.

Ponomar'	A member of the church staff at the parish level who rang the bell and led the choir during the Divine Liturgy and other services.
Prosfora	Also *prosvira*. The Eucharist bread or altar bread. Part of it is consecrated (i.e., it becomes the Body and Blood of Christ) and is distributed to the faithful at the Eucharistic celebration. The rest is blessed (but not consecrated) and is given out after the Eucharist. (*antidoron*).
Proskurnitsa	Also *prosvirnia* or *prosfornia*. A (female) member of church staff at the parish level who baked the Eucharistic bread.
Rassophore	"Robe-bearer." The first degree of monasticism following the novitiate (which is not binding), during which a novice is tonsured and bound to maintain the monastic life.
Riznichii	The person who oversees the *riznitsa*, the vestry or room where vestments are stored. The term *riza* is the general term for the vestments worn by the clergy.
Sakkos	The outer vestment worn by a bishop (instead of the priest's phelonion) in the Eastern churches. It is a long tunic with wide sleeves, fastened along the side with buttons or tied with ribbons. It was initially awarded by the Byzantine emperors to patriarchs as a mark of special distinction, but in the sixteenth century came to be worn by all Eastern bishops.
Schema	Also called the Great Schema. The highest degree or strictest form of monasticism in the Orthodox churches, often entered just before death and entailing a name change (from the one taken on entering the *Rassophore*).

Vladyka   "Master." A term used to refer to a bishop or archbishop in the Russian Orthodox Church (a direct translation of the term *"Despota"* used for a bishop in the Greek Church). It is also used in religious literature to refer to God (especially Jesus). The female equivalent, *Vladychitsa,* is used not infrequently to refer to the Mother of God.

Notes on Spelling and Terminology

The East Slavic polity or polities have been referred to as Rus' up to the time of Ivan the Terrible, after which they are referred to as Muscovy, Russia, Ukraine, or Belarus, etc., as appropriate. For the sake of convenience, I have used Rus' as both a noun and an adjective (as it appears in the Oxford English Dictionary). Writing "Rus'ian" or "of Rus'" all the time seem unwieldy. The Russian adjective for Rus' is "russkii," usually translated as "Russian," in the ethnic sense – as opposed to "rossiiskii" which means "of Russia." I try to avoid the term "Russia" or "Russian," since, particularly in this day and age, it could imply that the people, area, history, or culture of Rus' – which encompassed what is today parts of the Ukraine, Belarus, western Russia, and parts of the Baltic States, Poland, and Moldova – belongs exclusively to the modern Russian state or people. (I would add that Rus' heritage does not belong exclusively to Ukraine or Belarus either).

I have spelled the names of geographic features as they are spelled in the modern states in which they are situated. Thus, for example, Kyiv, Chernihiv, Volodymyr, and Halych, rather than Kiev, Chernigov, Vladimir-in-Volynia, and Galich or Galicia. Russian personal names have been rendered according to the Library of Congress transliteration system and diacritical marks have been maintained with a few modifications. Thus, for example, Sofia rather than Sofiia. I have also dropped the hard signs when they are no longer used after 1918, and the adjectival endings "-ago" are rendered with the modern "-ogo." Personal names have been maintained in their Russian form rather than anglicized.

I have at times use the term *bishop* to refer generally to all levels of the episcopal rank (bishop, archbishop, metropolitan, and patriarch), but use specific ranks when referring to particular individuals or when clarity requires it.

Archbishop Il'ia (r. 1165-1186) is also known as Ioann (and sometimes as Ivan), especially in the hagiographic literature. His brother, Archbishop Gavriil (r. 1186-1193), is also known as Grigorii. I refer to them as Il'ia and Gavriil, the names by which they are known in the *Novgorodian First Chronicle*, *Novgorodian Fourth Chronicle*, and a number of other major primary sources. Gavriil's name was spelled with one i in the chronicle. I have chosen to spell it in the modern way, with two i's.

Archiepiscopal tenures are given from their election rather than their date of consecration since several of them exercised the office but were never consecrated or held office for several years before being consecrated (e.g., Evfimii II, elected in 1429, but consecrated only in 1434.)

The term *sobor* is translated as "church" unless it is the cathedral church of a bishop, at which point it is called a "cathedral." Sofiiskii Sobor is rendered as "The Cathedral of Holy Wisdom," rather than "St. Sofia's." There are several female saints named Sofia in the Orthodox Church, but the cathedrals in Kyiv and Novgorod (as well as those in Constantinople, Polatsk, Tobol'sk, and Vologda) are not dedicated to any of them.

The term *papert'* (pl., *paperti*) is retained in discussing the architectural feature in the Cathedral of Holy Wisdom in Novgorod. The term is often translated as "porch," "gallery," or "vestibule," but this is unsatisfying when talking of Novgorod because the *paperti* there are integral to the building rather than additions or extensions.

Monetary units have been explained only very briefly. As currency values changed significantly over the period of this study, it is difficult to speak with any precision as to the worth of certain currencies at any given time. Furthermore, currencies had different values in different parts of Rus'; for example, a Novgorodian *grivna* was not the same as a Muscovite one.

Introduction

1. Upper register of the Mid-15th c. Novgorodian Battle with the Suzdalians icon, here depicting Archbishop Il'ia/Ioann presiding over the procession with the Icon of the Virgin of the Sign from the Trading Side of the city across the Volkhov River towards the Cathedral (Sophia) Side in 1169/70.

A history of the medieval Novgorodian archiepiscopal office needed to be written for several reasons. The episcopal office is a key one in the church, the most important institution in the medieval world, and the bishops and archbishops of Novgorod one of the most significant churchmen in the Rus' church, with some scholars even contending that the office was second only to the metropolitanate in importance. A history of the office advances our understanding of the Eastern episcopate and Eastern Christianity as it formed and grew in the Eastern Europe context. It reveals how bishops related to one another within the ecclesiastical metropolis (province) and across the broader Orthodox Church, how they interacted with other institutions outside the church, like the princes or the city authorities, how they related to the Western Christian and pagan communities around them, and clarifies the important contributions they made to religious and secular culture, including to the arts, architecture, hagiography, and historiography.

Greater understanding of the office also adds to our knowledge of Novgorod the Great's place in the history of Rus' and later Russia. The city was one of the key political, religious and ecclesiastical, cultural, economic, and commercial centers of Rus', the "Father of Rus' cities" just as Kyiv was the "Mother of Rus' cities,"[1] so that a better understanding of the office of archbishop, who was also as a key figure in the political, judicial, social, and economic life of the city, and of Rus' more broadly, seems natural and indispensable to a fuller understanding of the history of the city, of Rus', of Eastern Slavdom, and of the Eastern church.

The available evidence points to the Novgorodian archbishops being, perhaps, the preeminent patrons of the arts, architecture, chronicle-writing and the copying of important religious texts and other documents in Rus', including saints' lives and even folklore. As such, they were vital figures in the transmission of the history, culture, and faith of Rus' and later of Belarus, Ukraine, and Russia.

After the fall of Novgorod to Moscow, the Novgorodian bishops continued to play important roles in Muscovite, Imperial, and Soviet church history, so an understanding of where the office came from makes sense. In 1492 (7000 A. M.), when the Orthodox Church thought the world would end, Archbishop Gennadii (r. 1485-1504) commissioned the calculation of the date for Easter for the next thousand years. In 1499, he commissioned the first complete edition of the Bible in Slavic.[2] Metropolitan Makarii, who crowned Ivan IV tsar in 1547 and was one of his chief advisers early in his reign, had been archbishop of Novgorod (r.1526-1542). In Novgorod he commissioned the first editions of the *Velikie Minei Chet'i* and the *Stepennaia Kniga*,[3] two of the most important literary works of that period, and instrumental texts in Russian proto-nationalism. Patriarch Nikon, whose reforms in the 1650s led to the Old Believers' schism, had been metropolitan of Novgorod (r.1649-1652). Novgorodian Archbishop Iov (r.1698-1716) consecrated the Cathedral of Peter and Paul in St. Petersburg, the first church in St. Petersburg and the burial place of the Russian emperors. Feofan (Prokopovich) helped Peter the Great establish the Holy Governing Synod and write the "Spiritual Regulations" that governed the imperial church and afterward was made archbishop of Novgorod (r.1725-1736). When he wrote the "Spiritual Regulations," he was archimandrite of the Khutyn Monastery and assistant to Novgorodian Archbishop Feodosii III (r.1720-1725).[4] Archbishop Dimitrii (r.1757-1767) crowned Catherine II (r.1762-1796) and served as her spiritual adviser. Archbishop and later Metropolitan Arsenii II (r.1910-1933) was a candidate for the office of patriarch when it was reestablished in 1917.

In the Soviet period, Metropolitan Aleksei of Leningrad and Novgorod was one of the church leaders who met with Stalin in 1943 and oversaw the re-legalization of the church and its revival in the later Stalinist era. As archbishop of Khutyn (r.1926-1932) and metropolitan of Staraia Russa (r.1932-1933), he managed the Novgorodian eparchy during Metropolitan Arsenii's exile to Central Asia. He was then metropolitan of Novgorod for two months in 1933, then metropolitan of Leningrad from 1933 to 1943, and then metropolitan of Leningrad and Novgorod from 1943 to 1945 when the sees were merged (he famously remained in Leningrad during the Blockade rather than be evacuated). He served as patriarchal locums tenens (*patriarshii mestobliustitel'*), or acting head of the Russian Orthodox Church, upon the death of Patriarch Sergei on May 15, 1944 until he himself was elected patriarch on February 2, 1945.[5] Metropolitan of Leningrad and Novgorod Nikodim (r. 1967-1978) was the Patriarchal Exarch in Western Europe; Metropolitan of Leningrad and Novgorod Antonii (r.1978-1986) was an important figure in the church's relations with the outside world in the later Soviet period. Finally, Patriarch, Aleksei II (r. 1990-2008), was metropolitan of Leningrad and Novgorod (1986-1990) before his election as patriarch.[6] Many of these Imperial and Soviet era prelates were, admittedly absent from Novgorod, residing instead in St. Petersburg/Leningrad, with their ties to Novgorod rather nominal, although, for others, their time in Novgorod or their ties to the city and the archiepiscopal office were formative in their later personalities and policies.

This study focuses on the period from the establishment of the archiepiscopal office in 1165, because this that truly set the office apart from the other bishops in Rus'. It will, however, touch on the bishops prior to 1165 and the role they played in establishing the church and the Novgorodian eparchy in the almost two centuries before the establishment of the archiepiscopate. The study ends with the Muscovite Conquest of Novgorod in 1478 and the deposition of Archbishop Feofil (r.1470-1480), because these events are thought to have fundamentally changed the nature of the office, though there will be some discussion of archbishops and metropolitans of Novgorod after 1478, contrasting the office before and after 1478 or extrapolating how the earlier archbishops may have acted based on evidence or sources from after the Muscovite conquest.

Novgorod the Great and its Place in Russian History

Before laying out the organization and methodology of this study, a brief sketch of Novgorod the Great, its geography, its political and social structure, and its place in Rus', will help to set the archiepiscopal office in a clearer socio-political and spatial context. A survey of the traditional historiographical view of Novgorod and its archbishops also provides a historiographic context, and lays out the main theories and viewpoints that have dominated the scholarship for much of the last two centuries – and are still found in many general histories even today – and which have to be engaged in order to come to a fuller understanding of the office.

Novgorod is the other great urban center in Rus', known to scholars, but perhaps much less familiar to the broader public.[7] Kyiv was preeminent from the first organized state system as early as the tenth century up to the Mongol Invasion in the mid-thirteenth century. Moscow dominated the period from the end of the Golden Horde's power in the 1480s to the establishment of the Russian empire in 1700. And since Nikolai Karamzin's *Istoriia gosudarstva rossiiskogo*, published in twelve volumes between 1816 and 1829, set the tone of Russian historiography (or perhaps it was Vasilii Tatishchev's more questionable *Istoriia Rossiiskaia*), there has been a tendency to view much of Rus' and Appanage history in terms of the eventual, inevitable (or even proper) unification or "gathering of the Rus' lands" under Moscow's legitimate authority.[8] The Russian Empire is essentially Muscovy continued, which in their view was merely the continuation of Kyivan Rus' shifted to the northeast, to Vladimir-on-Kliazma, to Moscow (and eventually to St. Petersburg.) This, of course, is overly-simplistic and ignores the "appanage" principalities of Tver', Smolensk, Riazan, Novgorod and others, none of which necessarily thought unification under Moscow was all that legitimate, inevitable, or good. It also ignores western and southern Rus' which eventually became Ukraine and Belarus'. Today, both Kyiv and Moscow are huge, vibrant, modern cities and capitals of their countries. Novgorod the Great is not (nor, might I add, are Smolensk, Tver', Vladimir, Suzdal', or other former princely seats). Novgorod is a relatively small provincial city of about 200,000 people with about fifty lovely medieval churches scattered among drab Soviet-era buildings. The city and oblast gained some notoriety for their considerable economic growth in the 1990s, but in many ways, it seems history has long ago passed it by.

Novgorod was one of the largest cities in medieval Northeastern Europe, although medieval population figures are, of course, quite speculative and imprecise, so that the city's true population is, and probably will forever remain, unknown. Soviet academician and historian Mikhail Tikhomirov based his estimates on the sizes of armies mentioned in the chronicles, or of the number of victims of various plagues, conflagrations, or famines, but ultimately concluded that "It is practically impossible to determine the size of the population of towns in Medieval Rus'."[9] In the Kyivan period, Novgorod was surpassed in size and importance in Rus' only by Kyiv, and it was eclipsed by Moscow only at the end of the medieval period. Between the relative decline of Kyiv in the late twelfth century (and most certainly by the time of its sack by the Mongols in 1240) and the rise of Moscow in the fourteenth and fifteenth centuries, Rus' fragmented politically into several states know, inaccurately, as "appanage principalities," though they were not appanages in the medieval western sense of that word, but rather independent states.[10] It was during this period, when no one city held sway over all of what had been the Kyivan Rus' state, that Novgorod flourished and gained political independence. Since it never dominated Rus' politically, as did Kyiv, or as Moscow later did, Novgorod never gave its name to a historic period. However, from 1240 into the fifteenth centuries, it was the largest and most significant city in Rus', important politically, as Olga Sevastyanova put it, as "a stepping stone to power in Rus'" and "an object of rivalry" between the grand princes of Vladimir and Lithuania.[11] It controlled, albeit loosely, a territory stretching from the border with

Livonia (modern-day Estonia and Latvia) to the Ural Mountains, and from the Barents Sea south to the Volga River, making it one of the largest states in medieval Europe.[12]

Culturally, too, Novgorodian art, architecture, and literature were preeminent during this period, profoundly influencing Rus' and subsequent Muscovite and Russian culture. Novgorod was so important as a center for the arts in the medieval period, that Mikhail Tikhomirov concluded that "In the history of Rus' culture, Novgorod holds a place equal to that of Kyiv;"[13] Nikolai Dejevsky called the city "the most consistent and prolific center of culture in medieval Russia;"[14] and Viktor Bernadskii asserted that Novgorod's contribution to Russian art was on par with Florence's contribution to Italian art.[15]

Commercially, the city was the heart of the fur trade in Northern Rus' and the vast wealth from furs and other commodities sold in the market in Novgorod made the city an important source of tribute for the Golden Horde, the western portion of the Mongol Empire established in the 1240s and lasting into the fifteenth century. It made the princes of Moscow wealthy, since it was they who gathered the *dan'* or tribute for the khans in Sarai and, according to some scholars, may have skimmed as much as 6/7ths off the top for themselves.[16] The archbishops and the local boiars gained from this trade, and then lost out when the Hanseatic League cut silver to Novgorod and closed its merchant enclave (Peterhof) in the city for several years (1388-1392; 1443-1448). By the middle of the fifteenth century, trade shifted to Reval and Dorpat. The Muscovite grand princes also began to seize fur-bearing lands along the Dvina in the fifteenth century.[17] The city declined further under Muscovite rule, the wealth from the fur trade going to the grand prince and his boiars. Ivan IV "the Terrible" (r. 1533-1584) brutally attacked the city in 1571 and it was later surpassed by Arkhangelsk as the main western entrepôt into Muscovy.[18] It was finally eclipsed economically, commercially, and ecclesiastically in northwestern Russia by the founding of St. Petersburg in 1703.

Novgorod's economic importance was key to its political and cultural significance, and stems from its geographic location in northwestern Rus' close to Scandinavia and the Baltic. It stands astride the Volkhov River, 150 miles south of where that river debouches into Lake Ladoga, and a mile and a half north of where it flows out of Lake Il'men. The ermine, sable, black marmot, silver fox, and gray squirrel furs – sought-after luxury items in Europe and the Middle East – were brought to Novgorod from the forests that stretched to the northeast of the city along the shores of Lake Ladoga and Lake Onega all the way to the eastern coast of the White Sea and on to the Urals.[19] Other commodities included timber, wax, honey, and walrus tusks (called "fish teeth" in the sources), but fur was always the principal commodity. Sergei Platonov noted the city's importance as "the main trading point along the route 'from the Varangians to the Greeks'," that is, from Scandinavia to Constantinople.[20] From Scandinavia, traders traveled across the Gulf of Finland and up the Neva River to Lake Ladoga, then along the southern shore of the lake to the mouth of the Volkhov River and up the river to Novgorod. From there they traveled across Lake Il'men, up the Lovat or other rivers and then over short portages to the Western Dvina River and further south to the upper reaches of the Dnieper River. They then traveled south (around several cataracts) to the river's mouth, then along the west coast of the Black Sea to Constantinople. Other trade routes passed eastward down the Volga to the Caspian Sea and on to Persia, or westward from Novgorod, through Pskov, and on to the German cities of Livonia or into Lithuania and Poland. From there they linked up with the cities of northern Germany (which later formed the Hanseatic League). Novgorod's prime location meant that the city was one of the key entrepôts between Rus' and Western Europe throughout the medieval period. The Lithuanian specialist S. C. Rowell summed up the city's commercial importance when he called Novgorod not only "the dominant economic and political power" in Northwestern Rus', but also "the most important trading post in Northern Europe."[21]

The City's Geography, Administration, and Political Institutions

Despite its importance to the political, commercial, ecclesiastical, and cultural life of Kyivan and, particularly Appanage, Rus', medieval Novgorod remains an enigmatic place. Geographically, of course, it is much better understood than it is socially, economically,

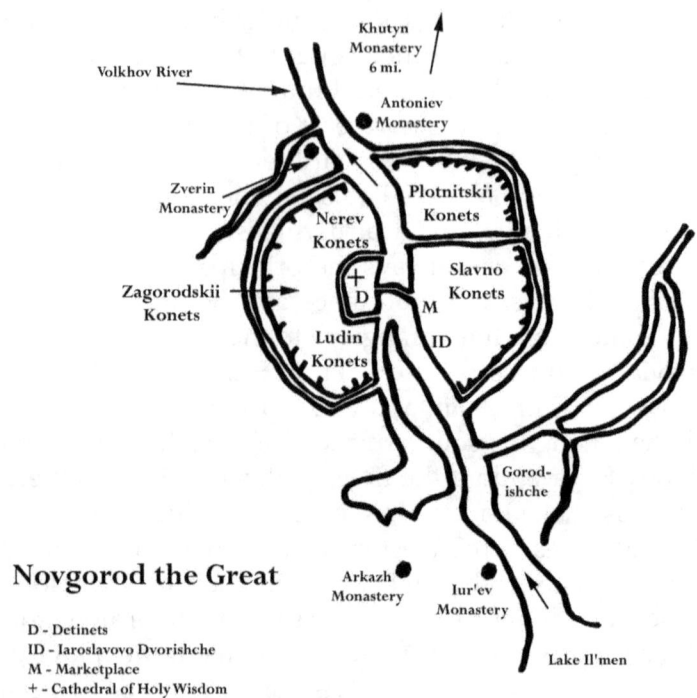

Novgorod the Great

D - Detinets
ID - Iaroslavovo Dvorishche
M - Marketplace
+ - Cathedral of Holy Wisdom

or politically. Much remains unknown, and probably unknowable due to the lack of substantial source material from the medieval period and the laconic nature of the sources that are available. But it is still possible to sketch the basic outlines of Novgorod's geography and major institutions, and thereby provide not only a feel for the physical space in which the archbishops lived and worked, but also construct a basic framework of their social, political, cultural and religious environment as well.

Novgorod is bisected by the Volkhov River into sides (*storona*): the Sofia Side on the left or west bank of the river, named for the Cathedral of Holy Wisdom (*Sviataia Sofiia* in Russian), and the Market or Trade Side on the opposite bank. In the medieval period a wooden bridge connected the two sides, stretching from the *Detinets* or kremlin, the fortified center of the city in which the cathedral and archbishop's palace stood, across to the market on the right bank.²² Administratively, the city was divided into five boroughs or "ends" (*kontsy* - sing., *konets*): the Zagorodskii ("Beyond the Fortress"), Nerevskii (Nerev), and the Liudin, also called the Goncharskii or "Potters", *kontsy* on the Sofia Side; and the Plotnitskii ("Carpenters") , and the Slavienskii ("Slavno" or "Slovene") *kontsy* on the Market Side. While some scholars have argued that this organization into five *kontsy* occurred only in the 1470s, at the very end of the period under study, others assert that the city originated as three separate settlements which became the Nerev, Liudin, and Slavno *kontsy*, with the Plotnitskii *konets* forming in 1168 and the Zagorodskii in the 1260s.²³

The traditional scholarship contends that each *konets* held its own *veche* (pl *vecha*) or public assembly and that a city-wide *veche* was also convened either in front of the Cathedral of Holy Wisdom, or at Iaroslav's Courtyard (*Iaroslavovo Dvorishche*) near the Church of St. Nicholas in the Marketplace,²⁴ or sometimes in both places at once. The *veche* or *vecha* then elected the city officials. Starting in the early twelfth century, the *veche* of each *konets* elected a single *posadnik* (pl. *posadniki*; i.e., mayor, so-called because they were originally placed – *posadi* – by the Kyivan grand prince). It also elected an elder (*starosta*) for the *konets*. The city-wide *veche* elected a *tysiatskii* (pl. *tysiatskie*; i.e., thousand-man) beginning in the late twelfth century. He was originally head of the city militia but evolved into a judicial and commercial official over the centuries. Other officials tied to the city's administration, courts, merchant associations, or who performed functions in the outlying regions and districts of the Novgorodian Land, were apparently either elected by the *veche* or appointed by the higher magistrates, but much remains uncertain as to the actual constitution of the state.²⁵

Originally, there was only one *posadnik* and one *tysiatskii*, but over the course of the centuries the number increased, so that by 1359 there were six *posadniki*, one representing each of the five *kontsy* or boroughs of the city and one acting as "*stepennyi posadnik*," the senior mayor or mayor of all Novgorod. By 1417, there were twenty-four *posadniki*, and by 1463, there were thirty-six, as well as several *tysiatskie*.²⁶ Former *posadniki* and *tysiatskie* continued to hold influence even after their term of office ended. They and their clans formed the *boiarstvo*, the city's nobility or aristocracy, or what was sometimes referred to in the chronicles and other sources as "the lords." Some scholars have also written of a "Council of Lords" (*sovet gospod*) being established after reforms in the first quarter of the fifteenth century. The current and former *posadniki*, *tysiatskie* and other town notables made up this council that ran the city. But there is very little in the primary sources to indicate such an institutionalization of the aristocracy in Novgorod ever existed. In fact, the "lords" appear to have been more institutionalized in Pskov than they were in Novgorod, although no formal "Council of Lords" is mentioned in sources from either city.[27] Indeed, while there is some evidence supporting that *vecha* were convened by the different *kontsy*, and there were multiple *posadniki* and *tysiatskie* created during the course of the Middle Ages, particularly following Posadnik Ontsifor Lukich's reforms in the 1350s, the city's exact political constitution is confused, and the neat and tidy organization and institutions found in the traditional historiography probably never existed. Furthermore, how the various *posadniki*, *tysiaskie*, and other town officials interacted with each other, with other officials and with the *vecha*, or how the offices of prince or, more importantly for our purposes, that of archbishop, fit into Novgorod's constitutional framework, is uncertain.

Dejevsky may have called Novgorod "the most important Riurikid seat after the grand princedom in Kyiv itself,"[28] but Novgorod was never the patrimony of a single princely dynasty. Prior to 1136, the grand prince in Kyiv placed a prince in Novgorod, often a son or other close relative, to administer the city on his behalf. The grand princes of Vladimir (almost always the grand princes of Moscow after 1317), was almost always titular prince of Novgorod after the first quarter of the thirteenth century. But from the late eleventh to the late thirteenth century, Novgorod could at times elect or dismiss its princes. Perhaps the *veche* did this, perhaps it was the *sovet gospod*, but the sources do not really tell us. The city usually chose the most powerful prince in Rus', or asked him to send a son or other close relative,[29] but after the second quarter of the twelfth century the princely office in Novgorod was a somewhat precarious one relative to the other princes in Rus'. Although individual princes usually held the office for only around a year at a time, the grand princes in Kyiv and Vladimir, and the princes of Chernihiv, Smolensk, and Halych, dominated the office. It was a lucrative one given the city's commercial wealth, so the princes fought over it and the Novgorodians played one off against another as best they could. This resulted in a somewhat elective princely office that kept a single hereditary dynasty from taking control in Novgorod, but the city never really shook off princely rule.[30] The city did establish de facto independence or autonomy, but really only in the early fourteenth century, so that by the last quarter of the 1300s it had come to see itself as "His Majesty Lord Novgorod the Great" (*Gospodin Gosudar' Velikii Novgorod*). The city itself was sovereign rather than having any sovereign prince or other ruler over it. This nomenclature not only served to distinguish Novgorod the Great from Nizhnii (or Lower) Novgorod on the Volga, but also to equate it with the Grand Prince (*Velikii Kniaz'* compared to *Velikii Novgorod*).[31] Independence lasted only until the end of the fifteenth century when, after a series of defeats by Muscovite armies, the local government fell to Grand Prince Ivan III "the Great" (r. 1462-1505) in early 1478. He had been the city's prince since 1462, as had his ancestors for more than 150 years, but he established direct Muscovite rule in the city only in 1478, ending Novgorod's unique political organization.

The archbishop took his place among the prince (or after the fourteenth century, the prince's *namestnik* (pl. *namestniki*), or lieutenant, and the local officials and the *vecha*, in governing the city. Some scholars have called him the head of state, but this term is anachronistic and problematic. There is no indication he was ever formally recognized as such by the Novgorodians, nor did he act alone in a civil capacity except in the rarest of instances.[32] Rather, the archbishop, the several *posadniki* and *tysiatskie*, and other members of the *boiarstvo* seem to have formed a collective leadership, although determining the specific purview of the archbishops within this collective is likely impossible. In part, the purpose of this study is to come to a clearer understanding of their place within the city elite and the roles it allowed them to play in the city's economic, political, and cultural life, and in the wider history of Rus'.

It must be stated, and will be reiterated, that the paucity and brevity of the sources likely make an understanding of the precise roles the archbishops played (politically as well as economically and ecclesiastically) extremely difficult if not impossible. Often what we have are later copies of documents found in sixteenth or seventeenth century *sborniki* (collections) now housed in archives or libraries in Moscow and St. Petersburg. The distance in time between these copies and the events they record, or how correctly or truthfully the copyists or compilers of these *sborniki* understood or recorded the originals they are purportedly based on, call their accuracy into question. Additionally, the chronicles and other sources were sometimes edited, if not by the chroniclers at the time, then later by the grand princely administration to paint the grand princes in a positive light and, subsequently, to paint independent Novgorod as treasonous, disorganized, irreligious or heretical ("Latin"), immoderate or unrestrained. Add to this the fact that the earliest Novgorodian chronicles were often written in an overly-concise style, as if in code; John Fennell wrote how events are "briefly and unsatisfactorily described by the sources," and of "the singular reticence of the chroniclers, who, as is often the case, appear to be deliberately concealing information."[33] What Roy Fletcher observed of the Chronicle of Ireland is also true of the Novgorodian chronicles: "With very rare exceptions, the annalists reserve judgement; they do not indicate the cause for events and do not make causal connections between different events;[34] or, as Timofei Guimon put it, they "prefer simply to describe events."[35] This may be due, at times, to the fact that the chroniclers were writing about events across town and assumed the reader (and not necessarily a large readership) was already aware of what had happened and which Church of the Transfiguration was being referenced. All this has led scholars to broadly differing interpretations of events.[36]

 Besides the degree of institutionalization of the *veche* and its role in electing the city's officials, there has been a long-standing debate as to its democratic or oligarchic nature. Eighteenth and nineteenth century historians and writers, including Aleksandr Radishchev and Mikhail Lermontov, as well as Vasilii Kliuchevskii, saw Novgorod as a democratic city-state ruled by the *veche*, and some twentieth- and twenty-first-century scholars maintained this general viewpoint.[37] It played well among those who opposed tsarist autocracy and clung to the idea that Russia was not foreordained to autocratic, arbitrary rule or lacked any history of popular governance, or who saw the people (*narod*) as communal and democratic at heart. In this way, the *veche* moved from history to political ideal, myth, and even verse. Thus, Lermontov wrote in 1832:

> Hail, sacred cradle of the warrior Slavs!
> Arrived from foreign lands, I gaze
> With rapture at the gloomy walls
> Through which the centuries of change
> Passed harmlessly; where the veche bell
> Alone did serve the cause of freedom,
> And then the end of freedom tolled,
> And many a proud soul with it did fall...
> Oh, tell me, Novgorod, are they no more?
> Is not your Volkhov what it was before?[38]

More recent scholarship rejects this romanticized, democratic view since democracy as we think of it is a modern development. It instead sees Novgorod as run by an oligarchy of land-owning families who controlled the office of mayor (*posadnichestvo*) and other secular offices, a governmental system not unlike the city-states of medieval Germany, Flanders and Northern Italy.[39] In this interpretation, either the *veche* was made up of the city elite or, if it included the common people, it was convened in order to give them a sense of participation in the government, or perhaps to build consensus, but was firmly controlled if not manipulated by the oligarchs.[40]

Novgorod's constitution and its oligarchic or democratic nature are beyond the scope of this study. I believe that the city was run by the elite with the common people having some say in matters through popular acclamation or sometimes raucous and violent demonstrations, but believe the sources are simply too scarce, laconic, or contradictory for historians to ever achieve any consensus on Novgorod's precise political make-up. This limits our ability to fully understand the archiepiscopal office, especially its political roles. If the city was democratic, then a bishop, even one elected by the *veche*, seems out of place. And if he did have a place at the political table or exercised political power in a democracy, it would be very different from that wielded by a bishop in an oligarchic city. And if he was respected and honored – influential rather than wielding true political power – his roles in the city's political, social, legal, economic, and cultural life would be different as well.

Organization of the Study

This study is organized thematically rather than chronologically in order to better focus on the various roles of the archbishops. It draws together as many of the available primary and secondary sources as possible to offer as complete a picture as possible of the archbishops, their office, and their importance to the history of Rus' and of the Russian church. But it also seeks to place Novgorod within its wider framework, in relation to Moscow, Kyiv, and the rest of Rus', and to compare archbishops with other episcopal sees in the Catholic and Orthodox lands around it, wherever possible, so as to show the unique aspects of the office, how it developed, and what it contributed to history and culture.

Thematically, it begins broadly before focusing in on the particular; moving from wider Christendom and narrowing to the church in Rus' and then the local church in Novgorod, and in so doing to look at the roles exercised by archbishops in terms of Christian, Orthodox, Rus', and Novgorodian ecclesiastical tradition, politics, economics, and culture. With this in mind, Chapter One looks at the theoretical understanding of the bishop in the Orthodox world in order to provide a conceptual framework for what the office should or was expected to be within the church and wider society. While theory often did not translate into practice – Rus' and later Russia was not a terribly theoretical in their religious mindsets – the institutional church and the laity often judged their bishops based on an idealized image of the bishop or what was demanded or allowed of him in biblical texts and canon law. The next two chapters look at the archbishop's ecclesiastical roles, since it was his position in the church that formed the basis of his historical activity. Chapter Two looks at the archbishop's place in the Rus' church, while Chapter Three deals with his position as head of the Novgorodian archeparchy. Chapter Four looks at the very unique electoral process as it developed in Novgorod from the late twelfth to the late fifteenth centuries and significant insofar as it was by this process that the men who became archbishop usually entered history. Through election they went from being obscure monks or hegumens – a few were mentioned in the chronicles prior to their episcopates – to being significant historical figures and city magnates. Chapter Five looks at the archbishops' political activity as part of the city's elite and how unique this power was not just in the Rus' church, but throughout the Orthodox world, although it must be kept in mind that Novgorod's bishops never attained the political power of many Catholic bishops nor were they, as some might contend, Novgorod's head of state. Chapter Six looks at the economic aspects of the office and the administration the archbishops supervised. This administration not only oversaw the religious or ceremonial aspects of the Novgorodian archeparchy, but also gathered in and oversaw the archbishops' enormous wealth, which in turn financed the archiepiscopal administration and allowed the archbishops to carry out all their other political, ecclesiastical, and cultural roles. Chapter Seven lays out the archbishop's cultural influence, among the most significant aspects of the office. Art historians have certainly recognized the archbishops as cultural patrons for a long time, but the extent and importance of their patronage has not been given proper emphasis in the previous scholarship. Furthermore, their patronage of the arts and of chronicle-writings is how they have lived on in the collective memory.

Methodology and Sources

This study relies on a great number of sources, and I have sought out primary sources – chronicles, princely charters, law codes, treaties, letters, ecclesiastical documents, icons, saints' lives, service books, legends, and tales – and have focused on material as close as possible in time and space to the events under study with the assumption that such sources are less corrupted by later additions or editing, the clouding of memories, or misunderstanding due to changes in meaning over time, or by cultural differences. Whenever possible, multiple sources have been consulted in researching particular events, to "triangulate" what took place and cancel out local inaccuracies, individual bias, mistakes, or gaps in information that might be found when relying on only a single source (though multiple sources sometimes give multiple interpretations that confuse rather than clarify). Reference to less historically-reliable sources such as icons, saints' lives, legends, and tales is understandably contentious. Many historians dismiss them as completely inaccurate or nearly worthless as historical sources. But I include them because they still provide useful information: the common perception of the archbishops and their office, or perhaps the image they or the church wished to convey, as well as their cultural importance. These sources have been used in conjunction with more-reliable, or at least more accepted, historic sources to ground the book in empirical evidence as much as possible.

Most of the primary sources for the period under study have been published in the last two centuries, but while researching the sixteenth century archbishops on a Fulbright Senior Scholar grant in 2006-2007, I came across documents in archives, libraries, and museums in Russia that, while often from after 1478 or copied out centuries later, shed light on the period under study or tell us how the Muscovite-appointed archbishops of Novgorod viewed their pre-Muscovite predecessors, and sometimes continued to invoke them or carry out their policies. The *Biblioteka Novgorodskogo Sofiiskogo sobora* (the Library of Holy Wisdom) now in the Russian National Library in St. Petersburg, has some volumes of which date back to the archiepiscopate of Moisei (r.1325-1330; 1352-1359). This collection was most useful in discussing the archbishops' patronage of the arts and culture and their promotion of the saintly cults of their predecessors in office, but archival documents have been used throughout the study to clarify some material in the published versions.

The basic primary sources are the chronicles gathered in the *Polnoe sobranie russkikh letopisei* (The Complete Collection of Rus' Chronicles) or published separately. The most important single chronicle is the *Novgorodian First Chronicle*,[41] although the *Novgorodian Fourth Chronicle*[42] and the *Sofia First Chronicle*[43] are also significant. These three are the oldest and most complete of the Novgorodian chronicles, compiled under the auspices of the archbishops themselves.[44] The *Novgorodian Second Chronicle*,[45] and *Novgorodian Third Chronicle*,[46] are utilized less often since they are much abbreviated and often repeat what is found in the *Novgorodian First Chron-*

icle or *Novgorodian Fourth Chronicle*. Despite shortcomings, all the Novgorodian chronicles provide an enormous amount of valuable information. The *Pskov First* and *Second Chronicles* give the history of the second most important city in the Novgorodian archeparchy and shed light on the archbishops' relationship with that city, which becomes particularly interesting after Pskov gained political independence from Novgorod in the fourteenth century.[47] Beyond Novgorodian and Pskov chronicles, *the Lavrentian Chronicle*,[48] *Hypatian Chronicle*,[49] and the *Moskovskii letopisnyi svod kontsa XV veka* describe events in the rest of Rus',[50] though they, understandably, have less material on Novgorod and the archbishops. Other annals tell us about other regions and provide a useful comparison with events and institutions in Novgorod.[51] The *Letopisnyi sbornik, imenuemyi Patriarsheiu ili Nikonovskoi letopis'iu*,[52] commonly called the *Nikon Chronicle*, is less reliable. It is a sixteenth century compilation of earlier chronicles heavily edited to give a pro-Muscovite slant to events. It can still provide useful information if carefully read, although wherever possible, I have referred to the earlier chronicles from which the *Nikon Chronicle* were drawn, such as the *Moskovskii letopisnii svod* and the *Sofia First Chronicle*.

Primary source documents published in the nineteenth and twentieth centuries include the *Gramoty Velikogo Novgoroda i Pskova* (The Charters of Novgorod the Great and Pskov)[53] and the *Novgorodskie pistsovye knigi*, the land registers or cadastres drawn up in the late fifteenth and sixteenth centuries on the orders of the grand prince of Moscow. While these date from just after the period under study, they provide significant information on episcopal and ecclesiastical (mainly monastic) landholdings during the later part of this study and show how the situation changed with Novgorod's loss of independence, as well as information on parish structures and church personnel not available from other sources.[54]

Many documents of the Rus' church have also been published in a number of publications, including volume six of the *Russkaia istoricheskie biblioteka*,[55] the first volumes of the *Akty istoricheskie*[56] and the *Dopolneniia k Aktam istoricheskim*,[57] the *Russkii feodal'nyi arkhiv*,[58] and, most recently, *Documentary Sources on the History of the Rus' Metropolitanate: The Fourteenth to the Early Sixteenth Centuries*.[59] In addition, the *Kormchaia kniga* or "Pilot's Book" and other church documents, most notably those edited by Vladimir Beneshevich,[60] have been consulted, as have biblical and patristic writings, the documents of the first seven ecumenical councils and several important local councils (which make up a significant part of the *Kormchie Knigi*), as well as other material found in the *Ante-Nicene Fathers* and *Nicene and Post-Nicene Fathers* series and Jacques-Paul Migne's awesome collection of documents.[61] Taken together, these provide insights into the religious and ecclesiastical world in which the archbishops and the archeparchy of Novgorod flourished and the theory of the bishop in the Orthodox world. The correspondence of the patriarchs of Constantinople also offers details about the relations between Novgorod, the metropolitans, and the patriarchs, although what survives only covers the fourteenth and fifteenth centuries.[62] Rus' law codes and other princely statutes have also been consulted, since they provided the legal basis for the church and the archbishops and their activities. These have been published in both Russian and, in some cases, in English, in several editions.[63]

A number of Western documents also shed light on the archbishops, particularly their relations with the West, and offer a comparison between the Catholic and Orthodox episcopate. Most notable among these are documents from the Livonian cities,[64] the Teutonic Knights,[65] the cities of northern Germany and the Hanseatic League,[66] and the chancellery of the grand princes of Lithuania.[67]

The archbishops themselves left relatively few documents beyond the chronicles, which, admittedly, were written at their behest and do not necessarily reveal their individual personalities. Bishop Luka Zhidiata left the *Sermon to the Brethren*, given to a group of monks at an unknown time and place. Although he lived prior to the establishment of the archiepiscopate, his sermon is discussed as an example of homiletic works by the prelates of Novgorod and compared to the works of later archbishops.[68] Archbishop Nifont left answers to a series of questions posed by members of the clergy, known as the *Voproshanie Kirika* (The Questions of Kirik).[69] Archbishop Il'ia left two sets of rules: one, sent in a letter to an unnamed Bishop of Bilhorod, was on the administration of the sacraments by the white clergy; the other addressed how monks should live.[70]

Archbishop Antonii wrote a famous description of Constantinople a few years before its sack in 1204.[71] Archbishop Vasilii Kalika left a letter to Bishop Feodor of Tver' concerning the existence of the earthly paradise.[72] These few sources give us some idea of the archbishops as preachers and writers.

Several archbishops are the subjects of saints' lives, legends, and folktales, particularly Archbishop Il'ia,[73] but also Evfimii II and Iona.[74] Others appear in the lives of other saints or as antagonists or supporting characters in the tales and legends of other protagonists. As noted above, these sources are of limited historical value, but can reveal common perceptions of how people understood the archbishops and their office at the time and sometimes show how the archbishops not only patronized the arts, but themselves became part of Novgorodian cultural life as venerated or fictionalized, mythical, or legendary figures. And since some of these were written by or at the behest of later archbishops, they can reveal the archbishops' thinking about their office, their predecessors (and how they wanted to portray them), the church, Novgorod, and the wider world in which they lived. These images influenced how people reacted to the real archbishops and may even have influenced how the archbishops were portrayed in more historically accurate sources; an archbishop who failed to live up to the ideal image painted in the legendary or hagiographic literature might suffer abuse at the hands of the Novgorodians, or chroniclers might use types or topoi from legends or the hagiographic literature to explain real events. Modern historians, again, dismiss accounts of miracles, omens, and prophesies as superstition, but the medieval Novgorodians believed in them, reacted to them, perhaps even expected them, and included them in the chronicles and liturgical books like the *Velikie Minei Chet'i*. Thus, while not everything in these legends, tales, or saint's lives (or even the chronicles) was factual or historically accurate, they may have been *real* and meaningful to the medieval Novgorodians and still tell us something of how the citizens of that foreign country that is The Past saw the world.

I have also made use of numerous secondary sources in undertaking this study. While not all can be discussed here, the most important merit mention. The numerous books and articles of Valentin Ianin, the dean of Novgorodian history and archaeology, have been invaluable in studying the political and social life of the city in the medieval period, in particular his work on the *posadnichestvo* and the study of the seals of the metropolitans, archbishops, *posadniki*, and other officials.[75] Archaeological studies by Ianin and others are also important in understanding the material culture of Novgorod, and point out where the physical evidence fills in or even contradicts the written record.[76] Archaeology is key to uncovering important artifacts, including sphragistic evidence that deepens to our understanding of the political roles played by the archbishops and the *namestniki* and other officials in their administration. Archaeology is also important in uncovering the art and architecture of the Cathedral of Holy Wisdom as it looked in the medieval period, including artifacts (clothing, liturgical and household vessels, etc.) and in excavating the archbishops' tombs. It also useful in revealing the architectural significance of the churches and other structures the archbishops patronized. Birchbark documents, leather and wooden articles and other artifacts also bring us closer to the city in which the archbishops lived and new artifacts are being uncovered with each excavation, adding new information not available in the reinterpretation of old, published sources.

Other important secondary sources include expansive histories of the Russian Orthodox Church written by Evgenii Golubinskii,[77] Metropolitan Makarii (Bulgakov),[78] as well as shorter works by Anton Kartashev,[79] John Fennell (left incomplete at his death),[80] and others (several similarly named *History of the Russian Church*) as well as the biographies of the archbishops written in the late nineteenth century by Aleksandr Tomilin, Konstantin Zdravomislov and Pavel Tikhomirov.[81] These ecclesiastical histories have been invaluable in placing the archbishops within the wider Russian Orthodox Church and the Orthodox community. They provide a solid overview of Russian ecclesiastical history although they often suffer from the same problem of some of the general histories in that they tend to be Moscow-centric and see early events in light of later Muscovite unification. The biographies have been most useful in providing a basic overview of the lives of the bishops, archbishops, and metropolitans of Novgorod, though they sometimes tend toward hagiography. Several post-Soviet studies of the Novgorodian church and the archbishops have been most informative, but they often focus on a limited aspect (politics, art, etc.) of the office, cover a short period,[82] or, in one case, is a very good collection of essays, but an incomplete history of the archbishop and their archeparchy.[83] More general studies of Russian and northeastern European history have helped place Novgorodian events into wider Russian and European history,[84] while more focused works on agricultural and economic history, art and architecture, literature, and Orthodox Christianity help place the archiepiscopal office in its Novgorodian, East Slavic, and wider Christian context.

Historiographic Issues

This historiographic review reveals that previous scholars have, by no means, ignored the archbishops of Novgorod. But a number of these scholarly works are either dated; cover a limited period, only touched on the archbishops secondarily while focusing on other topics such as Novgorod's political structure or relationship with Moscow, the wider church, interprincely competition, the socio-economic system, landownership, peasant resistance to the land-owning aristocracy, and so forth; or they focus on only one aspect of the archbishops, their land-ownership or economic roles, their political roles, or their alleged autocephalous tendencies, for example.

In other cases, earlier works, such as those by Tikhomirov and Zdravomislov, were thorough in their use of the chronicles and other sources, including published letters, charters, and saints' lives, and, thus, useful insofar as they went, but they are more narrative than analytic, and at times tended toward hagiography. This is an understandable inclination given that Tikhomirov was the archpriest of the Church of Our Lady of the Sign in Novgorod, but a more "scientific," empirical, or critical looks at the office and how it changed over time is needed. Furthermore, older works, of course, fail to take into account more recent scholarship, the exciting archaeological discoveries since the Second World War, or new historical interpretations. A number of works are also unavailable or difficult to find in the United States and Western Europe.

As noted, earlier studies have pointed out the vast size of the Novgorodian archeparchy and the important place of the archbishops within the church hierarchy, but what do the sources really tell us about that role in the Rus' church, and their activities in their own archeparchy? Much of the ecclesiastical historiography – the aforementioned works of Golubinskii, Makarii, Kartashev, Fennell and others – tend to focus on the metropolitans and the church's close relationship with the grand princes of Moscow. Discussions of the ecclesiastical position of the archbishops of Novgorod have at times been relatively slight, or else emphasize conflict between the metropolitans and the Novgorodian archbishops, often seen through a Muscovite lens. That is, the archbishops' interactions with the grand princes and the metropolitans have been discussed but have often been seen in terms of his friendliness or hostility toward Moscow within the context of the Moscow-Tver' or Moscow-Lithuania rivalries. Or they have been viewed from the perspective of obedience or defiance toward legitimate ecclesiastical or princely authority. Anti-Kyivan or anti-Muscovite behavior has been seen where it might not have existed, and was deemed uncanonical, illegal, immoral, or even treasonous. Ecclesiastical histories have also tended to see the Novgorodian archiepiscopal office as only a small part of the wider Rus' church, as a member at a council or a party in a dispute over who was rightful metropolitan.[85] But what were the reasons the Novgorodians themselves (the archbishops and others – as revealed in the chronicles and other sources) gave for their opposition to the princes or metropolitans? Aleksandr Nikitskii's *Ocherk vnutrennei istorii tserkvi v Novgorode* and his work on the church in Pskov, focused more on the broader Novgorodian church than on the archbishops, and emphasized canonical propriety – what should have happened according to the law or ecclesiastical custom.[86] But what actually happened, and what motivated the archbishops and the city to act as they did, even in violation of the law or customs?

The archbishops' political roles, particularly their position among the "lords" in Novgorod, and their often-antagonistic relationship with Moscow, has been a major focus of earlier scholarship. But as noted, to call the archbishop the most powerful political figure in the city, the city's head of state, and the main formulator of Novgorod's anti-Moscow foreign policy is weighted, judgmental, and anachronistic, probably saying more about modern concepts of institutionalized, post-Enlightenment government (separation of powers between different branches, à la Montesquieu), or modern notions of democracy, nationalism, church-state relations (separation of church and state), or even the powers of Western prince-bishops, than about what actually transpired in medieval Novgorod.[87] Marxist and Imperial Russian historians saw Novgorod, the church, and other aspects of Rus' history through the biases of their time or the limits of their theoretical or ideological approaches, the inevitability of Muscovite centralization or tsarist autocracy, Russian nationalism, how everything fit into Marx's stages of history, followed the alleged laws of history, or their emphasis on class conflict. These interpretations are understandable, but not very useful in clarifying the office in its medieval context. In going back to the sources, what do they tell us about the archbishops' political roles?

Because the archbishops were usually not the main focus of research, scholars have reached drastically different conclusions about them, which often are not supported by close reading of the evidence. Policies or actions that make perfect sense from the Novgorodian perspective or from the point of view of a Novgorodian archbishop, often seem obstreperous, apostate, or treasonous, when viewed from the standpoint of a grand prince or metropolitan. In some cases, scholars mention the archbishops in passing and a role or attribute gets assigned to them that is passed down in the historiography uncritically. For example, Edward Sokol, in writing about the *veche*, argued: "in the mid-twelfth century [the *veche*] began selecting the all-powerful archbishop, the nominal head of state."[88] He did not, however, elucidate on what made the archbishop "all-powerful," nor did he look at the actual process of election and how it changed over the centuries, or who said the archbishop was nominally head of state. Bernard Pares, in his general history of pre-Revolutionary Russia, was equally vague in his assessment of the archbishops, merely stating that they "came to have a strong local authority,"[89] but never explained what that meant.

Henrik Birnbaum wrote perhaps the most accessible and well-known series of essays on medieval Novgorod.[90] Although they are largely based on secondary sources and repeat previous assertions without necessarily assessing their accuracy, Birnbaum was more specific about the archbishops' political powers. In "presiding over the Council of Lords," the archbishop, he wrote, "may be considered the republic's formal head of the state," although he admitted that the *posadniki* and *tysiatskie* were really "the two most influential officials in Novgorod the Great."[91] Birnbaum's conclusions were similar to those of Sergei Platonov more than half a century earlier: "in the administration of Novgorod, the bishop had a great role,"[92] although he ultimately saw the *posadnik* as "the main executive power in Novgorod."[93]

Aleksandr Khoroshev, writing in the late 1980s, concurred with Platonov's assessment, namely that independent Novgorod was run by an alliance between the archbishop and the boiars,[94] but did not look at how the archbishop was different from the others among the city's elite due to his ecclesiastical position. Khoroshev's work, furthermore, is from a decidedly Marxist viewpoint, which seems anachronistic since the end of the Cold War, and tends to suffer from the herculean efforts of Marxists to cram past events into Marx's oversimplistic stages of history or see every instance of peasant discontent as a proto-revolution or some aspect of class warfare.

Joel Raba wrote several studies in the 1970s on the Novgorodian church, including one that looked at Archbishop Evfimii II (r. 1429-1458),[95] and another on the church's role in Novgorodian foreign policy at the end of the fifteenth century. In this latter study, Raba argued that the office of archbishop was "the sole well-developed and stable Novgorodian institution,"[96] contending that the long tenures of the archbishops made their position more stable than those of the *posadniki* and *tysiatskie*. Thus, it was the archiepiscopal office, rather than the secular political offices, which came to represent long-term Novgorodian state interests. However, the greater longevity of the archiepiscopal office vis-à-vis the *posadnichestvo* or the office of *tysiatskii* may be more apparent than real. Ianin, in his study in the 1960s on the Novgorodian *posadniki*, has shown that, although they were elected annually, individual *posadniki* often held office for a decade or more and passed the office down to their sons or other close relatives, not unlike what occurred in elected mayoralties in Venice or other city-states to the West. Thus, the *posadnichestvo* was actually also a very stable office.[97] The longevity of archiepiscopal tenures certainly contributed to the importance of that office, but this was not exclusive to the archbishops, and their importance may also be explained by the central place held by the church in medieval Rus' and the archbishops' place in it, a supranational organization of preeminent authority at the time. It may also be explained by the increasing number of *posadniki* and *tysiatskie* in the fourteenth and fifteenth centuries that led to the diffusion of power among the *boiarstvo*, while the political power or influence of the archbishop remained in the hands of one man.

Other studies fail to recognize changes in the archiepiscopal office over time. Thus, Khoroshev and others have written of an alliance between the archbishops and the boiars that began in the early twelfth century and lasted to the end of Novgorod's independence, but do not discuss how this alliance changed over the course of these three and a half centuries or how the archbishops' political position waxed or waned.[98] Furthermore, the terminology of "alliance," or "union," (the word is the same in Russian) or of the archbishops' "siding with" the rest of the city elite implies that they were different from the other members of the aristocracy, and that they worked with them for different reasons. In some sense this is true, since the archbishops were the only churchmen among the elite and had ecclesiastical interests that the *boiarstvo* did not. But the archbishops also had many interests in common with the boiars. According to Ianin and others, the Novgorodian aristocracy (or oligarchy) was based on land-ownership, and the archbishops were among the greatest landowners in Novgorod at the end of Novgorodian independence. Thus, due to their wealth and convergent interests, the archbishops were not simply allied with the Novgorodian aristocracy, they were part of it.

In other instances, scholars have reached erroneous conclusions in enumerating the archbishops' political functions, particularly the archbishop's role as the city's executive power. For example, Vasilii Kliuchevskii asserted that the archbishop of Novgorod was "the permanent president of (the *Soviet gospod),*"[99] or Council of Lords, which Birnbaum defined as "a delegated and executive organ of the *veche*."[100] These scholars argue that the Council carried out the day-to-day duties of the government when the *veche* was not in session, and usually met in the archbishops' "chambers" in the Palace of Facets.[101] Indeed, Birnbaum contended that the archbishop, "by presiding over the Council of Lords... came to occupy first place in the secular hierarchy of the city."[102] G. P. Fedotov, too, saw the archbishop as "the president of the Council of Masters" (*Soviet gospod*), explaining: "In effect, he was the one who was 'president' of the republic, to draw a modern analogy...The archbishop stood above parties and expressed the unity of the republic."[103] He noted that "immense wealth and even military force were concentrated in his hands. 'The House of St. Sophia' was the largest economic entity in Novgorod and 'The Bishop's Troops,' were a notable part of her civil guard."[104]

Ianin gave a fuller account of archiepiscopal power, blurring the lines between what belonged to the archbishop and what belonged to the state:

> Among the elected offices of Novgorod, the first place was held by the Novgorodian bishop. He was custodian of the Novgorodian state treasury and owner of extensive state lands, the primary part of which had been confiscated from lands owned by the prince, attached to the Cathedral of Holy Wisdom. To him belonged the right of the church courts and control over the merchant scales. Together with the boiar upper class, he took part in the foreign policy of the republic and in his court were compiled the Novgorodian chronicles. The Novgorodian bishop...having received in 1165 the status of archbishop, presided over the "Council of Lords" - the governmental organ of the boiar oligarchs. The political role of the archbishop was determined, first and foremost, on the basis of his being the greatest of the Novgorodian feudal (lords).[105]

All these scholars touch on important aspects of the office: its extensive lands and immense wealth (sometimes used for state purposes), its role in Novgorod's domestic and foreign policy, its role in the ecclesiastical courts, weights and measures, chronicle writing, and so forth. And while the primary sources confirm that the archbishop was one of the city's important political figures, that the archiepiscopal administration held enormous landed wealth, and oversaw the ecclesiastical courts, there are several problems in the historiography. It too is based on modern assumptions of governmental organization, or even western ideas of medieval episcopal secular powers, something largely if not totally unknown in the Orthodox East.

Furthermore, the primary sources do not seem to support some of the conclusions reached on the "Council of Lords" being established as a public body after reforms in the first quarter of the fifteenth century.[106] To describe it as the "executive council" of the *veche* and argue it effectively ran the city until the conquest by Moscow in 1478 is to read far too much between the lines.[107] While the *Pskov Judicial Charter* and some chronicle entries speak of "the lords," it is a stretch to form these "lords" into an organized, political institution that controlled the *veche* and ran the city. Furthermore, there is some evidence for a more inclusive polity with real power exercised by a *veche* whose membership was not limited to the aristocracy. If this is the case, then it cannot be said with any certainty that the archbishops presided over the Council of Lords or that the council was the "executive organ" of the city.

Third, some evidence cited as proof of the archbishops' secular political powers does not really reveal political power at all. The archbishops or their judges did sit on the civil courts to be sure, but to cite supervision of the ecclesiastical courts, which dealt with ecclesiastical cases, not secular political matters, is no evidence of secular power. And these courts were in no way unique: church statutes issued by Vladimir and Iaroslav in the late tenth and early eleventh centuries grant such powers to the metropolitans and the bishops, citing Byzantine precedents to justify this grant, and similar ecclesiastical courts operated across the Christian world. Other claims are also problematic: the Council of Lords may not have existed, at least as a formal body, the bishop did not have a cavalry unit, and the Palace of Facets was only built in the fifteenth century, toward the end of this period, so civil or court meetings held there may tell us little of what happened in earlier centuries. What, then, does the actual evidence tell us about the archbishops' political roles? And how did these roles develop and change over time?

Scholars have, likewise, looked at the archbishops' wealth and economic roles as the basis for their political power, but these discussions also have shortcomings. Some tend toward normative arguments as to the illegitimacy of this wealth, that churchmen should accept apostolic poverty or that the church ought to be merely a spiritual institution. Such works fail to comprehend the more-worldly aspects of the medieval church, nor do they try to understand the church as an important social and cultural or spiritual institution that very much created and directed medieval civilization. Consequently, they fail to place these economic aspects within the context of the archiepiscopal office, or even that this wealth may have been needed to finance the archeparchial administration and patronize arts and architecture, chronicle writing, and hagiography.

Thus, even in areas that have already been the topic of previous scholarship, there is considerable grounds for not only going back to look at the traditional primary sources, but also to incorporating new archaeological findings and new interpretations, in order to more fully understand the archbishops of Novgorod, the Rus' and Eastern Orthodox churches, and broader medieval Eastern European world. This study not only looks at areas already studied, such as Novgorod's political and economic history, but breaks new ground in areas that have been more overlooked, particularly the important contributions the archbishops made to Novgorodian and Russian art and culture. I also admit where the sources are too scant or unclear to draw firm conclusions as to specific roles played by the archbishops, and am sad to say this occurs all too frequently.

This discussion of problems in the historiography is in no way meant to disparage the efforts of previous scholars. This monograph owes a great deal to previous scholarship; problems in earlier scholarship are pointed out in an effort to correct and certainly not to dismiss earlier scholars or their works as being of little value. I do not believe I am rewriting the history of the Rus' church or of Novgorod the Great. Rather, my hope is to come to what a colleague called "a near approximation of the truth" in spite of the biases and shortcomings that I bring to the work, and add in some small way to our understanding of the archiepiscopal office and the great city and church of which it was so much a part.

Chapter One
The Bishop in Theory

2. The seven ecumenical councils of idealized bishops from the upper register of a 16th-century Novgorodian "Wisdom Builds her House" icon. Moscow.

Introduction

Before looking at the praxis of the episcopal office in medieval Novgorod, it is important to consider briefly the theory of the bishop as it was understood, especially in the medieval Rus' church. By "theory" is not meant the more organized or formal study or conceptualization of the episcopate developed over the course of the Middle Ages in the West by canon lawyers, theologians, papal, imperial, or royal apologists, and other writers and thinkers in response to the Investiture Controversy and the other disputes between the Papacy and various emperors and kings. Such a formal study did not exist in Rus'. Rather what is meant is something more akin to the word *theoria* as it was used in ancient Greek, meaning a "viewing" or "beholding." For our purposes, it means how Rus' –

and in particular Novgorodian – Christians, viewed or beheld their bishops. In their mind's eye, who should be bishop, how was he expected to act, and what was he supposed to do as bishop?

But even before we consider this Rus' conceptualization, several modern and Western preconceptions are worth pointing out, since these color our view of what a bishop is or should be and these preconceptions were not true of bishops in the Middle Ages. Additionally, we must bear in mind that the episcopate was and is different in its Eastern and Western variants.

The first preconception is that the bishop does not, or should not, generally hold temporal, secular political office or power,[1] certainly not as an aspect of his episcopal office. There are political dynamics to every office from which the episcopate is by no means immune. But bishops today do not govern secular states or territories, adjudicate secular court cases (and ecclesiastical courts have a much narrower competence than did medieval ecclesiastical courts), nor do they wield other temporal powers such as signing treaties, overseeing weights and measures, and so forth. Thus, while modern bishops are often important public figures, and can and do speak out on important issues of the day – human rights, the poor, nuclear war, the environment, and so forth – they have *influence* rather than real political *power* or authority. There are, of course, exceptions to this generalization: the Pope as head of the Vatican City-State being the major exception.[2] But overall, in the modern world there is much more of a "separation of church and state," with the modern bishop being much more confined to the spiritual realm than was the medieval bishop. There are no prince-bishops anymore.

A second preconception is that bishops should not possess earthly wealth and should not be "worldly" – they should live in this world, but not of it. Some bishops may still live in palaces (e.g., in Krakow, Munich, Strasbourg, Prague, and Nicosia, to name just a few), and a bishop may oversee sometimes sizeable diocesan properties, charitable funds to help the poor, unwed mothers, and so forth. He may also have secretaries and chauffeurs, but none of this is really his personal property to do with as he wishes, but, rather, belongs to the diocese. They also generally do not, as some medieval bishops did, hold huge tracts of land, engage in trade, raise horses or hunting dogs, oversee the markets, peddle church offices, charge for administering the sacraments, sell indulgences, have mistresses or illegitimate children, raise or lead armies, go hunting in a princely manner, or do other things that were sometimes all too common, and occasionally even quite acceptable in the medieval period, at least in the West, though some of these practices were frowned upon, if not technically forbidden, even then.

It is important to understand that the Eastern bishop was and remains different from his Western counterpart. The Eastern churches choose their bishops exclusively from the black or monastic clergy, a practice never found in the West. There were, of course, cases where someone from the white clergy was shorn a monk after his wife died or took the veil (Novgorodian archbishops Il'ia and Vasilii Kalika are two such examples).[3]

Despite the episcopate's origins in the monastic community, there was often tension between the monk, who had renounced the world, and the bishop, who had to go back into the world to administer the church and who, in turn, had to seek out suitable candidates to succeed him. This tension led one of the Desert Fathers, John Cassian (d. 435) – or at least a later copyist – to title a chapter of his *Institutes*, "That a monk should by all means flee women and bishops."[4] A number of saint's lives and Patristic letters indicate that Cassian was not alone in this sentiment. Thus, when the people of a vacant see appealed to Bishop Timothy of Alexandria that the monk Ammonius of Nitria (on the Nile Delta southeast of Alexandria) be made their bishop, Timothy sent a delegation to bring Ammonius for consecration. The monk firmly refused and when the envoys persisted, he is said to have cut off his left ear, since church tradition forbade a mutilated man from entering the clergy. When the delegates returned after Timothy had told them that the Old Testament proscription need not be followed if the man was otherwise worthy of ordination,[5] Ammonius threatened to cut out his own tongue. Rather than see the monk suffer further self-mutilation, the envoys withdrew.[6] Athanasius of Alexandria rebuked the monk Dractonius for refusing the episcopal calling, warning him not to "say or believe those who say that the bishop's office is an occasion of sin, nor that it gives rise to temptations to sin."[7] He apparently wore Dractonius down, since his name appears in both

Athanasius' *History of the Arians* and Jerome's *Life of St. Hilarion*, among the orthodox bishops exiled during the Arian persecutions under the Emperor Constantius in 356-357.[8]

Several Novgorodian archiepiscopal candidates also took office reluctantly, or willingly resigned, at least according to the chronicles. Moisei laid aside the episcopal office to return to monastic life in 1330, returned to the episcopate after Vasilii Kalika's death in 1352, and resigned again in 1359.[9] Aleksei resigned in 1375, only to take up the office again later that year. It is not clear whether they resigned because they disliked the worldliness of the office and desired the tranquility of the monastery (Moisei's building projects call this interpretation into doubt), or if Novgorodian factional politics or disagreements with the metropolitan were the cause.[10] Gail Lenhoff and Janet Martin note the custom of a Novgorodian archiepiscopal candidate denying the office three times before finally accepting it,[11] but I have found no such tradition specifically articulated in the sources and the custom was not often practiced.[12] Certainly archbishops Mitrofan and Antonii showed no reluctance or timidity, but fought hard to hold on to the office, taking their case all the way to the metropolitan in Kyiv. Thus, an expressed reluctance to take charge of an episcopal see is not necessarily a formulaic feigned-humility or literary topos. It is quite possible that a man who had sought isolation from the world in a monastery – who had legally and formally died to the world[13] – would not want to come back into it to deal with the administrative, political, financial and other burdens of the episcopal office.

The Origins of Episcopal Theory

With an awareness of these modern preconceptions, and of the differences in the Eastern episcopate (and its relationship to monasticism), we turn now to the views of the medieval Novgorodian archbishops and whence they originated. We have four main sources: biblical references to bishops, which are few and, admittedly do not refer to the office as it later developed; Apostolic and Patristic sources; and the canons of the first seven ecumenical councils and a number of local councils, mainly in the East (though, for example, the Synod of Carthage is also cited), many of which became the basis for the Eastern church's nomocanon, or code of canon law. We will consider each in turn.

Biblical Sources

Regrettably for the historian, bishops are already found in Acts and several of Paul's letters and these references provide almost no information as to the office's foundation or its function at the time, though they do give an idea of who Luke and Paul thought a bishop should be. A number of Christian churches with episcopal structures believe Jesus consecrated the Apostles as the first bishops, and they passed on this authority through Apostolic Succession to later bishops, although the term "bishop" is never used in the Gospels.[14] But this is rather a theological viewpoint and we see almost nothing of the office's historic origins – how the Apostles actually passed on the office to the second generation of Christians,[15] nor do we see how the episcopate separated from the priesthood and formed a distinct order in the hierarchy. Paul may have ordained bishops, but we only see him meeting with them later,[16] and he likewise wrote to or of them only later; we do not see the moment of their consecration or a lot of the practical knowledge of the office he may have passed on, though we know it was carried out by a sacramental laying on of hands.[17]

The office called *episkopos* in the Greek, meaning "supervisor" or "overseer,"[18] was not fully formed when the term is used in Paul's Letters to Timothy and Titus,[19] or in Luke's Book of Acts.[20] However, the letters do give us some ideas of what some of the earliest Christians – or at least Paul – thought of the bishops and these ideas influenced later Christians in thinking about the office. Paul lays out the qualifications for episcopal candidates in the *First Letter to Timothy*:

> The saying is sure: If any one aspires to the office of bishop (overseer - *episkopes*), he desires a noble task. Now a bishop must be above reproach, the husband of one wife, temperate, sensible, dignified, hospitable, an apt teacher, no drunkard, not violent but gentle, not quarrelsome, and no lover of mon-

ey. He must manage his own household well, keeping his children submissive and respectful in every way; for if a man does not know how to manage his own household, how can he care for God's church? He must not be a recent convert, or he may be puffed up with conceit and fall into the condemnation of the devil; moreover he must be well thought of by outsiders, or he may fall into reproach and the snare of the devil.[21]

Similarly, he writes in in the *Letter to Titus*:

For a bishop (overseer - *episkopon*), as God's steward, must be blameless; he must not be arrogant or quick-tempered or a drunkard or violent or greedy for gain, but hospitable, a lover of goodness, master of himself, upright, holy, and self-controlled; he must hold firm to the sure word as taught, so that he may be able to give instruction in sound doctrine and also to confute those who contradict it.[22]

Apostolic Sources

The early Apostolic sources, from the decades after the biblical age, continue the theory of the bishop for the early church. The first of these is the *Didache* ("Teachings"), which dates to around AD 50 to 120. It speaks of bishops in only four lines, calling on the church to "appoint for yourselves, therefore, bishops and deacons worthy of the Lord, men who are meek and not lovers of money."[23] It then explained that "for unto you they also perform the service of the prophets and teachers. Therefore, despise them not; for they are your honorable men along with the prophets and teachers."[24]

The *Didascalia Apostolorum*, ("The Teaching of the Apostles"), an early third century Syrian document thought by the early church to have been written by the Apostles at the time of the Council of Jerusalem,[25] is based in part on the *Didache*. It does not appear in the *Novgorodian Synodal Kormchaia of 1282*[26] or *Kormchaia* published by Beneshevich, nor did he include it in his collection of church documents before Peter the Great. But it is included here because its first chapters form the basis of the later *Apostolical Canons* and these and the later chapters provide us a glimpse of how the view of the bishop developed in the early church. These views are quite similar to and most certainly influenced Patristic and later views of the office, including the views held by the Rus' church. The *Didascalia* called on a bishop to choose as his successor "a man advanced in years of whom they give testimony that he is wise and suitable to stand in the bishopric,"[27] though a young man, if he showed maturity, could also be called to lead the church, just as Solomon (at twelve), Josiah (at eight), and Joash (at seven) reigned over Israel and Judah.[28] The episcopal candidate was to be "instructed and apt to teach."[29] Morally, he was to be "blameless, in nothing reproachable, one remote from all evil,"[30] meek, merciful, and a peacemaker in the spirit of the Beatitudes,[31] "clear of all evil, wrong, and iniquity,"[32] "watchful and chaste and staid and orderly."[33] He was to be "of a noble mind,"[34] "merciful, gracious, and full of love,"[35] a pattern "of righteousness," and "an example to the people,"[36] so that, as bishop, he could better "make inquisition of any man's misdeeds, or rebuke him and give sentence upon him."[37] Once bishop, he was "not to keep silent from them that sin, but rebuke and reprove and correct and admonish and afflict him that sins," then he would cast dread and fear upon other sinners and bring about their repentance.[38] He was to be kind and merciful to the poor and lowly, to watch over the laity as a mother bird would her eggs,[39] to seek out those who had fallen away and bring them back,[40] to exercise the power to bind and loose granted by Christ to the Apostles,[41] and be "a proclaimer also of the wrath to come in the judgment of God…threatening the grievous fire which is unquenchable and intolerable"[42] The bishop was also strictly warned of the dangers of failing to stamp out heresy or schism:

> …Have a care of all, that none may stumble and perish by reason of thee. For a layman has the care of himself alone, but thou carriest the burden of all. And very great is the load that thou bearest; *for to whom the Lord hath given much, much also will he require at his hand.* [Lk 12.48] As therefore thou carriest the burden of all, be watchful;[43]

Bishops were to be "the physicians of the church,"[44] and were warned "Do not then use force, and be not violent."[45] Rather, they were to be merciful and forgiving and be "priests and prophets and princes and leaders and kings and mediators between God and His faithful,"[46] and ultimately to exemplify and imitate Christ.[47] Ideally, they were seen as a *type* (*typus, typum* in the Latin translation) or archetype of God (the Father), whereas the deacon "stands beside" the bishop as an archetype of Christ, and the priest was "to be thought of" as an archetype of the Apostles.[48] The bishop was "the high priest, teacher, and father after God...(a) ruler and leader, (a) mighty king and God after God Almighty."[49]

As the *Didascalia Apostolorum* was based on, though much more expansive than, the *Didache*, so too the *Apostolical Canons*, particularly the first six chapters, are based on and are seen as a companion to the *Didascalia*.[50] A set of eighty-five rules originally also thought to have come from the Apostles, they are now believed to date to the fourth century. They deal in large part with the episcopate, but also touch on the priesthood and diaconate. They are included in the *Novgorodian Kormchaia*,[51] and, as such, more directly affect the medieval Rus' view of the bishop that interests us.

According to the *Apostolical Canons*, candidates for the episcopate were not to be recently baptized, nor were they to have led a wicked life up to the time of their consecration.[52] They were forbidden from gaining office by simony,[53] or to have used the "rulers of the world" to gain office.[54] Those who had done so were to be stripped of office. Once in office, on pain of deprivation of office, the bishop was enjoined to look after the spiritual needs of the clergy and people in his care, instructing them in piety and looking after the clergy's physical needs.[55] He was not "to undertake the cares of the world" or to engage in public administration,[56] nor was a bishop or other clergymen to enter the army or live for the world,[57] but was to focus on ecclesiastical affairs. In administering the sacraments, a bishop was to be deprived of office if he did not receive a repentant sinner back into the church, since Christ had said that "There is joy in heaven over one sinner that repenteth."[58] He and other clergy were forbidden from using violence against the faithful and unbelievers in their care,[59] and from ordaining brothers, sons, or other family members or "whom he pleases."[60] They were forbidden to rebaptize those truly baptized and warned to rebaptize those who were "polluted by the ungodly;" they were ordered to baptize according to Christ's command ("in the name of the Father and of the Son and of the Holy Spirit") by triple immersion.[61]

Administratively, bishops in each country were to "know who is chief among them" (i.e., who was their metropolitan-archbishop) and "not to do any great thing without his consent; but... to manage only the affairs that belong to his own parish [diocese], and the places subject to it."[62] They were to oversee ecclesiastical revenues in the diocese, but were strictly enjoined not to appropriate any for their own private use or give any to family members, or otherwise "alienate the revenues of the church."[63] The clergy, for their part, were to not "do anything without the consent of the bishop,"[64] and were forbidden from speaking ill of the bishop, since it is written "Thou shall not speak evil of the ruler of thy people."[65]

In their private lives, bishop and clergy were forbidden from playing dice or drinking, nor was a bishop to be one who "requires usury of those he lends to," nor were they to eat in taverns, all on penalty of deprivation of office.[66] They could certainly abstain from meat, wine, or marriage, but if one did so "because he abominates these things, forgetting that 'all things were very good,'[67] and that 'God made man male and female,'[68] and blasphemously abuses Creation," then he was to either reform or be deprived of office.[69] Bishop and clergy were furthermore, expressly forbidden, on penalty of deprivation of office, from engaging in fornication, stealing, or perjury. It was not that the laity was permitted such things, but the bishop and other clergymen were particularly admonished to avoid such vices because they were to serve as an example to the rest.[70]

Patristic Sources

The *Apostolical Canons* were long attributed to Pope Clement I (r. 88-99),[71] whose *First Epistle to the Corinthians* is found in the Rus' church's *Kormchie knigi*. In the letter, Clement claims that the episcopal office is mentioned in the Old Testament, when the Spirit says "I will appoint their bishops in righteousness and their deacons in faith."[72] Closer to his own time, the Apostles appointed bishops, and that office had been passed down to his time. Due to the office's biblical origins, the bishop was to be respected and could not be removed except for grave wrongdoing.[73]

Clement's Eastern contemporary, Ignatius of Antioch, (ca. 50-ca. 100) is more expansive, touching on the episcopate in a number of his letters. He extolls the importance of the bishop and clergy in his *Epistle to the Trallians* (i.e., Tralles, a city on the Aegean coast in southwest Asia Minor) equating the bishop with the church itself: "Let everyone revere the deacons as Jesus Christ, the bishop as the image of the Father, and the priests as the senate of God, for without them one cannot speak of the church."[74] In his *Epistle to the Ephesians*, he adjured Christians to "regard the bishop as the Lord Himself,"[75] and in Chapters 8 and 9 of his *Epistle to the Smyrnaeans*, he admonished them: "all of you follow the bishop, as Jesus Christ does the Father," to do nothing without the bishop, and "honor God and the bishop."[76]

Almost a century and a half later, Cyprian of Carthage (d. 258) laid out his views of the episcopate, listing qualifications similar to those found in *First Timothy* and the *Apostolical Canons* and echoing Clement in equating the bishop with the church. Cyprian adds that a bishop must not only "be able to teach," but must also learn, "because he who grows daily and profits by learning better things teaches better."[77] He then defined the church in this way: "the people united to their bishop, the flock clinging to its shepherd, are the church…The bishop is in the church and the church is in the bishop, and if anyone is not with the bishop, they are not in the church."[78]

This view of the bishop as the quintessential element of the church remains in both Catholic and Orthodox theology. Since the Truth of Christ is passed on through Apostolic Succession, that is, through the episcopate, the bishop plays an essential role as the "divinely appointed teacher of the faith" in his diocese.[79] The bishop was, and still is, the true dispenser or originating minister of the sacraments in his diocese in both Catholic and Orthodox teaching.[80] The priests and deacons are merely his assistants, dispensing the sacraments only by his authority and permission.

Basil the Great (d. 379) wrote several letters addressed to his *chorepiskopi* (auxiliary bishops of rural districts in the ancient Greek church). His *Epistle 13* forbids them from taking money for ordination,⁸¹ and even though this letter was in its *Kormchie knigi*, the Rus' church allowed such payments until the sixteenth century.

Ecumenical Councils and Local Synods

Much of the material in the *Kormchie knigi* that have come down to us consists of the documents of the first seven ecumenical councils that the Eastern Orthodox churches accept as canonical, as well as a number of local synods or councils that, though not ecumenical, are influential precisely because of their inclusion in Eastern Orthodox canon law. They also include a number of patristic writings, though, admittedly, not all the ones we have touched on. The several conciliar and synodal canons that touch on the episcopate add to our understanding of the Eastern church's conception of the office.⁸²

Thus, the Fifteenth Canon of the First Council of Nicaea and the Second Canon of the First Council of Constantinople forbid bishops from preaching in other dioceses or from moving from town to town.⁸³ The Second Canon of the Council of Chalcedon forbids simony in the ordination of priests.⁸⁴ Incidentally, the local Rus' church Council of Vladimir in 1274 confirmed this proscription,⁸⁵ but allowed bishops to still charge a fee of seven *grivnas*,⁸⁶ which was not considered simoniacal until the 1503 Council of Moscow,⁸⁷ and even then the practice continued. Chalcedon also made it clear that monasteries and alms houses were under the authority of the local bishop and local clergy were to have their cases heard in episcopal rather than secular courts.⁸⁸

Several regional synods addressed the duties of the bishop more extensively. Thus, the Twenty-fourth Canon of the Council of Antioch in Syria (341 AD) repeats the concept of the bishops as models for the laity and archetypes of Christ that we have seen in Clement, Ignatius, and Cyprian. The council declared that "the bishop... is entrusted with the whole people and with the souls of the congregation,"⁸⁹ and that the bishop should be bound to the opinion of the metropolitan, and should do nothing without his knowledge except diocesan matters (similar to Canon 35 of the *Apostolical Canons*). Among their tasks within the diocese, they were admonished to ordain men "free of blame" as priests.[90] The Council of Sardica (Sofia, Bulgaria), held in AD 343 or 344, also saw charitable works as a key component of the office, and decreed: "it is proper that bishops should intercede for persons suffering from violence and oppression, afflicted widows and defrauded orphans, provided, nevertheless, that these persons have a just cause or petition."[91] It adds that if "those who are suffering from injustice or who are condemned for their offenses to deportation or banishment…seek refuge with the mercy of the church, such persons should be succored and pardon be begged for them without hesitation [by the bishop]."[92] The Council of Carthage (AD 419) forbade presbyters (priests) from consecrating the chrism, by which the faithful are chrismated at their baptism (and also later confirmed in the Western church) and priests ordained, or from consecrating virgins, because these were prerogatives of the bishop.[93] It also confirmed the bishop's authority over his priests and anathematized those priests who made a schism against their bishops.[94] If a bishop was accused of wrongdoing well before the next scheduled synod, he was to be tried before twelve bishops.[95] As many bishops as possible were to consecrate a new bishop, but there should be at least three.[96] Once consecrated, a bishop was not to be received in another diocese except by the consent of that diocese's bishop,[97] and he had the right to ordain priests in his diocese whenever he wished.[98] He was to be excommunicated if he neglected his diocese,[99] and he was not to excommunicate others except for grave offenses.[100] The Council of Trullo, also called the Quinisext Council, held in 692 AD, also specified what was to be expected of the bishops; like Cyprian, it saw them as teachers or preachers:

> It behooves those who preside over the churches every day, but especially on the Lord's days, to teach all the clergy and people words of piety and of right religion, gathering out of the holy Scripture meditations and determinations of truth, and not going beyond the limits now fixed, nor varying from the tradition of the God-fearing fathers.[101]

The View of the Bishop in the Rus' Church and the Eparchy

These ancient sources provide a theoretical and canonical basis for understanding the bishop in the Eastern church, even if episcopal theory was never so fully articulated in Rus' as in the medieval West. Admittedly, the availability of the letters of Clement, Ignatius, Cyprian or other Christian writers to the medieval Novgorodians is uncertain. But the point here is not an extensive look at the sources of episcopal theory from Luke or Paul available to the medieval Novgorodians. Rather, the aim is to look at the view of the bishop found in the medieval Rus' church and see where that view came from, either directly (through *sborniki* and various redactions of the *Kormchie knigi*) or indirectly (as source material for those writers who were available in medieval Rus').

Although there is no treatise on the Novgorodian archiepiscopal office, chronicles, letters, and other documents provide some idea of how they thought of their archbishops. On a number of occasions in the chronicles, after an archbishop is elected, dismissed, or died, terms are used to describe the man that are very similar to those in the early Christian sources just reviewed. In 1228, when Archbishop-elect Arsenii was removed from office, the chronicler referred to him as "a modest and gentle man."[102] In 1299, the whole town "great and small" selected as archbishop "the man chosen by God, the good and humble man, the hegumen of the Holy Annunciation [Monastery] named Feoktist."[103] In 1330, Grigorii Kalika was also referred to as "a good and humble man" at his election.[104]

The metropolitans of the Rus' church wrote similarly of the bishop. Kiprian (r. 1381-1406; in Lithuania from 1375; in Moscow 1381-1382 and after March 1390),[105] a Bulgarian whose appointment to the Kyivan Metropolitanate was rejected by Muscovite authorities until 1381 and then again from 1382 to 1389, wrote to St. Sergei of Radonezh and Feodor, hegumen of the Simonovskii Monastery prior to his arrival in Moscow in July 1378:

> I am coming to my son, the grand prince in Moscow; I am coming, bringing peace and blessing as once Joseph was sent by his father to his brothers.[106] Whatever some say about me, I am a bishop, and not

a military man. I bring a blessing as the Lord who sent His disciples to preach, teaching them saying: "He that receiveth you receiveth Me."[107]

Kiprian's successor, Fotii (Photius, r. 1408-1431), a Greek by birth, wrote several letters to Pskov in the summer of 1416 trying to stamp out the *Strigol'niki*, a heretical movement of an uncertain nature; our only sources were written by opponents who quite probably never understood it, since their goal was to destroy, not study, it. Its adherents seem to have opposed fees for the administering of sacraments, which they considered bribery or simony. This complaint had wider implications, though. Opposition to simoniacal clerics cast doubt on the validity of sacraments they administered, the temporal power and authority they held, and the landholdings and other wealth of the church they led. In Pskov, it led to defiance of the Novgorodian archbishop. Patriarch Nilus (r. 1380-1388) had countered the complaint of simony in a 1382 letter to Pskov asserting that the church denounced the sale of church offices or sacraments for money, but that fees collected for ordinations, marriages, and other sacraments were not simony, but, as Aleksei Alekseev explained, were "necessary payment for reimbursement of expenses,"[108] and that "priests have a right to receive income from church services and that this collection of money is not simony."[109]

Metropolitan Fotii also defended payment for ordination, writing that the Byzantine Emperor Isaac Comnenus (r. 1057-1059) had allowed bishops to accept a payment of seven pieces of gold (*zlatnitsa*) for the consecration of a priest, and three for a deacon.[110] In a letter dated September 25, 1416, he supported the condemnation of usury by bishops, priests, and deacons expressed in the *Apostolical Canons* and elsewhere.[111] But in another letter sent that same day, he quoted a veritable litany of canons in defense of episcopal authority (in the face of Pskov's defiance of the Novgorodian archbishops): the Thirty-first Canon of the *Apostolical Canons* which ordered that a member of the clergy or laity who opposed his bishop unjustly was to be defrocked (in the case of the clergy) or suspended (i.e., excommunicated, in the case of the laity);[112] the *Fifth Canon* of Antioch that forbade the clergy from heading private assemblies (breaking from the established church) without the consent of their bishop;[113] the alleged Thirteenth Canon "of the first and second councils," which, according to Fotii, commanded that heretics, who "sprout up like tares" among the wheat,[114] "be excommunicated and imprisoned until they mend their ways and are obedient to their bishop;"[115] the Sixth Canon of the Council of Gangra which anathematized those who took "the fruits of the church" and gave them out without the bishop's permission,[116] and the Tenth Canon of Carthage, which forbade a priest from celebrating the divine liturgy or erecting an altar without episcopal consent.[117] He went on to quote St. Isidor of Pelusium, who defended the physical church, saying church buildings existed to save souls, not for worldly things,[118] and John Chrysostom's eleventh homily on the Letter to the Ephesians, in which he asserts that "even the blood of martyrdom cannot wipe away this sin" of those "who create a church heresy" (*raskolenie tserkovnoe tvoriashchikh*).[119] Both these texts had been available in Slavic translation since the ninth or tenth centuries.[120]

Thus, the metropolitan supported the local bishop and clergy against anti-clericalism and attacks on their temporal power, but also pointed to the ideal or theoretical view of the clergy – bishop, priest, and deacon – that the Rus' church held at the time, based on centuries of biblical, patristic, and conciliar texts. Fotii's use of these sources indicates their availability (or at least Fotii's assumption that they were available) in the Novgorodian eparchy. His remarks, and those of Kiprian before him, and of the Novgorodians in their chronicle, show us something of how the church at the time viewed their bishops. The rest of this book takes this as a starting point and examines what happened in actual practice.

CHAPTER TWO
The Archbishops and the Russian Church

3. Relief from the lid of the wooden casket of Il'ia/Ioann, dated 1559: from the Cathedral of Holy Wisdom, now in the Russian Museum, St Petersburg.

Introduction

Christianity existed in Rus' for several generations before an organized church or episcopate was formed.[1] According to chronicle accounts of early Rus', with the Baptism of 988 the official church was established and, with it, Christianity as an organized culture in Rus' came into being. The church hierarchy, canon law, doctrines – including the views of the role and behavior of the bishop – and other religious and ecclesiastical elements were, by this account, brought in from Byzantium and grafted onto Rus'. Thus, the *Lavrenteskaia Letopis'* claims that immediately after the Baptism, Prince Vladimir "began to found churches and to assign priests throughout the cities, and to invite the people to accept baptism in all the cities and towns."[2] Several later chronicles claim he established ten bishoprics, including in Novgorod (anachronistically referred to as an archbishopric even before 1165).[3] He then petitioned Byzantine Emperor Basil II Boulgaroktonos ("the Bulgar-slayer") (r. 976-1025), who sent him Byzantine bishops, priests, and deacon, to run those eparchies.⁴ Thus, according to these chronicles, the Kyiv metropolis (ecclesiastical province) was established under the Patriarchate of Constantinople and the Rus' episcopate came into being, including the office of bishop of Novgorod.⁵

Ioakim Korsunianin, the first bishop of Novgorod, would have been among those Byzantine bishops sent to Prince Vladimir in Kyiv and then dispatched to Novgorod and the other bishoprics. His surname points to ties to the Byzantine city of Korsun (Chersonesus or Cherson) on the Crimea where, according to several chronicles, Vladimir was baptized.⁶

However, the very early history of the Kyivan metropolitanate, and of these first Rus' bishoprics, is murky. According to some sources, Mikhail the Syrian, the first Kyivan metropolitan, only served about three years (988-991), and it was only under his successor, Leontii (r. 992-1008), that the bishops were sent out to their eparchies.⁷ It is not certain when Ioakim Korsunianin arrived in Novgorod,⁸ where, it is said, he built the first (wooden) Cathedral of Holy Wisdom "with thirteen tops" (cupolas)⁹ on the site of a pagan burial ground, thus superseding pagan rites and holy spaces with Christian ones, a not uncommon practice by Christian missionaries.¹⁰ He is said to have built other churches too, including the wooden Church of Ioakim and Anne, named for the grandparents of Jesus and his own patron saints (and where he and his successor, Luka Zhidiata,¹¹ are said to have been buried), and the churches of the Perun Monastery, south of the city, the first monastery in the Novgorodian Land.

But, again, all this is murky, and a number of scholars argue that the establishment of the church in 988 is largely legendary. Mikhail Priselkov wrote of "The Korsun Legend," arguing that the Byzantine-led church was never established under Vladimir. He argued, instead, that the church at the time of Vladimir was created from Bulgaria, not Constantinople, and it was only under Iaroslav Vladimirovich in the 1030s – after the fall of the First Bulgarian Empire – that a Byzantine hierarchy was brought into Rus' and a metropolis under the Patriarchate of Constantinople established.¹²

As for Novgorod, there is archaeological evidence that the cathedral was, indeed, built on a pagan site, but there is no archaeological evidence for the wooden cathedral or the church of Ioakim and Anne, and very little evidence of Ioakim Korsunianin aside from references to him in the chronicles. He was said to have been succeeded by Efrem, (though Efrem was apparently never bishop, but led the eparchy for five years until Luka arrived, then apparently left Novgorod.) Ioakim's and Luka's remains were said to have been transferred to the current cathedral, though archaeologists question whether the remains traditionally identified as Luka's are, in fact, his.[13]

If the Byzantine-led church was not established until half a century later than the earliest Kyivan and Novgorodian chronicles claim, then Luka, rather than Ioakim, was Novgorod's first bishop. But even then, we still know very little of him or much else about the early Novgorodian church. Stefan, Feodor, and German are little more than names on a list, historically speaking (though German has hagiographic writings about him).[14]

From these rather opaque beginnings, the Novgorodian eparchy did not stand out markedly from the others; we know almost nothing of them either. And this was the case in Novgorod for almost two centuries. It was somewhat remarkable in being the first eparchy headed by a native of Rus', Luka, but it was only when Metropolitan Ioann raised the office to the archiepiscopal dignity in 1165,[15] and Novgorod grew in economic, political, and cultural influence, that the office and the eparchy really began to stand out and our sources become somewhat clearer and more plentiful. The office remained the only archbishopric in the Rus' church up to the late fourteenth century.[16]

The Title of Archbishop in the Orthodox Church

The archiepiscopal title set Novgorod's prelates apart from the other bishops in Rus' though scholars have debated the precise meaning of the title. Understanding the title as it was used and understood in the Rus' church is, however, more than mere academic hair-splitting, since it helps determine the place of Novgorod's archbishops within the wider Rus' church. The title has sometimes been seen as granting independence to the Novgorodian church, and if this were true it would fundamentally change our understanding of the office, the eparchy, and the Kyivan province.

But the title did not grant independence. The misperception that it did is perhaps due to a greater understanding of and more extensive sources on the Western episcopate, where archbishops usually headed ecclesiastical provinces made up of several dioceses headed by (suffragan) bishops subordinate to them. Western archbishops were, and still are, what the Orthodox refer to as metropolitans. (Indeed, both are technically called "metropolitan-archbishops"). In the Orthodox church, however, the title of archbishop often meant something different, as it can on rare instances in the West. In the medieval Orthodox church, the title of archbishop commonly denoted a bishop who was "by special arrangement...exempt from the jurisdiction of the provincial metropolitan and depend[ent] directly on a patriarch: they were given the title of autocephalous archbishop,"[17] but did not have suffragan bishops. This definition has led Russian historians like Evgenii Golubinskii to argue that Novgorod's archbishops were autonomous from the metropolitan in Kyiv, answering directly to the patriarch of Constantinople.[18] Emil Herman concluded that *all* archbishops in the Orthodox church were autocephalous,[19] and Valentin Ianin argued that the inscription on the seal of Bishop Ioann Pop'ian (r. 1110-1130) showed the autocephalous status of Novgorod, in relation to both Kyiv and Constantinople, even before the creation of the archiepiscopate in 1165.[20]

Iaroslav Shchapov, however, clarified that there were two types of archbishops in the Eastern church:

> The title was well known in the Christian church, being granted to those episcopal sees which by virtue of historical conditions or some special relationship with the patriarchate were not subordinate to the geographically closest metropolitan and came directly under the hand of the patriarch. The enumeration of twelfth-century archbishoprics lists forty to fifty sees that possessed this advantage. But neither these nor later enumerations listed Novgorod as an archbishopric because the only Rus' archbishopric was merely titular, an honorary archbishopric, whose relationship with superior centers did not relieve it of subordination to Kyiv.[21]

These two types of archbishops in the Byzantine church exacerbate the confusion over the title: originally the archiepiscopal title designated certain metropolitans who presided over the most important sees in the empire, such as Rome, Alexandria, and Antioch. In this way the patriarch of Constantinople is still formally "The Archbishop of Constantinople, the New Rome, and Ecumenical Patriarch."[22] The title was associated with ecclesiastical autocephaly, and was thus later applied to autocephalous ecclesiastics, such as the primate of Cyprus. Such titular archbishops,[23] not dependent on any metropolitan but only on the patriarch, were elected by the patriarch and the *endemousa synodus*, or council of bishops, in Constantinople, and ranked below a metropolitan. However, in addition to the numerous autocephalous or titular archbishops, other important bishops, such as at Ephesus, Thessalonica, Caesarea in Cappadocia, and Athens, were also called archbishops, even though they remained answerable to their metropolitans.[24] The Novgorodian archbishop was this latter type, honored with the title but still always subordinate to his metropolitan.

In discussing modern Eastern Orthodoxy, Timothy Ware, (Kallistos, after taking monastic vows), writing in the 1960s, pointed out another source of confusion in the titulature of the Eastern church, namely that the terms "metropolitan" and "archbishop" were transposed in the Byzantine church from the medieval period to the present:

> Originally a metropolitan was the bishop of the capital of a province, while archbishop was a more general title of honor, given to patriarchs and bishops of special eminence. The Russians still use the titles more or less in the original way; but the Greeks at present give the name metropolitan to *every* diocesan bishop, and call by the title archbishop those who in ancient times would have been styled metropolitan. Thus, among the Greeks an archbishop now ranks above a metropolitan, but among the Russians the metropolitan is the higher position.[25]

Chronicles and other documents show that Novgorod's archepiscopal title was "a more general title of honor" and the

Novgorodian eparchy remained under the metropolitan of Kyiv at all times during the medieval period. Thus, in 1270, Metropolitan Kirill III sent a letter to Novgorod after they had recently dismissed Prince Iaroslav Iaroslavich (1230-1272, Prince of Novgorod r. 1255, 1264-1267, 1269-1272), telling the Novgorodians "God has made me [metropolitan-] archbishop[26] of the Rus' lands and you are to listen to God and to me."[27] The letters of Metropolitans Kiprian and Fotii and the visit by the Archbishop Dionisii of Suzdal' to Novgorod on behalf of the metropolitan and the patriarch, cited in the previous chapter, are further evidence that Novgorod remained part of the Kyivan metropolitanate (as did Rostov, which by that time also had an archbishop.)

Another misconception is that the archiepiscopal title made Novgorod's prelates second in power after the metropolitans, the metropolitans' *namestniki* (vicars) or *protothronoi*, or the next-in-line for the metropolitan throne.[28] The Rus' church had a very simple, three-tier episcopal structure consisting of the Patriarch of Constantinople, the Metropolitan of Kyiv and the archbishops and bishops subordinate to Kyiv. None of the archbishops, in Novgorod, Suzdal', Rostov, or elsewhere in Rus' ever oversaw suffragan bishops or provinces of their own. There were no known hierarchical rules or divisions of power or jurisdiction beyond the simple hierarchy of the metropolitan and the archbishops and bishops under him. Several scholars contend that the bishops of Iur'ev and Bilhorod, near Kyiv, were the metropolitan's vicars (*namestniki*), rather than the archbishops of Novgorod, and that they carried out the metropolitan's duties in his absence or during a vacant see.[29] This did not really place them above their fellow bishops when the metropolitan was present and was not a hierarchical distinction but rather a way of providing practical administrative continuity in the metropolitan's absence.

The Archbishops and the Metropolitans

The Novgorodian archbishops' subordination to the metropolitans in Kyiv, Vladimir, or Moscow did not mean that relationship was always smooth. After the Mongol conquest, the Novgorodian archbishops gained a considerable degree of *de facto* autonomy from the metropolitan, and, through the *veche* or sortition,³⁰ the archeparchy came to choose its own archbishop from among local candidates beginning in the twelfth century, rather than having the metropolitan or grand prince appoint someone and send them to Novgorod, as had been the practice up to that time. And while the metropolitans officially rejected episcopal appointment by lay officials (which would include the *veche*) in documents sent to the city in 1224 and 1395, the practice continued until the Muscovite conquest.

The archbishops were formally subordinate to the metropolitans and went to the metropolitan for consecration, but beyond this, there is surprisingly little interaction between the metropolitans and archbishops in the sources. Five Kyivan metropolitans visited Novgorod a total of nine times in the two centuries between the Mongol Invasion and 1448. Conversely, only seven of the twenty-one archbishops traveled to the metropolitans for reasons other than their own consecration. Beyond this, there are a few letters exchanged between the metropolitans and archbishops that have survived. Though scant, it does confirm the Novgorodian archbishops continued subordination to the Metropolitans of Kyiv and All Rus', even if that relationship was strained at times, and, by the 1350s, Novgorod did seek autonomy under the direct control of Constantinople, though that was never granted.

Luka, Nifont, and the Defense of Canon Law and Tradition

The first clash between Novgorod and the metropolitan predates the archiepiscopate by more than a century. The Younger Redaction of the *Novgorodian First Chronicle* reports that in 1051 "Iaroslav placed Larion (Hilarion) as Metropolitan of Rus' in [The Cathedral of] Holy Wisdom [in Kyiv], in agreement with the bishops,"³¹ but there is no indication that Novgorod, or any other Rus' bishopric, opposed this uncanonical appointment (since it was not made by the patriarch).³² Indeed, Aleksandr Khoroshev argues that Luka was clearly among the bishops who agreed to Hilarion's appointment.³³ After Hilarion, Efrem was appointed metropolitan around 1055.³⁴ That same year, Luka's slave, Dudika, denounced him and Efrem called Luka to Kyiv and condemned him, imprisoning him for three years, only to release him in 1058 when the denunciation was determined to be slanderous. The details of the slanderous denunciation are never explained; the Novgorodian chronicles merely report that "Archbishop (sic) Luka took [back] his seat in Novgorod and his authority (*oblast'*)"; Dudika was punished by having his nose and both his hands cut off, after which he fled to the Germans.[35] Khoroshev saw Luka's three-year detention at the hands of Metropolitan Efrem's as a "harbinger" of Novgorod's later autocephalous or autonomous tendencies,[36] though there is no way of knowing how Luka (or Novgorod) felt about this, since he died along the Kopys River in modern Belarus on October 15, 1060 on the trip back to Novgorod.[37]

His successor, Bishop Stepan, visited Kyiv in 1068, where he was "strangled by his slaves."[38] In 1095, Bishop German "went to Kyiv and died there."[39] Khoroshev suggests the deaths of these three in a 35-year span, may have been the result of what he calls "Byzantine methods" tied to their stay in Kyiv, that is, efforts by the metropolitan or grand prince to get rid of troublesome Novgorodian prelates.[40]

Khoroshev's conclusions are possible, and the deaths of three of four Novgorodian bishops between 1060 and 1095 either in or en route from Kyiv are not beyond suspicion, but we have no real evidence to support such a conclusion. The sources give no indication that Luka opposed the appointments of either Hilarion or Efrem, that he was arrested for this reason, or that he, Stepan, or German succumbed to any "Byzantine methods" for opposing the Kyivan secular or ecclesiastical authorities. Almost nothing is said of Stepan or German at all, in fact. The chronicles merely indicate that these bishops died, one by murder – and there is no indication his slaves were working on anyone's behalf – and the other two in or on the road from Kyiv. Luka and German were probably not in the prime of life (nor was Stepan for that matter). Luka had been bishop in Novgorod for twenty-five years and was not likely young when appointed to that office; he had been imprisoned for three years in Kyiv and only released shortly before his journey, and depending on the harshness of his imprisonment, might have been in poor health. We simply don't know.

Much more is said of Nifont in the sources. And this time

we know that his visit to Kyiv almost a hundred years later (1149-1150) was over the disputed consecration of the Kyivan metropolitan. Metropolitan Klim Smoliatich (or Kliment, that is, Clement), had been uncanonically appointed metropolitan by Grand Prince Iziaslav "with the bishops of the Rus' province,"[41] rather than by the patriarch and the episcopal council in Constantinople – just like Hilarion during Luka Zhidiata's episcopate. The *Novgorodian First Chronicle* relates that Nifont, having been summoned to Kyiv by the grand prince and the metropolitan, confronted Klim, saying "you were not fittingly appointed for you were neither blessed nor appointed by the great council (in Constantinople)."[42] For defending canon law and refusing to accept Klim, the metropolitan (and the grand prince) confined Nifont in the Kyiv Caves Monastery,[43] the chronicle noting that they "did not hurry to acquit him."[44] He was released when Prince Iurii Dolgorukii took Kyiv in July 1149, at which point Grand Prince Iziaslav fled to Volodymyr and took Klim with him.[45] Nifont returned to Novgorod in 1150 "and the Novgorodians were happy."[46] The *Novgorodian First Chronicle* reports that he died on April 21, 1156 and was buried in the Kyiv Caves Monastery. Immediately after that, it says he had gone to Kyiv "against the Metropolitan,"[47] meaning Klim, even though Patriarch Constantine IV Chliarenis (r. 1154-1156) had consecrated Konstantin (r.1155-1159) as Metropolitan of Kyiv in the autumn of 1155. Nifont went to Kyiv to await the new metropolitan with other bishops who opposed Klim (who was still ensconced in Volynia), but died before Konstantin's arrival.[48] For his defense of patriarchal prerogatives, Patriarch Nicholas IV Mouzalon sent charters elevating Nifont to the archiepiscopal dignity.[49]

Khoroshev argues that Nifont's confrontation with Klim was part of a concerted effort by the Novgorodian church to gain autocephaly.[50] However, Nifont's behavior can just as easily be interpreted as that of a defender of church unity, whereas Iziaslav's appointment of Klim was actually destroying that unity. Indeed, Khoroshev lists Nifont, along with the bishops of Smolensk and Polatsk, as constituting an anti-Iziaslav party opposed to the grand prince's efforts to create an autocephalous church in Rus'.[51] Despite this, and his citing Patriarch Nicholas Muzalon's decree granting Nifont the archiepiscopal title in gratitude for his support against

Iziaslav's autocephalous tendencies,⁵² Khoroshev still asserts Nifont (and Novgorod) sought autocephaly from Kyiv in the 1140s.⁵³

But Nifont was defending canon law and tradition in the face of the canonical illicit actions by the Kyivan grand princes and their chosen metropolitans.⁵⁴ Canon Twenty-eight of the Council of Chalcedon (AD 451) specifically grants the Patriarch of Constantinople the right to ordain or consecrate metropolitans in three Roman Dioceses:

> ...in the Pontic, the Asian, and the Thracian dioceses, the metropolitans only and such bishops as of the Dioceses aforesaid as are among the barbarians, should be ordained by the aforesaid most holy throne of the most holy church of Constantinople; every metropolitan of the aforesaid dioceses, together with the bishops of his province, ordaining his own provincial bishops, as has been declared by the divine canons; but that, as has been above said, the metropolitans of the aforesaid Dioceses should be ordained by the archbishop of Constantinople, after proper elections have been held according to customs and have been reported to him.⁵⁵

These three provinces were just west of Constantinople and just across the Bosporus and along the southern coast of the Black Sea in Anatolia, but as Christianity spread in the East, the prerogative came to be exercised in other, newly established ecclesiastical provinces in the Balkans and, after 988, in Rus'. Nifont knew this and stood not for Novgorodian autocephaly or autonomy, but for the maintenance of church law over the uncanonical actions of the grand prince.

From the Disputed Archiepiscopate (1210-1229) to the Death of Vasilii Kalika

The next major dispute occurred some six decades later, when the Novgorodians sent Archbishops Mitrofan and Antonii to the metropolitan in 1219, asking him to solve the problem of which one was rightful archbishop. In January 1211, Mitrofan had been unceremoniously thrown out of office and driven out of Novgorod to Toropets, and Antonii had been named bishop by Prince Mstislav the Daring and the Novgorodians and sent to Kyiv for consecration.[56] In 1218, Mitrofan returned "from Vladimir"[57] and was escorted to the Church of the Annunciation, possibly at the Arkazhskii Monastery south of the Sofia Side of the city.[58] The next year, Antonii left Novgorod but later came back and ensconced himself in the Church of the Savior on the Nereditsa, south of the Trade Side of the city, while Mitrofan was brought back as archbishop.[59] The prince and the Novgorodians then told the two rivals to go to the metropolitan to have him decide who was the rightful archbishop. Metropolitan Matfei ruled in Mitrofan's favor and sent Antonii to serve as bishop of Peremyshl' (Przemyśl).[60]

There is little indication of contact between the metropolitans and the archbishops again until the second half of the thirteenth century when, in the wake of the Mongol Invasion, two metropolitans visited Novgorod, each of them twice. Metropolitan Kirill III (r. 1242-1281)[61] visited in 1251 and 1256. On the first occasion, he consecrated Dalmat as archbishop in the Cathedral of Holy Wisdom;[62] in 1256, he arrived with Grand Prince Aleksandr Nevskii and remained in Novgorod while Aleksandr marched against the Yem, a Finnic tribe often at war with Novgorod, but the nature of his visit is otherwise unexplained.[63] Metropolitan Maksim (r. 1283-1305) visited Novgorod in 1285 and 1300. *The Novgorodian First* and *Novgorodian Fourth Chronicles* merely state that Maksim visited the city in 1285.[64] However, in 1300, he arrived with several other bishops and consecrated Feoktist as archbishop; the *znamenanie* or *narechenie* (appointment) was held in the Church of Boris and Gleb, and the consecration itself (*khirotoniia* – from Greek for "laying on of hands") in the Cathedral of Holy Wisdom.[65] A generation later, Moisei went to Moscow to be consecrated but was also at the funeral of Grand Prince Iurii Danilovich along with Metropolitan Petr, and bishops Varsonofii of Tver', Prokhor of Rostov, and Grigorii of Riazan'.[66] His relationship with Petr was short-lived since the metropolitan died the following year.[67]

Petr's successor, Metropolitan Feognost (r. 1328-1353), seems to have had a generally positive relationship with both Moisei (at least during his first tenure (1325-1330)) and Vasilii Kalika. He came to Novgorod in 1329, two years after the Tver' Uprising against the Tatars, and while there, excommunicated Pskov for harboring Grand Prince Aleksandr Mikhailovich (Prince of Novgorod r. 1325-1327; Prince of Tver', 1326-1327 and 1338-1339; Grand Prince of Vladimir, 1327), who had either led the uprising or not done enough in the Tatars' eyes to suppress it.[68] Moisei seems to have supported Feognost's decision – or at least there is no evidence he opposed it – but Vasilii Kalika was godfather to Aleksandr's son, Mikhail, brought him to Novgorod in 1341, and taught him to read and write, an act that could indicate tacit support for Aleksandr and Pskov, or even opposition to Moscow, though Vasilii's several visits to Feognost do not suggest hostility between the two men.[69] Besides being consecrated by Feognost in Volodymyr in 1331,[70] Vasilii traveled there to meet him again in 1334, although the chronicles do not give us any details of this visit.[71] Feognost himself visited Novgorod in 1341 "with many people," but the chronicler less-positively reported that "the feeding and gifts weighed heavily on the *Vladyka* and the monasteries" which had to support the metropolitan and his retinue while in the city.[72] Furthermore, the archbishops often lost the ecclesiastical court fees during a metropolitan's visit, since the metropolitan could adjudicate cases while in the city and received the fees from them.[73] Thus, Novgorod had to pay twice, once for the metropolitan's upkeep and twice in lost revenues from the ecclesiastical courts. We will visit the problem of ecclesiastical court fees again later.

Feognost seems to have maintained generally good relations with both of the men who sat on the archiepiscopal throne during his metropolitanate. When Vasilii went to Moscow in 1346 to accompany Grand Prince Simeon to his enthronement as prince of Novgorod, Feognost presented him with the gift of a *polystaurion* (*polystavriia* or *kreshchataia riza* in Russian),[74] a special *phelonion* (*felon* in Russian) – a liturgical cloak or chasuble covered with crosses.[75] The *polystaurion* was, according to John Meyendorff, "a privilege bestowed [by the patriarch] upon distinguished Byzantine prelates only," though he added in a footnote: "It appears, however, that in the fourteenth century a larger number of Byzantine ecclesiastical officials were granted this distinction and included dignitaries of the patriarchate without episcopal rank."[76] The *polystaurion*, therefore, was not necessarily a symbol of episcopal or archiepiscopal power, but was a significant sign of patriarchal favor.[77] That Metropolitan Feognost, and not the patriarch, gave the *polystaurion* to Vasilii,[78] the first Novgorodian archbishop so honored, indicates that it was not strictly in keeping with the Byzantine tradition. Although the patriarch may have granted Feognost, a Byzantine, the right to bestow it on suitable candidates in Rus'. The metropolitan might also have just taken the tradition and started using it in the Rus' church, although the fact that Patriarch Philotheus Kokkinos (r. 1353-1354, 1354, 1364-1376) mentioned it in a July 1354 letter to Archbishop Moisei would indicate at least tacit approval of the practice.[79] Its mention by the chronicle clearly indicates that it was an important, symbolic, gift. But it is important to note that the *polystaurion* was a personal privilege and did not extend to the office itself, since Philotheus reprimanded Archbishop Moisei for wearing it without permission after he returned to office following Vasilii's death in 1352.[80] Moisei obediently discontinued wearing it, waiting another two years before the patriarch granted him the privilege.[81]

Worsening Archiepiscopal-Metropolitan Relations after 1352

The death of Vasilii Kalika in 1352 seems to have been a turning point in the relationship between the archbishops and the metropolitans, with Novgorod apparently seeking autonomy from the Kyivan metropolitan twice in the next forty years. In 1353, Archbishop Moisei sent emissaries to Constantinople asking for the blessings of the emperor and the patriarch and complaining about "improper matters" Metropolitan Feognost had forced upon Moisei.[82] What those were is unclear, but we know Philotheus awarded a *polystaurion* to Moisei. Some scholars suggest Moisei demanded to be removed from the metropolitan's jurisdiction and the gift was a sop. Philotheus did not remove Novgorod from the Kyivan province and since Metropolitan Feognost had died the year before, Moisei's complaint would have been moot. But the incident indicates souring relations between Novgorod and the metropolitan. It is unclear if Moisei was on any better terms with Feognost's successor, Aleksei. Aleksandr Presniakov argues that Moisei rejected

Aleksei's appointment, or at least failed to send a letter to the patriarch acknowledging Aleksei as worthy of the office.[83] However, the absence of records may merely indicate the loss of historical source material over the centuries, rather than poor relations between Aleksei and Moisei.

Moisei's successor, Aleksei, seems not to have had very warm relations with his namesake either, suggesting that Presniakov may have been on to something and the archbishops may have been trying to stay at arm's length from the metropolitans and from Muscovite grand princes as well. In June 1370, Philotheus sent a letter to Archbishop Aleksei reproaching him for wearing the *polystaurion*, stating that it was an honor that could not be worn by any bishop or archbishop, but only by those on whom the privilege had been conferred. To do otherwise was not only inappropriate, but was canonically illegal and risked excommunication. This is similar to what Moisei had done in 1352, but what is more important for us is that, in the letter, the patriarch threatened excommunication not only for Aleksei's arrogating the *polystaurion* privilege when it had not been granted to him, but also for his disobedience toward the metropolitan and Grand Prince Dmitrii Ivanovich (Donskoi) (r. 1359-1389) of Moscow.[84]

How bad things got in the next several years is, as is often the case in the Rus' sources, debatable. The *Moskovskii letopisnii svod* tells us that rather abruptly that in 1376, Archbishop Aleksei retired to the Derevianitsa Monastery and the Novgorodians sent a delegation of boiars to Metropolitan Aleksei (r. 1354-1378) in Moscow to bring the archbishop back to the throne.[85] That August, Archbishop Aleksei went with several boiars and the archimandrite to Metropolitan Aleksei in Moscow, and remained two weeks, but the chronicles are again silent on the details of the meetings.[86] It seems that the archbishop's retirement was sour grapes at something the metropolitan had, or was perceived to have, done, since after the metropolitan complied with their request and sent his blessings, Archbishop Aleksei quit the monastery and returned to the archiepiscopate. The Moscow visit may have been related to his abortive retirement earlier in the year; he may have been angry that he did not receive a *polystaurion*. Or he may have tired of the office and wanted to go live a monk's life but was somehow persuaded to come back. The laconic nature of the sources offers little from which to draw firm conclusions..

There are other possibilities. The *Novgorodian Fourth Chronicle* mentions that several clergymen – *Strigol'niki* heretics – were thrown from the great bridge in Novgorod right before mentioning Archbishops Aleksei's visit to Moscow, so he may have gone to consult on the matter of heresy in the eparchy.[87] Or the visit might have had something to do with the appearance of Metropolitan Kiprian in Lithuania in 1375. Metropolitan Aleksei may have wanted to make it clear that Novgorod was under his, not Kiprian's, jurisdiction, but the chronicles are silent on what the two Alekseis discussed, other than to say that the metropolitan blessed the archbishop and sent him back to Novgorod. The *Novgorodian First Chronicle* mentions Kiprian at the end of the entry for 1376, after Archbishop Aleksei's summertime visit to Moscow, when he sent letters to Novgorod announcing his metropolitanate.[88] The Muscovite chronicle mentions his consecration in Constantinople in December, his arrival in Lithuania, and his missives to Novgorod. But, again, the two sources are silent on what the two prelates discussed in Moscow that August.[89]

Metropolitan Kiprian and Novgorod

Metropolitan relations with Novgorod grew markedly worse with Kiprian's arrival in Rus'. Much of his metropolitanate was a struggle for recognition from either the grand prince in Moscow or the church in Novgorod. It was a sad situation for one of the most energetic and capable churchmen of the fourteenth and fifteenth centuries who did much for the Rus' church despite great hardships: he brought a number of important texts from Constantinople and the Balkans, under his auspices a number of important ecclesiastical and literary works were translated or compiled, and he wrote several himself.[90] But he met serious resistance when he visited Novgorod in 1391 and again in 1395. In fact, a sharp clash occurred almost immediately after Patriarch Philotheus appointed Kiprian to the Lithuanian metropolitanate in December 1375.[91] Upon arriving in the north, Kiprian sent letters to Novgorod informing Archbishop Aleksei and the Novgorodians that he had been canonically elected and consecrated as metropolitan. Aleksei and the Novgorodians told him to send word to Moscow.[92] This has been interpreted as a rejection of both Kiprian and of Novgorodian subservience to the local metropolitan. However, it may have been neither of these. Rather, it was a rejection of Kiprian's personal authority over Novgorod since Kiprian had been named metropolitan of Lithuania, with the understanding that he was to take over as metropolitan of Kyiv and All Rus' upon Metropolitan Aleksei's death. Aleksei was still very much alive in 1375. Thus, Novgorod was not denying Kiprian's rights as a metropolitan of Lithuania or denying that they were subservient to a metropolitan; they were just arguing that Novgorod was not part of the ecclesiastical province of Lithuania, but rather of Kyiv, and as such they answered to Aleksei, not Kiprian.[93]

But after Aleksei's death,[94] Kiprian was still not accepted in Moscow, and instead Grand Prince Dmitrii named another metropolitan, Pimen, leading Kiprian to excommunicate the grand prince and his advisers.[95] Novgorod initially did not accept Pimen either; in 1385 he too was denied the right to receive appeals against the judgments of the archbishop of Novgorod and the lucrative court fees associated with them. During Lent 1385, the Novgorodian *posadnik, tysiatskie,* and all the boiars, *zhitye liudi, chernye liudi,* and all five *kontsy* of the city swore an oath (*tselovanie*) "at the *veche* at the prince's court" (the *Iaroslavovo Dvorishche*) to not allow appeals to the metropolitan, making the archbishop's ecclesiastical court the highest appellate court in the archeparchy.[96] Three years later, Archbishop Aleksei retired; the chronicler asserts he did so of his own free will,[97] though there are scholars who interpret this as Aleksei being forced out by a pro-Muscovite faction in the city, since Novgorod seems to have accepted Pimen because it sent Archbishop-elect Ioann II to be consecrated by him in Moscow (January 17, 1389). The metropolitan threw him a feast with Grand Prince Dmitrii in attendance, but the relationship soured considerably after Grand Prince Vasilii I took the throne and Kiprian was finally allowed to take the metropolitan throne in Moscow.[98] In fact, almost the entire first decade of Ioann's archiepiscopate, and Kiprian's metropolitanate in Moscow, were taken up with the crisis over the metropolitan's rights in Novgorod.

Dmitrii Donskoi died in 1389 and that same year Kiprian

traveled to Constantinople to meet the new patriarch, Antony IV (r. 1389-1390 and 1391-1397) and obtain a letter addressed to Novgorod requiring compliance with the tradition of the metropolitan sitting in judgment in Novgorod for a set period and collecting the court fees there.[99] Kiprian arrived in Moscow on March 6, 1390.[100] In the winter of 1391, he and the bishop of Riazan' were welcomed in Novgorod by Ioann and the hegumens of the Novgorodian monasteries, who met him with crosses and held a procession as was Novgorod's custom toward dignitaries visiting the city. The metropolitan and his entourage stayed two weeks, but despite Ioann's welcome (the insistence that he did welcome the metropolitan may just be a chronicler trying to exonerate the archbishop from culpability in defying the metropolitan), Kiprian was again denied the right to hold court in Novgorod. Posadnik Timofei Iur'evich and Tysiatskii Mikita Feodorovich "and all Novgorod" insisted that they had a charter exempting Novgorod from metropolitan jurisdiction over its church courts.[101] Who granted them this charter is unknown – it could merely mean the above-mentioned oath taken at the *veche* in Lent 1385 – but Kiprian apparently felt it illegal and left town "holding no love for Novgorod the Great."[102] In fact, he excommunicated the archbishop and the entire city. Novgorod responded by dispatching an embassy to the patriarch in 1392. The *Novgorodian Fourth Chronicle* merely states that Antony told them to "obey the Metropolitan of Rus',"[103] but Antony, in fact, replied with two letters in September 1393.[104] In one, he explained "we [the patriarch] hear this from you: 'we [the Novgorodians] will go over to the Latins.'"[105] He confirmed the excommunication and reasserted the metropolitan's authority over Novgorod.[106]

The whole conflict with Kiprian after his acceptance in Moscow is inexorably tied up in the politics of the period and was not just an obstreperous Novgorodian church opposing its rightful metropolitan, nor was Novgorod simply greedy to keep the money from court cases. At the time, the Muscovite grand princes were encroaching on the Novgorodian fur-bearing lands in the Northern Dvina basin, and thus Kiprian's quite legitimate effort to assert his rights in Novgorod was apparently seen as yet more encroachment by Moscow and was thus fervently opposed to the point of Novgorod suffering excommunication for it. Grand Prince Vasilii

I (r. 1389-1425) apparently saw the Novgorodians' actions as a denial not only of Moscow's ecclesiastical authority, but even of his political overlordship over the city, and thus he "broke the peace with Novgorod over the charter which Novgorod the Great had concluded not to be summoned by the metropolitan in Moscow."[107] It is interesting that the chronicle gives this as the direct cause of the war that broke out in 1393.[108] How much of this was heartfelt support for the legitimate rights of the church and indignation that the Novgorodians did not "Fear God...[and] honor the emperor,"[109] and how much of it was just a pretext to grab the fur-rich Dvina Lands Moscow had coveted since at least the reign of his father, is impossible to say; so often actions have more than one cause. But this was the beginning of the downward slide in political and ecclesiastical relations between Novgorod and Moscow that culminated in Novgorod's conquest 85 years later.

The war went back and forth; Vasilii took the city of Torzhok, and the districts of Volokolamsk and Vologda, "and ravaged many districts," while the Novgorodians "took Ustiug, Ustiuzhna, and many other districts from the grand prince," before the Novgorodians "not wishing to see more bloodshed between Christians," relented and turned over the charter to the metropolitan. Kiprian then absolved them of this (alleged) sin and blessed them, lifting the ban of excommunication from the city.[110]

But when he went to Novgorod in 1395, this time with patriarchal envoys, Kiprian was still denied his right to sit in judgment and collect the fee. He remained all autumn trying to exercise his right but to no avail, although he was honored by Archbishop Ioann and, despite their disobedience, blessed the archbishop and the city.[111] His spring 1395 letter to the Novgorodian clergy on liturgical practices suggests a more positive relationship with Novgorod,[112] but when he called Ioann to Moscow in 1396, Ioann stayed just two days.[113] The brevity of Ioann's visit seems to suggest that all was not well and the chronicler, in focusing on the honor and blessing that Ioann received, may yet again have been glossing over a failed effort by Kiprian to regain his right of jurisdiction or smooth over relations with Ioann and the city. It is hard to imagine that Ioann would have made such a journey lasting several days or weeks, to remain just two days. It seems, rather, that this visit must have been part of ongoing negotiations to resolve the crisis, or that some dispute occurred in Moscow leading to Ioann's sudden departure. Kiprian sent emissaries to Novgorod in 1397 and later that year Ioann traveled again to Moscow after the metropolitan's *stolnik*, Kliment, came to Novgorod to summon him: "Come to Moscow: your father, the metropolitan, calls you on episcopal business" (*o sviatitel'skikh delekh*).[114] The events leading up to 1397 and the political events of that year (Vasilii had sent his boiars into the Dvina Land), however, would tend to indicate it was more than sacred business. Indeed, in the *Novgorodian First Chronicle* this summons is wedged in between the grand prince's dispatch of his boiars to the Dvina and the arrival of the Novgorodian embassy (of which the archbishop was a member) to Moscow, suggesting that the metropolitan was calling Ioann to negotiate. If so, they failed, although the metropolitan is again reported to have dismissed the archbishop and the ambassadors with a blessing.[115]

By Eastertide 1398, the Novgorodians were frustrated by the drawn-out conflict and its failed negotiations, and, most notably, the loss of the Dvina Land. They asked for and received Ioann's blessing to campaign along the Dvina. That lasted most of the year and successfully wrested the region back from the grand prince's boiars. Ioann then blessed the embassy that set out for Moscow that autumn to end the conflict.[116] Having taken back the Dvina Land, Novgorod could negotiation from a position of strength, and Vasilii this time made peace with them "as of old" (*po starinoi*). Whether this meant that the metropolitan could have his right of jurisdiction is not known. Kiprian never went back to Novgorod. In fact, the next metropolitan to visit the city, Isidor, did not come for another 39 years and did not sit in judgment.

Kiprian did not forget the indignity suffered at the Novgorodians' hands. In 1401, he again summoned Ioann "on episcopal business," just as in 1396.[117] This seems part of a concerted effort by the metropolitan and the grand prince to try to recoup their losses of 1398, for at the same time Kiprian summoned Ioann, Vasilii sent his boiars back into the Dvina Land, but they were beaten back by a Novgorodian force. The grand prince sent another army against Torzhok, which seized lands held by the church there but then apparently withdrew.[118] In 1402, the grand prince let several Novgorodians return home from Moscow and, in 1403, Kiprian finally let Ioann leave after he had been held there three years and four months in the Monastery of St. Nicholas the Old.[119] The chronicle mentions that there was much rejoicing in Novgorod on Ioann's return, but nothing more is said about his apparent arrest, the war, or the dispute over metropolitan jurisdiction that led to it. No mention is made of Kiprian again until his death under the year 1406.[120]

Novgorod's Absence from Momentous Church Events

After this generation-long crisis, there is little evidence of the archbishops relationship with the metropolitans for the remainder of Novgorodian independence. Archbishop Ioann visited Metropolitan Fotii in the winter of 1411,[121] and several letters of safe passage (or copies of them) for the archbishops or archbishops-elect to come to Moscow are extant, though we don't know what transpired during these visits.[122] Indeed, there is no evidence in the chronicles of the archbishops visiting the metropolitans for reasons other than their consecration after 1411, and the sources are silent on the archbishop's participation in the two most important church matters of the fifteenth century: the Union of Florence in 1439 and the establishment of an autocephalous Rus' church nine years later.

Some of this is explained by the fact that Kiprian's successor, Metropolitan Fotii, was extremely peripatetic, traveling several times between Lithuania and Moscow in a concerted effort to keep his province united, but he never visited Novgorod, perhaps indicating a continued strain between Novgorod and Moscow. He sent a blizzard of letters to Pskov in September 1416 and February 1418, indicating he was kept abreast of events there by priests who were writing to him, as well as other missives to the eparchy at other times during his metropolitanate, but none were ever sent to the Novgorodian archbishops directly, at least none that have survived. He ordained the archbishop-elect Samson a deacon and priest and then consecrated him archbishop, giving him the name Simeon, in March 1416,[123] but he never consecrated Simeon's successor, Feodosii, who was elected archbishop in Novgorod but returned to monastic life two years later (Feodosii died in 1425).

Fotii then consecrated Evfimii I in 1424, but would not consecrate Evfimii II.[124]

Evfimii II was elected in 1429 but was consecrated only in 1434, and by Metropolitan Gerasim (r. 1433-1435) in Smolensk rather than Moscow.[125] This can partly be explained by the fact that Fotii had died in Moscow in 1431; Gerasim remained in Lithuania, and Isidor, did not arrive in Moscow until 1437, so there was no metropolitan in Moscow for six years. This, however, does not explain why Fotii did not consecrate Evfimii between Evfimii's election in November 1429 and Fotii's own death in February or July 1431. Fotii's procrastination certainly may have been a calculated effort to avoid consecrating an unacceptable, anti-Muscovite candidate, but perhaps not.[126] With the death of Grand Prince Vasilii I in 1425, Fotii sat on the regency council that ruled Moscow and oversaw Vasilii II's upbringing. Perhaps Fotii simply had his hands full with all this and consecrating Evfimii was not a top priority. Evfimii was elected and carried out the function of archbishop, and there is no indication that Fotii sought to remove him.

Gerasim may have been Fotii's successor as Metropolitan of Kyiv and all Rus'.[127] If so, it was correct for Evfimii II to go to him for consecration. But from Moscow's point of view,[128] Gerasim's nomination by a Catholic prince and his presence in Lithuania threatened to split the Rus' Church or even take Western Rus' over to the Catholic Church. This latter fear is probably unfounded, if not an unfair accusation, as there is no indication Gerasim was anything by Orthodox. Whatever the reason, Fotii's failure to consecrate Evfimii II and the latter's consecration by a Lithuanian metropolitan in Smolensk may not necessarily mean Fotii opposed Evfimii's archiepiscopate, and certainly not that Novgorod was "going Latin," although this has often been the interpretation.[129]

After Fotii's death and Gerasim's execution, the metropolitan see in Moscow sat vacant another two years, and it was only in 1437 that Metropolitan Isidor (r. 1437-1441) passed through Novgorod en route to the Council of Florence and the attempted union of the Eastern and Western churches. Indeed, his entourage arrived in Novgorod on October 9 and stayed seven weeks before moving on to Pskov, where it arrived on St. Nicholas Day.[130] He is the only metropolitan to visit Novgorod between 1395 and the establishment of Muscovite autocephaly, indeed the only one between 1395 and the end of Novgorodian independence in 1478. One of the two accounts of Isidor's travels to and from Florence tells us he was met by Archbishop Evfimii II "with great honor" when he arrived at the Iur'ev Monastery south of the city on 7 October. When he entered Novgorod itself two days later, he was met again by Evfimii along with all the citizenry, then celebrated a Divine Liturgy in the Cathedral of Holy Wisdom. The source then claims Isidor stayed seven days before going to Pskov and then on the Florence.[131] Despite the reportedly warm reception, it seems, Isidor may have placed little faith in Archbishop Evfimii II's ability to justly oversee the church in Pskov given the political separation of the two cities that had begun almost a century earlier.[132] Perhaps Moscow was trying to weaken Novgorod by separating Pskov from the Novgorodian eparchy. This may explain why Isidor gave episcopal powers in Pskov to Archimandrite Gelasi, apparently waiting until he was in Pskov to act. His seven-day sojourn in Novgorod may have included a meeting with Evfimii in which the latter agreed to this move for the duration of Isidor's absence (Indeed, Pskov was removed from Evfimii's control only temporarily, and was apparently returned to the archbishop's control in 1441 when Isidor returned)[133] but yet again the sources are silent. Isidor may have been acting diplomatically to thwart efforts by the Pskovites to gain their own bishopric, as they had tried to do earlier; his actions may, therefore, have been a compromise solution and may even have benefited Novgorod's archbishops, who did not have to face opposition from Pskov during Isidor's absence.

Isidor passed south of the city on his return, apparently through Vilnius and Smolensk,[134] a more direct route to Moscow and not necessarily an intentional effort to avoid an unpleasant altercation with Evfimii. What discussions (in person or via letters) he had about the union with Archbishop Evfimii II or the other bishops of the Rus' church are not known.[135] Thus Novgorod and its archbishop seem left out of one of the most momentous chapters in the history of Eastern and Western church relations and one of the main causes for Rus' autocephaly seven years later, which the Novgorod archbishop likewise seemed a distant observer.[136]

The archbishop of Novgorod and the bishop of Tver' sent

their written consent to the consecration of Metropolitan Iona in 1448, the first autocephalous head of the Rus' church, but were themselves absent from Moscow.[137] They were also absent from the elections of Metropolitan Feodosii (r.1461-1464) in 1461 and Metropolitan Gerontii (r. 1473-1489) in 1473, though they sent their written consent on these occasions as well.[138] Nor are the prelates of Tver' and Novgorod mentioned among those celebrating the consecration of Metropolitan Filipp (r. 1464-1473) in 1465, although the chronicle notes that that those who were not present sent their written consent.[139] So Novgorod seems to have distanced itself from the metropolitans and from the Russian church in general, at least in terms of personal interactions, but we ultimately do not know whether this seemingly dysfunctional relationship was by design - a concerted effort to attain ecclesiastical independence, or a sign of Novgorod's opposition to Moscow or to church autocephaly.[140] Their written consent tends to refute such a conclusion.

In the secular sphere, Novgorod's distrust of Moscow as the power dynamic clearly shifted in Moscow's favor over the course of the fifteenth century—with the grand princes continuing their effort to poach important fur-harvesting lands from Novgorod after Vasilii I's campaign of 1393—very likely contributed to the archbishops' personally distancing themselves from Moscow.[141] And the ecclesiastical and the political were by no means separate spheres, as has been noted: Vasilii attacked the Dvina Land because Novgorod denied Kiprian his rights in Novgorod and, earlier, in 1370, Patriarch Philotheus had warned Archbishop Aleksei against disobeying the metropolitan and the grand prince.[142]

Thus, we see a more direct or personal contact in the first half of the twelfth century was followed by a period of decline in such contact from the second half of the twelfth century to the second quarter of the fourteenth century, just as other archiepiscopal activities declined (as we shall see). This was probably due in large part to the Mongol Invasion. The relationship grew more personal again in the mid-fourteenth century but direct contact fell off again around the beginning of the fifteenth century. After 1411, personal contact with the metropolitan seems to have largely ceased aside from journeys to Moscow for consecration. Only one archbishop, Iona, visited Moscow – in 1463 – for a reason other than his own consecration.[143]

Letters continued to pass between the metropolitans and the archbishops, and in one instance, it appears Metropolitan Iona thought the Novgorodian prelate could have been a potential political ally when, in 1452, he wrote Archbishop Evfimii in an attempt to get him to intercede with Novgorod's civil authorities over Novgorod's harboring of Prince Dmitrii Shemiaka, Vasilii II's great nemesis in the latter part of the civil war that had raged on and off since 1425, but Shemiaka died in Novgorod the following year, the *Ermolinskaia Chronicle* noting that "popular rumor says he died from poison."[144] If Evfimii did try to intervene, it was unsuccessful.[145] So, the ties between the metropolitan and Novgorod were never severed, but in many ways, Moscow and Novgorod were politically and ecclesiastically distant, with Novgorod gaining *de facto* if not *de jure* autonomy after 1395 and especially after 1411, until the Muscovite conquest.

The relationship worsened over the course of the fifteenth century. This was due in part to the appearance of metropolitans nominated by the (Catholic) grand princes of Lithuania and the attempt to create a Metropolitanate of Lithuania. The first attempt led Metropolitan Fotii to send out the equivalent of an encyclical – an *okruzhnoe poslanie* – in 1415 or 1416, to all the bishops, priests, princes, and "Christ-named people of the Lord" in the Kyiv province (as such it was not specifically addressed to Novgorod) - warning that Grigorii Tsamblak (r. 1413-1420), nominated by Grand Prince Vytautas (Vitold) (r. 1392-1430) and consecrated by a local synod without the approval of Patriarch Euthimius II of Constantinople (r. 1410-1416),[146] was not a legitimate metropolitan.[147] In September 1416, Fotii wrote Pskov a vague missive couched in biblical and ecclesiastical language, before (to a degree) coming to the point: "I write to you lists taken from the divine scriptures and from the divine rules concerning the separation of the church of God from the unholy men."[148] Pskov was to understand that Grigorii was meant, based on the earlier encyclical letter. Grigorii's appointment by a Catholic prince, as well as his attendance at the Council of Constance, led to accusations by Moscow of his supposed "Latinism." Though there is no indication that similar accusations were leveled at Novgorod at this time, despite the threat the Novgorodians made to Patriarch Anthony in 1392-1393, these letters demonstrate a growing fear of splitting the province and ultimately of losing the western part of it to Catholicism. That fear – or pretext – would eventually be used to harry the Novgorodian archeparchy and justify the Muscovite conquest.

A similar situation arose some forty years after Grigorii Tsamblak, when with another "Latin metropolitan" in Lithuania threatening to poach eparchies from the province, and this time the metropolitans were very much afraid of Novgorod's defection from Orthodoxy. Thus, in 1458 or 1459 and again in 1461, Metropolitan Iona dispatched a slew of letters warning the Orthodox bishops of Lithuania, the Lithuanian princes and nobility, the city of Pskov, the bishops of Smolensk and Chernihiv,[149] and Archbishop Iona of Novgorod to reject Metropolitan Grigorii of Kyiv, Lithuania, and Lower Rus' (r. 1458-1472).[150] In July 1461, the newly-consecrated metropolitan, Feodosii, dispatched another such letter to Archbishop Iona.[151]

A decade later, Metropolitan Filipp and Grand Prince Ivan III still feared Novgorod's defection to Grigorii.[152] They particularly feared Archbishop-elect Feofil would go to Grigorii for consecration and that he and the Novgorodians would "go Latin," since Grigorii had been a Uniate placed by Pope Pius II (r. 1458-1464) in 1458, although he had subsequently returned to Orthodoxy. In the first part of 1471, Filipp wrote twice to Novgorod, addressing Feofil with other church officials, and calling on them not to defy the grand prince by joining with the King of Poland and abandoning Orthodoxy.[153] Whether or not these entreaties had any effect, or if it was the grand prince's decisively victory over the Novgorodian army at Shelon' River on July 14, 1471, a campaign justified in part by Novgorod's alleged planned defection from Orthodoxy,[154] Feofil did not go to Grigorii, but was consecrated by Filipp in Moscow on December 15, 1471 just as the grand prince and metropolitan had wanted.[155]

Moscow's fear and repeated accusations that Novgorod would Latinize is unjustified. Various remarks by the Novgorodian archbishops over the centuries, such as Archbishop Nifont's answer in the "Questions of Kirik" that a woman who took her children to a Catholic priest should be given the same penance as if they had taken them to a sorcerer,[156] or anti-Catholic remarks in the Novgorodian chronicles – composed in the archbishop's own scriptorium – such as those against the King of Poland for turning Orthodox churches in Volynia into Catholic ones,[157] and the several wars against the Teutonic knights, the Poles, the Lithuanians (after 1386), and Swedish crusaders in the thirteenth and fourteenth centuries, suggest no love for Catholicism on the part of Novgorod's archbishops, and there is no convincing evidence that in the fifteenth century, the archbishops or their flock had in any way changed their mind. In fact, a draft treaty from 1471 with the King of Poland and Grand Prince of Lithuania indicates Novgorod sought to protect both its Orthodoxy and its wealth. The king was not to interfere in the archbishop's court – that is, he was not to hear appeals from or sit in judgment in Novgorod's ecclesiastical courts or collect court fees there – nor was he to construct Catholic churches in Novgorod or its environs, and he had to appoint an Orthodox *namestnik*.[158]

Novgorod within the Rus' Church

This rocky relationship with the metropolitans is not the sum total of the archbishops' or Novgorod's relationship with the Rus' church as a whole. The changing political and ecclesiastical relationship between Novgorod and Moscow allowed Novgorod's archbishops to attain a level of autonomy unseen in any other eparchy of the Rus' church, but this was not linked to the archiepiscopal title or any formal grant from the patriarch, metropolitan, or grand prince. Nor was there ever a concerted effort by the Novgorodians and their archbishop to attain autocephaly in any formal sense, meaning that the Novgorodian church would have been administratively independent of the Kyivan or Muscovite church and the Novgorodian clergy themselves would have chosen *and consecrated* their head (the threat "to go Latin" notwithstanding). The archbishops did gain a large degree of *de facto* autonomy and, through their economic, political, and cultural resources, were able to maintain the Novgorodian archeparchy's relative autonomy for much of the fifteenth century in the face of serious threats from both the Muscovite metropolitans and grand princes. Novgorod did demand that the patriarch remove them from under the metropolitan in 1392-1393 (and apparently threatened to "go Latin" if their demand was not met), but this effort failed and there does not seem to have been any effort to gain autocephaly after that. The relationship was more indirect from the 1390s to the end of Novgorodian independence, and some archbishops have been alleged to have been anti-Muscovite, but others, namely Iona and Feofil (at least initially) seemed much more inclined toward Moscow.

It is not beyond the realm of the possible that Novgorod could have attained autocephaly, at least from the Kyivan ecclesiastical province, if not from the Patriarchate of Constantinople, though that latter achievement seems much less likely in the Rus' context. Autocephalous national churches had been successfully established in Bulgaria and Serbia, and several other countries during the medieval period as part of efforts to establish political - and thus also ecclesiastical – independence from the Byzantine Empire, a rather different situation than that found in Novgorod or Muscovy.[159] Tsar Boris (r. 852-892) of Bulgaria had made some overtures to Rome in 870 before accepting the authority of the patriarch of Constantinople. Bulgaria had established an independent state, but its church remained a province of the patriarchate of Constantinople until 927, when Tsar Symeon (r. 893-927) raised Archbishop Leontius of Preslav to the rank of patriarch. This, however, was never recognized by Constantinople, and Byzantine Emperor John I Tzimiskes (r. 969-976) formally abolished the See of Preslav when he conquered the city in 972;[160] Patriarch Damyan of Drista fled westward to Sredetz (Sofia).[161] In Western Bulgaria, Tsar Samuel (r. 976-1014, crowned 997) made Damyan patriarch of Ohrid, though Emperor Basil II reduced the see to an archbishopric in 1015 and the Bulgarian church only gained autocephaly again in 1185. A separate patriarchate of Trnovo (Ternovo) was established in 1234.[162]

Christian Serbia dates to the seventh century,[163] and the Serbian church remained under the patriarch of Constantinople until Sava (d. 1235), youngest son of Stefan Nemanja (Grand Župan, r. 1167-1196), when Patriarch Manuel II (r. 1217-1222), then at Nicaea, elevated Sava to the archiepiscopal rank in 1219 in exchange for Sava's recognition of him as rightful patriarch in the face of rival claims from Epirus in the Morea (Constantinople being under Latin control from 1204-1261). Tsar Stefan Dušan (king of Serbia r. 1231-1246, Emperor 1246-1255) elevated Ioannikii (Joanikje) to Patriarch of Peč on Easter (April 16) 1346.[164]

Thus, there seems to be a natural progression within Orthodoxy: a church is established as a province of Constantinople and, after several centuries, the province gains or is granted autonomy or autocephaly. Accordingly, the argument goes, Novgorod may have followed the Serbians, Bulgarians, Romanians (with separate metropolitanates in Muntenia – Greater Wallachia – and Moldavia), and others, and broken free from Kyiv or Moscow.

But in the fifteenth century, Constantinople continued to decline and eventually fell, and therefore could not keep the Rus', Bulgarians, or Serbians under the patriarchs, and language and cultural differences also played their part. The Golden Horde fragmented and Moscow's power grew as Novgorod's waned. But, not only did Novgorod fail to establish an autocephalous church – it was much more likely to have fallen under the metropolitans established in western Rus' in the fourteenth and fifteenth centuries than to have established autocephaly– but there is little firm evidence that the Novgorodians ever made a concerted effort to do so. Alleged autocephalous tendencies, as we have seen, can often be explained in other ways. The appeal to the patriarch in 1353 was a call for better behavior by the metropolitan, not autocephaly, and the rather crude threat to "go Latin" in 1392 (if they actually made such a threat) may have had more to do with Moscow's growing political pressure. Novgorod wanted to guard its freedom and wealth, but that did not necessarily want full-blown autocephaly.[165]

Conclusion

From the admittedly limited sources we have we can see that the Novgorodian church apparently defended patriarchal rights in the eleventh and twelfth centuries. But by the middle to late fourteenth century, the relationship between Novgorod and its metropolitan had become strained. From then on, Novgorod drew away from the metropolitans and, in a real way, achieved ecclesiastical autonomy for some eight decades before the Muscovite conquest.

This litany of disputes, admittedly, fails to consider other ways Novgorod was an important member of the Rus' church. To give just one example, the *Novgorodian Kormchaia of 1282* includes princely church statutes, the *Russkaia Pravda*, the Canons of Metropolitan Kirill (i.e., the decrees of the Council of Vladimir) and other documents, which might otherwise have been lost to history, as well as the "Questions of Kirik" and the Letter of Archbishop Il'ia to the Bishop of Bilhorod, so that the archbishops and the Novgorodian contributed in a unique way to medieval Rus' canon law and history.[166] The rest of this book will look beyond this tension between archbishop and metropolitan and consider the significant contributions the archbishops made to church art and architecture, historiography, and hagiography.

CHAPTER THREE
The Archeparchy

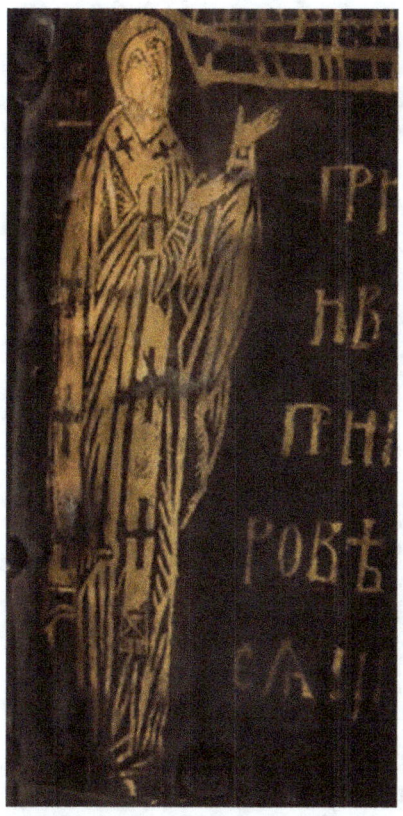

4. Depiction of Vasilii Kalika on the Vasil'evski Doors (Gates) from the Holy Wisdom Cathedral (1335/6), removed to Aleksandrovskaia Sloboda in 1570.

In discussing the bishop's authority in the Byzantine Empire, the principles of which would have been passed on to the Kyivan metropolitanate, the Byzantine scholar Emil Herman wrote:

The bishop had complete control over the diocese in ecclesiastical affairs; clergy and monasteries were normally subordinate to him. Above all, he was responsible for preaching the revealed truth to the faithful committed to his care and for ensuring that no false doctrine led his flock away. It was his right and his duty to inflict heavy penalties, even excommunication, whenever either divine commands or the rulings of the Church were disobeyed.[1]

This succinctly sums up the bishop's role at the eparchial or diocesan level. He was the chief administrator, head teacher, and

The Novgorodian Land

defender of the faith against all threats, internal and external. Complete control over the eparchy meant no priest could administer a sacrament, preach or teach, or build a church without his approval. The bishops were not merely Christian exemplars to their flock, nor were they just the administrative heads of their diocese, but it is worth reiterating Cyprian of Carthage's summation of the office, that "the bishop is in the church and the church is in the bishop, and if anyone is not with the bishop, they are not in the church."[2]

This episcopal authority was at the heart of who the bishops and archbishops of Novgorod were – they were appointed or elected to lead the church in Novgorod so that their political, economic and cultural roles, while extremely significant, were in some ways ancillary to their roles as overseers of the archeparchy. And the archeparchy itself was huge, stretching from the Livonian border just west of Pskov up to the White Sea and Arctic Ocean and over to the Urals. And yet, despite their preeminence as head of the archeparchy and the archeparchy's immense geographic expanse, the sources tell us relatively little of the archbishops' administrative activities, their teaching and preaching, their administration of baptism, ordination, or other sacraments, or their consecration of churches. What little they do reveal is mostly confined to a small geographic area in and around the city of Novgorod itself. Furthermore, there are long gaps in activities presented in the sources, indicating not only the impact of the Mongol invasion on Rus' (though Novgorod itself was never attacked), but also economic and political crises and the waxing and waning of archiepiscopal power and influence throughout the medieval period, which may have impacted the ability to manage affairs and even dispense the sacraments throughout the entire archeparchy.

Defenders of Orthodoxy: Paganism

The presence of pagan Finno-Ugric tribes in the archeparchy, along the southern coast of the Gulf of Finland and to the northeast around Lake Ladoga, Lake Onega, and up to the White Sea, meant that Novgorod's archbishops had to address the issue of either converting them or fending them off, and they did so probably for almost the entire period under study, not just at the time of the initial baptism of Rus'. Furthermore, in overseeing an eparchy that stood on both the Catholic-Orthodox and Christian-pagan frontiers, Novgorod's bishops may have had to concern themselves with conversion and the defense of Orthodoxy in ways that their brethren in other Rus' eparchies might not. The land cadastres and other sources indicate that the bishops from the beginning (whether that was in the 980s or 990s or later in the 1030s) faced a daunting task and may not have succeeded in making significant inroads into some pagan tribes during the entire Kyivan and Appanage periods, so that there might have been very little in terms of a Christian presence in large parts of the archeparchy even at the end of the fifteenth century.

The initial introduction of Christianity in the Novgorod Land seems to have met serious resistance as we shall see, so despite hagiographic literature which often paints the saintly missionaries, especially the apostles to the various nations or lands as supremely confident and larger-than-life men, it was most certainly a difficult and at times discouraging calling. Ioakim Korsunianin, if he is not merely legendary, was a Greek-speaker from the warm Mediterranean climate that graces the Crimea, sent to a land that must have been very strange to him: a cold, marshy region where in summer, the sun seems never to set, yet in December barely cuts through the murk of what Arab-speaking travelers called "the Land of Darkness."[3] He had been sent from Constantinople, the New Rome and Queen of Cities, to establish the church in a pagan land then almost utterly devoid of cities.[4] How well he knew Slavic is impossible to say. And those he, Luka, or the princes sent out to convert the Novgorodian land must have experienced similar fears and difficulties.

As noted in the last chapter, the earliest years of the eparchy are extremely sketchy,[5] with the founding date only known to within a few years (somewhere between 988 and 992), though it could have been as late as the 1030s. Whenever it occurred, it is by no means clear how well things went for the missionaries. Some sources repeat the legend that Ioakim boldly tore down the idol of Perun and threw it in the river, just as Vladimir had done in Kyiv,[6] but the legend goes on to say that Perun left his cane on the bridge and cursed it as the place the Novgorodians would forever quarrel, calling into question its usefulness as a historic source.[7] More reliable accounts tell us almost nothing about the first several decades of the conversion of the Novgorodian Land. Vasilii Tatishchev relates that Bishop Ioakim and Posadnik Dobrynia, Prince Vladimir's uncle, faced a violent uprising soon after their arrival,[8] a not uncommon occurrence for missionaries. But Tatishchev's historiography is rather suspect. Most other accounts are sparser and give little indication of the actual conversion process.

Ioakim is said to have served 42 years in Novgorod, dying in 1030, "and then his student Efrem, who taught, was in his place."[9] There is, however, serious doubt that Ioakim, and especially Efrem, even existed. Vadym Aristov argues that the reference to Efrem was a misunderstanding by a later chronicle writer or compiler (repeated by later historians) of an earlier reference to St. Ephrem (Ephraem) the Syrian, a fourth century hymnographer.[10]

Luka Zhidiata arrived from Kyiv in 1035, but very little is known even at this point. Luka consecrated the current Cathedral of Holy Wisdom, the mother church of the eparchy, but his efforts at evangelization are not known. Nothing is known of Stepan (if he existed) except the violent nature of his death already discussed.[11]

Stepan's successor, Feodor, however, faced serious difficulties in Novgorod. In 1071, a pagan sorcerer led an uprising that threatened the bishop, who was supported only by Prince Gleb Sviatoslavich (Prince of Tmutarakan, r. 1064-1065, 1067-1068 Prince of Novgorod, r. 1068-1078) and his retinue. Feodor's exhortation to the Novgorodians to be true to the Christian faith fell on deaf ears and it was only the violent and cunning action of Prince Gleb that ended the revolt: he asked the sorcerer to prophesy the future, and when the man boasted that he would do great things that day, Gleb chopping him in two with an ax, at which point the uprising collapsed.[12] The incident shows that Christianity had only a meager foothold in Novgorod almost a century after Ioakim's alleged arrival.

The uprising was, in fact, part of a general pagan revival or upheaval that occurred at that time throughout Rus' as well as in Poland and elsewhere. Indeed, scholars note that pagan traditions never really went away in Rus', but lurked just below a thin veneer of Christianity.[13] Priests complained for centuries that people went to pagan festivals but not to church,[14] and a number of documents, such as the *Statute of Vladimir* and *Statute of Iaroslav*, both purportedly from the eleventh century but, in their present forms at least, dating as late as the fourteenth century,[15] handed over prosecution of pagan offenses to the church, indicating paganism was still a problem then. The *Statute of Vladimir* specified offenses such as "witchcraft; [the making of] potions; [the making of] charms; sorcery; magic… or [if] someone prays [to a pagan god] beneath a grain-drying bin, or in a copse of trees, or by the water,"[16] and the subsequent *Statute of Iaroslav* noted similar pagan practices.[17] In the twelfth century *Voproshanie Kirika* (the *Questions of Kirik*), the monk Il'ia, perhaps the later archbishop of that name, asked Archbishop Nifont what was to be done about women who took their sick children to pagan sorcerers rather than to Orthodox priests to be prayed over, again indicating the persistence of paganism in the Novgorodian eparchy almost two centuries after the Baptism.[18] That four sorcerers were burned at the stake in Novgorod's *Iaroslavovo Dvorishche*, the princely compound on the Marketplace, as late as 1227; and twelve witches (*zhonke veshchikh*) executed in Pskov in 1411, indicates paganism's persistence in the archeparchy.[19] Indeed, as late as the 1533, Archbishop Makarii (r. 1526-1542) wrote a letter to Grand Prince Vasilii III (r. 1505-1533) and his son Ivan (the future Ivan IV) indicating that he was sending priests and monks out to the Vodskaia Fifth to convert the region:

> To the Chud and the Izhorians,[20] and around the towns of Ivangorod, Iamgorod, Korela [Keksholm], Kopor'e, Ladoga, Oreshek [Orekhov], and along all the coast of the Variag [Varangian] Sea [the Gulf of Finland] in the Novgorodian Land, and along all the rivers of the Pomore from the German shore of Livonia at the Narva River to the Neva River and from the Neva River to the Sespri River on the Swedish shore, and in all the Karelian Land, and from the Konevii Vod to the Great Lake of the Neva [Lake Ladoga] and from Kaiaanst on the German coast and around the Pereiskii Sea and from the Lesk River to Lopi to the wilds around the Great Lake of the Neva [Ladoga][21]

Makarii asserts that all the land of Rus' had been baptized at the time of "the faithful (*blagovernogo*) Grand Prince Vladimir" and pagan sites had been destroyed in the Chud, Izorian, and Karelian lands "and in many cities in Rus'," but the Chud, Izhorians, Karelians, and others had clung to pagan rituals even to the time of Vasilii III, and continued to worship "forest and stone and rivers and swamps (*blata*), springs and mountains and hills, the sun and the moon and the stars and lakes. And it is simple to say - they bow down to all creatures as if to God and honor and sacrifice blood to the Devil (*k besom*) - of oxen and sheep and all cattle and birds."[22]

The letter casts doubt on the success of Makarii's predecessors, at least in the eyes of the sixteenth century Muscovite church establishment, in converting the pagans in the areas between Novgorod and the Gulf of Finland, along the Neva, and up along the southern and western shores of Lake Ladoga. This, again, suggests that much of the archeparchy was never Christianized in the medieval period. A subsequent letter sent by Makarii's successor, Archbishop Feodosii (r. 1542-1551), to the clergy of the Votskaia Fifth in 1548 (it quotes verbatim from Makarii's letter and called on the clergy there to convert the local inhabitants) indicates that even Makarii's activities had not been completely successful and paganism still persisted in much of the Zavoloch'e.[23]

And while it may seem from Makarii's and Feodosii's letters that the Novgorodian bishops and archbishops were remiss in their duty to fulfill to "Go, therefore, and make disciples of all nations, baptizing them in the name of the Father, and of the Son, and of the Holy Spirit,"[24] there is some evidence that Christianity had spread to these very regions around the Neva River and lakes Ladoga and Onega in earlier centuries. It is sometimes unclear the precise role the archbishops played in this process, but there are clues. A proviso in the 1339 treaty with the Swedes and Swedish sources on King Magnus' crusade up the Neva River in the 1340s and early 1350s indicate there were Orthodox converts among the Izhorians living along the river, since Archbishop Vasilii Kalika tried to protect them in the treaty, and the Swedish sources tell us that the Catholic Swedes had "shaved their beards," meaning they forcibly converted the Izhorians to Catholicism.[25] In 1395, the Swedes invaded Karelia again and took the *pogosty* of Kiureskii and Kiulolaskii and burned the churches there,[26] although these could just have been Christian outposts in an otherwise pagan country. Archbishop Simeon's and Evfimii II's visitations to Karelia and the Zavoloch'e regions in the fifteenth century also indicate that there were Christians in those regions, especially since the chronicle notes that the reason for Evfimii's visitation was to "bless his Novgorodian *votchina* [proprietary estates] and his archbishopric, and his [spiritual] children."[27]

Archaeological evidence from the region also suggests Christianity had spread into the Vodskaia *Piatina* (along the Gulf of Finland, where Makarii sent his missionaries in 1533) by the mid-thirteenth century; and had spread east of Lake Ladoga and along the southern coast of Lake Onega shortly before that.[28] There are other indicators that Christianization in the regions north of Novgorod did not merely consist of Rus' communities surrounded by pagan Finno-Ugrian tribes. The Rus' had colonized the Izhora region as early as the eleventh century, and some Izhorians converted to Christianity.[29] The late thirteenth-century *Life of Aleksandr Nevskii* indicates Christians among the Izhorian elite by the 1240s,[30] and archaeological evidence points to "an increasing number of baptized natives among the Votians and the Izhorians from the middle of the thirteenth century."[31] Grave artifacts such as cross pendants suggest that the local populations outside the Russian towns or fortresses of (Staraia) Ladoga, Kopor'e, Orekhov, and Keksholm had accepted Christianity not much later than this, although there are scholars who believe these items were worn as trinkets by pagan populations unaware of their true religious significance.[32] Aleksandr Musin rejects this idea but admits that the Izhorians and other tribes in the region never fully Christianized in the medieval period, thus explaining the missions in the 1500s.[33]

Other records indicate Christianity spread north across Lake Ladoga to northern Korela (Karelia) with Efrem, a monk from Mount Athos, who founded the Valaamskii Monastery on Holy Island in Lake Ladoga in 1389. Monks from the monastery founded the Konevskii Monastery on Konevets Island under Arsenii Konevskii around 1395.[34] *The Tale of the Valaamskii Monastery*[35] relates that hostility from the pagan Karelians led Efrem to leave Valaamskii (he later founded the Perekomskii Monastery south of Novgorod in 1407), but Sergei Valaamskii remained, soon turning to Novgorodian Archbishop Ioann for help in efforts to enlighten the "demon-worshipping Karelians." Ioann enthusiastically supported the effort, issued charters giving Sergei full control of the Valaamskii Monastery, and appealed to the Novgorodian *posadniki* and *tysiaskie*, who dispatched armed forces (called "envoys" in the *Tale*). These carried out what John Lind called "a virtual Russian counter-crusade against the Karelians,"[36] killing many of them, and driving the rest from the island.[37] Though a particularly violent and unpleasant episode, it shows a Novgorodian archbishop spreading Christianity into the pagan hinterland. It also underscores the persistence of paganism so late after the Baptism, and at least some pagans' unwillingness to quietly accept Christianity.

Defenders of Orthodoxy: The Catholic Crusades

Beyond the persistence of paganism, Teutonic Knights and Swedish crusaders in the thirteenth and fourteenth centuries launched several crusades against the Novgorodians. Even within the archeparchy, the "heresy" of Catholicism threatened the archbishops' Orthodox flock.[38]

Following a two-year war (1337-1339), the Swedes and Novgorodians agreed to peace in 1339 on the terms of the old Treaty of Noteborg (Orekhov) of 1323, though the chronicle adds, "concerning the Kobylich Korel [Karelians, i.e., Christians among the Karelians], they agreed to send envoys to the Prince of the Swedes [King Magnus Eriksson],"[39] Novgorod sent several envoys northward who found the king at Lyudovl, "in the Murman country"[40] and concluded a treaty with him there. The chronicle notes that "the *Vladyka* [Archbishop Vasilii], on his behalf, sent his nephew [*sestricha*, his sister's son], Matvei"[41] and while it does not specifically say what part Matvei played in the treaty, a proviso concerning the Karelians – absent from the earlier treaty – indicates he was sent to save the Orthodox converts among them. Of the pagan Karelians, the treaty stipulated: "if ours escape to you, slay or hang them, if yours to us; we will do the same to them; that they make no treachery between us." The Novgorodians then insisted: "But these we will not deliver, [those among the Karelians] who have been baptized into our faith; there are but few of them; the rest have all died by the wrath of God."[42]

Several decades later, Vasilii's successor Ioann II, as we have seen, used force against the Karelians northwest of Lake Ladoga, indicating the archbishops were still trying to convert the region, but relying on more violent means to do so.[43] In fact, the violent "counter-crusade"[44] was a reaction to the threatening inroads Catholicism was making into the region at that time. Should the region have converted to Catholicism, the Karelians would have sent their tribute to the West, and Catholicism would press on Novgorod not just from the west, but from the north as well.[45]

Though perturbed by the Catholic threat, the archbishops did not engage in any "conspiracy of silence" as the Rus' bookmen allegedly employed toward their (pagan and later Muslim) Mongol overlords,[46] whose immunity charters (*iarlyki*) to the church flew in the face of the bookmen's worldview.[47] The archbishop's chroniclers wrote rather little about the goings on in Catholic world right on their Western border. But charters show the archbishops among the Novgorodian officials negotiating with envoys from the Catholic kingdoms and cities, as well as interacting with the (Catholic) merchants in the German and Gothic courts in Novgorod.[48] There are also indications that the archbishops fought off Catholic encroachment within the archeparchy itself. In the *Voproshanie Kirika*, Archbishop Nifont assigned the same penance to women who took their children to be blessed by "Varangian" (Catholic) priests as he did to those who took them to sorcerers.[49] When the Swedes came up the Neva River and landed at the mouth of the Izhora "with their prince and their bishops" almost a century later, Aleksandr Iaroslavich, duly blessed by Archbishop Spiridon,[50] marched an army out and defeated them, killing their *voevoda* (who also had the name of Spiridon).[51] When the Swedes returned a century later, and King Magnus Ericsson called on the Novgorodians to debate with his "philosophers," or Catholic theologians. Archbishop Vasilii told them to go to Constantinople if they wished to debate.[52] Four years later, the archbishop oversaw the reconstruction of the fortress at Orekhov, which had been briefly taken by the Swedish crusaders and then recaptured by the Novgorodians, and which not only protected Novgorod against Catholic crusaders, but also protected the city's vital trade route out of Lake Ladoga and down the Neva into the Baltic.[53] The pressure exerted on Novgorod to convert to the faith of the Scandinavians, Livonian Germans, Poles, and Lithuanians (after 1386) was thus a considerable threat at various points throughout the thirteenth, fourteenth and fifteenth centuries. And, as we have seen, the Novgorodians specified in a 1471 draft treaty that Polish King Casimir IV (Grand Prince of Lithuania, r. 1440-1492; King of Poland, r. 1447-1492), with whom they were negotiating to make their prince, could not build Catholic churches in Novgorod and had to appoint an Orthodox *namestnik*.[54] Despite this centuries-long fending-off of Catholicism, we noted the grand princes' and metropolitans' assertions that the Novgorodians would abandon the faith and "go Latin," a pretext to justify war in the 1390s and, ultimately, the conquest of the city in the 1470s.[55]

Defenders of Orthodoxy: Heresy

The Novgorodian archeparchy was the epicenter of the only two heresies found in medieval Rus': the *Strigol'niki* in the mid-fourteenth century and the *Judaizers* in the late fifteenth and early sixteenth centuries. The standard view is that archbishops prior to the Muscovite conquest were negligent in dealing with these heresies. Most writings against the *Strigol'niki* that have come down to us are not from the archbishops but, as noted above, were from Metropolitan Fotii, Archbishop Dionisii of Suzdal, the patriarch in Constantinople, and others. And Archbishop Gennadii seems to have stumbled upon the Judaizing heresy quite by accident and was most desirous to stamp it out when it was uncovered, so much so that in a letter to the Moscow sobor of 1490, he insisted that a church council be convened not to debate with those accused of heresy, but "only for one purpose: to punish the heretics, that is, to burn them and hang them."[56] Natalia Kazakova and Iakov Lur'e wrote that Vasilii Kalika had "looked through his fingers" at the *Strigol'niki* heresy spreading in Novgorod during his tenure, and the sense in Muscovite sources seems to be that that Archbishops Feofil and Sergei (r. 1483-1484) ignored the "Judaic-Reasoning Novgorod heretics" (more commonly called the Judaizers).[57] But these accusations are unfair. Vasilii Kalika fought hard to defend Orthodoxy from encroaching Swedish crusaders,[58] and while this did not consume his entire archiepiscopate, it was the focus of attention for the last few years his life. The *Strigol'niki* heresy first appears in the sources in Patriarch Nilus' 1382 letter to Pskov, thirty years after Vasilii's death, so it is unknown how widespread it was during Vasilii's archiepiscopate if it even existed at that time.[59] Boris Rybakov claims Archbishop Moisei battled the *Strigol'niki* after Vasilii's death,[60] and the chronicles note that under Aleksei five heretics were thrown from the Great Bridge and drowned in the Volkhov River in 1375,[61] though whether this was a judicial execution or a public lynching is unclear.[62] Since princely statutes placed heresy within the purview of the ecclesiastical courts, and two of the heretics were deacons, that is, church people, they would have been subject to the ecclesiastical courts under Aleksei's jurisdiction,[63] if they were not lynched. As for the later Judaizing heresy, it is said to have begun only in 1470-1471 and was not discovered until 1487, almost a decade after the fall of Novgorod to Moscow.[64]

Letters and documents from patriarchs, metropolitans, and other bishops over the course of the fourteenth and fifteenth centuries seem to support actions taken by the archbishops rather than attempts by other churchmen to override the archbishops or fight a heresy the Novgorodian prelates were ignoring.[65] Patriarch Nilus' 1382 letter to Pskov was probably conveyed by Archbishop Dionisii of Suzdal' to Aleksei,[66] who arrived with "charters" from Constantinople and taught "the laws of God and the true faith to Christians in Pskov."[67] The chronicle clearly indicates this was done with Archbishop Aleksei's permission, confirming the archbishop worked with other churchmen to fight the heresy. Metropolitan Fotii's letters from the early 1400s, quoted at some length in the first chapter, called on the Pskovites to be faithful and obedient to their bishop, again showing the wider church working with the archbishops to stamp out the heresy.

Some scholars argue that it took Gennadii, a Muscovite appointee, to root out and destroy the Judaizing heresy in the wake of inaction by Novgorod's locally-elected archbishop, Feofil. However, as noted above, the heresy was not uncovered until 1487.[68] Moreover, by Gennadii's own account, Skhariya the Jew, the alleged founder of the movement,[69] arrived in the city from Kyiv only in the winter of 1470-1471, in the entourage of the Lithuanian Prince Mikhail Aleksandrovich (or Olel'kovich), and thus would have only affected the archiepiscopate of Feofil, in no way indicating general indiscipline on the part of the pre-Muscovite archbishops.[70]

The fact that the *Judaizers* were not dealt with until a Muscovite appointee arrived may suggest the real problem was one of differences in ritual or administrative practices between the Muscovite and the Novgorodian churches.[71] That some of those removed for heresy (a number were executed) were members of the church administration in the final years of Novgorodian independence, including the head of the white clergy, Archpriest Gavriil of the Cathedral of Holy Wisdom, suggests that accusations of heresy may merely have been a pretext to remove undesirables in the wake of the Muscovite take-over of the Novgorodian church,[72] destroy the old Novgorodian church administration, and remake it in the image of the Muscovite church. The vague descriptions of the heresy cast further doubt on the reality of the problem.[73] It seems churchmen took the standard complaints against heresies found in the Patristic writings, a not uncommon practice in the medieval period, and dusted them off for use against what they were finding – or claiming to find – in and around Novgorod at the turn of the sixteenth century.[74] We again have only the church's account of the heresy, so we cannot be sure of the full nature of the heresy, if it, in fact, existed.

Episcopal Prerogatives

The Novgorodian archbishops had several prerogatives within their archeparchy. Their approval was required for churches to be consecrated, for the Gospel to be preached and Christian doctrine taught, and for any sacraments to be administered by the priests and deacons who acted on their behalf. Like other aspects of the office, the evidence of these activities in chronicles and other documents is exiguous, though still enough to draw some worthwhile conclusions.

Church Consecrations

Church construction was one of archbishops' main activities and one of the few activities the archbishops carried out fairly consistently from the twelfth to the fifteenth century and that are attested to regularly in the sources, although there was a decline in this activity similar to that seen in other archiepiscopal activities during the thirteenth century.[75] Hegumens, princes, merchants, *posadniki*, *tysiatskie*, and boiars also built churches, but archiepiscopal church construction far outpaced that of any other office in Novgorod and, perhaps, anywhere else in Rus'. The archbishops' role as builders will be discussed in a later chapter as part of their cultural patronage.

Tradition and canon law hold that bishops have to consecrate all churches in their diocese, either in person or through a designated representative.[76] But between 1153 and 1445, only twenty-one church consecrations were noted in the *Novgorodian First Chronicle* and the Pskov chronicles. There were four consecrations up to 1201, then we see the same thirteenth-century drop off in activity seen in other archiepiscopal activity, with no consecrations mentioned between 1201 and 1294.[77] There were then four consecrations between 1294 and 1324, another, shorter gap between 1324 and 1364, then thirteen consecrations up to the archiepiscopate of Evfimii II beginning in 1429, after which there is a real fall off in church construction and consecrations until the archiepiscopate of Makarii in the 1520s. Of the archbishops before the Muscovite Conquest, ten are never cited in the chronicles consecrating any churches,[78] and eight others only consecrated one church each.[79] It is probable, given the requirement under canon law, that consecrations often took place but simply are not mentioned in the sources, the chroniclers presupposing that their readers would take for granted that church consecrations were a normal part of the archbishops' duties, and if a church's construction is mentioned, it must have been consecrated soon afterwards. If this is the case, it is not clear why some consecrations were mentioned but not others. Some churches were large and important enough to warrant mention, but others that are mentioned seem small and of less interest. But this is likely a post-Enlightenment demand for organization or consistency that is often absent in medieval sources.

Teaching and Preaching

According to the Nineteenth Canon of the Quinisext Council, one of the primary duties of the bishop was "to teach all the clergy and the people words of piety and of right religion."[80] This view of the bishop as teacher and preacher did not start with Quinisext, but went back to the very first years of the church. Indeed, Paul wrote to the Corinthians that "Christ did not send me to baptize but to preach the gospel."[81] The *First Letter to Timothy* states that episcopal candidate must be "an apt teacher,"[82] and the *Second Letter to Timothy* exhorts the recipient to "preach the word."[83] Teaching was such an important aspect of the episcopate that the office was formerly referred to as "the preaching office" (*officium predicationis*). In the *Lives* of Sts. Cyril (also called Constantine the Philosopher) and his brother Methodius, the Apostles to the Slavs repeatedly stressed the importance of learning (and by extension teaching). Cyril supposedly had a dream when he was seven years old where he chose Sophia, the Wisdom of God, to be his wife.[84] He later remarked: "For me nothing is greater than learning."[85] The *Life of Methodius* noted that: "Merciful God, who will have all men saved, and to come unto the knowledge of the truth, roused *our teacher*, the blessed Methodius, to do a good deed in our age for the sake of the people about whom none ever cared."[86] The importance of preaching, teaching, and learning (and of the bishop as teacher), was, therefore, apparent in early Christian and later Orthodox tradition.

Despite this, the bishops and archbishops of Novgorod left little evidence of this activity in the sources. It may be assumed that they taught, but a historic argument cannot be based simply on what is supposed to have happened. There is some evidence, though. The library that has survived along with references to several archbishops as bookish and learned, suggest they were teaching. The Novgorodian First and Fourth Chronicle notes that after Ioakim Korsunianin's death, "his student Efrem, *who taught*, was in his place,"[87] indicating that Ioakim taught Efrem, who then taught the other Christians in the eparchy.

But, again, Ioakim may be legendary and Efrem a misinterpretation, and in terms of solid documentary evidence we have only a rather simple homily from Bishop Luka Zhidiata (r.1035-1060), the *Voproshanie Kirika*, of Archbishop Nifont (r.1131-1156),[88] The Rules of Il'ia,[89] and Vasilii Kalika's letter to Bishop Feodor of Tver' concerning the earthly nature of paradise.[90] There are also a few references to teaching in the *Novgorodian First Chronicle*. In 1341, Prince Mikhail Aleksandrovich, the infant son of Prince Aleksandr of Tver', came to Novgorod to be taught by Archbishop Vasilii Kalika to read and write, which would have meant learning to read Scripture.[91] Perhaps teaching and preaching, like church consecrations, were so clearly a function of the archiepiscopal office in the minds of the chroniclers that they did not warrant specific mention: the archbishops may have given homilies frequently, but almost none have survived. This is somewhat problematic though, since several Rus' bishops were famous preachers – Metropolitan Hilarion's Sermon "On the Law and Grace" is recognized as a beautiful example of Kyivan Rus' religious literature as are the sermons of Bishop Kirill of Turau (Turov) from the twelfth century – and while there is no Novgorodian archbishop during our period famous for his homilies, there is no reason to believe that they did not preach or teach at all.[92] But there are few extant sermons from Rus', thus few preachers are known, and thus the homiletic silence from Novgorod is not unique.[93] Orthodox Christianity's emphasis on ritual over doctrine may also explain the lack of archiepiscopal teaching and preaching, since they may have been more focused on liturgical ritual or the construction of churches and monasteries where these were performed.[94]

Luka Zhidiata's *Homily to the Brethren*, first read to monks of an unknown monastery in the mid-eleventh century, reveals no deep exegetical or theological understanding. Indeed, John Fennell and Anthony Stokes called the homily "little more than a catalogue of the most elementary and basic tenets of Christianity."[95] It calls on the monks to "scrupulously keep the commandment: to believe in one God, glorified in the Trinity, in the Father, and the Son, and the Holy Spirit, as the Apostles have taught and the holy Fathers affirmed…"[96] Luka then calls on them:

> to believe in the Resurrection and everlasting life, and in the everlasting torment for sinners. Be not idle in going to church, both to matins, and to Divine Liturgy, and to vespers, and in your cell, wanting to sleep, only go to bed after having worshipped God. Be present in church with the fear of God; do not converse, nor muse, but beseech God with all (your) mind that He will forgive your sins. Have charity toward every man, but above all toward the brethren.[97]

His teachings on how the monks should live the Christian life are merely a list of bible verses, which, while showing a knowledge of Scripture, do not probe deeper: "do not render evil for evil,"[98] "be meek and humble," "do not swear by God's name,"[99] "fear God, honor the prince,"[100] "do not kill,[101] do not steal,[102] do not lie,[103] do not bear false witness,[104] do not hate,[105] do not covet,[106] do not slander, do not commit adultery either with a slave or with anyone else,"¹⁰⁷ and so forth.

Fennell and Stokes describe the homily as "of the simplest nature" in which "no explanations are given, no examples…. nothing is done to help the listener understand why he should obey these instructions." It is a "gaunt and artless" address and a "strange hotch-potch of doctrinal commands and ethical advice," suggesting that "perhaps it is nothing more than a set of precepts written down by Luka for the edification of the clergy of Novgorod, short sermon notes on which their teaching might be based."¹⁰⁸ That is, Luka's sermon was perhaps deeper and fuller and we are left only with a few talking points. It is worth noting that Christianity, at least as an organized, institutionalized church, had only been present in Novgorod for perhaps seventy years and while the chronicles claim Ioakim Korsunianin built the Perun Monastery, the first monastic foundation in the Novgorodian Land, in 995, it is not clear how extensively monasticism had spread by Luka's episcopate.¹⁰⁹ If Ioakim was, in fact, legendary and Luka was the real founder of the eparchy, he may have been teaching some of the first monks – and the first Christians – in the eparchy and may, therefore, have needed to teach them very basic Christian tenets. Additionally, Eastern Orthodox monasticism did not emphasize the need for a monastic clergy trained in theology, as monasticism in Western Christianity did, especially beginning in the early thirteenth century with the creation of the mendicant orders and the increasing clericalization of monks. Orthodox monks, especially in the medieval period, were meant to withdraw from the world and play their part in salvation history by praying for humanity.

Despite its simplicity, Ivan Evseev noted that the homily bears similarities to Cyril of Jerusalem's addresses to catechumens and concluded that Luka used at least the first of Cyril's addresses in drawing up his homily.¹¹⁰ So, while he may have not been a great theologian or exegete, he does show his familiarity with biblical texts (not surprising for a bishop) and some Patristic writings.¹¹¹

But if the homily's simplicity was due to the newness of Christianity in Novgorod, it must be said that no great theological work or exegetical treatise ever appeared there in the medieval period, even as the Christian faith took deeper root. The writings of the archbishops that are still extant show that their message remained simple and straightforward. The *Voproshanie Kirika,* a series of 152 questions from the archiepiscopate of Nifont, are fairly limited in a theological or exegetical sense, but do show Nifont's understanding of the Nomocanon or *Kormchaia.*[112] Named for the monk Kirik, who posed one hundred and one of the questions, though another 24 were posed by the priest Sava, and 28 by Il'ia, who, again, may have succeeded Nifont to the archiepiscopal throne.[113] The questions deal with relatively simple procedural issues, such as what penance to assign for certain sins,[114] proper conduct during fasts,[115] and the correct way to celebrate the liturgy.[116] However, some have argued that the *Voproshanie* shows not only basic tenets of the Orthodox faith, but also a rudimentary form of episcopal training, that is, if in fact Archbishop Il'ia and the priest Il'ia mentioned in the *Voproshanie* are one and the same.[117] It is also interesting that a certain Arkadii is mentioned, who might have been bishop between Nifont and Il'ia.[118]

Besides the *Voproshanie,* Nifont is also shown in the *Novgorodian First Chronicle* combating un-Christian or improper behavior through the withholding of sacraments. In 1136 he forbade his priests from presiding over the marriage of Prince Sviatoslav Ol'govich of Chernihiv, though it is not clear why Nifont concluded that "it behooves him not to take her to wife."[119] That the marriage was within prohibited degrees of consanguinity is highly unlikely since the bride was the daughter of a *posadnik,* and several historians have discussed the possibility that Sviatoslav was already married, but the chronicle simply does not say why Nifont forbade the marriage.[120] Whatever the reason, the marriage was technically non-canonical, since the marriage document had to be issued by the bishop. Furthermore, all priests are subject to the local bishop and priests from outside the eparchy are forbidden from performing sacraments except in dire emergencies. In 1145, Nifont also forbade his priests from presiding over the funerals of two drowned priests, perhaps because they had committed suicide, although, again, the chronicle does not specify.[121]

Like Nifont's answers and Luka's homily, Archbishop Il'ia's rules are simple and practical. There are, in fact, two sets of instructions: Pavel Tikhomirov wrote that the first set was drawn up by a domestic in the House of Holy Wisdom named Kirik, based on Il'ia's earlier teachings to the white clergy,[122] but according to Konstantin Kalaidovich, these were part of a letter sent to the bishop of Bilhorod Kyivskii (Belgorod).[123] The second set was Il'ia's own rules to the monastic clergy.[124] In the instructions to the white clergy, the administration of sacraments are addressed: what to do if it is uncertain whether a person has been baptized (baptize them again), and on confession, what to do if the priest forgets to put water or wine in the chalice during the Divine Liturgy, or

> If it happens that a mouse begins to gnaw at the Eucharistic bread (*agntsa*,[125] nom. sing. *agnets*, lit. "the Lamb") during the service [of the Divine Liturgy] and the priest sees it before the transfer or during the transfer of the holy gifts [i.e., before or during the Great Entrance – MP], then having cleaned it with a knife, let the service continue, but do not take out new Eucharistic bread; put the piece (*krokhi* – piece, crumb) on the *eiliton*[126] (and then drop it in the water).[127]

The instructions to the monastic clergy ("*Pravila Chernorriztsem*") call on them to live away from the world, avoid secular people as much as possible, not be drawn into worldly affairs, not allow women inside the monastery, obey the hegumen, not store away gold or silver, and be a monk at all times and in all places.[128] Il'ia cites a number of biblical passages: The Second Letter of Timothy, explaining that soldiers (for Christ) did not get involved in business affairs;[129] The Letter to the Romans, the Gospel of John, and the Psalms on being children of God, etc.[130] He also refers to the Third and Fourth Canons of the Council of Chalcedon,[131] again showing at least some knowledge of the Bible and *Kormchaia*. But, just like his predecessors, none of this is particularly profound theologically.

Vasilii Kalika's Letter to the Bishop Feodor of Tver' (*Poslanie Vasiliia Novgorodskogo Feodoru Tverskomu o rae*) is a much more interesting piece, and one which has led to lively debate among scholars as to its meaning.[132] Bishop Feodor apparently doubted the existence of a physical, earthly paradise, saying that only a spiritual one existed. Vasilii, having heard of Feodor's doubts, wrote to convince him that an earthly paradise had, in fact existed, and still does. He used several arguments, some of them understandable for a clergyman, but one of them also quite interesting. First, he quoted the Bible. An earthly paradise must have, and must still exist, he wrote, because the Book of Genesis states that the Tigris, Euphrates, and Nile Rivers flowed from it.[133] Adam had also been expelled from paradise, so again, it must have existed.[134] Adam's bones were in Jerusalem,[135] which Vasilii had likely seen during his pilgrimage there,[136] and after the Resurrection, God had commanded Adam to enter paradise, so it still existed at that time.[137] Vasilii also wrote that the dead who had been raised up and entered Jerusalem on Good Friday had come from this earthly paradise.[138] Second, he cited examples from the saints: St. Macarius had lived 20 *poprishches* from paradise,[139] St. Ephrosinius, called Evfrosim in the letter, had received three apples from paradise,[140] and St. John Chrysostom had written that paradise was in the East and Hell was in the West.[141] It was, thus, an earthly place one could travel to, and take apples from; it had a geographic location (in the East.) and was not merely a spiritual realm.[142] Vasilii also argued that those destined for heaven would remain in the earthly paradise until the Second Coming, and that Mary, as well as Enoch, Elijah, and other Old Testament prophets and saints were in the earthly paradise.[143]

Vasilii went on to write that God did not allow men of his day to see paradise, but that "many of my children (i.e., his spiritual children) the Novgorodians" had seen the entrance to hell, in the West – in "the Blowing Sea" (*na Dyshuchem' mori* – as the Rus' called the White Sea and the Arctic Ocean), guarded by a great serpent, where the river Morg flows into the underworld three times a day.[144] If God allowed this place of torture to continue in existence, Vasilii asked, how much more must He have allowed paradise to still exist? In fact, he wrote that God's "words and deeds are everlasting." He went on to argue that "this place, holy paradise, was found by Moislav the Novgorodian and his son, Iakov"[145] (contradicting his earlier statement that God no longer allowed men to see paradise); Moislav and Iakov, with others, traveling in three boats, were blown off course with one boat lost; the remaining two came after a long time to a beautiful mountain, "and they saw on that mountain an image of a Deesis, painted with wonderful azure and decorated beyond measure, as if not created by human hands."[146] And though they never saw the sun, they saw that the place shone by its own light and they heard joyful singing. When they sent a man up to the top of the mountain, he began laughing and clapping his hands and ran away toward the singing. A second did likewise, so they sent up a third man with a rope tied around his leg, and when he tried to run away, they pulled him back down the mountain but found him dead, so they fled from the place. Vasilii assured Feodor that these men's children and grandchildren still lived in Novgorod.[147]

A physical paradise, and the saints in it were, thus, a physical reality to Vasilii Kalika. Scripture and the saints told him this was so, and members of his own Novgorodian flock had seen it with their own eyes during journeys to the East.

While this is the liveliest of the documents revealing the teaching role of the bishops and archbishops of Novgorod, only four men: Luka Nifont, Il'ia, and Vasilii Kalika left us admittedly rather scant and unsophisticated documents compared to what we find in Byzantine and Latin literature of the same time. Novgorod or the wider Rus' church had no Photius or Gregory of Palamas, no Anselm, Bonaventura, or Thomas Aquinas. The bishops and archbishops of Novgorod took the basic doctrines and rituals that Ioakim Korsunianin or Luka Zhidiata and their brother bishops, and the missionaries under them, had taught around the turn of the eleventh century and seem not to have ventured many new ideas about them. That Archbishop Gennadii, at the turn of the sixteenth century, complained that "ignorant men are instructing children," and called on the metropolitan to set up a system of schools to train priests,[148] and half a century after that, the Stoglav Council noted that village priests throughout Muscovy were often uneducated and even illiterate,[149] unfortunately indicate that the archbishops of Novgorod, and indeed, the bishops throughout the Rus' church, had not succeeded in even teaching their own clergy, let alone the laity over the entire medieval period.

The Sacraments

The sacramental and holy nature of the archiepiscopal office is seen throughout the chronicles and other medieval sources. In times of distress or pestilence archbishops prayed for the Christians in their care, they prayed for peace when the city was attacked or the army away on campaign, cared for the sick, comforted the dying, and buried the dead. In happier times, they christened and enthroned princes and celebrated their marriages, established churches and monasteries, celebrated the Divine Liturgy in the cathedral, and led processions around the city. Miraculous powers were attributed to them. In 1169, Archbishop Il'ia prayed for the city, then besieged by Prince Andrei Bogoliubskii's Suzdalian army, and, through the intercessions of the Mother of God, saved the city.[150] In 1238, Archbishop Spiridon prayed for the city's deliverance from the Mongols, who turned away still 100 *versty* from the city.[151] The chronicles credit the archbishops with saving Pskov from the plague in 1360 and 1389, as well as Novgorod in 1390.[152] When a massive fire swept through Novgorod in 1342 and looting ensued, "the *Vladyka* (Vasilii) with the hegumens and the priests ordered a fast and made processions with crosses to the monasteries and churches throughout the city, praying to God and to His Immaculate Mother, that He might avert from us His just wrath."[153] In 1421, when the Volkhov River overflowed its banks and inundated nineteen monasteries, Archbishop Simeon and the clergy made tearful prayers in the Cathedral of Holy Wisdom for divine deliverance.[154]

Beyond these extraordinary events, the archbishops would have regularly administered the sacraments, but chroniclers mention this only on special or extraordinary occasions, such the celebration of the Divine Liturgy upon arrival in the city after their consecration, or when princes were baptized, a *posadnik* married, or boiars or hegumens buried. Thus, Archbishop Il'ia, the hegumens, and the clergy celebrated a Divine Liturgy and funeral service in the Cathedral of Holy Wisdom for Prince Mstislav Rostislavich in June 1180.[155] Vasilii's baptism of Prince Mikhail, infant son of Prince Aleksandr Mikhailovich of Tver', in Pskov in 1333 has already been mentioned, but he also baptized Narimont, the adult son of Lithuanian Grand Prince Gedymin (Gediminas) (Narimont received the Christian name of Gleb) also in Pskov.[156] The chronicle also indicates that in 1342 Vasilii presided over the funeral of Posadnik Varfalomei Iure'vich in the presence of the hegumens and priests of Novgorod.[157] The chronicles never mention the archbishops administering the sacraments to the common people.

The apparent favoritism might suggest the archbishop associated only with the elites and eschewed the common people. Indeed, scholars like Khoroshev and Karger – the latter admittedly an art and architectural historian – claim the archbishops were drawn from the upper classes, despite some evidence to the contrary.[158] But the archbishops may just as likely have administered the sacraments to all the people, rich and poor alike, but chroniclers only noted special occasions involving important people. The chronicles, like modern newspapers or news broadcasts, pointed out the extraordinary and the unusual, when princes or *posadniki* were baptized or buried, but not the less interesting, everyday activities of the common people.

Administration of the Archeparchy

The importance and wealth of the archeparchy required an ecclesiastical administration to managed important legal, financial, and economic activities (the economics of the archiepiscopal office will be discussed more fully of Chapter 6). Like other archiepiscopal functions, these are somewhat confined to a relatively small area of the archeparchy, suggesting archiepiscopal power was not as great as some scholars would have us believe.

Pastoral Visits

Over the entire period under study, the chronicles report only ten archbishops making twenty-three pastoral visits or visitations (*poezdka*, pl. *poezdki*) outside the city of Novgorod itself. Eighteen of these were to Pskov, the remaining five to Karelia, Ladoga, Staraia Russa, and the Zavoloch'e. All but three of these took place after 1330. In the twelfth century, Nifont, Gavriil, and Martirii traveled to Pskov, Ladoga, and Staraia Russa, respectively. After that, there was a period of more than one hundred twenty years in which no *poezdki* are reported.¹⁵⁹ This gap in activity is again, seen in other spheres of activity and is explained in part by the dispute between Mitrofan, Antonii, and Arsenii over the archiepiscopal office, which switched hands five times between 1211 and 1229.¹⁶⁰ The Mongol Invasion of 1237-1240 also explains the lack of visitations outside the city for part of this period. However, no *poezdki* took place from the election of Spiridon in 1229 and the Mongol Conquest, or for almost a century after that. Rus' may have been physically, economically, and psychologically devastated for some time after 1240, but the Mongol Conquest cannot completely explain this, or other such breaks in activity, which lasted to the beginning of the archiepiscopate of Vasilii Kalika in 1330.¹⁶¹

Whatever the cause, Vasilii revived the office after this nine decades of decline,¹⁶² and it is with him that pastoral visits resumed. He visited Pskov in 1330, 1333, 1338, and 1352. It was a lucrative destination since the fees of its ecclesiastical courts were supposed to go to the archbishop while he was in residence (just as they went to the metropolitan when he visited Novgorod, though Pskov often denied the archbishops the right, just as Novgorod did to the metropolitans). As the second city in the archeparchy, which had its own school or style of icon-painting and was an important market center on the road to Livonia and Lithuania, its size and cultural and economic importance explain why the archbishops visited more frequently than other towns in the archeparchy. But beyond lucrative court fees, Vasilii was called by the Pskovites themselves in 1352, a mission of mercy that failed and cost Vasilii his own life.¹⁶³ Aleksei visited Pskov thrice, in 1360, 1373, and 1384,¹⁶⁴ and the chronicler notes that Aleksei's 1360 visit was also made to bless the city during an outbreak of plague.¹⁶⁵ Aleksei also consecrated the Church of Sts. Peter and Paul there, accompanied by the choir (*svoim krilosom*) of the Cathedral of Holy Wisdom.¹⁶⁶ His successor, Ioann, visited Pskov four times. His 1389 visitation was, like Vasilii Kalika's and Aleksei's earlier visits, to pray for the city's deliverance from the plague, in this case successfully.¹⁶⁷ The sources record only two other archiepiscopal visits outside the city of Novgorod from Ioann's archiepiscopate to 1478, when Archbishop Simeon visited Karelia, in 1419,¹⁶⁸ and Evfimii II traveled to the Zavoloch'e region (the land "Beyond the Portages"), the vast, unorganized territories comprising the northeastern part of the Novgorodian Land, in 1446.[169]

The archbishops must certainly have passed through a number of districts on the way to Kyiv, Volynia, Moscow, or other places outside the archeparchy, when they journeyed to their consecration or on "church business," though the sources only offer a few specific instances, as when Archbishop Mitrofan went to Toropets after being expelled from Novgorod in 1211,[170] or when his successor, Antonii, went to Torzhok in 1219 after the Novgorodians brought Mitrofan back and brusquely told Antonii: "Go where you want."[171] To be fair, these were not "pastoral visits," but the archbishops must have also visited other places on state business, as when Archbishop Moisei (and the metropolitan) threatened Pskov with excommunication for harboring Grand Prince Aleksandr Mikhailovich.[172] The chronicles note that Grand Prince Ivan Kalika, the metropolitan, and Archbishop Moisei remained in the village of Opoki east of Pskov.[173] Vasilii Kalika's 1352 journey to rebuild the fortress at Orekhov, where Lake Ladoga empties into the Neva River, is another rare example of an archbishop visiting districts outside Novgorod itself, though that was not a "pastoral visit" in the spiritual sense.[174]

The infrequency of visits may indicate the archeparchy was organized well enough to not need direct personal intervention by the archbishops. Archaeological evidence suggests several towns in the *Piatiny* – the more populated and organized western part of the Novgorodian Land, such as Ladoga and Torzhok – may have been administered by the archbishops' *namestniki* who might have reported to him by messenger or traveled to Novgorod, thus making archiepiscopal visitations to those towns unnecessary.[175] Conversely, it may also be that Novgorod, Pskov, Ladoga, Staraia Russa, and a few other towns were Christian islands in an otherwise pagan sea, so that there were neither many parishes outside Novgorod, nor an extensive ecclesiastical administration (especially outside the *Piatiny*) necessitating archiepiscopal visitations. That is, the vast eastern hinterland of Novgorod, and perhaps much of the rural parts of the *Piatiny* themselves, had no churches to administer or Christians to visit or teach.[176] Being sparsely populated, it may not even have had that many pagans to convert (though, as has been noted, there was some missionary activity).

The Parish Structure in the Fifths

It is extremely difficult to say much at all about the parish structure in the Novgorodian archeparchy during the medieval period. The Novgorodian land cadastres (*Novgorodskie Pistsovye Knigi*) do provide some indication of the parish structure outside the city itself, but they date from only the 1490s at the earliest,[177] more than a decade after the period under study. They therefore do not necessarily indicate the parish structure from before 1478, nor do they show how it changed (and grew) from the twelfth to the late fifteenth centuries. However, they provide at least a general outline of the church at the local level outside the city of Novgorod.

Based on his study of the parish clergy from the *Pistsovye knigi*, Dmitrii Balovnev counted 823 churchmen serving the 349 churches registered in the cadastres,[178] not a huge number of personnel to oversee, and thus perhaps explaining the seeming confinement of archiepiscopal activities to the city of Novgorod itself. Balovnev explains that each parish was supposed to have six staff-members: a priest, a deacon, a *d'iak* or *d'iachka* (who, while not counted among the church hierarchy, carried out important functions such as acting as the parish clerk and picking readers and the choir), a *ponomar'* (who rang the bell and sang in the choir), a *storozh* (watchman), and a *proskurnitsa* (*prosvirnia, prosfornia*) who baked the Eucharistic bread (called the *prosvira* or *prosfor*).[179] The cadastres indicate that in the late fifteenth and into the sixteenth century the churches in the *Piatiny* were understaffed. If all had been fully staffed, there should have been 2,094 church personnel in the *Piatiny* (349 churches x 6 staff members each). As it is, only 82% of the churches had a priest, only 60% had *d'iaki* or *d'iachki*, only 24% had *ponomaria*, only 26% had *storozhia*, 40% had *poskurnitsy*, and a mere 3.4% had deacons.[180] (See Table 3:1 in appendix)

Not only were they understaffed, there is also little indication that the archbishops had contact with these rural parishes. They may have been overseen by archiepiscopal *namestniki* or *volostiteli*, as these officials are mentioned in the chronicles for various districts and some of their seals have been found in archaeological excavations. According to tradition and canon law, the bishop would ordain priests and deacons (less than 300 men according to the cadastres), but how much contact he had with them after their ordination is unknown, and it seems unlikely he would have any contact at all with the *ponomar'ia, proskurnitsa, d'iaki,* or *storozhi* who would have been answerable to the local priest or, at most, the district *namestniki*. Thus the cadastres reveals the vast archeparchy was, to a certain extent, devoid of Christians for much of the period under study. There was no powerful archbishop overseeing a vast and influential church administration in one of the most important eparchies of the Kyiv province. This is certainly not to argue that the archbishops were insignificant. For one, we do not know the number of Christians, priests, or parishes in other eparchies of Medieval Rus', so relative to others, the Novgorodian archbishops may have been powerful, but it seems their church, in terms of clergy and believers, was much smaller and less influential than earlier scholarship seems to suggest.

Relations with Pskov

The archbishops' oversight of Novgorod's "Little Brother," Pskov, seems strangely circumscribed. While Pskov was the destination of most of their visitations outside Novgorod the Great, relations were strained for significant periods and the archbishop's ability to exercise episcopal authority over the church in Pskov was limited. The archbishops were often unable to sit in judgment (and receive the court fees) in Pskov, so that the second most important city of the archeparchy was *de facto* autonomous from the archbishop in Novgorod just as Novgorod was from the metropolitans. The patriarchs of Constantinople and the metropolitans of Kyiv and All Rus' dispatched letters directly to the Pskovites against the *Strigol'niki*,[181] and not to the archbishops in Novgorod, another indication of the strange relations between the archbishops and their flock in Pskov. And while these letters called on the Pskovites to be obedient to their bishop, they suggest Pskov had attained a considerable degree of ecclesiastical independence at some point in the fourteenth or fifteenth century just as it had been politically independent since the Treaty of Bolotovo in 1348.

There are yet more indicators that the church in Pskov operated independently of its bishop or that the Novgorodian archbishop's authority was limited there, and metropolitans not only approved this, but initiated it. Around 1395, Metropolitan Kiprian sent a letter to the clergy in Pskov (dated April 17, but without any year) explaining that he had consecrated antimensions in Novgorod and ordered the archbishop (Ioann) to send them to Pskov,[182] but Kiprian later heard that Ioann had gone to Pskov and given them the antimensions, but told the Pskovites to cut them into four pieces (to consecrate more churches without needing the metropolitan to consecrate more antimensions). This angered Kiprian, since it was not right to cut up the cloths after they had been consecrated. He sent another 60 antimensions with the letter to the clergy of the Trinity church (the current cathedral in Pskov), and told them to use them to consecrate churches but not to cut them into pieces. He also instructed them on the proper way to baptize and distribute communion, and other church practices which were apparently being improperly done in Pskov (and possibly Novgorod as well).[183] But more importantly for our discussion, he was instructing the Pskov clergy to carry our sacraments and consecrate churches without the participation or approval of their archbishop in Novgorod.

Metropolitan Isidor's removal of Pskov from Novgorod's episcopal jurisdiction, mentioned in the previous chapter, is another such instance of Pskov ecclesiastical autonomy from Novgorod. And despite Oskar Halecki's argument that Isidor returned Pskov to the archbishops' control upon his return from Florence in 1441,[184] other evidence indicates that later metropolitans maintained Pskov's special status. The lack of archiepiscopal visitations to Pskov until Evfimii II visited in 1453 and 1457 is highly suggestive.[185] His successor, Iona, despite Pskov's refusal to pay the tithe to Novgorod and its demand for its own bishop in 1463-1464, forgave the city and visited there in 1466 and again in 1468, the latter in response to a plague outbreak.[186] This shows that Pskov was still under the archbishop's ecclesiastical jurisdiction, but also that the relationship remained irregular.

Other metropolitans' letters also suggest Pskov's autonomy from its archbishop. Fotii's letters, in particular, dealt not only with the *Strigol'niki*, but also with the remarrying of nuns, even those who had taken the *schema*, laicization of the clergy, laymen changing confessors, neglect of fasting and communion rules, lack of discipline in the monasteries - including monks wearing "German" (i.e., foreign or even Catholic) garb – and dancing and "diabolical" games on the part of the laity. All these things would have been the prerogative or duty of the Novgorodian archbishop to address (or left to him to deal with) rather than the metropolitan writing the local clergy in Pskov, unless, that is, Pskov was ecclesiastically autonomous of Novgorod.[187]

Pskov's attempts to establish *de jure* independence from Novgorod on at least three occasions – in 1307, 1331, and 1463-1464 – also highlight the atypical ecclesiastical status of Pskov within the archeparchy.[188] In 1331, Lithuanian Grand Prince Gedymin (ca. 1316-1341) and Pskov Prince Aleksandr Mikhailovich even sent emissaries to Metropolitan Feognost in Volodymyr asking that a certain Arsenii be made bishop of a newly-created episcopate at Pskov.[189] The metropolitan included Arsenii among the three candidates for archbishop of Novgorod, from which Vasilii Kalika was chosen, thus denying the princes' request.[190] This probably goes far in explaining the sometimes-turbulent relationship Vasilii had with Pskov He visited the city in 1333, when he baptized Mikhail Aleksandrovich and Narimont,[191] but when he visited again in 1337, he was denied the traditional right of jurisdiction and he left, "having cursed them."[192] He only visited again when the Pskovites summoned him after plague broke out in the city in 1352.[193]

At roughly the same time the archbishops were losing their power over Pskov, their title changed to explicitly include Pskov and emphasize their ecclesiastical oversight of that city. Prior to 1400 the archbishops are formally titled "Archbishop of Novgorod the Great" or "The Novgorodian archbishop." But in 1400, the title "Archbishop of Novgorod the Great and Pskov" first appears. Interestingly, it is the *Pskov First Chronicle*, rather than a Novgorodian one, that first refers to Ioann II as "Most Holy (*preosviashchennyi*) Archbishop of Novgorod the Great and Pskov."[194] The title, however, is not found again in the Pskov chronicle until 1448, and is not even used consistently thereafter,[195] and the title "Archbishop of Novgorod the Great," without reference to Pskov, is still found in many documents after 1400.[196] Furthermore, the *Novgorodian First Chronicle*, compiled in the archbishops' own scriptorium, uses the titles "*Vladyka*," "archbishop," or "Novgorodian archbishop;" and never refers to Pskov in the archbishops' titles. It would seem more likely for Novgorod to use the title in an effort to assert its ecclesiastical authority over Pskov, or to cover up the fact that it was actually losing control over that city, while Pskov should have denied the addition of their city to the Novgorodian archbishop's title since it would undercut Pskov's striving for a politically and ecclesiastically independence.

The addition of the city of Pskov in the archbishop's title appears in the sphragistic evidence more than a half century after its appearance in the Pskov chronicles. All legible archiepiscopal seals prior to Iona's (r. 1458-1470) refer to "the Archbishop of Novgorod the Great;" Iona's is the first seal to bear the inscription "Archbishop of Novgorod the Great and Pskov."[197] This is just as independent Novgorod is declining in the face of Muscovite encroachment, a mere two years after the humiliating Treaty of Iazhelbitsy. Scholars see Iona as rather pro-Moscow and thus it seems odd for him to make such an assertion of Novgorod's independence and power (over Pskov). It is, ultimately unknown why the title was adopted. It may merely be that, as the metropolitans were styled "of Kyiv and All Rus',"[198] other churchmen were taking on similar styles (e.g., the Bishop of Tver' and Kashin). Novgorod may have simply been following suit, and it may not have meant much more than that.

In some ways, Pskov became ecclesiastically autonomous around the time of the Treaty of Bolotovo in 1348, when Novgorod recognized Pskov's political independence and granted a charter to its "Younger Brother."[199] The Novgorodians also agreed to the Pskovites' demand that the archbishop appoint a Pskovite to sit in judgment there, rather than send a Novgorodian *namestnik* or *tiun*, and not to extradite Pskovites to Novgorod for judgment.[200] This, however, merely limited the archbishop's powers; it did not deny him the right to sit in judgment himself, although, as we have seen, Vasilii Kalika had been denied that right in 1337, more than a decade before the treaty, and the Pskovites were displeased in 1411 when Ioann tried to send a *namestnik* rather than go to Pskov himself.

The *Pskov Judicial Charter* confirms the archbishops' continued authority in Pskov even while it shows that city's abnormal status within the archeparchy. The charter is not blessed by the archbishop, but rather by "our fathers, the priests of all five great churches [in Pskov], and the hieromonks, deacons, and the priests, and the entire clergy of God..."[201] It says little about the ecclesiastical courts and almost nothing about the rights of the Novgorodian archbishops, but does confirm that the archbishop still oversaw the church in Pskov since it stipulated that "Neither the prince, nor the *posadnik*, nor the archbishop's *namestnik* is to retry a trial."[202] It goes on to stipulate the cases to be heard by the ecclesiastical courts:

> The archbishop's *namestnik* is to judge priests, deacons, Eucharist bread makers, monks and nuns. If a priest or deacon [comes before a court] or [if litigation is instituted] against a monk or nun, so that both [litigants] are church people, and not ordinary [citizens], then the prince is not to judge them, nor is the *posadnik*, nor are any other [secular] judges to judge [them], for [they are subject to] the court of the archbishop's *namestnik*. If one of the litigants be an ordinary citizen, a layman, and is not a churchman, then the prince and the *posadnik* are to judge the case in common with the archbishop's *namestnik*.[203]

So, the available evidence shows Pskov's awkward position within the archeparchy, just as Novgorod had an irregular status within the ecclesiastical province of Kyiv. While always formally part of the archeparchy during the period of study – it did not gain its own bishop until 1589 – Pskov exercised considerable autonomy in the fourteenth and fifteenth centuries and at times ran its own ecclesiastical affairs, though the "Archbishop of Novgorod the Great and Pskov" remained its formal hierarch.

The Ecclesiastical Courts

Beyond the sacraments, the ecclesiastical courts were one of the most significant ways the archbishops had a real impact on peoples' lives. Princely statutes, law codes, and other documents give some indication of their competence, court officials are mentioned in the *Russkaia Pravda*, the *Novgorod Judicial Charter*, the *Pskov Judicial Charter*, and various charters and treaties,[204] but judicial rulings (judgment charters) and other court documents themselves are, sadly, no longer extant.[205]

The bishops' and the church's status in early Rus', episcopal authority to try certain crimes or civil infractions, and their authority over "church people" originate from Byzantine canon law. Judicial authority in Rus', however, actually derived from the *Russkaia Pravda*, princely statutes, and other documents promulgated in the years after the baptism of Rus', and the earliest Rus' chronicles confirm this.[206] Princely support for the church and its role in Rus' society was guaranteed in the Shorter Redaction of the *Russkaia Pravda*, drawn up in the mid-eleventh century: it provided a tithe to the church: of every *grivna* fine, 15 *kuny* were to go to the church; from a fine of 12 *grivny*, 2 went to the church.[207]

But the *Pravda* does not mention the bishops' specific political or legal rights or duties. These are set forth in a number of princely charters. Prince Vladimir is traditionally credited with issuing the first of these sometime prior to 1011,[208] the *Statute of St. Prince Vladimir*, which granted the ecclesiastical courts in Rus' all cases involving:

> ...Fornication; adultery; rape; abduction [of women]; [disputes] between a husband and wife over an inheritance; [cases which arise] if [a man and a woman] marry within the prohibited degrees of consanguinity or spiritual relationship [which stem from acting as godparents for someone]; witchcraft; [making of] potions; [making of] charms; sorcery; magic; these three dishonors: [accusation of] fornication and [making of] poisons, heresy; fighting [in which a man bites another]; or [cases in which a son beats his father or [if] a daughter [beats] her mother, or a daughter-in-law [beats her] mother-in-law; if brothers or children bring suit over an inheritance; church theft; [cases in which] people uncover a [buried] corpse; [if some people] cut down a cross or carve [mutilate?] a cross on the walls; or [if some-

one] leads cattle, or dogs, or fowl [into church] without good reason, or does anything else not fitting for church; or [if] two friends fight and the wife of one grabs the other by the genitals and crushes [them]; or [if] they catch someone with a four-legged animal [about to sacrifice it? committing bestiality?] or [if] someone prays [to a pagan god] beneath a grain-drying bin, or in a copse of trees, or by the water; or if an [unmarried] girl aborts a fetus.

All these cases are given to the church. The Prince, his boiars and their judges are forbidden to interfere in these courts.

I have given all [these cases to the church courts] according to the regulations of the first [Christian] emperors and according to [the canons of] the seven holy ecumenical councils of the great hierarchs [of the church].[209]

It went on to forbid the prince's judges (*tiuny*, sing. *tiun*) from interfering in the church courts and ordered them to give a tenth of the prince's court fees to the church.[210] It also declared:

From of old it was established and entrusted to the holy bishops to supervise all town and trade scales, weights, and dry measures;[211] from of old it was established by God [that] the bishop is to supervise [these scales and measures] without trickery, neither diminishing nor increasing [the weights and measures], [since] he is to give account of all [these things] on the Day of Judgment, just as [he will] for men's souls."[212]

It furthermore enumerated the church people to be tried not by the princely (or civil) courts, but only by the ecclesiastical courts:

...The abbot, the priest, the deacon, their children, the priest's wife, and whoever is in the choir, the abbess, the monk, the nun, the woman who bakes the

Eucharist bread, the pilgrim, the physician, the freed [debt] slave, the manumitted slave, the wanderer, the blind and the lame; [also all church people] in monasteries, hospitals, inns [and] refuges for wanderers and pilgrims.[213]

The statute explains that "these are church people, those who do God's work. The metropolitan or bishops hold jurisdiction [in disputes] between them, whether [it be a case of] insult, or quarrel, or physical harm or inheritance."[214] Cases involving a church person and another not among the church people were to be presided over jointly by the prince's judge and an ecclesiastical judge, as is seen in the later *Pskov Judicial Charter*.[215] The statute prescribed no legal punishment in the event that the ecclesiastical courts were not established in this manner. However, those guilty of violating the statute were to be "cursed in this age and in all the next by the seven ecumenical councils of the holy Fathers,"[216] which to the medieval mind, may have counted for more than any legal punishment the prince could have meted out.

Many of the same provisions are found in *the Statute of Prince Iaroslav* (r. 1019-1054), the oldest extant copy of which dates only to the fifteenth century, though its similarities to Byzantine legislation and the *Statute of Vladimir* suggest an earlier origin.[217] Both Vladimir's and Iaroslav's statutes recognize the rights or privileges of "the metropolitan and the bishops," so that, while issued in Kyiv, they also applied to Novgorod and the other eparchies.[218] Iaroslav's went beyond his father's statute to specify what fines were to be paid to the metropolitan or bishop and gave them jurisdiction over the following: "divorce [cases] in all towns; the customs duty each tenth week [is to go] to the church and the metropolitan; and his people are not to pay the customs duty anywhere, nor the duty on goods entering a town; and I have given [the church the revenues from] the 'eighth' [exacted from weighed goods brought into town for trade]."[219]

The fines for various crimes went to the metropolitan or bishop: if the daughter of a boiar was abducted or raped, ten gold *grivny* were levied, with five going to the metropolitan. If she was the daughter of a lesser boiar, two *grivny* were levied with one going to the metropolitan. If she was the daughter of the "good people," the fine was two silver *grivny*, with one ruble going to the metropolitan. Those abetting in the crime were to each pay sixty *nogaty* to the metropolitan. Punishment was left to the prince.[220] If a man put aside his wife and she was the daughter of a boiar, the man was fined three hundred *grivny* (paid to the wife) and a fee of five gold *grivny* was paid to the metropolitan.[221] Women sent to convents for adultery or for killing their newborn babies, or for other offenses, could be redeemed by a payment to the metropolitan.[222] Rapists paid a fine to the metropolitan and were punished by the prince.[223] A godfather having intercourse with a godmother paid a fine to the metropolitan,[224] as did adulterers,[225] arsonists,[226] those guilty of incest or who married within prohibited degrees of consanguinity[227] or polygamy,[228] Jews or Muslims or non-Orthodox foreigners who married Rus' [Orthodox Christian] women,[229] those who had sex with nuns[230] or engaged in bestiality,[231] as well as fornicators,[232] thieves,[233] those guilty of pagan practices,[234] fighting,[235] and so on.

This statute also gave the metropolitan or bishop jurisdiction over cases involving church people – specifically identified as monks, nuns, priests, priests' wives, widows (of priests), the women who bake the Eucharist bread, and the sextons – and he was to judge them separately from laymen, "and [he is] free to condemn them to whatever [he pleases]."[236] Priests, monks, or nuns who got "drunk at an inappropriate time [e.g., during Lent]" were guilty before the metropolitan or bishop,[237] as were priests who christened children outside their own districts except in dire emergencies.[238] A monk or nun who renounced their vows paid 40 *grivny*.[239] The statute also decreed that "whatever goes on among monastery people and among church people, and in the monasteries themselves, neither the prince nor the rural judge [is to] interfere in that, and the metropolitan's *volosteli* have jurisdiction over these [matters], and their escheated estates go to the metropolitan's *volostel'*."[240] Those guilty of interfering in the episcopal courts were, as in the earlier statute, to be cursed: "to stand with me at the Judgment before God and be cursed by the three hundred and eighteen holy fathers who were in Nicaea" and by all the saints.[241] But unlike the earlier statute, they were to be judged and punished severely according to the temporal law as well, though the exact punishment is not specified.[242]

Both statutes indicate that the princes recognized that the metropolitan and ecclesiastical courts held, or were at least legally entitled to hold, jurisdiction over many areas, mainly dealing with family law, inheritance, heresy, witchcraft, pagan practices, as well as those involving church people. The *Statute of Iaroslav* also indicates that the metropolitans and bishops gained monetarily from the court fees assessed for each case.

Several local princes also issued statutory charters for their principalities, granting jurisdiction similar to what we see in Vladimir's and Iaroslav's statutes, even though they had already granted authority and jurisdiction "to the metropolitan and the bishops."[243] The earliest of these local statutes is the *Statutory Charter of the Smolensk Prince Rostislav Mstislavich*, issued on the occasion of the founding of the Smolensk eparchy (sometime between 1137 and 1150), though it survives in only a sixteenth century copy.[244] Like Vladimir's and Iaroslav's statutes, it gives ecclesiastical courts jurisdiction over cases involving family and marriage law and criminal offenses connected with the church or committed by church people.[245] Novgorod's local ecclesiastical charter was issued by Prince Vsevolod Mstislavich around 1136. Given that he was dismissed so soon after issuing it, "The Statute of the Novgorod Prince Vsevolod [1135-1137] on Church Courts, [Church] People, and Trade Measures" may have never gone into force.[246] It was similar to other statutes from Kyiv and other eparchies, and likely served as precedent for the archbishops' later authority. It forbade the prince's children, his *namestniki* and *tiuny*, or his boiars, from interfering with the church, specifically with the collection of fees by the House of Holy Wisdom, the Church of St. John's, and the church courts.[247] The charter also declared that "the archbishop of Novgorod together with the hundred-men are to supervise the House of St. Sophia [Holy Wisdom], while the elders are to answer to the archbishop, or to whomever of our lineage shall be prince in Novgorod, and are to support the house of St. John."[248]

The fifteenth century *Novgorodian Judicial Charter* laid out other legal powers enjoyed by the Novgorodian archbishops. Although dating only 1470 or 1471,[249] it speaks of the legal functions of the archbishops in terms similar to those set out in earlier statutes and speaks of these functions being carried out "according to custom," suggesting it was a confirmation of earlier practices, perhaps carried out since the time of Vsevolod's charter.[250]

The charter states that "Hieromonk Feofil, who was appointed to the archbishopric of Novgorod the Great and Pskov, is to conduct his own court, the church court, according to the canons of the Holy Fathers, and according to the Nomocanon; and he is to judge everyone equally, whether boiar, [a man of] middle means, or a poor man."[251] Furthermore, it forbade anyone "to remove the *posadnik, tysiatskii,* the archbishop's *namestniki,* and their judges from [their] court[s],"[252] and the *posadniki, tysiatskie* and the archbishop and all their judges were protected from slander.[253] The archbishop, his *namestnik,* and the steward who affixed the seal to documents, were to receive 1 *grivna* for each ruble (10% of the penalty) for each case that went to court, and 3 *dengi* for each case which did not go to court (e.g., because a defendant failed to appear).[254] The *posadnik, tysiatskii,* archbishop's *namestnik,* and their judges were also ordered to finish their cases within a month.[255] Other sections mentioned the archiepiscopal role in the courts, including his bailiff,[256] stipulated that referral hearings were held in the archbishop's chamber;[257] and that if an archbishop's *namestnik* was to leave town for an extended period and not finish a case, he was to pay a fine of fifty rubles to the grand prince.[258]

These charters show a progressive development of the bishop's judicial roles. The *Statute of Vladimir* gives the church courts jurisdiction over certain cases and over certain people. The *Statute of Iaroslav* repeats these areas of jurisdiction and stipulates the fines to be levied in each case. The statutes of the Smolensk and Novgorodian princes were issued for specific localities. The *Novgorodian Judicial Charter* and the *Pskov Judicial Charters* confirm the earlier laws of these cities and provide specific details on judicial personnel and court administration. All of them show that from the twelfth to the fifteenth century there was an understanding that certain cases and people ("church people") were the exclusive purview of the church. They also show that the church and its bishops played important roles in Rus' jurisprudence and society, and that the church was supported through tithes and judicial fees, which made the church and its bishops wealthy.

It is important to note, however, that the canons and statutes, like all laws, were not always followed. George Weickhardt wrote that in spite of statutory grants, "the bishops' courts nonetheless had to struggle constantly to preserve their jurisdiction over clergymen."[259] He noted that in 1395, Metropolitan Kiprian complained that lay judges in Pskov were hearing cases involving church people, and Archbishop Simeon prohibited such cases again in 1418, under penalty of excommunication for the lay judges, a penalty which Metropolitan Fotii confirmed.[260] In 1416, Simeon had reminded the hegumen and monks of the Snetogorskii Monastery of the Mother of God, just north of Pskov, that the hegumens, and not Pskov's secular judges, had jurisdiction over the monasteries.[261]

The Monasteries

Simeon's letter brings us to the question of the archbishop's jurisdiction over the monasteries in the Novgorodian archeparchy. As monasticism was an extremely important aspect of both Eastern and Western Christianity during the Middle Ages, understanding how the monasteries fit into the administrative structure of the archeparchy would add much to our understanding of the archiepiscopal office. But what we know of the archbishops' relationship with the monasteries, like many of their other activities, is limited. We know, of course, that most of the archbishops were drawn from the monasteries, and that they founded at least sixteen monasteries prior to or during their archiepiscopates and built and repaired a number of monastic churches in already-extant monasteries.[262] They granted land to monasteries and, in a few instances, helped nominate and consecrate hegumens and hegumenias (mothers superior), and presided over their funerals.[263] Luka's *Sermon to the Brethren* and Il'ia's rules show that the archbishops were interested in monastic organization, education, and discipline (as does Simeon's letter). Several archbishops also retired to monasteries and several were buried in monasteries. But beyond that, it is hard to say the particular administrative apparatus by which the archbishops oversaw the hegumens and their monasteries, or if they did so at all.

We must, again, venture into canon law and hazard some speculation as to the archiepiscopal authority over the monasteries. The Fourth Canon of the Council of Chalcedon in 451 declared:

> It is decreed that no one anywhere build or found a monastery or oratory contrary to the will of the bishop of the city; and that the monks in every city and district shall be subject to the bishop… and they shall meddle neither in ecclesiastical nor in secular affairs, nor leave their own monasteries to take part in such; unless, indeed, they should at any time through urgent necessity be appointed thereto by the bishop of the city…But the bishop of the city must make the needful provisions for the monasteries.[264]

The Eighth Canon further ordered: "Let the clergy of the poor-houses, monasteries, and martyries remain under the authority of the bishop in every city according to the tradition of the Holy Fathers; and let no one arrogantly cast off the rule of his own bishop,"[265] while the Twenty-fourth Canon stated that monasteries erected at the consent of the bishop shall remain monasteries forever.[266]

The Rus' church's familiarity with ecumenical and certain regional councils that made up a sizeable part of its *Kormchie knigi* has already been discussed. They and the princely statues also helped define the relationship between the bishops and the monasteries. The *Statute of Prince Iaroslav* declared that "whatever goes on among monastery people and among church people, and in the monasteries themselves, neither the prince nor the rural judge [is to] interfere in that, and the metropolitan's [and bishops'] *volosteli* have jurisdiction over these [matters], and their escheated estates go to the metropolitan's *volosteli*."[267] The *Pravosudie mitropolich'e*, an early Muscovite ecclesiastical law dated to the 1380s or 1390s, though its earliest extant copy is only from the sixteenth century,[268] decreed that the bishop alone has jurisdiction over the monasteries.[269] However, none of these statutes clarify what exactly episcopal or archiepiscopal jurisdiction over the monasteries actually entailed, nor is it clear if the *Pravosudie mitropolich'e* was ever in force in Novgorod the Great.

There are later indications of archiepiscopal control over the monasteries which may also have been true in an earlier period. Thus, in 1509, Archbishop Serapion I (r. 1506-1509) was removed from office when he vociferously opposed the removal of the Volokolamsk Monastery from his control. Iosif of Volokolamsk had founded he monastery in 1479 under the patronage of Prince Boris Vasil'evich of Volotsk (r. 1462-1493), but later argued with Boris' son, Fedor, (who maintained material jurisdiction over the monastery) and, in 1507, Iosif requested Grand Prince Vasilii III take the monastery under his direct protection, which he did with Metropolitan Simon's blessing (who would have then assumed spiritual jurisdiction while the grand prince would have had material control).[270] Serapion, who obviously took his spiritual jurisdiction over the monasteries seriously, protested.[271] In 1543, archbishop Feodosii II wrote to the hegumen of the Pskov Caves Monastery telling him to forgive the elder (*starets*) Savatii, who had been thrown out of the monastery, since a Christian should always strive to forgive, as God forgave King David.[272] These incidents are, of course, outside the timeframe of this study, but they clearly indicate that the archbishops in the sixteenth century, basing their argument on earlier precedent (Serapion cited numerous canon laws and Church Fathers to support his claim; Feodosii quoted Scripture), had control over the monasteries, did not want them taken from under their jurisdiction (in the case of Serapion), and involved themselves in internal disputes when they deemed it appropriate (in the case of Feodosii).

Despite these examples, overall the evidence seems to indicate that the monasteries were largely independent of the archbishops. This cannot be explained simply by saying that the monasteries were far afield – out in the rural districts where the archbishops rarely went – since, contrary to the common image of medieval monasteries as rural establishments far from cities, medieval monasteries, especially in the Novgorodian Land, were largely urban. Numerous monasteries stood within the city itself and still more in its immediate environs. In fact, only a handful were founded in the hinterland of Novgorod or Pskov. Still, Simeon's letter which stressed the hegumens' authority over cases involving monks in their monasteries (rather than his own authority over the monasteries), as well as land charters and other documents, all suggest the monasteries were largely self-administered in day-to-day economic activities, legal jurisdiction, and disciplinary matters. The archbishops had appellate jurisdiction and could step in during extraordinary crises, but there is little evidence of this, particularly prior to 1478. In fact, the archbishops issued immunity charters granting particular monasteries freedom from the appellate jurisdiction of the church courts without a specific summons from the archbishop.

These land and judicial immunity charters date to as early as the mid-twelfth century. During the archiepiscopate of Nifont, Prince Iziaslav Mstislavich, with Nifont's blessing, granted "the villages of Vitoslavits and Smerd and the field of Ushkovo" to the Panteleimon Monastery.[273] The charter prohibited subsequent princes, boiars, and archbishops from interfering with the monastery thereafter.[274] While kept from interfering with the Panteleimon Monastery, whatever that meant, the archbishops maintained ecclesiastical and judicial authority over it and could still summon the hegumen or other monks to court. In other instances, the archbishops waived or modified the right of summons, such as in the mid-fifteenth century charter Evfimii II granted the Spassko-Verendovskii Monastery which gave the monks the privilege of appearing in court only when summoned by the archbishop himself;[275] the archbishop's *namestnik* or other judicial official could not summon them, even when acting on behalf of the archbishop. Archbishops Iona and Feofil later confirmed this privilege.[276] The monastery also received fishing rights on the Verenda River "by the grace of God the Holy Savior and the blessings of archbishop of Novgorod the Great *Vladyka* Ivan."[277] In granting immunity from appellate jurisdiction, the archbishops indicate that they had that right of jurisdiction in the first place since you cannot give away what you do not have, and again, they maintained judicial oversight in maintaining the right to summon the monks personally.

Documents also reveal that hegumens made land transactions without referring matters to the archbishops.[278] Furthermore, the Novgorodian *veche*, or the *vecha* of the different *kontsy*, as well as the *posadniki* and *tysiatskie* granted land to monasteries with no apparent reference to the archbishops, as when the Slavno *konets* granted land to the Savvino-Visherskii Monastery in the mid-fifteenth century.²⁷⁹ Posadnik Ivan Lukinich granted land to the Ostrovskii-Nikolskii Monastery at about this same time, again with no reference to the archbishops.²⁸⁰ Furthermore, Hegumen Sergei of the Monastery of the Intercession of the Mother of God and St. Nicholas the Miracle-worker and the priests and elders of the Ostrovskii Monastery bought land from a certain Karp Vasilev, again with no apparent need for archiepiscopal oversight or approval.²⁸¹ These land transactions would suggest the archbishops, again, left the monasteries alone to run themselves, not surprising since if the archbishops wanted to micromanage the monasteries there would have been no need for monks to elect their hegumens to lead them.

In addition to the ambiguity in documents as to the archbishop's actual authority over the monasteries, traditional historiography asserts that the "archimandrite of Novgorod" was the second most important official in the archeparchy and oversaw the Novgorodian monasteries, thus taking the black clergy largely out of the hands of the archbishops,²⁸² This claim, however, is rather like the claim that the archbishop was the second most important official in the Rus' church after the metropolitan. In both cases, it is hard to speak of a hierarchical order given the simplicity of both the monastic and ecclesiastical hierarchy. There is almost no evidence archimandrites controlling the black clergy in the sources, and the archbishops had *namestniki* or vicars who acted on their behalf and could have overseen the white as well as the black clergy. Normally in the East, an archimandrite could oversee either several hegumens and their monasteries, much as a Western abbot does, but he could also just oversee a large and important monastery with no subordinate monasteries. So, it is not clear how much the "archimandrite of Novgorod," was merely head of the Iur'ev Monastery, the most important of the early Novgorodian monasteries, or if he oversaw other monasteries. While referred to as the "archimandrite of Novgorod" – indeed there is a list at the back of the Novgorodian First and Fourth Chronicles, much like the lists of princes, *posadniki*, and archbishops²⁸³ – this may have merely meant that he was only archimandrite in Novgorod for several centuries,²⁸⁴ rather than indicating that he supervised all the monasteries in the archeparchy.²⁸⁵ That said, Archimandrite Sava was buried in the Antoniev, rather than the Iur'ev Monastery,²⁸⁶ and several archimandrites built churches in other monasteries,[287] suggesting their authority over other monasteries, or perhaps the Novgorodian monasteries as a whole.[288] But it could also be that they had been monks at these monasteries before becoming archimandrite of the Iur'ev Monastery. Sava had, indeed, been hegumen of the Antoniev earlier, so his burial there would not have been unusual or necessarily indicative of the archimandrite's authority over all Novgorodian monasteries.[289]

The apparent autonomy enjoyed by the Novgorodian monasteries may not be that unique within Eastern Orthodoxy, nor was there need of an archimandrite to oversee all the monasteries. Aristeides Papadakis argued that the Orthodox monastic tradition "paralleled the clergy's own institutional and sacramental functions," and these parallel traditions were often in conflict, as we have seen in John Cassian's warning to monks to avoid bishops and women, and Ammonius' exertions to avoid episcopal office.[290] While monasticism in the West became almost completely coenobitic (i.e., communal) and underwent clericalization, with the monks becoming part of the institutional church, Papadakis notes that the Orthodox monk technically remained outside the institutional church. The Eastern Orthodox monk was often eremitic (i.e., a hermit) and technically was not a member of the clergy, but held a mixed status because of his monastic vows; only those few who became priests (*hieromonks*) were members of the clergy. The rarity of clergy among the monks was likely the norm in the Benedictine monasteries (including the Cluniac and Cistercian orders) in the West, but the canons (like the Premonstratensians), and later the Franciscan and Dominican friars, were often ordained, so that Western monasticism had much greater institutional and disciplinary structure and greater clericalism than in the East.[291] The less-structured nature of Eastern Orthodox monasticism may therefore partly explain the apparent looser control the archbishops exercised over the Novgorodian monasteries.

In addition, certain monasteries in the Byzantine Empire had special status. Aristocratic or imperial foundations were more closely tied to their founders than to the local bishop and maintained some level of autonomy long after their founding. They, like other Eastern monasteries, based their monastic regime on a *typikon* (also *typicon*, pl. *typika*) or foundation charter, usually approved by the local bishop, which served as the *regula* or rules for the monastery, much as St. Benedict's rules served the Benedictine Order and St. Augustine's rules served other Western monastic communities, except that *typika* were usually unique to each monastery.[292] There were also s*tauropegial* monasteries,[293] which were at first answerable to the local bishop but over time came to be answerable directly to the patriarch.[294] While Rus' had no *stauropegial* monasteries until 1383, when the Simonov Monastery became the first,[295] there were earlier princely, aristocratic, and merchant foundations, and each monastery had its own *typikon*. In the Novgorodian archeparchy, the archbishops apparently approved every new monastery,[296] and the different circumstances behind each monastic foundation and their unique development meant that some monasteries had more autonomy than others.

The archbishops also consecrated monasteries or monastic churches, indeed the approval of monastic foundations and the consecration of churches were traditionally the exclusive purview of the bishop.[297] Most references to monastic church consecration in the archeparchy date to the twelfth century, but later ones also appear in the chronicles, which often name the church being consecrated but do not necessarily indicate that it is a monastic church.[298] Sometimes the chronicles are clearer, as under the year 1399, when Ioann consecrated the Church of the Intercession at the Zverinets Convent of the Intercession or when he established the Transfiguration Monastery on the Verenda River in 1407, "and consecrated it himself."[299] Thus, there are indications monastic consecrations likely went on over the entire period, although there is less information on them than for church construction and consecration.[300]

The archbishops also sometimes named the heads of monasteries or convents: in 1131, Archbishop Nifont (rather than Nikita in 1117, as the legend would have it) named Antonii hegumen of the Monastery of the Holy Mother of God (i.e., the Antoniev Monastery).[301] In 1195, Martirii named a new hegumenia of the Convent of St. Barbara in cooperation with the nuns,[302] After Martirii, Archbishop Antonii "and the whole of Novgorod" removed Sava from the hegumenate of the Iur'ev Monastery and replaced him with Arsenii, formerly hegumen of the Khutyn Monastery.[303]

The archbishops also presided over the funerals of hegumens, as Spiridon did in 1243 when he, along with Hegumen Sidor (Isidor) and Prince Aleksandr Nevskii, buried Varlaam, founder and hegumen of the Khutyn Monastery.[304]

However, the chronicles are sometimes vague in their terminology, and so it is ambiguous whether the archbishops always appointed the hegumens of Novgorodian monasteries. Thus, while Nifont made Antonii hegumen of the Antoniev Monastery, Dionisii (Deonisii) was appointed hegumen of the Iur'ev Monastery in 1158, presumably by the *veche* or some group of people within Novgorod; in any event, the bishop of Novgorod did not appoint him so far as can be determined.[305] When Dionisii died in 1195, after 35 years as hegumen of the Iur'ev Monastery (he was also called the "Novgorodian archimandrite" by the chronicles), Savatii was appointed hegumen in his place,[306] but it does not appear that the archbishop placed him, rather he was placed by the Novgorodian *veche*.

Of the archbishops who retired to monasteries, at least one was forcibly removed from office and imprisoned in a monastery. Four apparently retired due to ill health.[307] Ioann Pop'ian retired in 1130 but died 14 years later, so ill health is unlikely the cause for his retirement.[308] Arsenii was removed in 1229, having never been consecrated, and went on to become hegumen of the Iur'ev Monastery.[309] Moisei left office in 1330 and entered an unnamed monastery but returned to office after the death of Vasilii Kalika in 1352; he retired again in 1359, this time to the Kolomtsy Monastery, which he had founded in 1334, and died there in 1363.[310] Feodosii was removed from office in 1423, also without having been consecrated, and sent to the Trinity Monastery where he died two years later.[311] Feofil, the last archbishop of an independent Novgorod, was forcibly removed from office in 1480 by the orders of Grand Prince Ivan III and imprisoned in the Chudov Monastery in the Moscow Kremlin, where he died sometime in the first half of the 1480s.[312]

Five archbishops were also buried in monasteries. Nifont was buried in the Kyiv Caves Monastery.[313] Moisei died at the Kolomtsy Monastery on January 25, 1363 but was buried "in St. Michael's in the Monastery on the Skovorodka which he had founded eight years before."³¹⁴ Ioann was buried in the Church of the Resurrection in the Derevianitskii Monastery.³¹⁵ Evfimii II was buried in the Viazhitskii Monastery outside of Novgorod.³¹⁶ Iona was buried in the Otenskii Skete where he had been hegumen prior to his archiepiscopate.³¹⁷ And Feofil died in Moscow, where he had been imprisoned, but was buried in the Feodosiev Cave in the Kyiv Caves Monastery.³¹⁸

The relationship between the archbishops and the monasteries is thus a complex one. Bishop Ioakim Korsunianin is alleged to have founded the first monastery in the 990s, and his successors came out of the monasteries and built and patronized other monasteries over the centuries. They consecrated monastic churches (katholicons or conventual churches) and appointed monastic heads, and they could summon monks to the ecclesiastical courts. Several archbishops resigned and returned to monasteries, not always voluntarily. But they also appear strangely hands-off about the monasteries in the archeparchy. There may be several explanations for this: primary sources have certainly been lost, but perhaps too, no such material was ever kept. Monasticism may not have been as extensive in the archeparchy as one might think given the vastness of the Novgorodian Land, just as Christianity was, perhaps, not as extensive or deeply rooted in the archeparchy. In fact, while studying monasticism in the Byzantine Empire, Peter Charanis estimated that the black clergy probably only made up a mere one percent of the entire population of the Empire, that is, around 150,000 to 200,000 out of a population of perhaps 15 to 20 million.³¹⁹ He also concluded that, while the monasteries in the empire may have been numerous (in 964, Emperor Nicephoros II Phocas (r. 963-969) had written of "myriads" of them already in existence in his novel banning new monastic establishments),³²⁰ the number of monks per monastery was usually quite small. The great monasteries may have housed one hundred and eighty or two hundred monks each,³²¹ but "the vast majority of the Byzantine establishments housed between ten and twenty monks."³²² Charanis concluded that around the year 1000 there were some 150,000 monks in 7,000 monastic establishments or an average of twenty-one monks per monastery.³²³

If monasticism in Rus' was at all comparable to that of the Byzantine Empire, the sparse population of the Novgorodian and

Pskov lands would mean a very small monastic community indeed. The archeparchy had some ninety monasteries during the period under study: 81 monasteries in the Novgorodian Land and 9 in the Pskov Lands.[324] Of these, eighteen date from the twelfth century, with three built before 1165. Only nine were founded in the thirteenth century – the thirteenth century downturn yet again. The fourteenth century saw the foundation of forty-two monasteries and, in the fifteenth century, twenty-one, however, five of these may have been founded after 1478. Thus, an average of 23 monasteries were founded each century between the twelfth and the end of the fifteenth centuries.

Based on these figures, there were probably around 1,900 monks and nuns in the archeparchy by the late 1470s (21 monks or nuns each for some 90 monasteries or 1,890 monks or nuns in all). But for the first half of the period under study, only 32 monasteries existed. Thus, for roughly half of the period of Novgorodian independence, there were perhaps a mere 672 monks (21 monks or nuns each in 32 monasteries) in the archeparchy. Even if the monasteries housed 100 monks each, significantly more than their Byzantine counterparts, there would only be around 9,000 monks and nuns in the 1470s and maybe 3,200 in the mid-fourteenth century, not huge numbers for such a vast territory. This probably explains the archbishops' apparent inactivity toward the monasteries.

But Russian scholars have concluded that Rus' monasteries were actually *smaller* than those of Byzantium. Aleksandr Nikitskii believed most monasteries in Rus' housed only six or seven monks on average, and only two or three in the *sketes*, well below the Byzantine average.[325] If the higher of Nikitskii's figures are used, then only 630 monks and nuns inhabited the ninety monasteries in the archeparchy at the end of the fifteenth century. Since some of these monasteries were *sketes* with only two or three monks, the figure is probably lower than that, and even lower in the earlier period when there were fewer monasteries.

Thus, the number of monks and nuns in the archeparchy was relatively small even if generous estimates are used, and even smaller in earlier periods: a few hundred. This helps to explain the looser, less extensive, church administration in Novgorod, the lack of documentation and references to personnel found in what sources we do have, as well as the lack of direct or personal oversight by the archbishops than might seem natural in the vast expanses of such an allegedly important archeparchy.

The archbishops also probably made so few visits outside Novgorod because, of the eighty-one monasteries in the Novgorodian Land, a third of them were in the city or its immediate environs. Another ten were within 50 *versty* of the city. Of the remainder, four were in Kirillov or on Beloozero, two in Staraia Russa, and one each in Tikhvin, Chereponets, and on the Shelon' River. Of the nine in the Pskov Lands, five were in Pskov itself, one was on Lake Pskov, and the rest were from 5 to 25 *versty* from the city. The locations of the rest are not clear. Taken together, the monasteries' small size and their close proximity to Novgorod or Pskov made a large administration or personal archiepiscopal visitations unnecessary.

Conclusion

The archbishop of Novgorod oversaw one of the most important eparchies and held the second most important position in the Russian church due to the honorary title of archbishop and the importance of Novgorod in the cultural and economic life of Rus'. But evidence of their teachings and preaching, church and monastic consecrations, liturgical and sacramental activities, pastoral visits, oversight of monasteries, and judicial roles indicate the church administration of the Novgorodian archeparchy was not as extensive as might have been expected given its vast geographic expanse and the city's importance. Activities were largely confined to Novgorod and Pskov and their immediate environs. Nikitskii long ago noted the difficulty in determining church affairs outside Novgorod itself, and argued the archbishops had personal administration in the city of Novgorod, and only rarely in other towns.[326] That said, the bishop alone had the authority to consecrate churches, distribute the antimension that every parish needed to celebrate a Divine Liturgy, approve marriages, ordain priests,[327] and oversee the church courts in his diocese. That the Novgorodian archbishops deputized others to act in their name did not mean this power or authority was diminished, merely that it was delegated. Activity was limited because there were few clergymen and not many believers in a geographically-expansive but sparsely-populated archeparchy that seems not to have been fully converted. Despite this, the archbishops, personally or through deputies, adjudicated cases in the ecclesiastical courts, oversaw the white and black clergy, taught, preached, administered the sacraments, and protected Orthodox Christianity against the inroads of paganism, heresy, and Roman Catholicism pressing upon the flock they kept watch over.

CHAPTER FOUR
Election

The Absence of Background

5. Archbishop Aleksei (r. 1360-1375, 1375-1380), as depicted in the Volotovo Dormition Church in 1363 (destroyed in World War II)– here an 1894 copy by F. M. Fomin. Following Archbishop Mosei's retirement, Aleksei was elected by sortition. Retiring in 1375, he resumed his office with the blessing of Metropolitan Aleksei and a petition from the *veche* (NPL: 365, 373).

In Rus', as elsewhere, princes were significant historic figures simply due to their station in life, and were born into that station; thus, their births were noted in the chronicles and significant events in their youth or adolescence were also sometimes mentioned. Similarly, Novgorodian notables – the boiars who became *posadniki* and *tysiatskie* – were born to lead, and sometimes are mentioned prior to taking office as well. But the archbishops of Novgorod were not born into that office, nor were they historic figures simply due to birth or inheritance. While some of them appear in the chronicles when they were archimandrites or hegumens and founded monasteries and built churches, most entered the historic scene with their elections.

There are accounts of the early lives of a number of archbishops found in saints' lives (*zhitie*, pl. *zhitiia*), and Pavel Tikhomirov and Konstantin Zdravomislov compiled books of the biographies of the Novgorodian hierarchs in the late nineteenth and early twentieth centuries.[1] They made use of chronicle sources and other, more reliable primary documents, but also relied on the saints' lives and traditions, which most historians view skeptically. The lives were often written long after their subjects had died in order to advance their candidacies for sainthood, promote already-established saintly cults, and inspire religious devotion, not to reveal the historic truth. So, they are valuable as literary, hagiographic and cultural documents, but are often of limited value as historic sources especially if unsupported by other, more reliable, documents. Still, they can be of some use.

Thus, the saint's lives reveal Archbishop Moisei (in life, Mitrofan) to have been the son of a wealthy man named Filipp,[2] that Evfimii II was named Ioann prior to his taking monastic orders and was the son of the priest, Feodor, and his wife Anna,[3] and that Archbishop Iona's baptismal name was Ioann. We also learn that Iona was orphaned at age seven and raised by a woman named Natalia Medovartseva, "the mother of Iakov Dmitrievich Medovartsev, the grandmother of Mikhail," who, although poor, had a *d'iak* teach him reading and writing;[4] Iona himself remembered that, in his youth, "Due to poverty, I was quiet."[5] All this serves to flesh out these men and may give us something of their personality and background.

But sadly, sources historians accept as more reliable often tell us practically nothing of the archbishops' families or early lives. The chronicles reveal little about Moisei; they tell us that Archbishop Ioann II was the son of a Novgorodian named Porfirii and that he had a brother named Vasilii who died in the *schema* at the Lisitskii Monastery in 1400;[6] they also report that Mikhail Klopskii prophesied in 1408 that Iona would become archbishop half a century later, but say nothing of Iona's poverty or of his being orphaned.[7] And while there is not necessarily any reason to discount the baptismal names or other facts given in saints' lives, such as their parents' names, the fact that this information is interwoven with legends and hagiographic topoi means historians must treat it with caution.

And so, we are left with scant information prior to their elections and consecrations. Even when we do have historical evidence, it often reveals little of the men themselves. For example, Archbishop Antonii's *Kniga Palomnik* (Pilgrim's Book) tells us nothing of Antonii himself, his early life, his family, his religious training, his class background, his spiritual views, and so forth. Rather, it gives interesting and historically important details of Constantinople prior to the Fourth Crusade.[8] Iona's Life, as we have just seen, states he was a poor orphan and had a quiet temperament, but are these the actual attributes of the man himself, or merely Orthodox topoi (quietude and humility) or a rags to riches tale – the medieval Novgorodian version of the boy born in a log cabin growing up and becoming president – meant to flesh out an otherwise unknown life prior to his entry into the historic record?

Because of the lack of reliable information on their early lives, we must start with their election, well after they were mature men and had shown leadership promise in the church. How they were elected was not only the starting point, in many ways, of their historic lives, but it was also a unique process in medieval Christendom. Indeed, it was one of the most striking aspects of the office. A look at this process reveals fascinating patterns not only about the electorate and the pool of candidates, but also how the Novgorodians thought of the office of archbishop and the men who held it.

Ecclesiastical Election

The traditional view in the historiography is that the *veche* elected Novgorod's secular and ecclesiastical officials – the prince, the *posadnik*, and the *tysiatskii* among the secular officials and the archbishop, archimandrite, and the hegumens, and hegumenias among the ecclesiastical officials.[9] Thus Aleksandr Nikitskii wrote that the *veche* usually elected the archbishop, but in cases where it could not decide, lots were placed on the altar in the Cathedral of Holy Wisdom.[10] Georgii Fedotov wrote that "the *veche* elected the entire [city] administration, not excluding the archbishop, and had the power to check it and judge it," elaborating further that "The archbishop stood above parties and expressed the unity of the republic. To make him really independent, his name was drawn from those of the candidates elected by the *veche*. The three lots on the altar symbolized the divine will for the fate of the city-state."[11] Iaroslav Shchapov revealed how this process changed over time: "The chronicle reports changes in the procedure of consecrating the head of the Novgorod eparchy in the course of the twelfth century." Before that, the metropolitan of Kyiv consecrated the bishops in Kyiv and then sent them to Novgorod, but Shchapov noted that "new principles of electing the Novgorod prelate on the spot" developed in the late twelfth century and that "Later, too, archbishops were elected and ordained in Novgorod, on the spot as it were."[12] Stephen Rowell concluded simply "the *veche* maintained the right to elect the nominal head of state, the archbishop."[13] He added that "uniquely among the bishops of Rus' the Novgorodian hierarch was elected from a list of three local candidates by the city *veche*. The metropolitan merely invited the 'God-chosen' man to consecration; he took no part in the election."[14] Edward Sokol also wrote that the *veche* came to elect the prince, the *posadnik* and the *tysiatskii*, and "In the mid-twelfth century, it began selecting the all-powerful archbishop, the nominal head of state,"[15] to which Aleksandr Nazarenko concurred when he wrote that "Beginning with St. Arkadii (1156/58-1163), the Novgorodian prelates were invariably chosen at the *veche*."[16]

In fact, the *veche's* role in episcopal elections was more complex and the electoral process changed over the centuries. Although the *veche* most certainly played a role, it appears sometimes to have elected the archbishop (although who comprised the *veche* is often unclear) and at other times to have merely acclaimed the archbishop-elect after his election. Indeed, the sources indicate considerable changes in the electoral process from the middle of the twelfth to the end of the fifteenth centuries. In the earliest years, the grand princes or metropolitans appointed the bishops and archbishops; tradition claims Grand Prince Vladimir sent the first bishop to Novgorod in the late 980s or early 990s,[17] and the Kyivan grand princes and metropolitans continued to appoint them until 1156 when the Novgorodians, faced with a vacant metropolitan see, convened a *veche* and chose Arkadii as their bishop. After this, Novgorod's archbishops were, with two exceptions, elected locally until Ivan III conquered the city in 1478 and, even after the conquest, Muscovite authorities tried to maintain the tradition of election by lots (sortition or aleatoric democracy) that had developed in the late fourteenth century: Archbishop Sergei was elected by lots in Moscow on July 17, 1483 and installed on September 4, only to be removed on July 27 of the following year after a disastrous tenure;[18] he was replaced by the grand prince's appointee, Gennadii. From that time on the grand prince and the metropolitan again chose the archbishop of Novgorod.

But the system of election not only evolved from one of appointment by the grand prince or metropolitan to one of election by the Novgorodians themselves (and back again), the precise method of election also changed. In 1156 "All the townspeople gathered together and decided to appoint as their bishop, Arkadii, a man chosen by God."[19] This is apparently a reference to a *veche*; Maiuki Eizo argued that the term "chosen by God" and similar terminology found in accounts of other elections indicates election by lots even though the chronicles do not specifically say this.[20] If Eizo is correct, then Arkadii was the first of seventeen archbishops elected by lots, though use of lots is actually mentioned in only nine of those instances. But this interpretation is based on slim evidence. That a candidate was "God-chosen" could simply mean that God's will was carried out and need not refer to the actual electoral process itself.[21] God could choose His candidate by influencing the *veche* or by influencing the person who drew the lots, though the latter method may have been seen as more direct divine intervention. In any event, a two-step process developed in the middle of the fourteenth century where a number of candidates, usually three, were selected, their names were written on lots, which were then placed on the altar of the Cathedral of Holy Wisdom, then, or so the Novgorodians believed, God Himself, acting through an impartial agent, chose who He wanted to be archbishop.

Before delving deeper into the progression of Novgorod's electoral system, it is important to clarify the term "election". The Russian word often translated as "election" is *izbranie*.[22] However, the modern verb *izbrat'*, which has the same root, is usually translated as "to choose; to select," but usually not "to elect" (which would be *vybirat'*; election would be *vybory*). Furthermore, the word "election" has in the last two centuries been infused with democratic overtones that are anachronistic for the medieval period. The term "election" was used in the medieval period for both ecclesiastical (e.g., papal, abbatial, or episcopal) as well as secular offices (e.g., the election of the Frankish kings or the Holy Roman Emperors). Regarding secular offices, the term meant the selection of a candidate rather than their hereditary accession to office. It was used in the Catholic Church to refer to the selection of a pope by the College of Cardinals, the principles of which were established by Pope Nicholas II and the Council of 1059. More commonly it referred to the selection of a bishop, initially in a "primitive" election by the "clergy and the people" (*electio per clericum et populum*),[23] and later by a cathedral chapter. It was also used to refer to the selection of an abbot or prior by the monastic community. Election was in contrast to the appointment of bishops, abbots, or priors by the pope, the archbishop or bishop, or the local prince.[24] In this study, the term is used to mean the local selection of an archbishop by the Novgorodians (or some portion of them), or by the drawing of lots, rather than his appointment by the grand prince or metropolitan.

Episcopal Election in the Orthodox Churches

In discussing episcopal election in Novgorod, many scholars have noted that they were uncanonical, though uncanonical elections were, in fact, common throughout the Middle Ages. Golubinskii wrote: "according to canon law, the election of a bishop should have been carried out by a council of bishops of the province, under the leadership of the metropolitan without the influence of local authorities." However, in Rus', "contrary to canon law, the selection of candidates for bishop was not made by the metropolitan with a council of bishops, but by the appanage (*udel*) princes."[25] Vernadsky echoed these sentiments, writing: "Bishops were nominally appointed by the metropolitan. Actually, the prince of Kyiv, and later the princes of each land in which a bishop's see was situated, exerted considerable influence on the nomination of the bishop."[26] More recently, Khoroshev contended that, regarding the archbishops of Novgorod: "the Kyivan metropolitans must have waived several church dogmas in the face of the practical arrangement of forces."[27] This might be considered what the Orthodox churches call "economy" (*oikonomia* in Greek), defined as: "an exercise of her stewardship by the Church whereby that which by the strict letter of her law is forbidden, is permitted."²⁸

Though seldom achieved in practice, the church did, in fact, establish from its earliest years at least the principle that episcopal elections were to be carried out by the bishops assembled in a council and were not to be interfered with by secular or lay authorities. The electus was then to be consecrated by at least two other bishops. These principles were found even in the *Apostolical Canons*, where the First Canon proclaimed: "Let a bishop be ordained by two or three bishops"²⁹ and the Thirtieth Canon (or Thirty-first depending on the numbering used by certain scholars) declared: "If a bishop obtains possession of a church by the aid of the temporal powers, let him be deposed and excommunicated, and all who communicate with him."³⁰ The First Apostolical Canon strongly influenced the Fourth Canon of the First Council of Nicaea, which stipulated:

> It is by all means desirable that a bishop should be appointed by all bishops of the province. But if this is difficult because of some pressing necessity or the length of the journey involved, let at least three come together and perform the ordination, but only after the absent bishops have taken part in the vote and given their written consent. But in each province the right of confirming the proceedings belongs to the metropolitan bishops.³¹

These two principles of election by an episcopal synod and prohibition of secular interference (the Thirty-First Apostolical Canon was quoted verbatim) are repeated in the Third Canon of the Second Council of Nicaea that declared:

> Any election of a bishop, priest, or deacon brought about by the rulers is to be null and void in accordance with the canon that says *'if any bishop, through the influence of secular rulers, acquires responsibility for a church because of them, let him be suspended and let all those who are in communion with him be excommunicat-*

ed.' It is necessary that the person who is to be advanced to a bishopric should be elected by bishops, as has been decreed by the holy fathers at Nicaea in the canon that says *'It is by all means desirable that a bishop should be appointed by all bishops of the province. But if this is difficult because of some pressing necessity or the length of the journey involved, let at least three come together and perform the ordination, but only after the absent bishops have taken part in the vote and given their written consent. But in each province the right of confirming the proceedings belongs to the metropolitan bishops.'*[32]

Clearly, Novgorod and the wider Rus' church were familiar with these canons which were part of their *Kormchaia kniga*.[33] Several Kyivan metropolitans even cited them in decrees and letters opposing un-canonical elections, though they – *economically* – tolerated princely appointment of bishops and elections by the Novgorodians despite these official declarations to the contrary.[34] Metropolitan Kirill decreed in 1224 that lay interference in episcopal elections was punishable by immediate excommunication.[35] Metropolitan Kiprian, in his *Life* of Metropolitan Petr, echoed Kirill's prohibition, as well as those of earlier canon law.[36] Grand Prince Olgerd of Lithuania, who, though a pagan, nonetheless had a significant Orthodox population to govern, opposed Petr's candidacy and put up his own candidate – Gerontii. Both candidates traveled to Constantinople hoping to be consecrated by the patriarch, but due to God's favor, Petr was sped along by favorable winds and weather while storms held Gerontii back. When Gerontii finally arrived in the imperial city, Patriarch Athanasius I admonished him, saying "laymen are not allowed to carry out the election of bishops, nor may anyone dare to reach for such a title on his own, not before he is elected by the Holy Assembly, and first of all marked by the sign of the Most Holy and Life-giving Spirit."[37]

As hagiographic literature, this is, again, of questionable historic value. Given the Byzantines' usual skill in diplomacy, it is doubtful the patriarch ever spoke these words to Gerontii. However, the Life, written by Kiprian himself, reveals the metropolitan's view of lay interference in episcopal elections (though it ignores the role the Prince of Moscow played in Petr's nomination – or the emperor's role in patriarchal elections). Indeed, in a letter to Sergei of Radonezh, Kiprian made similar remarks:

> Canon seventy-six of the Holy Apostles reads: 'A bishop should not allow a brother, or son, or another relative, or a friend to appoint whoever they want to the episcopal dignity; it is not right to appoint heirs of one's episcopacy and make God's gift into human preference'....How could such men transmit episcopacy itself to others, as successors of their pastoral authority....out of human preference, or friendship, or because of blood-relationship, the things that were consecrated by God? If any such gift occurs, the action is invalid according to the canons, and the perpetrator is to be excommunicated. For it has been ordained that bishops would be appointed by synods...Also Canon Twenty-three of the Council of Antioch says 'Even at the end of his life, a bishop is not permitted to establish another as his successor'... The thirtieth Canon of the...Holy Apostles says...'If a bishop acquires the high priesthood with the help of civil authorities, let him be deposed and excommunicated, as well as those who cooperate with them...'[38]

Kiprian's preoccupation with lay interference in episcopal elections probably sprung from his own fifteen-year struggle to gain acceptance in Moscow, but the beliefs expressed are similar to his predecessors' as well as the "Regulation on the Election and Installation of Bishops" dating to 1423,[39] which confirmed election of new bishops by a council of bishops (i.e., an episcopal synod) called by the metropolitan "according to the tradition of the holy Apostles and the God-fearing Fathers."[40] In fact, the opening lines of the *Regulation* are very similar to the Fourth Canon of First Nicaea and the Third Canon of Second Nicaea, as well as the Thirty-first Canon of the Apostolical Canons. All declare that all bishops in an ecclesiastical province should have a say in the election of a new bishop but, if dire need requires it, three bishops can meet and, with the written approval of those absent, elect a bishop who is then confirmed by the metropolitan by the laying on of hands. Those defying episcopal synods, or over whom "diabolical bitterness comes...and in disobedience fall into the ditch (*rov*)[41] with princes and rulers...[a reference to lay election?] are to be stripped of the episcopal honor and office [and] expelled from among the number of bishops."[42] Thus the ecclesiastical province of Kyiv, over the course of the thirteenth, fourteenth, and fifteenth centuries, maintained, at least as its official policy, a standard of episcopal election very much in keeping with the canons of the church from the earliest years of Christianity. It was, obviously, not heeded either in Novgorod or elsewhere in Rus'. Lay interference, in fact, continued to be widespread throughout Orthodox and Catholic Europe, probably far beyond what could be considered prudent *oikonomia*.

Indeed, despite this policy, Kiprian's rival in Moscow, Metropolitan Pimen, seems to have approved the election by lots of Archbishop Ioann in 1388, sending word to the Novgorodians to "choose three men that God will give to you," and then consecrating Ioann in Moscow the following year.[43] That Novgorod's archbishops-elects were almost always consecrated by the metropolitans after election in Novgorod provides further evidence that the metropolitans allowed election by uncanonical methods, though after 1359 the use of lots could, as the chroniclers seemed to claim, be seen as God choosing His archbishop rather than impermissible election by the laity, since no human agent had directly chosen the archbishop. That said, the metropolitans seem to have made no distinction between election processes before or after 1359.

There was, in fact, one apparent instance of an archbishop of Novgorod being elected in a canonically-acceptable manner. A Greek-language registry kept during the tenure of Metropolitan Feognost (r. 1323-1358) mentions the election of thirteen bishops by episcopal synod between 1328 and 1347, one of them being Vasilii Kalika, in Volodymyr (in Volynia) in 1331.[44] In each of these elections, at least three bishops chose a candidate to fill a vacant see with the consent of the other bishops in the province, after which the metropolitan consecrated the nominee. In the case of Vasilii's election, the registry states:

On August 25th, the 14th year of the indiction, in the year 6839 (1331 AD). The election of the God-saved city of Great Novgorod. In the presence of the God-loving bishops Afanasii of Volodymyr, Feodor of Halych, Grigorii of Kholm [Chelm], and Mark of Peremyshl [Przemyśl], and by agreement of the other bishops, three worthy people were chosen in accordance with the canonical regulations: the hieromonk Arsenii, the hieromonk Vasilii, and the Archimandrite Lavrentii. And the hieromonk Vasilii was preferred and chosen; Vasilii was consecrated archbishop by the laying on of hands.[45]

This version of events clearly shows a canonical election, but it is contradicted by the *Novgorodian First Chronicle*, which states that Vasilii was elected not by a council of bishops in Volodymyr, but by the Novgorodians themselves:

The Novgorodians, having deliberated much, were without a bishop for about eight months; and all Novgorod (from small to great) and the abbots and priests chose Grigorii Kalika a good, (gentle) and humble man, who had been designated by God.... In January [he] was shorn a monk, having received the name Vasilii; he was then installed in the archbishop's palace until they should send him to the metropolitan.[46]

Despite the arguments of Eizo and Meyendorff that "designated by God," meant election by lots,[47] the rest of the entry indicates election by the abbots and priests, acting as sort of a cathedral chapter, although the term is anachronistic for the Eastern church, and the vague formulae of "the Novgorodians" and "all Novgorod" may indicate participation of not just secular officials but the wider population as well. Meyendorff attempts to explain the apparent contradiction between the chronicle and the metropolitan's registry by arguing that Vasilii was elected (by lots) in Novgorod and then "[o]bviously Theognostos [Feognost] went through the motions of a regular election by the bishops, but he had no real alternative to the consecration of Basil [Vasilii] who had already been chosen and installed as acting-archbishop in Novgorod."[48] However, Vasilii Vasil'evskii perhaps better explains Feognost's behavior; having received word of Vasilii's election in Novgorod, the metropolitan added two other candidates in Volodymyr so that a canonical election could be carried out.[49] The bishops meeting in Volynia found no fault with Novgorod's *electus*, and consecrated him archbishop.

There may, however, be another explanation for the events of 1331. The *Novgorodian First Chronicle* reports that emissaries from the exiled Prince Aleksandr Mikhailovich of Tver' and his protector, the Lithuanian Grand Prince Gedymin, "and all the Lithuanian princes" arrived in Volodymyr with their own candidate to be created Bishop of Pskov.[50] Their candidate, Arsenii, may be the same one mentioned in Feognost's list. Thus, the election in Volodymyr may have been carried out to deal with Pskov's demand for the creation of its own bishopric, which Feognost thwarted by adding the Pskovite candidate to the candidates for archbishop of Novgorod. When Vasilii was "elected," or more properly speaking, his election in Novgorod was confirmed by the bishops' synod in Volynia, the Pskovite embassy was defeated. Eizo finds this theory interesting, but admits it cannot be definitively proven based on available source material.[51] Rowell further contends that, since Vasilii was not first on the list in Feognost's registry, he was probably not Novgorod's first choice, since in seven of the thirteen elections, the first-named was consecrated, and in only two cases was the second candidate ordained. Details are lacking in the other four instances.[52]

The debate surrounding Vasilii's election suggests that, despite Meyendorff's claim that Feognost had no real alternative than to consecrated Vasilii, the metropolitan was not powerless in the face of Novgorod's choice of archbishops, nor of Pskov's demand for its own bishop. Metropolitans had, of course, placed their candidates in Novgorod prior to Arkadii's election in 1156, and they were also able to place Il'ia and Dalmat after 1156. That the metropolitans rarely rejected Novgorod's candidate did not mean they could not, though they seem to have never done so directly, but instead ignored an unfavorable archbishop-elect by not summoning him for consecration, as in the case of Evfimii II, who kept the archbishopric by going to another metropolitan for consecration in 1434 (there being no metropolitan in Moscow by that time). But only two archbishops-elect were never consecrated and the metropolitan's views in those specific instances are unknown. Arsenii, a monk at the Khutyn Monastery was elected in 1223 and carried out the functions of that office until 1225 and again from 1228-29 before being driven out of office by the Novgorodians, blamed for "an exceptionally rainy autumn," and accused of having deposed Antonii by bribing the prince;[53] he never returned to the archiepiscopate, nor was he ever consecrated, though he is thought to have become hegumen of the Iur'ev Monastery.[54]

It is not known whether Arsenii was unacceptable to the metropolitan. The metropolitanate was vacant when Arsenii was elected, and there is no information on what Metropolitan Kirill II felt about the Novgorodian after Kirill's arrival in Kyiv (he was consecrated on January 6, 1224 or 1225). He arrived just after the disastrous battle on the Kal'ka River (May 31, 1223), in which the Mongols captured and killed three princes on the battlefield, including Kyivan Grand Prince Mstislav Romanovich, killed another six in headlong flight trying to cross back over the Dnieper, and are said to have slain seventy boiars;[55] The *Nikonian Chronicle* claims 60,000 Rus' warriors were killed in the battle, not including the casualties among the Polovtsy allies, though this figure is not to be believed.[56] The clearly-stunned Novgorodian chronicler explained that "the Tatars turned back from the river Dnieper, and we know not whence they came, nor where they hid themselves again; God knows whence He fetched them against us for our sins..."[57] the Rus' princes then seemed to have forgotten the Tatars, and the interprincely wars that had long devastated Kyivan Rus' continued unabated. The *Suzdalian Chronicle* shows Kirill trying to bring peace between the princes for the rest of his tenure.[58]

Similarly, in 1421, Hegumen Feodosii of the Klopskii Monastery was elected archbishop, but the Novgorodians removed him in 1423 before he was ever consecrated.[59] Whether Metropolitan Fotii opposed Feodosii's candidacy, as he is later said to have opposed Evfimii II's, is hard to say. In fact, there is no case of a candidate elected in Novgorod being sent for consecration only to be replaced by a candidate of the metropolitan's own choosing. Thus, the metropolitan could, apparently ignore a candidate (if he was far off in Novgorod), which he may have done in the case of Evfimii II, but usually Kyiv and Moscow seem to have accepted Novgorod's method of election as a prudent concession.

The Pool of Candidates and the Role of the Monasteries

In most of Novgorod's episcopal elections only the winners are known and we have information on the other candidates in only seven of the nineteen elections.[60] There were three candidates in six of these seven elections, but only two are mentioned in the election of 1274. Thus, we know something about twenty candidates. Eleven of them were hegumens, two were *kliuchniki* of the previous archiepiscopal administration, one was bishop of Volodymyr, one was the *dukhovnik* (confessor) of the previous archbishop, one the priest of St. Barbara's Church (i.e., a member of the white clergy), one was a monk, and two were Greeks (Byzantines) of uncertain status. Of the winners in these seven elections, four were hegumens, one was *kliuchnik* of the previous archbishop, one was the previous archbishop's *dukhovnik*, and one was a monk (it is not known if he was also a hieromonk at the time).[61] While little is known of the candidates themselves, especially those not elected, beyond the ecclesiastical office they held at the time of their election or the monastery from which they came, the elections do reveal several things.

First, the candidates were not limited to the Novgorodian Land since a bishop of Volodymyr was among the candidates, although Novgorodian candidates were clearly favored and how seriously a bishop from southwestern Rus' was actually considered is debatable. Second, candidacy was limited to the clergy. It is not certain the Greek candidates were clergymen, but it seems a reasonable assumption that a Greek in Novgorod or Rus' would have been a cleric, though there were also Greek merchants and artists (though the artists were often monks engaged in iconography). Third, the black or monastic clergy was favored, not surprising given the Orthodox tradition of drawing the episcopate from the black clergy. In fact, in 1470, the candidates were chosen at the *veche* only "from among the hieromonks," mainly from among the hegumens, though, in other instances, members of the white clergy were also candidates. In three cases, secular or parish clergy were elevated to the archiepiscopate after they took monastic vows: two priests and one archdeacon (Il'ia, Vasilii, and Feofil).[62] There is no indication that they were married at the time of their election (which would have forced their wives to enter a convent); they were likely widowers.[63] The Rus' church required widowed priests to enter monastic orders,[64] though the Moscow Synod of 1503 indicates that plenty of widower-priests had not done so, and had concubines (*nalozhniki*), and this practice had likely been going on for some time.[65]

In addition to the favoritism toward the monastic clergy, and the heads of monasteries, the importance of certain monasteries can also be seen. Of 183 monasteries listed in the Novgorodian land cadastres (*Novgorodskie pistsovye knigi*)[66] at the turn of the sixteenth century, and another sixteen in the Pskov Land, eight unsuccessful and thirteen successful archiepiscopal candidates came from only thirteen monasteries and monks and hegumens from only nine ever became archbishops. Another four candidates came from the archiepiscopal administration, of which two were elected archbishop.

Of the thirteen winning monastic candidates, four (Antonii, Arsenii, Ioann, and Simeon) came from the Khutyn Monastery and two from the Iur'ev Monastery (Spiridon and Moisei). The rest came from the Starorusskii Spasskii Monastery (Martirii), the Blagoveshchenskii [Annunciation] Monastery (Feoktist), the Trinity-Klopskii Monastery (Feodosii), the Derevianitskii Monastery (Evfimii I), the Lisitsa Hill Monastery (Evfimii II), and the Otenskii Skete (Iona). Nifont, placed by the Kyivan metropolitan in 1130, came from the Kyiv Caves Monastery.[67] The unsuccessful monastic candidates came from the Annunciation Monastery (Parfenii in 1388 and Zakarii in 1421), the Iur'ev (Ioann in 1274), the Antoniev (Sava in 1359), the Lisitsa Hill Monastery (Arsenii in 1421), The Nativity Monastery (Afanasii in 1388), St. Michael's Monastery at Skovorodka (Mikhail in 1415), and the Kholomskii Monastery (Lev in 1415). Two others, Varfonofev and Puinov (both candidates in 1471), came from Iona's archiepiscopal administration: Varfonofev had been Iona's *dukhovnik* (confessor), and Puinov his *kliuchnik*.[68]

It is hard to say why candidates came from so few monasteries. Some scholars speculate that the largest or wealthiest monasteries dominated the elections, but the land cadastres, admittedly covering only the last decades of the period of study, do not bear this out. It is not clear how much land monasteries held during earlier periods, indeed scholars argue that Rus' monasteries only acquired large landed estates in the fourteenth century, so it would seem Novgorodian monasteries did not have large land-holdings until the last century of independence.[69] In any event, since only the winning candidate is known in most elections, one cannot say the candidate from the wealthiest monastery always or usually won, even if data from the cadastres are used as a rough estimate of the relative wealth even for the early centuries. In three of eight elections (1388, 1415 and 1421), we know the names of at least two monastic candidates, allowing us to compare the relative wealth of their monasteries, but for the elections of 1193, 1229, 1274, and 1359, there was only one monastic candidate; in the election of 1471, none of the candidates were monastic but were part of the House of Holy Wisdom, the archiepiscopal administration, at the time of the elections.

In only two elections (1388 and 1415) was the winner from the monastery with the most land. In both cases, they were from the Khutyn Monastery, the largest monastic landholder in the Novgorodian Land with 1,815 *obzhi* of land at the end of the fifteenth century.[70] In 1421, however, Feodosii, hegumen of the Trinity Monastery at Klopskii, with a mere 85 ½ *obzhi* of land, was elected over candidates from monasteries with significantly more land: Hegumen Zakarii was from of the Annunciation Monastery, which controlled 458 *obzhi* of land, while Arsenii was the archbishop's *kliuchnik* at the Listitsa, a monastery with 175½ *obzhi* of land.)[71] All told, there is simply not enough information to say definitively that the deck was stacked (or the lots weighted) in favor of candidates from wealthier monasteries, or that factors other than chance (or the will of God) were responsible for the election of Novgorod's archbishops, particularly when election was by lots (if the archpriests who drew the lots during the elections of 1388 and 1415 skewed these elections it is impossible to say). The largest monasteries never monopolized the archiepiscopate and it is difficult to say what role politics played in elections, though it seems the reforms of 1354 led to sortition being the mechanism for elections after Moisei's retirement in 1359.

The Khutyn and Iur'ev Monasteries were the wealthiest in the Novgorodian Land and placed six of their monks or hegumens in the archiepiscopate (four from Khutyn and two from Iur'ev) while no other monastery placed more than one candidate in the episcopate. The Kyiv Caves Monastery had candidates placed in the eleventh and early twelfth centuries, but this is outside the scope of this study.[72] This is certainly not a lock on the office which saw 30 bishops and archbishops between 988 and 1478. Indeed, candidates from the wealthiest monasteries vied for the office for a relatively brief period. The three from the Iur'ev Monastery all date from the thirteenth and fourteenth centuries, while candidates from Khutyn Monastery were elected in 1211 and 1223, when Mitrofan, Antonii, and Arsenii vied for the office; another Khutyn monk did not become archbishop until 1388 (another was elected in 1415). Some very wealthy monasteries never competed for the archiepiscopal office. For one, the Arkadievskii (Arkazh') Monastery, founded by Bishop Arkadii in 1153, before his elevation to the episcopate, possessed 1,537½ *obzhi* of land, making it the third largest monastic landowner after the Khutyn and the Iur'ev monasteries,[73] yet after Arkadii, none of its monks or hegumens was ever candidates for the archiepiscopate.

Overall, then, whoever the electorate may have been, human or divine, it showed a preference for archimandrites and hegumens of important monasteries.[74] These men would have been experienced ecclesiastical administrators with managerial experience over a community of monks, economic experience with sometimes sizeable land-holdings, and political experience dealing with previous archbishops, archimandrites, neighboring land-owners, tenant-farmers on their monastic lands, and even boiars or princes who granted them land in return for commemorative prayers. They had also served as spiritual leaders of the monks of their monasteries and perhaps even local laity or pilgrims to the monastery, and could use that experience as the spiritual leader of the eparchy. They were likely more qualified than any other candidates, except for other bishops.

The Evolution of Episcopal Election and the Origin of Election by Lot

The use of sortition as the electoral mechanism of Novgorod's bishops was fully adopted only in the last half of the fourteenth century and survived a little over a century before the fall of Novgorod and the return to the appointment of Novgorod's archbishops. Prior to this, the chronicle describes the process at the time of the first election in 1156:

> Archbishop Nifont died...that same year all the townspeople gathered together and decided to appoint as their bishop Arkadii, a man chosen by God; and all the people went and took him out of the Monastery of the Holy Virgin [in the presence of Prince] Mstislav Iur'evich, all the clergy of Holy Wisdom, all the town priests, and all the hegumens and monks; and they installed him, entrusting him with the bishopric in the court of Holy Wisdom, until there should be a metropolitan in Russia and then he should go be consecrated.[75]

It isn't clear who comprised the electorate. "All the townspeople" (*vs' grad liudii*) is a vague term. Did all the citizens or inhabitants gather (in a *veche*) and pick Arkadii, or were they represented by the *posadnik* or the boiars ("the best people")? Or did the clergy pick him and "all the townspeople" then acclaim him at the *veche*? It is far from certain. Thirty-seven years later, the Older Redaction of the *Novgorodian First Chronicle* describes a similar election, adding that the Novgorodians consulted with Prince Iaroslav Vladimirovich (Prince of Novgorod r. 1182-1184, 1187-1196, and 1197-1199),[76] the clergy – the abbots, *sof'iane* (the cathedral chapter as it were) and the priests – (all of which may have taken place in 1156, insofar as the clergy made up part of "all the townspeople" mentioned in the chronicle):

> Gavrilo [Gavriil], archbishop of Novgorod died, and the Novgorodians, having consulted with Prince

Iaroslav, the hegumens and the *sof'iane* [the Men of Holy Wisdom], and the priests, decided on Martirii, chosen by God, and sent for him from [Staraia] Russa, and installed him as bishop; and they sent [word] to the metropolitan and he sent for him with honor; and he [Martirii] went [to Kyiv] with the foremost men; and Prince Sviatoslav and the metropolitan received him with love; and they consecrated him on December 10.[77]

There is a discrepancy in the two versions of the chronicle. While the Older Redaction, quoted above, mentions an election apparently by the *veche*, the Younger Redaction's describes the more fully evolved election by sortition: "some wanted Mitrofan, and others Martirii, and others wanted a Greek...And they laid three lots on the holy altar of Holy Wisdom," sending in a blind man to bring the lots out to the *veche*. Martirii's lot remained on the altar, and he was placed in the archbishop's palace to await consecration by the metropolitan.[78] This election by lots may be a later interpolation based on the memory of later elections by lot.

The first indisputable election by lots was in 1229, described in the chronicle in terms similar to the 1193 election in the Younger Redaction:

> The same year, Prince Mikhail said: "Behold, you have no bishop and it is not seemly for this town to be without a bishop...you should look for a suitable man whether from among priests, hegumens, or monks" And some said to the prince: "There is a monk, a deacon at St. George's [Monastery] named Spiridon; he is worthy of it!" And others named Ioasaf, bishop of Volodymyr, and yet others [named] a Greek: "Whomever the metropolitan shall give, that one shall be our father." And Prince Mikhail said: "Let us cast three lots; let it be whom God will give us." And having written out the names, they laid them on the altar and sent out young Prince Rostislav from the bishop's council chamber [to draw

lots]. God chose a servant for Himself and a shepherd for the flock in Novgorod and in its entire region, and Spiridon was drawn; and they sent to the monastery for him, and having brought him, they installed him in the court of Holy Wisdom, until he should go to Kyiv to be consecrated.[79]

Sortition was not employed again until 1359. *The Novgorodian First Chronicle* notes that Archbishop Moisei played a role in choosing his successor, telling the Novgorodians to "choose a man for yourselves, whomever God gives you." The chronicle then says that, "having deliberated much, the *posadnik* and the *tysiatskii* and all Novgorod and the hegumens and priests decided not to make a choice for themselves by human means but decided to accept God's decision and to trust in His mercy, and let God designate whomever He and Holy Wisdom should desire."[80] Picking three candidates, "they placed three lots on the altar in [the Cathedral of] Holy Wisdom, saying 'Whomever God and Holy Sophia, the Wisdom of God, may desire to have as a servant at His altar, his lot will He leave on His altar.'"[81] The decision not to resolve the matter themselves but to rely on sortition likely had a more pragmatic reason than just trusting in God. Five years earlier, Posadnik Ontsifor Lukich had reformed and greatly expanded the *posadnichestvo* and this seems to have diluted secular power in the city. Rather than touch off an argument among several boiar clans or factions, election by lot was deemed less divisive.[82]

But in this instance, Moisei merely suggested that the Novgorodians choose candidates themselves; he did not select them. In 1274, however, the dying Archbishop Dalmat actually named two candidates to succeed him: Kliment, his *dukhovnik*, and Ioann, the hegumen of the Iur'ev Monastery.[83] The Novgorodians elected Kliment and he was consecrated in 1276. Thus, the chronicles show that a previous archbishop could chose his successor. Conversely, in 1470, the *Vologodsko-Permskaia Chronicle* reveals that the *veche* elected the candidates, choosing three from among the hieromonks and then drawing lots, although we don't know the composition of the *veche*, and it is worth repeating that in episcopal elections, the *veche* may not have comprised the entire population but only secular officials or the Novgorodian clergy, particularly the archimandrites, hegumens, and the *sof'iane*.[84] The participation in episcopal elections of these groups is sometimes specified in the chronicles, but there is no proof that the clergy alone elected the archbishop. In fact, in the elections of 1192 and 1359, the clergy consulted with the men of Novgorod and the city officials and together they chose the archbishop.

If the general population and city officials did not actually elect the archbishops, they at least oversaw or acclaimed the election. In 1388, Posadnik Mikhail Danilovich placed his seal on the lots and then laid them on the altar in the cathedral.[85] The actual drawing of the lots was carried out by someone who was for some reason considered incapable of fraud or guile or beyond reproach, someone somehow touched by God. During the Divine Liturgy, he took two of the lots off the altar one by one and carried them out to the *veche* assembled in front of the cathedral. An unnamed blind man drew the lots in 1193.[86] In 1229, Prince Rostislav, the infant son of the Prince Mikhail Vsevolodovich, drew them.[87] In 1388, it was the archpriest Izmailo, and in 1415, the old archpriest Vasilii.[88] The lot remaining on the altar was that of the man "chosen by God,"[89] acclaimed by the *veche* and sent to the metropolitan for consecration.

The sources never explain where this tradition of election by lot came from. In addition to the canonically-acceptable election by an episcopal synod, a parallel tradition developed in the early Church of election by the clergy and the people (*electio per clericum et populum*). This latter tradition dates to at least the late fourth century when, we find that St. Augustine was chosen by the people of Hippo Regius in AD 395 to be coadjutor to Bishop Valerius, though Augustine himself did not want the office.[90] (Later canons established that serious reluctance or refusal by a candidate invalidated the election, even if the candidate later changed his mind.)[91]

Election by the clergy and the people is also found in the One Hundred Thirty-Seventh Novella of Justinian's *Corpus iuris civilis*:

> We decree that every time it may be necessary to consecrate a bishop in any city, the clergy and prin-

cipal citizens of the said city shall assemble, and issue proclamations by which they nominate three persons, and then make an oath on the Holy Gospels, in conformity with the Scriptures. This oath, inserted in the proclamations, shall be worded as follows: "That they did not select the three persons whom they have nominated in consideration of any gifts or promises made to them; nor through friendship, nor induced by any affection whatsoever, but for the reason that they knew that the candidates whom they have chosen are steadfast in the Catholic [Universal] Faith, and of honorable life; that they have passed the age of thirty years, and have neither wives nor children; and that they have had neither concubines nor natural children, nor have any at present; and if any of them formerly had a wife, he had but one, and she was neither a widow, nor separated from her husband, and that his marriage with her was not prohibited, either by the sacred canons, or by secular laws; that neither of the three candidates is charged with the duties of any public office. ..."

Following election, the three candidates were to be sent to the metropolitan, who would choose one in consultation with the other bishops of the province.[92]

Election by the clergy and the people was gradually replaced in the West by royal appointment, beginning in at least the sixth century, and later by papal appointment in the twelfth. And intriguing though the similarities are between Novgorod's electoral process and this so-called primitive election "by the clergy and the people", there is no indication the Novgorodians were even aware of this early tradition or the section from Justinian's code let alone that they based their electoral process on them. Novgorod's electoral process arose centuries after this method had been abandoned elsewhere in Europe. And Novgorod did not follow Justinian's Novella. They may have selected three candidates, but sent only one to the metropolitan.[93]

Another possibility is that sortition had biblical origins. The practice of using a game of chance to determine the will of God is found at several places in the Old Testament. The *Book of Exodus* described the *Urim* and *Thummim*, sacred lots cast to ascertain the will of God, that were kept in the *Ephod*, called the "Breastplate of Decision," worn by the high priest and used by the king or the priests to reach important decisions.[94] In the *Book of Joshua*, God apparently told the Israelites to cast lots to find out who had sinned and thus caused their defeat at Ai, near Bethel.[95] In the *First Book of Samuel*, the tribes of Israel assembled and chose King Saul by lots.[96] A few chapters later, Saul consulted the *Urim* and *Thummim* before attacking the Philistines and to determine who was to blame for God's negative reply.[97] King David later used the *Urim* and *Thummim* to ascertain whether he should pursue Amalekite raiders who had captured his two wives.[98] In the *Book of Jonah*, when the prophet set sail from Joppa (modern Jaffa or Yafo) "to flee to Tarshish from the presence of the Lord,"[99] God cast a violent storm on the ship and the crew decided "Come, let us cast lots, so that we may know on whose account this calamity has come upon us."[100] The lot fell on Jonah, who was then thrown into the sea to be swallowed up by the large fish that the Lord had "provided."[101] One of the *Proverbs* summed up this recurrent theme of a game of chance as the way God made His will known, asserting: "the lot is cast into the lap, but the decision is the Lord's alone."[102] Similar sentiments appear in the *Novgorodian First Chronicle's* accounts of the elections of 1229 and 1359.[103]

The drawing of lots is also found in the New Testament, where in the first chapter of the *Acts of the Apostles* two candidates are nominated to replace Judas Iscariot, Joseph Barsabbas called Justus, and Matthias.[104] Following prayer, the apostles drew lots and the lot fell to Matthias who joined the Apostles.[105] While the Novgorodian churchmen must have been aware of these biblical uses of lots, there is no indisputable proof that they the basis for the election of the archbishops by lots, although the similar rationale, that God's will was manifest in the lots, is highly suggestive. If so, it is odd that lots were used for the first time only in 1229, some 330 years after the establishment of the office, and then again only 130 years later in 1359.

While the Bible most certainly served as a guide to the Novgorodian archeparchy, the custom of sortition was probably drawn from more direct, and less divinely inspired, influences, namely Byzantine traditions (which themselves may have had biblical origins.) There are numerous instances of the Byzantines drawing lots to help make important decisions and these are much closer in time to the Novgorodian practice. Byzantine princess Anna Comnena (Komnene), wrote that when her father, Emperor Alexius I Comnenus (r.1081-1118) debated whether he should go to war against the Polovtsy (known as the Cumans in Byzantine sources):

> Unable to trust his own judgment and unwilling to rely on his own unaided calculations, [he] referred the whole matter to God and asked Him to decide. All the churchmen and soldiers were summoned to an evening meeting in [Hagia Sofia]. The emperor himself attended and so did the Patriarch Nicolas. On two tablets Alexius wrote the question, "Should I go out to attack the Cumans?"; on one "Yes" was added, on the other "No." They were then signed and the patriarch was commanded to place them on the Holy Table. After hymns had been sung all through the night, Nicolas went to the altar, picked up one of the papers and brought it out. In the presence of the whole company, he broke the seal and read aloud what was written there. The emperor accepted the decision as though it derived from some divine oracle.[106]

The reasoning behind both Alexius' and the Novgorodians' use of lots is identical: namely, they do not trust their own judgment and thus refer the matter to God to decide; indecision in going to war is also similar to Saul's and David's uses of lots in the Old Testament. The method the emperor used – lots chosen during or after a religious service – also matched that of the Novgorodians. It is quite possible, given Novgorod's ecclesiastical and cultural ties with Constantinople, that the method was adopted from Constantinople, although there is no indication that Novgorod used the method to determine issues of war or peace. Alexius' method is also much closer in time than the biblical sources and may have made its way to Novgorod in the century or so after his death.

Closer still in time to the Novgorodian use of lots is the Nestorian Patriarch (Catholicos) Denha's (r. 1266-1281) use of lots not to elect a prelate, but to determine the Syriac name that would be given to a Uighur monk he had appointed metropolitan-archbishop. In 1280, when two Uighur monks arrived in Baghdad en route to pilgrimage in Jerusalem, Denha appointed one of them, Markos, Metropolitan of Cathay (North China), and the other, Sawma, as Visitor-General. He told Markos:

> "Hitherto no man hath called Rabban Mark 'Mar Mark,' but I wish to call him by this name. And moreover, I have thought out a plan [for doing so]. We will write down [on slips of paper a number of] names, and lay them upon the altar. And whichever name shall go forth [from among them] with some clearly recognizable indication, by that we will call Mark." And he did this, and the name of "Yahb-Allaha" came forth, and the Catholicos said "this is from the blessed Lord."[107]

While this is not the Byzantine Church, per se, and it seems highly unlikely that Novgorod adopted election by lots (on the altar) from a Nestorian source, indeed, Denha's use of lots post-dates Novgorod's first use, the similarities between Alexius', Denha's, and the Novgorodians' use of lots, particularly writing names or other information on slips of paper or parchment (or perhaps birchbark in the case of Novgorod) or tablets and placing them on the altar, suggest a common tradition in the Eastern churches of using lots to determine God's will concerning important issues, just as was done in biblical accounts.

It seems more likely that Byzantium was the source of the Novgorodians' use of lots. The Byzantine episcopate was apparently never elected by lots, but there are Byzantine monastic *typika* that indicate lots were used to elect monastic superiors for a number of monasteries in the empire. The *typikon* of Athanasios Philanthropenos, drawn up in November 1158 for the Monastery of St. Mamas in Constantinople,[108] stated that if the superior's death was expected, he was to write the name of three candidates on a piece of paper, seal it, and have it deposited in the sacristy of the monastic church until after his death;[109] if the monks could agree on one of those candidates, he was to be named superior. But if the superior died suddenly without naming three candidates, then the whole monastic community should decide on a new superior; if they could not agree, then three lots were to be drawn.

> Both the choice of the three [candidates] who are about to be selected and their installation will be carried out in this manner. On three pieces of paper of the same size, the following words will be written:
> "Master, Lord Jesus Christ, our God, Thou who knowest the hearts [of men], by the intercession of the all-pure Lady, the Mother of God, and the holy celebrated among the martyrs Mamas, reveal to us sinners whether thou has judged our brother so-and-so worthy of the position of our superior."
> The same words [will] be written again on the other pieces of paper and the names of the three candidates inscribed on them. When the papers have been stamped with the seal – that of the protector if he is present, and in case he does not want to be or is somehow unable to be, by the seal of [a representative] whom the [protector] will assign by means of a written and signed statement – they will be placed on the holy table during vespers on Saturday or that of a feast of the Lord, or that of the holy great martyr Mamas, if it should occur at that time. A vigil shall be performed and a whole-hearted supplication with a contrite heart shall be made by you, my most venerable fathers, because the matter for which we make the supplication is important. On this hangs the maintenance of the monastery and, equally, its destruction, which I pray does not happen, and the hope of your salvation.

On the next day, after the divine liturgy has been celebrated and after its completion, while the priest is still dressed in his priestly vestments, a *trisagion* will be performed by you and these *troparia* will be sung: "Have mercy on us, O Lord, have mercy"; "Lord turn to us from heaven and behold" (Ps. 79:14): "Glory"; "By your God-given staff, Holy One"; "And now"; [and] "Only-begotten One, of the same substance." The deacon will make and *ektenes* declaiming that after the other petitions: "We again beg that the Lord Our God reveal to us the one worthy of our Leadership." You will respond, "Kyrie eleison," thirty times and perform fifteen deep bows, saying also to yourselves, while you raise your hands to God: "God, thou who knowest the hearts [of men], show to us sinners the one worthy of our leadership." After these bows, when the priest himself has performed three similar bows before the holy table, and while still dressed in his priestly vestments, as we said, is repeating the same invocation, he will lift up on of the three pieces of paper. When it has been offered in the presence of the whole community by the priest himself to the one who placed his own seal upon it, he will recognize his own seal and the piece of paper will be opened, as all watch, and the owner of the name written on it will enter with the priest into the holy sanctuary with his head uncovered. Then as our *typikon* and the staff are lying in the place before the holy altar, he [the superior-elect], after making three bows, will take them, pondering and considering with himself from where he takes them and to whom he promises to protect them, and that angels are recording his promise, who are going to lead him to that fearful place of judgment to give account of the fulfillment of his promise.

After the whole brotherhood has responded three times "worthy," he shall come out and stand in a place assigned to the superior, and everyone will offer him the divine greeting [with a kiss], and glory will be offered to God, and the dismissal will follow with the customary prayer of the priest. He will be your superior thereafter, whom you are to revere as a father, and have an obedient attitude toward him as one appointed by God.[110]

These instructions were taken almost word for word from the *typikon* of the Empress Irene Doukaina Komnene (Comnena) for the Convent of the Mother of God *Kecharitomene* (Full of Grace) in Constantinople, composed during the second decade of the eleventh century;[111] they are similar to other *typika*.[112] The laying of three lots on the altar during or after the Divine Liturgy and the reference of the superior as "one appointed by God," as well as the use of the protector's seal on the lots, are strikingly similar to terminology and manner of election in Novgorod, albeit election in the Byzantine case was of the first-chosen and not the last-remaining. The Novgorodians' repeated references to their archbishops as men "chosen by God" sounds remarkably similar to the Byzantine *typika*; all point toward Novgorod's episcopal election by lot coming out of twelfth century Byzantine monastic traditions, understandable given that Rus' monasticism drew its earliest rules from Byzantine *typika*,[113] and that the earliest bishops of Rus' came from Byzantine monasteries. Churchmen, such as Metropolitan Kiprian, also brought Byzantine church literature from the empire into Rus' over the course of the medieval period.

Sortition occurred only nine times. Martirii and Spiridon were elected in 1193 and 1229 respectively, with another seven sortitions from 1359 to 1482. The only exception during this latter period was Iona, who was unanimously elected by the *veche* on March 19, 1458, just 8 days after his predecessor's death.[114] The earlier elections by lots in the twelfth and thirteenth centuries were apparently an effort to resolve disputed elections, particular the election of 1229, which ended the almost two-decades-long dispute among Mitrofan, Arsenii, and Antonii over the archiepiscopal throne. In some sense, these earlier elections by lot seem outliers and Joel Raba is certainly correct in tying the use of lots after 1359 to Ontsifor Lukich's 1354 reforms and the evolution of a "ruling collective" of the various *kontsy*,[115] or what Valentin Ianin called a "collective *posadnichestvo*."[116] Raba did not recognize that elections by lots had occurred earlier than 1359, and he might be right in doing so, as these earlier elections may not be the basis for election in 1359 and thereafter. These later sortitions seem more based on Byzantine traditions and the political situation that arose in Novgorod after 1354 than the reintroduction of practices from the late twelfth or early thirteenth centuries.

The Consecration of the Archbishop-elect

After election, the archbishop-elect was acclaimed by the entire city: the *posadniki* and *tysiatskie* "with the Novgorodians," brought him from his monastery or church and placed him in the archiepiscopal palace until the metropolitan summoned him.[117] The *Novgorodian First Chronicle* explains that the Novgorodians "led him up to the canopy" or he "sat at the canopy."[118] His activities do not appear to have been limited prior to consecration, as they were in the Catholic Church, which had an intermediate stage of *confirmation* during which the pope or metropolitan-archbishop dispatched a letter confirming the election, after which the *electus* could then be consecrated. The medieval Rus' Church lacked the legal intricacies of the Catholic Church, which even limited what garb the archbishop-elect could wear (they could not wear the *pallium* until installed), what seals they could use (it was to bear the title "*electus*" until confirmation but not afterward, and could not bear the title of archbishop until consecration), and what powers they could wield (for example, they could not alienate archdiocesan property, install suffragan bishops, or consecrate churches).[119]

Despite the lack of obvious limits on what they could do as *electus*, the term archbishop-elect is used in reference to two of the archbishops, indicating that the distinction was not unimportant.[120] Evfimii II was referred to as a hieromonk in the preamble to a treaty, rather than archbishop-elect or archbishop as he is in the *Novgorodian First Chronicle* in 1433.[121] In a treaty signed before June 24, 1434 (i.e., before his consecration) he is referred to as "the Archbishop-elect Evfimii,"[122] just as he is in the chronicle when it mentions that: "Archbishop-elect Evfimii built himself a house in his court and it had thirty doors, and German (*nemechkii*, i.e., foreign) masters from overseas made it with the masters of Novgorod;"[123] only after his consecration is Evfimii referred to as archbishop.[124] Feofil, too, was referred to as "archbishop-elect" between his election in early 1470 and his consecration on December 15, 1471. In a 1471 treaty, Feofil is referred to as "the hieromonk Feo(f)il, elected to the archbishopric,"[125] and as "Feofil, elected to the *vladichestvo*..."[126] In the *Novgorod Judicial Charter*, he is also referred to as "archbishop-elect."[127] But the Novgorod's archbishops-elect still carried out the archiepiscopal duties apparently unencumbered by their legally-ambiguous status: Evfimii built an archiepiscopal palace while still archbishop-elect, thus alienating archdiocesan property (or wealth), and Feofil took part in negotiating and concluding treaties. Furthermore, Efrem, Arsenii, and Feodosii carried out the duties of the episcopal office for several years each (five in the case of Efrem; two or three years in the case of the other two) without ever having been consecrated. Usually an archbishop-elect was consecrated within six months to a year, but there were exceptions: Arkadii was not consecrated until August 10, 1158, almost two years after his election, and Evfimii II's four-to-five-and-a-half-year wait has already been discussed.[128]

Consecration consisted of a two-part ceremony: the designation, called the *znamenanie* (lit. sign or banner) or *narechenie (naming)*, was followed by the consecration (*khirotoniia*) itself, held in a different church.[129] In most cases the archbishop-elect traveled to the metropolitan who consecrated him in the presence of several other bishops.[130] Thus, in 1331, Metropolitan Feognost consecrated Vasilii Kalika in Volodymyr in the presence of the bishops of Polatsk, Volodymyr, Halych, Peremyshl (Przemyśl), and Kholm (Chelm),[131] while in 1388, the metropolitan consecrated Ioann II in Moscow in the presence of the bishops of Smolensk and Riazan;[132] in 1416, the bishops of Rostov, Suzdal', Tver', Sarsk (Sarai), and Perm', as well as the grand prince and his brothers, were present at the consecration of Archbishop Simeon. In Moscow, the first part of the consecration took place in the Dormition Cathedral (*Uspenskii sobor*) in the Kremlin, and the second was held in the Church of St. Michael (*Arkhangelskii sobor*), across Cathedral Square.[133] Twice, the consecration took place out in Novgorod itself: in 1251, Metropolitan Kirill III consecrated Dalmat in Novgorod, but there is no indication in which church the *narechenie* took place, though the consecration almost certainly took place in the Cathedral of Holy Wisdom.[134] In 1300 Metropolitan Maksim came to Novgorod with the bishops of Rostov and Tver' and consecrated Feoktist. The *narechenie* was held in the Church of Boris and Gleb in the Detinets, while the *khirotoniia* took place in the cathedral.[135]

Conclusion

A unique electoral system developed in Novgorod by the latter half of the fourteenth century whereby, at least in the Novgorodians' spiritual view, God Himself chose their archbishop from among three candidates whose lots were placed on the altar of the Cathedral of Holy Wisdom. Sortition was used in the elections of 1193 and 1229, but fell into disuse for more than a century before being revived in 1359 in the wake of political reforms and the diffusion of power in the city after 1354. The Novgorodians apparently took sortition from Byzantine monastic traditions, which itself probably had biblical origins. It is often not clear how the three candidates were chosen, although the *veche* or the previous archbishops sometimes chose them. Following election, the electus was led "to the canopy" and seems to have carried out the office from the moment of election, although sacramentally they were sent to the metropolitan (or, rarely, he came to them) and consecrated in the presence of several other bishops in accordance with canon law.

This uniquely Novgorod system outlived independent Novgorod by seven years. The last independently-elected archbishop, Feofil, was arrested, taken to Moscow, and imprisoned in the Chudov Monastery.[136] The date of his resignation,[137] date of death, and place of burial,[138] are not known for certain.

His successor, Sergei, an elder in the Troitse-Sergiev Monastery, was elected by lots on July 17, 1483, apparently in Moscow, though the sources do not say. (The two other candidates were Elisii, archimandrite of the Savior Monastery, and Gennadii, archimandrite of the Chudov Monastery – Feofil's jailer).[139] Lots were laid on the altar according to tradition, but this time the metropolitan drew them in the presence of Grand Prince Ivan III, his son Grand Prince

Ivan Ivanovich, the archbishop of Rostov, and the bishops of Riazan, Kolomna, and Sarai.[140] Sergei was consecrated on September 4,[141] but was removed from office on June 27, 1484 and imprisoned in the Trinity Monastery, where he had been a monk before his election.[142] His successor, Gennadii, an unsuccessful candidate in the 1483 election, was not elected by lots, but rather "placed" in office on December 12, 1485.[143] After this, the metropolitan or grand prince appointed the Novgorodian prelate just as had been done before 1156. The process had come full circle.

CHAPTER FIVE
Politics

Introduction

The political roles of Novgorod's archbishops are probably the aspect of the office most analyzed by historians, since much of the traditional historiography argues that the archbishops were heads of the medieval Novgorodian Republic. However, the political roles are actually one of the more difficult parts of the office to reach definitive answers on given the sparse sources and the traditional historiography's portrayal of both Novgorod's constitution and the archbishop's place within it that is tantalizingly and satisfyingly clear-cut, but not necessarily true. This traditionalist view has been discussed some in the introduction, but is worth repeating briefly here since it needs to be addressed, if not refuted, in order to come to a truer understanding of the archbishop's political position.

In this traditional view, the archbishop headed the city; he oversaw the city's treasury – kept in the alcoves in the upper galleries of the Cathedral of Holy Wisdom – and chaired the "Council of Lords" made up of the *posadniki* and *tysiaskie*. The council acted as an executive organ of the all-city *veche*, which elected local officials, including the archbishops, invited and dismissed Novgorod's princes (at will), and oversaw the *vecha* of the five *kontsy* that made

6. The Aleksiev Cross named after Archbishop Aleksei and said to have been commissioned to commemorate Grand Prince Dmitrii Donskoi's victory over Mamai at Kulikovo Field in 1380. It is now just inside the north entrance of the Cathedral of Holy Wisdom.

up Novgorod. Each *veche* of the *kontsy*, in turn, oversaw one of the *Piatiny*, the five organized territories into which the Novgorodian Land was divided, while the all-city *veche* oversaw the unorganized Zavoloch'e region to the north and east of the *Piatiny* (See map). The archbishop was also said to have been one of the heads of the city's judiciary, overseeing judges in the ecclesiastical and municipal courts. He acted as the republic's foreign minister or ambassador-at-large, insofar as he frequently headed embassies to the grand prince or other princes. He acted as a symbolic focal point for popular patriotism and "stood above the political fray" like a president or constitutional monarch in a parliamentary system, and brought peace to warring factions within the city. He built fortresses and other buildings of a purely secular nature. He mustered armies and commanded his own "banner" or cavalry squadron. He supervised weights and measures in the marketplace and thereby had oversight of mercantile activities in this very mercantile republic. He also headed the local church. His *namestniki* ran outlying towns like Staraia Ladoga and Torzhok. Taken together, the archbishop of Novgorod was apparently little different from the prince-bishops (*Fürstbischof*, or *Fürstarchbischof* – Prince-archbishops) of the Holy Roman Empire or similar bishops who were secular lords in the West.[1]

There were variations in this interpretation to be sure: Imperial-era or Russian nationalist historians saw Moscow's "gathering of the Rus' lands" as a legitimate, even an inevitable occurrence. Thus, Novgorod was a rebellious – if not treasonous – republic, led by its very partisan archbishops and defying its legitimate sovereign. Some Soviet-era histories were written from a Marxist perspective, which argued that the archbishops worked with the city's secular authorities to oppress the lower classes, using religion as a tool or weapon wielded, in keeping with Marx's idea of religion as "the opium of the people,"[2] to maintain power structures in the city.

This view of the archbishops as "heads of state," "presidents of the republic," Novgorodian nationalists, or classist elites is, however, anachronistic, and doesn't help in clarifying matters. Indeed, to see such a neat and tidy political structure in Medieval Novgorod is to read a lot into the relatively few available sources and impose a post-Enlightenment order and modern sentiments on an often-messy medieval political milieu. Frankly, a clear, neat picture that is true to the limited source evidence is and will likely remain impossible, a point made often enough in this study already. The true picture is likely much more muddled. What can be gleaned from the sources is that the archbishops were not Novgorod's princes, presidents, prime ministers, treasurers, foreign ministers, military commanders, ministers of justice, ministers of commerce, or chief legislators in any formal or institutionalized sense of these terms. They did play very important roles in the city's political life and their political activities did touch on what modern people would call the city's executive, legislative, judicial, military, financial, and commercial spheres. Indeed, they probably had greater political influence or secular power than any other bishop in the Rus' Church with the exception of the metropolitans. In fact, they may have had greater political power than almost any other bishops in all of Orthodox Christendom save for the patriarchs and a few other metropolitans or autonomous archbishops. The problem remains, though, that their political powers, like so much of what they did, was de *facto* power and almost never formalized, institutionalized, *de jure*, or *ex officio* power.

The constitution of the Novgorodian government more broadly – and by that, I mean the basic principles, traditions, and laws that determine the powers and duties of the Novgorodian government and state – remains ambiguous. Frankly, it is sometimes impossible to tell where the powers or authority of, say, the *posadniki* left off and that of the *tysiastkie* (or the archbishop) picked up. The political powers of the archbishops were never written down in a formal document, institutionalized, or legally or theoretically recognized, as were, by comparison, the secular political power of medieval Catholic prelates. For example, for several decades beginning in the 1230s, Archbishop Albert Suerbeer of Riga fought for his rights in Riga against the Teutonic Order; his successor, Archbishop Jens Grand of Lund, Bremen, and Riga (d. 1327) then appealed to Rome against the King of Denmark in the late thirteenth and early fourteenth centuries; he brought charges before Pope Clement V against the Teutonic Knights in 1305, and two years later asked the pope to suppress the order on grounds of heresy.³ There are no such cases of disputed authority between Novgorod's bishops and the secular officials that were appealed to the metropolitan or patriarch. There isn't even a sense that they could or should have done this.

That said, the archbishop's place in the church and in Novgorodian life, as well as the city's place in wider Rus' make a truer understanding of their political roles important. If they had *de facto* rather than *de jure* power, or influence rather than formal, enumerated power, that would significantly alter our understanding of the city's political make-up. A city ruled by consensus among oligarchs would also be quite different from one overseen by a prince-bishop. In trying to reconstruct or better understand the archbishop's placed in Novgorodian politics, it is important to avoid seeing the archbishops as prince-bishops like their Catholic counterparts, with clearly-articulated secular powers. It is equally important to realize that the Novgorodian archbishops' powers were not typical of the Orthodox episcopate as a whole.

What we have is a much looser, more complex, if not ambiguous, constitution in which the archbishops shared power with the city's secular officials and governed based on influence rather than on real power that anyone had granted them. To draw on a Latin legalistic distinction, they had *auctoritas*, that is, (moral) authority or influence, rather than *potestas*, or power,⁴ what one scholar called "more than advice and less than a command,"⁵ or *de facto* as opposed to *de jure* power. This authority developed gradually from the tenth through the thirteenth centuries, declined (as did their other activities) and then revived again and reached its fullest form in the middle of the fourteenth century.

In fact, the second and third quarters of the fourteenth century is a crucial period in Novgorodian history. Vasilii Kalika (r. 1330-1352) revived the archiepiscopal office. Around the same time, a number of local and regional events took place that would prove fateful for Novgorod. The power of the *posadnichestvo* fragmented as the number of *posadniki* grew due to Ontsifor Lukich's reforms in 1354. Moscow took firm control of the grand princely office under Ivan Kalita (r. 1325-1340), and the relationship with Novgorod grew strained as Ivan sought more and more Novgorodian silver to pay the *dan'*. Under Dmitrii Donskoi (r. 1359-1389), Moscow began its slow encroachment on Novgorodian territory, especially the northern fur-bearing regions, culminating in the final conquest of Novgorod in 1478. The metropolitanate also settled in Moscow in 1325, and Pskov achieved independence from Novgorod in 1348. Thus, Novgorod's archbishops achieved the acme of their power and importance just as other local powers were becoming diffused and Muscovite grand princely and ecclesiastical power was coalescing. Novgorodian archiepiscopal power and influence lasted a little over a century before it succumbed – along with the Novgorodian Republic - to Muscovite grand princely autocracy.

Indeed, that all these developments occurred at roughly the same time may indicate a relationship between the rise of Moscow, the fragmentation of secular power in Novgorod, and the rise of archiepiscopal political power there.[6] Thus, understanding the archbishop's powers may be crucial to understanding Rus' history at this time. It may be that the archbishop's increased political power was a reaction to the growing power of the grand princes of Moscow and/or the weakening of the *posadnichestvo*, though whether this was intentional, or grew to fill a vacuum, may never be known. Be that as it may, the archbishop's growing political activities, and the changes in the Novgorodian secular power-structure, suggest that the "gathering of the Rus' lands" was not seen as inevitable or legitimate by the Novgorodians, or, indeed, by inhabitants of other principalities like Tver', Nizhnii Novgorod, or Riazan, and that those who opposed Moscow were not traitors either to the grand princes or to their religion. To argue otherwise is, in some sense, to interject modern ideas of Russian nationalism into the medieval period or even to buy into the grand princely propaganda of the 1470s. Indeed, the Novgorodians (including the archbishops) tried vigorously to fend off Moscow from the late fourteenth and throughout the fifteenth centuries. The political powers amassed by the archbishops may have helped them hold out as long as they did.

Before going into these particular political powers, it is important to differentiate the place of the Orthodox episcopate in the secular world from the more familiar and better documented secular powers of the Western episcopate if we are, again, to understand what powers the archbishops of Novgorod really exercised and how unique these were in the Orthodox milieu.

The Bishop in Politics: Divergent Catholic and Orthodox Viewpoints

The Western Episcopate: Princes and Warriors

Perhaps most problematic in trying to understand the Novgorodian archbishops' political powers is the tendency to see them in terms of the much better documented, studied and even familiar – at least to Western scholars – Catholic episcopate. Among the key differences between the medieval Catholic and Orthodox churches is the role of the bishop in politics. This stems from the different histories in the Eastern and Western Roman Empires that meant different developments in the Eastern and Western churches since Late Antiquity. Catholic bishops stepped into the political void left by weak Western emperors and barbarian invasions that ultimately led to the fall of the Empire in the West at the end of the fifth century. Western bishops took on significant political roles which came to be an accepted aspect of their office, even if it might be formally denied them in canon law. Western bishops served as chancellors and advisors to emperors and kings or ruled over ecclesiastical fiefs, the Papal States and the ecclesiastical principalities of Cologne, Trier, Mainz, Strasbourg, and Salzburg, just to name a few.

The East never saw a comparable rise in political power in the Orthodox episcopate. The Eastern Empire survived another thousand years after the fall of Rome, and the Byzantine emperors, their civil service, and their army maintained political stability and authority giving little opportunity, or little need, for churchmen to assume secular political powers. Orthodox bishops were certainly not apolitical nor was there was a strict separation between church and state, or religious and secular life, in the Orthodox world. Such separation was foreign to the medieval mind in both East and West. Scholars speak of the Church-State "Symphony," a relationship between the Byzantine emperor and the patriarch of Constantinople much closer than seen between king and bishop in the West. Others refer to "Caesaropapism" by which the emperor ruled both empire and church. Neither concept allowed for an independent church to develop as gradually occurred in the West over the course of the Investiture Controversy and other disputes which led to the concept of "The Two Swords" articulated as early as the papacy of Pope Gelasius (r. 492-496).

Until the Age of Reason, Christendom, including Byzantium and Rus', understood the political order as ideally based on Divine Will: the duty of an emperor, king, prince, or city official was to preserve and defend Christendom and establish a just rule that mirrored the Kingdom of Heaven.[7] In doing so they enforced Christian morals and doctrinal homogeneity in their domains, supporting and being supported by the church. Many appointed bishops, so that the traditional view of Caesaropapism as an Eastern phenomenon is probably overstated; most European princes were Caesaropapist to a degree, though the West did establish a tradition of the church being separate, even if this was not always honored in practice. In part this was necessary. Clergymen were sacerdotal figures who were assumed to be more trustworthy than the average peasant or townsman, hence in many law codes, they could prove their innocence by compurgation rather than trial by ordeal or combat. They were also among the only literate people in society and thus were called upon by kings and princes to carry out administrative tasks of a decidedly secular nature, especially in the West.[8]

But Western bishops – as well as other clergymen and monks – were also warriors or military commanders. They raised and led troops and fought in battle themselves,[9] this despite occasional condemnations of the practice,[10] as when Gregory of Tours' (ca. 538-594), an archbishop, criticized two brothers, both bishops – Salonius of Ebrun and Sagitarrius of Gap – who he complained engaged in "physical assaults, murders, adultery, and every crime in the calendar,"[11] dispatching mobs to attack Bishop Victor of St. Paul-Trois-Chateaux "with swords and arrows,"[12] and, "instead of seeking protection in the heavenly Cross, they were armed with the helmet and the breastplate of this secular world and, what is worse, they are said to have killed many men with their own hands."[13] Gregory was so disturbed that he returned to the brothers later his history, complaining that they "armed themselves like laymen and killed many men with their own hands."[14]

A few more examples illustrate this phenomenon that existed throughout Latin Christendom. In the Holy Roman Empire, the Archbishop of Mainz and the Bishop of Metz fought the Vikings,[15] Archbishop Philip of Cologne and Bishop-elect Conrad of Worms led armies into Italy to aid the Emperor Frederick Barbarossa in

April 1176,[16] and Archbishop Christian of Mainz (d. 1183) killed nine opponents in the Lombard War and knocked out the teeth of thirty more.[17] Odo of Bayeux,[18] half-brother of William the Conqueror, and Archbishops Roger and Geoffrey of York were warrior-bishops in England, to name just three.[19] Philip of Dreux, bishop of Beauvais (r. 1175-1217), warred with and was captured by King Richard the Lionheart (r. 1189-1199) in Northern France; when the pope asked for his release, Richard sent the bishop's bloody mail shirt and the mocking reply: "We found this. Is it not your son's coat?"[20] Archbishops Hugolin (or Ugolin) of Kolocza and Matthias of Gran (Esztergom) in Hungary, were killed with three other bishops fighting the Mongols at the Battle of Sajo River (Mohi) on April 11, 1241.[21] Pope John XXII (r. 1316-1334) and Pope Julius II (r. 1503-1515) personally led troops in battle.[22] So too did Cardinal Robert of Geneva (later Antipope Clement VII; r. 1378-1394), who personally led troops against Cesena while a papal legate in 1377, and upon its surrender, massacred 4,000 of the city's inhabitants despite having sworn on his galero to spare them.[23] When some of his own men objected to the wanton slaughter, he cried out for "Blood and more blood!"[24]

The Eastern Episcopate

Novgorod came into contact with Catholic warrior-bishops along its Northern and Western frontiers. In 1196, Berthold of Uexküll, second bishop of Livonia, assembled the first crusading army in the Baltic States only to be killed in battle against local tribes two years later.[25] His successor, Bishop Albert von Buxhoeveden, entered Livonia in 1200 at the head of an army and founded the Brothers of the Sword, which later merged with the Teutonic Order.[26] Archbishop Anders Sunesen of Lund in Scania (r. 1201-1228) along with Bishop Theoderich von Treyden of Estonia (r. ca. 1211-1219), helped Danish King Valdemar II (r. 1202-1241) lead a crusading army into Estonia in 1219 and fought at the Battle of Lyndanisse near Tallinn (Reval, Kolyvan), where Theoderich was killed.[27] These early incursions into Livonia are not noted in the *Novgorodian First Chronicle*, though the chronicle does note when, in 1240, Bishop Albert's brother, Bishop Hermann of Dorpat (Derpt, Iur'ev, modern Tartu, Estonia), accompanied the Teutonic Knights as they marched on the fortress of Izborsk guarding the western approaches to Pskov,[28] as well as the presence of a bishop with a Swedish prince and his troops at the battle on the Neva where Aleksandr Nevskii earned his sobriquet.[29] Two years later, Hermann sent troops to fight Aleksandr at the Battle on the Ice.[30] A little over a century later, the chronicler noted German bishops with the master and commander and the Teutonic Knights encamped below Izborsk in 1368.[31]

The appearance in the chronicles of Catholic bishops acting as men of war, or at least accompanying armies into Rus', suggests how alien this behavior was to the Novgorodians. By contrast, the only case of a Novgorodian archbishop playing any role in military affairs is an entry in the *Novgorodian Fourth Chronicle* under the year 1471, in which Archbishop-elect Feofil limited the use of his cavalry when Grand Prince Ivan III marched against Novgorod and met the Novgorodian forces in battle on the Shelon River on July 14; Feofil allowed the cavalry to attack the Pskovite troops but not the grand prince's. However, Feofil did not lead troops or even accompany them on campaign, and there may be other explanations for why he acted in this matter.[32]

That the idea of churchmen personally bearing arms or leading men into battle was abhorrent to Orthodox sensibilities, at least to the Byzantine Orthodox, can be found in the writings of several Byzantine notables. Anna Comnena, writing in the 1140s, described an incident in which Byzantine marines boarded a crusading ship crossing the Adriatic, led by one Marianus, son of the Byzantine admiral. Mistaking the Byzantines for the Syrian fleet, the crusaders tried to fight them off, including a priest who shot at Marianus with a bow. When he ran out of arrows, he threw slingstones, one of which knocked Marianus unconscious for a time. When he ran out of sling-stones, he threw barley cakes until the Byzantines overwhelmed him. He was carried ashore grievously wounded and, just before dying, boasted "If you had met me on dry land, many of you would have died at my hands." Anna wrote:

> The Latin customs with regard to priests differ from ours. We are bidden by canon law and the teachings of the Gospel, "Touch not, grumble not, attack not - For thou art consecrated." But the Latin barbarian

will at the same time handle sacred objects, fasten his shield to his left arm, and grasp a spear in his right. He will communicate the Body and Blood of the Deity, and meanwhile gaze on bloodshed and become himself "a man of blood," (as David says in the Psalm). Thus, the race is no less devoted to religion than to war. This Latin, then, more man of action than priest, wore priestly garb and at the same time handled an oar and ready for naval action or war on land, fought sea and men alike. Our rules, as I have just said, derive from Aaron, Moses and our first high priest.[33]

Around the same time, an unnamed Byzantine ambassador on his way to the court of the Holy Roman Emperor Lothair complained to Peter the Deacon, the official chronicler of the abbey of Monte Cassino in Italy, that "Your pope has become the emperor," adding that he disapproved of the Roman Catholic Church whose "bishops (pontifices) rush into wars, as your Pope Innocent [II] is doing, distributing money, assembling soldiers, and generally assuming the purple."[34] While these sentiments were from Byzantine sources, Rus' churchmen held similar beliefs that they had learned from their Byzantine teachers and there are a few times when we find them in the sources. Metropolitan Kiprian, a Bulgarian who had been a monk on Mount Athos in northern Greece as well as a close associate of the patriarch of Constantinople, and thus, familiar with Byzantine views, emphasizes in a letter to Sergei of Radonezh and Hegumen Fedor we have already discussed: "I am a bishop, and not a military man."[35] This view seems to have been held widely enough that there are no instances of Rus' warrior bishops.

Aleksandr Musin and Olga Kuzmina argue, however, that priests in Novgorod (or the Novgorodian archeparchy) fought in the town militias, with Musin even arguing that the practice was common throughout Rus' over the medieval period.[36] He asserts that priests in the "street churches" – smaller ones that did not hold daily liturgies – had to find other work to survive and this included service in the town militia. But there are just three references in the chronicles of priests being killed in battle or fleeing with a defeated army,[37] and in only one of those does it appear that the priest personally bore arms. In that case, after the Livonians defeated the Pskovites in 1343, "a certain Ruda, priest of the Church of Boris and Gleb, threw down all his weapons to escape from the battle, and ran to Izborsk and told them: 'the Germans have beaten everyone' before rushing off to report the same in Pskov."[38] The other instances could easily be priests who accompanied (and thus fled with) the army as chaplains, or being killed in the crossfire, as it were, rather than taking up arms personally.[39] Musin argues the prohibition on priests taking up arms only dates to the Muscovite period. This seems unlikely, but if the Rus' had not adopted the clear Byzantine and canonical prohibitions against priests taking up arms, they certainly knew of them as attested a response dated August 12, 1276 from the patriarchal synod in Constantinople to Bishop Feognost of Sarai.[40] In question 31, Feognost asks whether a priest in the army (*"pop na rati"*) who killed someone could continue to serve, to which the patriarchal synod replies that it "is withheld" by the holy canons.[41] Canon 83 of the Apostolical Canons cited in Chapter One, above, ordered that any bishop, priest (presbyter), or deacon "who goes into the army and desires to retain both the Roman government and the sacerdotal administration, be deprived,"[42] as had the Council of Chalcedon, whose Seventh Canon forbids the clergy from departing on military service or secular office on pain of anathema.[43] Both canons, of course, are found in multiple editions of the Rus' *Kormchaia kniga*, so they were known to Rus'. In any event, if the priests were fighting in the army, there is no indication that the Rus' bishops ever did so.

As the Byzantine ambassador's complaint to Peter the Deacon reveals, Orthodox sensibilities not only considered it inappropriate for bishops to be military men, but saw many other political activities as likewise unbecoming. Joan Hussey, citing the Third and (the aforementioned) Seventh Canons of the Council of Chalcedon, underscored this point in noting that "by canon law episcopal office was incompatible with secular office." However, she went on: "this did not debar a bishop from participation in non-ecclesiastical affairs, but he was considered to be acting in an advisory capacity for moral reasons."[44] Thus, Byzantine bishops carried out political tasks but did so wielding authority, not power, to again use the old Roman distinction.⁴⁵ That said, the line between religion and secular politics was very thin at best, as demonstrated by Patriarch Anthony IV of Constantinople's 1393 letter to Grand Prince Vasilii I of Moscow, in which he rebuked the grand prince for having caused the metropolitan to omit the emperor from the diptychs (the list of those to be prayed for during the Divine Liturgy) of the Rus' church, as well as several disparaging remarks Vasilii is said to have made about the emperor.⁴⁶ The patriarch reprimanded Vasilii for saying of Russia that "we have the church but not the emperor," an unacceptable stance for Anthony:

> It is not possible for Christians to have the church and not have the empire. For church and empire have a great unity and community; nor is it possible for them to be separated from one another…The holy emperor is not as other rulers and governors of other regions are… He is anointed with the great myrrh and is consecrated *basileus* and *autokrator* of the Romans –to wit, of all Christians.⁴⁷

Other so-called kings (the patriarch saw the use of the title by mere princelings as an arrogation) were merely local authorities, not like the Byzantine emperor who was "lord and ruler of the *oikoumene* (*oikoimenis kiros kai archon*)⁴⁸ …the universal emperor…the natural emperor (*physikou Basileos*) …"⁴⁹

Thus, the patriarch and the emperor, church and state, were inextricably linked in Byzantine thought – as we have already seen in the concept of *symphonia*. In this particular instance the patriarch was certainly concerned with ecclesiastical matters, specifically his loss of control over the Rus' church, but he was also speaking for the emperor in a political matter. Civil disobedience was disobedience to God's will in the Orthodox view, since God had ordained the existing political order and the emperor was the "vice-regent of God on earth." The patriarch employed a churchman as his envoy: Archbishop Michael of Bethlehem, accompanied by Alexius Aaron, a Byzantine official representing the emperor's interests (the latter's presence highlights the political aspects of the embassy). Additionally, Michael carried a letter to Novgorod about its rejection of Metropolitan Kiprian's right of jurisdiction – a largely religious or ecclesiastical matter[50] - instructing the archbishop to address the *veche* before handing the letter to the town officials, apparently hoping that that the archbishop or the *veche* might persuade the city's leaders to change their behavior toward Kiprian.[51]

The Archbishops' Unique Position in Politics

Considering the disparate views of the episcopate in the Catholic and Orthodox worlds, it is worth noting that, in their secular or political activities, the Novgorodian archbishops often seem closer to Catholic bishops than to their Orthodox brethren. This may be due, in part, to Novgorod's unique political structure, the Novgorodian church and state being *de facto* independent from the grand prince and metropolitan in Moscow. The prince remained the nominal executive power in Novgorod but was usually absent, particularly after the fourteenth century.[52] In his absence, a political void developed in Novgorod in some ways similar to the one in the Western Empire after the fall of Rome. Local secular officials – the *posadniki*, the *tysiatskie*, and the boiarstvo in general – filled this void in the course of the twelfth and thirteenth centuries, but toward the end of the fourteenth century political changes, including Ontsifor Lukich's reforms in 1354, led to an increase in the number of *posadniki* and *tysiatskie*, and increased political fragmentation. This may have led to growth in archiepiscopal political power and influence. Or perhaps Vasilii Kalika and his successors, through their own personalities and drive, actively sought power when no other single office or individual stood at the apex of power. The citizens looked to the archbishops and the church as moral authorities or as the symbolic fathers of the city, and, as the House of Holy Wisdom had an independent administration which could carry out the governance or serve as the bureaucracy of the republic, the church and archbishops rose up to assume real political powers not seen in any other Rus' principality or eparchy.

Novgorod, located on what Eric Christiansen called "the Catholic frontier,"[53] could have adopted Catholic ideas of the secular political roles of bishops found across that frontier. If so, the sources are silent on this matter. Indeed, they are largely silent about the Catholic bishops in Riga, Dorpat, Kolyvan, Courland, and Oesel. (The Livonian and Estonian sources likewise say very little about the Novgorodian archbishops.) Episcopal envoys from Kolyvan and Dorpat appear in Novgorodian chronicles and treaties, but there is no apparent sense of affinity felt by the Catholic and Orthodox bishops toward one another. Indeed, the envoys from the German bishops are apparently treated the same as the envoys of any secular lord.[54] Furthermore, the Novgorodian sources cover the crusades launched by the Teutonic Knights and the King of Sweden across the border into the Novgorodian Land; they note the political and commercial treaties concluded between Novgorod and Western European states; and they show the archbishops calling in artisans and other experts from Catholic Europe to cast bells, build the Palace of Facets, and undertake other artistic projects, but never indicate there was any significant transfer of Western European political, theological, or philosophical ideas until after the period under study. In October 1490, Archbishop Gennadii forwarded a report from the ambassador of the Holy Roman Empire about the Spanish Inquisition to Metropolitan Zosima suggesting similar methods to suppress heresy in Novgorod, marveling: "Truly, what firmness the Franks (*friazov*) maintain for their faith! The emperor's envoy told me how the Spanish king purges his land."[55]

Although it is not clear where the thought of the archbishops assuming secular political power came from, or even if it was a conscious process, it is clear that the archbishops assumed real, personal, secular political power. They became members of the political elite on par with the *posadniki*, *tysiatskie*, boiars, and other important people in the city, joining them to form an aristocracy[56] that governed Novgorod the Great for the last century or so of its independent existence.[57]. And while they almost never acted alone in their secular activities, their behavior was certainly not in keeping with Orthodox sensibilities voiced by Byzantine and Rus' writers.

Some of their political activities were in keeping with their roles as overseers of Christians in their care and as peacemakers. They welcomed and hosted foreign dignitaries, ransomed captives, made peace between various factions during internal disputes, offered sanctuary or protected individuals from bodily harm, and generally sought to unify the Novgorodians in Christian charity.

These were not actions unbecoming of an Orthodox bishop. Indeed, it was their duty traditionally to appeal for clemency for the convicted and to ransom captives, so while these duties certainly had political ramifications, they were not strictly secular political activities.

The archbishops, however, did take on other powers that were, strictly-speaking, secular: they patronized construction projects of a clearly secular nature, such as fortifications in and around the city and elsewhere in the Novgorodian Land, they functioned as Novgorodian ambassadors to the grand princes of Moscow and Lithuania, and to other princes in manners far more extensive than that of other bishops and well beyond the role of ransomer of captives or as peacemaker standing above the fray, and most significantly, they were parties to treaties between Novgorod and other powers: Riga, Dorpat, the Hanseatic League, Sweden, Lithuania, Tver', and Moscow, all of which reveals them to be deeply involved in Novgorod's partisan, secular, politics in ways not seen of any other Rus' bishop with the possible exception of the metropolitan.

The Archbishop as Ambassador

A medieval city's cathedral was often the largest building in town and the local bishop's moral authority made him a natural symbol of the city. Novgorod was no different. Due to the city's economic and cultural importance, visitors were fairly frequent to Novgorod, and the archbishops were often there to greet them. Archbishop Dalmat and the clergy welcomed Grand Prince Aleksandr Nevskii to the city in 1255, bearing crosses and blessing him as he arrived to be their prince yet again.[58] The archbishop also welcomed the Flemish traveler Ghillebert de Lannoy, one of the few Westerners to have seen and commented on the archbishops during the period of this study, when he visited in 1415.[59] Lannoy concluded that the archbishop was the real power in the city and wrote how he and his cathedral symbolized the city.[60] Novgorod was free, with a communal government, but "there is a bishop here who is like their sovereign."[61] Furthermore, he wrote of the church's importance and the archbishop's wealth and authority. The city boasted 350 churches and "a castle situated on the bank of the aforementioned river [the Volkhov], and in it stands the Cathedral of Holy Wisdom, which they revere, and their aforementioned bishop lives there."[62] During his nine-day visit, Lannoy met the archbishop and the town officials (*seigneurs*, or "lords"), the *tysiatskii* (whom he called "*dux*") and the *posadnik* ("*bourchgrave*"), and every day, the archbishop (it would have been Archbishop Ioann or Simeon) "sent more than thirty men to me with bread, meat, fish, hay, oats, beer, and mead," while the *tysiatskii* and *posadnik* honored Lannoy with "the strangest and most remarkable banquet I have ever seen."[63] The ostentatious display of wealth and the archbishop's role as host, add to the impression that the he held considerable political and economic power or influence. The archbishops also greeted other guests, such as Sophia, the niece of the last Byzantine Emperor, who passed through the city in 1473 en route to her wedding to Grand Prince Ivan III in Moscow.[64] Archbishop Feofil welcomed Ivan III when he arrived in the city several times in the 1470s;[65] his predecessors had welcomed numerous other princes over the centuries,[66] as well as the metropolitans,[67] and several Byzantine bishops when they came to Novgorod.[68]

The archbishops also went to other cities. Their ambassadorial service was among their earliest political roles and extended their political power beyond their own archeparchy. The earliest such embassy took place in 1135 when Archbishop Nifont went to make peace between Kyiv and Chernihiv.[69] Despite churchmen often being sent on embassies for essentially apolitical reasons, to bring peace and to ransom hostages, acts seen as a bishop's Christian duty, Nifont's mission was clearly of a political nature. Indeed, he went only after Posadnik Miroslav's effort to make peace a year earlier had failed, indicating he was not their first choice and perhaps adding a bit of desperation to the embassy. The Novgorodians were clearly fed up with Novgorodian Prince Vsevolod Mstislavich's inability to bring several years of fighting, which had flared up after Grand Prince Mstislav's death in 1132, to a successful conclusion for Novgorod, or indeed, to any conclusion at all. Nifont's mission was successful both because it was his Christian duty to seek peace, but also because it politically benefited Novgorod.[70]

Nifont went with "the best men," indicating he was working with the other city officials. Indeed, most other embassies consisted of the archbishop and several city officials or boiars; the archbishop almost never acted alone.[71] In 1141, Nifont went with the "best men" to bring Prince-elect Rostislav Iurievich to Novgorod.[72] In 1148, he and others went to Vladimir to make peace with Prince Iurii Dolgorukii,[73] and many of his successors went with city officials on other embassies up to the end of Novgorodian independence.[74] Antonii and Arsenii never acted as ambassadors, most certainly because of the long and confused dispute over the archiepiscopal throne. There also seems to have been a lapse in embassies during the tenures of Archbishops Simeon and Feodosii (1415-1423), in Feodosii's case probably because he was never consecrated,[75] but the inaction by several other archbishops fits no discernible pattern.

Ecclesiastical embassies were by no means unique to Novgorod, and it was a churchman's duty to be peacemakers, to ransom captives, and (especially for bishops) to appeal to princes for clemency toward prisoners. Churchmen were also called on to be ambassadors due to their literacy, a useful skill in drawing up documents. Their role as spiritual leaders or as men "chosen by God" may have given both those who sent them and those who received them the confidence – or at least the hope – that they would be fair and impartial. It would also mean that they would be treated with deference and respect by princes or other city officials with whom they met and negotiated. This was true not just in the Orthodox world, but across the Catholic frontier, and it was even true among the Mongols, who were first pagan and then Muslim but who maintained a tolerant policy toward the church, granting several immunity charters.[76] As churchmen, Novgorod's archbishops would have had ties with churchmen in other cities, at least within Rus' and the Orthodox world, and these could be used to bring about a successful embassy.

The *Novgorodian First Chronicle*, the *Lavrentian Chronicle*, the *Hypatian Chronicle*, and other chronicles give numerous examples of ecclesiastical embassies beyond Novgorod.[77] While Nifont's embassy in 1135 was political in nature, as were other embassies, they are not invariably indicative of political power being wielded by Novgorodian and other Rus' bishops. Iaroslav Shchapov explained: "It was traditional for the highest members of the church organization to act in the capacity of envoys, negotiators, and representatives of a prince or city,"[78] adding that "the use of metropolitans and bishops in the capacity of ambassadors is found repeatedly in the political history of the early Russian [sic] principalities,"[79] including in a footnote the following examples: metropolitans in 1210 and 1230, a bishop in 1154, a bishop and an abbot in 1206, and priests in 1185 and 1229.[80] He added:

> This role was first of all traceable to their spiritual status and the medieval notion that clergymen, especially of the upper ranks, had the special support of the Lord and were therefore less exposed to danger in secular conflicts. On the second hand, they were less committed and less involved in these conflicts than the prince's men and the city aristocracy, who were, indeed, directly involved. At the same time, however, the function of metropolitans and bishops as envoys or negotiators was confined only to the technical side of representing the interest of the conflicting parties and nothing more.[81]

The archbishops may have carried out embassies impartially at times, but at other times they were not "less committed and involved in these conflicts." They were just as involved as the city nobility, and acted in agreement with the *posadniki*, *tysiatskie*, and "the lords." Thus, in 1328, Archbishop Moisei together with Tysiatskii Avraam sent envoys to Pskov,[82] probably because Pskov was harboring Prince Aleksandr Mikhailovich of Tver' after the Tver' Uprising against the Mongols the year before. This episode, already mentioned above, will be discussed more fully later, but in the present discussion it shows that there were both religious (the threat of excommunication) and political ramifications (the very real threat of Muscovite and Mongol reprisal against northwest Rus'). Vasilii Kalika's dispatch of his nephew as part of the 1339 embassy to Magnus Eriksson of Sweden has also already been cited for the religious nature of the dispute, but he also acted in concert with the secular officials."[83] In 1434, a Pskovite embassy to Novgorod paid homage to "their father" Archbishop Evfimii II while in the city to conclude peace with Pskov's "Older Brother." The embassy was successful, and peace was concluded on the old terms with the archbishop's blessing. Later that year, Evfimii "and all Novgorod" sent Antip, son of Prince Aleksei of Kopor'e, to Pskov and the Pskovites kissed the cross in front of the envoy to abide by the old treaty.[84] In January of the following year, Evfimii himself went to Pskov to hold court according to the old terms, but the Pskovites fought with the *sof'iane* and refused to pay the *obrok* (quitrent) owed the archbishop, causing him to depart in anger.[85] In the waning months of the republic, Archbishop Feofil sent Ivan Ivanov Markov to Grand Prince Ivan III on October 16, 1477 (the grand prince was then in Torzhok approaching the city) asking for safe-passage for Feofil to negotiate with the grand prince, negotiations which, it turns out, would lead to the end of Novgorodian independence early the following year. The archbishop was, again, not acting alone; Markov accompanied several other ambassadors, including several *posadniki*.[86]

Sometimes their ambassadorial activities included the payment of ransom or tribute. The former activity fulfilled the requirements of Christian charity,[87] but the payment of tribute (*dan'*) was certainly a political function (rendering unto Caesar). In 1317, the Novgorodians sent Archbishop David "with supplication" (*s molboiu*) to Grand Prince Mikhail Iaroslavich to try to ransom "their brothers" Mikhail had seized,[88] but he refused. The Novgorodians sent Vasilii Kalika to Grand Prince Ivan I at Pereiaslav in 1333 and offered Ivan 500 rubles if he would renounce his privileges over Novgorod, but he refused.[89] In 1386, Archbishop Aleksei made peace with Grand Prince Dmitrii at Iamnii, at which time the grand prince took 8,000 rubles.[90] In 1427, Archbishop Evfimii I met Lithuanian Grand Prince Vytautas, who was then besieging Novgorod. The next year he went to Porkhov with several Novgorodian envoys and paid Vytautas 5,000 rubles in tribute and 1,000 more to ransom Novgorodian captives.[91] In 1441, Evfimii II was sent with several boiars to Grand Prince Vasilii Vasilevich at Demian to make peace. There he paid 8,000 rubles to the Grand Prince.[92] That 8,000 rubles were paid to the grand prince in 1386 and 1441 suggests this was Novgorod's tribute that it had withheld. It isn't known if any money paid was from the archiepiscopal treasury or city coffers, if the archbishop was sent because he was rich and could afford such ransoms and tribute, if the money was raised by donation, especially if it was ransom money, or if it was merely conveyed by the archbishops. If it was tribute – and 8,000 rubles was a very large sum in the fourteenth and fifteenth centuries –the money was unlikely the archbishop's own.

The Archbishop as Domestic Peacemaker

The archbishops sought to bring peace to their city, especially when disagreements between factions led to riots or civil unrest. Thus in 1342, Archbishop Vasilii Kalika and (his?) *namestnik*, Boris, brought peace after the *chernye liudi* rose up against Ondreshko and Posadnik Fedor Danilovich, accusing them of killing Luka Varfolomeyev, son of Posadnik Varfolomei Iurievich and brother of Posadnik Matvei Varfolomeevich,[93] while he had been campaigning in the Dvina Land.[94] When Ondreshko and Fedor fled to Kopor'e, Ontsifor Lukich, the decedent's son, appealed to the archbishop, who sent the archimandrite along with several boiars to bring them back to Novgorod. When the two men denied any role in killing Luka, Ontsifor and his uncle, Matvei Varfalomeevich (also called Koska), convened a "Vladyka *veche*" in front of the Cathedral of Holy Wisdom while Ondreshko and Fedor convened a counter-*veche* at the *Iaroslavovo Dvorishche* across the river. The following morning, Ontsifor and Matvei sent the archbishop over the great bridge to negotiate with the *veche* on the Market Side. While Vasilii Kalika was still in talks with Ondreshko and Fedor, Onstifor and his *veche* took up arms and crossed over to attack the two men and their *veche*. It seems though, that Ontsifor and his followers were bested in the fight and, in the ensuing confusion, Matvei and his son, Ignat, had to take refuge in one of the churches on the market while Ontsifor fled the city. The archbishop and *namestnik* managed to bring peace.[95] It seems Vasilii Kalika initially sided with Ontsifor and Matvei, first sending the archimandrite and other men to Kopor'e to bring Ondreshko and Fedor back and then being sent by Ontsifor and his uncle to the other side of the river to the opposing *veche*. He also seemingly sided with the family since he presided over Posadnik Varfolomei's funeral with the hegumens and the priests of Novgorod, which Aleksandr Khoroshev argues is proof of the archbishop's close ties to and political support of the boiars of the

Nerev *konets*, which included Varfolomei Iurievich and his family.⁹⁶ That said, Varfolomei had been *posadnik* for sixteen years and his family had held the *posadnichestvo* going back to 1272, and there is no cause that we know of for the archbishop to have refused to preside at his funeral, Vasilii's presence may not necessarily indicate favoritism of Varfolomei's family but merely the honoring of a respected Novgorodian official from a respected family.⁹⁷ His actions after the funeral can easily be seen as an effort to bring two accused murderers to justice and keep the dispute from getting (further) out of hand. Several scholars have also argued that Vasilii and other archbishops showed pro- or anti-Lithuanian or Muscovite leanings, which may be true, but not necessarily. They could have wanted to bring peace to their city as a good bishop or Christian should. Furthermore, their support for one policy or another could be for matters of church, not state. They could have opposed Lithuania because it might split the Rus' church into several provinces or, after 1386, might lead to the spread of Catholicism. They could have opposed Moscow because it was seizing fur-bearing lands along the Northern Dvina and Vechegda rivers and might confiscate ecclesiastical lands. Political support of certain boiar clans or pro- or anti-Lithuania or Moscow factions did not have to enter into it.⁹⁸

Vasilii's predecessor and successor, Archbishop Moisei, also acted as domestic peacemaker. After retiring to the Kolomtsy Monastery in 1359, he came out again and, taking Archbishop-elect Aleksei, the archimandrite, and several hegumens,⁹⁹ quelled a disturbance between armed groups from the Sofia Side and the Slavno "Side" (actually, a *konets* of the city on the Market Side) that had destroyed the great bridge and led to a tense, three-day standoff. Moisei blessed the Novgorodians and told them: "Children, do not cause strife among yourselves, exultation to the pagans, and the devastation of the sacred churches, and this place; engage not in battle." The *Novgorodian First Chronicle* reports that the crowd "accepted his word, and dispersed" but only after sacking several houses in the Slavno *konets*.¹⁰⁰ The incident suggests that Aleksei, new to the job, did not yet have the authority to act alone, probably not because he was still just archbishop-elect, but because of his inexperience, and it took Moisei, who had held the office for a number of years spanning several decades, to come out of retirement and put a stop to the violence.

The archbishops also protected individuals, often important civil officials, threatened with bodily harm during civil unrest. In 1209, Posadnik Dmitrii Miroshkinits and his clan (the chronicle calls them "his brethren") angered the Novgorodians by levying taxes and fees on Novgorodian and foreign merchants in the city. Although Dmitrii died in Vladimir, when his body was brought back for burial, the Novgorodians wanted to throw it from the bridge into the Volkhov River, a postmortem lynching (throwing still-living people from the bridge was often how mobs disposed of enemies) and denial of Christian burial. Archbishop Mitrofan, however, would not allow this, and Dmitrii was buried in the Iur'ev Monastery, alongside his father.[101] Politically, Mitrofan calmed the hatred between opposing factions and ensured that the *posadnik* was treated justly. But in religious terms, Mitrofan was carrying out one of the corporal works of mercy by ensuring that a member of his flock received a proper burial. In another episode, rioters attacked the former *posadnik*, Smen Mikhailovich, in 1287. He fled to Archbishop Kliment and was given sanctuary in the Cathedral of Holy Wisdom,[102] an act of Christian mercy and not necessarily evidence of archiepiscopal favoritism for a *posadnik* or his clan.

The Archbishop as Civil and Military Builder

Just as the archbishop's relations with boiar families or political factions are sometime ambiguous, being interpreted by some as indicating favoritism for one faction or family over others, their building projects are also sometimes ambiguous. A number of fortification projects carried out by the archbishops may indicate partisan support for a certain faction or policy, but they may also simply have been efforts to defend their flock. They certainly indicate the archbishops exercising political power unlike other Orthodox bishops. Most construction projects the archbishops patronized were ecclesiastical in nature and will be discussed in the next chapter. The (more) secular or civil projects, including those of an ambiguous nature, relate to the Detinets (the "Young Man's Compound"), the fortified compound at the heart of Novgorod, built and maintained by the archbishops and filled with churches and chapels, the Cathedral of Holy Wisdom, and the archiepiscopal palace. They include fortifications in other parts of the city and elsewhere in the Novgorodian Land.

The Detinets

The Detinets' walls served as defense works around the archiepiscopal compound, but the whole space served a dual religious and secular role. The archbishops' role in building and renovating the Detinets is quite clear: In the fall of 1044, Prince Vladimir Iaroslavich "laid out and made Novgorod."[103] In 1116, Prince Mstislav Vladimirovich "laid out a Novgorod larger than the first."[104] It is not clear if Vladimir and Mstislav built only the Detinets, and if so, whether they were wooden palisades atop earthen embankments, or stone walls. Perhaps Mstislav merely enlarged the Detinets, but these entries seem to suggest that the two princes built the fortifications around the entire town, or significant parts of it, and not just the Detinets itself. In fact, any work on the Detinets would indicate princely encroachment on what had been, up to that point, the archiepiscopal compound. This is certainly possible. Vladimir built the second cathedral after the one Ioakim Korsunianin had built burned down. We know that in 1302 "a stone city" (*kamennyi gorod*) was built, another ambiguous term as "gorod" can mean either fortress or fortified city, so it could mean that the Detinets was rebuilt in stone, or that the entire city, or sections of it, were enclosed by a stone wall.[105]

In any event, no archbishop is named as patron of these projects. In 1331-1334, Archbishop Vasilii Kalika, built stone walls for at least part of the Detinets, from the Church of St. Vladimir, next to the Vladimir Tower, to the Church of Boris and Gleb, that is, the northeastern section of Detinets wall along the river. It seems this section was finished in 1331. The rest of the Detinets was completed over the next three years.[106] Archbishop Moisei's silver was used to repair the walls in 1361.[107] Over the centuries, each of the fortress' six gates was also topped by a chapel, four of them patronized by an archbishop.[108] In 1400, Archbishop Ioann rebuilt the northern Detinets wall in stone,[109] and in 1439, Evfimii II rebuilt the belfry and the Detinets wall that had been destroyed when the previous belfry collapsed into the wall after floodwaters undermined its foundation. Less martial projects within the Detinets include a stone house (*terem*) "where the waters are blessed" and a stone bakery, possibly for the baking of Eucharistic bread, built by Ioann in 1409.[110] Evfimii II's Palace of Facets, an addition to the archiepiscopal palace, was built in 1433,[111] a clock tower "in the garden," in 1436,[112] and a granary (*kliuchnitsa*)[113] and a new archiepiscopal residence in 1443.[114]

The Detinets was the heart of Novgorod the Great and served as an inner defense for the city as well as the archbishops. Several structures in the compound certainly served both ecclesiastical and civil functions, boiars lived in the southern part of the compound,[115] and *vecha* were held in front of Holy Wisdom. The Palace of Facets, part of the archiepiscopal palace just northwest of the cathedral, is the alleged meeting place of the Council of Lords, probably because it was one of the largest chambers in the city, useful for receiving ambassadors, signing treaties, hosting dinners, and holding other civic or secular events. The *Novgorod Judicial Charter* notes that referral hearings for court cases were to be held "in the archbishop's chamber," which may refer to the Palace of Facets. Thus, it was

7. From The Vision of the *Ponomar'* Tarasii From Spaso-Preobrazhenskii Sobor of Khutyn Mon. (last third of the 16th c.), now in The Novgorod Historical Museum. Note the Palata (lower left) has both the roof church (removed in 1930) and steps. The clock tower (upper right) appears somewhat more as in a pre-1917 postcard than the current restoration does.

8. Aerial view of the Detinets. -- shows three of Evfimii's constructions in their current state: the Palace of Facets, the belfry, and the clock tower.

a multi-purpose structure serving the entire community and not merely a hall in the archiepiscopal palace.[116]

The chronicles also record the archiepiscopal compound being used for other political purposes, even as a jail on several occasions. Thus, in 1136, Prince Vsevolod Mstislavich, his wife, children, and mother-in-law were held in the Detinets for two months before being expelled from the city.[117] In 1210, Prince Sviatoslav Vsevolodovich, placed on the Novgorodian throne by his father the year before, was "placed" in the Detinets with his men when Prince Mstislav Mstislavich came and took the throne; Mstislav sent Sviatoslav back to his father the next year.[118] In 1314, Grand Prince Mikhail's *namestniki* were confined to the archbishop's palace (literally "courtyard") in the Detinets.[119] We do not know whether these episodes indicate active archiepiscopal support for a certain policy – they certainly indicate passive acceptance of them – or whether the archiepiscopal compound was merely deemed the most secure place to hold a deposed prince and his entourage, denying them use of the *Iaroslavovo Dvorishche* or the *Gorodishche*, but still allowing them to remain in some comfort, perhaps secure from angry

9. Novgorod, Palace of Facets. As of the 2006-2013 partial restoration of the Brick-Gothic exterior. (Top of Clock Tower in background.)
10. Interior in the 1880s. Photograph: Ivan F. Barshchevskii (1881-1886)
(Current restoration reveals brickwork.)

mobs or opposing factions, until they were "shown the road." Since Novgorodian princes were at times deposed and brought back, and were normally clients of much stronger princely patrons in Kyiv, Suzdalia, Smolensk, or elsewhere, it was politically inexpedient to cast a prince into a dungeon, assuming Novgorod had such a thing, so confinement in the archbishop's palace may have been deemed sufficient to depose them without unduly humiliating or harming their person.[120]

Around the City

The archbishop's military construction projects were not limited to the Detinets, though they did not undertake such projects until the second quarter of the fourteenth century.[121] As he was the first bishop mentioned building the Detinets, so too Vasilii Kalika is the first to build city walls beyond the Detinets, when, in 1335, he built a wall on the Market Side from "St. Il'ia's to St. Paul's"[122] in cooperation with "his children, the Posadnik Fedor Danilovich and the Tysiatskii Ostafii, and all Novgorod."[123] Three years later, "the damaged bridge [over the Volkhov River] was repaired by order of the *Vladyka* Vasilii, for he urged on the work himself; he began and finished it with his own people."[124] The bridge was one of the most important civil construction projects because it linked the two Sides of the city. Archbishop Aleksei had a stone wall built along the road to Luga in 1384.[125] We do not know why the archbishops patronized these projects; it is unlikely that they were exercising secular powers, including the responsibility of maintaining the city's defenses and roads, as a prince-bishop would. Rather, they probably did so out of enlightened self-interest, to defend themselves, their city and their economic interests. They could also show their importance through patronage, or could have been done out of Christian charity. The bridge also might have been one of the few to span the river for miles around, and therefore was necessary for trade and to bring in payments in kind from the outlying estates to the archbishops and other landowners living in the city. Furthermore, the entry from 1335 attests that the archbishops had their own builders who could be set to work not only on building churches, but on non-ecclesiastical structures as well.

Beyond Novgorod

The archbishops also patronized civil edifices well beyond the city and its immediate environs. The greatest example of this is when "the Novgorodians and the boiars, and the *chernye liudi* [lower class free people in Novgorod] appealed (literally "beat their foreheads on the ground") to the archbishop of Novgorod, *Vladyka* Vasilii" and told him: "Go, lord (*gospodine*), and establish a fortress at Orekhov," which he did.[126] Orekhov, an island in the middle of the Neva River where it flows out of Lake Ladoga, protected the important trade route up the Neva River into Lake Ladoga that the Hanseatic merchants traveled to Novgorod. The fortress, first built by Grand Prince Iurii Danilovich 29 years earlier to defend against Swedish encroachment,[127] had been destroyed in recent fighting with King Magnus Eriksson's crusaders, and since it was so important, its upkeep was crucial. That the archbishop was given this task shows his important political position in Novgorod, even though Orekhov was not an archiepiscopal foundation, and Vasilii's commission to rebuild it is the only known instance of an archbishop playing a role at Orekhov. Furthermore, the archbishops had, so far as we know, nothing to do with Orekhov or other fortresses in the region like Kopor'e, Iamburg (modern Kingisepp), or Korela (modern Priozersk)[128] before 1352.[129] In fact, Vasilii rebuilt the fortress followed the crusade of Swedish King Magnus Erickson in the region and after Novgorod appealed to Lithuanian and Muscovite princes to come to their aid. Only when these appeals went unheeded, did Vasilii step to patronize the rebuilding of the fortress. He was well suited to the task: fabulously rich, with a workforce already experienced in building the Detinets and Novgorod's city walls, as well as numerous churches, and having the authority of a man "chosen by God" who had led the archeparchy for more than two decades.[130] Furthermore, his activities up to that point, such as sending his nephew as part of the 1339 embassy, show him protecting Orthodox converts in the area, and rebuilding the fortress would also serve this purpose.[131] Thus, his actions, while certainly not ecclesiastical in a strict sense, had religious overtones and cannot be separated from his roles as overseer of his archeparchy. Grand Prince Vasilii II "wishing our [the Novgorodians] good and by the command of Archbishop Iona and on the order of all Novgorod the Great," strengthened (*pokrepil*) the fortress in 1460,[132] so what may have been an ad hoc or emergency action on Vasilii Kalika's part was maintained by his successors.

These non-ecclesiastical construction projects (they are mainly military in nature) certainly indicate the archbishops' involvement in Novgorod the Great's secular affairs. They are not necessarily indicative of the powers of a prince-bishop or head of state so much as they show the archbishop's efforts to defend Orthodoxy, protect his city – which was supposed to mirror the heavenly Jerusalem (as there was no clear delineation between secular and religious affairs in the Middle Ages), and preserve his economic, political, and administrative interests and the souls under his care. It is worth stressing that this power or influence only arose in the first half of the fourteenth century, with Vasilii Kalika's archiepiscopate, and was wielded inconsistently thereafter. Indeed, only four archbishops – Vasilii Kalika, Aleksei, Ioann, and Evfimii II – undertook civil or secular construction projects, though many of these were tied to the Detinets, the archbishop's own compound.

The Archbishop in Novgorod's Civil Administration

The archbishops also carried out important duties in Novgorod's civil administration. Their role as overseers of the ecclesiastical courts was discussed in the previous chapter, but they were, according to George Weickhardt, "probably involved in judging many purely secular disputes" as well.[133] They appear in land transaction documents and their seals are found on deeds between laymen that are not of an ecclesiastical or religious nature.[134] Weickhardt noted that "from this evidence Ianin concluded that the archbishop's court was well established in secular matters by the mid-fourteenth century," though he noted that it was uncertain whether the evidence indicated the archbishop acting as judge or merely as a registrar of deeds."[135] He also observed that the *Novgorod Judicial Charter* listed the archbishop among the members of the referral (*doklad*) court, along with a boiar and a member of the *zhitye liudi* from each *konets*.[136] These were the referral cases heard "in the archbishop's chamber," that is, the Palace of Facets.[137]

The *Pskov Judicial Charter* notes other secular or civic roles the church and the archbishop played in that city, although it must be remembered that archiepiscopal authority was limited there. The charter declared that litigants summoned to court were to "come to the church in the local district for the reading of the summons." If they hid or failed to appear, the bailiff (*pozvonik*) was to read the summons before the priest of that church.[138] Thus, at least in Pskov, the local churches served as a place of summons to civil court, and the priests as witnesses in the event the litigant failed to appear. The Church of the Holy Trinity, the main church in Pskov, also served as the city's archives (as the Cathedral of Holy Wisdom seems to have done in Novgorod).[139]

Among the more unique political activities Novgorod's archbishops carried out was their appearance in charters in which they represented the city in negotiations with other Rus' cities and principalities as well as with Livonia, Lithuania, Sweden and other Northern European polities. Only one other churchman appears in such a document: Lavrentii, the *namestnik* of the Bishop of Smolensk, was among the witnesses to a 1284 commercial treaty between Riga and Smolensk, although there is no evidence his bishop ever held political powers like those wielded by Novgorod's archbishops.[140] Even the metropolitan, who sat on regency councils in Moscow, do not appear in charters and treaties the way Novgorod's archbishops do. In this sense, the archbishops stood out markedly. They were not merely witnesses and their participation in these treaties increased through the thirteenth to the fifteenth centuries. In fact, they began appearing in such documents only in 1264, during the archiepiscopate of Dalmat (r. 1249-1274),[141] that is, relatively late in the period under study, but right in the middle of the period where we find an interruption in other activities, such as pastoral visits and church construction. Only in 1301, during the tenure of Archbishop Feoktist (r. 1299-1308), were archbishop's blessings invoked for the first time, in that instance in a treaty with the German and Hanseatic city of Lübeck. Unfortunately, though, the precise nature of archiepiscopal participation in these treaties never comes into sharp focus. The archbishops do not appear consistently in the documents, and when they do, the terminology used is vague. It is not certain what is meant when the treaty invokes "Blessings from the *Vladyka* [and] greetings from the *posadnik*...and from the *tysiatskii*...and from all the greater and lesser men, and from All Novgorod the Great to the Prince..."[142] Perhaps the archbishops merely invoked God's blessing for the success of the negotiations, in which case they were little more than an authoritative witness, or maybe they were in some ways signatories or parties of the treaties, or they oversaw the oaths taken by the signatories, sealed by the kissing of crosses or icons of the saints, much as people swear oaths on the Bible today.

A few documents clearly show that the archbishops were parties to the treaties and did not simply bless them or oversee the administering of oaths. In addition to the 1339 treaty, known from the chronicles but the full text of which is not extant, a treaty dated February 10, 1316, clearly states that: "the Grand Prince Mikhailo [Mikhail Iaroslavich of Tver'] concluded this [treaty] with the *Vladyka* David, and with the *posadnik*, and with all Novgorod."[143] The treaty also refers to "Feoktist's treaty," showing that Feoktist had been party to an earlier treaty with the grand prince.[144] The 1316 treaty bears the seals of Grand Prince Mikhail and Archbishop David, one of sixteen treaties bearing an archiepiscopal seal. Much later, in 1470-1471, the city drew up a draft treaty with Casimir IV

11. A close-up of a late nineteenth century full-length fresco of Archbishop Feoktist [Photograph Michael C. Paul]

(noted above), in which Archbishop-elect Feofil was party to the treaty for religious reasons (as in 1339) and not as a political representative of Novgorod the Great. In the preamble, Casimir declared (or would have had the treaty been ratified) "I, the illustrious King of Poland and Grand Prince of Lithuania, have concluded a treaty with the Archbishop-elect Feofil and with the *posadniki* of Novgorod, and with the *tysiatskie*, and with the boiars, and with the *zhitye liudi* and with the merchants, and with all Novgorod the Great."[145] The treaty then addressed Casimir's rights as prince of Novgorod, how he should hold court, including how his judge (*tiun*) should sit with the Novgorod constables (*pristavy*), how his *namestnik* should hold trial with the *posadnik* in the archbishop's courtyard, and how he should not interfere with cases heard by the archbishop. Furthermore, to preserve Novgorod's Orthodox faith in light of Casimir's Catholicism, the draft demanded that Casimir's *namestnik* in Novgorod be of the Orthodox faith,[146] and:

> You, illustrious king, shall not take our Greek Orthodox faith away from us, and we shall appoint our *Vladyka* of our free will, whomever it pleases us, Novgorod the Great, in our Orthodox Christianity.
> And you, illustrious king, shall not erect Roman [Catholic] churches in Novgorod the Great, nor in the dependent towns of Novgorod, nor in all the Novgorodian land.[147]

The difficulty in drawing broad conclusions about these treaties lies in the fact that only sixteen documents bear the seals of only eight archbishops,[148] and although Daniel Kaiser notes that the *Pskov Judicial Charter* permitted the archbishop's seal to serve as the prince's equivalent,[149] in the case of the treaties of 1316 and 1470-71, the archbishops were acting on their own, concluding treaties with, not on behalf of, the princes. The inconsistent archiepiscopal presence in these treaties makes drawing firm conclusions incredibly difficult. Certainly, some charters refer to the archbishops or bear their seals because the prince or other officials were away from the city when the treaties were concluded, as in the case of the treaty drawn up between Dalmat, Grand Prince Aleksandr Iaroslavich and his son, Dmitrii, the Novgorodian *posadnik*, *the tysiatskii*, and "all Novgorod" on the one hand, and the Gotland Shore on the other. The treaty makes no reference to Dalmat, but bears his seal.[150] Ianin argues that the archbishop sealed the document because Aleksandr (Prince of Novgorod from 1257 to 1263) had gone to the Horde in 1262 (he died on the return journey). Aleksandr had placed his son, Dmitrii, as his *namestnik* in Novgorod in 1259, but Dmitrii, too, was absent from the city, having led an army off to Iur'ev (Tartu, Estonia). Aleksandr's brother, Iaroslav, and other princes who might have spoken for Novgorod, were also investing Iur'ev, and thus the archbishop was probably the only one left to seal the document, though it is written in the name of the grand prince.[151] A later treaty bears Feoktists seal, and Ianin argues he sealed this document because Grand Prince Andrei Aleksandrovich, Prince of Novgorod at the time, was likewise absent from the city.[152] These are only two of 54 treaties in which the archbishops appear, and we cannot explain their participation in most treaties by saying they were merely standing in for the princes.[15

Indeed, the archbishops acted independently of the princes and concluded treaties on Novgorod's behalf, almost always in cooperation with the *posadniki, tysiatskie,* and other city officials. Feoktist sealed two versions of the same *riad* (an agreement reached between Novgorod and its prince, enumerating the princes rights in the city, in this case with Grand Prince Mikhail of Tver'), and then sealed a third *riad* in 1307 or 1308, also with Grand Prince Mikhail (apparently a renegotiation or renewal of the earlier *riady*).[154] Thus, he acted in a secular political capacity for the city, speaking collectively on its behalf, with the *posadnik* and *tysiatskii*, although it is not possible to say definitively if one or another official stood above the rest in stature or power or where one's authority ended and another's began.[155]

Conclusion

The evidence of the Novgorodian archbishops' political roles is sparse and at times vague, but it does show they were unique among the Orthodox episcopate in the political powers they wielded, particularly in their participation in international (interprincely, intercity) treaties, their construction of fortifications and other civil projects, and their participation in other secular affairs (such as judicial proceedings). They were not, however, as powerful as the traditional historiography suggests. They did not hold the formal secular powers of prince-bishops of the Catholic West and were not "presidents of the republic" in any formal or institutionalized sense of that term. They certainly stood among the city fathers since they were part of the land-holding aristocracy and they oversaw or represented the city in concert with the other aristocrats. It is not possible to see where their powers ended and that of other officials began since such delineations were never written down or otherwise formalized. That they acted in accordance the others could suggest a wariness toward, or even a sense of illegitimacy, in acting alone.

These political powers developed over time. A brief period of political activity during Nifont's archiepiscopacy gave way to a long period of inaction that ended with the archiepiscopate of Vasilii Kalika almost two hundred years later. After that, the archbishops played important political roles up to the end of Novgorodian independence. Indeed, after Ivan III ended the *posadnichestvo* and closed down the *veche* in 1478, it was Archbishop Feofil, the only local political or religious figure of any stature left in the city, who paid homage to the grand prince and handed over all power to him, ending the Novgorodian Republic.[156]

CHAPTER SIX
The Economics of the House of Holy Wisdom

12. The Church of St. John the Forerunner at Opoki (also known as the Church of St. John in Petriatin Court) just north of the Marketplace, first built by Prince Vsevolod Mstislavich in 1127-1130 and locus of the the city's official weights and measures. This is the reconstruction by Archbishop Evfimii II "on the old foundations" in 1453. [Photograph Michael C. Paul]

Introduction: Novgorod's Importance in the Economic Life of Rus'

From Kyiv's decline in the late twelfth century to the consolidation of Muscovite power over the once-independent Rus' principalities, largely accomplished at the end of the fifteenth century, Novgorod was the wealthiest commercial city in Rus', and the archbishops were key figures in its commercial and economic activity. Their economic roles were played out in a city long recognized as one of the wealthiest and most important commercial centers in Rus' and Eastern Europe more broadly. Therefore, it makes sense to begin discussion of the economic aspects of the archiepiscopal office with a brief overview of Novgorod's importance in the economic and commercial life of Rus' and the archbishops place within it.

Janet Martin explained the basis of the city's great wealth:

> Novgorod controlled a major portion of the foreign trade conducted by Kievan [sic] Rus', particularly with Scandinavia and, increasingly through the eleventh century, German traders from the Baltic Sea community... Novgorod dominated the Volga trade with the non-Rus' commercial centers of Bulgar-on-the-Volga and those on the Caspian Sea.[1]

Indeed, the Vikings, called *Rus'* or *Varangians* (*Variag*) in Russian parlance, came to northwestern Rus' to access furs, honey, and other commodities to trade in the West. Ultimately, they came for the Middle Eastern silver *dirhams* being brought up the trade routes from Persia and Constantinople, along the Volga and Dnieper rivers and into the region around Novgorod.[2] According to the legendary beginnings found in the Rus' Primary Chronicle, the Rus' established political control first at Novgorod, under Riurik in the mid-ninth century,[3] and only later moved on to Kyiv and founded the Riurikid Dynasty that ruled Russia until 1598.[4]

The real foundation of Novgorod as a city most likely dates to the late tenth century around the time of Ioakim's perhaps-legendary arrival. We know very little of these early years, particularly economic or mercantile developments, but by the twelfth century, Novgorodian merchants had set up a trading community on the island of Gotland in the Baltic Sea between Finland and Sweden and were carrying on a brisk Baltic trade.[5] In the thirteenth and fourteenth centuries, the Novgorodians curtailed their foreign travels and Scandinavian and German traders instead came to Novgorod twice a year to trade in the marketplace. The Scandinavians set up their own enclave around the Church of St. Olaf, called the "Varangian Church" in the *Novgorodian First Chronicle*, the focal point of the Gothic Court or *Gotskii Dvor*. Germans affiliated with the Teutonic Order and the Hanseatic League established a similar commercial enclave at Peterhof (Peter's Court or the German Court or *Nemetskii Dvor*) around the Church of St. Peter. There they traded Flemish wool cloth, beer, wine, dried or smoked fish, and other goods in exchange for Novgorodian furs, wax, timber, and silver.[6]

Riurik's descendants moved on to establish dynasties in other cities, but the Rus' princes remembered Novgorod's economic and commercial importance, and this perhaps explains why a local dynasty was never established in the city. The most important and powerful princes vied for control of the city and its wealth, and this competition effectively kept Novgorod independent until, in the late fifteenth century, Moscow had outstripped the other Rus' princes in wealth and power and was able to conquer Novgorod.[7] Even before this, silver collected in Novgorod was key to securing or maintaining the grand princely throne, especially in the early fourteenth century when Tver' and Moscow vied for the khan's *iarlyk* or patent of office.

Thus, in 1318, Grand Prince Iurii Danilovich of Moscow gained the *iarlyk* from Khan Uzbek by promising to gather more tribute than his rival, Grand Prince Dmitrii Mikhailovich of Tver'. (Dmitrii's father had earlier lost the *iarlyk*, in part, by alienating Novgorod.) In 1321, Iurii marched against Tver', but the bishop of Tver' helped bring peace between the princes when they met on the Volga,[8] whereupon Dmitrii handed over 2,000 silver rubles, apparently as tribute to the khan. But rather than deliver the tribute to Sarai, Iurii spent much of the next four years in Novgorod, having been "summoned" there by the Novgorodians, according to the chronicle.[9] He fought off attacks on Novgorod's northern frontiers, leading a military expedition against the Swedes (called *Nemtsy* in the chronicle) who had attacked Korela, and bombarding the Swedish-held town of Vyborg for a month with six catapults (*porokov*).[10] It was only after the khan grew weary of Iurii's long delay in Novgorod and granted the *iarlyk* to Dmitrii Mikhailovich in 1322 – and apparently had summoned Iurii – that Iurii finally begin to make his way toward Sarai, only to be waylaid and robbed of his treasure by Dmitrii's brother, Prince Aleksandr Mikhailovich, in the Rzheva district (*"na Udrome"*).[11] Iurii fled to Pskov and, rather than go back to the khan empty-handed, he returned to Novgorod to gather a new treasure. While there, he shored up the source of Novgorod's immense wealth: he signed a treaty with King Magnus of Sweden, and built the fortress at Orekhov to defend Novgorod and the trade route down the river should the treaty not hold. He also led a campaign against Ustiug to reestablish Novgorodian control over that city and the vital fur-trading routes passing through it. At the conclusion of this campaign, in 1324 or 1325, Iurii left the Zavoloch'e district for Perm' and traveled down the Kama and the Volga to Sarai.[12]

The princes were not the only ones aware of the city's great wealth. The forests where the Novgorodian harvested furs were said to be teaming with animals; squirrels, martens, and sables are said to have rained from the sky.[13] This brought people from far afield to Novgorod, and not just traders. Byzantine churchmen arrived on several occasions seeking aid as their empire and church lost ground to the Ottomans. Metropolitan Mark from the Monastery of the Mother of God on Mount Sinai and Archimandrite Vnifantii of the Monastery of St. Michael's in Jerusalem arrived in 1376 "seeking charity,"[14] and Bishop Theodoulus of Trebizond came from Constantinople in 1407 seeking alms.[15] The Kyivan metropolitans' efforts to gain the considerable ecclesiastical court fees in Novgorod, discussed above, is further indication of the fame and importance of Novgorod's wealth.

The Archbishops' Fabled Wealth

The archbishops drew on this great wealth. In fact, their own wealth was legendary. They came to be among the richest landowners in the city, and though they were not always so protective of this wealth as they were with Kiprian and other metropolitans, tales survive of their greed and miserliness. The *Novgorodian First Chronicle* repeated the rumor that Archbishop Nifont fled to Constantinople in 1156 after he had "plundered Holy Wisdom,"[16] and other sources reported that Grand Prince Ivan III required 300 carts to carry off the archiepiscopal treasury of gold, silver, furs, precious stones, fine silk cloth, and other valuables, along with all the valuables he had confiscated from the boiars when he conquered the city in 1478.[17] Although it is not known how much of this was the archbishop's personal treasury and how much belonged to the archeparchy, the city, particular townspeople, or the monasteries, the archbishops' treasure must have been considerable since they were among the wealthiest men in the city.

Less historically reliable tales speak similarly of archiepiscopal avarice. *The Tale of the Shchil Posadnik of Novgorod*, tells of Archbishop Il'ia's crude attempt to extort money from Shchil the hegumen of the Shchilov Monastery.[18] *The Tale of Mikhail Klopskii* tells of Evfimii I's exaction of a black horse from the Trinity Monastery at Klopskii in addition to the regular monastic payments to the archbishop,[19] leading Aleksandr Khoroshev to call Evfimii "an extortionist and blackmailer."[20] Another legend tells that in 1478, Archbishop Feofil hid (at least a portion of) his treasure from Grand Prince Ivan III in the right-hand wall of the staircase leading up to the choir of the Cathedral of Holy Wisdom, where Tsar Ivan IV "the Terrible" discovered it in 1547.[21]

Additionally, the *Strigol'niki* condemned the clergy in Novgorod for its "love of silver" and other vices, attacking not only the Novgorodian archbishops but their priests and deacons as well.[22] It is impossible to say how much wealth in land, specie, or in other property they accumulated over the centuries, or even if they were too wealthy or too greedy, as the *Strigol'niki* and some of the legends contend. Apostolic poverty was never much practiced in medieval Christendom, and we must abandon the notion that because a bishop or priest took a vow of poverty, that meant the church was poor; and many churchmen, especially among the episcopate, were from noble families and were as wealthy as their secular brethren. Somewhat in their defense, though, many churchmen, including the Novgorodian archbishops, used their wealth to oversee the archeparchial administration, carry out charitable works, and fulfil other ecclesiastical tasks and Christian duties that enriched Novgorodian and Rus' cultural life, as will be seen in the next chapter.

The Archiepiscopal Administration

Expenses

It is worth providing a few examples of some of the archiepiscopal administration's personnel and activities to give some idea of the costs involved. We discussed in the previous chapter the archbishop's jurisdiction over church people, which went far beyond priests, deacons, monks, and nuns to include the bakers of Eucharistic bread, members of church choirs, priests' wives, widows, freedmen (manumitted slaves), illiterate priests' sons, and bankrupt merchants. He also had jurisdiction over "monasteries, hospitals, inns and hostels for pilgrims."[23]

Having jurisdiction over them in the church courts does not necessarily mean the archbishops supported them financially, but it seems that at least some church people, such as widows, freedmen, and bankrupt merchants, as well as some institutions, such as hospitals and hostels for pilgrims, may have required money from the archiepiscopal coffers for their maintenance. Having jurisdiction did mean he headed a judicial system that dealt with cases involving these church people, and this system included *tiuny* (judges) and *podvoiskie* (bailiffs) which were either paid out of the archbishop's coffers, or were granted land for their maintenance or a right to raise a levy from the district in which they worked.

We have also mentioned archiepiscopal patronage of construction projects (more on that later). We know Vasilii Kalika sent his own master builders ("his own men") to work on the fortress of Orekhov in 1352,[24] so that the archbishop had to provide for them and probably for other construction personnel, such as stonecutters, masons, carpenters, smiths, and various other craftsmen and artisans. Other projects, such as churches the archbishops patronized, would have required additional craftsmen, such as glaziers, iconographers and fresco-painters, bell-makers, skilled metalworkers, and even bridge-builders, and these might have been paid by the archbishop.

The archbishops wined and dined princes and their entourages and carried out other diplomatic and political functions, all of which were expensive undertakings. In 1421, Archbishop Simeon and the *posadniki*, *tysiatskie*, and boiars bestowed gifts on Prince Konstantin, the grand prince's brother, as he departed Novgorod. Konstantin had arrived in 1419, and had been granted estates and the right to collect a tax for his maintenance, all of which cost either the city or the archbishops (depending on whose estates they were) in lost income.[25] When Grand Princess Sophia Paleologa's entourage passed through Novgorod in October 1473 en route to her wedding in Moscow, Archbishop Feofil and the boiars received her with honor and presented her with numerous gifts.[26] In 1476, her husband, Ivan III, arrived in the city "with many people," and was greeted by the archbishop and the Novgorodian boiars, during which Feofil gave him gifts on several occasions until the grand prince left for Moscow on January 26. At a dinner Feofil hosted in the grand prince's honor on November 17, 1476, he gave Ivan three rolls of Ypres cloth,[27] 100 *korabliki*,[28] and an unspecified number of walrus tusks, as well as bottles of red and white wine.[29] On December 14, the archbishop presented the grand prince with 100 more *korabliki*, 5 more rolls of Ypres cloth, several more bottles of wine, and 2 bottles of honey.[30] On January 19, 1477, he gave the grand prince yet more gifts, including 300 more *korabliki*, 2 gold *grivny*, 12 silver *grivny*, 5 *soroka*[31] of sable fur, and 10 more rolls of Ypres cloth.[32] These were luxurious gifts (sable is certainly fit for a king), and showed not only the archbishop's wealth, but also Novgorod's active trade with the West since the Ypres cloth and *korabliki* could only have come from the Low Countries and England, and the wine likely from France. Whether the House of Holy Wisdom engaged in this trade itself or merely bought these goods on the market is not always known. The Ypres cloth was listed as a payment to the archbishop for entry into the wax-merchants' association tied to the Church of St. John at Opoki at the northern end of the Marketplace,[33] but it could also have been bought in the market. Other gifts such as the sables and bottles of honey more than likely came from the archbishops' own estates, and walrus tusks came from the far north.

An inventory from a later period also illustrates the complexity and scale of the Novgorod archiepiscopal administration's economic activities,[34] and while costs or the size of the administration may have been different from the period under study, we can still get a sense of the scale of the Novgorod's archbishops' administration. The inventory shows the House of Holy Wisdom was purchasing significant amounts of goods, including foreign goods, for every aspect of the administration and the wider church in Novgorod. According to Andrei Gnevushev's calculations, the archiepiscopal administration included 191 houses (literally "courtyards") in the city and 130 *sof'iane* in the first part of the sixteenth century, a number that increased to 156 *sof'iane* in 1547, and then declined to 59 in the 1590s.[35] These figures are, again, from at least seventy years *after* the Muscovite conquest, and the office had probably changed considerably by then, but we can compare this with Feofil's activities just mentioned, since the House of Holy Wisdom likely had more wealth, expenditures, and personnel, prior to the grand princely confiscations of land and the archiepiscopal treasury and imposed direct Muscovite control on the city, all of which likely considerably reduced archiepiscopal activity.[36]

Boris Grekov's study of the archiepiscopal administration in the sixteenth and seventeenth centuries revealed a large administration carrying out a number of important and fascinating economic activities, as exemplified by an inventory from 1547 showing that the archiepiscopal administration bought gold satin cloth from the Germans that the archbishop then turned around and presented to Prince Iurii Vasil'evich, the brother of Tsar Ivan the Terrible. It also bought 16 *arshiny* of yellow satin cloth, six logs for the well in the archiepiscopal courtyard, a ream of writing paper for the archiepiscopal treasury and two of cotton paper (the latter for framing icons), 800 *veds* of firewood,[37] two shanks[38] of iron, three padlocks, 39 golden icons from unknown iconographers, five icons from the iconographer Morozok Davydov, 38 icons from the iconographer Fedka (Fedor) Tarasov (16 of them golden), 64 golden *korableniki* (*korabliki*) from Griban Artiuship, 53 Ugrian (Hungarian?) gold pieces bought in Pskov, 486 *pudy* of fresh (*presnyi*) honey or mead, one barrel of German honey or mead, one *pud* of regular honey or mead, one barrel of fish, four barrels of salmon, ten *arshiny* of taffeta, six *portishchy* of silken damask, one dugout canoe or small boat, 300 Cretan lemons, 174 barrels of hops, one *pud* of copper, and unspecified amounts of silk, gold, silver, fat, oil or butter, ammonia and tin (for tinning cookware), coal, bricks, axes, saws, nails, and boards. The total cost of all the goods was more than 765 rubles, a fantastic sum at that time.[39]

Beyond these purchases, we have some sense of other expenditures by the House of Holy Wisdom before 1478, although exact figures are lacking. We know too that the archbishop and the monasteries had to maintain the metropolitan and other church officials when they visited the city since the chronicler complained that when Metropolitan Feognost visited the city in 1341 with an extensive entourage, their "feeding and gifts weighed heavily on the *Vladyka* [Vasilii Kalika] and the monasteries."[40] When Novgorod sent envoys to the metropolitans and patriarchs, their expenses en route had to be provided for. Thus in 1353, when Moisei sent envoys to the Byzantine emperor and the patriarch of Constantinople, "asking for their benediction and for redress in improper matters forced upon him by the metropolitan,"[41] the expenses of the journey down through modern-day Russia and Ukraine (the precise route is not known) to the Black Sea and then along its shore to Constantinople and the subsequent return to Novgorod the following year, all had to be paid for. The archbishops' own journeys to the metropolitan to be consecrated and for other "church business" had to be paid for as well, and some of these were rather lengthy trips, such as Vasilii Kalika's journey to Metropolitan Feognost in Volodymyr in 1331.[42]

We know some archiepiscopal officials were not paid out of the archiepiscopal coffers, since the *Novgorod Judicial Charter* listed the fees for certain such officials who traveled circuits for the ecclesiastical courts; for each 100 *versty* traveled outside the city, the *pristavy*, *podvoiskie*, and the *sof'iane* received 4 *grivny*, apparently paid by each district through which they passed.[43] There were also land stewards and other officials (e.g., *volostiteli*) who oversaw archiepiscopal estates, and they needed either to be paid or else granted land or a right to gather fees for their maintenance from the estates they worked on or those attached to the churches where they worked.

There were archiepiscopal tithe collectors (*desiatinnik*), known from complaints by the clergy of Pskov that they were being overtaxed by them, which led to the creation in 1343 of the position of senior priest (*popovskii starost*) to oversee and protect the priests in that city against the *desiatinnik*.⁴⁴ It is not clear whether they were paid directly by the archbishop, drew a percentage of the tithe they gathered for their own upkeep, or were granted land or other provisions.

We have also seen that several archbishops paid tribute and ransom,⁴⁵ though we do not know whether these payments were drawn from their own treasury or if they were merely delivering funds from the Novgorodian state treasury, though a number of scholars see the two as indistinguishable. It seems the tribute would have been a state expense gathered from throughout the Novgorodian Land, though the archiepiscopal and monastic estates might have paid it too, especially after the Golden Horde declined, since we know the Orthodox grand princes taxed the church while the pagan and later Muslim khans had granted it at least six immunity charters (*iarlyki*).⁴⁶ Ransom might have been gathered by the city or from the families of those to be ransomed, but it could also have been paid by the church, since ransoming captives was traditionally seen as an act of mercy carried out by the bishop.

Personnel

A number of personnel, referred to in the chronicles and other sources as the *sof'iane*, "the men of Holy Wisdom," oversaw the archiepiscopal administration.⁴⁷ One of the most important of these, already discussed to a considerable extent, was the *namestnik* (pl. *namestniki*), usually translated as "lieutenant" when referring to the prince's official, but sometimes as "vicar" with regard to the archiepiscopal official.⁴⁸ According to the Novgorod and Pskov *Judicial Charters*, the archbishops' *namestniki* usually carried out judicial functions,⁴⁹ and they were assisted by other court officials mentioned in the charters, including *pristavy* (sing. *pristav*), *podvoiskie* (sing. *podvoiskii*) (different terms for the archbishop's bailiffs), the *sof'iane* (listed among the bailiffs), *d'iaki* (secretaries), *birichi* (town criers), and *izvestniki* (those who issue the summons).⁵⁰ The *namestniki* also carried out non-judicial tasks, as has been noted,⁵¹ and archaeological excavations have uncovered their lead seals in Torzhok (Novyi Torg), Ladoga, Korela, Obonezhye, and the Dvina Land, leading Valentin Ianin to conclude that, at least for a time, archiepiscopal *namestniki*, rather than Novgorodian city officials, administered these cities and districts. But it is difficult to conclude from just a few seals what the *namestniki* whose inscriptions they bore were doing there. They may very well have run the civil administration in these towns and districts, or they may have just been supervising the ecclesiastical courts there. Or, if the archeparchy was divided up into vicariates (to use a western term), each may have been administered by a *namestnik* residing in a certain town, much as *vicars forane* in the Catholic Church today.[52] If Ianin's conclusions are correct, though, it must be noted that archiepiscopal control of Ladoga was short-lived, and that of Torzhok lasted only about a century, from the late thirteenth to the early fifteenth centuries.[53]

The archbishop's *kliuchnik* (pl. *kliuchniki*; from *kliuch* meaning "key," and usually translated as "steward") was also a judicial official; they are referred to in the *Novgorod Judicial Charter* as the one who affixed the archbishop's or his *namestnik's* seal to the judgment charters.[54] Archbishop Aleksei had been *kliuchnik* of the House of Holy Wisdom prior to his election, and Arsenii, the archiepiscopal *kliuchnik* at Lisitsa, was an unsuccessful archiepiscopal candidate in 1421.[55] Other archiepiscopal officials appear in the sources, though sometimes their precise duties are unknown. In 1228, the house of the archbishop's *stolnik*, Andrei, was plundered during the rioting that broke out around the time Archbishop Arsenii was driven from office.[56] The title (from the Russian word *stol*, meaning table) would indicate a servant who oversaw the archbishop's table, brought dishes and served the archbishop and others of his entourage, although in Moscow in later periods there were also *stolniki* who served in the *prikazy* (government departments), so the title might have been kept while the office changed function. Chronicles also mention archiepiscopal *d'iaki* (clerks or secretaries),[57] one of whom drew up the document that Archbishop Feofil signed and sealed on behalf of the city recognizing the direct rule of the grand prince in January 1478.[58] A number of *kliuchniki*, *stolniki*, and *d'iaki* were attached to the House of Holy Wisdom. Officials with these titles were tied to other churches, monasteries, and princely or boiar households as well.

Chroniclers note still other personnel attached to the church, though they may not have held a formal office or been counted among the *sof'iane*. As churches often served as warehouses,[59] watchmen (*storozhi;* sing. *storozh*) were hired to guard them; there were also watchman of the archbishop's wine and root cellars. The *Novgorodian First Chronicle* reports that during a fire in 1299, looters killed a *storozh* at the Church of St. John while another was burned to death at the Church of St. James.[60] During another fire in 1340, two *storozhi* were murdered by looters at the Church of the Forty Martyrs, and a priest was possibly murdered watching over the precious objects in the "Church of the Mother of God in the Marketplace" (the Church of the Dormition), although the chronicler admits he may have died in the fire, while a *storozh* and his son were burned to death in the Church of Paraskeva-Piatnitsa right next door.[61] The chronicle also notes that Andrei, the *storozh* of the Church of the Holy Mother of God by the town gate, was struck by lightning and killed on April 9, 1419.[62] These watchmen may not have been paid by the archbishop, but rather by the parish whose premises they guarded.

The chronicle mentions others who were in some other ways attached to the archiepiscopal administration: the choir of the Cathedral of Holy Wisdom is noted many times participating in the consecration of churches.[63] In 1313, Archbishop David attached monks to the stone Church of St. Nicholas in the monastery he had built in the Nerev *konets*.[64] Most monasteries were apparently self-sufficient and were not provided for out of the archiepiscopal coffers; rather the archbishops received a tax from them, so that the archiepiscopal administration was in some sense maintained by the monasteries, not the other way around. But in this case, David patronized the monastery and provided for its monks, though this might have only been a temporary measure at its founding. There were also men hired on an ad hoc basis, as in 1230, when Archbishop Spiridon hired a man to bury more than three thousand famine victims in a mass grave behind the Church of the Holy Apostles on Prussian Street.[65]

Boiars were also attached to the archiepiscopal administration. Thus, the *Novgorodian First Chronicle* notes in 1418 that Archbishop Simeon sent his priest and one of his boiars to bring peace during a disturbance at a *veche*.[66] Boris Grekov mentions *koniushnye* boiars, that is, boiars who oversaw the stables, as well as *druzhniki* (members of the *druzhina* or armed retinue raised by the archbishop for the defense of Novgorod or as a bodyguard for the archbishop and his administration); these *druzhniki* would have been boiars.[67] This information comes from the sixteenth or seventeenth centuries, but we know that there were similar people before 1478, since a cavalry unit raised by the archbishop was ordered not to attack the grand princely army at Shelon' River.[68] Grekov also noted other personnel paid out of the archiepiscopal coffers in the sixteenth century: cooks (*povary*), bakers,[69] cowherds, brick-makers,[70] and personnel working in the archiepiscopal stables in the city, including, the aforementioned *koniushnie* boiars, but also grooms (*koniushii, koniukhi*) and *deti boiarskie* attached to the House of Holy Wisdom,[71] as well eighty-six other personnel, including bread-makers, millers, clerks, carpenters, blacksmiths, stonecutters, silversmiths, priests, sacristans, and bell-ringers.[72] Personnel also worked in the archbishop's cellar; collectively known as the *pogrebnye striapchie*, including an elder or cupbearer (*chashnik*), brewers, water carriers, and *storozhi* of the courtyard and cellar.[73] Again, this is after the fall of independent Novgorod, but similar personnel were certainly attached to the House of Holy Wisdom in earlier centuries: Evfimii II built a granary and bakery, suggesting there must have been cooks, bakers and others attached to them; we know that Vasilii and Evfimii hired (or sought to hire) bell-makers, and other artisans, some of them Germans or foreigners who hung doors in the cathedral or helped build the Palace of Facets.

The archbishops patronized construction of numerous churches and possibly provided for the priests assigned to some of them. No patronage of the white clergy is mentioned specifically, but Archbishop David's support of the black clergy in a monastery he founded suggests this may have happened. Petr Stefanovich argues that the person who founded, commissioned, sponsored, or patronized a church or monastery (*ktitor*) had certain prerogatives over it, possibly including the appointment or support of the priests or monks there, though, admittedly, his study also covers a later period.[74] Furthermore, the Stoglav Council (1551) indicates that priests in the archeparchy (and probably other eparchies) were often chosen by and provided for by their own parishioners – since the council condemned Novgorodian parishioners in particular for taking bribes from candidates for the priesthood before sending them to the archbishop for consecration.[75] We do not know how widespread this practice (of parishes appointing and paying their own priests) was before 1478, though it seems likely not uncommon– and by no means limited to Novgorod (or even the Rus' Church, since Jack Kollmann noted Byzantine precedents).[76] All this shows that the upkeep of the archeparchy's priests was not an archiepiscopal expense. Nor was their education. Candidates for the priesthood were often educated, if at all, by the village priest – often their own father – and while there has been some references to literacy and education in the chronicles, it is too scant to say much of any organized or formal educational system or schools – *uchilishcha*.[77] The Stoglav asserted that "prior to this in the Russian tsardom – in Moscow, in Novgorod the Great, and in other cities – there were numerous schools (*uchilishcha*) [in which] letters, writing, singing [i.e., conducting services,] and reading were taught, and therefor there were many more who were literate, who could write, sing, and read,"[78] but the evidence for this (at least in the Novgorodian archeparchy) is scant and, for our purposes, there was no training at the archeparchial level and the local priest often remained ignorant and unlettered.[79] In a 1503 letter, Archbishop Gennadi complained that "ignorant men are instructing children and are corrupting their speech," that many priests remained illiterate, and he appealed to Metropolitan Simon (r. 1495-1511) to set up schools to (better) train clergymen.[80]

Bishop Luka's problems with his slave Dudika, and Bishop Stefan's murder at the hands of his slaves, discussed in Chapter Two, indicate the bishops owned slaves at least in the eleventh century. The *Novgorod Judicial Charter* also refers to "the archbishop's man," which Daniel Kaiser notes may have meant his slave, although it probably referred to a member of the *sof'iane*.[81] These slaves, of course, needed to be fed, clothed, and housed. Several charters note that Novgorodian bishops were granted land with tenants already on them.[82] These people were probably not provided for out of the archbishops' resources as they were, like all serfs, there to provide income to their landlord, not the other way around. They harvested or produced goods like grains, cheeses, eggs, and so forth, and were allowed to keep a percentage of what they made or collected, while the rest was either given as payment in kind or sold to make a cash payment to the House of Holy Wisdom. Each estate would have had an archiepiscopal overseer paid by the archiepiscopal administration or taking sustenance from the estate.

The archbishops needed a considerable income to pay for these expenses. If the legends are to be believed, they succeeded in amassing an enormous treasure, which placed them not just among the city's elite, but among the most important clergymen in the Rus' church, as already noted. This wealth led to criticism of the archbishops as greedy, un-Christian misers, but it also allowed them to patronize great works of art and architecture, oversee a scriptorium from which the Novgorodian chronicles and important religious texts came. Before we look at this cultural patronage, let us consider the sources of this wealth.

Sources of Income

Princely Charters

Just as the church across Europe grew to be the wealthiest landowner over the course of the Middle Ages so too it was in the Novgorodian Land. Isaak Budovnits contends that church landownership in Rus' dates only to the thirteenth century,[83] thus in the first several centuries under study, the House of Holy Wisdom had to rely on other sources of income. Indeed, in the earliest years of organized Christianity, the Rus' church relied on the princes for support. Thus, in 996, Prince Vladimir patronized the construction of the Church of the Mother of God in Kyiv, known as the Church of the Tithe because he decreed that a tenth of the incomes of his estates and towns would go to support it.[84] Statutory charters long attributed to Vladimir and his son, Iaroslav, also established a system of tithes for the church. Scholars debate whether these charters applied to all of Rus' or just in the vicinity of Kyiv and contend the charters date only from the thirteenth or fourteenth centuries,[85] significantly after Vladimir and Iaroslav. The *Rus' Primary Chronicle*, however, mentions an income-providing charter at the time of the founding of the Church of the Tithe, indicating that there were some princely provisions for the church even then, although whether its provisions were as extensive as the church statues of Vladimir and Iaroslav is impossible to say.[86]

The tithe that Vladimir and Iaroslav granted was drawn from princely revenues, namely court fees, princely incomes from every tenth week of trading at the market, and tribute collected "from all the herds and all the animals," "from all properties," "from all one's cattle...and from the crops for all time," and "from a tithe from all the towns."[87] The charters also handed control over weights and measures to the bishops, so that they received the fees for their use in the marketplace,[88] since

> From of old it was established and entrusted to the holy bishops to supervise all town and trade scales, weights and dry measures; from of old it was established by God [that] the bishop is to supervise [these scales and measures] without trickery, neither diminishing nor increasing [the weights and measures], [since] he is to give his accounting for all [these things] on the Day of Judgment, just as [he will] for men's souls.[89]

Besides providing tithes to the church and exempting the metropolitan's people from paying customs, Iaroslav's statute established the judicial competence of the ecclesiastical courts, enumerating the crimes to be tried by the church and the fines to be paid to it,[90] and it applied "to the metropolitan and the bishops," while local charters, most dating to the twelfth century, enumerated specific episcopal powers and privileges in eparchies beyond the metropolitan center.

The local charters granted to Novgorod by Prince Vsevolod Mstislavich (Prince of Novgorod r. 1117-1136) and his immediate replacement, Prince Sviatoslav Ol'govich (Prince of Novgorod r. 1136-1138, 1139-1141)[91] were issued around 1136 or1137, that is, during Nifont's tenure, just as Novgorod was, according to tradition, shaking off princely rule. Vsevolod's Charter, which Daniel Kaiser dates to between 1135 and 1137, but which must have been granted before Vsevolod's arrest in late May 1136 and his dismissal a month and a half later,[92] provides several sources of support for the church:

I consulted with the Novgorodian archbishop, and with my princess, and with my boiars, and with the ten hundred-men, and with the elders court and [responsibility for supervising the trade] measures which are in the market to the Holy Mother of God [Cathedral] in Kyiv[93] were given to the metropolitan; and to Holy Sophia [Cathedral] in Novgorod, and to the bishop and to the elder of the merchant corporation of St. John and to all Novgorod [I have given responsibility for and income from] the trade measures, the wax scales, the honey weights, and ruble weights [for weighing true metals], and the cloth measures [kept in the Church of John the Baptist], and the fees [deriving from measuring the cloth I entrust] to the monks, and the priest [who serves] the merchant corporation of St. John [shares] with the priest of the Boris and Gleb Church [the fee for writing [sales documents], and the guard of the merchant corporation of St. John is entrusted with the brand [for horses] and ten buckets of salt.[94]

This grant of control over weights and measures echoes Iaroslav's charter and added significantly to the Novgorodian archbishop's influence and wealth. Precious metals (silver), bundles of luxury and squirrel fur,[95] pots of honey, balls of wax, and other commodities were traded in the marketplace in Novgorod, and the archbishops earned a fee for weighing and measuring these commodities.

The exact amount of revenue is never stated in the charter or other primary sources, though a very rough estimate is possible. In her discussion of the fur trade in Novgorod, Janet Martin calculated that a minimum of 200,000 squirrel pelts a year flowed through Novgorod in the late fifteenth century. In earlier years, at the height of the squirrel pelt trade, perhaps as many as 400,000 to 600,000 squirrel pelts flowed through the city annually.[96] In the late fifteenth century when 1,000 squirrel pelts were valued at 6.5 Novgorodian rubles,[97] the 200,000 squirrel pelts passing through Novgorod would have been valued at 1,300 rubles or 20,057 silver *grivny* or 80,228.5 *grivny kun*. If the archbishop took a tenth (a tithe) of the value of the furs being measured, he would have earned 130 rubles (2,005 silver *grivny* or 8,022 *grivny kun*) in annual fees at the end of the fifteenth century and considerably more at the height of the fur trade, perhaps as much as 390 rubles or 6,017 silver *grivny*.

Sviatoslav's charter began with a reference to "the statute which we had in Rus' from our great-grandfathers and grandfathers" that "gave to the bishop a tenth [part] from the tribute, the bloodwite, and fines, [and from] everything that comes into the prince's household,"[98] indicating that grants to the bishops of a tenth of certain revenues was a well-established practice. The charter went on: "here in Novgorod, I found established by the princes who came before me (i.e., Vsevolod, whom he replaced in 1136, but also others) a tithe [given to the church] from the tribute. I saw [that the church received] as much of a tithe from the bloodwites and fines as [came all the?] days into the prince's hands, into his storeroom."[99] Sviatoslav decreed: "the bishop takes in place of the tithe from the bloodwites and fines 100 *grivny* of new *kuny*" paid by the revenue collector in the Onega lands,[100] and "if the revenue collector does not pay a full 100 [*grivny*] but gives 80 [*grivny*] instead, then take the additional 20 *grivny* from the prince's treasury."[101] The charter then enumerated tribute be given to the archbishop from particular *pogosty* (sing. *pogost*), or administrative centers that collected taxes from the district around them. This totaled 37 ½ *sorochky* of (luxury) furs (sables and martens), or 1,500 luxury furs per year. (See Table 6.1 in the Appendix).

This was significant tribute. Furs were to Novgorod what coal was to Newcastle or steel to Pittsburgh, and were extremely valuable. Brought from the north they (along with honey, timber, and other commodities) came to Novgorod and from there passed on to Constantinople and the Hanseatic League where they were purchased by the royal courts of Western Europe and the Middle East.[102] Thus, the fur tithe was an important concession to the church on the princes' part. And it is worth stressing that these are luxury furs, much more valuable than the more numerous squirrel pelts or other furs also collected. The *pogosty* listed were located along the main fur harvesting routes stretching far to the northeast of Novgorod to the Kuloi River just south of where it empties into the White Sea, indicating the extent of territory Novgorod controlled even in the twelfth century.[103] The charter also reveals the Cathedral of Holy Wisdom owned one district on the Vel' or Vel'ia River where it emptied in to the Vaga River.[104] Janet Martin pointed out that this meant the archbishops controlled "a main segment of one of the main trade routes crossing Novgorod's northern possessions,"[105] and from this, she concluded that the archbishops participated in Novgorod's fur trade, at least indirectly "by safeguarding, and perhaps exacting tolls on, fur traffic passing through their possessions on Novgorod's trade routes, as well as by accumulating luxury furs through rents and selling it."[106] The archbishops also received salt from the sea district "from the salt kettles and boilers by weight"[107] as well as monetary payments from the Obonezh'e districts all told equaling 36 ½ *grivny* and 20 *kuny*. (See Table 6.2 in the Appendix).

To put all this in perspective, in the early 1500s, income from a service estate of 300 *chetverti* (roughly 400 acres or 162 hectares though the size of a *chetvert* varied considerably since it was based on "good land") would have been approximately 5 to 8 rubles annually, while in the late 1500s, the cost of equipping a cavalryman was 5 to 7 and a half rubles, and the expense for a horse and rider on campaign was an additional 7 rubles.[108] In 1547, the highest paid member of the *pogrebnye striapchie* in the House of Holy Wisdom was paid 400 *dengi* (2 Muscovite rubles), another earned 300 *dengi*, and most people in the archbishop's service earned from 72 (for Ignash the brewer) to 180 *dengi* (for Levka the water-carrier). The *storozh* of the cellar earned 120 *dengi*,[109] while a blacksmith earned 200 *dengi* or 1 Muscovite ruble.[110] A *druzhnik* attached to the House of Holy Wisdom was paid 90 *dengi*; cowherds earned 112 *dengi*.[111] In the late sixteenth century, the daily wage of a carpenter (an important trade in Novgorod where the majority of buildings, as well as roads, drainage pipes, and bridges were all made of wood) was 1 *altyn*, increasing to 2 *altyny* by 1661. A tanner earned 23 *dengi* a day in 1593 and 80 in 1661.[112] In 1552, when Ivan the Terrible established the *strel'tsy* (harquebusiers) in Moscow, they were paid, or were at least entitled to, 4 rubles annually, though this was supplemented through farming or trade.[113]

Admittedly, comparing wages and prices over centuries is extremely inexact. These prices and wages are from well after the period under study and are not all from Novgorod. In the intervening years there was considerable inflation, so that wages and costs in earlier centuries were, generally, lower, though wars, famines, and other events would have driven them up from time to time.[114] Bearing this in mind, these figures provide at least a basic sense of the considerable archiepiscopal income just from the fees for overseeing weights and measures and from tithes granted in these two princely charters.

The archbishops also drew income from one more provision of Vsevolod's charter, which decreed that "Anyone who wants to join the St. John merchant association will give a fee of fifty silver *grivny* to the merchant elders and [a bolt of] Ypres cloth to the *tysiatskie*...[and on the feast of St. John] the elders and [ordinary] merchants are to give the bishop a silver *grivna* and Ypres cloth."[115] Thus, the archbishops earned a silver *grivna* and a bolt of valuable cloth from Ypres every feast of St. John the Baptist. Archbishop Feofil's gifts of 5 or 10 rolls of Ypres cloth to the grand prince on two occasions in 1476 and 1477 would likely have come from this payment, though a later inventory shows the archiepiscopal administration also purchased bolts of Ypres cloth.[116]

These are impressive incomes, but Vsevolod was driven from office in 1136 and died in Pskov in 1138, and the Novgorodians dismissed Sviatoslav in 1138, though they called him back in 1139, only to see him leave for Kyiv of his own accord in 1141.[117] Due to the brevity and instability of their reigns, scholars wonder just how long these princely charters were in force, especially as princely power declined overall, at least in the traditional historiography, at just this time.

Land

As noted, the Rus' church does not seem to have come into possession of significant amount of land until the thirteenth century and, according to Iaroslav Shchapov, the monasteries became landowners even before the bishops. In 1062, and again in 1073, Prince Iziaslav granted lands to the Kyiv Caves Monastery, the first such grant recorded in the chronicles.[118] Episcopal landownership is not found in the sources until the twelfth century, and in Novgorod not before the fourteenth.[119] Even then, we only get a general sense of landownership and its economic importance to the Novgorodian archiepiscopal office due to the fragmentary nature of the sources. What evidence there is indicates that from at least the early twelfth century, the bishops and archbishops of Novgorod had considerable wealth, though not in land. They were able to build churches and monasteries upon their arrival in the city (though the exact date of this arrival is uncertain), yet the princes probably paid for these earliest churches and monasteries, as there was no ecclesiastical administration to gather tithes or other income before or so soon after the Baptism.

Stone church construction prior to the twelfth century was limited to princes and hegumens in Novgorod, perhaps indicating that the bishops lacked their own economic resources at that time. That the hegumens were able to undertake such projects suggests that the Novgorodian monasteries had wealth, possibly from land, as early as the mid-eleventh century. Wealthy patrons granted land so the monks would pray for their or their relatives' salvation or provided funds to monasteries where they would live out the last years of their lives, or for the upkeep of younger sons or daughters who became monks or nuns. Since the bishops did not provide this spiritual welfare, the wealth first went to the monasteries and only later to the bishops. Thus, it was Prince Vladimir who rebuilt the Cathedral of Holy Wisdom in 1045-1052, rather than Bishop Luka,[120] while several hegumens were able to build stone churches for their monasteries around this time.

Novgorod's bishops begin to play their own part in stone church construction or decoration only in 1108, when Nikita's money was used to have the cathedral painted. In 1135, Nifont built the Church of the Mother of God in the marketplace, but he was not the only patron; he acted in cooperation with Prince Vsevolod. In 1144, he had all the porches of the cathedral frescoed, and in 1151 had the roof covered in lead and the outer walls plastered in lime. In 1153, he had the first stone church built entirely under archiepiscopal patronage: the Church of St. Clement in Staraia Ladoga.[121] Three years later, he had the main church in the Mirozhskii Monastery in Pskov built. We do not know the source of Nifont's income or how much land the House of Holy Wisdom held at this time, but the princely charters date to the beginning of Nifont's tenure. Thus, it seems that Nifont accumulated the fees from weights and measures and the fur tribute granted by these charters and used that to build the first real architectural projects sponsored solely by a Novgorodian hierarch only at the very end of his tenure.[122]

The greatest source of information on actual archiepiscopal landownership is the *Novgorodskie pistsovye knigi*, or land surveys, compiled at the end of the fifteenth and beginning of the sixteenth centuries, the earliest from 1495, nearly twenty years after the Muscovite Conquest. This is rather too late for our interests, and they are incomplete. However, study of them by Liudmila Danilova and earlier scholars reveals the archbishops to be the wealthiest landowners in the Novgorodian Land even after Ivan III's land confiscations. They held 2,132 towns and villages, 6,292 courtyards (houses), 8,201 peasants, and 6,880 7/12ths *obzhi* of land.[123] While useful in determining the wealth of the archbishops in the late fifteenth century, there is little information for earlier years.

Despite this shortcoming, there are indications the church, and specifically the archbishops, held extensive lands in earlier centuries. For one, Novgorod lost extensive holdings in the Dvina Land, along the Pingega River and along a strip of White Sea coast to the Muscovite grand princes in the late fourteenth and early fifteenth centuries and was never able to regain them. These were among the most important fur harvesting districts in all the Novgorodian Land. In losing these, Novgorod's archbishops, boiars, and merchants lost not only the wealth that could have been gained by selling the fur from them, but also taxes and other fees levied there.[124] This was the beginning of Novgorod's slow decline and fall as an independent city-state. Indeed, the grand prince continued to poach land from the Novgorodians, and we see in the *Dvina Judicial Charter* that Ivan III issued, that the archbishop and other Novgorodian landowners were stripped of considerable holdings along the Vaga, Veli, Pezhme, and Kuloiu Rivers, which were then taken over by the grand prince.[125] When he finally took Novgorod in 1478, Ivan confiscated even more land from the archbishop, the six largest monasteries, and a number of important boiar families. Aleksandr Shapiro calculated that the archbishops in fact lost 79% of their lands in the confiscations of the late fifteenth and early sixteenth centuries.¹²⁶ This suggests the vast wealth found in sixteenth century sources may have paled in comparison to what they had in the fifteenth century and before, although land could have been returned or bought after 1478, especially after Archbishop Makarii returned with the treasury in 1527.

So, the *Novgorodskie pistsovye knigi* do provide some information on archiepiscopal landholdings before 1478. In fact, they list both the old and new receipts of landowners, that is, landownership from before and after the fall of Novgorod. Comparing these two lists, Danilova noted 6,880 *obzhi* listed as belonging to the archbishops were from the new receipts, that is, from after the end of Novgorodian independence. The old receipts, from before 1478, listed incomes from only 2,731 *obzhi*, indicating the archbishops actually held more land after the Muscovite Conquest than before. From these 2,731 *obzhi* of land:

> The archiepiscopal residence received 151 rubles, 9 *dengi* (minus one *denga*) in *obrok* [quitrent] (equivalent to more than 30,000 rubles at the beginning of the twentieth century), 3,000 *koroby* of grain, 68 sheep, ram's shoulder-blades [of mutton], 91 *poloty* of meat, 17 dishes and 19 cups of butter (around 30 kg), 156 cheeses, 20 chickens, 1,210 eggs, 540 loaves of bread, 27 *bochky* and 17 ½ *koroby* of hops, 71 ½ *koroby* of hemp seeds, 3 *chetvertki* of salt, a *bochka* of beer, 24 *koroby* of turnips, 1,450 squirrel pelts, 85 *piatky* (minus one *gorst*) of flax (minus 2 *funty*, 5 *pudy*), and 80 wagonloads of hay.¹²⁷

Based on studies of archiepiscopal landownership carried out by Gnevushev in the early twentieth century, Danilova in the 1950s, and Shapiro in the 1970s, Ianin, Khoroshev, and others have concluded that the archbishops stood among Novgorod the Great's landowning elite. But how they used their land, and whether it was utilized differently than other landowners such as the monasteries or the boiarstvo, is not apparent from a mere listing of their holdings. Danilova noted that much archiepiscopal land was in the Derevskaia and Bezhetskaia *Piatiny*, in the south, the most fertile of the *Piatiny* and breadbasket of the Novgorodian Land. She also found that the archbishops not only held land astride the trade routes running northeast of Novgorod, as Martin and others have noted, but also held land to the south, along the Lovat' and Pola rivers, which served as trade routes leading to Tver', Moscow, and the rest of Rus'.[128] In fact, the *Novgorodian First Chronicle* refers to Molvotitsy (in the Dervskaia *Piatina* about 125 miles south-southwest of Novgorod) as "the *Vladyka's* town."[129] And on some estates, horses were raised for the archbishops. The stableboys in the village of Markovo on the Volkhov River owed service to the archbishop and herds of horses were pastured near the village and the villagers had to provide 700 bales of hay for their fodder. Danilova saw this as indicative of the archbishops' participation in trade, since the horses were used to carry goods to market.[130] The hay and other fodder collected was also used to feed horses for archiepiscopal embassies to Moscow, Kyiv, Lithuania, and elsewhere. It also fed horses used by *namestniki, druzhniki*, bailiffs, *kliuchniki*, and other officials of the House of Holy Wisdom, and fed cavalry mounts for the Novgorodian army (admittedly not the same type of horse as those used for travel or as draft animals). Because the archbishop's banner made up part of the Novgorodian army, and the archbishops apparently provided cavalry mounts or even levied cavalrymen with their mounts from their estates, the archbishops played an important role in Novgorod's defense. This probably explains Feofil's ability to order the Novgorodian cavalry not to attack the grand prince's troops at Shelon' River, but to limit their attack to the Pskovite troops.[131]

Later Novgorodian archbishops and metropolitans (after 1589) left instructions for subordinates on gathering duties (*poshlina, sbor*). These and the registers of payments from peasants to the archiepiscopal administration show how the archbishops used their land.[132] The cadastres suggest similar processes prior to 1478. They indicate archiepiscopal officials gathered much of the revenue from his estates in monetary payments rather than payments in kind. Danilova concluded from her study, that more than half of the rent was monetary.[133] In the Mikhailovskii *Pogost*, for example, monetary payments made up 54% of rent payments to the archbishop; in the Zabolotye Volost of the Luzhskii *Pogost* they made up 39%, and in the village of the Zabolotye itself, 42%.[134] Shapiro noted that this differed from the practices of secular landowners. Thus, in the Udomolia region, 95% of the archbishop's rents were monetary payments, whereas other estate-holders there received only 43% of their rents in money. And it is interesting to note that after the confiscation of archiepiscopal land in the Zabolotye *Volost*, the new owners, the grand prince and his Muscovite retainers, changed their rents to monetary payments (since grain, cheeses, eggs and other payments in kind would have spoiled before reaching Moscow).[135] This difference between archiepiscopal and secular rents was found throughout the entire Shelonskaia *Piatina*. On archiepiscopal estates there, where the majority of rent payments had been in kind, almost all were changed to monetary payments after the Conquest.[136] So before 1478, the archbishops received most of their rents in money, and this difference seems to be due to the fact that the archbishops were essentially absentee landowners and could not receive in-kind payments before they went bad, whereas local landowners prior to the confiscations by Moscow might have lived on the estates (or at least visited them enough) to allow for payment in kind. It could also be that the archbishops had so much land, they did not need all of them to pay rents in kind, as they could not use that much grain, that many eggs or chickens, and so forth, so some paid in kind, but most paid money. That the grand princes changed much of the rest of the in-kind rents to cash payments is likely for the same reasons: his absence from Novgorod and the huge amount of land he owned, and the fact that, if gathered in-kind, he could not use all of it before spoilage. Furthermore, his *pomeshchiki* needed to buy and equip a horse and its rider, so that money was more useful than payment in kind.

Most payment in kind was in grain or bread, enough in Danilova's view, to feed several hundred people.[137] These were probably the *sof'iane*, who included the previously mentioned *volosteli, poselskie, kliuchniki*, the administrators of the archbishops' vast land holdings, as well as other archiepiscopal officials like the *namestniki* and lesser servitors such as stable boys, honey and flax producers, and so forth. Danilova also concluded that honey and flax production must have been under the archbishops' control since they never taxed these occupations.[138]

In discussing the fur trade, Martin found other indications of different land-use between archiepiscopal and secular estates in the same districts. She concluded that ecclesiastical estates in the Ermtsa district and the Dvina Land did not exploit their lands the same way their lay neighbors did. Namely, they did not collect the squirrel tax (called the *bel*, after *belka*, the Russian word for squirrel). Instead, they collected the *gornostal* (from *gornostai*, the Russian word for ermine) at a higher rate than neighboring lay estates.[139] Thus the archiepiscopal administration collected a tax on a luxury fur, rather than on less valuable squirrel pelts. The *pistsovye knigi* show other differences. Peasants on archiepiscopal land in the Krechnevskii *Pogost* in the Votskaia *Piatina*, close to Novgorod, owed the archbishop 180 eggs and a third of the grain (*khleb*), whereas those in the area holding lands from the monasteries or the grand prince owed monetary payment and a third of the grain, but not eggs.[140] These eggs could have been used merely as food, but then the neighboring monastic and grand princely lands would probably also have demanded them as payment as well. That the archbishops alone demanded eggs may be explained by the fact that he patronized an icon workshop: iconographers mix egg yolks with tempera paints to give the icons a glossy, mother-of-pearl sheen.[141] Monasteries without icon-workshops, or lay estates, would not need as many eggs. In other districts, lay estates collected eggs as well,[142] but it is not so much that monastic and lay landowners also received eggs as payment in kind, but that neighboring secular and even monastic landowners in the same *pogost* did not demand eggs as payments while the archiepiscopal estates did.

There are still more examples of differences in rent collection between archiepiscopal and neighboring lay estates. The peasants on the grand princely and other lay estates in the Zaveriazh Uezd of the Shelonskaia *Piatina* paid *obrok* (quitrent) and a set portion of the grain, usually between a third and a half,[143] while the peasants on archiepiscopal lands also paid monetary rent, but their grain payments were set at 165 ½ baskets (*koroby*) of rye, 70 ½ baskets of barley, 10 baskets of wheat, and 11 baskets of oats, as well as 24 baskets of turnips, rather than a third or a half of just the grain.[144] Because the receipts do not give the total number of *koroby* harvested in rye, barley, wheat, or oats, but only those actually paid to the archbishop, it is not clear what portion of the grain crop this constituted.

The available evidence, therefore, indicates the Novgorodian archbishops were not simply the greatest landowners in the Novgorodian Land, but that their land utilization differed from that of their secular and even monastic neighbors and that they and their administration consciously husbanded their resources and were not merely absentee landlords.

Fines and Court Fees

The archbishops also earned fees from the ecclesiastical courts they supervised. These were usually divided between the princes and the church, although Rus' canon law required wrongdoers to pay fines to the bishop's treasury with nothing going to the prince.[145] Thus, the Shorter Redaction of Iaroslav's Statutes stipulated that "weddings and mass fights and killings, should they occur, and manslaughter [i.e., maiming or death resulting from tournaments or other pagan marriage rituals], are paid for with bloodwite to the prince and hierarch half and half,"[146] while certain types of tribute and matrimonial payments went entirely to the bishop.[147] Shchapov also noted that these statutes held parents legally liable if their daughters remained unmarried, with boiars fined 5 *grivny*, lesser boiars 1 *grivna*, and commoners 1 ruble, with these fines going to the bishop.[148] The plaintiff would probably have to pay for a judge to hear a case or for the issuance of a judgment charter. The *Expanded Russkaia Pravda* indicates still other fines: "These are court fees: from the bloodwite nine *kuny*, nine *vekshy* to the prince's man, 30 *kuny* for beehives, and for all other matters four *kuny* to [whoever] helps, and six *vekshy* to the prince's man."[149] Fees were also paid to churchmen who oversaw the "kissing the cross" or of icons of the Virgin or the saints by which oaths were sealed: "And these are the fees for administering the oath: [for cases] involving homicides 30 *kuny*, [for cases] involving beehives 27 *kuny*; and the same [for violations] of plowland [borders]. And [for cases] involving manumission [of slaves] nine *kuny*."[150] Although the *Pravda* does not specifically deal with fees to ecclesiastical courts, since the archbishops also heard appeals in the secular courts, they must have received income from court fees similar to those enumerated in the *Pravda*.

At the local level, the *Novgorod Judicial Charter*, issued at the very end of Novgorodian independence, also had provisions for court fees, including for the ecclesiastical courts:

> From [each] ruble [penalty prescribed by a] court, the archbishop and his *namestnik*, and the *kliuchnik* for [affixing] the seal take one *grivna*, and from [each] ruble [penalty prescribed for a decision] without a [full] court hearing [because one litigant did not appear at court], the archbishop and his *namestnik* and the *kliuchnik* are to take 3 *dengi* for [issuing] the charter [about the land]. And the *posadnik* and *tysiatskie* and their judges and [any] other judges are to take from [each] ruble [penalty prescribed by] a court 7 *dengi* [= 3.5 percent], and from [each] ruble [penalty prescribed for a decision] without a [full] court hearing 3 *dengi*.[151]

The charter also provided for fees to the archbishop's judicial personnel for traveling to issue summons,[152] as well as for issuing judgment charters.[153] These provisions were similar to those in other charters such as Grand Prince Vasilii Dmitrievich's statutory charter to the Dvina Land, issued in 1397 or 1398,[154] as well as Ivan III's *Sudebnik* promulgated in 1497.[155]

No one knows how much these court fees brought into the archiepiscopal coffers, but it must have been significant since the archbishops and the Novgorodians as a whole were willing to suffer excommunication rather than allow the metropolitan to exercise his right to hear cases and collect judicial fees in the city.[156] Had they been only token payments, the Novgorodians would have certainly yielded to the customs.

Other Sources of Income

The archbishops had still other sources of income including payments for the performance of religious rites such as weddings, the ordination of priests, and the presentation of antimensions to new churches. All of these practices were, technically speaking simoniacal, though the medieval church allowed them for quite a long time.

The Moscow Council of 1503 forbade the collection of fees for priestly ordination, but Gennadii had attended the council and signed the document condemning the practice,[157] and then went right back home and continued to collect the fee (*mzda*), and "even higher fees than before."[158] Metropolitan and grand princely officials investigated, and he was removed from office in disgrace.[159] It was claimed the fees covered the cost of the ceremony, for the wine or the candles, as the Emperor Justinian had argued, or to defray the expense of the archbishop's journey, if the ordinations were not held in the cathedral. They were not for the sacrament itself. More than two hundred years earlier, the first article of the Council of Vladimir allowed the bishops to collect at ordinations "some recompense up to 7 *grivny* according to the practice of the Greek Church based on Justinian's Novella 123 and Novella 1 of Isaac Comnenus."[160] The practice apparently continued even after Gennadii's removal, and the Stoglav Council of 1551 allowed it to continue,[161] and clergymen still had to pay for their ordination documents.[162]

In turn, the laity paid their priest the marriage fee (*venechnaia poshlina*). Jack Kollmann explains that "In the Byzantine and early Kievan [sic] churches, a prelate was supposed to issue his written authorization to a priest for each marriage. This authorization, affixed with the prelate's seal or *znamia*, itself became known as the *venechnaia znamia*."[163] The fee would have been paid for receipt of the *venechnaia znamia*. There were also the tithe-collectors (mentioned earlier) noted in the documents of the Stoglav Council, who administered local justice prior to 1551; how much they gathered in the archeparchy prior to 1478 (or for their other activities there) are unknown. Additionally, we know the Stoglav Council accused the Novgorodian archbishop's *namestnik* and other officials in Pskov of selling church offices,[164] but we, again, do not know how prevalent these practices were before 1478, or even how much it was known or approved of by the Novgorodian archbishops.

Rus' bishops also charged for each antimension presented to a church at its consecration.[165] Not only was this a way for the bishops to make still more money, but it was a way for them to control the local parishes, since new churches required an antimension to carry out Divine Liturgies. Like ordination fees, the collecting of fees for the antimension (necessary to carry out the Eucharist) was technically simoniacal, but was allowed. The fathers of the Stoglav Council were apparently not of one mind on the matter, as they at one point forbade the practice, but at another provided a schedule of fees to be charged for the antimension.[166]

The bishops also collected tithes (*desiatina*) or fees (*poshlina, dokhod*) from the parishes throughout the eparchy.[167] These were collected from the priests, who had collected it from their parishioners. With regard to the Novgorodian archeparchy, an expenditure book from 1557 has excerpts from such registries,[168] and archiepiscopal charters making reference to such fees all date to after 1478.[169] But chroniclers indicate that the archbishops were collecting similar duties before this, since Archbishop Sergei, the first Muscovite archbishop, was much disliked for levying higher fees than his predecessors.[170] The Stoglav Council was apparently trying to address long-held practices.

The archbishops also received valuable gifts from monasteries, or when they visited Pskov or other towns or districts in their eparchy. Indeed, the metropolitan and other bishops received a traditional visitation fee, called a *zaezd*, when they visited a region.[171] The archbishops were also presented with gifts when they went to Moscow to be consecrated, on other "ecclesiastical business," or when they were part of an embassy.[172] Some were more important as symbols, like the gifts of *polystaurions* given to Vasilii Kalika and Moisei; the Ostromir Gospels seem to have been a gift to the archiepiscopal library, and Kostia's and Bratilo's kraters were also gifts to the archbishops, all of which are now important cultural artifacts.

Gifts are, of course, always welcome. Not only did they add to the prestige of the office, but the gift of an icon, chasuble, chalice, vestment, panagia, miter, book, or other such item meant that the archiepiscopal administration did not have to purchase the item or hire an artisan to make it. But gifts were not a constant or reliable source of income, and it is hard to determine whether the archiepiscopal administration gained all that much from them, since it presented similar gifts to princes, metropolitans, archimandrites, hegumens, and other notables.

Conclusion

Over the centuries, the archbishops grew to become the greatest landowners in Novgorod. Before confiscations by the grand prince in the late fifteenth century, their wealth, and the purported greed of some archbishops, was legendary. Major fur-harvesting and trade routes passed through their lands, allowing them to play an important and lucrative role in the economy. They earned huge incomes from these vast landholdings, court fees, tithes, payment for the use of weights and measures in the marketplace, payments for marriages, ordinations, and other sacraments, monastic fees, gifts, and other sources. Their greed, if real, cannot be excused, nor can their immense riches be explained away as merely sufficient for their upkeep or that of their personnel and the archiepiscopal administration. They did have needs "just as the prince had needs," to paraphrase Sviatoslav's charter of 1130, but they had wealth well beyond their needs. From this treasure, they supported church people and various officials in the archiepiscopal administration to maintain the physical fabric of the church in Novgorod. They used it to supervise a system of ecclesiastical courts, carry out diplomatic missions to distant cities, provide for military forces, and protect widows, orphans, and the downtrodden under their care. They built fortresses and erected and decorated numerous churches great and small, some of which are among the most famous examples of Rus' architecture. They were among the greatest builders in Rus', and also great patrons of the arts and literature. They were, in fact, among the greatest figures in all of Rus' history.

CHAPTER SEVEN
The Archbishops and Rus' Culture

13. The Church of the Twelve Apostles near the embankment enclosing the Sofia Side of the city. Archbishop Evfimii II rebuilt this church in 1455 on the site of a church originally built or rebuilt in 1358. [Photograph: Michael C. Paul].

Introduction

The three great periods of Rus' history, the Kyivan, Appanage (or Mongol), and Muscovite periods, each saw a different center of art, architecture, and culture. As the name indicates, Kyiv was the dominant cultural center of the Kyivan period, which saw its golden age under Iaroslav the Wise (r. 1019-1054), and Moscow rose in prominence with artists like Andrei Rublev and Dionisii in the fifteenth century and achieved cultural preeminence under Ivan the Great (r. 1462-1505) and his successors. But during the Appanage period from the thirteenth to the end of the fifteenth century, it was Novgorod the Great that stood at the center of Rus' culture.[1]

The profoundly religious nature of Rus' culture meant that it was only natural that the archbishops of Novgorod were the preeminent cultural patrons during these centuries, and they are, in fact, among the most important patrons of art and culture in all of Rus' history. The churches they built and decorated influenced church architecture throughout Rus'. Chronicles written, collected, and edited under archiepiscopal auspices – and redactions of them held in suburban monasteries – incorporated earlier Kyivan chronicles, added Novgorodian elements, and were later incorporated into later all-Russian chronicles. They are crucial sources on Rus' history. Books written or copied in the archiepiscopal scriptorium and housed for centuries in the archiepiscopal library, in the upper galleries of the cathedral, are themselves important sources for understanding the spread of ideas from Byzantium and the South Slavs to Rus' and are some of the earliest books in Rus'. Their workshops produced beautiful icons and illuminated manuscripts which show the development of Rus' art, liturgies, and theological thought.

The archbishops also promoted the veneration of saints, another key aspect of medieval culture. They brought to Novgorod the saintly cults from Kyiv, Moscow, Constantinople, and other centers of the Orthodox world, but they also promoted the veneration of local saints, many of them their own predecessors as archbishop, several of whom later became important saints in the wider Rus' Church, even after the Muscovite takeover. In this way, the archbishops promoted Novgorod as a key religious and cultural center, a holy and "God-saved" city, and in so doing tied the Novgorodian church spiritually and culturally into the broader Rus' and Orthodox community and salvation history.

Taken together, it is no exaggeration to say that the archbishops' creation and sponsorship of art, architecture, book-writing, historic writing, and other aspects of culture is their greatest contribution, far greater than their political and economic influence which has long since passed away. Despite this, their cultural patronage has been somewhat overlooked. Art historians have certainly recognized the icons and churches the archbishops' commissioned as hallmarks of Rus' culture, and they have remembered certain archbishops.

Olga Popova and Viktor Lazarev, for example, noted Archbishop Vasilii Kalika's patronage of several illuminated manuscripts, the Vasilii Gates in the Cathedral of Holy Wisdom, and other important works of art.[2] William Craft Brumfield, an authority on Rus' architecture, noted that "the city of Novgorod is, by a fortunate set of circumstances, the great repository of medieval Russian [sic] art, with more than fifty churches and monasteries extending from the eleventh through the seventeenth centuries,"[3] adding that "the city rapidly developed an indigenous architectural style in churches commissioned by its princes during the twelfth century as well as in the 'commercial' and neighborhood churches of the fourteenth and fifteenth century."[4] He then names five Novgorodian bishops and their architectural contributions. First, he points out Ioakim Korsunianin's (possibly legendary) construction of the Church of Ioakim and Anne and the oaken Cathedral of Holy Wisdom,[5] followed by Luka Zhidiata's commissioning the Cathedral of Holy Wisdom along with Vladimir Iaroslavich and Iaroslav the Wise (Luka is left out as a patron in some chronicles, as is Iaroslav).[6] Then he discusses Nifont's "energetic support of church construction," and collaboration with Prince Vsevolod Mstislavich in building the Church of St. John on Opoki, which he calls the Church of John the Baptist at Petriatin Court (the same one Evfimii rebuilt in 1453), in building the Church of the Dormition on the Market, and in endowing the Church of the Transfiguration in the Savior Mirozhskii Monastery in Pskov.[7] He then points out Il'ia, for commissioning of the Church of the Annunciation at Miachino in 1179.[8] And, finally, he notes "the final state of Novgorod's history as an independent political and cultural center is dominated by the figure of Evfimii (Euthymius), archbishop of Novgorod from 1429-1458,"[9] who rebuilt churches "in an earlier medieval styles,"[10] particularly the aforementioned Church of St. John at Opoki and the Church of the Dormition. He also commissioned eighteen new churches and other buildings, among them the Church of the Twelve Apostles and the Palace of Facets, "as a means of reaffirming Novgorod's glorious past in the face of an uncertain future."[11]

In addition to these great builders, Gennadii's Bible is important as the first complete biblical corpus in any Eastern Slavic language.[12] Makarii, more famous as metropolitan of Moscow than archbishop of Novgorod, is noted for his abundant bookish activities, including the commissioning of the *Velikie Minei Chet'i* and the *Stepennaia Kniga*.[13] But these last two are outside the scope of this study and they and their predecessors have not been seen as part of a wider phenomenon: the Novgorodian archiepiscopal office in creating and patronizing Rus' art, architecture, culture, and history.

The art and architectural historians ultimately fail to capture something of the scale of the Novgorodian archbishops' contribution to culture: the number of churches, icons, books and other cultural objects and their role as the main patron of culture in medieval Novgorod and Rus', perhaps greater patrons than any other office over the three and a half centuries under study.

Religion and Novgorodian Culture

It is not surprising that the archbishops would have had such a profound role in Novgorod's cultural life given the extent which religion dominated life in Rus' – and later Russia – for almost its entire history. To be sure, religion infused human existence for much of its history and secularization and the retreat of religion to the private sphere are very modern phenomena. Rus' and Russia, though, were in some ways more deeply religious than other (religious) societies around it, particularly medieval Western Europe and even the Byzantine Empire. Catholic Europe and Byzantium had secular spheres: literature and the arts were not exclusively religious in nature: the Byzantines had philosophy and secular literature including a tradition of secular historic works, such as the histories of Michael Psellas, John Skylitzes, Leo the Deacon, George Hamartolos, and even the Patriarch Photius the Great, who referred to or epitomized Herodotus, Ctesias, Arrian, Josephus, Diodorus Siculus, Cassius Dio, and many other secular (ancient) historians.[14] The West had histories like Gregory of Tours' *History of the Franks*,

Bede's *Ecclesiastical History of the English People*, medieval romances, troubadours, secular Latin poetry such as the Goliards, epic poetry like the Icelandic sagas, Aristotelian philosophy translated from the Greek and Arabic, Marco Polo, and so forth. Even Rus' was not completely devoid of non-religious culture. It had its *skomorokhi* or minstrels,[15] its *byliny*,[16] its epic poetry: "*Slovo o polku Igoreve*," ("the Lay of Igor's Campaign") – admittedly replete with pagan imagery – and "*Zadonshchina*."[17] However, in many ways, these were aspects of popular or folk culture, often berated by the clergy as sinful or, at best, a waste of time, and "high culture" remained almost exclusively religious to the extent that Russia did not see the development of truly secular art and literature until the seventeenth and eighteenth centuries.[18] The Rus' acquired Christianity from the Byzantine Empire (though also from the Bulgarians and, later, from the Serbs), but did not receive the secular literature, historiography, philosophy, or other non-religious aspects of Byzantine and Greco-Roman culture. Lacking these secular models to draw from, they focused instead on religion. In this way, Rus' and Russia remained in some sense more deeply religious than the rest of Europe well into the early modern period.

    The importance of religion in Rus' and Russian life over almost a millennium meant the church had a prominent place in culture, just as it did in the medieval West. It was the premier patron of literature, fine arts, architecture, and other cultural activities throughout Latin and Eastern Christendom throughout the Middle Ages. Arguably the church kept Western Civilization alive during the Dark Ages that followed the fall of the Western Roman Empire. And while the Eastern Roman Empire never experienced the Dark Ages, the Byzantine church was still one of the greatest patrons of the arts and culture in Eastern Christendom. And in the lands that came under Byzantine's cultural influence, the church played a role as cultural and political unifier not dissimilar to its role in the West. In Rus' after the Mongol Invasion, it was the Orthodox Church that kept Rus' culture, and even just the idea of a single Rus' polity or cultural space, alive in the face of political, and possible ecclesiastical, fragmentation. Metropolitans Petr, Aleksei, and others did this by continued use of the title "Metropolitan of Kyiv and All Rus'" and they fought to keep their ecclesiastical province unified in the face of attempts by the Lithuanian grand princes and the Poles to create separate metropolitanates in Northwestern Rus' and Halych in the fourteenth century.[19] Churchmen wrote the chronicles that called on the Kyivan princes to unite in Christian brotherhood, to unite against the Polovtsy or the Mongols, and, later on, reminded the people that there was once a single Rus' state and that there was still a single church and Rus' cultural affinity that made the Rus', in their divided (Riurikid) principalities, culturally similar to one another and different from the other peoples living around them.[20]

But this religious preeminence was not merely in the rituals and teachings of the institutional church or in its efforts to maintain unity in the face of political fragmentation and invasion. The world was understood and defined in profoundly religious terms – a worldview very alien to the modern one. The earliest Rus' chronicle begins with Noah's Flood and the division of the world among Noah's sons (a common medieval explanation of the various ethnicities and cultures of the world). It then turns to legends as to the beginning of the Slavs and how they spread out in Eastern Europe, and then the arrival of the Rus'.[21] In this way, the people of Rus', like other medieval peoples, fit themselves into salvation history. The Rus', for their part, divided the people into Christians (i.e., the Orthodox) and the "godless" or "pagan" which included the Catholics of the Polish, Livonian, German, and Scandinavian lands, the Lithuanians (converted to Catholicism in 1386) and the Tatars (despite their conversion to Islam under Khan Uzbek in the early fourteenth century they remained "pagan" to the chroniclers), as well as the actual pagans among the Finno-Ugrian tribes around them.[22] The Rus', like other medieval people, explained political and economic events, natural disasters, and other occurrences in terms of the will of God or the machinations of the Devil.

We have seen this already in Novgorodian sources where plagues, heavy frosts, long hot spells, floods, famines, invasions, the levying of especially heavy taxes, defeats in battle, riots, murder, and other civil unrest occurred "because of our sins,"[23] or they were blamed on "the accursed and all-destroying Devil who from the beginning wished no good for the human race."[24] God punished the Novgorodians "according to our deeds," or showed mercy on them, for example, by sending ice floes down the Volkhov River to destroy the bridge and keep violent factions on opposite banks of the river and thus unable to shed Christian blood.[25] He filled the sky with signs in the moon and the stars and the sun,[26] caused the earth to quake as an omen,[27] caused icons to weep or made chrism (*miro*) flow from them.[28] Angels and saints appeared in prophetic dreams and visions and churches collapsed as portents of impending calamities.[29] Good things happened by the intercession of the saints or because of the grace of a merciful God, who, for example, helped the Novgorodian *Voevoda* Yarun in battle in 1216,[30] and in 1231 watched over the holy churches and protected them while much of the rest of the city burned. When the Novgorodians constructed a great church or monastery, it was "a joy to the angels and perdition to the Devil;"[31] when there was peace among them, it was to the exaltation of the Cross and the disgrace of the Devil;[32] when the Novgorodians fought among themselves, it was due to the accursed and all-destroying Devil who schemed constantly, seduced people to do evil, and put sin into their hearts.[33] Artifacts, too, point to the deep religiosity of the Novgorodians; for example, bundles of wax bore seals declaring that they were *"tovar' bozhii"* ("God's goods") either because they were destined for use as church candles or because the wax had been harvested from apiaries on ecclesiastical estates.[34]

Earlier we saw how this deeply religious world-view naturally led the Novgorodians to turn to their archbishop for comfort, aid (or sometimes blame), as they did when the Suzdalians appeared below the city walls in 1169 and Il'ia prayed and, through the miraculous intercession of the Mother of God of the Sign, brought the Novgorodians victory,[35] or when "God and the great and sacred apostolic cathedral church of Holy Wisdom, and St. Cyril, and the prayers of the holy and Orthodox *Vladyka* [Spiridon], the faithful princes, and the very reverend monks of the hierarchical assembly"[36] interceded and the Mongols turned away before attacking Novgorod. There are other examples of a less miraculous nature where the archbishop stood as a moral authority for the city or were blamed when things went bad, (because he had sinned, or had not interceded enough for God's blessing, though the Devil was ultimately blamed). We see this when *Voevoda* Andrei marched an army out to the Iugra Land, between the Pechora River and the northern Ural Mountains[37] in 1193 and besieged one of the Iugrian towns there. The Iugrian "prince" lured the *voevoda* into the town with the "bigger men" (*viachshikh*) under the pretense of surrendering the city and paying them tribute, only to kill them; he then invited in 50 more of the army's "bigger men" and slaughtered them too, then another 30 more, after which the Iugrians sallied from the town and attacked the remainder of the Novgorodians, killing all but 80 of the besieging army. Novgorod the Great, however, heard nothing of this disaster all winter, and so "the prince and the archbishop and all Novgorod mourned."[38]

In 1228, after Archbishop Antonii retired to the Khutyn Monastery and Arsenii took up the archiepiscopate again, "the accursed Devil, who from the beginning desired no good for man and, jealous of him because he [mankind, or Archbishop Arsenii?] drove him [the Devil] away by nightly vigils, singing and prayer, stirred up a great tumult among the common people against Archbishop Arsenii a modest and gentle man."[39] The mob not only blamed Arsenii for the hot weather that withered the crops, but saw it as divine retribution because Novgorod had allowed Arsenii to remove Antonii and sit again on the cathedra himself. With this in mind, the *veche* (in this case a mob) locked Arsenii up in the Cathedral of Holy Wisdom and brought Antonii back.[40]

Novgorod the Great itself was inextricably tied to the institutional church. Froianov and Dvornichenko may have called Novgorod "one of the oldest and most powerful cities of Rus',"[41] a view found in most of the primary sources and repeated in the traditional historiography,[42] but recent archaeological excavations contradict this, revealing cultural layers going back only to the middle or end of the tenth century, that is, to the time of the Baptism.[43] That they reach their greatest depth in the northwestern end of the Detinets where the Cathedral of Holy Wisdom and the archiepiscopal palace now stand is intriguing, suggesting Novgorod – and not the legendary one mentioned in earlier entries, which probably referred to the *Gorodishche* – may owe its existence if not to the perhaps-legendary Ioakim Korsunianin, then to Christian missionary – and probably Rus' state – activity, since the two worked hand-in-glove. This likely took place over several generations, from 988 to the arrival of Luka in 1035. There is evidence of settlement in the region prior to the Baptism, and some cultural layers in the Nerev *konets* and the Market are as deep as those in the Detinets, but nothing takes on the appearance of a city before Ioakim's (or Christianity's) arrival.[44] The intervening years saw numerous churches, monasteries, and chapels built throughout the city, increasing its importance as an ecclesiastical and cultural center.[45] Indeed, church buildings stood so thick on the ground that Henrik Birnbaum asserted that "at one time the concentration of church structures per square mile within the bounds of the Volkhov city is thought to have been higher than anywhere else in Europe east of the Elbe and north of the Danube."[46]

Given the deeply religious nature of Medieval Rus', it is only natural that the head of the church in the most important city of the Appanage period would be among the most important, if not the most important, patron of art and culture, not just in their city, but in Rus'. The archbishops were by no means the only patrons of Novgorodian culture, but their religious and political authority, and oversight of so many churches, chapels, and monasteries throughout Novgorod and its hinterland, with their libraries, scriptoria, and icon workshops, with the immense economic wealth at their disposal, were able to patronize Novgorodian cultural in ways the princes, *posadniki*, *tysiatskie*, merchant elders, and other notables never could. In fact, Novgorod's bishops and archbishops came to hold a place in Russian cultural life as important as that of any grand prince, patriarch, metropolitan, bishop, great boiar, merchant, hegumen, or gifted iconographer.

Archiepiscopal Cultural Patronage

Architecture

Just as they were not alone among the Novgorodian elite in patronizing the arts, the archbishops were likewise not alone among the Rus' episcopate in patronizing architecture; indeed, the chronicles mention a number of bishops sponsoring church-construction throughout Rus'. The *Nikonian Chronicle* reports that in 1008 Metropolitan Ioann I (fl. ca. 1020) built a stone church dedicated to the apostles Peter and Paul in Kyiv and, in Pereislav, he built a stone church to the Exaltation of the Cross.[47] Bishop Mikhail of Iur'ev (modern Bila Tserkva, southwest of Kyiv) and Hegumen Feodosii built the first church in the Kyiv Caves Monastery in 1073 while the metropolitan was away in Constantinople.[48] In 1108, Bishop Stefan of Volodymyr finished the Church of the Mother of God in Klov (the Klovskii Monastery).[49] In the late eleventh century, Metropolitan Efrem (titular metropolitan of Pereislav)[50] oversaw a number of building projects: in Pereiaslav itself he built the Church of St. Michael and consecrated it in 1091.[51] He also built the chapel of St. Feodor over the city gates, the Church of St. Andrew, a bath, and a hospital, and he began work on the city walls, a rare example of a bishop outside Novgorod building city walls or fortifications. He also built other churches in the city of Militino,[52] and, in cooperation with Prince Vladimir Monomakh, built the Church of the Dormition in Suzdal' in 1096.[53] His successor, Bishop Ioann, erected the Church of the Dormition in Smolensk beginning in 1101, also in cooperation with Vladimir Monomakh.[54] In 1187, Bishop Luka of Rostov ordered the Cathedral of the [Dormition of the] Mother of God in Rostov be decorated with icons;[55] in 1194, his successor, Ioann, ordered the renovation of the Church of the Mother of God in Suzdal' and "looked for masters among the Germans," but found them in his own bishopric instead;[56] two years later, he began the Chapel of Joachim and Anne above the gates (the city is not specified) on May 1.[57] And in 1230, Bishop Mitrofan of Vladimir and Suzdal' ordered frescoes painted in the Church of the Mother of God in Suzdal'.[58]

But Novgorod's hierarchs stood apart in the sheer volume of patronage, and the importance of these works to Rus' art and culture outstrips the patronage of other prelates. No other Rus' bishop seems to have ever come close to Novgorod's in architectural or artistic patronage, but this may be due to the lack of source material on other eparchies – indeed, only a few other eparchies kept chronicles,[59] and a number of those likely didn't survive – and bishops outside the metropolis and Novgorod make relatively rare appearances in the chronicles. Given Novgorod's wealth, its bishops could afford to patronize the arts at levels that bishops of less wealthy cities would have only dreamed of. Furthermore, we know from study of the Novgorodian chronicles, that during certain periods, the chronicler did not keep track of church construction at all; at other times, another chronicler kept track of only stone constructions, while still another would mention both stone and wooden church constructions.[60]

What is available suggests that, outside Novgorod the Great, most churches in Rus' were princely constructions, such as Prince Vladimir's Church of St. Basil (his patron saint), built at the time of the Baptism in 988,[61] and of the Church the Tithe (built in 996) both in Kyiv;[62] Prince Iaroslav's Cathedral of Holy Wisdom (1036-1045),[63] also in Kyiv, Prince Andrei Bogoliubskii's Cathedral of the Dormition in Vladimir, northeast of Moscow, begun in 1158,[64] and the churches of the Moscow Kremlin built and rebuilt by several grand princes over the centuries, most recently by Ivan III (using Italian architects) in the late fifteenth century.[65] These are only the most prominent examples, but there are other, less well-known princes,[66] such as Prince Konstantin Vsevolodovich of Rostov, who rebuilt the Church of the Mother of God in Rostov in 1213 after it had collapsed.[67] He laid the foundation of the stone Church of Boris and Gleb in 1214, and began the Church of the Dormition and the Church of the Transfiguration in Iaroslavl' in 1215.[68] In Novgorod, too, princes were prominent cultural patrons in the eleventh and twelfth centuries, but the bishops and archbishops of Novgorod eclipsed them, beginning with Nifont's archiepiscopate, to become the greatest patrons of Novgorodian architecture and culture.

The Cathedral of Holy Wisdom

Not surprisingly, much archiepiscopal patronage was lavished on their own cathedral (just as their patronage of non-ecclesiastical buildings was often centered on the Detinets). According to the legendary beginnings of the church in Novgorod, upon arriving in the city ca. 988, Ioakim Korsunianin built his cathedral and episcopal palace right on top of a pagan cemetery.[69] The first stone church he built was not the cathedral, but, allegedly, the Church of Sts. Ioakim and Anne.[70] It was dedicated to his patrons and where he was initially buried in 1030.[71] A wooden Church of Holy Wisdom "with thirteen tops,"[72] and the Church of the Twelve Apostles were also built during his episcopate, the former possibly south and east of the current cathedral, along the Detinets' riverside wall where the Church of Boris and Gleb was later built;[73] this wooden Holy Wisdom burned in 1045,[74] after which the current, stone cathedral was built to the northwest.[75] The entire compound around that new cathedral, called "the House of Holy Wisdom" by later chroniclers, became the center of Novgorodian cultural and religious life.[76] The cathedral, or its patron, Christ as the Holy Wisdom of God, came to represent the city itself, just as St. Mark came to symbolize Venice, or other saints symbolized the cities they patronized.

The cathedral's name tied Novgorod to the wider Orthodox world. The cathedrals in Kyiv (1037-1039) and Polatsk (completed in 1066) were also dedicated to Holy Wisdom all at roughly the same time. These three cathedrals harked back to the cathedral in Constantinople (Hagia Sophia, built between 532 and 537)[77] and called by Rowland Mainstone "the supreme architectural expression of Eastern Christianity and...one of the greatest architectural and structural achievements of all times."[78] Kyiv had its Golden Gate too, just as Constantinople and Jerusalem did (later on, Vladimir-on-the-Kliazma did as well – Novgorod did not), and clearly Iaroslav the Wise, in his building of Kyiv, was consciously emulating Constantinople, one of the greatest cities in the world. It is likely that his son, Vladimir, built the new Holy Wisdom in Novgorod (1045-1050) to emulate Kyiv, the greatest city in Eastern Slavdom, then experiencing its golden age, and by extension, he imitated Constantinople[79] and even Jerusalem.[80]

All these Holy Wisdoms not only tied the Orthodox world together mystically or symbolically, but also indicate that there was perhaps something of a cult of Holy Wisdom in eleventh-century Kyivan Rus'.[81] It is worth taking a bit of an aside here to note too that the Polatsk Holy Wisdom had a much more direct link to the one in Novgorod. Vseslav Briacheslavich (Prince of Polatsk r. 1044-1101; Prince of Novgorod 1067 – not formally but by force of arms – and Grand Prince of Kyiv 1068-1069),[82] patron of the cathedral in Polatsk, burned the Nerev End in 1067 and looted the Novgorodian cathedral to enrich his own Holy Wisdom, taking, among other things, a bell,[83] which he hung in his cathedral.[84]

As for the Novgorodians, they themselves frequently drew attention to their cathedral and their divine patron, so that it was not only a link to their Orthodox brethren in Polatsk, Kyiv, or further afield, but was a focus of local, civic pride. When the Novgorodians fought foreign foes, they were not merely defending their homes and liberties or fighting for their princes, they were "fighting for Holy Wisdom" and their Orthodox faith.[85] On several occasions they voiced a willingness "to lay down their heads for Holy Wisdom" or "to die honorably for [the Cathedral of] Holy Wisdom and the angelic houses."[86] On one occasion, they even declared: "Where Holy Wisdom is, there is Novgorod."[87] They also summoned and dismissed their princes with reference to Holy Wisdom. Thus, in 1215, they called Prince Iaroslav Vsevolodovich to "Come to your patrimony – to Holy Wisdom."[88] In 1270, they quarreled with Prince Iaroslav Iaroslavich and would not accept him back as their prince, telling him: "we have no prince: only God, the Truth, and Holy Wisdom!"[89] The princes learned to pay homage to Holy Wisdom to gain the favor of the Novgorodians; when they arrived they often "bowed down to Holy Wisdom," as Prince Mstislav Mstislavich did in 1210,[90] and again in 1218,[91] and Prince Iaroslav did in 1270 when his quarrel with Novgorod was finally resolved with the help of the metropolitan.[92]

Although the cathedral and its archbishops symbolized Novgorod (indeed, the city's present coat of arms depicts the archiepiscopal throne and staff), ironically it was a prince rather than a bishop who built the cathedral.[93] Mikhail Karger, one of the major historians of Novgorodian medieval architecture, pointed out that the renovation and adornment of the cathedral became the exclusive purview of Novgorod's hierarchs only in the twelfth century.[94] The first such instance was in 1108 when the "acquisitions of the holy *Vladyka* [Nikita]" (*stiazheniem sviatogo Vladyky*) were used to pay for the frescoing of the cathedral just after Nikita's death.[95] Archbishop Nifont ordered the *paperti* painted in 1144 and at some point he had the interior of the cathedral proper painted as well.[96] Archbishop Vasilii Kalika had an iron fence put up around the building and hung gilt brass doors in 1336;[97] he repaired the iconostasis and icons after 1341 fire,[98] and a year later, ordered a bell cast by Muscovite masters.[99] In 1408, Archbishop Ioann had the main cupola gilded.[100] In the waning years of the republic, Evfimii II hung the so-called Sigtuna or Magdeburg Gates (also known as the Płock

14. The variously termed Sigtuna, Magdeburg, or Płock Gates which now hang at the western entrance to the cathedral. According to legend they were taken as booty from Sigtuna, Sweden in 1187, but in fact they were wrought in Magdeburg for the Archbishop of Płock and somehow made their way to Novgorod and were installed in the cathedral probably sometime during Evfimii II's tenure. Copies of them now hang in the cathedral in Płock, Poland. [Photograph: Michael C. Paul]

Gates) at the west entrance to the cathedral, perhaps harking back to the glory days of the twelfth century when the gates were created and (allegedly) brought to Novgorod.[101]

In addition to serving as an architectural and artistic workshop and exhibition hall for the archbishops and the sacramental and religious heart of the city, the cathedral was also Novgorod's great necropolis. Thirty-three Novgorodian bishops, archbishops, and metropolitans are buried in the cathedral, seventeen from before 1478.[102] Of these, eleven are canonized saints, ten from before 1478.[103] There are also several canonized princes and a princess buried in the cathedral,[104] making it the shrine of local saintly cults. It is quite understandable, then, that the Novgorodian archbishops would take care to maintain their cathedral and emphasize the importance of their own office, since not only were they head of a great eparchy, but also successors to a long line of saints.

Church Patronage

Patronage extended far beyond the cathedral; Novgorod's archbishops built, renovated, completely rebuilt, and decorated many churches, monasteries, and chapels throughout Novgorod and its environs, in Pskov, Staraia Russa, Staraia Ladoga, and elsewhere.

Exact figures on the number of churches in Novgorod and the Novgorodian Land in the medieval period are very difficult to come by for several reasons. First, as we have noted, not all constructions are reported in the sources; certain chroniclers did not see church buildings as important enough to include in the annals. Second, a number of archbishops patronized projects that were not churches but still deserve mention, though such projects (roads or large, public buildings) do not appear at all in the sources. Most village churches are not mentioned in the chronicles either. Third, no patron is named for most projects (115 of 295 or forty percent of those appearing in the chronicles).

The terminology is also sometimes problematic: some churches were built "under the archbishop" or "at the time of" a certain archbishop (*pri arkhiepiskope*) which does not mean that an archbishop had anything to do with its constructions. The Turks were said to have conquered Constantinople "at the time of (*pri*) Patriarch Athanasius, Grand Prince Ivan Vasil'evich of Moscow and All Rus' and Archbishop Evfimii of Novgorod the Great and Pskov," though it would be awkward to say it took place "under" them, since they were not responsible for the conquest.[105] Add to this the fact that there are quite a few churches with the same name in and around Novgorod: several "Churches of the Mother of God," several more "Churches of the Transfiguration of the Savior," a number of Churches of St. Michael or Sts. Peter and Paul, and so forth, and it is not always clear which one is being referred to in certain chronicle entries.

Likewise, a church is sometimes mentioned twice under two subsequent years in the chronicle; this may be a scribal error as the chroniclers knitted together several sources to compile their annals, but there also might be two churches, or a church and a monastery or chapel of the same name built or rebuilt around the same time. Or it may be the same church was built and then collapsed and had to be rebuilt the following year, as happened to the Church of St. John Chrysostom in the Detinets built under Evfimii II. Or it could be that one entry refers to the laying of the foundation and the latter to the church's completion a year or so later.

Sometimes the chronicler specifically mentions the archbishop consecrating a church, but this does not mean he built it, though some historians have taken it to mean just that.[106] Since church consecration was an archiepiscopal prerogative, he, at least in theory, would have had to consecrate every church, even those he did not patronize, although this was often done by members of the cathedral clergy and not by the archbishop himself; I have only found fifteen specific references to archiepiscopal blessing or consecration of a church.

Despite these shortcomings, the Novgorodian First, Second, Third, and Fourth Chronicles, and the *Avraamki* Chronicle show that the Novgorodian archbishops patronized 112 of 295 projects, or thirty-eight percent of the total. There may be another six that the archbishops patronized but the chronicles are too vague to say this for certain;[107] this would mean they patronized 118 or 40% of the total. This compares with only sixty-eight projects (23%) patronized by named Novgorodian boiars (including a *posadnik*, three sons of a *posadnik*, and a *tysiatskii*), eight by archimandrites, hegumens and monks (other than those who later became archbishop),[108] eleven by princes (and one by a princess), three by merchant groups, and three by streets or neighborhoods, and others.[109] Thus, named patrons other than the archbishops were responsible for a little more than a quarter of the projects. All princely patronage falls before 1198,[110] and archbishops were involved in several of these princely projects, including the Church of the Assumption on the Marketplace, built in 1135 by Prince Vsevolod Mstislavich and Archbishop Nifont;[111] in 1342, "*Vladyka* Vasilii erected the Church of the Holy Annunciation in the *Gorodishche* commissioned on the instructions of Grand Prince Semen (Simeon) Ivanovich."[112]

Archiepiscopal church construction falls into three periods. The first is during archiepiscopates of Nifont, Il'ia, Gavriil, and Martirii, in the late twelfth century. These men patronized nineteen projects. The second encompasses the archiepiscopates of Moisei, Vasilii Kalika, Aleksei, and Ioann, from the second quarter of the fourteenth century into the early fifteenth century, when these archbishops patronized thirty-two projects. The third is the archiepiscopates of Evfimii II and Iona, from 1429-1470, when the two men patronized 48 projects. Indeed, Evfimii alone patronized thirty-four projects, including twenty-three churches and chapels.

Earlier scholars have recognized five great archiepiscopal patrons: Il'ia and his brother Gavriil, Vasilii, Moisei, and Evfimii II, thus, overlooking Nifont, Martirii, Ioann, and Iona. In fact, Iona was the second most prolific patron of architecture, sponsoring fourteen projects, twelve of them churches and chapels. Ioann patronized nine, tying Vasilii and surpassed only by Evfimii II and Iona. By contrast, Mitrofan, Arsenii, Spiridon, Feoktist, and Feodosii are not known to have patronized any projects at all. Indeed, there were only five archiepiscopal projects between the death of Martirii in 1199, and the beginning of Moisei's archiepiscopate in 1325. Thus we observe the same decline in archiepiscopal cultural activity that we saw in their political activities and pastoral visits.

Some scholars contend that archbishops not only patronized (that is, paid for or ordered) the erection of architectural edifices, but personally influenced the style of Novgorodian art and architecture, though I would argue it is too hard to tell the personal involvement of most bishops or archbishops. Nikita, the first bishop mentioned as a patron of the arts, was dead by the time Holy Wisdom was painted (*p'sati* - frescoed), in 1108, and only his money was used. Whether he had personal input in the project prior to his death as to how it should look is not, and probably cannot, be known. The archbishops began to personally patronize art and architecture on a wide scale only with Nifont, who apparently had not been so thrifty as Nikita, and left no money behind. Rather, he was accused of "plundering Holy Wisdom" and fleeing to the south, though the chronicler of the *Novgorodian First Chronicle* at the time, defended him by listing the projects he had patronized:

> About this each one of us should reflect: which bishop painted (*ukrasi*) Holy Wisdom, painted (*isp'sa - frescoed*) the *paperti*, made an iconostasis[113] and painted the whole outside (*vsu izv"nu ukrasi*- i.e., whitewashed), and in Pskov erected a stone church

to the Holy Savior and another in Ladoga to St. Clement?[114]

Art historians tend to see a change in Novgorodian architectural styles beginning around Nifont's archiepiscopate. From a few large and elaborate edifices before Nifont, often patronized by princes, the Novgorodians turned to smaller, more intimate and more numerous churches; some even attribute this change to Nifont's personal artistic tastes.[115] But this change could be attributed to the fact that by Nifont's tenure there were already several large churches and the city did not need any more. There was already the Church of the Nativity of the Mother of God, the main church of the Antoniev Monastery, north of the Market Side, built by Prince Vladimir in 1039 that Hegumen Antonii rebuilt in stone in 1117;[116] the Cathedral of Holy Wisdom (re)built in stone in 1045-1052; the Church of St. Nicholas in the the Market, begun by Prince Mstislav Vladimirovich in 1113; the Church of Saint George in the Iur'ev Monastery that Hegumen Kiuriak and Prince Vsevolod had built in stone in 1119;[117] and the Church of St. John the Forerunner on the Opoki at the north end of the Market, built in stone by Prince Vsevolod in 1127-1130.[118]

That said, several of these larger churches served the monastic communities in the area (and were outside of the city, sometimes at a distance). Others served the princes, their families, and retainers. The cathedral was, of course, the seat of the (arch)bishop. The smaller (parish) churches, served the rest of the community. Thus, the change in style may indicate the establishment of parishes and the archbishops' efforts to (more-fully) Christianize the Novgorodians under their care – a maturation of the eparchial structure – more than (merely) a new architectural style based on Nifont's own tastes. Or it may indicate an economic downturn, which made large churches too costly, or where Nifont and his immediate successors were not yet wealthy enough to build huge churches (they may have only just begun earning income from the princely charters issued in the 1130s). Or perhaps Nifont really had absconded with funds and fled to Kyiv. Given how little the bishops and archbishops come across as distinct personalities in the sources, it is probably not a good idea to attribute certain architectural styles to certain bishop's individual artistic tastes, just as it might not be a good idea to attribute personal greed to any of them, despite what some legends may tell us.

Many of his churches may have been smaller than those built a generation earlier, but Nifont still patronized several imposing edifices, the just-mentioned Church of the Transfiguration in the Mirozhskii Monastery in Pskov, the Church of St. Clement in Ladoga, the Church of the Dormition in the Market (with Prince Vsevolod),[119] as well as the painting of Holy Wisdom, some of which survive. The frescoes of the Church of the Transfiguration have survived rather better, and show that Nifont built, according to William Brumfield, a "Greek church," which has been seen as a deliberate political statement to demonstrate opposition of Kliment, a Rus' churchman installed as metropolitan in defiance of patriarchal prerogatives. The architectural form certainly is Greek, and the iconography is Byzantine rather than anything local.[120] As such, so the argument goes, it shows not only his political leanings, but perhaps his cultural ties to the Byzantine world.

This is an interesting argument, but I would reiterate that the precise artistic tastes of the archbishops, with the possible exception of Vasilii Kalika (see below) and perhaps Evfimii's taste for architecture imitative of an earlier period, are rather difficult to determine given the scarcity of surviving examples and the fact that, even if works do survive (and were not heavily modified in later years), iconography and church architecture in the Orthodox world are quite formulaic and leave rather little room for personal creativity. Furthermore, that a bishop in an ecclesiastical province founded by Byzantine missionaries would employ Byzantine-style architecture and Byzantine iconography and iconographers is not necessarily a significant discovery and may tell us nothing of his personal tastes.

After the formal creation of the archiepiscopate in 1165 (again, Nifont held the title personally) the brothers Il'ia (r.1165-86) and Gavriil (r.1186-1193) made a unique team of archiepiscopal patrons, sponsoring five churches between 1179 and Il'ia's death in 1186.[121] Il'ia never patronized a church without his brother, although it is unclear why this is. Perhaps, again, the archiepiscopal treasury had not grown enough to pay for these projects on its own, or it had been emptied by Nifont, either by his alleged "plundering" or by the expenses incurred by his projects, and Il'ia needed to tap the resources from Gavriil's monastery to carry out his building program. Perhaps Gavriil was more interested in church patronage, architecture, and the like, and used his brother's position as archbishop to push his program. After Il'ia's death, Gavriil patronized two churches on his own.[122] Martirii followed Gavriil and patronized seven projects, including one while still hegumen.[123] Besides building churches, Martirii had Petrovits the Greek paint the Church of the Mother of God in 1196,[124] and three years later, "the *Vladyka's* Church of the [Transfiguration of the] Savior in Russa" was also painted. While not certain, it is probable that the *Vladyka* patronized "the *Vladyka's* Church" in the monastery he had founded several years earlier.[125] There is no mention of co-patrons in any of Gavriil's or Martirii's projects, suggesting that by this time archiepiscopal incomes were sufficient and stable enough to pay for church-construction without resorting to either the princes or hegumens.

The dispute over the archiepiscopate among Mitrofan, Antonii, and Arsenii that took up the second and third decades of the thirteenth century apparently kept Mitrofan and Arsenii from sponsoring any church projects, while Antonii managed just two. After the Novgorodians deposed Mitrofan in 1211, Antonii converted Mitrofan's palace into a church and named it after St. Antonii, his own patron saint,[126] a rather arrogant insult to his predecessor.[127] He then built the stone Church of St. Barbara in the convent of St. Barbara in 1218.[128]

After this, we see the already-noted thirteenth and early-fourteenth century interruption in archiepiscopal activities. That Archbishop Spiridon patronized no major architectural or artistic projects, after the Mongol invasion is understandable; why he patronized none in the nine years beforehand is less clear. The construction of two churches by other patrons in 1233 and 1238, (the patron of the former is not identified; the wife of Simeon Borisovich patronized the latter), demonstrates that external factors were not preventing all construction activities at that time, but the dispute over the archiepiscopal office in the 1210s and 1220s may have weakened it and left the treasury bare.

It was only with Archbishop Dalmat, more than two decades after the Mongol invasion, that a Novgorodian archbishop began to sponsor church construction again, and it was a rather modest one: he covered the Cathedral of Holy Wisdom in lead in 1261. It was only in 1296, almost eighty years after Antonii's Church of St. Barbara, and fifty-eight years after the Mongol conquest, that Archbishop Kliment started a new project, constructing a chapel over the gates of the Detinets, although it was a relatively small undertaking (a chapel and not a large church). Thus, we have to go on all the way to the archiepiscopate of David, ninety-four years after the Church of St. Barbara, to find a large stone edifice sponsored by a Novgorodian archbishop.[129] This is the Church of St. Nicholas "in his court" in the Nerev End, built in 1312.[130] Even then, this is an isolated project, and it is only with Archbishops Moisei and Vasilii Kalika, in the 1320s and 1330s, that archbishops returned to artistic and architectural sponsorship on the scale seen in the twelfth century.

Moisei patronized just one project during his first tenure, but sponsored five more during his second term, including the Church of the Assumption in Volotovo Field just east of Novgorod, built in 1352, which we will come back to shortly. After his second retirement in 1359, he patronized yet another project in 1362, the year before his death.

Then there was Vasilii Kalika. In addition to work on the Cathedral of Holy Wisdom already discussed, he may have laid the foundations of the Church of the Most-Pure Mother of God (the Church of the Dormition) in the Zverin Monastery in 1335, north of the Detinets on the Volkhov just outside the walls of the Sofia Side.[131] In 1348, he ordered the frescoing (*povele podpisati*) of the Church of the Resurrection in the Derevianitskii Monastery, which either he or Moisei had built in 1335.[132]

While built by Moisei in 1352, the Church of the Dormition in Volotovo Field was only painted with icons in 1363, under Moisei's successor Aleksei. Art historians believe the chronicle entry of 1363 refers only to the paintings of the sanctuary walls, while the remainder of the church was not painted until 1380 (still under Aleksei).[133] That Aleksei did not order the frescoes painted until shortly after Moisei's death may indicate that Moisei owned or

15. Copy in the State Russian Museum, St. Petersburg, of a fresco depicting Archbishop Moisei as donor of the Church of the Dormition in Volotovo Field. The original, on the south wall of the church, was destroyed along with the rest of the church during World War II and then rebuilt. Some of the frescoes were restored in the early 2000s.

16. Zverin Monastery Church of Symeon the Receiver of God with Archbishop Iona as founder-donor and wearing the white cowl.

controlled the church and Aleksei respected this while Moisei was alive. Both Moisei and Aleksei were depicted on the south wall of the church (the first for building it, the second for having it painted), the only known contemporary or near-contemporary painting of any of the medieval Novgorodian archbishops. They were shown haloed and wearing the white cowl then unique to the archbishops of Novgorod. Moisei, on the left, presented a model of the church to the Virgin Mary (a standard depiction of church patrons in religious art), while Aleksei, on the right, held out his hands in prayer toward her.[134] Sadly, during the Second World War, the front lines ran right through Novgorod for several years and the church was destroyed by artillery bombardment along with many other priceless monuments of medieval art and architecture in and around the city (interestingly, always blamed on the Germans; the Soviets apparently never shelled a church either by accident or design?)[135] Thankfully, photographs were taken of the frescoes in the 1920s, and a series of paintings of the interior was also made, preserving at least a glimpse of them for posterity.[136]

Aleksei's successor, Ioann, often overlooked by art historians, was actually among the most prolific of the archiepiscopal architectural patrons, sponsoring nine projects, including the painting of the Church of the Resurrection in 1400.[137] After his retirement, archiepiscopal patronage declined under Simeon, Feodosii, and Evfimii I. Indeed, Feodosii sponsored no projects whatsoever, perhaps because he was never consecrated and thus had limited authority – or limited control over the archiepiscopal treasury – while Simeon sponsored only two or three projects,[138] and Evfimii I only one.

Evfimii II was the greatest archiepiscopal and perhaps the greatest of all cultural patrons in medieval Novgorodian history, and historians have long recognized this. He patronized by far the most projects: thirty-four, twenty-three of them churches, including the construction and then reconstruction of the Church of St. John Chrysostom, which collapsed immediately upon completion in 1435 and had to be rebuilt the next year. He patronized the painting of two archiepiscopal palaces and three churches, had the great clock tower, a belfry, a granary, and a root cellar and storerooms (*chashnitsa i molodechnaia*)[139] constructed in the Detinets, and rebuilt the walls of the fortress (*gorod*) of Iam (present-day Kingisepp) on the border with Estonia.[140] Only a few of these survive: the Church of the Twelve Apostles, the Church of St. John at Opoki, the Palace of Facets, and a few others, and those have often been significantly altered over the years. Thus, scholarly claims that Evfimii used older Novgorodian styles from the fourteenth century and earlier, perhaps to hark back to a Novgorodian Golden Age during the waning years of Novgorod's independence, cannot be confirmed.[141]

Iona, the last of independent Novgorod's great episcopal builders, sponsored fourteen projects, including such non-ecclesiastical projects as the strengthening of the earthen embankments

17. The Belfry, rebuilt by Archbishop Evfimii: current state as strengthened for heavier bells in the 18th century. [Photograph Michael C. Paul]

around Novgorod[142] and the reconstruction of the fortress at Orekhov,[143] but he mostly built or rebuilt churches, including the Church of St. Nicholas at the Otenskii Skete, where he had earlier been hegumen.[144] He also built the Church of St. Lazarus,[145] perhaps the Church of St. Simon in the Zverin Monastery,[146] and the Church of the Transfiguration in Orekhov.[147] He also had the Church of St. Sergei of Radonezh in the Detinets painted; those frescoes still exist.[148]

It is possible that the archbishops gave the onion dome, called *lukovitsa* (from *luk*, meaning onion) to posterity, that quintessentially Russian symbol. Some art historians believe it was first developed in Novgorod in the fourteenth century, and from there spread to Moscow and beyond, although we ultimately do not know who was responsible for its development.[149]

Cross-cultural Ties

The archbishops did not limit themselves to the admittedly skilled local artisans in their artistic and architectural patronage.[150] They brought in iconographers and other craftsmen from Moscow, Byzantium, Serbia, and even Western Europe. The chronicles as well as modern analysis of the artistic styles in surviving iconography indicate they also maintained close ties with iconographic schools elsewhere in Rus', most notably Polatsk and Smolensk.[151] This interaction began with the first churches and cathedral in the Novgorodian Land – perhaps Ioakim, himself from the Byzantine Empire, or possibly Luka and Vladimir Iaroslavich when they built the current cathedral in 1045-1052, though the first direct chronicle reference to episcopal sponsorship of foreign artisans only dates to 1196, when Martirii hired the Greek Petrovits (Olisei Petrovich Grechin) to paint the Church of the Mother of God at the Gate.[152] Petrovich also painted the Church of the Savior on Nereditsa Hill (completed in 1198 under the patronage of Prince Iaroslav Vladimirovich, great grandson of Vladimir Monomakh).[153]

According to Valentin Ianin, though, Olisei has an even more interesting link to the archbishops. Ianin asserts Grechin became priest of the church of Constantine and Helena (though Ianin admits there were three churches of that name in the city at the time), then became hegumen (under the name Savva) of the Iur'ev Monastery and, finally was an unsuccessful candidate in the archiepiscopal election of 1193.[154] The theory is thought-provoking, and certainly not beyond the realm of the possible, but is ultimately unpersuasive, since it rests on a number of assumptions: that Grechin must be a surname rather than a reference to a clergyman of Greek origin, of which Ianin also notes there were several in the city at the time; that the Church of Constantine and Helena where Grechin (or a Greek priest) was appointed is the same church whose priest was elected hegumen of the Iur'ev Monastery that same year; and that he was then among the candidates for the archiepiscopal throne in 1229 (and had been a candidate thirty-six years earlier as well).[155] Again, none of this is completely implausible, but we just cannot say for certain that it was the case.

Following the thirteenth century interruption, Archbishop Vasilii hired Isaia the Greek to paint the frescoes in the Church of the Entry into Jerusalem in 1338.[156] Forty years later, Theophanes the Greek (Feofan Grek), said to have painted a considerable number of churches in Constantinople before becoming a towering figure in Rus' art,[157] was brought to Novgorod to paint frescoes in the Church of the Transfiguration on Il'ina Street. The *Novgorodian Third Chronicle* notes that it was "thanks to the boiar Vasilii Danilovich" that the frescoes were painted, even though the church housed the famous Icon of the Mother of God of the Sign, associated with the archbishops since Il'ia used it to inspire the troops in 1169, when Mary was said to have miraculously saved the city from the Suzdalians.[158]

In 1380, Serbian masters frescoed the Church of the Transfiguration of the Savior at Kovalevo, and around that time Serbian artists also painted the frescoes in the Church of St. Theodore Stratelates "on the Brook" (on the Market Side),[159] but there is no indication the archbishop sponsored Feofan or the Serbs.[160] The Serbian presence in the city is an example of the great Serbian (or Second South Slavic) influence on Orthodox art and culture in the fourteenth century. Another example is the illuminations in the *Novgorodian Lectionary*, dated to the first third of the fourteenth century and based on models found along the Treska River in Serbia and at the Hilandar Monastery, a Serbian foundation on Mount

Athos in northern Greece that was an important center of medieval (Slavic) Orthodoxy.[161]

In addition to important Byzantine and Serbian influences on Novgorodian and Rus' culture at this time, the transfer of craftsmen across the Catholic frontier is more intriguing, particularly given the confessional hostility that occasionally led to war between Orthodox Novgorod and Catholic Sweden, the Teutonic Knights and Livonian bishoprics. Also of interest is what role the Novgorodian archbishops played in this transfer. Notwithstanding Nifont's equation of "Varangian" (Catholic) priests with pagans,[162] of Vasilii Kalika's efforts in the 1339 treaty with Sweden to protect the Orthodox Karelians who remained after the war, or of the proviso in the draft treaty of 1471 forbidding a Catholic *namestnik* or Catholic churches in the Novgorodian Land, these cultural ties indicate a more peaceful interaction between Novgorod (and its archbishops) and the West.

Evfimii II maintained particularly close cultural ties with the West. In 1433 he brought in "German" (Western European) masters who worked with local ones to create the distinctly Gothic-styled Palace of Facets just northwest of the Cathedral of Holy Wisdom, referred to in the *Novgorodian First Chronicle* as "a palace in his court with 30 doors."[163] Two years after the palace was completed, He sent a letter to "our dear neighbors the Rigan mayors, the councilmen, and the dear people" informing them he was sending his servitor, Peter, to ask them to "send a good master of the bell-making craft to us," and promising "in return...(to) perform a favor for you."[164]

These projects show Evfimii's love for Western European culture,[165] a greater appreciation than that shown by any other archbishop.[166] The ultimate extent of cultural exchange across the Catholic Frontier is unknown, though it was certainly not only craftsmen or artistic styles that crossed over. Ideas also came from the West, including the Judaizer heresy in the late fifteenth century, which came in the entourage of a Lithuanian prince (although the alleged heresiarch was from Kyiv).[167] Political or economic ideas, which may explain the greater powers wielded by Novgorod's archbishops compared to other Orthodox prelates, may have come from the West, where bishops had considerably more secular powers.[168] Vast trade and commercial activity crossed the frontier, as did artistic exchange, so it is certainly possible political ideas also came over the frontier, although Westerner merchants seem to have been confined in the city to Peterhof and the Gotland Court, and the sources are virtually silent on ideas (aside for heresy) passing across the cultural divide.[169]

Literary and Artistic Patronage

The Archbishops' Scriptorium

The archbishops oversaw one of the great centers in Rus' for writing, editing, and copying liturgical texts, saint's lives, biblical and patristic works, and other literature, as well as manuscript illumination. They sponsored the writing, editing, and copying of the Novgorodian chronicle – at least the so-called "Novgorodian Archiepiscopal Annals" that scholars speculate is the basis for the extant copies of the *Novgorodian First Chronicle* – among our main sources on the archbishops, medieval Novgorod, and broader Rus' history.[170]

The archbishops also gathered an extensive collection of books, quite large by medieval standards. Indeed, when the library of the House of Holy Wisdom was moved to the St. Petersburg Spiritual Academy in 1859,[171] it amounted to 1,585 volumes spanning the period from the eleventh to the nineteenth centuries, though admittedly only about 200 are from before the Muscovite Conquest.[172] These included the Ostromir Gospels (*Ostromirovo Evangelie* – the oldest dated East Slavic book),[173] Gospel aprakoses (lectionaries), *menaion* readers (pl. *menaia*; Russian *mineia*, pl. *minei*),[174] scores of service books (*sluzhebniki*), copies of canon law (including the oldest *Kormchaia kniga* in Rus', discussed in Chapter One above), and miscellanies (*sborniki*) containing copies of some of the oldest extant princely and archiepiscopal charters, biblical excerpts, saint's lives, and other documents, which are not infrequently cited as the primary sources for Rus' history.[175] Many of these are from the sixteenth century or later and originally came from monasteries or other churches in the Novgorodian Land.[176] Several bear colophons identifying the archbishop under whom they were copied or written in the archiepiscopal scriptorium, including Gospel aprakoses from the archiepiscopates of Moisei and Aleksei,[177] the latter with an inscription identifying it as coming from the Church of the Resurrection in "the archiepiscopal court."[178] Several *menaion* readers are from the archiepiscopates of Aleksei, Evfimii II, Iona and Feofil, and compiled under their auspices.[179] A fifteenth century service book from the library already includes prayers to two Novgorodian archiepiscopal saints, Ioann (Il'ia) and Iona.[180] We know many more books did not survive, since the *Novgorodian Second Chronicle* tells us that Archbishop Moisei "sought out many copyists (*pistsa*) and wrote out many books" (*mnogy pistsa isyskal i knigi mnogie ispisal*) and died "leaving many writings,"[181] but just the single Gospel lectionary is all that remains.[182]

There is little of the archbishops themselves in what survives. A few documents written by archbishops will be discussed below. Probably the only book-length text, though, is Archbishop Antonii's *Kniga Palomnik*, a travel account of his journey to Constantinople in 1200, eight years before he became archbishop, (it is not from the Novgorodian cathedral library.) Evgenii Golubinskii dismissed it as "a guidebook, and not a very good one."[183] Others have noted, if not complained, that "Antonii is extraordinarily laconic in his reports and his pilgrimage is little more than a simple catalog of numerous holy sites and relics."[184] Be that as it may, his point was to tell future Rus' pilgrims what to see in Constantinople not write about himself or compose great literature with literary critics (or modern historians) in mind. It is historically important as one of the few remaining accounts of Constantinople from just before the Fourth Crusade,[185] and despite its laconic nature, Gail Lenhoff gleaned four rhetorical devises from the work, which she claimed represent Antonii's own artistic contribution.[186] There is little of the other archbishops' own personalities in the other remaining books or chronicles. After years of study, I have found just a single page actually written by an archbishop, and that is a smudged colophon penned by Feodosii II in his *formularnik*, long after the period under study.[187]

The Archbishops and the Novgorodian Chronicles

The various manuscripts of the *Novgorodian First Chronicle*[188] along with the later Novgorodian-Sophian group of chronicles[189] are among our most important historical sources, not only on the archbishops and their city, but of Rus' more broadly. The *Novgorodian First Chronicle*, however, is a copy of a no-longer-extant "Annals of the Archbishops of Novgorod." Vasilii Tatishchev claims to have discovered a chronicle written by (or under the aegis of) Ioakim Korsunianin, known as the *Ioakimovskaia Letopis'*, which would mean chronicle writing dates to the very beginning of the eparchy, but most scholars reject this claim, believing it relates to Patriarch Ioakim (r. 1674-1690), who, prior to his patriarchate, was Metropolitan of Novgorod (r. 1672-1674).[190]

Over the last century, historians and textual analysts have studied the Novgorodian chronicles and refined the dates of the various redactions, adding much to our understanding of the circumstances of their compilation.[191] The general scholarly consensus is that the earliest chronicle-writing in Novgorod dates to the eleventh century, since the Kyivan chronicle mentions uniquely Novgorodian events such as the Volkhov River flowing backwards for six days in 1063,[192] as well as Prince Vseslav of Polatsk's sack of Novgorod in 1067,[193] showing the Kyivan chroniclers copied from a Novgorodian source (of at least annalistic notes, if not of a longer chronicle text). The first extant copy we have, not just of a Novgorodian chronicle but of any Rus' chronicle, is the Synodal Recension of the *Novgorodian First Chronicle* (GIM Sin. 786), also known as the Older Redaction (written by one scribe around 1234; a second scribe added the entries from 1234 to 1330).[194] It was made for and continued by the Iur'ev Monastery.[195] There are two versions of the Younger Redaction: the Commission manuscript, written in 1439 and added to in the mid-1440s, and the Academy manuscript, written shortly thereafter.[196]

Research carried out by Aleksei Gippius has revealed "boundaries" in the text of the *Novgorodian First Chronicle* which generally correspond with changes in the archiepiscopal office, suggesting the new archbishop (or someone in his administration) chose a new chronicler when he entered office,[197] perhaps an archiepiscopal secretary who was also a cleric at one of Novgorod's monasteries or churches.[198] Based on these boundaries, Gippius listed twelve chroniclers or annalists appointed by Prince Vsevolod Mstislavich (1117-1132) Archbishop Nifont (1132-1156), Bishop Arkadii (1157-1163), Archbishop Il'ia (1164-1186), Archbishop Gavriil and Bishop Martirii (1187-1199) and Archbishops Mitrofan (1200-1211), Antonii (1211-1226), Spiridon and Dalmat (1226-1274), Kliment (1275-1298), Feoktist and David (1299-1310), a second annalist for David (1311-1324), and Moisei (1325-1330).[199] Guimon, noting Gippius' research on the topic ends in 1330, adds annalists for the tenures of Vasilii Kalika (1330-1352), Moisei's second tenure (1352-1359), Aleksei (1359-1388), Ioann (1388-1415) (whom he identifies as Ioann III), and Simeon (1415-1421).[200]

We probably know the names of three of these chroniclers: The deacon Kirik Novgorodets (b. 1110), chronicler for Nifont (1132-1156), the priest German Voiata of the Church of St. James (or Jacob), chronicler for Il'ia (1164-1186), and Timofei, the sexton (*ponomar'*) also of the Church of St. James (mentions himself s.a. 1230), chronicler for Spiridon and Dalmat (1226-1274).

Kirik Novgorodets has been mentioned before in discussing the *Voproshanie Kirika* (for whom they were named).[201] He was originally a deacon and domestic (i.e., head of the monastic choir) in the Church of Nativity of the Virgin in the Antoniev Monastery on the Market Side. Kirik's involvement is suggested by the more sophisticated way of telling time in the Synodal or Older Recension of the *Novgorodian First Chronicle*, s.a. 1136:

> In the year 6644 (A.M.), the fourteenth year of the Indiction…In that same year, in the month of July, on the 19th, previously called the fourteenth Calends of August, on the Sunday of the Council of St. Euthymius [the Great – i.e., the Council Chalcedon], in the third hour of the day and on the 19th day of the celestial moon…[202]

That same year, Kirik wrote the *Uchenie o chislakh*, which some have called the first "mathematical treatise" in Eastern Slavdom, but which is actually a chronological work, looking at how many weeks, hours, cycles of the sun and moon, and so forth have transpired from the creation of the world to Kirik's own time, and giving him a knowledge of chronology that he apparently wanted to show off in the entry of 1136.[203] Beyond that, he is known for translating the works of Patriarch Nikephoros I of Constantinople and the Pentateuch into Slavic. He was later ordained a hieromonk and may have referred to his own ordination by Archbishop Nifont under the year 1144, although some scholars believe this is a later chronicler.[204] He entered the archiepiscopal administration, where he was part of Nifont's entourage to Kyiv in 1149 that confronted Metropolitan Klim (Kliment).[205] He then disappears from history.

Kirik's compilation and those of other early chroniclers have not survived, but were apparently incorporated in to a rearrangement of the annals under Archbishop Il'ia around 1167.[206] This, again, is the oldest extant copy of the *Novgorodian First Chronicle*, the *Synodal Copy*, the rearrangement of which is attributed to German Voiata, a priest of the Church of St. James in the Nerev *konets*, who may be the chronicler who mentioned his own ordination in 1144.[207] He also wrote the defense of Nifont in 1156,[208] and his death is mentioned under the year 1188.[209] This copy was continued by Timofei, the *ponomar'* of the same Church of St. James, who mentions himself as "the sinful Timofei the *ponomar'*" in the entry for 1230.[210] Scholars believe this redaction was supplemented by entries from an archiepiscopal chronicle composed around the same time.

This redaction was rearranged under Archbishop Vasilii Kalika between 1330 and 1335, probably prompted by Metropolitan Petr's compilation of an all-Rus' chronicle around 1310, which included the earlier Novgorodian chronicles.[211] Vasilii's rearrangement apparently borrowed entries such as the first (brief) Tatar invasion and the Battle of Kalka River in 1223 and the Tatar Conquest of Eastern and Southern Rus' in 1238-1240 from the all-Rus' chronicle.[212] Vasilii's chronicle, however, has not survived, but the *Synodal Copy* of the *First Novgorodian Chronicle*, thought to have been made for the Iur'ev Monastery, is a near-contemporary and may be based on it.[213] Parts of Vasilii's chronicle made their way into the Younger Redaction of the *Novgorodian First Chronicle* when it was rearranged and amended at some time during the archiepiscopate of Simeon,

Feodosii, Evfimii I, or in the first year of Evfimii II's tenure, that is, sometime between 1420 and 1430. In the mid-fifteenth century, the metropolitan patronized a new arrangement of an all-Rus' chronicle, again influencing similar chronicle-writing or editing in Novgorod, known as the *First Sofiia Chronicle* and the *Novgorodian Fourth Chronicle*. The former was composed by Matvei Mikhailov Kusov during the archiepiscopate of Evfimii I.[214] A new arrangement of the *Sofiia Chronicle* was made under Evfimii II at some time in the 1450s. The *Novgorodian Fourth Chronicle* is found in two copies, the older dating to before 1437 and borrowing from the archiepiscopal redaction, and the later from before 1447, compiled in Evfimii II's scriptorium.[215] It was later continued into the sixteenth century in the *Novgorodskaia letopis' Dubrovskogo* with significant re-editing to burnish Moscow's image vis-à-vis Novgorod.[216]

Textual analysis of the chronicles, particularly the "boundaries" discovered by Gippius, shows the archbishops, beginning with Nifont, were deeply involved in chronicle-writing and redacting, quite possibly personally picking a new chronicler – drawn from local ecclesiastical houses - when they came into office. The segments of Kyivan chronicles copied into Novgorodian chronicles (particularly before ca. 1115), and the inclusion of parts of the Novgorodian chronicles in later Muscovite chronicler, underscores the importance of Novgorod in wider Rus' culture.

Icons and the Decorative Arts

Just as the archiepiscopal scriptorium was key to chronicle-writing in Novgorod and wider Rus', so too the archbishops' icon workshop was key to icon painting (*pisati*) in the city and among the Eastern Slavs. As such, the archbishops had a huge impact on wider Rus' culture throughout the medieval period.[217] The art historian Viktor Lazarev argues the archbishops oversaw the largest iconography workshop in Novgorod and employed iconographers and others known as the "*Vladyka's* men" (*vladychnyi parobok*) or the "*Vladyka's* boys" (*vladychnyi robiata*).[218] In the fourteenth century, iconographers began to cater to the needs of a wider part of the community, so much so that inexpensive icons could be commissioned by men of fairly modest means.[219] That said, we have little information on the workshop itself or any archiepiscopal oversight of icon-painting. We do know that the Stoglav Council in 1551 ordered tighter episcopal/ecclesiastical control over icon-painting throughout Muscovy because depictions of the life of Christ and the saints have theological ramifications. The council specifically ordered that icon-painters answer to master artists who were directly accountable to the local bishop.[220] However, we do not know if this was a reaffirmation of earlier practices or a new rule established by the council.

Relatively few icons survive from the period under study. Catalogs and art history books often identify them as merely belonging to the "Novgorodian School" and do not, and may not be able to, trace them back to the archiepiscopal (or any specific monastic or private) workshop. We know private icon workshops existed – we have already discussed the case of Aleksei Petrovich (Olisei Petrovits) Grechin,[221] and archaeologists have excavated his icon-workshop where several birchbark documents were discovered between 1973 and 1977.[222] These documents might suggest little regulation of iconography at this time, with individual priests ordering icons from a private studio with no apparent oversight by the archiepiscopal administration.[223] But as clergymen, Grechin and several of his clients could have faced judgment in the ecclesiastical courts were they to run afoul of acceptable theological norms, though we have no evidence icons of an unauthorized nature ever led to charges of heresy in Novgorod.[224]

Several icons were painted for Archbishop Vasilii Kalika when he refurbished the cathedral after the fire of 1341. The feast-day icons on the iconostasis are easily distinguishable from more typical Novgorodian icons of the period and, according to Lazarev, contain many Byzantine features. They are also similar to icons in the Church of the Mother of God at the Zverin Monastery, which Vasilii had built beginning in 1335.[225] Lazarev argues there is a "Byzantine current" flowing through these icons, which can also be seen in the Vasilii Gates, the Likhachev Gates, and a fourteenth century Gospel aprakos, but he ultimately concluded this current was absorbed into local Novgorodian trends and "did not play any decisive role in the art of Novgorod in the fourteenth century." It is safe to say, however, given Vasilii Kalika's patronage of all of these works, he was a Graecophile, just as scholars say Nifont was, based on the much-earlier frescoes of the Church of the Transfiguration in the Mirozhskii Monastery in Pskov. Vasilii also commissioned the Greek monk Isaia to paint the frescoes in the Church of the Entry into Jerusalem in 1338-1339, showing these were not merely Russian iconographers mimicking Constantinopolitan styles, but an actual Byzantine presence in the city.[226] Elissa Gordienko writes that Vasilii not only hired iconographers, but painted icons himself and, while it is intriguing to think that some of these icons were from his own hand, there is no proof.[227]

Frescoes painted under archiepiscopal sponsorship, already discussed some in the section on architectural patronage, would certainly have met with some sort of archiepiscopal approval, and could have served as examples of acceptable iconographic themes or patterns for private workshops. While the technical craft of fresco and icon painting differ, theologically and stylistically they are not so very different. But we do not know how much the archbishops themselves controlled or influenced the art. Iconographers were brought from as far away as Serbia and Constantinople to paint in the archbishop's workshop or decorate churches, and the city was, in earlier years, tied to iconographic schools in Smolensk and Polatsk as noted before, but none of this says much about archiepiscopal oversight.

The most famous iconographer to have worked in Novgorod was Feofan Grek (Theophanes the Greek). His frescoes in the Church of the Transfiguration on Il'ina Street in 1378, make use of rich reds, much darker than the usual bright red hues for which Novgorodian iconography is famous (Pskov, conversely, made greater use of blue). Only in the city for a brief time to paint a few projects, he must have influenced other Novgorodian iconographers, just as he influenced those in Moscow and other parts of Rus',[228] though it seems Feofan never worked for the archbishops.

Just as he was the greatest archiepiscopal builder, Evfimii II was also the most prolific supporter of iconography and decorative arts of all the archbishops. He was so significant that scholars refer to the Evfimian (Euthymian) Workshop, which endowed among other places, the Viazhishche and Khutyn monasteries. Of the many works produced, still extant are an icon of the Archangel Gabriel in the second tier (or range) of the Great (Dormition) Iconostasis in the Cathedral of Holy Wisdom (with an inscription that it was painted by the monk Aaron Feofanich, who painted four other icons in the iconostasis in 1438),[229] the Puchezh Shroud (*plachanitsa*) in the Kremlin Museum, the Khutyn Shroud in the Novgorod Museum,[230] and an embroidered Deesis now in the Tretiakov Gallery.[231]

The archbishops also sponsored the creation of sacred vessels for their cathedral and other churches and monasteries they endowed. Two twelfth century kraters (or craters) from the Cathedral of Holy Wisdom were sponsored by couples who had their names inscribed on them. "Petrilov and his wife Barbara," that is, Posadnik Petrilo Mikulchich and his wife, were the donors of "Bratilo's crater", while "Petr (Mikalkovich) and his wife Mar'ia" sponsored "Kostia's crater."[232] Whether they were made at the archiepiscopal workshop, they were, in any event, used in the cathedral for centuries. The cathedral's Great and Little Sions, tabernacles modeled after the tomb of Christ or of the "mother of all churches," Jerusalem's Church of the Holy Sepulcher (or Church of the Resurrection as it is known in Orthodoxy),[233] were made in the twelfth century by an unknown artisan or artisans and may be tied to the legend of Il'ia's nocturnal journey to Jerusalem from which he returned with the measurements of the Holy Sepulcher.[234] Other works, such as the *panagiarion* of Master Ivan, are more obviously products of archiepiscopal patronage; it bears an inscription indicating Archbishop Evfimii II's sponsorship in 1435.[235] Whether he personally patronized a particular work or not, the fact remains that he presided over one of the greatest periods of architectural and artistic flourishing in the city and Viktor Lazarev noted that Novgorodian iconographic styles from this period (undoubtedly influenced by the Euthymian workshop) greatly influenced later iconography and even modern artistic genres.[236]

The Archbishops as Cultural Subjects

The Archbishops' Saintly Cults

With twenty-two of its bishops and archbishops numbered among the saints, Novgorod the Great has far more episcopal saints than any other eparchy in the Rus' church, including Kyiv and Moscow.[237] In fact, Novgorod had sixty-eight saints, according to one manuscript, and not just bishops, but also princes and princesses, archimandrites, hegumens, and hegumenesses, monks and nuns, holy fools (*iurodivye*), and others, more than any other Rus' city except Kyiv (with 184).[238] Novgorod's episcopal saints outnumber the metropolitans and patriarchs by more than a fifth.[239] There are thirteen metropolitans canonized as saints,[240] three Muscovite metropolitans after 1478 (excluding Makarii),[241] and one patriarch (Germogen) (not counting Iov), as well as three bishops of Tver' (one from after 1480), two bishops each from Kazan', Riazan (including Iona, who was later metropolitan), Perm', Vologda,[242] Minsk and Turau (the latter two now in Belarus), and one bishop each from Vladimir-Suzdal, Pereiaslav, and Tobol'sk.[243] Novgorod had fully forty percent of all Rus' and Russian episcopal-saints from the pre-modern period. Our focus will be the seventeen Novgorodian bishop-saints from before the Muscovite Conquest.[244]

As saints, these men went from being patrons of culture and promoters of saintly veneration to subjects of culture and foci of veneration. Evfimii II began promoting the veneration of his episcopal predecessors and was the most significant archiepiscopal promoter of local saintly cults before 1478.[245] He used his extensive architectural and artistic patronage in conjunction with the canonization of local saints – especially his predecessors in the archiepiscopal office – to enhance the prestige of the archiepiscopal office and celebrate Novgorod's unique civic and ecclesiastical history and culture. This includes the legend of Archbishop Il'ia and the miraculous icon of the Mother of God of the Sign (*Znamenie*) and the Novgorodians' victory over the Suzdalians in 1169, emphasizing Novgorod as a holy city with a holy archbishop, and harkening back to Novgorod's golden age at the same time the city decline vis-à-vis Moscow in the 1450s.[246] One of the two famous icons of the *Battle of the Novgorodians with the Suzdalians* dates to Evfimii's archiepiscopate.[247]

Evfimii II and his successors' promotion of Novgorod's saints include the writing of saints' lives (*zhitiia*), a key element of the Orthodox canonization process. Archbishop Iona commissioned the *zhitiia* of Archbishops Moisei and Evfimii II.[248] The *zhitiia* of Il'ia and Iona were included in a late fifteenth century collection in the archiepiscopal library.[249] But for all his promotion of the Novgorodian archiepiscopal saints, none appear in the extant *menaion* readers or *sluzhebniki* from Evfimii's own archiepiscopate.[250]

Official veneration of Novgorod's bishop-saints could be said to begin on October 4, 1439, when the *ponomar'* of the Cathedral of Holy Wisdom claimed to have seen several of the bishop-saints walking around in the cathedral singing hymns.[251] The sources are very particular: "One night the *ponomar'* of Holy Wisdom, the monk Aaron, saw, not as in a dream, nor as an apparition, but in reality" ("*ne vo sne ni prividenii, no v iavu*"). The next morning, he told the archbishop, who received the news with great joy and wrote a decree marking that day as a feast commemorating those who had appeared: Bishops Luka, German, and Arkadii.[252]

That same year,[253] a piece of masonry fell from the cathedral's ceiling and broke open an unmarked tomb. Evfimii was summoned, approached the tomb with a candle, peered in, and saw the incorrupt body of a man in monkish garb, whom no one could identify. Shortly afterwards, a man in episcopal garb appeared to Evfimii in a dream and identified himself as Ioann (Il'ia), whose remains had been uncovered.[254] Evfimii then canonized him along with nine other Novgorodian prelates: the aforementioned Luka, German, and Arkadii, as well as bishop Ioakim and archbishops Gavriil (Grigorii), Martirii, Antonii, Vasilii and Simeon, assigning February 10 (O.S.) as their feast day.[255] He then transferred or "translated," the bodies of Prince Vladimir Iaroslavich and his mother, Anna, to a different location within the cathedral, a process that effectively canonized them.[256] These princely canonizations also promoted the Novgorodian archbishopric since Vladimir had built the cathedral.[257]

Evfimii's decrees only applied to the Novgorodian archeparchy; only the metropolitan or a church council could decree the veneration of saints across the entire Rus' church.²⁵⁸ Hence, Evgenii Golubinskii's study of canonizations in the Russian Church lists only two Novgorodian archbishops among the saints before the Councils of 1547 and 1549 (for those whose dates of canonization are known): Il'ia, canonized in 1439 by Evfimii II, and Evfimii II himself, canonized sometime before 1494, since a service for him drawn up that year was found in a *sluzhebnik* from the Solovetskii Monastery.²⁵⁹ The nine others canonized by Evfimii were not venerated by the entire church until much later. Feoktist and Moisei were apparently canonized at some point in the fourteenth century.²⁶⁰ Eleven more, including the nine whom Evfimii venerated (i.e., Ioakim, Luka, German, Arkadii, Gavriil, Martirii, Antonii, Vasilii Kalika, Simeon) as well as Gennadii (r. 1485-1504), and Pimen (1553-1570), were venerated by the entire Rus' church only in the sixteenth century.²⁶¹

After 1478, the archbishops continued to venerate their saintly episcopal predecessors. Archbishop Makarii (r. 1526-1542) included several Novgorodian archbishops in his *Velikie Minei Chet'i*, the first edition of which was compiled in Novgorod.²⁶² He included the tale of Il'ia's journey to Jerusalem on a demon in the September volume of the Novgorodian edition.²⁶³ Once metropolitan, he convened church councils in 1547 and 1549, during which several Novgorodian saints were officially recognized by the entire church.²⁶⁴ In 1547, Il'ia was again listed among the saints, and declared a wonderworker or miracle-worker. Nikita was also listed among the saints. Evfimii II, however, was not.²⁶⁵ He was added only in 1549, along with Nifont and Iona.²⁶⁶ The 1564 council, convened following Makarii's death in December of the previous year, invoked several saints, including Metropolitans Peter, Aleksei, and Iona (probably not the Novgorodian archbishop, since he was listed with the metropolitans), Archbishop Ioan (Il'ia) and Bishop Nikita of Novgorod, as well as Leontii, Isaiia and Imatii of Rostov. When confirming the right of the Novgorodian archbishop to wear the white cowl, it was noted that Il'ia among other wonderworkers (Metropolitans Peter and Aleksei, etc.) had worn white cowls – thus the privilege was a particularly holy one and amplified the stature of the Novgorodian archbishop.²⁶⁷

In addition to invoking his saintly predecessors at the 1564 council, Archbishop Pimen had written to Tsar Ivan IV and Metropolitan Makarii in 1551 asking to open the tomb of Bishop Nikita after Nikita had appeared in a dream to a holy man in Novgorod named Issaki. Permission was not granted until eight years later, 550 years after Nikita's death, at which time the body was found incorrupt, still dressed in a simple cassock with an omophorion. It was dressed in new clothes and reinterred.[268] The chronicle reported that on the day the tomb was opened several miracles occurred in Narva (Rugodiv), then under attack by a Swedish army: a beardless man in bishop's vestments (Nikita is always depicted beardless in icons) was seen along the riverbank holding aloft a cross. At the same time, several icons thrown into a fire by Lutheran iconoclasts did not burn.[269]

After the unrest of Ivan's later reign, including the 1571 sack of Novgorod, the untimely death of Pimen in 1571, the execution of Archbishop Leonid in 1575,[270] and the Swedish occupation of Novgorod, Novgorodian Metropolitan Makarii II (r. 1619-1626)[271] sent a letter to Tsar Mikhail Fedorovich in early November 1619 inviting him to a prayer service that was to take place at the Church of the Mother of God of the Sign in Novgorod on November 27, the Feast of the Mother of God of the Sign.[272] In the letter, Makarii noted that, in addition to prayers to Mary under her title of the Mother of God of the Sign, as well as other saints, several Novgorodian bishops and archbishops, would be invoked during an evening and all-night service, specifically Nikita, Ioann (Il'ia; closely tied to the miracle of the Icon of the Mother of God of the Sign in 1169), Evfimii II, and Iona.[273] In another letter written that same year to the Archdeacon Iosif, Makarii again invoked the names of Nikita, Ioann (Il'ia), Evfimii II, Iona, and, he adds, Moisei.[274] He also wrote to Patriarch Filaret in an undated letter, wishing him well during an illness, and saying he would be holding a prayer service in December, during which the Wonderworkers of Moscow and Novgorod (*nofgorodskikh*), Metropolitans Peter, Aleksei, and Iona, Bishop Nikita, and Archbishops Ioann (Il'ia), Evfimii II, and Iona, would be invoked.[275] In a 1671 letter to Archimandrite Iona of the Tikhvin Monastery, Novgorodian Metropolitan Pitirim (r. 1664-1672, afterwards Patriarch of Moscow and All Rus' to 1673) likewise invoked several

Novgorodian episcopal saints: Bishop Nikita, and Archbishops Nifont, Ioann (Il'ia), Evfimii II, Iona, and Moisei, as well as well as one other later archbishop, Serapion I (r. 1506-1509; d. 1516).[276] Thus, the process Evfimii II had started in the late 1430s was carried on by his successors, despite their Muscovite backgrounds. Under Makarii, the archbishops of Novgorod, venerated locally since the 1430s, came to be venerated throughout the entire Rus' church.

Iconographic portrayals of Novgorod's prelates were sometimes painted centuries after their deaths. We cannot discuss even all of the more important iconographic portrayals here, but several examples illustrate the importance of these saintly cults in the life of the church, even after 1478. The fresco of Moisei and Aleksei and the icon of Il'ia and the Battle of the Novgorodians with the Suzdalians have already been mentioned, dated from the late fourteenth through the early sixteenth centuries, but several important later depictions, indicate the Novgorodian bishops' continued, indeed growing, importance. Bishop Nikita and Archbishop Il'ia appear on several panagias now on in the collection of the Novgorod State United Museum, one from the Iur'ev Monastery and another worn by Metropolitan Makarii.[277] Nikita also appears along with five fourteenth-century Novgorodian saints in the top register of an early-eighteenth century icon of the Alfanov Brothers, one of whom had Nikita as his patron saint.[278] An icon pattern book from the seventeenth century includes a group icon of sixty-eight Wonderworkers of Novgorod.[279] Twelve of the seventeen bishop-saints appear,[280] but there are also individual icon patterns for Bishops Nikita and Arkadii,[281] and Archbishops Nifont,[282] Il'ia (Ioann),[283] Moisei,[284] Simeon,[285] Evfimii II,[286] and Iona.[287] Il'ia and Nikita are also depicted in full-length portraits (dated to the seventeenth century) over the south portal of the Dormition Cathedral in the Moscow Kremlin, the patriarch's cathedral and mother church of Russia since the fourteenth century, indicating that they were no longer local sons promoted by the Novgorodian bishop, but were important all-Rus' saints.[288]

The archbishops and metropolitans also venerated the relics of these archbishop-saints. Wooden sarcophagal effigies of Il'ia and Evfimii II sculpted and painted under archiepiscopal auspices, the former in the first half of the sixteenth century (under Makarii or Feodosii) and the latter under Pimen, cover their tombs in the Cathedral of Holy Wisdom and the Viazhishche Monastery respectively.[289] Interestingly, a later Novgorodian prelate, Metropolitan Kiprian (r. 1626-1634), was denounced to Tsar Mikhail Fedorovich (r. 1613-1645) and Patriarch Filaret (Mikhail's father) for a number of very serious crimes including harboring murderers and excommunicants in several monasteries in the metropolis, corruption, including nepotism involving a brother and, more scandalously, a son, who, along with other family members, were systematically looting the eparchial treasury, and keeping a mistress, his brother's widow, in one of the Novgorodian convents. But the *chelobitie* denouncing him began not with these egregious sins, but with the charge that he had covered up the relics of Archbishop Ioann (Il'ia) the Wonderworker in a coffin and then covered that with a cloth so pilgrims could not see the relics anymore! It even cites Prince Dmitrii Pozharskii, one of the saviors of Russia at the end of the Time of Troubles, who visited Novgorod and "marveled that this [the "hiding" of the relics] had never happened before."[290]

The Archbishops in Legend

Beyond official commemorations in icons and *zhitiia*, Novgorod's archbishops were also the subjects of popular legends and folktales (*povesti*) parts of which were worked into their saint's lives or the chronicles, so the modern distinction between history, official saintly veneration, and popular legends and folktales is an artificial one. The presentation of the archbishops in these stories demonstrates their importance and influence, sometimes long after their deaths, and what the common people may have thought of them. While it is not possible to discuss all the tales here, several of them deserve mention.

Far and away the most popular archbishop in the tales is Archbishop Il'ia (almost always referred to as Ioann), the first formal, and in some ways, the quintessential archbishop of Novgorod.[291] Some tales are based on actual events, for example, the *Tale of the Founding of the Dormition Monastery in Novgorod*, which he and his brother, Gavriil, had built in 1180.[292] Many tales have been embellished, like Il'ia's role in saving Novgorod from the Suzdalians in 1169. The *Novgorodian First Chronicle* merely recounts that it was through his prayers, and that of other saints, that the city was saved.[293] The later fifteenth century *Tale of the Victory of the Novgorodians over the Suzdalians* and the iconographic depiction of the event, show Il'ia leading a procession with the Icon of Mother of God of the Sign from the Church of the Transfiguration on Il'ina Street across the great bridge into the Detinets to raise Novgorodian spirits and to appeal to the Mother of God to save the city.[294]

Similarly, the *Tale of the Posadnik Shchil* has a historic basis. There was an historic Olonii Shchil' upon whom the main character is based, and the Shchilov Monastery he founded on the Dubenka River appears in the *Novgorodian First Chronicle* under the year 1309, more than one hundred twenty years after Il'ia's death. The tale is thus, not historical, though it includes *realia*, elements of historic truth, woven into a fictional tale.[295] While not useful as a historic source, it still shows us what the original storytellers, and perhaps later copyists, remembered about earlier archbishops, what duties the archbishop presumably carry out, and what was deemed proper episcopal behavior.

Other tales were clearly more fanciful. The *Tale of the Travels of Ioann of Novgorod*,[296] which scholars believe Pakhomii the Serb (Pachomius Logothete) reworked under Evfimii II's patronage after Il'ia's body was discovered in 1439. Indeed, Evfimii gathered a number of tales that had probably circulated orally for some time before being written down.[297] The tale shows how much the Euthymian workshop and the House of Holy Wisdom worked to resurrect the image of the great archbishop and hark back to a golden age as Novgorod declined.

Il'ia appears in the tale as a humble man of prayer and miraculous powers who spoke of his own holy experiences as if they were those of another man so as not to appear presumptuous.[298] Returning to his chambers one evening, he found a demon splashing around in a washing bowl.[299] Saying a prayer, he trapped the demon in the vessel and only agreed to release it after it promised to take him that very night to the Church of the Resurrection in Jerusalem.[300] Compelled by the power of God, the demon promised, transforming itself into a horse. "Retaining his power over the demon" and "having armed himself with the Cross and grace,"[301] Il'ia then rode the demon to Jerusalem, left it "still under his power" in front of the church while he went into the Holy Sepulcher to pray; the doors opened on their own and the candles in the tomb miraculously burned without anyone having lit them.[302]

Upon returning to Novgorod, the demon took vengeance by making it appear as if prostitutes were visiting Il'ia. The Novgorodians, incensed by their archbishop's sinful and unbecoming behavior, sought to depose him, taking him down to the great bridge and placing him on a raft (perhaps a reference to the several killing of people by being thrown from the bridge found in the chronicles).[303] But God favored His archbishop and the raft moved upstream (south) against the current to the Iur'ev Monastery, where Lake Il'men empties into the Volkhov.[304] The miracle convinced the Novgorodians that Il'ia was blameless and they begged his forgiveness for their unjust treatment.[305]

Pakhomii the Serb continued his work under Iona's aegis,[306] perhaps even into the archiepiscopates of Sergei or Gennadii - for almost half a century, completing *zhitiia* of several archbishops, including the *Tale of the Moisei, Archbishop of Novgorod*,[307] the *Tale of Evfimii, Archbishop of Novgorod*,[308] and at least one redaction each of the *zhitiia* of Ioann (Il'ia) and Iona.[309] He is credited with eleven *zhitiia*, though many were for other patrons. He also wrote fourteen services, including ones for the Mother of God of the Sign, and another for Evfimii, twenty-two canons, including ones for the Mother of God of the Sign and two for Evfimii, as well as a number of hagiographic tales.[310] In the sixteenth century, the Pskovite monk, Varlaam (in life, Vasilii) continued in Pakhomii's footsteps. In 1558, he wrote the *Tale of Nifont, Bishop of Novgorod*,[311] probably based on the *Paterik of the Kyiv Caves Monastery*, to commemorate Nifont, who founded the Mirozhskii Monastery in Pskov. That same year, he wrote the *Life of Nikita, Bishop of Novgorod* under the auspices of Metropolitan Makarii.[312]

In some tales, the bishops play supporting roles, as when Bishop Nikita appears in *Tale of Antonii Rimlianin*,[313] or when, in the *Prophesy of St. Varlaam*, Varlaam, founder of the Khutyn Monastery, visited Archbishop Antonii and foretold a frost and snow during the fast before St. Peter's Day.[314] Vasilii Kalika appeared in the *Life of Lazar of Murmansk*.[315] Four Novgorodian archbishops also appear in the tales surrounding Mikhail Klopskii, a famous Novgorodian *iurodivyi*.[316] Three appear in the *Tale of Mikhail Klopskii* itself.[317] Feodosii, appears as the wise and holy hegumen of the Holy Trinity Monastery at Klopskii where Mikhail resided, and Mikhail tells him that he would sit on the archiepiscopal throne one day, but would serve only two years.[318] Archbishop Evfimii I is portrayed in the same tale in a most unbecoming light, as an avaricious man whose behavior was antithetical to those of the ideal bishop. Not satisfied with the customary taxes levied on the monastery, he took "a horse as black as a raven" as additional payment,[319] after which Klopskii confronted him, telling him "You will live but a short time and leave everything behind." Evfimii sickened and died shortly thereafter.[320]

Evfimii II appears, by contrast, as a prayerful and holy man, much as Feodosii was. Visiting the monastery while still archbishop-elect and eating with the monks, he asked Mikhail during the meal to pray that he would be "invested by Grand Prince Vasilii," that is, that he would go to Moscow and be consecrated, since he had waited more than four years after election (the tale says three). Mikhail unexpectedly snatched a handkerchief from the archbishop-elect's hand and placed it on Evfimii's head, telling him "You will go to Smolensk and be consecrated into the archbishopric."[321] Evfimii II was, indeed, consecrated by Gerasim in Smolensk in 1434.[322]

Klopskii also appears in the *Tale of Archbishop Iona*.[323] In the tale, Iona, while still an adolescent (the tale says the event occurred during the archiepiscopate of Ioann II who died in 1415), watched as other boys abused a *iurodivyi* (i.e., Mikhail). The man, however, ignored the boys' bullying, ran up, grabbed Iona by the hair, pulled him close and, although not knowing him at all, called him by name, telling him: "Ivane! [or Ivanets, a diminutive of Ioann or Ivan, Iona's baptismal name – MP] Study your books diligently, for you will be archbishop of this great city."[324] This incident made its way into the *Novgorodian Third Chronicle*, which dates the event to 1408, fifty years before Iona became archbishop: "In the year 6916 [1408], Mikhail Klopskii...prophesied that Iona would be archbishop and about the conquest of Novgorod [by Ivan III]."[325]

In placing the (white) handkerchief on Evfimii II's head, Mikhail hints at the white cowl, the special monastic hood the archbishops of Novgorod wore.[326] While other bishops wore the black cowl typical of the monastic clergy, the white cowl was long unique to Novgorod's prelates, and through the *Tale of the White Cowl*,[327] composed according to tradition sometime in the late 1480s or 1490s on the orders of Archbishop Gennadii,[328] came to symbolize the pure Orthodox faith of Rus'.

The tale, though it dates to at least a decade after the fall of Novgorod, calls to mind traditions from prior to 1478. It relates how the white cowl made its way from Rome via Constantinople to Archbishop Vasilii Kalika in Novgorod.[329] And while its origin is transformed into legend here, the white cowl was very much real: when Vasilii's tomb was opened during the 1946 excavations in the Cathedral of Holy Wisdom, his body was found still wearing the white cowl and the *polystaurion* referred to in the tale.[330] The fresco painted in 1380 in the Church of the Dormition in Volotovo Field also depict Archbishops Moisei and Aleksei wearing the white cowl. (Evfimii II is usually depicted in icons wearing it as well).[331] Thus the tale deals with the regalia of the archiepiscopal office from at least the middle of the fourteenth century, showing that the memories of the archbishops of Novgorod lived on long after them.

The tale opens with the Emperor Constantine (r. 306-337 AD) afflicted with a deadly and incurable disease. Pope Sylvester, who had been in hiding during the Great Persecution (303-313), appeared and cured the emperor by the power of the Holy Spirit. In gratitude, and recognition of the true faith Sylvester revealed, Constantine gave him the white cowl, revered by popes for centuries after until, according to the tale, they fell away from the true faith in the ninth century and wished to destroy it. But a youth (i.e., an angel) appeared to the pope and commanded him to send it to Constantinople. There, Patriarch Philotheus (r.1353-1355, 1364-1376) had several visions in which the angel told him to receive the cowl and, although Philotheus wanted to keep the miraculous gift for himself after it had cured him of an eye disease, the angel commanded him to send it on to Novgorod to be worn by Archbishop Vasilii Kalika "so that he may glorify the Holy Apostolic Cathedral of Holy Wisdom and praise the Orthodox."[332] Vasilii, "who distinguished himself by fasting and virtuous ways," also saw the angel in a dream, appearing in monastic garb and wearing and the white cowl. He told Vasilii that the next day a Byzantine bishop would arrive with the cowl and a *polystaurion* from the patriarch.[333]

Vasilii led a procession with all the clergy of Novgorod in their vestments to meet the bishop and, receiving the gifts, took them to the cathedral and put them on. The moment he put on the white cowl, the icon of the Pantocrator painted in the main cupola cried out "Holy, Holy...*Ispola eti despota!*" ("Long live the bishop!")[334] In celebration of this miraculous gift, Vasilii "feasted all the priests, deacons and clergy of the city of Novgorod the Great for seven days...offered food and drink to the poor, to monks, and asked that the prisoners be released."[335] He presented the patriarch's messengers great gifts and sent still more for the patriarch and emperor.

The tale portrays Vasilii as a holy man blessed with a miraculous gift and generous to the poor, to churchmen, and to prisoners – the ideal Orthodox bishop – whose fame spread as far as Constantinople. It also shows the archbishops' legendary wealth. It is among the first in a series of works such as the monk Filofei's letter to Grand Prince Vasilii III, laying out the Theory of the Third Rome, and Makarii's *Velikie Minei Chet'i* and *Stepennaia Kniga*, collected and compiled in Novgorod and Moscow during the reign of Ivan IV, that helped in the formation of a Muscovite national consciousness.[336] According to the legend, the White Cowl was not simply a prerogative of the Novgorodian archbishops setting them apart from the other bishops, but claimed a special place for Rus' (and later Muscovy) in salvation history. The First Rome passed the miraculous gift to the Second Rome, which, in turn, passed it on, strangely, by way of Novgorod, to The Third Rome, Moscow, which had subjugated Novgorod by the time the tale was composed.[337]

The archbishops also appear in legends foretelling the fall of Novgorod, such as those surrounding the Church of St. John Chrysostom. Built in the Detinets in 1435 on the orders of Archbishop Evfimii II, the church collapsed almost immediately after completion, an event seen as an omen of city's own demise. Though Evfimii probably denied the validity of the legend (and ordered

18. Detail of Ecclesiastics from Tysiachiletie Rossii, the nineteenth century Millennium of Russia monument south of the cathedral. Included among them are Archbishop Feofan Prokopovich (on the right wearing a mitre and holding a staff in his left hand with his right raised in blessing, Patriarch Nikon (next to Feofan holding a staff and hooded rather than mitred) and Metropolitan Makarii (in profile to the left of the printing press behind the seated figure with the book and scrolls in his lap), all three of whom were at one time archbishops or metropolitans of Novgorod. None of the pre-1478 prelates are depicted in the monument. [Photograph: Michael C. Paul]

the chapel rebuilt the following year), the series of humiliating defeats at the hands of Moscow in 1456, 1471, and finally in 1477-1478, made the Novgorodians look back to possible portents of their demise.

Conclusion

Archiepiscopal patronage of art, architecture, iconography, bookish and literary activities – including writing, compiling, and editing chronicles – and their veneration and promotion of Novgorod's saints, especially their own predecessors, reveal the archbishops were among the most significant cultural patrons in Novgorod and perhaps in all Rus'. This patronage has left a few remaining beautiful architectural ensembles and works of art. Their chronicles are.

key historic sources, and the saints' lives and popular legends reveal something of the popular view of the archbishops, adding to Novgorod's sacred image and prestige. Their role in cultural creation and promotion was their greatest role.

Conclusion

How does the evidence in the available sources compare to the powers or roles sometimes ascribed to Novgorod's archbishops in various monographs and articles? The archbishops stand out among Eastern prelates and their significance has long been recognized by historians. Novgorod has likewise been known as one of the most important political, cultural, economic, commercial and ecclesiastical centers in Rus'. But a number of assertions are not supported by the historical evidence.

The archbishops played a greater role in their city's political life than did any other bishop in Rus' or perhaps more than most other bishops in the Orthodox world, though this fell short of the secular roles the Prince-Bishops of the Empire and other Catholic prelates played. The archiepiscopal administration was the largest landowner not only in the Novgorodian Land, but throughout Northern Europe in the High and Late Middle Ages, and this enormous wealth gave the archbishops considerable influence, permitting them to stand out among the city's elite and interact with princes and prelates throughout northeastern Europe.

The archbishops led an administration that performed important church sacraments and ceremonies, but also undertook the education of young princes, fed the poor and carried out other charitable work, ran the ecclesiastical courts and sat on the civil court, controlled weights and measures in the marketplace, gathered tribute on church lands and other fees across broad stretches of the Novgorodian Land, and supervised church people, which included not just priests and deacons, but also parish choirs, priests' sons, and others. Their wealth was fabled, perhaps even scandalous, with several bishops becoming legendary for their greed and corruption.

Ecclesiastically, there is no evidence the Novgorodian archbishops were the second most important prelate in the Rus' church, and certainly not the next in line to the metropolitan, serving as a locum tenems when the metropolitan see was vacant. The church had no real hierarchical structure; it was a single province headed by a metropolitan where all prelates were subordinate to him and essentially equal. If the see was vacant, bishops much closer to Kyiv – in Southern Pereislav or Iur'ev – oversaw the province. The archiepiscopal title gave an honorary status but no additional powers or duties. It did not indicate the Novgorodian church was independent from the metropolitan, nor is there evidence to support assertions that Novgorod was consistently seeking ecclesiastical independence from Kyiv or Moscow. Nifont opposed Metropolitan Klim, but that was because Nifont supported the patriarch's right to appoint the metropolitan, not because he sought Novgorodian autocephaly. Several archbishops fiercely opposed Metropolitan Kiprian in the last quarter of the fourteenth century, after which the ecclesiastical relationship between Novgorod and Moscow became more distant, but these actions, too, can be explained in ways other than a striving for ecclesiastical or political independence. They wanted to protect their income from court fees, and not see them go to Moscow at a time when the grand prince was threatening their holdings in the Dvina Land, and they may have seen the metropolitan doing the grand prince's bidding – acting as a Muscovite partisan rather than head of the Kyivan ecclesiastical province. But there is no evidence Novgorod wanted to set up an autocephalous church—or even "go Latin"—despite Muscovite claims to the contrary.

Thus, while medieval politics cannot be divorced from economics and religion, the traditional, Moscow-centric view of a centuries-long rebellious-streak in Novgorod's policy toward Moscow, is overly-simplistic at best. The reality, as it so often is, was more complex than a simple desire for political and ecclesiastical independence against the lawful grand prince and metropolitan. The metropolitan remained the Novgorodians' pastor and the grand prince their lord, though the Novgorodian church did attain a level of ecclesiastical autonomy. It elected its archbishop from among local candidates, and sent the electus to the metropolitans for consecration, but in many ways maintained a distance from the metropolitan center – especially in the fifteenth century – that other eparchies seem never to have achieved,.

Several scholars have asserted that the archbishops oversaw the largest eparchy in the Rus' church. Geographically, the Novgorodian archeparchy was vast, stretching from just south of Lake Il'men northeast to the Arctic Ocean and from the border with Estonia to the Urals. It was the largest in the Rus' church, larger than many states at the time, but evidence indicates the archbishops focused their activities almost exclusively on Novgorod and Pskov, making few visitations to outlying towns. The hinterland was sparsely populated and, anyway, was not fully Christianized during much of the period under study. Parishes in the towns – Ladoga, Staraia Russa, and so forth – as well as in *pogosts* in rural districts, were largely left to their own devices ecclesiastically-speaking. They chose their own priest and provided for him. They sent him to the archbishop to be ordained (and paid a fee for it). If they were lucky, he had been educated by the previous priest, often his father. The archbishops sent each new church an antimension to demonstration his authority over them. Besides that, it seems the archbishops had little to no interaction with parishes outside Novgorod. They did not oversee a large or impressive church administration that reached out into the country parishes. Thus, the physical vastness of the archeparchy did not translate into vast power or influence for the archbishops.

Politically, Novgorod's archbishops certainly played a role in Novgorod's achievement of local autonomy in the twelfth century (though we do not know whether they personally took part in, say, the dismissal of Vsevolod Mstislavich or other princes). They participated in governing the city, and sought to preserve Novgorod's freedom as Moscow's power grew in the fourteenth and fifteenth centuries. When that failed, Feofil handed over power to Grand Prince Ivan III. The office survived, while the other local offices, the *posadniki*, the *tysiatskie*, were suppressed. As eccleastics, they were unique among Novgorod's elite. In the way they came to power and the level of political and economic power they wielded, they were also unique among Rus' and Orthodox bishops.

The evidence does not support claims that the archbishops were the Novgorodian republic's "head of state." The archbishops oversaw courts that adjudicated secular cases which other church courts in other cities did not. They participated in embassies to princes, and oversaw treaties with the German cities to the West, though their exact role in these activities is uncertain. Their *namestiki* may have governed Ladoga and Russa for a time, but the evidence is inconclusive. and they had influence which gave them something of the status of an elder-statesman (though most bishops would have had similar influence given the church's profound importance in society). But the prince was the head of state and he placed a *namestnik* to see to his interests in the city. Novgorod's secular officials – the *posadniki* and *tysiatskie* – ran the city, though the exact constitution of Novgorod – where one official's power left off and another's began – will likely never been fully understood due to the brevity and paucity of the sources. The archbishops did have more political power than almost any other Orthodox bishop, and this is certainly noteworthy, but calling them "heads of state" seems to go too far.

Economically, the archbishops' wealth can be more firmly understood from land cadastres and other documents, but many of these date to (just) after the period of study. They do show considerable wealth, but we do not know how much land or other wealth the archbishops had before 1478, since they lost a considerable amount through Ivan III's confiscations. Nor is it clear how archepiscopal wealth expanded or contracted from the twelfth to the fifteenth centuries. Ultimately, the archbishop's apparently vast wealth, while legendary, remains elusive.

Time and again I have had to concede that we simply cannot know what happened in the past with regard to Novgorod's archbishops; the source material is lacking or too brief or too vague (with the chronicles providing the barest facts but often giving no context or explanation) to allow scholars to reach firm conclusions.

Many scholars have tried, to overcome these uncertainties, and in doing so, have provided valuable insight into the archiepiscopal office and the city it served. But I fear some have reached conclusions not borne out by the evidence, seeing modern organization and institutionalization not present in the medieval period. I have tried to focus more on the archbishops than many others who wrote more generally of the church or of the political rivalry between Novgorod and Moscow, to take a multi-faceted approach looking at a number of sources and using a number of disciplines

– art and architecture, archaeology, literature, politics, economics, and religion – to return whenever possible to the primary sources to find what they actually tell us, without the Imperial Russian, Marxist, or other filters, and, as best as can be done, to lay modern biases aside. With this in mind, hopefully this study does give a fuller, more nuanced view of a complex and dynamic office over the course of several centuries, and its importance to our understanding of Eastern Christianity and to Novgorodian and Rus' history and culture.

The old, confident image of the Novgorodian archbishop as something akin to a prince-bishop with clearly-delineated powers, the veritable president of the Novgorodian Republic, overseeing a very institutionalized *veche* and Council of Lords, is not borne out by the primary source evidence, nor is the image of them as rebels against church and state, hell-bent on establishing their own church with themselves at the helm or, worse still, "going Latin", as they broke political and ecclesiastical rank with their legitimate Muscovite suzerain. Again, the situation was more complex. The church and state in Rus' not centralized until later, and a Rus' or Muscovite identity, with Novgorod (or Tver', or Riazan', or other principalities) as integral parts of the state, likely did not exist until the grand princes and their supporters invented it.

The archbishops were, perhaps, the rational actors that political scientists hope to find. They were deeply committed to their faith and their city, prayed to save the city from invading armies and pestilence, worked to see it at peace and enriched economically, artistically, and spiritually, and filled with churches and icons. They fought, quite understandably and justifiably, to defend their city and their office against those who sought to take away or diminish their wealth, power, and authority. But this did not mean they opposed the metropolitans or grand princes at every turn; when they stood up to Kyiv or Moscow, cursed Pskov, or opposed heresy, there were often perfectly reasonable theological and ecclesiastical justifications for doing so, explained by the situation at the time rather than an overall program of rebellion or independence.

But, in another sense, the archbishops were not typical churchmen defending their city. There were several exceptional aspects of the office. Their election was unique among the Rus' episcopate. While many earlier histories simply state that the archbishops were elected by lot from among three candidates, this study shows a more complex electoral process, one evolving considerably from the twelfth to the fifteenth centuries, with election by lots not coming fully into use until the middle of the fourteenth century, with the election of Aleksei, apparently based on Byzantine monastic traditions.

Similarly, we find that many economic, political, and cultural aspects of the office were not fully-developed until the mid to late fourteenth century and thereafter, beginning really with the archiepiscopate of Vasilii Kalika (election did not begin with his death due to the fact that Moisei was on the scene to take up the office again), so that the electoral process was part of the growth in power of the office and probably due to a dilution of power among the city's elite following Ontsifor Lukich's reforms in 1354. As the more numerous *posadnichestvo* could not decide on a candidate, they left it up to a game of chance, God's will as they saw it, to pick an archbishop for them; this "man chosen by God" then had considerable powers that his predecessors never had when fewer *posadniki* held power.

This secular power was far greater than that of other bishops in Rus' or the Orthodox world, but again, it was concentrated in Novgorod, and not exercised in much of the rest of the Novgorodian land, and it really flourished only beginning with Vasilii Kalika. Nor was it firmly held, legally recognized, or well-enumerated compared to the powers exercised by Catholic bishops to the West, although their location along the Catholic Frontier may have meant ideas from their non-Orthodox neighbors crept into Novgorod. And even though the archbishops' position within the city's ruling elite does not come into clear focus in the sources, they, or their cathedral, came to symbolize the city; they served as ambassadors and peacemakers, adjudicated cases in the secular courts, and on occasion drew up and signed treaties. But their political activities, particularly their roles in treaties, were exercised inconsistently, even after the mid-fourteenth century and a clear pattern of political activity is difficult to discern. Even after they became much more politically significant in the late fourteenth century, they seem to have acted in concert with the *boiarstvo* and *posadnichestvo*.

The archbishops' most enduring contribution was their patronage of chroniclers, bookmen, and artisans, and even through a few works they created themselves. Indeed, this cultural activity place them among the greatest cultural patrons in Rus' and Eastern Europe. The sheer number of works produced for Novgorod's archbishops established long-lasting artistic and architectural trends that influenced later art in Moscow and other Rus' cities, and far outshone the cultural contributions of other bishops.

Accordingly, Novgorod's archiepiscopal office was among the most important offices in medieval Novgorod, involved in activities from the church to the market to the landed estate to the court, from cradle to grave, from the border with Estonia to the Ural Mountains, from the White Sea to the Volga and even throughout the wider Rus' and Orthodox world.

Appendix

Bishops and Archbishops of Novgorod 989-1478

St. Ioakim Korsunianin	(ca. 989 - 1030)
Efrem*	(1030 -1035)
St. Luka Zhidiata	(1035 - +10/15/1060)
Stefan	(1060 - 1068)
Feodor	(1069 - 1077)
St. German	(1078 - 1095)
St. Nikita	(1096 - 01/30/1108)
Ioann Pop'ian	(1110 -1130) (+1144)
St. Nifont	(1130 - + 04/21/1156)
St. Arkadii	(1156 - +09/19/1163)
Il'ia (St. Ioann)	(3/28/1165 - +9/7/1186)
Gavriil (St. Grigorii)	(1186 - +5/24/1193)
St. Martirii Rushanin	(1193 - +8/24/1198)
Mitrofan	(1198 - 1211, 1219 - +7/3/1223)
St. Antonii (Dobrynia Iadreikovich)	(1211 - 1219, 1226 - 28, +10/8/1229)
Arsenii*	(1223 - 1225, 1228 - 29)
Spiridon	(1229 - +1249)
Dalmat	(1251 - + 10/21/1274)
Kliment	(1274 - +5/22/1299)
St. Feoktist	(1299 - 1308) (+ 12/23/1310)
David	(1308 - +02/05/1325)
St. Moisei	(1325 - 1330, 1352 - 1359) (+1/25/1363)
St. Vasilii Kalika (Grigorii Kalika)	(1331 - +7/3/1352)
Aleksei	(9/13/1359 - 1388) (+ 2/3/1390)
Ioann	(1388 - 1415) (+6/24/1417)
St. Simeon (Samson)	(8/11/1415 - +6/15/1421)
Feodosii*	(9/1/1421 - 1423) (+ 9/29/1425)
Evfimii I (Emelian Bradatii)	(1423 - 11/1/1429)
St. Evfimii II (Ioann Viazhitskii)	(11/13/1429 - +3/20/1458)
St. Iona	(1458 - 11/8/1470)
St. Feofil	(1471 - 1/24/1480?) (+1482/84?)

(Archbishops in bold; dates are those of election, not necessarily consecration)
* Never consecrated

Bishops	Burial
St. Ioakim Korsunianin	Holy Wisdom
Efrem*	
St. Luka Zhidiata	Holy Wisdom (?)
Stefan	
Feodor	
St. German	Holy Wisdom
St. Nikita	Holy Wisdom
Ioann Popian	Holy Wisdom
St. Nifont	
St. Arkadii	
Il'ia (St. Ioann)	Holy Wisdom
Gavriil (St. Grigorii)	Holy Wisdom
St. Martirii Rushanin	Holy Wisdom
Mitrofan	Holy Wisdom
Antonii	Holy Wisdom
Arsenii*	
Spiridon	Holy Wisdom
Dalmat	Holy Wisdom
Kliment	Holy Wisdom
Feoktist	Annunciation M.
David	Holy Wisdom
Moisei	Skovorodka, then Holy Spirit M.
Vasilii	Holy Wisdom
Aleksei	Derevianitsa Resurrection M.
Ioann	Derevianitsa Resurrection M.
Simeon	Holy Wisdom
Feodosii*	Trinity M. (?)
Evfimii I	?
Evfimii II	Vyazhitskii M.
Iona	Otya Pustina
Feofil	Chudov M.

Table 3.1: Parish staff in the Novgorodian Fifths

Piatina	Churches	Priests	D'iaki	Ponomarii	Storozhi	Proskurnitsy	Deacons
Derevskaia	59	54	42	14	24	28	0
Votskaia	60	51	40	1	25	9	2
Shelonskaia	90	75	62	8	33	50	5
Bezhetskaia	90	65	35	47	0	44	5
Obonozhskaia	50	40	32	15	9	8	0
Total[1]	349	285	211	85	91	139	12

Source: D. A. (Dmitrii Anatol'evich) Balovnev, "Prikhodskoe dukhovenstvo XV-nachala XVI veka po Novgorodskim pistsovym knigam (chilennost' i osobennosti sostava)," *Otechestvennaia istoriia* 4 (Jul.-Aug. 2004): 131-139.

---

[1] By my calculations, Balovnev's figures for each of the Fifths should add up to 211 d'iaki, 85 ponomari, and 139 proskurnitsy, but he gives their totals as 217 d'iaki, 94 ponomari, and 140 proskurnitsy. Thus, the total should be 823 churchmen, rather than the 839 Balovnev gives.

Table 6.1: Tribute Granted to the Archbishop of Novgorod by Princely Charter.

Pogost	sets of 40s (sorochky) of fur
Voldutov in the Onega lands	2
Tudorov in the Onega lands	2
Ivan district	3
Rakula	3
Kegrel	3
The Mouth of the Emtsa River	2
The Mouth of the Vaga River	2
Puite	1
Chiudin	½
Ligoui	1[2]
Vavdit,	2[3]
Vel'	2
Vekshenza River	2
Borka	1
Otmina	1
Toima	1
Poma	½
Tosh'ma	1
Penenich	1
Porogopustitsy	½
Valdit	2
Volotsk on the Mosha River	2
Ema	1
Turov	1

Source: "The Statutory Charter of the Novgorod Prince Sviatoslav Olgovich," Art. 4, in ZDR, 225; PRP, 2: 117; Martin, *Treasure of the Land of Darkness*, 54-55.

---

[2]Plus all the duties from that district.
[3]Plus all the duties from that district.

Table 6.2: Tribute Granted to the Archbishop of Novgorod from the Obonezh'e and Bezichiche Districts

District	Payment in Grivny
Onega District:	
Olonets	3
Svera	1
Iuskola	3
Tervinichi	3
V'iunitsa	1
The Mouth of the Pasha River	½
Pakhitok on the Pasha River	1
Koukuev Hill	1
Permin	1
Kokorok	½
The Masiega Lowlands of the Sias' River	½[4]
Lipsouevich	½
Toivot	1
Lipna	½
Bezichiche (Bezhetskii Verkh) Districts:	
Bezhichi	6 and 10 kuny
Gorodetsk	2 ½
Zmen'	5
Ez'ska	4 and 10 kuny
Rybansk	1 Volga grivna
Iz'sk	½ Volga grivna

Source: "The Statutory Charter of the Novgorod Prince Sviatoslav Olgovich," Arts. 6, 7, ZDR, 225; PRP, 2: 118.

---

[4]The charter also added that "for the journey through all the land 10 grivny to the archbishop and 2 grivny for the priest. Ibid., Art. 6, in ZDR, 225; PRP, 2:118.

Notes

Introduction

1 Upon seizing Kyiv from the Varangians Askold and Dir, Prince Oleg declared it the "Mother of Rus' cities". *Lavrent.,* 23. The chronicler plays on the Greek word *metropolis* – "mother city". Dal' (1957), 329.
2 GIM Sinod. No. 915, *Gennadievskaia Bibliia.*
3 The *Velikie Minei Chet'i* is also rendered *Velikie Chet'i-Minei* and, in the pre-1918 orthography, *Velikiia Minei Chet'i.* I have chosen to use the modern, *Velikie Minei Chet'i,* but have left the pre-1918 orthography for the titles of archival manuscripts.
4 Feodosii (Feodor Mikhailovich Ianovskii) was deposed for opposing the Empress Catherine I's control over the church after Peter's death, and perhaps for opposing Peter's church reforms. The Synod, led by Prokopovich, condemned him in May 1725, and he was imprisoned in the Nikolo-Korelskii Monastery (now in Severodvinsk) where he died in early February 1726. Cracraft, 163-169 (where he is referred to by his anglicized name, Theodosius, or his surname, Yanovskii).
5 On Aleksei and the church's concordat with Stalin, see Dickinson, 337-346. On Antonii, see Tel'pis, 15. On Aleksei II, see Russkaia pravoslavnaia tserkov, "Mitropolit Leningradskii i Novgorodskii Aleksii," ZhMP (1989) No. 7:7; Logachev, 11-13; Pimen (Patriarch of Moscow and All Rus'), 10.
6 On the archbishops and metropolitans to 1892, see Pokrovskii, 63-72; Zdravomislov, 31, 41-42, 47, 60-61, 90. P. Tikhomirov (1891-1900), passim.
7 Sevastyanova and Frison, eds., 7.
8 Karamzin (1969), passim; Tatishchev, passim.
9 Tikhomirov (1956), 138-139. Other scholars have attempted to determine the city's size. R. W. Davies claimed that in the eleventh century, Novgorod had 10,000-15,000 inhabitants and had reached 46,000 by the end of the twelfth. Davies, 125. Henrik Birnbaum gave Novgorod's medieval population at its height at around 25,000, slightly larger than medieval Vienna, Nuremberg, Augsburg, or Strasbourg, but smaller than Kyiv's 40,000 inhab-

itants during its golden age in the mid-eleventh century, and much smaller than the northern Italian cities with populations around 50,000. By comparison, Paris and London are thought to have had 80,000-100,000 inhabitants at this time. Birnbaum (1987), 6-7. Petr Tolochko asserted that Kiev reached 50,000 residents prior to the Mongol conquest, while Novgorod had around 30,000 people. Tolochko, 89. See also Goehrke, (1973), 25-53. A. L. Shapiro claimed Novgorod's population was 32,000 at its height, based on analysis of the *Novgorodskie pistsovye knigi*, the land surveys or cadastres of the late fifteenth and early sixteenth centuries. The total population of the major towns of the Novgorodian Land is thought to have been around 48,400, and the entire Novgorodian Land reaching 520,000 people. Shapiro, 322, 326. See also Pronshtein, 30; Bernadskii, 136; NPK, 3:494, 879-885, 957-960, 5:230, 261-262. Some primary sources point to a rather large population. Thus, Ghillebert de Lannoy a Flemish visitor to the city in the fifteenth century, mentioned a Novgorodian army of 40,000 men. Potvin and Mouzeau, eds., 33. Chronicle accounts claim the grand prince's army defeated 40,000 Novgorodians at the Battle on the Shelon' River in July 1471. *Nikon*. (PSRL 12), 135; *Stepennaia kniga*, 2:538; PskL 2:182. This would indicate a large population (perhaps as many as half a million) from which to muster such a sizeable army. Most modern scholars believe these figures are greatly exaggerated, a typical problem of medieval sources throughout Europe. See Baiov, 22, 79; Razin 2:314.

10 The scholarly debate as to whether Kyivan Rus' was a unified state or merely a confederation of principalities is ongoing. Recent archaeological and historical research suggests southern Rus' (Kyiv, Chernihiv, and Pereislav) did not suffer economic decline from Polovtsy (Cuman) raids, and the alleged migration to Suzdalia in the twelfth century may have been an invention of Vasilii Kliuchevskii. Kliuchevskii (2000), 1:264ff. Thus, Kyiv's decline was only relative, and Rus' remained culturally, ecclesiastically, economically, and politically united. Martin (2007), 102-105; Miller (1986), 224-225; Hellie, 73.

11 Sevastyanova and Frison, eds., 109, 125.
12 Ianin, (1990): 84-91.
13 M. Tikhomirov (1956), 383.
14 Dejevsky (1984), 206.
15 Bernadskii, 26.
16 This is based on tribute calculated at 5,000-7,000 rubles annually. In 1480, Ivan III only sent 1,000 rubles, thus keeping 4/5ths to

6/7ths for himself. This, however, was at the end of Mongol rule and not indicative of earlier tribute amounts or how much the grand princes kept for themselves. Charles Halperin discounts direct embezzlement, since the khans considered it a capital offense, and argues instead for the grand princes exempting their own land from taxation. Halperin (1985), 78, 84.

17   Martin (1985), 81-84.
18   Ianin (2006), 1:210; Paul, "Continuity and Change," 300-301, 304-305.
19   On the fur trade and its importance to Novgorod, see Martin (1985), esp. 61-85, 130-140, 152-163; idem, (1978): 401-421; Franklin and Shepard, 331-333; Kerner, Chapters 2 and 3. For the fur trade in a wider European context, see Postan, 119-256.
20   Platonov, (1997), 136. Tikhomirov points to its strategic position along this trade route as the reason for it becoming "a giant of a city in comparison with the other towns in the northern part of medieval Rus'." M. Tikhomirov (1956), 375.
21   Rowell, 22.
22   A modern footbridge spans the river just north (downstream) of where medieval wooden bridge once stood. Troianovskii (2009): 61, 101.
23   Vernadsky (1976), 199. Langer, 47; Ianin, "Problemy," 49; idem, (2006), 192.
24   This is noted on a plaque on the Church of St. Nicholas in the Market and a map south of the Church of John the Forerunner on Opoki. (Visit, May 13, 2007).
25   For more on the geographic and political structure, see Halperin (1999), 350-51; Ianin (2006), 195-197; Sevastyanova and Frison, eds., 109-197.
26   Ianin (2006), 203-204.
27   Birnbaum (1981), 86, 89-90, 96; idem (1996); Goehrke (1981); Ianin (2003), 236-273; Kliuchevskii (1994), 172-206; idem, (1957), 2:68-69; Leuschner (1980); Nikitskii (1869): 294-309; Paul (2008), 75, 77, 78; Platonov (1997), 135-144, esp., 137; Vernadsky (1976), 98, 197-201; Zernack (1967); idem (1973), 9-23, esp. 15. There is no direct reference to the *sovet gospod* in the Rus' sources; the term is a modern invention. However, there are references to "the lords" in both Novgorodian and, particularly, Pskovite documents. See, Grekov, ed. (1940), 237-54, esp. Articles 10, 18, 24, 25, 26, 27, 29, 73, 106, 108, and 111, pp. 238-241, 248, 252-254; "Pskovskaia sudnaia gramota," ZDR, 1:332-334, 338, 341. Daniel Kaiser translates the term as "the Council," but in Russian it is "gospod" – "lords". Whether this is a reference to the Council of Lords, the boiars more gener-

ally, or even to "Lord Pskov" is unclear. Kaiser, ed. (1992), 88-104. Two reports by Hanseatic emissaries from 1292 and 1331, mention *"der heren rade,"* but it is not clear if this is an institution of government or an informal grouping of boiars. Napierskii, ed. (1868), also published as RLA, 75:61; Bunge, 1.546:683. Jonas Granberg rejects the existence of the *sovet gospod* entirely, contending "the sources presented so far are insufficient to support the conclusion that an institution such as the sovet gospod existed." Granberg, "Sovet Gospod," 396-401, esp. 401. Cf. Lukin (2014), 458-503. See also Chapter Four below.

28 Dejevsky (1984), 208.
29 On the Novgorodian princely office, see Paul (2008).
30 Halperin (1985), 50; Paul (2008), 82-83.
31 Halperin (1999), 347-348.
32 Iaroslav Shchapov wrote that Vasilii Kalika was "in reality the head of the Principality of Novgorod." Shchapov, "Vasilii Kalika," in MERSH 41:224. On the archbishop's political activities, see Halperin (1999), 361-362; Paul, (2007), 231-270; idem, "Vasilii Kalika," 253-271.
33 Fennell (1968), 101-102.
34 Fletcher, 424.
35 Guimon, 227.
36 On the rewriting of the chronicles, see Lur'e, (1994).
37 Radishchev (1961), 38; Kliuchevskii (2000), 1:401-403; Sergeevich, passim. Nikolai Karamzin also saw Novgorod as a democracy, but thought democracy unstable and dangerous. Karamzin (1969), 4:47, 48, 75-76, 110-111, 142-144; Black, 106, 111-112. For twentieth-and twenty-first century views, see Froianov (1974); Froianov and Dvornichenko; M. Tikhomirov (1956), 217-225; Lukin (2016), 279-306; Sevastyanova, 1-23. For more nuanced discussions of the various views of Novgorod see Halperin (1999); Levin (1989), 128, 129; Paul (2015), 229-242; idem (2008), 75.
38 Lermontov, 1:260. I am grateful to Jason Merrill for pointing me to the citation.
39 Ianin (2003), passim; Iushkov, *Ocherki*, 216; Idem, *Obshchestvenno-politicheskii stroi*, 360; Bernadskii, 154-161. For comparisons with other medieval cities, see Hansen, passim; Nicholas, *Growth of the Medieval City*; idem, *Later Medieval City*; Hamm, ed., passim.
40 For further discussion of the *veche*, see Granberg, "Political and Administrative Structure," 98-108; idem (2006); Paul, "Iaroslavichi," 39-59; Platonov (1916).
41 NPL.

42	*N4* (PSRL 4).
43	*Sof. 1* (PSRL 6, pt. 1); *Sof. 2* (PSRL 6, pt. 2).
44	For analysis of the chronicles, see Lur'e (1994); Bobrov (2001), as well as the introductions to the various volumes of PSRL.
45	*N2* (PSRL 3).
46	N3 (PSRL 3).
47	PskL 2 vols. (PSRL 5).
48	*Lavrent.* (PSRL 1.1). Also called the *Povest' vremennykh let and the Russian (or Rus') Primary Chronicle* up to the year 1108, it is continued to 1377 in the *Suzdalian Chronicle (Suzdal.)* (PSRL 1.2).
49	*Ipat.* (PSRL 2.1), (PSRL 2.2), (PSRL 2.3).
50	*Mosk.* (PSRL 25).
51	*Vosk.* (PSRL 7); *Prodol. Vosk.* (PSRL 8); *Ermolin.* (PSRL 23); *Ermitazh.* (PSRL 25); VPL, (PSRL 26); Zimin and Levina, eds.
52	*Nikon.*, (PSRL 9-13).
53	GVNP; see also Marasinova.
54	NPK; PKOP; Gusev, ed. (1908); Baranov, ed.
55	RIB 6.
56	AI, 1:1334-1598.
57	DAI.
58	RFA (1986-1992); RFA (2008).
59	DSHRM.
60	Beneshevich, ed. (1915); idem, DSK, (1905).
61	AAE; Žužek; Tanner, ed.; NPNF, vol. 9: Chrysostom; Percival; Athanasius, *Historia Arianorum* and *Letters*, NPNF, vol. 4; Basil The Great, *Letters*, in Way, trans., Deferrari, et al., eds.; Cyprian of Carthage, *Letters*, in ANF vol. 5; Connolly; Funk; PL; PG.
62	MM.
63	PRP; ZDR; Kaiser, ed. (1992).
64	RLA; Napierskii (1857). The *Livonian Rhymed Chronicle* also gives some insight into the relations between Rus' and its Catholic neighbors to the West. See L. Meyer, ed.
65	Joackim and Hubatsch; Strehlke.
66	Adam of Bremen; MGH *Nova Series*, 9.8: 32-33; see also Napierskii (1857), as well as several documents from PL and PG; Jaffe, ed.
67	*Akty otnosiashchesiia k istorii zapadnoi Rossii*, vol. 1 (1361-1598); Pashuto and Shtal, eds.
68	Bugoslavskii, ed., 194-237; Evseev, ed., 14-16; Thomson (1992), 205-217.
69	RIB 6:21-62; Fennell and Stokes; Fennell (1995).
70	Filaret 3:21-25; Kalaidovich, ed., 243; Il'ia (a.k.a., Ioann, Archbishop of Novgorod) "Pravila Chernoriztsem," in Nevostruev, ed. (1862-1863), 2:31-36.

71	Antonii (Dobrynia Iadreikovich, Archbishop of Novgorod), (1877); idem, (1899).
72	For analysis of the letter, see Klibanov (1960), 138-49; Gurevich, 3-27. See Chapter Two, below.
73	"Povest' o pobede Novgorodtsev nad Suzdal'tsami," in Kushelev-Bezborodko and Kostomarov, eds., 1:241-222; "Skazanie o bitve Novgorodtsev s Suzdal'tsami," PLDR, 4:448-453; "Povest' o postroennii blagoveshchenskogo monastyria v Novgorode," in Kushelev-Bezborodko and Kostomarov, eds., 1:255-256; "Povest' o Blagoveshchenskoi tserkvi," PLDR, 4: 464-467; "Povest' o puteshestvii Ioanna Novgorodskogo," in Kushelev-Bezborodko and Kostomarov, eds., 1:245-248; "Povest' o puteshestvii Ioanna Novgorodskogo na bese," PLDR, 4: 454-463; "Povest' o Shchile Posadnike Novgorodskom," in Kushelev-Bezborodko and Kostomarov, eds., 1:21-26. A number of these works are reprinted in BLDR, especially vols. 6 and 7.
74	"Povest' o Moisee, Arkhiepiskope Novgorodom," "Povest' o Evfimie, Arkhiepiskope Novgorodom," and "Vospominanie o blagoslovennom Ione," in Kushelev-Bezborodko and Kostomarov, eds., 4:10-15, 16-26, 27-35; The Vospominanie is also known as "Povest' ob Ione, arkhiepiskope Novgorodskom," PLDR, 5:334-349; BLDR, 7:232-253.
75	Ianin (2003); idem (1970); idem (1990), 84-91; idem, (1988); idem (1991); idem (1992); idem (1998); Ianin, and Gaidukov, 283-314.
76	See Dejevsky (1984), 206-223; idem (1977); Thompson; Kovalev (2002), 38-50; Musin (1996), 147-58; Porfiridov (1958), 222-225.
77	Golubinskii (1995); idem (1903); idem (1871).
78	Makarii (Bulgakov), *Istoriia*.
79	Kartashev.
80	Fennell (1995),
81	Tomilin, passim; Zdravomislov, passim. See also the lives of Moisei and Arsenii in P. Tikhomirov, ed. (1890); idem, (1891).
82	Kuzmina.
83	Musin (2016).
84	Crummey; Fennell (1983); idem (1961); Franklin and Shepard; Martin (2007); Riasanovsky; Rowell, passim; Vernadsky (1965); idem (1947); idem (1965); idem (1953); idem (1959).
85	In addition to narrative histories, lists of Russian hierarchs have been drawn up over the years, fitting the Novgorodian archeparchy into the wider Rus' church. See Amvrosii (Ornatskii, Archbishop of Penza and Saratov); Durnovo (1892-1898); Stroev.
86	Nikitskii (1879); idem (1883), 1-15; idem (1871), 1-70.

87	Birnbaum (1996); idem (1981).
88	Sokol, "Veche," in MERSH, 41:241.
89	Pares, 73.
90	Birnbaum (1996); idem (1981).
91	Birnbaum (1981), 95.
92	Platonov (1997), 139.
93	Ibid., 140.
94	Khoroshev (1989), 36.
95	Raba (1977), 161-173.
96	Raba (1979), 52.
97	Ianin (2003).
98	Khoroshev (1989),15, 22-23, 27, 32, 33, 37, 47, 63, 83, 84-86.
99	Kliuchevskii (2000), 1:405; idem, (1856-1859), 2:72-73.
100	Birnbaum (1981), 86.
101	See Vernadsky (1959), 38.
102	Birnbaum (1981), 87.
103	Fedotov, 2:191.
104	Ibid., 2:192; Dmitri Obolensky noted that Novgorod was the wealthiest ecclesiastical establishment in Eastern Slavdom. *XI Congrès International de Sciences Historiques*, 1:92, cited in Billington, 81. See also Grekov (1957-1960), 3:40-191.
105	Grekov, Cherepnin, and Pashuto, eds., 351. Emphasis added.
106	Ianin (2003), 236-273.
107	Rasmussen (1979), see also idem, (1977).

Chapter One

1	Canon 285 §3 of the current Code of Canon Law of the Roman Catholic Church forbids clerics from assuming "public offices which entail a participation in the exercise of civil power." *Code of Canon Law*, 100-101. This prohibition goes back to the first centuries of the church. See Canons 6, 81 and 83 of the *Apostolical Canons*, DSK 1:63, 79, 80. See below.
2	Twenty-six Anglican bishops sit in the House of Lords ("the Lords Spiritual"), but this is largely honorific. They give speeches in the house but do not hold government portfolios or otherwise carry out political functions, and do not normally vote in the House. The Church of England, the Church of Norway, the National Church of Denmark, the National Church of Iceland, and a number of others, are state churches. Catholicism is the state religion in Argentina, Bolivia, Costa Rica, Slovakia and several other states. The Russian Orthodox Church has a special status in Russia as well.

	The bishops in these churches may be influential, but still do not hold actual political power.
3	On Il'ia see NPL 31, 219; N2, 125; N4, 160; *Sof. 1*, 233-234. The *Novgorodian Third Chronicle* says he was consecrated bishop in 1163 and made archbishop in 1167; most others say he was consecrated in 1165 and made archbishop later that year. N3, 215. The *Rospis', ili kratkii letopisets novgorodskikh vladyk*, a supplement to the *Novgorodian Second Chronicle*, and the *Dubrovskii spisok* of the *Novgorodian Fourth Chronicle* says that prior to his episcopate he was priest at the Church of St. Blaise on the Sofia Side. *Priblav.* N2, 180; N4, 472. Vasilii, whose original name was Grigorii Kalika, was priest at the Church of Sts. Cosmas and Damian on Slave Street. NPL, 99, 342.
4	"*Quod monachus mulieres et episcopos vitare debeat.*" John Cassian, *De coenobiorum institutis*, Book 11, Chapter 18, in PL 49:418; Sterk, 13.
5	Leviticus 21:16-24 forbids the mutilated from entering the Judaic priesthood.
6	On Ammonius, see Palladius, *Historia Lausiaca*, chapter 12; Sterk, 2.
7	Athanasius, *Epistola ad Dracontium*, sect. 7, PG 25:531-532.
8	Athanasius says Dracontius has been exiled "to the desert places about Clysma." *Historia Arianorum ad monachos*, sect. 72, PG, 25:779-780. Jerome writes he was exiled to the fortress of Theubatus. *Vita Sancti Hilarionis*, 30, PL 23:44. He is listed as bishop (in fact, his replacement is listed) in Athanasius' *Festal Letter* of AD 368; Sterk, 16-18. Only an excerpt is available in Greek and Latin in Migne, PG, 26.2:1439-1440. The entire letter is translated from the Coptic in Brakke, 334.
9	NPL, 342, 365.
10	NPL, 373.
11	Lenhoff and Martin, 359n74.
12	Paul (2007), 258.
13	Hence the forcible tonsure of people to get rid of them politically, such as Byzantine Emperors Theodosius III, Artabasdos and Michael I, the boiars Ivan and Vasilii Patrikeev, and Grand Prince Vasilii III's first wife, Solomonia Saburova, to name just a few.
14	Mt. 16:18 is seen by the Catholic Church as establishing the Papacy, along with Jn 21:15-19. Mt 18:18 (the power to bind and loose) and Mt. 28:18-20 are often cited as the source of the episcopate.
15	The choice of Matthias to replace Judas Iscariot is perhaps the closest example. Acts 1:15-26.
16	We know that Paul met with the elders (*presbetyroys* – usually

	rendered "priests") of Ephesus at Miletus in Acts 20:17. He, however, also addresses the bishops (apparently there were more than one at Ephesus), telling them: "Keep watch over yourselves and over all the flock, of which the Holy Spirit has made you overseers (*episkopoys*), to shepherd the church of God that he obtained with the blood of his own Son." Acts 20:28.
17	"Rekindle the gift of God that is within you through the laying on my hands." 2 Tim 1:6. The first seven deacons were also ordained by the laying on of hands. Acts 6:6.
18	*Episkop* in Russian. The Greeks also use(d) the term *archiereus* (in Russian, *arkhierei*), literally "high priest." See below.
19	While modern biblical scholars consider the letters to Timothy and Titus to be Pseudo-Pauline, they remain useful for our purposes since they were considered to be authentically Pauline and canonical by the medieval Rus' church. For the sake of convenience, I will continue to refer to Paul, rather than "Pseudo-Paul."
20	The term bishop probably did not denote a specific ecclesiastical office at this time. Paul addresses his letter to the Philippians "to all the holy ones in Christ Jesus who are in Philippi, with the bishops (overseers - *episkopois*) and deacons (ministers - *diakonois*)" (Phil 1:1). indicating several "overseers" at Philippi. Since the Emperor Diocletian did not establish the diocesan administrative structure for the Empire until the late third century, from which the church took it, a clear administrative structure, with bishops overseeing separate cities or dioceses, could not have existed earlier than that.
21	1 Tim. 3:1-7.
22	Titus 1:7-9.
23	*Didache*, 15.1; Beneshevich, ed. (1915), 1:11. They are not in the *Novgorodian Synodal Kormchaia* of 1282 (GIM Sinod. No. 132), or in DSK.
24	*Didache*, 15.2-4; Beneshevich, ed. (1915), 1:11.
25	Connolly, xi.
26	According to its colophon, the *Novgorodian Synodal Kormchaia of 1282*, (GIM Syn. 132) was made under the patronage of Prince Dmitrii Aleksandrovich and given to Archbishop Kliment. Sreznevskii (1897), 85.
27	Connolly, 4.ii.1:30. Specifically, the bishop was to be no younger than 50; see Connolly, 28.
28	Ibid. See also Chapter 3 of Ignatius of Antioch's *Epistle to the Magnesians* (*Iz poslaniia k Magniisitsam*) in which he addresses the issue

	of familiarity versus respect for a young bishop. (In the letter he also refers to God the Father as "the bishop of us all"); Beneshevich, ed. (1915), 1:20
29	The instructions go on to say that he ought to be lettered, but if not, he was to be at least "versed and skilled in the word." Connolly, 4.ii.1:30.
30	Ibid., 4.ii.1:28.
31	Ibid., 30.
32	Ibid., 31-32.
33	Ibid., 32.
34	Ibid., 4.ii.5:35.
35	Ibid., 4.ii.3:32.
36	Ibid., 4.ii.5:36.
37	Ibid., 7.ii.18:56.
38	Ibid., 6.ii.17:54.
39	Ibid., 7.ii.19:60, 62.
40	Ibid., 63.
41	Ibid., 7.ii.17:55.
42	Ibid., 6.ii.17:54.
43	Ibid., 7.ii.18:56.
44	Ibid., 7.ii.20:64.
45	Ibid.
46	Ibid., 8.ii.25:80.
47	Ibid., 7.ii.24:76.
48	Ibid., 9.ii.26:88-89. Similarly, Ignatius of Antioch's saw the bishop as an archetype of the Father in his *Epistle to the Trallians*. (*Iz poslaniia k Tralliitsam*), Section 3.1 in Beneshevich, ed. (1915), 1:21.
49	Connolly, 9.ii.26:88. The bishop is also likened to God Almighty or called "God after God" several other times in the text, see Chapters Five and Six, sections ii.11-ii.12:40; and 7.ii.19:60.
50	On dating the *Apostolical Canons*, see ANF, 7:388 (in which they treat the *Apostolic Constitutions* as a whole). For the canons themselves, see pp. 500-505; PG 1:509-517. The numbering of the canons is slightly different in DSK.
51	The *Novgorodian Kormchaia* has an exposition on the *Apostolical Canons*. I. Sreznevskii (1897), 90-91.
52	Canon 80, DSK 1:79.
53	Canon 29, DSK 1:67.
54	Canon 30, DSK 1:67.
55	Canons 58 and 59, DSK 1:74.
56	Canons 6 and 81, DSK 1:63, 79;
57	Canon 83, DSK 1:80.

58	Canon 52, DSK 1:73. Lk 15:7.
59	Canon 27, DSK 1:66-67. Theologically, the bishop is entrusted with all souls in his diocese, not just the Christian ones.
60	Canon 76, DSK 1:78.
61	Canons 47, 49, and 50, DSK 1:72-73. The Trinitarian baptismal formula is from Mt 28:19.
62	Canon 35, DSK 1:69.
63	Canons 38, 40, and 41, DSK 1:70.
64	Canon 39, DSK 1:70.
65	Canon 55, DSK 1:74. The quotes are from Exodus 22:28 and Acts 23:5.
66	Canons 42, 44, and 54, DSK 1:71, 74.
67	Gen. 1:31.
68	Gen. 1:27.
69	Canon 51, DSK 1:73.
70	Canon 25, DSK 1:66.
71	Ukazatel' Kanonov, DSK 1:57.
72	Clement of Rome, *First Epistle to the Corinthians*, 42.5, PG 1:291-294; *Iz poslaniia k Korinfianam (okolo 96 goda)*, in Beneshevich, ed. (1915), 1:15. A footnote in the *Ante Nicene Fathers* notes that Clement has altered the text of Isaiah 60:17. ANF 1:16. The verse from Isaiah actually says "I will make your overseers peace and your taskmasters righteousness." The Greek word for overseer is, again, "*episkopos*," from which English gets the word "bishop," but is used symoblicly, not as an office or institution.
73	Clement, *First Epistle to the Corinthians*, 44.1, PG 1:296-300; *Iz poslaniia k Korinfianam*, in Beneshevich, ed. (1915), 1:16.
74	Ignatius of Antioch, *Ad Trall.*, 3.1, PG 5:677-678; Chapter 2 is entitled *"Be subject to the bishop."* PG 5: 675-676; *Iz poslaniia k Trallitsam*, in Beneshevich, ed. (1915), 1:21-22.
75	Ignatius of Antioch, *Epistle to the Ephesians (Epistula Ephesios)*, PG 5:649-650; *Iz poslaniia k Efesianam* in Beneshevich, ed. (1915), 1:19.
76	Ignatius of Antioch, *Epistle to the Smyraeneans (Epistula Smyrnaeos)*, PG 5:713-714; *Iz poslaniia k Smiriianam*, in Beneshevich, ed. (1915), 1:22.
77	Cyprian of Carthage, *Epistle 73* (Number 74 in PL) (*Ad Pompeium contra Epistolam Stephani de Haeretici Baptizandis*), sect. 10; There is a brief summary of it in PL 4:412-413 and it does not appear in Beneshevich, ed. (1915). See also Cunningham, 36.
78	Cyprian of Carthage, *Epistle* 68 (Number 79 in PL) (*Ad Florentium Pupianum de obtrectatoribus*) sect. 8, PL 4:406. This section is reproduced in Latin in Beneshevich, where it is numbered Epistle 66. Beneshevich, ed. (1915), 1:49.

79 Ware (1963, 1964), 255.
80 The Greek church says that the bishop serves the church "in place and as a type of Christ" (*"eis topon kai typon Xristoy"*). See, for example, Metropolitan Germanos of Il'ia.
81 Basil the Great, DSK 1:509-510, 512-514. These are in the *Novgorodian Kormchaia*. I. Sreznevskii (1897), 97.
82 There is no single accepted text of the *Kormchaia kniga*, but rather several *Kormchie*, though most redactions have many of the same documents. These include the *Efremovskii* redaction of Bulgarian origin, the Serbian *Ilovitskii* redaction of 1262, the *Novgorodian Synodal Kormchaia* (ca.1280-1282), and the Riazan *Kormchaia* of 1284. There must have been *Kormchie* before this, though, since Žužek demonstrates that the Questions of Kirik (*Voproshanie Kirika*), from the archiepiscopate of Nifont, utilized the *Kormchaia kniga*, indicating it was available in mid-twelfth century Novgorod. Žužek, 38; DSK 1:iii; M. N. Tikhomirov, and Milov, 8-9. On the manuscript tradition of early Russian *Kormchie*, see Beliakova, Moshkova, and Oparina, esp. 46-50.
83 First Council of Nicaea, Canon 15 and First Council of Constantinople Canon 2, DSK 1: 90, 96. Canon 5 of the Council of Chalcedon confirms this. DSK 1:115. The canons of First Nicaea are in the *Novgorodian Kormchaia*. I. Sreznevskii (1897), 91. Archbishop Dionisii of Suzdal' preached against the *Strigol'niki* in the Novgorodian eparchy in the 1380s, but he had been sent there with letters from the patriarch and orders to root out the heresy. RIB 6.22: 191-198; AfED, 230-234; NPL, 378-379.
84 Council of Chalcedon, Canon 2, DSK 1: 112-113. The canons are included in the *Novgorodian Kormchaia*. I. Sreznevskii (1897), 93.
85 The decrees of the Council of Vladimir were included in the *Novgorodian Kormchaia* under the title: "Pravilo Mitropolita Kiurila Rouskogo," I. Sreznevskii (1897), 108; they are published in full in RIB 6:84-102.
86 Apparently, the gold *grivna* is meant rather than the silver one. Cf., Fotii's letter below.
87 AAE 1.382:484-485.
88 Council of Chalcedon, Canons 8 and 9, DSK 1:116-17.
89 Council of Antioch, Canon 24, DSK 1:263.
90 Council of Antioch, Canon 9, DSK 1:256.
91 Council of Sardica, Canon 7, DSK 1:286. The Canons of Sardica are in the *Novgorodian Kormchaia*. I. Sreznevskii (1897), 93-94. One of the demands made by Ivan IV for him to return to Moscow after his "abdication" in 1564-1565 was that he be allowed to condemn

those he wished, without the metropolitan, archbishops, bishops, archimandrites, or hegumens interceding on their behalf. *Nikon.* (PSRL 13), 2:392.
92 Council of Sardica, Canon 7, DSK 1:286.
93 Council of Carthage, Canon 6, DSK 1:314-315. The Canons of Carthage are included in the *Novgorodian Kormchaia.* I. Sreznevskii (1897), 94.
94 Council of Carthage, Canons 10 and 11, DSK 1:317-318.
95 Council of Carthage, Canon 12, DSK 1:318.
96 Council of Carthage, Canon 13, DSK 1:319. Similarly, Canon 4 of First Nicaea decreed that all the bishops of a province should consecrate a new bishop, if possible, but at least three must do so, with the consent of the others and the approval of the local metropolitan. See NPNF, 14:11.
97 Canon 53 (57 in the Greek text) of the Council of Carthage, DSK 1:348-349. Hence the canonicity of Dionisii's activities in the Novgorodian archeparchy in the 1380s.
98 Canon 55 (59 in the Greek text) of the Council of Carthage, DSK 1:353-354. In this originally Latin canon, the right is specific to the bishop of Carthage (See PL 76:198-99), mistakenly called Karkhidon here in the Greek text, and then Kalkidon (Chalcedon) in the Slavic.
99 Canon 123 (125 in the Greek text) of the Council of Carthage, DSK 1:427.
100 Canon 133 (134 in the Greek text) of the Council of Carthage, DSK 1:438-443. The canon is in the form of a letter to the bishop of Rome granting him appellate rights over accused priests in the Carthaginian church.
101 Canon 19 of the Quinisext Council, DSK 1:158. The Canons of Quinisext are included in the *Novgorodian Kormchaia.* I. Sreznevskii (1897), 94-95.
102 NPL, 67, 272. Arsenii later became hegumen of the Khutyn and then the Iur'ev monasteries.
103 NPL, 90, 330.
104 NPL, 99, 342. or "good, gentle, and humble" in the Younger Redaction.
105 Kiprian had been a Bulgarian monk on Mount Athos and acted as Patriarch Philotheus' envoy to Russia and Lithuania. Droblenkova and Prokhorov, "Kiprian (ok. 1330-16.IX.1406) Mitropolit Kievskii i vseia Rusi," in SKKDR, 2.1:471-472.
106 Gen. 37:12-14.
107 The letter is not included in RIB volume 6 or AI. It is printed in

Pravoslavnyi sobesednik (1860), pt. 2, 84-85, as well as Prokhorov (1978), 195. DSHRM, No. 14. "He that receiveth you receiveth Me." is from Mt. 10:40 and Jn. 13:20.

108 A. Alekseev (2012), 56; AfED 1:233; RFA (2008), 119:400; AI 1.4:5.
109 A. Alekseev (2012), 58.
110 AI 1.21:44. He claimed several patriarchs supported the emperor.
111 AI 1.22:47; He quotes Canon 44 of the *Apostolical Canons*; DSK 1:71.
112 AI 1.2:42-43; RIB 6.42: 365-376, esp. 367-368; Canon 31 in DSK 1:67; AfED 3:244; DSHRM No. 6.
113 AI 1.21:43; Canon 5 of the Council of Antioch, DSK 1:255; AfED 3:244. Canon 5 (6 in the *Kormchaia kniga*) of the Council of Gangra forbids the clergy from holding assemblies without the consent of the local bishop. The canons of the Councils of Antioch and Gangra are included in the *Novgorodian Kormchaia kniga*. I. Sreznevskii (1897), 92.
114 The imagery is taken from Mt. 13:24-30.
115 AI 1.21:43; RIB 6.42:369-370: AfED 3:244-245. The misnumbering appears in several manuscripts. See RGB F. 256 Sobranie rukopisnykh knig N. P. Rumiantseva, No. 204, fols. 406v-407; GIM Sinod. No. 562, Sbornik mitropolich'ikh gramot, fol. 319. There is no Canon 13 of the First Council of Constantinople and Canon 13 of First Nicaea deals with Viaticum. DSK 1:89-90. It is unclear to which canon Fotii was actually referring.
116 AI 1.21:43; it is actually Canon 7 of the Council of Gangra, DSK 1: 246; AfED 3:245.
117 AI 1.21:43; DSK 1:317; AfED 3:245.
118 AI 1.21:43; AfED 3:245; Epistle 246, PG, 78:685-686. Scholars debate the attribution of these letters to Isidore. On their availability in Slavic translation, see Thomson (2018), 46.
119 AI 1.21:43-44; AfED 3:245-246; PG, 62:85.
120 Thomson (2018), 46.

Chapter Two

1 The seventeenth-century *Hustyn Chronicle* identified five "conversions" of Rus': 1.) by St. Andrew in the first century, 2.) Under Patriarch Photius in the 860s, 3) Sts. Cyril and Methodius's mission to Crimea and Khazars in 860, the Conversión of Princess Olga ca. 955, and the Baptism of Rus' under Vladimir in 988. *Gustyn.*, 39-41.
2 *Lavrent.*, 118; Labunka (1988-1989), 159-193
3 *Sof. 1*, 105, 106; *Ermitazh.*, 365. On the earliest bishoprics, see Shchapov (1989), 33-37.

4	Several chronicles claim Patriarch Photius of Constantinople (r. 858-867, 877-886; d. 893) played a part. See N4, 90; *Sof. 1*, 105; *Ermitazh.*, 365; *Vosk.*, 313. The *Hypatian Chronicle* mentions Basil and Constantine, but not the patriarch. *Ipat.* (PSRL 2.2), 94-106. Basil II was indeed emperor in 988, often mentioned along with his brother Constantine VIII, co-emperor until Basil's death in 1025, then sole emperor until 1028. However, Patriarch Nicholas II (r. 979-991) was patriarch at the time of the Baptism. The Emperor Constantine VII Porphyrogenitus claimed in his *Life of Basil I* that Photius' successor, Ignatius (r. 847 to 858 and 867-877), converted Rus'. Bekker, ed. (1838), 344.
5	Poppe (1997), 311-392.
6	*Ipat.* (PSRL 2.2), 96-97; *Sof. 1*, 100-101; *Ermitazh.*, 362-365. Often written as "Akim" in the chronicles.
7	Amvrosii, 1:45. Iaroslav Shchapov does not list Mikhail or Leontii among the Kyivan metropolitans, arguing they and several later metropolitans were probably legendary. He and Pavel Stroev list Feofilakt (r. 988-ca.1018) as the first Kyivan metropolitan. Shchapov (1989), 191-192; Stroev, 1. See also Poppe, "Political Background of the Baptism of Rus'," 202-204, 224, 228.
8	Dates for the establishment of the Novgorodian eparchy range from 988 to 992. N3, 207 (s.a. 988); N2, 179 (s.a. 989). *Ipat.* (PSRL 2.1), 258 (s.a. 990). Others give the year as 991. *Sof. 1*, 121; *Vosk.*, 313; *Stepennaia kniga*, 1:113-114. Tatishchev wrote that Ioakim arrived in Rus' in 991. Tatishchev, 1:107. Amvrosii, Durnovo, Kalinnikov, and Pavel Tikhomirov all give the date as 992. Amvrosii, 1:67; Durnovo (1892-1898), 1:35; Kalinnikov, 5, 16.; P. Tikhomirov (1891-1900), 1:9-10. Stroev gives no start dates for Ioakim or Luka. Stroev, 33.
9	N3, 208; Golubinskii (1995), 1.2:107-108; P. Tikhomirov (1891-1900), 1:14-15. Kenneth Conant interprets the "tops" as different roof levels rather than cupolas. Conant, 77, 79. Tikhomirov writes they were cupolas representing Christ and the Twelve Apostles. P. Tikhomirov (1891-1900), 1:14-15. The wooden churches of Northern Russia, such as the Church of the Transfiguration at Kizhi, on an island in Lake Onega (in what once was the Novgorodian Land), may show how multiple cupolas would have looked, although it dates to 1714 and has twenty-two cupolas. "Wooden Architecture," in Voyce, plates XXXIV-XXXVIII, esp. the churches of Kizhi, plates XXXVI-XXXVII; Brumfield (1983), 366-384; idem (1993), 501-520. See also the wooden Church of the Dormition in Varzug in the Murmansk Oblast', in Grabar', 195. There is also

the Novgorodian Museum of Popular Wooden Architecture, just north of the Iur'ev Monastery, with reconstructions of wooden churches and chapels from different historic periods and districts of the Novgorodian Land. None of these, however, have more than two or three cupolas and are of a later period.

10   On Novgorod archaeology and the site of the Cathedral of Holy Wisdom, see Thompson.

11   Malyshevskii contends Luka's surname may indicate Jewish origins but Evseev and Sobolevskii argue it is a Novgorodian variant of the name Georgii Malyshevskii, 2.1:49-52; Evseev, ed., 7-24; Sobolevskii, 255-256; Tvorogov, "Luka Zhidiata, episkop novgorodskii," in SKKDR, 1:251.

12   Priselkov (2003), 37-53.

13   Ianin (1988), 169-178.

14   Vadym Aristov argues that Ioakim (Akim), Stefan, Feodor, and German were "fictitious souls" invented in the fifteenth century to fill gaps in the historical record from the earlier years of the eparchy. Aristov, 50.

15   NPL, 31, 219; *Sof. 1*, 234. The archiepiscopal title was a personal honor bestowed on Nifont, but came to be tied to the eparchy with Il'ia. After 1165, and prior to creation of the Novgorodian metropolitanate in 1589, Martirii (r. 1193-1198) is the only prelate to have not held the title. The chronicles refer to him as such, but his three lead seals that have been discovered never bear the archiepiscopal title. Ianin (1970), 1:56. The title seems an honorific in the Rus' metropolis, since the patriarchs never refer to the Novgorodian prelates as "archbishops". See MM, 1.156:348; 1.267:522; 2.444:177; 2.446:181. Patriarch Antony IV, in a letter dated to between 1388 and 1395, refers to the "bishop of Novgorod," but then writes that Pskov was under the Novgorodian bishops' "archiepiscopate." (*"o bogoliubivii Episkope velikogo Novgoroda i poderzhashchaisia tvoei arkhiepiskope Plskove grade i prochikh predel"*). He refers to Dionisii of Suzdal' as "archbishop" a little later in the same letter. AI 1.6:9.

16   In 1382, Dionisii was created archbishop of Suzdal' and served there two years until Grand Prince Dmitrii nominated him as Metropolitan of Kyiv and all Rus'. He was never consecrated by the Patriarch. Makarii, *Istoriia*, 3:643. Feodor was archbishop of Rostov from 1390 to 1394. Another twenty-one Rostov archbishops oversaw the see until it became a metropolitanate in May 1589. Makarii, *Istoriia*, 4.2: 357; Golubinskii (1995),1:251. Historical and archaeological evidence indicate an archbishop in Rostov in the

mid-twelfth century and another at Tmutarakan' in the eleventh or twelfth centuries. On Rostov, see Ianin and Gaidukov, 3:29-36, picture 62a; Ianin (1970), 2:299, 666, 679. On Tmutarakan', see PG, 119:884-885, referred to as "Bishop of the Goths," since that tribe had occupied the Crimea in late antiquity.

17 Strayer, ed., 3:446.
18 Golubinskii (1995), 1.1:286; see also Khoroshev (1989), 30; Vernadsky argues there were two classes of archbishops in the Byzantine hierarchy, the majority being directly answerable to the patriarch, the remaining exercising essentially autocephalous powers. Vernadsky (1976), 67.
19 Hussey, ed., (1967), 4.2:110.
20 Ianin (1978), 9:47-56. Vitalien Laurent, in publishing the metropolitan seal of one of the Kirills (it is not clear if it is Kirill II (r. 1225-1233) or Kirill III (r. 1242-1281) – in fact, it is not clear if there was a Kirill I (ca. 1040)) – argued that the inscription, "Archbishop of the Metropolis of Rus'," instead of the usual "Bishop of the Metropolis of Rus'," indicates the Rus' church was headed by an archbishop and, therefore, autocephalous of Constantinople. Laurent. vol. 5 *(L'eglise*; 1975), plate 108, No. 792.
21 Shchapov (1989), 62.
22 MM, 1.151:340; 1.270:525; 1.319:580; 2.337:18; 2.404:129; 2.409:137; 2.426:157.
23 Poppe (1979): 15.
24 Kazhdan et al., 1:155-156.
25 Ware (1963, 1964), 299-300.
26 Metropolitan Petr also called himself "Archbishop of Kyiv and all Rus'." *Stepennaia kniga* 2:321.
27 NPL, 89, 321; *Mosk.*, 149; *Ermolin.*, 88.
28 Henrik Birnbaum referred to the Novgorodian archbishops as the *protothronos* of the metropolitan and argued Novgorod "ranked second only to the southern capital" in the church hierarchy, citing Andrzej Poppe as his source. Birnbaum (1988-1989), 522. See Poppe (1968), 158-164. Cf., Podskalsky, 281. The *protothronos* or *protothronus* is "the first bishop of an ecclesiastical province; he holds the first rank after the patriarch or after the metropolitan" in the Byzantine church (or, our case, in the Rus' metropolis). But "at the death of either of these latter dignitaries [the patriarch or metropolitan], the *protothronus* assumes his jurisdiction until a successor is installed." The Novgorodian archbishops were second in honor in the Kyiv metropolis, but never assumed the administration of the Rus' church, or exercised the metropolitan's

29	Golubinskii (1995), 1.1:668-669; Maksimovich, 1:113-114.
30	Paul (2003): 251-275; see also Chapter Four below.
31	NPL, 181. The Older Redaction does not include the statement on the bishops' agreement, merely noting that Iaroslav placed Hilarion. NPL, 16. Obolensky argues the appointment had patriarchal approval. Obolensky (1956), 61-62.
32	Several scholars argue Hilarion's appointment was, in fact, canonical, and thus not precedent-setting for the later, uncanonical, appointment of Klim. See, for example, Poppe (1970), 108-124.
33	Khoroshev (1989), 19.
34	Khoroshev argues that this Efrem may have been the same caretaker of the Novgorodian eparchy from 1030 to 1035. Ibid., 17. The year of Hilarion's death is uncertain, as was whether Iaroslav or Iziaslav was grand prince at the time. There are several theories on Hilarion's ultimate fate. Mikhail Priselkov argued that he left office on Iaroslav's death and became a monk in the Kyiv Caves Monastery, taking the name Nikon, under which he composed the earliest Rus' chronicles. Priselkov (1911), 188-201.
35	NPL, 182-183; N2, 122; N4, 118. Some scholars see this episode as a later embellishment by the chronicler of the *Sofia First Chronicle* based on similar events in Germany. See Nazarenko (2015), 293-301; Aristov, 53.
36	Khoroshev (1989), 19.
37	N4, 120; *Nikon.* (PSRL 9), 91.
38	N4, 125; *Sof. 1*, 142; Grekov, *Izbrannye trudy*, 4: 7-436; here 59.
39	N4, 137.
40	Khoroshev (1989),19-20, 29; Golubinskii (1995), 1.1:812. On Stefan, Luka, and German, see NPL, 473; N2, 179; N3, 212, 213.
41	NPL, 28, 214.
42	Ibid., 214.
43	The monastery was raised to the rank of a lavra in 1688, an honor given to the most important monasteries which made it directly subordinate to the Moscow patriarch. Prior to that, it was stauropegial, making it directly subordinate to the patriarch of Constantinople, from 1592-1688. It was directly subordinate to the patriarch of Moscow from 1688, and to the Metropolitan of Kyiv in 1786. Mitsik and Federova, "Kyivo-Pecherska lavra, Sviato-Uspen'ska Kyivo Pecherska lavra," in Smolii, ed., 4:191, 192. It is referred to here as a monastery, the status it held during the period under study.

(Note: item 28 continuation at top: jurisdiction during any vacancy in the metropolitan office, so that referring to them as *protothronus* is, strictly speaking, incorrect. See McClintock and Strong, eds., 696.)

44	Ibid., 28, 214. On the politics of Nifont and Klim's conflict, see Khoroshev (1989), 23-29; Makarii, *Istoriia*, 2:290-292.
45	*Ipat.* (PSRL 2.2), 383.
46	NPL, 215.
47	NPL, 216-17, 473. The *Novgorodian Fourth Chronicle* dates his death to April 18. N4, 155.
48	*Ipat.* (PSRL 2.2), 483. Klim attempted to return to the metropolitanate following Iurii Dolgorukii's death in 1157 and again in 1163. Ibid., 503, 522.
49	*Ipat.* (PSRL 2.2), 484 (s.a. 1156). On Nifont's title, see Sokolov, 327; Onasch, 26; I. Sreznevskii (1882), 59. Two lead seals bear inscription indicating his archiepiscopal rank. Shchapov (1989), 63, 65-67. For arguments the title was granted in recognition of his support of the patriarch, see Golubinskii (1995), 1.1:310, 443-44; Priselkov (2003), 383-384; D. Likhachev, "'Sofiiskii vremennik'," 240-265. Filaret claims Iurii Dolgorukii referred to Nifont as archbishop, but the patriarch or metropolitan never recognized the title. Filaret, 1:522n174; cf., Beliav, 3:72, 115.
50	Khoroshev (1989), 28-33.
51	Ibid., 28-29.
52	Ibid., 29.
53	Ibid., 20.
54	DSK 1: 67, 78, 263; Meyendorff (1981), 40.
55	NPNF, 14:287.
56	NPL, 52, 250. Denis Krustalev argues Mstislav removed Mitrofan because of the Novgorodian archeparchy's uninspired conversion efforts among the Chud following Mstislav's 1209-1212 campaigns in Livonia, after which Catholic missionaries were more successful in converting the region. Krustalev, 1:76-77.
57	I.e., Vladimir-on-Kliazma, rather than Volodymyr (Vladimir-in-Volynia). Grand Prince of Vladimir Vsevolod "Big Nest" had nominated Mitrofan while Vsevolod's son, Sviatoslav, was prince of Novgorod (though Sviatoslav was only three years old at the time). NPL, 44, 238.
58	Ibid., 57-58, 259.
59	Ibid., 60, 261.
60	NPL, 60, 261; N4, 199-200.
61	Grand Prince Daniil Romanovich of Halych chose Metropolitan Kirill II in 1242, just after the Mongol Invasion but before Batu (also Baty) Khan's return from Hungary. He was not sent to the patriarch (then residing in Nicaea during the Latin Empire) for consecration until after Batu Khan confirmed Daniil as grand

prince of Halych at the end of 1245 or the early 1246. Thus, while his metropolitanate is dated from 1242, he did not really take up his duties until returning from Nicaea in 1249. Golubinskii (1995), 2.1:50-53.

62 NPL, 80, 304; N3, 220; N4, 230.
63 NPL 81, 309; N4, 597; *Mosk.*, 141, 143.
64 NPL, 326; N4, 246.
65 NPL, 91, 330.
66 NPL, 97, 340; *Mosk.*, 167. The *Novgorodian Fourth Chronicle* mentions Moisei's trip to Moscow after Iurii's funeral. N4, 260.
67 N4, 260.
68 Fennell (1967), 161-179.
69 NPL, 354. Vasilii had baptized Mikhail in Pskov in 1333. NPL, 345.
70 NPL, 343; *Mosk.*, 170.
71 N4, 266. It must have been an important meeting given the hazards and expense of traveling between Novgorod and Volynia at the time. The lands along the route were unstable and under threat from Poland and Lithuania. Prince Feodor of Kyiv "and a Tatar basqaq" had attacked Vasiliii's party returning from his consecration in 1331. NPL, 346; N4, 264. By Vasilii's death, the king of Poland (called the "king of Krakow" in the chronicles) conquered Volynia, and he had "done much evil to the Christians (or peasants)" and turned the Orthodox churches into Catholic ones. NPL, 361; N4, 279.
72 NPL, 353; N4, 270; *Mosk.*, 173.
73 It is not clear if the metropolitan had the right to hear all cases or only appeals during visitations. Based on the later conflicts with Kiprian and Pimen, it seems Novgorod denied the metropolitan the right to hear appeals against the archbishop's judgement.
74 *Kreshchataia riza* – "cross-covered vestment" (in Greek, *polystaurion*: "many crosses"). *Riza* is the general Russian term for clerical vestments. The *riznitsa* is the vestry or sacristy overseen by a *riznichii*. Before becoming archbishop, Feofil had been Iona's *riznichii*. On Novgorod's *polystaurion* privilege, see Ianin (1988), 62.
75 NPL, 358; N4, 276; Meyendorff (1981), 84, 246, 277. When archaeologists excavated the cathedral tombs in 1946, Vasilii Kalika's remains were found still wearing his *polystaurion* and the white cowl. Mongait, 99-104. However, Valentin Ianin initially noted that, while Mongait identified the remains in Burial #5 as those of Vasilii, they could also be those of either Simeon or Evfimii I. Ianin (1988), 64, 70. However, there is no indication Simeon or Evfimii I were granted the *polystaurion*, which would mean the remains are

	Vasilii Kalika's. On the identification of the remains as those of Simeon, see Iakunina, 105-107.
76	Meyendorff (1981), 84-85. See also Rowell, 164; Kazhdan et al., 3:1647, 1696.
77	The specific symbol of episcopal power in the Eastern Church is the *omophorion*, a long scarf marked with crosses worn around the shoulders and draping down in front. See Kazhdan et al., 3:1526. The *panagia* ("all holy" in Greek), a medallion worn around the neck and bearing an icon of Jesus and the Mother of God (called the *engolpion* in Greek) is also a symbol of the episcopate. Archbishops, metropolitans, and patriarchs wear two of them as a symbol of their elevated status. It was, apparently, also worn by hegumens, at least in Rus', Moisei's *panagias* from when he was a hegumen are kept in Palace of Facets in Novgorod. See Gordienko (1991), 89, 90, 93, 95.
78	The white cowl (Museum No. NGM KP 3766), a large piece of a *polystaurion* (Museum No. NGM KP 7543/6) and fragments of an *omophorion* (Museum No. NGM KP 7543/1) excavated from Vasilii Kalika's assumed grave are on display in the Palace of Facets. Novgorodskii gosudarstvenyi ob"edinenyi muzei-zapovednik. Ekspozitsii: Palata arkhiepiskopa Evfimiia II na Vladychnom dvore Novgorodskogo Kremlia, (https://novgorod-iss.kamiscloud.ru/entity/OBJECT?exposition=3827568). Accessed June 11, 2023.
79	MM, 1.156:347-350, esp. 348; RIB 6.Pril.10:55, 56. Philotheus mentions Feognost had granted the *polystaurion* ("*felon* with four crosses") to "the previous bishop" (Vasilii Kalika), but not Moisei.
80	RIB 6.Pril.10:55, 56. Cf., Ianin (1988), 64.
81	Rowell, 164. The *polystaurion* that Patriarch Philotheus sent to Moisei in 1354 could still be seen in Novgorod in the middle of the nineteenth century. Makarii (Miroliubov) (1860), 2:323, 330; Elissa Gordienko notes "the Vladyka's Court" received Moisei's *polystaurions* and a chrysobull from the patriarch as signs of Novgorod's independence from the metropolitan. Gordienko (1991), 63. See also Gormina, 10 and plate 17. An omophorion, embroidered with Moisei's name (Museum No. NGM KP 3765) is on display in the Palace of Facets along with a *felon* said to have belonged to him (Museum No. NGM KP 2126). though not a *polystaurion*. Novgorodskii gosudarstvenyi ob"edinenyi muzei-zapovednik, Ekspozitsii g. Velikii Novgorod Palata arkhiepiskopa Evfimiia II na Vladychnom dvore Novgorodskogo Kremlia, (https://novgorod-iss.kamiscloud.ru/entity/OBJECT?exposition=3827568). Accessed February 12, 2022.

82 NPL, 363; N4, 286; Meyendorff (1981), 163; S. Solov'ev (1959-1966), 4:595. The chronicles indicate Feognost died prior to Moisei's embassy, suggesting the embassy may have been sent over concerns that Feognost, a Byzantine, would be replaced by a pro-Muscovite candidate, since there was a tendency to alternate between Byzantine and Rus' candidates.
83 Presniakov, 200; Sokolov, 346-347.
84 MM 1.267:522-523; RIB 6.Pril.19:115-118; Meyendorff (1981), 84, 189. Cf., Makarii, *Istoriia*, 3:178-179; P. Tikhomirov (1891-1900), 1:195-196.
85 *Mosk.*, 192. NPL, 373, (s.a. 1375).
86 NPL, 374; N4, 305.
87 N4, 305.
88 Aleksei visited Moscow for two weeks beginning on August 13. NPL, 374.
89 *Mosk.*, 192-193.
90 Droblenkova and Prokhorov, "Kiprian," in SKKDR 2.1: 471-472; Prokhorov, "Kiprian," in TODRL 39 (1985): 53-71
91 Golubinskii (1995), 2.1:214.
92 NPL, 374; *Mosk.*, 192-193.
93 On the dispute over Kiprian's creation as Metropolitan of Lithuania, and the plan for him to succeed Aleksei, see Meyendorff (1981), 246-7; Golubinskii (1995), 2.1:214-15, 226-62, 297-356, esp. 343-345; Presniakov, 242-256.
94 NPL, 375.
95 "Poslanie mitropolita Kipriana igumenam Sergiiu i Feodoru," RNB. Solov. No. 858, Kormchaia, 1493g., fols. 527-536; BLDR, 6: 412-423; DSHRM No. 15.
96 N4, 342.
97 NPL, 381.
98 Ibid., 382-383.
99 MM 2.446: 181-187; N4, 367-368, 370-371; *Sof. 1*, 508; cf., Meyendorff (1981), 246-247.
100 *Mosk.*, 281.
101 N4, 371.
102 NPL, 384-385; Meyendorff (1981), 247. The *Moskovskii letopisnii svod* mentions Kiprian's visit but not his conflict with Novgorod. *Mosk.*, 219.
103 N4, 372.
104 MM 2: 177-180. The Greek letter and a modern Russian translation are in RIB 6.Pril.37:235-252 and 38.253-262. The genuine Rus' version is in RNB F.IV.3, fols. 399v-401v; DSHRM, No. 26.

105	MM 2.444: 178; RIB 6.Pril.38:255-258, esp. 257; Nikitskii (1879), 113–114. This is the only instance of the Novgorodians actually threatened to "go Latin," and it is from a patriarchal letter, which may indicate a misunderstanding or misrepresentation by the patriarch rather than an actual threat by the Novgorodians.
106	AI 1.7:16-17 (s.a. 1391-1397); MM 2.444:177-180, 2.446:181-187; RIB 6.Pril.38:253.
107	NPL, 385.
108	Ibid., 385-386.
109	1 Peter 2:17.
110	NPL, 385-386; N4, 374-375; Weickhardt, 418; Nikitskii (1879), 111-115.
111	NPL, 387; N4, 375. Weickhardt argues that after 1393, the metropolitans apparently had appellate jurisdiction over all episcopal courts, including Novgorod's. He, however, does not discuss the events of 1395. Weickhardt, 419. See also F. Dmitriev, 93.
112	RIB 6.29:235-238; AI 1.11:19-20; DSHRM, No. 30.
113	NPL, 387.
114	Ibid., 389-90.
115	NPL, 390; N4, 382.
116	NPL, 391, 393.
117	Ibid., 396.
118	Ibid., 396-397.
119	NPL, 398; *Mosk.*, 233.
120	NPL, 399.
121	NPL, 403; *Mosk.*, 241
122	AI 1.73:124 (s.a. 1462-1464); 1.279:511-512 (s.a. 1470); DSHRM, Nos. 166 and 181.
123	NPL, 406.
124	NPL, 415; *Mosk.*, 246.
125	NPL, 417; Lithuanian Grand Prince Svidrigailo (r. 1430-1432) sent Gerasim to Constantinople for consecration in 1432, but had him burned at the stake in Smolensk in 1435 for supporting Sigismund, a rival grand prince. PL, 2:43-45; Nikitskii (1879), 118; Alef (1961), 393.
126	See Golubinskii (1995), 2.1:417-418.
127	Golubinskii discusses Gerasim's title, noting that it is not clear whether he was the Metropolitan of Lithuania or of Kyiv and All Rus'; he concludes he was likely Metropolitan of Lithuania, and that the Metropolitanate of Kyiv and All Rus' was thus vacant from 1431 to 1437. Golubinskii (1995), 2.1: 416-421. See also Vodov, 236-238.

128   A charter between Novgorod and Ivan III drawn up on August 11, 1471 with "the blessings of the hieromonk Feofil, nominated (*narechennogo*) to the archiepiscopate of Novgorod the Great and Pskov," affirms that the *vladyka* would not do anything contrary to the wishes of the Moscow-based Metropolitan of all Rus', and would be consecrated "at the House of the Most Pure [the Dormition Cathedral in the Moscow Kremlin] at [Metropolitan] Petr the Wonderworker's tomb…on the Moscow." GVNP, doc. 26, pp. 45-48, esp. p. 46; DSHRM No. 178.

129   PskL 1:42; PskL 2:129.

130   NPL, 419; N4, 436; PskL 1:44 (s. a. 1438).

131   This is from the anonymous "Khozhenie na Florentiiskii sobor." See DRV, 4:293-321. The text apparently combines the beginning of one account of Isidor's travels with the ending of Simeon of Suzdal's *Tale of the Council of Florence*, both found in *Sbornik istoricheskii* from the first half of the sixteenth century (RNB Sof. 1464, No. 1469), which has two (rather condemnatory) accounts of Isidor's journey to Florence and back. The first part found in DRV is from the second account (fols. 404-438), while the ending is from the first account (fols. 368-393v.) See also, BLDR, 6:464-473; Popov, 344-359; On Isidor and Evfimii, see Bobrov (2001), 194-217.

132   For more on the interaction between Isidor and Novgorod, see Bobrov, "Novgorodsko-pskovskie otnosheniia" 359-373, esp. 359-361.

133   NPL, 419; Halecki, 62. Khoroshev (1989), 106.

134   *The Pskov First Chronicle* says Isidor arrived back from Florence on the feast of the Intercession of the Mother of God (October 14) but does not say where exactly he was. He arrived in Moscow from "Lithuania…in the spring, in Palm Week" (the week before Holy Week, April 2-8 in 1441). PskL 1:45. Kartashev notes Isidor was in Vilnius in August 1440 and Bobrov argues he remained in Smolensk in the winter of 1440-1441. Kartashev, 1:364-365; Bobrov, "Novgorodsko-pskovskie otnosheniia," 364-365.

135   That the monk Simeon of Suzdal', who accompanied the metropolitan to Florence and back, wrote his strongly anti-Union "Selections of the Holy Writings Against the Latins and the Tale of the Eighth Latin Council," in the scriptorium in Novgorod suggests Evfimii II opposed the Union. There are some suggestions, however, that it was written as late as 1458-1462, during Iona's tenure, so it is unclear if Evfimii openly broke with Isidor in 1441. Cherniavsky, 349-350; Delektorskii, 132ff.; Popov, 90f.

136   Bobrov argues Evfimii's building and art projects and promotion

of local saintly cults beginning in the 1430s were expressions of opposition to the Union. Bobrov, "Novgorodsko-pskovskie otnosheniia," 368-371.
137 *Mosk.*, 270.
138 Ibid., 277, 301.
139 Ibid., 279.
140 Gustav Alef concluded from Iona's request that Evfimii convince the Novgorodian civil authorities not to harbor the excommunicated Shemiaka that the Novgorodians did not recognize Metropolitan Iona's election as legitimate. Alef, (1961), 400. For Iona's letter, see AI 1.53:101-103.
141 Paul (2007), 258.
142 MM, 1.267:522-523; RIB 6.Pril.19:115-118.
143 N2, 141; N4, 498. No reason is given for the trip.
144 *Ermolin.*, 155. See also Bobrov (2014), 516-540.
145 AI 1.53:101-103 DSHRM, No. 111. Metropolitan Fillipp also sent a letter to Iona in April 1467 telling him not to allow the alienation of land granted to monasteries for the commemoration of the dead. AI 1.82:130-133; RIB 6.101:713-722; DSHRM, No. 175.
146 Rowell, 168. Patriarch Joseph II's (r. 1416-1439) letter to Metropolitan Fotii regarding Grigorii is published in RIB 6.40: 357-360.
147 AI 1.19:27-40; RIB 6.39:315-356; DSHRM No. 58.
148 AI 1.20:41; RIB 6.40:364-365.
149 AI 1.63:112-114; RIB 6.81:619-626 (to the Orthodox bishops of Lithuania); DSHRM No. 134; RIB 6.85:635-640 (to the Lithuanian princes and nobles); RIB 6.87:645-658 (to the Orthodox bishops of Lithuania); RIB 6.88: 657-670 (to the bishops of Smolensk and Chernihiv); RIB 6.89: 671-674 (to a loyal Rus' bishop in Lithuania); 6.90: 673-678 (to Pskov on loyalty to Orthodoxy and Grand Prince Vasilii II).
150 AI 1.65:116-118; RIB 6.86:639-644; DSHRM No. 133. (Met. Iona to Archbishop Iona, 1459).
151 RIB 6.95: 689-694.
152 AAE 1.80:59-60; AI 1.280-281:512-518; DSHRM Nos. 183-184; AI 1.282
153 *Mosk.*, 284-286; *Sof.* 1, 7-8; AI 1.280:512-514; 1.281:516-517; 1.282:518-519; AAE 1.80:56-60; Halecki, 85-97; Lenhoff and Martin, 346-47, 361. Grand Prince Ivan III also wrote to Iona warning him to have no relations with Metropolitan Grigorii. RIB 6.100:707-712.
154 Filipp wrote a letter to the grand prince asking him to show mercy if the Novgorodians returned to loyalty. AI 1 282: 518-519; DSHRM No. 185.

155 *Mosk.*, 293, (s.a. 1472); N4, 498.
156 RIB 6.2:32, question 33.
157 NPL, 361; N4, 279.
158 GVNP, doc. 77, pp. 130-132. Cf. Paul (2007), 262.
159 For a discussion of Bulgaria and Serbia, see Steindorff, 7-24, esp. 16-21.
160 Preslav was listed only once in the *notitiae* of the Patriarchs of Constantinople and then as a suffragan of Ternovo, which was listed not as a patriarchate, but only as a metropolitanate (the original five patriarchates are the only ones listed). The list, however, is from the Ottoman period, well after the period of the Preslav Patriarchate. Darrouzès, 197-198, 420.
161 On Tzimiskes and Preslav, see Leo Diaconus, Book 9, Sect. 12, p. 157. Patriarch German resided consecutively in Moglen, Voden (Edessa) (in present-day north-western Greece), and Prespa (in present-day southern Republic of Macedonia). His successor, Filip, moved to Ohrid ca. 990. See Curta and Stephenson, 241.
162 Golubinskii (1871), 6, 33-46; Runciman (1930), 174; Fine (1983), 192.
163 Constantine Porphyrogenitus, 124-127, 152-161; Golubinskii (1871), 444.
164 Golubinskii (1871), 433-443, 449-456, 472-473. Fine dated Joannikje elevation to the patriarchal rank to Easter, 1346; Obolensky considers that as the day of Dušan's coronation, and dated Joannikje patriarchate to 1345 or early 1346. Fine (1987), 116-117, 309; Obolensky, *Byzantine Commonwealth*, 314-15, 329-330.
165 Novgorod was not the only bishop wanting autonomy. Cf., F. Dmitriev, 93.
166 I. Sreznevskii (1897), 108-109.

Chapter Three

1 Herman, "The Secular Church," 112.
2 Cyprian of Carthage, *Epistle 68* (*To Florentius Pupianus, on Calumniators; Ad Florentium Pupianum de obtrectatoribus*) sect. 8, PL 4, col. 406.
3 Ibn Battutah, 127; Martin (1985), 21-22.
4 Notwithstanding the Old Norse name for Rus': *Garðaríki*, that is, "realm of cities." See Jackson, 170-179.
5 On the dubious nature of the fragmentary account of the Baptism of Novgorod that Ioakim allegedly left, and which Tatishchev claimed to have discovered, see Tvorogov, "Ioakim," in SKKDR 1:204-205. Cf., Tatishchev, 1:107.

6	Vladimir ordered the idol of Perun be tied to a horse's tail and dragged through the streets, with men beating it with staves. It was then thrown into the Dnepr River where it was forbidden for it to come to rest along the riverbank until it had gone over the cataracts to the south. *Lavrent.*, 117-118; *Sof. 1*, 101.
7	*Novgorodskaia vtoraia (arkhivskaia) letopis'*, 169.
8	Tatishchev wrote that the Novgorodians attacked Dobrynia, burned his home, and killed his wife and other family members. Tatishchev, 1:112-113; see also S. Solov'ev (1959-1966), 1.1:185-187.
9	NPL, 473; N4, 113; *Novgorodskaia vtoraia (arkhivskaia) letopis'*, 196.
10	Aristov, 49-60, esp. 59-60.
11	NPL, 473.
12	NPL, 191-96, especially 196; *Mosk.*, 7.
13	Levin (1993); Rock, 26.
14	RIB 6.2:32.
15	Of more than 90 manuscript versions of the "Statute of Iaroslav", none date from before the fourteenth century. On the various manuscripts, see Zimin's discussion in PRP, 1:257ff. For an attempt to reconstruct the original text, see Shchapov (1972).
16	"The Statute of Saint Prince Volodimir," Art. 9-11, ZDR, 149; Art. 6 in the First Redaction and Arts. 6-7 in the Third Redaction in PRP, 1:238, 245.
17	See the Longer Redaction of "The Statute of Prince Iaroslav [on] Hierarchs' Courts," ZDR, 28-132, 191; PRP, 1:71-205; 259-262.
18	RIB 6.2:32, question 33; Rock, 26.
19	NPL, 65, 270; PskL 2:36; Zguta (Dec. 1977), 1189-1190. Zguta links the periodic rise of witch-hunts to famines and other disasters.
20	The Izhorians are also known as Ingrians or Ingermans.
21	N4, 564-565. Cf., DAI 1.28:27-30. See also Kochkurkina, Spiridonov, and Jackson, 97; Makarii (Veretennikov) (2002), 39-40.
22	N4, 565.
23	DAI 1.43:57-60. For Feodosii's copy of his predecessor's missive, see RNB Q.XVII.50, *Formuliarnik novgorodskogo arkhiepiskopa Feodosii (II)*, fols. 116v.-120v.
24	Mt. 28:19; cf., Mk. 16:15; Lk 24:47.
25	NPL, 359-60; Klemming, ed., 1:177, line 168; Christiansen, 186; Paul, "Vasilii Kalika," 267.
26	NPL, 387.
27	Evfimii left August 7, 1446 and returned to Novgorod the following January 23. NPL, 426-7; N4, 442-443; Nikitskii (1879), 64.
28	Musin (2002), 91- 121, esp. 97, 107, 109, 115-116.
29	Nazarova, 177.

30 "Zhitie Aleksandra Nevskogo. Pervaia redaktsia, 1280-gody," in Begunov and Kirpichnikov, 191-192; Gadziatskii, 100-148; Nazarova, 178.
31 Nazarova, 187; see also Riabinin, 24.
32 Franklin and Shepard point to burial practices as indicators of the extent of Christianization, such as inhumation rather than cremation and the decline of potsherds in graves, showing that pagan funerary feasts or the leaving of gifts for the dead were no longer practiced. They note, however, that in some burial grounds, both Christian ornaments and pagan amulets are found and that "the bearer or donor of these objects, which are sometimes placed together in the same grave, need not have been aware of their divergent associations." Franklin and Shepard, 174-175, 176, 228.
33 Musin (2002), 97.
34 Amvrosii, 3:480; N3, 233; Musin (2002), 109. John Lind dates the founding to 1393. Lind (2001), 148.
35 Okhotina-Lind; Okhotina, 124-135. The manuscript dates to well after the events in question. John Lind dates it to 1556-1558 and attributes it to the Novgorodian archiepiscopal administration, rather than the monks of the monastery. Lind (1992), 1-30; Okhotina-Lind, 21-23, 30, esp. 23 and 30; Lind (1986): 115-133. For discussion of the events and the historic usefulness of the document, see Paul (2007), 254-256.
36 Lind (2001), 148-149.
37 Okhotina-Lind, 168-169.
38 The Catholic Church, at least in recent centuries, defines Orthodoxy as a *schism*: the churches are divided over administrative prerogatives –the supremacy of the Popes – rather than a *heresy*: division over improper doctrine. However, Cardinal Humbert of Silva Candida, whose misuse of his papal legatine authority in 1054 helped bring about the Great Schism, wrote tracts against the "heresy" of omitting the *Filioque* (even though it was the Catholics who had *inserted* it) into the Creed. He wrote of differences in practices and theology as heretical as well. The Catholics in Livonia apparently saw the Russians as heretics or even as non-Christians. See Urban (1975); Christiansen.
39 NPL, 349; Paul, "Vasilii Kalika," 265.
40 NPL, 350.
41 Ibid.
42 Ibid., 350. Paul, "Vasilii Kalika," 253-254; Lind (2001), 145.
43 On Ioann and the Karelians, see Paul (2007), 254-256.

44	The term is John Lind's. Lind (2001), 148-149; Paul (2007), 256.
45	Paul (2007), 256.
46	Halperin (1984): 442-466. Halperin also discusses the Ideology of Silence in *Russia and the Golden Horde*. Halperin (1985), 1-9, 61-74. See also idem (1998-1999) 98-117.
47	Six immunity charters are printed in PRP 3:463-480. A seventh, thought to be a forgery (allegedly from Khan Uzbek to Metropolitan Petr), appears in Sakharov, ed., 184-185. See also *Drevneishii spisok. Kratkoe sobranie iarlykov, dannykh ordynskimi khanami russkim mitropolitam*, RFA (1987) 3:571-594.
48	On Novgorodian (and archiepiscopal) relations with the German merchants, see Lukin (2022), 117-142.
49	RIB 6.2:32, question 33; Rock, 26. That they are Christian rather than pagan priests is indicated by use of the word "*pop*" rather than "*zhrets*."
50	*Mosk.*, 132, (s.a. 1241); *Sof. 1*, 306.
51	NPL, 77, 291, 293.
52	NPL, 359. Donald Ostrowski argues this was not due to any inability to debate, but to an outlook among the Orthodox that "If all of truth has already been revealed in the Bible, the Seven Ecumenical Councils, and the writings of the Church Fathers, and we can know it as well through our souls by using these writings as a guide, then clearly anything new, any new ideas that are not already contained therein, must, by definition, be wrong and not truthful." Ostrowski (2018), 78.
53	Paul, "Vasilii Kalika," 253-271; idem (2007), 249, 254.
54	GVNP, doc. 77, pp. 129-32; Halecki, 85-97; Golubinskii (1995), 2.1:533-534.; Lenhoff and Martin, 346-347, 361.
55	On Moscow's reaction to Novgorod's supposed Catholic tendencies, see RIB 6.94:689-694; 6.102:721-732; AI 1.280:512-514; 1.281:516-517; 1.282:518-519; *Sof. 1*, 7-8. DSHRM, Nos. 183-185.
56	AfED, 373-382, esp. 381; RIB 6.115:763-784, esp. 784; Pliguzov (1992), 276; Paul, "Continuity and Change," 282-283.
57	Khoroshev (1989), 67-68; cf., AfED, 331, 333-338.
58	Paul, "Vasilii Kalika," 253-271.
59	A. Alekseev (2005), 285. Moisei blamed the heresy for certain problems during his second tenure (1352-1359), but this account was written by Pakhomii the Serb around 1470, more than a century after the events in question. Idem., 287. See also "Povest' o Moisee, Arkhiepiskope Novgorodskom"," in Kushelev-Bezborodko and Kostomarov, eds., 4:11; Pechnikov, "Spornye voprosy istorii strigol'nichestva v Novgorode," in Ianin, ed., *Stolichnye i periferiinye goroda Rusi*, 138-139.

60 Rybakov calls Vasilii "a less strict pastor than his successor (*smenivshii*) Moisei." Rybakov (1993), 202.
61 NPL, 373; N4, 305. Paul, "Continuity and Change," 282-283. Khoroshev argues Archbishop Aleksei was undoubtedly tied to the executions. Khoroshev (1989), 74. Pavel Tikhomirov and Boris Rybakov both argue the heretics were lynched without Aleksei's support. P. Tikhomirov (1891-1900), 1:203; Rybakov (1993), 4-11, esp. p. 8. Rybakov used the word "*rasprava*," which could mean "execution," or "punishment" but also "reprisal" or "violence." See also Alekseev (2005), 285.
62 "Ustav kniazia Vladimira Sviatoslavicha o desiatinakh, sudakh i liudiakh tserkovniykh," Arts. 9-11, in ZDR, 140, 149; PRP, 1:238, 241-242, 245.
63 "Ustav kniazia Vladimira Sviatoslavicha," Art. 16, in ZDR, 149; Art. 8 in PRP, 1:238. "The Statute of Prince Iaroslav," in ZDR, 191-192; PRP, 1:238, 242, 246. Grekov, ed. (1940), Art. 109, p. 254; ZDR, 341-342; PRP, 2:322-323.
64 On the *Strigol'niki*, see AfED, 34-71; A. Alekseev (2012), 11-207; Klibanov (1960), 118-136; Flier, 121-158; Poppe (1966), 204-208. A less reliable assessment of the *Strigol'niki* is found in Rybakov (1993).
65 MM 2.347:31-34.; 2.516:282-285; RIB 6.22:191-198; 6.42:365-376; also AI 1.21:42-45: *AfED* Pril. 3:243-247; DSHRM No. 60; RIB 6.55:475-482; 6.56:481-488.
66 RIB 6.22: 191-198.
67 NPL, 378-79.
68 AfED, 115, 318.
69 Moshe Taube describes Zechariah ben Aharaon ha-Kohen (called Skhariya the Jew in the church writings against the Judaizing movement in the early 1500s) as "a copyist and annotator of scientific and philosophical texts between 1454 and 1485," who, after working in Kyiv in the 1460s and accompanying Prince Mikhail to Novgorod in 1470, reappears in Damascus based on a colophon from 1485. Taube (2003), 57, 59. See also Taube (1993-1996), 3:168-198.
70 Pliguzov (1992), 269-288; Vernadsky (1933), 436-454. On Mikhail, see Lenhoff and Martin, 346, 347, 349, 363, though they do not discuss his ties to the Judaizers.
71 On the handling of the Judaizers, see AfED, Priloz.12-16, 18-20:309-320, 373-386.
72 RNB F. IV. 165, fols. 660v-663v; *Sof. 1*, 49-50; AfED, 155, 380, 385, 426-29, 471-473, 479. 506. Two Novgorodian priests were transferred to the Cathedral of the Dormition and the Church of St. Mi-

chael the Archangel in the Moscow Kremlin after the annexation of Novgorod in 1478, where they spread the heresy. Goldfrank (1998), 18-19; Metropolitan Zosima was himself accused of sodomy and rejecting the general resurrection, but was never tried. Goldfrank (1998), 19.

73 For more on the Judaizers, see RIB 6.114:759-764, 6.115:763-784, and 6.116:785-88; *Prosvetitel'*, esp. Slova 1-11, pp. 1-464; AfED, 74-220; Priloz.14-15:313-315, Priloz.18-19:373-382; A. Alekseev (2012), 211-496; Zuckerman, 72-99; Wieczynski (1972), 374-389; Fennell (1951), 486-509; Halperin (1975): 141-155. On the use of accusations of heresy for political reasons, see Lur'e (1960), passim, esp. 75-203.

74 On Jewish influence in the movement, see A. Alekseev (2012), 211-496; Ostrorski (2017), 123-139. See also Taube (2016); and Ryan and Taube; Lur'e and Klibanov downplay any Jewish influence. Lur'e, *Ideologicheskaia bor'ba*, 73-203; Klibanov (1960), 187-200. See also Goldfrank, 64-91, here, 73-80.

75 Miller (1990), 321-355; idem (1989), 360-390.

76 In 1365, the Pskovites consecrated the Trinity Cathedral in the kremlin (Krom) with Archbishop Aleksei's permission. NPL, 369. On the bishop's role in church consecrations, see Sokolof, 11.

77 Paul (2007), 252.

78 Martirii, Antonii, Arsenii, Spiridon, Dalmat, Vasilii, Feodosii, Evfimii I, Iona, and Feofil.

79 Il'ia, Mitrofan, Kliment, Feoktist, David, Moisei, Simeon, and Evfimii II. Gavriil consecrated two churches while Ioann and Aleksei consecrated five and six churches respectively.

80 NPNF, 14:374.

81 1 Cor. 1:17.

82 1 Tim. 3:2.

83 2 Tim. 4:2. Paul also encourages Timothy "what you have heard from me before many witnesses entrust to faithful men who will be able to teach others also." 2 Tim. 2.2.

84 Kantor and White, trans., 5.

85 Ibid., 10-11. In the *Proglas to the Gospels*, Constantine of Preslav, often mistaken for St. Cyril (also called Constantine) in the medieval period, emphasized the importance of learning, declaring: "People are naked without books." Constantine of Preslav in Dinenkov, Kuev, and Petkanova, eds., 51-57, esp. 53 and 56.

86 Kantor and White, 72-3. Emphasis added.

87 NPL, 473; N4, 113, *Novgorodskaia vtoraia (arkhivskaia) letopis'*, 196. Emphasis added.

88	Bugoslavskii, 194-237; Fennell and Stokes, 60-61; Thomson (1992), 205-217. For the text of the *Voproshanie Kirika* (The Questions of Kirik), see RIB 6.2:21-62; Fennell (1995), 73-77; Giraudo, 743-760.
89	"Postanovlenie Il'ii, arkhiepiskopa Novgorodskogo," in RIB 6.4:75-78; Fennell (1995), 77. Filaret, 3:21-25; Kalaidovich, ed., 223-224; Il'ia, "Pravila Chernoriztsem," in Nevostruev, ed., (1862-1863), 2: 31-36; P. Tikhomirov (1891-1900), 1:95-97.
90	Scholars are divided over what Vasilii's letter actual says: some see it as heretical, while others see it as promoting Hesychasm, the most important form of Eastern Orthodox mysticism. See AfED, 33, 37; Klibanov (1960), 3-27; Terras, 52-53. Veselovskii, 91-104; Panchenko, 24-26.
91	NPL, 354.
92	TODRL 11:342-367; 12:340-461; 13:409-426; 15:331-348; Franklin, trans. (1991); Ponomarev, (1894), 88-104; Nadson, 4-15; Fennell and Stokes, 40-43, 61-63.
93	There are also the eight sermons of Hegumen Feodosii of the Kyiv Caves Monastery, but there is little else. See TODRL 5:168-184.
94	See Runciman (1955), 7-8.
95	Fennell and Stokes, 61.
96	Evseev, ed., 14; Thomson (1992), 216-217. The text is also published in Bugoslavskii, 194-237; and in Makarii, *Istoriia*, 2.Pril.6:539-540.
97	Evseev, ed., 14.
98	1 Thes. 5:15; Rom. 12:17-21; Evseev, ed., 15.
99	Ex. 20:7; Lev. 19:12; Deut. 5:11; Mt. 5:33-3; Evseev, ed., 16.
100	2 Pet. 2:17; Evseev, ed., 16.
101	Ex 20:13; Deut. 5:17; Evseev, ed., 16.
102	Ex. 20: 15; Lev. 19:11; Evseev, ed., 16.
103	Lev. 19:11; Evseev, ed., 16.
104	Ex. 20:16; Deut. 5:20; Evseev, ed., 16.
105	Lev. 19:17; Evseev, ed., 16.
106	Ex. 20:17; Deut. 5:21; Evseev, ed., 16.
107	Ex. 20:14; Deut. 5:18; Evseev, ed., 16.
108	Fennell and Stokes, 61.
109	P. Tikhomirov (1891-1900), 1:15.
110	Evseev, ed., 13; Fennell and Stokes, 61.
111	Luka's homily is similar to a number of monastic rules found in Rus', including Il'ia's "Pravila chernoriztem." See Nevostruev (1862); idem, (1862-1863); idem, (1866). Cf. Terras, 33.
112	Fennell (1995), 73-77; Giraudo, 743-760; Žužek, 134-138. The *Voproshanie Kirika* (or *Kirikovo*) is found in the *Novgorodian Synodal Kormchaia of 1282*. GIM, Sinod., No. 132.

113	RIB 6.2:21-62.
114	Ibid., 6:21, 62.
115	Ibid., 6:25.
116	Ibid., 6:30.
117	Ibid., 6:21-22.
118	Ibid., 6:62.
119	NPL, 24, 209.
120	Tikhomirov noted Karamzin's argument that the marriage was within prohibited degrees of consanguinity, but also Tatishchev's claim that Nifont opposed the marriage because it was Sviatoslav's second (the first had been to a Polovtsian princess) and because the prince's servitors had killed the bride's father in Rostov shortly before. P. Tikhomirov (1891-1900), 1:55; Karamzin (1969), 2:121-122; Tatishchev 2:148n393, 265-266.
121	NPL, 213.
122	P. Tikhomirov (1891-1900), 1:94.
123	It is not known to which bishop of Bilhorod the letter was sent. Kalaidovich speculates it may have been Bishop Makarii, who died in 1190. Kalaidovich, ed., 221. The instructions are published in RIB 6.4:75-78.
124	Nevostruev wrote that the *Pravila Chernoriztsem* were written down under Archbishop Kliment and Prince Dmitrii Aleksandrovich, at the end of the thirteenth century, but were originally from Il'ia. Nevostruev, ed., (1862-1863), 2:31. Just as Archbishop Il'ia may be the same Il'ia who drew up 28 of the *Questions of Kirik*, it is possible that this Kirik is the same one writing down the rules for Il'ia after he became archbishop.
125	In Kalaidovich, it is referred to as the *diskos* (paten), since the bread has not yet been consecrated (i.e., it has not yet become "the Lamb") at the time of the Great Entrance. Kalaidovich, ed., 224.
126	The *eiliton* (also spelled *iliton*, or *liton*, as it is written in the rules) is a cover or wrapping for the antimension, the special altar cloth with saintly relics sewn into it required in order to hold a Divine Liturgy. Kalaidovich, 224; On the antimension, see also *Polnyi pravoslavnyi bogoslovskii entsiklopediicheskii slovar'*, 1:174-176; Nikol'skii (1907), 8; "Antimins," in Dal' (1978), 1:18.
127	Kalaidovich, ed., 223-224, esp. 224. RIB, 6.4:78; Filaret, 3:21-23. P. Tikhomirov (1891-1900), 1:94-96, esp. 96. In some versions, the instructions to drop the fragment into the water are left out. There are no instructions to what to do with the mouse; it simply disappears from the historic record.
128	Ili'a, "Pravila chernoriztsem," in Nevostruev, ed., (1862-1863), 2:33; Filaret, 3:23-25; P. Tikhomirov (1891-1900), 1:96-97.

129	2 Tim 2:4.
130	Rom. 8:14, Jn. 1:12, Ps. 81:6.
131	Il'ia, "Pravila chernoriztsem," in Nevostruev, ed., (1862-1863), 2:34. The Third Canon forbade the clergy from managing secular property or engaging in worldly business. The Fourth Canon subjected the monasteries to the authority of the local bishop. NPNF, 14:269-271.
132	The letter is found in several manuscripts: RNB, F. 550, *Osvnovnoe Sobranie Rukopisnoi Knigi*, Q.IV.298, fols. 437-442v.; RNB F.550, Q.XVII.50, *Formuliarnika novgorodskogo arkhiepiskopa Feodosiia*, fols. 174-180; RGB, F. 304.I, Glavnaia Biblioteka Troitse-Sergievoi Lavry, No. 39, *Sbornik XVI v.*, fols. 239-242v. Printed editions include: *Sof. 1*, 422-428; *Stepennaia Kniga*, 2:387-390; PLDR, 1:42-49, 531-534; BLDR, 6: 42-49; P. Tikhomirov (1891-1900), 1:180-190, esp. 186-190. See also Shevyrev, 4:122-124.
133	*Sof. 1*, 423; BLDR 6:44-45; P. Tikhomirov (1891-1900), 1:180, 187. The description of the rivers flowing out of paradise is from Gen. 2:10-14.
134	*Sof. 1*, 423; BLDR 6:42-43; P. Tikhomirov (1891-1900), 1:180, 187. Adam's expulsion from paradise is from Gen. 3:23-24.
135	Daniil, hegumen of a Chernihiv monastery, visited Jerusalem in 1106-1107 and wrote of his travels, including his visit to the Church of the Holy Sepulcher, the grave of Adam, and the legend surrounding it. Scores of manuscripts of his account are available; most dating to the fifteenth and sixteenth centuries including RNB F. 728, Sof. Sobr., No. 1295; RNB Q.XVII.88 *Sbornik smeshannogo soderzhaniia*, fols. 1-48; GIM, Sinod. No. 181; GIM Chudov. No. 270. Earlier manuscripts might be the source of Vasilii's belief that paradise and Gethsemane were the same. For a published version of Daniil's account, see Prokhorov, ed. "Khozhdenie igumena Daniila," PLDR 2:24-115, 627-645; Venevitinov, 1-138. See also Tvorogov, "Daniil," in SKKDR 1:109-112; Baldi, 6n946.
136	Vasilii also wrote that he had seen the "hermitage" Jesus had stayed at when he fasted in the desert near the Jordan River and the 100 date trees Christ had planted there. They survived, so, by implication, paradise survives "because all God's works are everlasting." *Sof. 1*, 425.
137	*Sof. 1*, 425-426. According to a tradition dating back to at least Origen, the Garden of Gethsemane, on the western slope of the Mount of Olives to the east of Jerusalem (where Jesus prayed and sweated blood before his arrest, according to Mt. 26:36-56; Mk. 14:32-52; Lk. 22:39-53; Jn. 18:1-14 – though it is not called Geth-

semane in the last two Gospels), is the remnant of the Garden of Eden. The skull beneath the cross, often depicted in Orthodox and Catholic iconography (hence the Aramaic name "Golgotha" or the Latin "Calvaria" - "the Place of the Skull;" see Mt. 27:33; Mk. 15:22; Jn. 19:17; Luke refers to it as "the Place of the Skull," but does not give the Aramaic name for it; Lk 23:33), is said to be Adam's, out of whose dead mouth grew the tree that became the cross; thus the crucifixion happened on the very site of the original sin. Since Vasilii Kalika ("the Pilgrim") had made a pilgrimage to the Holy Land and had probably visited Jerusalem and the garden, he could have considered himself an eyewitness to paradise. Since at least the eighth or ninth century there has been a Chapel of Adam in the Church of the Resurrection (also called the Church of the Holy Sepulcher) to mark Adam's tomb. See Origen, *Matthaeum Commentariorum series*, in PG, 13:1777-1778, Sect. 126b-c; Nilus, "Letters," PG, 79:83; Eutychius, *Annales*, PG, 111:911-918; Ambrose, *Epistle 71*, PL, 16:1241-1243; Pseudo-Cyprian, *Ad Flavium Felicem de resurrectione mortuorum*, in von Hartel, ed., 3.3:322. St. Jerome did not believe the story, as he makes clear in his *Commentary on Matt. 27:33* in PL, 26:217-218, and *Commentary on Ephesians 5:14* in PL, 26:526a-b. Other Patristic and medieval writers likewise denied the two sites were identical, but some believed the legend into the Renaissance. Pseudo-Athanasius wrote that the Jews believe Adam was buried in Hebron. Pseudo-Athanasius, in PG, 28:297-208. For the Jewish tradition, see *Babylonian Talmud, Erubin* 53a.

138 *Sof. 1*, 425; BLDR 6:44-45; P. Tikhomirov (1891-1900), 1:188. The resurrection of the dead at the time of the Crucifixion is from Mt. 27:52.

139 BLDR 6: 44-45. A *poprishche* (also *pop"rishche*) is a unit of distance calculated by the church for the purposes of travel per diem. It is equivalent to 20 *versty* or 13 miles. See Dal' (1978), 3:306; Bogatova, et al., eds., 17: 99; Shevyrev, 3:123, 160n18. On Macarius, see "O Sv. Makarii i o rae," in Kushelev-Bezborodko and Kostomarov, eds., 3:135.

140 BLDR 6: 44-45. On Ephrosinius (Evfrosinii), see Russkaia Pravoslavnaia Tserkov', *Kniga zhitii sviatykh*, vol. 1 (for September), fols. 125v.–127r., esp. fol. 126v.

141 BLDR 6:44-45. Vasilii probably takes this from one of John Chrysostom's Homilies on Genesis. The Thirteenth Homily addresses God planting paradise in the East (and refutes the idea that paradise is not a physical place.) See PG 53:108-109. In his

	Eighteenth Homily, Chrysostom addresses the expulsion of Adam and Eve from Paradise. PG 53:150-151. I have not found the precise quote Vasilii uses in his letter.
142	See also *Sof. 1*, 424; P. Tikhomirov (1891-1900), 1:181, 187.
143	BLDR 6:44-45; *Sof. 1*, 423; P. Tikhomirov (1891-1900), 1:180, 187; Mary, Enoch, and the Prophet Elijah did not die. Mary "fell asleep" and some say she was assumed into heaven body and soul (although the Orthodox Church has never declared a definitive doctrine to this effect, as the Roman Catholic Church has). Enoch, the father of Methuselah, lived 365 years and while the other nine antediluvian patriarchs (from Adam to Noah) died, "Enoch walked with God; then he was no more, for God took him." Gen. 5:24. Elijah rose to heaven in a whirlwind on a fiery chariot. 2 Kings. 2:11 (Fourth Kings in the Septuagint and the Latin Vulgate as well as in Orthodox Old Testaments). Since they did not die, they must be in a physical and not merely a spiritual paradise. According to Orthodox tradition, Enoch and Elijah are the guardians of paradise, and are thus mentioned here. Enoch and Elijah are also sometimes identified as the two witnesses in Rv. 11:3-12, whose corpses will lie in the street for three days, and again, since they have bodies, they must be in a physical place. Elijah may also be specifically mentioned because while on the cross, Jesus' lament that God had forsaken him was erroneously thought by the bystanders to have been addressed to Elijah, who would (physically) return to help Jesus. Mt. 27:46-49; Mk 15:34-36.
144	BLDR 6:46-47; *Sof. 1*, 424; Filaret, 1: 192; Shevyrev, 3:123-124; P. Tikhomirov (1891-1900), 1:181, 187-188.
145	BLDR 6:46-47; *Sof. 1*, 426.
146	BLDR 6:46-47; *Sof. 1*, 426.
147	BLDR 6:46-47; *Sof. 1*, 427.
148	AI 1.104:146-148.
149	RGB, Fond. 304.I, № 215 *Stoglav (Postanovlenie Moskovskogo sobora 1551 g.)*, Chapter 25, fols. 89v-90r. Kozhanchikov (1863), 91-92; Emchenko, Chapter 25, pp. 285-286.
150	"Povest' o pobede Novgorodtsev nad Suzdal'tsami," in Kushelev-Bezborodko and Kostomarov, eds., 1:241-242
151	NPL, 33, 76, 221, 289. The thawing of the marshes around Novgorod may have caused the Mongol cavalry to turn away from the city. Saunders, 83.
152	NPL, 376, 383-384. On other occasions, however, the archbishops' prayers failed to halt the plague. Archbishop Vasilii's visitation to Pskov in 1352 at the behest of its citizens to pray for deliver-

ance from plague failed and he died en route back to Novgorod, probably of the plague. Members of his entourage then apparently brought the plague to Novgorod. NPL, 100, 362. Incidentally, Metropolitan Feognost, Grand Prince Simeon, his brother Andrei, and two of his sons also died of the plague that year in Moscow. NPL, 363; *Sof. 1*, 431; Golubinskii (1995), 2.1:170. In 1417, Archbishop Simeon was unable to save Novgorod from the plague, but led a procession around the city, personally celebrated Divine Liturgies, and gave extreme unction to the dying. NPL, 408.

153 NPL, 355.
154 *Mosk.*, 245.
155 Mstislav Rostislavich of Smolensk was called to Novgorod and arrived in the city on November 1, 1179; that winter he led the Novgorodians against the Chud in Ochela (Atzele, a medieval principality now part of the Latgale district of northeastern Latvia bordering Russia and Estonia) and died in Novgorod on June 14, 1180. NPL, 36, 225-226; *Suzdal.*, 387; *Ipat.* (PSRL 2.2), 609; Paul (2008), 90. As Georgii, his baptismal name, he is recognized as a saint by the Russian Orthodox Church; his relics lie in a gypsum sarcophagus along the south wall of the Chapel of the Nativity of the Mother of God in the Cathedral of Holy Wisdom across from the sarcophagus of Bishop Nikita.
156 NPL, 345.
157 Ibid., 355.
158 Khoroshev (1989), 36; Karger, 62-63. Henrik Birnbaum claims the white clergy were mostly lower class while the black clergy came largely from the upper classes. Birnbaum (1981), 75. But, several archbishops (e.g., Il'ia, Gavriil, Vasilii Kalika, and Evfimii II) were either of the white clergy themselves or were sons of priests, and The *Life* of Archbishop Iona states that he was a poor orphan. "Vospominanie o blagoslovennom Ione," in Kushelev-Bezborodko and Kostomarov, eds., 4:27-35.
159 In 1153 Archbishop Nifont consecrated the Church of St. Clement in Staraia Ladoga, the only reported visit by an archbishop to that city. The church stood just south of the fortress but is no longer extant; fragments of its frescoes are now in the Ladoga History Museum. The parish was transferred to Novaia Ladoga when Peter I built that town in 1704. According to a plaque in the Church of the Nativity of John the Forerunner in Staraia Ladoga, it was built in 1276 "with the blessings of Archbishop Kliment through the donations of the Slaves of God Ivan and Mar'ia." (Visit, May 11, 2007). However, there is no indication that Kliment personally

visited that church and consecrated it. Cf. NPL, 29, 215; Nikitskii (1879), 64. Nifont built the stone Church of Christ the Savior in the Mirozh Monastery in Pskov and had its interior frescoed. He is assumed to have visited there to consecrate it. NPL, 29, 216. That church is still extant, and although it has been significantly altered over the centuries, the twelfth-century frescoes have been recently uncovered. Additionally, Archbishop Gavriil traveled to Pskov in 1188, where one of his priests died. NPL, 39. A decade later, Bishop Martirii had the stone Church of the Transfiguration built in his monastery in Staraia Russa and consecrated it on the feast of the Dormition. The church was painted the following year, probably on Martirii's orders. Evfimii II had the church rebuilt in 1442, but there is no indication that the bishops visited the city on those occasions. NPL, 43-44, 237; 44, 238, 422.

160   See Paul (2007), 252.
161   John Fennell argues that the devastation described in the chronicles is probably overstated and that many cities, including Novgorod, actually escaped ruin, while the economy rebounded relatively quickly after the invasion. Fennell (1983), 86-90. Saunders writes that the Mongols "inflicted upon her [Rus'] a permanent injury." Saunders, 82. David Miller argues, based on church construction, that the Mongol Invasion did have a significant immediate impact, but that the economy had recovered sufficiently by the end of the thirteenth century to support large church constructions. With this in mind, it is possible that the archiepiscopal office, if impacted by the Mongol invasion, as it likely was, could have recovered by the beginning of the fourteenth century. Why it took another generation is unclear. Cf. Miller, (1989), 360-390.
162   NPL, 100, 362.
163   NPL, 362, (s.a. 1352); Mikhailov, 315-320.
164   NPL, 367; PskL, 2:105, 106.
165   NPL, 367.
166   PskL, 2:105.
167   NPL, 383. A decade later he was given jurisdiction for a month "according to custom," after which he blessed the city and returned to Novgorod. Ibid., 396.
168   N4, 426; Avgustin (Nikitin; Archimandrite), 54; Nikitskii (1879), 64; P. Tikhomirov (1891-1900), 1:235-236.
169   NPL, 426-7; N4, 442; Nikitskii (1879), 64. The number of pastoral visits after 1330 indicates an apparent increase in archiepiscopal activities within the archeparchy just before interactions with the wider Rus' church declined in the fifteenth century.

170	NPL, 52, 250; *Sof. 1*, 262; *Mosk.*, 109.
171	NPL, 60, 261.
172	PskL, 2:23 (s.a. 1330).
173	The village of Opoki, where the Udokha flows into the Shelon' River, is about fifty miles east of Pskov and now just inside the Pskov Oblast'. In 1346, Grand Prince Algirdas of Lithuania conquered the village and others along the Shelon'. NPL, 358.
174	NPL, 100; Paul (2007), 249, 254. Paul, "Vasilii Kalika," 253-271.
175	Seals of these *namestniki* found during archaeological digs and are presented in Ianin (1970) and Ianin and Gaidukov, *Aktovye pechati*, 2:51-67, 179-188, 267-273; 3:79-86, 181-189, 286-290. The Pskov Chronicles also indicate the archbishops sometimes sent *namestniki* to act on their behalf in that city. Thus, in 1411, Archbishop Ioann II sent the archpriest (*protopop*) Timofei to Pskov to carry out his *poezdka*, but the Pskovites sent him back saying the pastoral visit was the duty of the archbishop alone. Ioann went himself two years later. Khoroshev claims he sat in judgment for two weeks rather than the usual month, though the chronicles do not actually say how long he visited. NPL 404; N3, 119; N4, 413; PskL, 1:33, 2:119; Khoroshev (1989),105. Ianin argues Ladoga was politically administered by the archbishop's *namestnik*, possibly explaining why the archbishop almost never visited the city himself. I don't find this assertion convincing. These towns may have been ecclesiastical administrative centers similar to vicariates in the West, explaining the significant number of the *namestniki*'s seals found. Ianin (1960), 252-256; idem, (1970), 2:60; Paul (2007), 244.
176	Stefan of Perm' converted some pagans in the far eastern reaches of the Novgorodian archeparchy and a new bishopric was created at Perm' in the late fourteenth century.
177	The last of the Novgorodian *pistsovye knigi* date to the 1560s.
178	Balovnev, 131-139. The cadastres are incomplete, and do not include all of the Obonezhskaia Fifth.
179	Ibid., 132.
180	Ibid., 137. There are discrepancies in several of Balovnev's totals and I have modified the percentages for the *d'iaki* and *ponomari* based on my calculations. The additional *proskurnitsa* that Balovnev counted did not alter the percentage he gave (40%).
181	AI 1.4:5-7; 1.6:9-16.
182	This suggest that the archbishop did not have the authority to consecrate antimensions (and thus consecrate churches – specifically their altars), at least in Pskov, at this time. However, there

is an antimension in the State Hermitage Museum dated September 1, 1148 for an altar "consecrated by Nifont, Archbishop of Novgorod, by command of the Bishop of Rostov Nestor," indicating that the archbishops had the authority, at least for a time, to consecrate churches in the archeparchy. Zagraevskii, 179-189. The antimension was found in the Church of St. Nicholas in the *Yaroslavovo Dvorishche*, but Aleksandr Musin argues it is actually for the nearby Church of St. George in the Marketplace based on the reference to St. George in the inscription. Musin (2016), 77-78. The bishop of Rostov's "command" was a commission for the construction of the church; he did not command Nifont to consecrate the antimension. See Nikolskii (1872), 29.

183 RIB 6.30:239-242; AI 1.8:17-18.

184 The *Novgorodian First Chronicle* noted that he "appointed Archimandrite Gelasi (as their *Vladyka*) and gave him the *Vladyka's* [i.e., the archbishop's] jurisdiction and all the taxes." NPL, 419; Halecki, 62. On various interpretations of this act, see Bobrov (2001), 194-196, esp., 194; Khoroshev (1989), 90; Pliguzov and Semenchenko, 11; Zimin (1991), 87.

185 PskL, 2:139-140, 143. Despite never visiting, several archbishops still interacted with Pskov. Ioann's dispatch of a *namestnik* to Pskov in 1411 has been noted, and Kiprian's letter noted above suggests Ioann may have visited the city around 1395; Simeon wrote a letter to Pskov in 1419 and Evfimii I issued a charter to the city in 1426. In 1477, Feofil also issued a charter. RIB 6.56:473-476; 6.47:401-402; 6.108:741-744. Based on Isidor's actions in 1437, if he had granted Pskov ecclesiastical autonomy from Novgorod, it had apparently been rescinded (perhaps after Novgorod's excommunication was lifted).

186 PskL 1:72; 2:157-158, 161-162, 166.

187 RIB 6.27:231-234; 6.28:233-236; 6.30:239-242; 6.41:361-366; 6.42:365-376; 6.43:375-384; 6.44:385-388; 6.48:403-418; 6.51:427-438; 6.53:466-472; 6.55:475-482, 6.56:481-488; 6.58:491-498; DSHRM Nos. 27-29, 59-62, 68, and 80; AI 1.21:42-45; 1.33:63-65; 1. 34:65-67; AfED Pril. 2:234-243; 2:247-251. Pril. 4:247-251; Pril. 5:251-253. Fotii's letters on liturgical and administrative practices are in DSHRM, No. 57, 63, 65, 72, 75. See also Stefan of Perm's letter against the *Strigol'niki* in RIB 6.25:211-228; AfED Pril. 3:234-243; Rybakov (1993), 150-222.

188 PskL, 2:151-159, (s.a. 1463-1464). In 1463, Pskov refused to pay fees to Novgorod and demanded their own bishop. Metropolitan Feodosii denied the request and ordered them to pay the fees. AI 1.277:508-510.

189	NPL, 343, (s.a. 1331).
190	Vasilii had already been elected in Novgorod. NPL, 342-343. For a discussion of his election and consecration, see Chapter Four, below.
191	NPL, 345.
192	Ibid., 348.
193	NPL, 100, 362; PskL 2:102.
194	PskL, 1:26 (s.a. 1400). *Preosviashchennyi* is sometimes translated as "Right Reverend."
195	PskL 1:48 (s.a. 1448), 1:49 (s.a. 1449), 1:50 (s.a. 1453), 1:54 (s.a. 1457), 1:55 (s.a. 1458), 1:72 (s.a. 1466).
196	AI 1.24:50 (s.a. 1416-1421); 1.31:61 (s.a. 1426); 1.44:87-88, (s.a. 1448-56); 1.77:126 (s.a. 1463); 1.269:500 (s.a. 1458); 1.274:506 (s.a. 1461); GVNP, doc. 48 A and B (s.a. 1405), pp. 85-86; doc. 50 (s.a. 1410-1411), p. 88, doc. 51 (s.a. 1411), p. 89; doc. 52 (s.a. 1411), p. 90; GVNP doc. 54 (s.a. 1417), p. 92; doc. 57 (s.a. 1418-1421), p. 95; doc. 60 (s.a. 1421), p. 99; doc. 66 (s.a. 1436), p. 109; doc. 67 (s.a. 1436), p. 110; doc. 71 (s.a. 1441), p. 117; doc. 72 (s.a. 1448), p. 118.
197	Ianin (1970), 2:49, 178, 284-285.
198	The metropolitans kept the title "Metropolitan of Kyiv and All Rus'" even after moving to Vladimir in 1299 and Moscow in 1325. For several examples of the continued use of the title after 1299, see RIB 6.26:229 (Metropolitan Kiprian to Archbishop Ioann in 1392); 6.42:365 (Metropolitan Fotii to Pskov in 1416); 6.64: 139 (Metropolitan Iona to the Lithuania Princes and nobles in 1448). However, this usage was not consistent and Kyiv was sometimes dropped, so they were titled "Metropolitan of All Rus'." Kyiv seems to have finally been completely dropped from the title under Metropolitan Feodosii (r.1461-1464). For examples without Kyiv in the title, see RIB 6.13:139; 6.18:163. 6.19:167; 6.20:173; 6.86:639; 6.95:689; 6.101:713. For a fuller discussion on the title, see Pliguzov (1991): 340-353.
199	See Ianin, "'Bolotovskii' Dogovor," 3-14.
200	*Sof.* 1, 226. S. Solov'ev (1959-1966), 2.3:258. This is similar to the 1393 Novgorodian charter giving Novgorod freedom from the Kyivan metropolitan's appellate jurisdiction, as noted in the previous chapter.
201	Grekov, ed. (1940), 237. The charter is also published in ZDR, 331-343; PRP, 2:302-324; Kaiser, ed. (1992), 88f., The term *sobor* (pl. *sobory*) is usually translated as "cathedral," but in Russian usage it means a large church (sometimes called a "main church") where daily liturgies are celebrated. In this sense, there were up to seven

sobory in Novgorod and six in Pskov by the end of the fifteenth century. A bishop's seat is currently translated as a *kafedral'nyi sobor*, though that term is not found in the sources until 1676. DAI 7:58; Bogatova et al., eds., 7:94; 23:79-80.

202 Grekov, ed. (1940), Art. 2, p. 237.
203 Ibid., Art. 109, p. 253.
204 Kaiser (1980), 101-114.
205 In addition to princely and judicial charters, the tale, "Novgorodskii sud i sviatyi Varlaam," speaks of the Novgorodian ecclesiastical courts. See Kushelev-Bezborodko and Kostomarov, eds., 1:273-274.
206 *Lavrent.*, 121, 124-125; *Sof. 1*, 105-111.
207 "The Short Russkaia Pravda," Art. 41, PRP, 1:84. Technically a tithe is one-tenth, while some fees are obviously more than that. The Longer Redaction of the *Pravda*, dating from the twelfth-century, and the Abbreviated Redaction do not mention the church.
208 The statute is not dated, but makes reference to Prince Vladimir consulting with his princess, Anna, who died in 1011. PRP, 1:237, 240, 244. Textual inconsistencies call into question the statute's eleventh century origin, and it survives in manuscripts only from the thirteenth and fourteenth centuries and was certainly used by the church at that time. Kaiser (1980), 50-51.
209 "The Statute of Saint Prince Volodimir," Art. 6 in the First Redaction, Arts. 6-7, PRP, 1:238, 245. Translation from Kaiser, ed. (1992), 42-3.
210 Ibid., Art. 9 in the Third Redaction, PRP, 1:245.
211 The entrusting of weights and measures to the bishop is perhaps drawn from Proverbs 16:11: "A just balance and scales are the Lord's; all the weights in the bag are his work." Though the proverb emphasizes justice, a literal interpretation in the medieval period might justify the bishop, as God's representative in the eparchy, overseeing them.
212 Ibid., Art. 6 of the Second Redaction and Art. 11 of the Third Redaction, PRP 1:242, 245-246. Translation from Kaiser, ed. (1992), 44.
213 Ibid., Art. 8 of the First Redaction, Art. 7 of the Second Redaction, Art. 12 of the Third Redaction, PRP, 1:238, 242, 246. Translation from Kaiser, ed. (1992), 44.
214 Ibid., Art. 8 of the Second Redaction; Art. 13 of the Third Redaction, PRP, 1:242, 246. Translation from Kaiser, ed. (1992), 44.
215 Ibid., Art. 8 of the Second Redaction; Art. 13 of the Third Redaction, PRP, 1:242, 246.

216	Ibid., Art. 14 of the Third Redaction, PRP, 1:246. Such anathemas are not uncommon in Russian and other Orthodox formal documents.
217	Kaiser (1980), 54.
218	The phrase appears in the various recensions of Vladimir's statute and most copies of Iaroslav's. See Shchapov (1976), (Vladimir's statute): 15, 18, 19, 21, 23, 31, 37, 43, 46, 55, 60 (in Latin), 62 and 66 (both mention the bishops of Rus', but not the metropolitan specifically – who is, in any event, a bishop), 70-71, 74, 77; (Iaroslav's statute): 86, 91, 93-94, 100, 110, 116, 121, 125 (in Latin), 128, 133. The Archival Recension refers to "hierarchs" (*sviatitel'em*) rather than to the metropolitan and bishops separately; Ibid., 103. The recension known as the "Svitka Iaroslavlia" does not have the exact phrase, but applies to the metropolitan and the bishops. Ibid., 137. The Ustiug redaction grants freedom to the metropolitan, bishops, priests, and deacons in all the cities. Ibid., 139. A church statute appearing after the Commission manuscript of the *Novgorodian First Chronicle* provides a list of church people similar to those enumerated in Vladimir's and Iaroslav's statutes, and recognizes the metropolitan's and bishops' authority over them. Copies of Vladimir's and Iaroslav's statutes follow, with Iaroslav's statute entitled "And behold, the Statute of Iaroslav (on the) Courts of the Hierarchs (*sviatitel'skaia*);" both recognize the rights of the metropolitan and the bishops over church courts. SPbII RAN F. 11, Sobranie Arkheograficheskoi komissii, No. 240, Komissionyi spisok Novgordoskoi pervoi letopisi, fols. 268v.-269v.; NPL, 478, 480, 481.
219	"The Statute of Prince Iaroslav," Prologue, PRP, 1:265.
220	Ibid., Art. 1, PRP, 1:266.
221	Ibid., Art. 2, PRP, 1:266.
222	Ibid., PRP, 1:267.
223	Ibid., Art. 8 in the Short Redaction; Art. 7 in the Longer Redaction, PRP, 1:260, 267.
224	Ibid., Art. 9 of the Short Redaction; Art. 11 of the Longer Redaction, PRP, 1:260, 267.
225	Ibid., Art. 7-8 in the Short Redaction; Art. 8-9 in the Longer Redaction, PRP, 1:260, 267.
226	Ibid., Art. 10 in the Short Redaction; Art. 12 in the Longer Redaction, PRP, 1:260-268.
227	Ibid., Arts. 11-12, in the Short Redaction; Arts. 13-14 in the Longer Redaction, PRP, 1:260, 268.
228	Ibid., Art. 13 of the Short Redaction; Art. 15 of the Longer Redaction, PRP, 1:260, 268.

229 Ibid., Art. 17, PRP, 1:268.
230 Ibid., Art. 15 in the Short Redaction; Art. 18 in the Longer Redaction, PRP, 1:260, 268.
231 Ibid., Art. 19, PRP, 1:268.
232 Ibid., Arts. 21-26, PRP 1:268-269.
233 Ibid., Arts. 25-27 of the Short Redaction; Arts. 30-32, of the Longer Redaction, PRP, 1:261, 269. The theft of white cloth and other items may have also been part of outlawed pagan rituals.
234 Ibid., Art. 33, PRP, 1:269.
235 Ibid., Arts. 28-31 of the Short Redaction; Arts. 37-43 of the Longer Redaction, PRP, 1:261, 269-270.
236 Ibid., Art. 43, PRP, 1:270.
237 Ibid., Art. 33 in the Short Redaction; 45 in the Longer Redaction, PRP, 1:262, 270.
238 Ibid., Art. 48, PRP, 1:270.
239 Ibid., Art. 52, PRP, 1:270.
240 Ibid., Art. 54, PRP, 1:271. A *volostel'* oversaw a *volost* or rural district.
241 Ibid., Art. 35 in the Shorter Redaction; Art. 54 of the Longer Redaction, PRP, 1:262, 272.
242 Ibid., Art. 35 of the Shorter Redaction; Art. 54 of the Longer Redaction, PRP, 1:262, 272.
243 PRP, 1. 237, 241, 244.
244 "Smolenskie ustavnye gramoty," PRP, 2:39-52.
245 Kaiser (1980), 58.
246 Paul (2008), 84-85.
247 "Statute of the Novgorodian Prince Vsevolod," Art. 4 in PRP, 2:162-163.
248 Ibid., Arts. 4 and 5 in PRP, 2:162-163. St. John's was where the weights and measures were kept as well as the fees collected for their use.
249 "Novgorodskaia sudnaia gramota," PRP, 2:212; AAE, 1.92:69-72.
250 Ibid., Art. 3, PRP, 2:212.
251 Ibid., Art. 1, PRP, 2:212.
252 Ibid., Art. 6 in PRP, 2:212.
253 Ibid., Art. 6 in PRP, 2:213.
254 Ibid., Art. 8, PRP, 2:213.
255 Ibid., Art. 9, PRP, 2:213; The Russian text mentions "the archbishop's *posadnik*," which Kaiser notes, is probably a scribal error. Kaiser, ed. (1992), 80.
256 Ibid., Art. 23, PRP, 2:215.
257 Ibid., Art. 26, PRP, 2:215. This is thought to be the Palace of Facets, built by Evfimii II in 1433.

258 Ibid., Art. 28, PRP, 2:215-216.
259 Weickhardt, 420.
260 Weickhardt, 420-421; F. Dmitriev, 93.
261 AI 1.24:50; Weickhardt, 421.
262 Two of these monasteries were founded prior to their episcopates: Arkadii founded the Arkadievskii (Arkazh') Uspenskii Monastery in 1153, remnants of which still stand along the road to the Iur'ev Monastery south of Novgorod. Martirii founded the Spaso-Preobrazhenskii (or Transfiguration) Monastery in Staraia Russa in 1192. NPL, 29, 215; 40, 231.
263 In 1131, Nifont "placed Anton" as hegumen of the Antoniev Monastery. In 1195, following the death of the hegumenia Khristina, Martirii and "all the nuns" of the convent of St. Barbara "chose and appointed" Varvara Giurievna Olekshinitsa as the new hegumenia and Martirii consecrated her on St. Euphemia's day (July 11 or September 16; since this episode appears after the building of a church begun May 4 and completed on August 2, Varvara's consecration would likely have been on 16 September.) In 1226, Archbishop Antonii, Posadnik Ivanko, and all the Novgorodians chose an unnamed Greek priest of the Church of Constantine and Helena to succeed Savatii as archimandrite (and hegumen of the Iur'ev Monastery). In 1230, Sava was removed as archimandrite and Archbishop Spiridon and all the Novgorodians led Arsenii out of the Khutyn Monastery and made him archimandrite. NPL, 22, 207 (s.a. 1131); 42 (s.a. 1195); 65, 269 (s.a. 1226); 70, 278 (s.a. 1230). On February 15, 1461, Archbishop Iona placed German ("an honest and good man") as the archimandrite of the Khutyn Monastery (indicating there was a second one in the archeparchy by this time, since the "Archimandrite of Novgorod" was at the Iur'ev Monastery.) *Avraamki*, 204. In most instances, however, the chronicles merely state that a hegumen died and "they placed" another in his place, which could mean the monks of the monastery or the Novgorodians more broadly.
264 Council of Chalcedon, Canon 4, in Percival, 270.
265 Council of Chalcedon, Canon 8, in Percival, 273.
266 Council of Chalcedon, Canon 24, in Percival, 284.
267 "The Statute of Prince Iaroslav," Art. 54 of the Longer Redaction, in ZDR, 192. Cf., The Eastern Rus' Redaction in PRP, 1:271.
268 Kaiser (1980), 59; PRP, 3:438.
269 "The Pravosudie mitropolich'e," Art. 38, in RFA (1948 or 1951), 2 vols. (Moscow: AN SSSR, 1948-1951), 2: 25-29; PRP, 3:428, 432.
270 Zimin and Lur'e, eds., 239-240.

271 N2, 184; N3, 247; N4, 537; *Zhitie sviatitelia Serapiona Arkhiepiskopa Novgorodskogo*; P. Tikhomirov (1891-1900), 2.1:90-91; Zdravomislov, 29; Paul, "Continuity and Change," 285-286.
272 DAI 1.55:36-38. He wrote the hegumen after receiving a letter on the matter from Metropolitan Makarii.
273 GVNP, doc. 82, p.141.
274 Archbishop Simeon granted land to the monastery in the early fifteenth century. Ibid., doc. 90, p. 147.
275 Ibid., doc. 94, pp. 149-150.
276 Ibid., doc. 97, p. 153; doc. 100, p. 155.
277 Ibid., doc. 107, p. 164. See also doc. 108, pp. 164-165; doc. 109, pp. 165-166; doc. 115, p. 174.
278 Ibid., doc. 102, p. 159; doc. 104, p. 161.
279 Ibid., doc. 112, p. 172.
280 Ibid., doc. 114, p. 173.
281 Ibid., doc. 117, pp. 175-176. See also doc. 118, p. 176; doc. 119, p. 176-177; doc. 120, pp. 177-178; doc. 121, p. 178; doc. 123, p. 182; doc. 124, p. 183; 125, p. 183; doc. 126, p. 184.
282 Granberg (2006), 31-32; Ianin (1963), 118-127.
283 NPL, 465-475; N4, 623-627. Kirill ("Kiur'iak") is listed as the first archimandrite, but these lists do not correspond very closely to the Stroev's list, and thus may not be the same office.
284 As noted above, there was a second archimandrite at the Khutyn Monastery by 1461.
285 In towns with no bishop, the archimandrite or hegumen of the town's chief monastery was ceremonial head of the local clergy. When the archbishop was absent from Novgorod – during a vacant see or while was away on "church business" in Kyiv or Moscow or on visitation, the archimandrite of the Iur'ev Monastery may have played this same role. This, however, did not necessarily make him "head" of the black clergy while the archbishop was in the city, and certainly not in any formal sense.
286 Sava was also one of the candidates for archbishop in 1359. NPL. 365, 375.
287 In 1310, Archimandrite Kirill built the Church of the Dormition at Kolomtsy. In 1410, Archimandrite Varlaam erected the Church of St. Varlaam of Khutyn over the gate of the Lisitsa Monastery. NPL, 93, 333; 402.
288 The first archimandrite mentioned in the chronicle, Savatii, died in 1226, where he is called both hegumen of the Iur'ev Monastery and archimandrite of Novgorod, as is Varlaam in 1270, suggesting the offices were not synonymous. NPL, 65, 269; 88, 319. That said,

Stroev lists Kirill (archimandrite from 1295-1310) as the first archimandrite, and thus the earlier references may be later, anachronistic interpolations, much as early Novgorodian bishops are sometimes referred to as archbishops long before 1165. The next monastery to have an archimandrite was the Khutyn Monastery, but that was only in formally established in 1608. See Stroev, 45, 50.

289 For a discussion of these traditional assessments of the archimandrites, see Nesin, 44-139. See also Kuzmina, 97-103.

290 Papadakis, 39. The monks of Mt. Athos have often stood in opposition to the Byzantine or Greek hierarchy during heresies or other conflicts, such as the efforts to implement the Union of Florence. See Gill, 394.

291 Papadakis, 39-40.

292 They may, however, be based on the *typikon* of a more famous monastery. The liturgical *typikon* of the Studion Monastery in Constantinople served as the basis for a number of later monastic foundations, including the Kyiv Caves Monastery. Standardization of monastic worship began under St. Sabbas the Sanctified (439-539), who compiled earlier teachings into what is variously called the *Jerusalem, Palestinian,* or *Sabbaite typikon,* revised by Patriarch Sophronius of Jerusalem (r.634-638) and then added to by St. John Damascene (676-749). See "Sabas: Founder's Typikon of the Sabas Monastery near Jerusalem" in Thomas and Hero, eds., 1311-1318. See also Herman, "Byzantine Monasticism," in Hussey ed. (1967), 4.2:169-170. On the *typika* in Rus' see Vernadsky (1976), 206. It should be noted that Vernadsky may have overlooked the distinction between *liturgical* and *disciplinary typika*.

293 Michael Angold noted: "The founding of every monastery required a *stauropegion*, or 'blessing over the foundation.' This took the form of the planting of a cross, whence the name *stauropegion*. It was normally performed by the local bishop and was an earmark of the rights that he would subsequently exercise over the monastery." Angold (1995), 338. See also Herman, "Byzantine Monasticism," in Hussey ed. (1967), 4.2:170.

294 Angold (1995), 337-345.

295 Davidenko, "Moskovskii Simonovskii Monastyr'," *Pravoslavnaia entsiklopediia* 47:479.

296 The chronicles mention instances where the archbishops helped found monasteries or blessed a foundation, such as when Moisei founded the Derevianitskii Monastery north of the Market Side in 1335 and the Monastery of St. Michael the Archangel at Skovorod-

ka southeast of the Novgorod ca. 1350 (he built a stone church in the monastery in 1355). Both were founded between his tenures as archbishop. NPL, 346; 364. Beyond the chronicles, the "Tale of Shchil', Posadnik of Novgorod," tells of an apocryphal confrontation between Shchil' and an Archbishop Ivan at the founding of Shchil"s monastery. In one version, two men are sent to the archbishop to request that he bless the monastery's main church. The *Novgorodian First Chronicle* notes that the Shchilov Monastery was founded in 1310; in the Older Redaction the founder is not referred to as Shchil' or Sshchkil', but as Olonia, his monastic name; in any event, there was no Archbishop Ivan (either Il'ia or Ioann) in 1310; David was archbishop. NPL, 93, 333. "Povest' o Shchile posadnike novgorodskom," in Kushelev-Bezborodko and Kostomarov, eds., 1:21-24. The "Tale of the Founding of the Annunciation Monastery" mentions Archbishop Feoktist blessing the founding. See "Povest' o postroenii Blagoveshchenskogo monastyria v Novgorode," in Kushelev-Bezborodko and Kostomarov, eds., 1:255-256. The monastery was founded in 1170 under Il'ia and his brother, Gavriil; Feoktist was not archbishop until 1299. NPL, 33, 222. The "Tale of Antonii Rimlianin" notes that Antonii had Bishop Nikita bless the founding of the Antoniev Monastery in 1117. See "Povest' ob Antonii Rimlianine," in Kushelev-Bezborodko and Kostomarov, eds., 1:263-270, esp. 265-267. Nikita, however, had died in 1108; Ioann Pop'ian was bishop in 1117. NPL, 19, 203. While not historically accurate, these legends reveal that the Novgorodians who composed and listened to them recognized the role of the archbishops in blessing new monastic foundations.

297   As noted above, stauropegial monasteries take their name from the bishop planting a cross, signifying his approval of the monastic foundation. The Russian term is *stavropegiia*. The sixty-sixth chapter of the Stoglav Council gave prelates jurisdiction "in accordance with the sacred canons [over] all holy coenobitic and idiorhythmic (*obshche i osob'sushchie*) monasteries and also maiden's convents, and over all archimandrites, hegumens, hegumenesses, priors (*stroiteli*), the entire sacerdotal and monastic orders, and all unordained church servitors." Kollmann (1978), 475. As such, the bishops would have had to approve the founding of new monasteries. The Stoglav considered church consecration an episcopal prerogative that had been infringed upon by the cathedral clergy and the Moscow Council of 1667 specifically ruled that only a prelate could consecrate a church, strengthening his control over

	the monasteries, since he would have to approve the erection of monastic churches. How much these prerogatives were maintained, or eroded, before the seventeenth century is unknown. See Kollmann (1978), 370-371.
298	In 1173, Il'ia consecrated the Church of the Holy Savior at the Gates of the Iur'ev Monastery. Il'ia and his brother, Gavriil, founded the stone church of the Annunciation in the monastery by the gates seven years later, and after Il'ia's death, Gavriil consecrated the Church of the Dormition in the Arkadii Monastery on June 4, 1189. In 1192, Gavriil consecrated the Khutyn Monastery. In 1195, Martirii consecrated a church in the Resurrection Monastery and in 1196 the Church of St. Kirill in the Monastery of St. Kirill on Liubianin Street. NPL, 34, 223; 36, 226; 39, 230; 40, 231; 42, 234; 42, 235.
299	Ibid., 400.
300	Ibid., 394.
301	Ibid., 20, 22; 204, 207.
302	Ibid., 42, 234.
303	Ibid. The chronicle later states that Sava died that same year, so his replacement may have been due to ill health rather than some offense.
304	Ibid., 364, 365, 368.
305	Ibid., 30, 217.
306	Ibid., 41, 234.
307	Antonii retired to the Khutyn Monastery in 1228. His death is listed sub anno 1232, with the comment that he had gone mute on March 17, 1228, the feast of St. Aleksei the Man of God (d. 411). NPL 72, 281. Feoktist retired to the Monastery of the Annunciation in 1308 and died two years later just before Christmas; and Aleksei and Ioann both retired to the Derevianitskii Monastery. NPL, 92, 270; 332, 381, 383, 405. Paul, "Continuity and Change," 306.
308	NPL, 22, 207.
309	NPL, 272; Stroev, 35.
310	NPL, 99, 342, 368.
311	Ibid., 414; Paul, "Continuity and Change," 306.
312	*Nikon*. (PSRL 12), 197; Zimin and Levina, eds., 119; Stroev, 35; Makarii, *Istoriia*, 4:353-354. On the different dates for Feofil's death, see Chapter Four, below.
313	Stroev, 33.
314	NPL, 99, 365, 368. See also Paul, "Continuity and Change," 279-280. In 1686 his remains were reburied at the Dukhov Monastery. Stroev, 35.

315	Stroev, 35.
316	Indeed, he is known as Evfimii Viazhitskii. Golubinskii (1903), 82.
317	Stroev, 35.
318	Ibid.
319	Charanis (1971), 73.
320	Von Lingenthal, ed., 3:292-296, Novel 19; Charanis (1948), 56-58; idem (1971), 73. The Emperor Basil II also wrote against the proliferation of monasteries in a novel in 996. Charanis (1948), 63.
321	According to some accounts, the Studion Monastery under the direction of Theodore Studite grew from twelve monks to more than a thousand. Charanis (1971), 69, 72.
322	Ibid., 72.
323	Ibid., 73.
324	Makarii, *Istoriia*, 2:668-674, 3:649-662; Stroev, 42-130; 385-412. Stroev lists 100 monasteries in the Novgorodian Land, of which only thirty-nine were known to have been founded prior to 1478. Another three monasteries were founded at the end of the 15th century, but it is not clear if they were founded before 1478. Another eleven monasteries not listed by Stroev are found in the *Novgorodian First Chronicle*. NPL, passim. Stroev listed forty-five monasteries in the Pskov eparchy, of which six are known to have been founded prior to 1478 and another three by the end of the fifteenth century. Gnevushev counted 138 monasteries in the Novgorodian Land listed in the land cadastres, but it is not clear when 48 of them were founded. Cf., Stroev; Gnevushev.
325	Nikitskii (1873), 205. The *Novgorodian Fourth Chronicle* notes that in the 1520s, there were, according to statute, between 2 and 7 monks or nuns per monastery. N4, 545; Makarii (2002), 42. This, however, was well after the Conquest of Novgorod and a seventeen-year vacant see, so these figures may not reflect the size of monasteries in the pre-Conquest period. The *Zhitie of Archbishop Iona* claims 7,650 monks and nuns died along with 300 parish priests during an outbreak of the plague in 1466 (out of a total of 220,652 deaths throughout the Novgorodian Land), indicating a monastic population significantly larger than the seven monks or nuns per monastery suggested by Nikitskii. See P. Tikhomirov (1891-1900), 1:292.
326	Nikitskii (1879), 63-64.
327	Ordination by the archbishop is mentioned only once in the sources, sub anno 1144, when the chronicler referred to his own ordination by Archbishop Nifont. NPL, 27. Tikhomirov suggests this is the future archbishop, Il'ia; others believe it is German Voiata.

P. Tikhomirov (1891-1900), 1:77. O. V. Tvorogov, "Ioann (v miru Il'ia)," in SKKDR 1:209. Gennadii's removal in 1504 for charging fees for ordination (and a higher fee than usual) indicate the archbishop conducted ordinations, but there are few other examples. Outside Novgorod, there is one document noting the ordination of a priest by the bishop of Perm'. RIB 6.105:737-738; 6.6:92.

Chapter Four

1 P. Tikhomirov (1862); idem, (1891-1900), passim; Zdravomislov, passim.
2 "Povest' o Moisee, Arkhiepiskope Novgorodom," in Kushelev-Bezborodko and Kostomarov, eds., 4:11; Taisiia, *Zhitiia sviatykh*, 1:71-73; P. Tikhomirov, ed., (1890).
3 Taisiia, *Zhitiia sviatykh*, 1:151. Tikhomirov says his father's name was Mikheia, and he was the priest of the Church of St. Theodore the Great Martyr (the Church of Theodore Stratelates on the Brook). P. Tikhomirov (1891-1900), 1:245.
4 Filaret writes that Iona was taught letters by "a *d'iak*," called a "former deacon" in the published version of Iona's *Life* (where his stepmother is not named). See Filaret, 1:309; "Vospominanie o blagoslovennom Ione," in Kushelev-Bezborodko and Kostomarov, eds., 4:28.
5 "Vospominanie o blagoslovennom Ione," in Kushelev-Bezborodko and Kostomarov, eds., 4:27-35; Filaret, 3:308-309; P. Tikhomirov (1891-1900), 1:272-273. The recollections are given in the first person in Filaret and Tikhomirov, but in the third person in Kushelev-Bezborodko and Kostomarov. The first-person account appears to be from RNB Q.XVII.50 (see for example fol. 358), which Karamzin identified in his *Istoriia rossiskogo gosudarstva* as *Zapiska Volokolamskogo Monastyria* No. 666. On the identification of No. 666 as RNB Q.XVII.50, see Zimin (1977), 16n16, 23n75; see also Abelentseva (2002), 40-47, esp. 42.
6 N4, 390.
7 N3, 235.
8 Antonii, (Dobrynia Iadreikovich [Andreikovich]; Archbishop of Novgorod), "Kniga Palomnik"; Belobrova, 225-235.
9 Vernadsky (1976), 185-6; idem (1965), 18; idem (1959), 37; Karamzin (1959) 7, 8; Platonov (1997), 139; Froianov (1980), 150; Froianov and Dvornichenko, 168, 171-172, 187-188; Sergeevich, passim; Iu. Alekseev, 242-274; Rowell, 22; Fedotov, 2:186-194; Igor Froianov argues that all bishops in Kyivan Rus' were elected by the city

10 Nikitskii (1879), 54-57. In five elections (Archbishop Aleksei's in 1359, Ioann's in 1388, Simeon's in 1415, Feodosii's in 1421, and Evfimii I's in 1423) the lots were "laid on the throne" (*na prestole*). In 1192 and 1229, they were laid "on the holy altar" (*na sviatei triapeze*). In the last two cases of election by lots (the election of Evfimii II in 1429, and Feofil in 1470), it is not said where the lots were laid. NPL, 68, 232, 275, 365, 381, 405, 414, 415; *Mosk.*, 284; *Nikon.* (PSRL 12), 125. The altar (*triapez; altar'* in modern Russian) was sometimes referred to as the throne (*prestol*), and in modern Orthodox teaching, is still sometimes referred to as such. See, for example, Belovinskii.

11 Fedotov, 2:190-191.

12 Shchapov (1989), 63-64. He also writes that the archbishops were "elected on the spot, and subsequently endorsed in Kiev." He does not discuss the change from *veche* election to sortition.

13 Rowell, 22.

14 Ibid., 174.

15 Sokol, "Veche," in MERSH, 41:241.

16 Nazarenko (2000) 1:47.

17 Eparchies were supposedly established in Kyiv, Novgorod, Polatsk, Bilhorod (a suburb of Kyiv), and Chernihiv soon after the conversion in 988 (or 992). However, *The Rus' Primary Chronicle* does not say this, but merely that "He [Vladimir] began to found churches and to assign priests throughout the cities, and to invite the people to accept baptism in all the cities and towns." *Lavrent.*, 118. Several chronicles report Metropolitan Leon arriving in Kyiv and Ioakim Korsunianin ("Archbishop Akim") being sent to Novgorod "and to other cities bishops and priests and deacons who baptized all the Rus' Land". *Sof. 1*, 105-106; *Ermolin.*, 15; *Ermitazh.* 365.

18 N3, 243; N4, 525; *Mosk.*, 330; Kloss (1998), 131-132; Paul, "Continuity and Change," 277-281.

19 NPL, 29, 216.

20 Eizo, 208n8. John Meyendorff notes that "the selection of Basil [Vasilii] by lot is indicated by the conventional expression 'designated by God' ('Bogom naznamenana')." Meyendorff (1981), 84n39. The nine elections where lots are specifically mentioned are of Martirii, Spiridon, Aleksei, Ioann, Simeon, Feodosii, Evfimii I, Evfimii II, and Feofil. The eight instances where bishops or archbishops were "chosen by God," "by the will of God," or were

assembly, though he provides no evidence to support this claim. Froianov (1980), 135-37. Eizo, 207.

"God-designated" are of Arkadii, Mitrofan, Antonii, Kliment, Feoktist, David, Moisei, and Vasilii.

21   Metropolitan Kiprian, wrote in a letter dated June 23, 1378, addressed to Sergei of Radonezh and Fedor, hegumen of the Simonov Monastery in Moscow, that he had been appointed metropolitan "through the will of God," though he also wrote that this election had been carried out "through election of the great and holy synod, through the blessing and installation by the ecumenical patriarch..."   RIB 6.20:173-86; DSHRM, No. 15; Meyendorff (1981), Appendix 8, 293.

22   For example, see "Chin izbraniia i postavleniia v episkopy," in Beneshevich, ed., (1915), 24-41; The *Novgorodian First Chronicle* also uses the word *izbrati* when writing of the selection of the archbishops. NPL, 29, 216, 365.

23   The term was used by the early church, including Popes Celestine I (r.422-432) and Leo I (r. 440-461), and later by the Second Canon of the Council of Aix-la-Chapelle in 857, and elsewhere. See Parsons, 9-26, 40.

24   On episcopal election in the Western Church, see Barnes, "Cathedral," in Strayer, ed., 3:191-192; Green, "Elections, Church," in Strayer, ed., 4:421-425; Heintschel, passim; Parsons, passim; Warren, "(Cathedral) Chapter," in Strayer, ed., 3:265-266.

25   Golubinskii (1995), 1.1:360.
26   Vernadsky (1976), 205.
27   Khoroshev (1989), 35.
28   Douglas, 40.
29   DSK 1:62. See also Chapter One above.
30   Ibid., 1:67-68.
31   Ibid., 1:84-85.
32   Ibid., 1:208.
33   See Chapter One, above.
34   Aleksandr Musin argues that popular election of the bishop was canonically-permissible and that claims to the contrary are ahistorical, but later notes that archiepiscopal election in Novgorod "had certain differences from the requirements of the canons," most notably election by lot and the lack of three candidates, but he then insists "all features have their own explanations that do not go beyond the limits of permissible deviations from church canons." Musin (2016), 83-85, 96, 97.

35   The decree is published in RIB 6.5:79-84; Fennell (1995), 51.
36   Kliuchevskii attributes the *Life of Metropolitan Peter* to Prokhor of Rostov, but Børtnes rejects this, attributing it to Kiprian based on

	"the earlier Life...written by an anonymous Muscovite around 1327." Kliuchevskii, (1871, reprinted, 1968), 74ff; Børtnes, 116; Kuchkin, 59-79.
37	*Stepennaia kniga*, 1:325; Kiprian (Metropolitan of Kyiv and All Rus'), 1629; Børtnes, 122.
38	RIB 6.20:176-178; DSHRM, No. 15.
39	AAE dates the document to 1456, but Pavlov, in his introduction in RIB 6:437-438, dates it to 1423, as does Pliguzov in DSHRM, No. 73.
40	"Chin izbraniia i postavleniia v" episkopy," in RIB 6.52:437-464, esp. 437-439.
41	This is probably a reference to Ps. 7:15 (verse 16 in the Old Church Slavic Bible: "They make a pit (*rov*), digging it out, and fall into the hole (*iama*) that they have made." It could also refer to Prov.28:10: "Those who mislead the upright into evil ways will fall into pits of their own making, but the blameless will have a goodly inheritance" or Mt. 15:14: "Let them alone; they are blind guides of the blind. And if one blind person guides another, both will fall into a pit." However, the word *rov* is not used in the verses in Proverbs or Matthew in the Old Church Slavic Bible, *zapadnia* – trap, snare, pit – is used in Proverbs, and *iama* – pit, hole – is used in Matthew.
42	RIB 6.52:439-440.
43	The election was carried out on the instructions of "the Metropolitan of the Rus' Land," and Ioann was consecrated by "Metropolitan Pimen of all Rus'" (*"mitropolitom Puminom vseia Rusi"*). NPL, 381-83 (s. a. 1388).
44	Regel, ed., doc. 12, pp. 52-56, esp. 56; Vasil'evskii, 445-463; Meyendorff (1981), 81-85.
45	Regel, ed., doc. 12, p. 56; Vasil'evskii, 452.
46	NPL, 99, 342-43. The Younger Redaction adds "from great to small" and "gentle" in describing, respectively, the Novgorod assembly and Vasilii.
47	Eizo, 209; Meyendorff (1981), 84. Musin likewise suggestion that the term denotes sortition. Musin (2016), 99.
48	Meyendorff (1981), 84.
49	Vasil'evskii, 211.
50	NPL, 343; Rowell, 173-176; Eizo, 213-215. NPL, 343; N4, 264; *Sof. 1*, 219.
51	Eizo, 215.
52	Rowell, 174.
53	NPL, 67; 272. See also Majeska, 29.
54	NPL, 61-68; 263-74; Stroev, 35: A. Alekseev (2005), 296.

55	NPL 62-63, 265-267; *Suzdal.*, 446-447; *Ipat.* (PSRL 2.2), 741-745; *The Nikonian Chronicle* speaks of "seventy great and brave bogatyrs" being killed, along with many "*tysiaskie, voevody*, most of the boiars" and many common soldiers. *Nikon.* (PSRL 10), 92. Mstislav Mstislavich the Daring (*Udaloi*) is the only prince specifically named as having escaped by the *Novgorodian First Chronicle*, but Fennell notes half the princes actually survived the battle and the Mongols' pursuit. Fennell (1983), 66-68.
56	*Nikon.* (PSRL 10), 92. Fennell rejects this as implausible, as he does the *Novgorodian First Chronicle's* figure of only a tenth of the Russians surviving or of "countless numbers" slaughtered and the *Suzdalian Chronicles* figure of 10,000 killed. NPL, 63, 267; *Suzdal.*, 446-447; Fennell, (1983), 66-68.
57	NPL, 267.
58	Kirill's consecration is listed sub anno 1224 in the *Suzdalian Chronicle*. *Suzdal.*, 448; *Ipat.* (PSRL 2.2), 753. Stroev gives the year as 1225 and lists no metropolitan in Kyiv between 1214 and 1225. Stroev, col. 2.
59	NPL, 413-4; Khoroshev (1989), 85.
60	These are the elections of 1193, 1229, 1274, 1359, 1388, 1415, and 1421.
61	Of all the archbishops whose backgrounds are known (and again, many of their backgrounds are found in saints' lives), whether they were elected or not, we find that six were hegumens, five were monks, two were priests, two were specifically *dukhovniki*, one was an archimandrite, one was a *kliuchnik*, and one was an archdeacon (*protodeacon*). Of the bishops prior to 1165, two were Greeks whose office before their episcopate is not known, two were hegumens, and two were monks. The backgrounds of three are unknown, and of another all that can be said is that he was Rus' and not Greek.
62	While early church councils recognized this occurrence, they called for a timely period of training. That said, the candidates from the white clergy in Novgorod were sometimes advanced through the clerical ranks within a matter of weeks, as noted above in the case of Aleksei in 1359. This phenomenon was not exclusive to Novgorod; Patriarch Photius of Constantinople was a layman at the time of his election and was advanced through the ranks of deacon and priest and shorn a monk all within a week of his election. See Norwich, 64-65; "Photios," in Kazhdan et al., 3:1669.
63	The *Novgorodian First Chronicle* refers to Vasilii as "the former

	priest of Sts. Cosmas and Damian Church on Slave Street," and says he was tonsured in the Holy Angel's Monastery in January, 1331 after his election. NPL, 99, 342-343, 344, 346. Cf., Regel, doc. 12, p. 56; Vasil'evskii, 452; Eizo, 210. The *Novgorodian First Chronicle* mentions Vasilii's "children" several times, probably used in the sense of "spiritual children" as it is used during Evfimii's visit to the Zavoloch'e, where there is indication that he was ever a member of the white clergy prior to his archiepiscopate. NPL, 426.
64	Metropolitan Petr (r. 1308-1326) ruled that parish priests retire to a monastery when their wives died and Metropolitan Fotii (r.1408-1431) reiterated this. RIB 6.17:161; 6.51:434-435. There is precedent for this in Byzantine canon law, as noted in a complaint from the early sixteenth century. See Bodianskii, ed., 45-50. The Church Council of 1667 abrogated this rule. See Subbotin, ed., pt. 2, pp. 86v-87.
65	DSHRM, No. 80.
66	Gnevushev, 348-359. As noted above, a review of sources, including lists of monasteries in the 1995-1997 edition of Makarii's *Istoriia russkoi tserkvi* and Stroev, reveal only 90 monasteries in the Novgorodian and Pskov lands, of which 85 are known for certain to have existed before 1478. Makarii, *Istoriia*, 2:668-674, 3:649-662; Stroev, 42-130; 385-412. Other sources list only 55 monasteries in the Novgorodian archeparchy in the fifteenth century, up from 17 in the thirteenth century. Kul'pinova, Zherve, and Strakhova, eds., 9.
67	Prior to the archiepiscopate, German and Nikita also came from the Kyiv Caves Monastery.
68	Feofil, came out of the archiepiscopal administration as well, so that the House of Holy Wisdom monopolized the election of 1471.
69	Budovnits, 47-48.
70	Gnevushev; Danilova, 46; Podvigina, 44.
71	Gnevushev, 348-359.
72	Leontii and Isaiia of Iaroslavl' were monks at the Kyiv Caves Monastery in the late eleventh and twelfth centuries. Stroev, 329; Serapion, Archimandrite of the Kyiv Caves Monastery, became Bishop of Vladimir in 1274. Golubinskii (1995), 2.1:65; Stroev, 653.
73	Gnevushev, 348.
74	Metropolitan Feognost's registry shows a similar preference for hieromonks. Twenty-nine of thirty-seven candidates in thirteen elections were hieromonks, two were archimandrites, and six were either not named, or their clerical office not given. Regel, 52-56.

75	NPL, 29-30, 216.
76	Paul (2008), 91, 110.
77	NPL, 40 (s.a. 1193).
78	Ibid., 231-232 (s.a. 1193).
79	NPL, 68, 274-275. Prince Mikhail Vsevolodovich was Prince of Novgorod from 1225 to 1226 and again from 1229 to 1230. See Paul (2008), 93.
80	NPL, 365.
81	Ibid., 365.
82	On Ontsifor's reforms, see Ianin (2003), 262-287, esp. 270-272.
83	NPL, 322-323.
84	VPL, 230. The *Okonchanie Spiska Stroevskogo* of the *Novgorodian Fourth Chronicle* does not mention the *veche*, only reporting that Archbishop Feofil was chosen by lots during a liturgy at the Cathedral of Holy Wisdom, N4, 446.
85	N4, 349.
86	NPL, 232.
87	NPL, 68. 275. Tatishchev claims Rostislav was seven years old at the time of his *postrig*, the ceremony where he was shorn Prince of Novgorod, in spring 1230. Tatishchev, 4:369. There is no way of knowing if Rostislav was coached to pick his father's candidate. Martin Dimnik argues all the candidates were supporters of Prince Mikhail. Dimnik, 31.
88	There is no indication that the archpriests were blind or in other ways incapable of guile. Indeed, given their position as leaders of the white clergy, they seem likely to have had a conflict of interest in seeing certain (non-monastic) candidates over others, although it might have been thought they had the archeparchy's overall interests in mind rather than parochial or monastic interests. As clergymen, they may have been considered more trustworthy than a layman, a common sentiment in medieval law codes. On the election of 1388, see NPL, 381-382; N4, 349; Nikitskii (1879), 56. On the election of 1415, see NPL, 405-406; N4, 414.
89	NPL, 40.
90	Macauley-Jackson and Loetscher, eds., 1:368. Much later, Archbishop Anselm of Canterbury (r. 1093-1109) is also said to have been a reluctant candidate. See Vaughn, 240-250.
91	Parsons, 175-178. Thrice-denying the archiepiscopate before accepting was said to be a tradition in Novgorod. See Chapter One, above.
92	John Meyendorff attributes the clauses on episcopal election to Novella 6, but that novella deals with the moral character and

	marital status of possible candidates for the episcopate. Meyendorff, "Clergy, Byzantine," in Strayer, ed., 3:446. Novella 137 dealt with the procedures for election. Justinian, Novella 6, pp. 35-47; Novella 137, pp. 695-699.
93	Regel, doc. 12, p. 56; Vasil'evskii, 452.
94	Ex. 28:6-30.
95	Josh. 7:13-8:26. How God would "designate" the guilty is not specified, but some scholars believe it was by means of the *Urim* and *Thummim*.
96	1 Sam. 10:17-22.
97	1 Sam. 14: 36-42; cf. Ex. 28:30; Deut. 8:8.
98	1 Sam. 30:7-8.
99	Jon. 1:3.
100	Jon. 1:7-8.
101	Jon. 1:8-2:1.
102	Prov. 16:33.
103	NPL, 68, 274-275; 365.
104	Acts 1:18.
105	Acts 1:15-26, esp. verses 25-26.
106	Comnena, Book 10, Section 2, pp. 297-298.
107	Budge, ed. and trans., 147-148. Yahb-Allaha was elected Patriarch (Catholicos) following Denha's death in 1281.
108	Eustratiades, ed., 245-314, esp. 260-263; Thomas and Hero, eds., 1: xxix-xxx; 3: 995.
109	Thomas and Hero, eds., 3:973, 982, 994-995.
110	Eustratiades, ed., 261-2621; Thomas and Hero, eds., 3:995-996.
111	Thomas and Hero, eds., 2:649, 655, 674-675.
112	The *typikon* of Emperor John II Komnenos (r. 1118-1143) for the Monastery of Christ Pantokrator in Constantinople (drawn up in October 1136) indicated that after three days of prayer, an unlettered person was to carry the lots to the altar the night before the election, and another unlettered person should take one of the lots from the altar and the person named on the lot would be superior-elect. Ibid., 2:731, 751.
113	As noted above, the Kyiv Caves Monastery's liturgical *typikon* may be based on the liturgical *typikon* of the Studion Monastery in Constantinople, though not necessarily its disciplinary *typikon*. That said, Theodore Studite's Testament for the Monastery of St. John of Studion does not indicate election by lots, but merely calls on the monks to "elect someone by a common vote in a godly fashion and in a manner which the fathers have established." Ibid., 1:77. The monastery's *typikon* does not indicate how the superior is to be elected either. Ibid., 1:84-119.

114	Several chronicles fail to mention Iona's election in 1458, merely saying that he was placed in office. Most chronicles mention Evfimii's death in 1458. *N2*, 141; *N4*, 445, 455, 491, 609. As for Iona's election and consecration, the *Novgorodian Second* and *Third Chronicles* note that he was sent to Novgorod. N2, 141; N3, 241. The *Novgorodian Fourth Chronicle*, the *Nikonian Chronicle*, and the *Sofia First Chronicle* also note that Iona was placed in the archiepiscopate, but mention no election. *N4*, 455-456, 492, 609; *Sof. 1*, 272; *Nikon*. (PSRL 12), 112; *Mosk.*, 276. Both Stroev and Makarii list Iona as having been elected in May 1458, with his consecration taking place the following February. Stroev, 35; Makarii *Istoriia*, 4:353. Golubinskii notes that Iona was consecrated in February 1459, but does not mention an election. Golubinskii (1995), 2.1:504. Filaret notes Iona was elected by the Novgorodians in late 1458 and consecrated in February 1459. Filaret, 3:310. Pavel Tikhomirov, however, clarifies that Evfimii II died on March 11 and Iona was chosen unanimously by the *veche* on March 19; the speed and unanimity of the Novgorodians suggest that election by lots (often used to end disputes among factions) was not necessary and was therefore not used. Tikhomirov, (1891-1900), 1:274. See also *Zhitie sviatitelia Iona arkhiepiskopa novgorodskogo*, 4.
115	Joel Raba argued that the "lots" were actually the scepters of the various candidates (who were usually hegumens). Raba (1979), 52-53. There are, however, other indications that the lots were in fact strips of paper, parchment, or birch bark with the candidates' names written on them (hence Posadnik Mikhail Danilovich was able to attach his seal to them in 1388). In one of the tales surrounding Sadko the Merchant, he and his men draw lots to decide which of them would be sacrificed to the King of the Sea, after writing their names on the lots. While difficult to date, and probably later than the fifteenth century, the tale's use of lots may be based on the historical reality of episcopal elections. R. Smith, "Some Recent Discoveries in Novgorod," *Past and Present*, No. 5. (1954): 10. On Sadko, see Rybnikov and Gruzinskii, 134; Astakhova, 2:638.
116	Raba (1979), 53. For discussion of Novgorodian inter-boiar politics in the early thirteenth century, see Ianin (2003), 270-273, 276-281.
117	E.g., NPL, 405 (s. a. 1415); 414 (s. a. 1421).
118	Robert Michell and Neville Forbes define the *sen'* (literally "canopy" but which they translate as "threshold" - which would be *porog* in Russian) as a platform placed in a church and used in

consecration ceremonies. Michell and Forbes, ed., 123n7. In the case of Moisei, the Novgorodians "led him to the canopy" in 1324 before sending him to the metropolitan to be consecrated. In 1415, Archbishop-elect Simeon was "raised...honorably to the canopy at his election in August 11 and consecrated in Moscow the following March 22. In 1429, when Evfimii I died, the *Novgorodian First Chronicle* noted he "sat at the canopy" one year and two weeks between his election and consecration. Thus, it would seem that the ceremony "at the canopy" took place at the time of election and was not part of the consecration. NPL, 97, 340, 405, 415.

119   On the powers and rights of the *electus*, see Benson, 167-189
120   Some scholars think one treaty refers to Evfimii II as archbishop-elect and date it to 1435, but others argue it refers to Evfimii I, and date it to 1424. Ianin (2003), 340, 343; Zimin supports a date between April 1433 and March 1434. Zimin (1956), 318-320. See also Khoroshev (1989), 89.
121   GVNP, doc. 19, p. 34. Valk dates the treaty to 1435, after Evfimii II's consecration, which is not likely since it does not mention Evfimii's archiepiscopal rank. Ianin dates it to August or September 1424, during the tenure of Evfimii I. Ianin (1991), 173-77, esp. 174; NPL, 416.
122   GVNP, doc. 64, p. 107; Ianin (1991), 109-110. Ianin, noting Evfimii's elect status, dates the treaty before Evfimii's consecration in Smolensk on March 26, 1434. Valk dated it merely "earlier than June 24, 1434."
123   NPL, 416.
124   NPL. 418 (s.a. 1435); GVNP, doc. 22, p. 39.
125   GVNP, doc. 26, p. 45; PRP, 2:251.
126   GVNP, doc. 77, p. 130; PRP, 2:247; AI, 1.279:511-512; 1.280-281:514-518.
127   PRP, 2:212, 219; Vernadsky (1965), 83; ZDR, 1:304. The charter is also published in AAE, 1.92: 69-72. See N4, 447.
128   NPL, 417. See also Golubinskii (1995), 2.1:417.
129   Nikitskii (1879), 58-9. See NPL, 91, 330.
130   Canon law suggests the presence at episcopal consecrations of "many bishops" if possible, but requires at least three. See Canon 13 of the Council of Carthage, in Percival, 448.
131   NPL, 343; *Mosk.*, 170. All the bishops present were from southwestern Rus', i.e., present-day western Ukraine and Belarus. The bishops mentioned in the chronicles are the same as those listed in Metropolitan Feognost registry, except the bishop of Polatsk, who is not in the registry. Regel, doc. 12, p. 56; Vasil'evskii, 452;

Eizo, 210. Meyendorff states that the consecration took place in Volodymyr, not in Kyiv. Meyendorff (1981), 84. In 1332, Bishop Feodor of Halych, present at Vasilii's consecration, was elevated to the rank of Metropolitan of Halych. Makarii, *Istoriia*, 3:643.

132   NPL, 281-283; *Sof. 1*, 491; *Mosk.*, 214.

133   *Mosk.*, 214; *NPL*, 382, 406; *Sof. 1*, 243, 491; Nikitskii (1879), 59. Archbishop Simeon was consecrated in the Church of St. Michael the Archangel in 1415, but it does not say in which church the *narechenie* took place. *Mosk.*, 242. P. Tikhomirov (1891-1900), 1:231. A document of 1431 indicates that it was standard by that time for the Novgorodian archbishop to be consecrated in the Dormition Cathedral and the Church of St. Michael the Archangel in the Moscow Kremlin. AAE, 1.91:99.

134   Cf. N4, 230; P. Tikhomirov (1891-1900), 1:131.

135   NPL, 91, 330; Nikitskii (1879), 58-9. Of the other bishops and archbishops, Ioakim through Spiridon were consecrated in Kyiv (except for Efrem and Arsenii, who were never consecrated.) Kliment was consecrated in Kyiv, David and Aleksei in Vladimir-on-Kliazma, and Moisei and Ioann II, and all archbishops after him, in Moscow except for Feodosii, who was never consecrated, and Evfimii II, who was consecrated in Smolensk.

136   Several chronicles date his removal to January 19, 1480. N3, 243; *Sof. 1*, 19, 34-35; *Nikon.* (PSRL 12), 197. The *Moskovskii letopisnyi svod kontsa XV veka* dates his arrest to September 9, 1480 and his confinement to the Chudov Monastery to September 24. It says he died there after a year and a half (*pol tretia let*). *Mosk.*, 326. The *Sofia Second Chronicle* says he was removed in 1479 and died in 1483. *Sof. 1I*, 221, 235. The *Ioasafovskaia Letopis'* says he was removed on January 19, 1479, sent to Moscow on January 24, and died there after three and a half years, in mid-1482. Zimin and Levina, eds., 119. The Continuation of the *Voskresenskaia Chronicle* dates his removal to 1480 but gives no date of death. Prodol. Vosk., 204. A manuscript listing burials in the Kyiv Caves Lavra gives Feofil's date of arrest as September 1480. RNB Titov No. 2727, *O moshchakh sviatykh pochivaiushchikh v kievskikh peshcherakh*, fols. 10-10v.

137   AAE dates Feofil's resignation charter to 1479; AAE vol. 1, doc. 378, pp. 476-77. However, there are three such charters in RNB Q.XVII.50, the apparent source for AAE, and only Gennadii's is dated and bears his signature. RNB Q.XVII.50, *Formuliarnik novgorodskogo arkhiepiskopa Feodosiia* [II], fols. 227v.-230. Feofil's charter is included in two other manuscripts but his name does not appear in the body; rather it is from "N., archbishop of

Novgorod." He is named in the conclusion where he confirms that he has signed it with his own hand. See BAN 16.17.29, Sbornik XVII veka, fols. 89-91; GIM Sinod. Sobr. No. 997, Minei Chet'i Mitropolita Makariia, Avgust', fols. 1550-1550v. The published version in RIB also lacks a date, although the introductory note refers to its placement in various texts between 1479 and 1482-1483. RIB 6.110:745-748, esp. 745-746. Stroev writes that he resigned in July, 1482. Stroev, 35. Pliguzov dates it to between December 25, 1482 and March 25, 1483. DSHRM, No. 210; cf., Paul, "Continuity and Change," 274, 306.

138   The *Novgorodian Third Chronicle* says he died October 26, 1482 "and was buried in Novgorod." N3, 293. The *Sofia First Chronicle* says he sat a year and a half (*poltret'ia let*) in the Chudov Monastery before he died. *Sof. 1*, 19. The *Nikonian Chronicle* says he sat three and a half years (*pol sema let*). Nikon. (PSRL 12), 197. Another manuscript dates his death to October 26, 1484. RNB Titov No. 2727, *O moshchakh sviatykh pochivaiushchikh v kievskikh peshcherakh*, fols. 10-10v. The list of prelates in the back of the 1996 edition of Makarii's *Istoriia russkoi tserkvi*, gives the date of his confinement in the Chudov Monastery as January 24, 1480, his res- his resignation as June 1482, and his death as October 26, 1482. Makarii, *Istoriia*, 4:353-354. Stroev gives his death as October 26, 1482, the date given in the *Novgorodian Third Chronicle*. Stroev, 35. In two earlier articles, I cited chronicle and secondary sources that gave two different dates for Feofil's removal: January 19 and January 24, 1480; I also dated his resignation to sometime in June 1482, and his death as October 26, 1482. I have since come to see that the sources do not agree and it is difficult if not impossible to give a firm date. See Paul (2003), 274; idem (2007), 267.

As to his place of burial, Tatiana Panova cites the *Novgorodian Second Archival Chronicle* that he died in 1483 and was buried in the Chudov Monastery. After the Chudov and Voznesenskii (Ascension) monasteries were destroyed in 1929, Feofil's remains were lost ("*utracheno*") with those of Archbishop Gennadii, and 194 of 324 other burials in the Moscow Kremlin. T. D. (Tatiana Dmitrievna) Panova, passim, esp. 20, 26. Cf. *Novgorodskaia vtoraia (arkhivnaia) letopis'*, 200. The *Novgorodian Third Chronicle* says Feofil was buried in Novgorod. N3, 293. Amvrosii agrees with this, but he also has Feofil listed among those buried in the Kyiv Caves Monastery. Amvrosii, 1:76, 313. Filaret say Feofil was buried in the Kyiv Caves Monastery; Filaret 3:113-114. Tikhomirov mentions both traditions; P. Tikhomirov (1891-1900), 1:334. Petr

Solov'ev writes he is buried in the Cathedral of Holy Wisdom; see P. Solov'ev, 114-118. However, Ianin does not list Feofil among those buried in the cathedral. Ianin, *Nekropol'*, 192-193. Several manuscript lists of saints from the sixteenth, seventeenth, and eighteenth centuries count Feofil among the Kyivan rather than the Novgorodian saints as they are categorized according to where the saints are buried (although a number of other Novgorodian archiepiscopal saints are also missing from the list, so he could simply be absent from the Novgorodian list). In two lists from the seventeenth century there is a "Bishop Feofil" listed among the Kyivan saints, although his eparchy is not indicated. RNB Sobranie Mikhailovskogo Q.351, *Kniga ob derzhashchaia viede sobranie vsekh rossiiskikh sviatykh*, fol. 5; BAN Sobranie F. Kalikina No. 29 *Ukazatel' rossiiskikh sviatym s nachala Russkoi zemli po XVII veke*, fol. 4v. In another list, a certain Feofil is listed, but no ecclesiastical office is indicated. BAN Sobranie Druzhina No. 83, *Kniga glagolemaia o rossiiskikh sviatykh*, fol. 5. A list from the mid-eighteenth century lists a Bishop Filipp in the left column (where the saints are named), with "Feofil" written in the right column (which is usually left blank). Whether any of these is Feofil of Novgorod is not clear. RNB HCPK Q. 36, fol. 171v. Feofil is, however, listed among those buried in the Feodosiev Cave of the Kyiv Caves Monastery in RNB Titov No. 2727, fol. 10v. He is not found in a list of Novgorodian saints from the seventeenth century but, again, this is probably because the lists are based on the place of burial, so if Feofil was buried in Kyiv, he would not appear on the Novgorodian list. See RNB Mikhailov. Q.348, *O sviatykh Velikonovgorodskikh episkopex arkhiepiskopekh prepodobnykh chudotvortsekh*. (Likewise, on one list, Stefan of Perm' is included among the Muscovite saints since he was buried in the Moscow Kremlin – his remains were also "lost" in the 1920s – while on another list, Novgorodian bishops Nifont and German are counted among the Kyivan saints since they are buried there. See BAN Druzhin. No. 83, fol. 18; On a third list Bishop Nikita and Archbishop Nifont are found among both the Kyivan and Novgorodian saints. RNB Mikhailov. Q. 351, fols. 4v., 9v.)

139 *Mosk.*, 330; *Nikon.* (PSRL 12), 214-215; Kloss (1998), 1:131. None of the candidates are from Novgorodian monasteries.
140 *Mosk.*, 330; *Nikon.* (PSRL 12), 214-215.
141 *Mosk.*, 330; *Nikon.* (PSRL 12), 215; Kloss (1998), 1:131. Sergei is called "elder of the Trinity Monastery" and then "the former Archpriest Simeon of the [Church of the] Mother of God." N4, 525; *Nikon* (PSRL 12), 215.

142   *Pribavl.* N2, 184; N3, 244; N4, 525; *Mosk.,* 330; *Nikon.* (PSRL 12), 216; Stroev, 35; Makarii, *Istoriia,* 4:353-4. Amvrosii, 1:76. Stroev and Makarii give the year of his election as 1483, and the year of his deposition as 1484. Kloss gives the date of Sergei's death as April 9, 1495. Kloss (1998), 1:132. The cause for Sergei's brief tenure is ultimately uncertain. Zdravomislov says that the Novgorodians saw him as "weak in soul and body" and thus disliked him. He also mentions the incidents of madness. Zdravomislov, 27-28. Pavel Tikhomirov went into greater detail on the various chronicle accounts of madness, which were seen as divine retribution for violating the ancient customs of Novgorod. P. Tikhomirov (1891-1900), 2.1:9-11. See also N2,183-184; N4, 525; "Povest' o Moisee, Arkhiepiskope Novgorodom", in Kushelev-Bezborodko and Kostomarov, eds., 4: 12; Paul, "Continuity and Change," 280-281.

143   N2, 143; N3, 244; N4, 525; *Sof. 2,* 320; Stroev, 35; Makarii, *Istoriia,* 4:353-354; P. Tikhomirov (1891-1900), 2.1:12, 15.

Chapter Five

1   Paul (2007), esp. 235, 244. The bishops of Cetinje, Montenegro are the only prince-bishops of the Orthodox/Ottoman world that I know of, but this began only in 1516, after the period currently under study. See Stevenson, 162-180; Attwater, 2:83. The role the patriarchs of Constantinople played as ethnarch in the Ottoman Empire was also a political role, but that began only with the Ottoman conquest in 1453, at the very end of our period of study.

2   Karl Marx, "Introduction to 'A Contribution to the Critique of Hegel's Philosophy of the Right,'" in Marx and Engels, 3:175.

3   Helle, Kouri, and Jansson, 1:365; Menache, 215.

4   Cicero, III, XII, 28, p. 131.

5   Arendt, 123.

6   Power-sharing may not indicate weakness; a collective might be able to establish consensus among important families or clans and, therefore, govern better than a single ruler. Many historians, however, contend that clan infighting and class factionalism made it impossible for Novgorod to make decisions and disputed authority led to multiplication of the *posadnichestvo*.

7   On Western Europe, see Reynolds, 323; Barber, 25-6, 432-34; Mundy, passim, esp. 221-242. On Eastern Christianity, including Caesaropapism and the Church-State Symphony, see Runciman (1977), 1-2, 22; Angold (1985, 1997), 145.

8	A bishop's word, like the king's, was incontrovertible, according to Article 16 of the *Dooms of Wihtred of Kent* (r. 690-725) and a priest or other cleric could clear himself by swearing an oath before the altar (Articles 18 and 19). Douglas and Whitelock, eds., 363. See also Paul (2007), 238.
9	For a list of warrior-bishops, see Hurter, 2:292; Johnson, 206-222.
10	Another notable example is Thomas Aquinas' assertion that "warlike pursuits are altogether incompatible with the duties of a bishop and a cleric." ST, SS, Q. 40, Art. 2, 9:505. For a fuller look at Western warrior-bishops, see Paul (2007), 238-241.
11	Gregory of Tours, Book 5, Sect. 20, p. 285.
12	Ibid.
13	Ibid., Book 4, Sect. 42, p. 237.
14	Ibid., Book 5, Sect. 20, p. 286
15	Hirsch, Pabst, and Bresslau, eds., 1:49.
16	Oman, 1:446, 449.
17	D. Schaff, 797-798.
18	Odo is depicted several times on the Bayeux Tapestry, including in one scene in which he wears a helmet and chainmail and wields a war club under the caption: *"Hic Odo episcopus bacalum tenens confortat pueros."* ("Here Bishop Odo, holding his staff, comforts the boys." Bernstein, Chapter 9, esp. 138-139, 141-143; 264-265.
19	D. Schaff, 798.
20	Ibid., 797. The quote is from Gen. 37:32.
21	Gabriel, 41.
22	D. Schaff, 797. Julius led a campaign against the Venetians to retake Perugia and Bologna in 1506. See Shaw.
23	Leader-Temple and Marcotti, 119-122.
24	Lot, 1: 417; Sismondi, 4: 422.
25	Henricus Lettus, 2.6:14-15; L. Meyer, ed., line 502, p. 12.
26	D. Schaff, 432. The Brothers of the Sword (*Fratres militiæ Christi Livoniae* in Latin, *Schwertbrüderorden* in German) were practically wiped out on September 22, 1236 in the Battle of Schaule (Saule) against the Samogitians (Lowland Lithuanians) and the Semigalians, after which they became a branch of the Teutonic Order known as the Livonian Order. Christiansen, 102-103; Urban (2000), 142-147.
27	Nielsen, in Murray, ed. (2001), 95-117.
28	NPL, 77, 294; Henricus Lettus, 2.6: 29-30, 31; L. Meyer, ed., lines 2065-98, pp. 48-49; line 2229, p. 52.
29	NPL, 77, 291.
30	Henricus Lettus, 2.6:29-30, 31; L. Meyer, ed., pp. 48-49, lines 2065-2098; line 2229, p. 52.

31	NPL, 370.
32	N4, 446; Tomilin, 23; Fennell (1961), 43. No other Novgorodian or Rus' chronicle refers to this event and it is hard to imagine such a pivotal incident would go unnoticed by most chroniclers. For further explanation for the archbishop's control over the cavalry, see Paul (2007), 260-261 and Chapter Six below.
33	Comnena, Book 10, Sect. 8, p. 317. On the battle with the priest, see 315-318. Sewter notes that Anna misquotes Colossians 2:21 ("Touch not, taste not, handle not"); Runciman (1955), 83, 105; Angold (1985, 1997), 166.
34	Peter Diaconus, 7:833.
35	DSHRM, No. 14; *Pravoslavnyi Sobesednik* (1860), pt. 2, 84-85; Prokhorov (1978), 195; Meyendorff (1981), 209, 292. On Kiprian's background, see Droblenkova and Prokhorov, "Kiprian (ok. 1330-16.IX.1406) Mitropolit Kievskii i vseia Rusi," in SKKDR 2.1: 464-465.
36	Musin (2005), 60; Kuzmina, 70-72. See also Kleimenov and Tikhokin.
37	In 1193, the Novgorodian *voevoda* Iadrei had led an army out against the Iugra country, captured one town and besieged another for five weeks. The Iugrians convincing the Novgorodians to send their twelve "most outstanding men" to parley in the town, at which point which the Novgorodian envoys were killed, among them the priest Ivanko Legen. NPL 40-41. In 1234, the Lithuanians raided Staraia Russa, making it "as far as the marketplace" before being driven back outside the town, at which point the priest Petrila was killed along with three other townsmen. NPL, 73; PskL 1:181-182.
38	PskL 2:26; 98.
39	There is also the case of Aleksandr Peresvet, a monk from the Holy Trinity monastery who, according to the *Skazanie o Mamaevom poboishche*, was killed in single combat with the Tatar champion, Temir Murza (Chelybei) at the Battle of Kulikovo on September 8, 1380. His fellow monk, Rodion Osliabia, was also killed in the battle. BLDR 6:153, 177, 187. Both also appear in *Zadonshchina*; PLDR 4:96-111; BLDR 6:104-119, esp. 113. The two fought because of their past experience as warriors (prior to taking monastic vows), not because monks or clergymen usually took up arms. Andrei Nikitin argues Peresvet's monasticism, his duel with Temir Murza, and Sergei's blessing are all ahistorical. Nikitin, 494-530.
40	Musin, Kleimenov and Tikhokin, and Artem Grachev date this to 1272, though Kleimenov and Tikhokin give the 1276 date in a footnote. Musin (2005), 60; Kleimenov and Tikhokin, 46.

41	RIB 6. 12:129-140, esp. 138. Kleimenov and Tikhokin misnumber this as question 21. Kleimenov and Tikhokin. Musin notes that most manuscripts up to the sixteenth century says that the clerical state is not to be withheld in such an instance; that is, the *"se"* is altered to read *"ne."* Musin (2005), 60-61.
42	*Apostolical Canons*, Canon 83, DSK 1:80. See Chapter One, above.
43	Council of Chalcedon, Canon 7, DSK 1:115.
44	Hussey (1986), 326-327.
45	This distinction between "the sacred authority of the priests and royal authority" (*"auctoritas sacra [al. sacrata] pontificum, et regalis potestas"*) is seen, for example, in Pope Gelasius I's letter known as *Famuli vestræ pietatis* or *Duo Sunt*, to the Emperor Anastasius I Dicorus in 495 AD. See PL 59, Epistola VIII, col. 42.
46	Presniakov, 250.
47	MM, 2.447: 188-192, esp. 190-191; RIB 6.Pril.40:265-276.
48	*Archon* is usually translated as "prince," though it could mean other rulers, especially in the classical period. *Basileus* is usually translated as "emperor" when the Byzantines referred to their own ruler, but the term is problematic. It is used to refer to Jesus as "King of the Jews" in the New Testament. In the archaic and classical periods, it was used to mean kings of various states, including the kings of Israel and Judah in the Septuagint.
49	MM, 2.447:188-192, esp. 190-191; RIB 6.Pril.40:265-276. For discussion of this incident, see Barker, 194-196; Obolensky (1979), 299-315, reprinted in Obolensky, *Byzantine Inheritance*; idem (1978), 123-132, also reprinted in *Byzantine Inheritance*. Christian Raffensperger notes that the Byzantines saw themselves as universal overlords, but does not believe Vasilii I or other so-called vassals within the Commonwealth necessarily accepted this notion. Raffensperger, 159-174.
50	MM, 2.446:181-87.
51	The patriarch used the Greek term *synakseos* (synaxis) – meeting, gathering, assembly - for the *veche*. MM, 2.450: 195. The *veche* might have been addressed so that the contents of the letter could not then be hidden by the city officials.
52	Paul (2008), 74, 100.
53	Christiansen.
54	GVNP, doc. 72, p. 118; doc. 73, p.120. Other treaties mention envoys from Riga, Kolyvan, and Dorpat, but they were apparently sent by the civil officials and not the bishops of those cities. See GVNP, doc. 71, p. 117; doc. 74. p. 124.
55	AfED 18: 378. For more on the Judaizers, see Goldfrank, (2017):

	1-25; P. Tikhomirov (1891-1900), 2.1:39. The Judaizers were said to have arrived from Lithuania in 1471, an admittedly unwanted and perhaps negative transfer of ideas in the view of at least the Rus' church. See Paul, "Continuity and Change," 280-283.
56	Aristotle used the term *aristocracy* to indicate just rule by a small group, as opposed to the deviant form of rule by a small group, which he called *oligarchy*. Aristotle, Book 3, Part 7, lines 1279a32, p. 190; Book 4, Part 2, ln. 1289a26, p. 239.
57	Paul (2007), 236-237.
58	NPL, 81, 308; *Sof. 1*: 333; *Mosk.*, 142.
59	Stéfane Mund dates Lannoy's sojourn in Novgorod and Pskov to 1413. Mund, 47.
60	Potvin and Mouzeau, eds., 33; Thompson, x; Kochin, 69; Paul (2007), 235-236.
61	Potvin and Mouzeau, eds., 33; Thompson, x. The Russian translation uses the word *nachalnik*: "leader". Kochin, 69.
62	Potvin and Mouzeau, eds., 33; Kochin, 69-70.
63	Potvin and Mouzeau, eds., 34.
64	*Mosk.*, 298.
65	Ibid., 305.
66	NPL, 412-413; *Mosk.*, 244-245.
67	NPL, 353; *Mosk.*, 172.
68	NPL, 373-374, 399; *Mosk.*, 244-245. The *Novgorodian First Chronicle* claims (incorrectly) that Byzantine Emperor "Aleksa Manuilovits'" (Alexios II Komnenus; r. 1180-1183) visited the city in 1186. NPL, 38, 228. Alexius, however, had been strangled with a bowstring under orders from Andronicus I in October 1183. See "Alexius Manuelis Filius," in Niketas Choniates, *Histories*, in PG 139, cols. 625-627.
69	NPL, 23-4, 208; N4, 146.
70	Vsevolod's dismissal from Novgorod was due, in part, to his failings in fighting the Suzdalians. NPL, 24, 209; N4, 146-147; *Ipat.* (PSRL 2.1), 14; *Sof. 1*: 157; P1, 176; Paul (2008), 85.
71	Paul (2007), 249n65.
72	NPL, 211. He and the best men did likewise in 1154, when they brought in Prince Mstislav Iur'evich. NPL, 29, 216; Paul (2008), 85, 110.
73	NPL, 28, 214.
74	There is no evidence in the sources that Archbishops Gavriil, Antonii, Arsenii, Feoktist, Simeon, Feodosii, or Iona ever carried out embassies.
75	NPL, 414; N4, 431.

76	On Mongol relations with the Church, see Fuhrman, 166-172; Weickhardt, 418; PRP, 3:466, 470; Pliguzov and Khoroshkevich, 84-102; Okhotina (1990), 67-84. There were some Nestorian Christians among the Mongols, but they were a minority. See also the missions of the Franciscans John of Plano Carpini and William of Rubruck in Dawson, ed., 3-76; 89-220.
77	NPL, 96, 338, 373; *Lavrent.*, 263-264; *Suzdal.*, 344; *Ipat.* (PSRL 2.2), 237-238, 299, 302-303, 476; Shchapov (1989), 45-46, 179-180; RLA, 2 and 3: 2-4; 38: 19-20; Thietmar von Merseberg, 32-33; Rapov and Tkachenko, No. 3, pp. 65-66; Rowell, 78.
78	Shchapov (1989), 179.
79	Ibid., 180.
80	NPL, 29; *Suzdal.*, 425, 435, 455; Paul (2007), 249; Shchapov, 180n62
81	Shchapov (1989), 179.
82	NPL, 341.
83	NPL, 350; Paul (2007), 253.
84	PskL, 1:43.
85	PskL, 2:130-131. The *Pskov First Chronicle* merely says Evfimii came to Pskov, celebrated a liturgy in the Church of the Holy Trinity, and left at the end of January. The dispute between the archiepiscopal administration and Pskov is not mentioned. PskL, 1:43.
86	*Mosk.*, 311; Paul (2007), 265.
87	See Canon Seven of the Council of Sardica, NPNF, 14:422.
88	NPL, 95, 337; N4, 257.
89	NPL, 345.
90	Ibid., 380.
91	Ibid.,415.
92	Ibid., 421.
93	Varfolomei was *posadnik* of the Nerev *konets* from 1316-1332; Matvei succeeded him and served from 1333-1345. Ianin (2003), 260-261.
94	The chronicle does not explain who Ondreshko was and Ianin refers to him as "a certain Andrei" ("*kakogo-to Andreiia*"). Ianin (2003), 259. Fedor Danilovich was *posadnik* of Prusskaia Street (in the Detinets) from 1329-1346, and then of the Liudin and Zagorodskii *kontsy* from 1346-1351. Ianin (2003), 261, 269, 288.
95	NPL, 355-356; Ianin (2003), 259-260, 262-263. It is not clear from the chronicle if Boris is Vasilii's vicar or the *namestnik* of the grand prince.
96	NPL, 355; Khoroshev (1989), 59. The charge of archiepiscopal favoritism may be overstated. Vasilii had been priest of the Church

of Sts. Cosmas and Damian on Slave Street in the Nerev *konets* and he may have remained close to the Nerev boiars after his archiepiscopal election; thus, there may not have been any untoward political ties or machinations between the archbishop and the Nerev boiars and other archbishops may not have had similar close, personal ties. Thus, when the Liudin and Zagorodskii *posadnik* Vasilii Fedorovich (in office 1384-1392), son of Fedor Iur'evich (*posadnik* of those *kontsy* in the 1340s) died in 1392; he was buried in the Church of St. Nicholas, but Archbishop Ioann did not officiate at the funeral. Neither did he officiate at the funeral that same year of Posadnik Mikhail, Fedor Danilovich's brother (*stepennyi posadnik* in 1372-1373 and *posadnik* of the Liudin and Zagorodskii *kontsy* from 1372 until 1392), even though Mikhail had died in monastic orders. NPL, 385. Ianin (2003), 269, 289, 293-294.

97   Varfolomei's uncle, Mikhail Mishinich, had been *posadnik* in 1272 and 1273-1280; Varfolomei's father, Iurii Mishinich, had been *posadnik* of the Nerev *konets* from 1300 to 1315. Varfolomei himself was *posadnik* from 1316 to 1332; his brother, Matvei, from 1333 to 1345, and his grandson, Ontsifor, from 1347 to 1350. Ianin (2003), 252, 260-261, 268-269.

98   Ianin (2003), 261-262, 270; Paul (2007), passim.

99   Aleksei was elected in 1359, prior to the disturbance, but not consecrated until July 12, 1360 (in Vladimir). NPL, 365-366.

100 NPL, 366. Ianin (2003), 279.

101 NPL, 51, 248.

102 Ibid., 326.

103 These walls were likely destroyed (at least partially) when Prince Vseslav of Polatsk sacked the city and looted the cathedral in 1067 (The attack is listed under different years in the Older and Younger Redactions and under 1067 in other chronicles). NPL, 17; 186; *Lavrent.*, 166; *Ipat.* (PSRL 2.2), 155.

104 NPL, 20, 204; N4, 142.

105 NPL, 181; N3, 222; N4, 252. Troianovskii argues from archaeological evidence (the historic sources are silent on the matter) that this construction consisted merely of stone towers overlooking earthen embankments topped by a wooden palisade. Troianovskii (1998), 59.

106 NPL, 99-100, 343; Bernadskii, 25; Karger, 64; Troianovskii (1998), 59.

107 N4, 290. Similarly, after a fire devastated both Sides of the city in 1391, the Novgorodians took 5,000 pieces of silver "from Holy Wisdom...from the accumulation of Archbishop Aleksei," and another 1,000 silver pieces from each of the city's *kontsy* to rebuild.

Ibid., 370. Both projects used the archbishop's silver about two years after they had retired, just as Bishop Nikita's silver was used after his death in 1108 to fresco the interior of the cathedral, suggesting this was perhaps the bishop's personal wealth and not part of the church treasury; possibly it was earmarked for the projects and had to be used soon after his retirement or death. NPL, 19; N3, 233.

108   In 1195, Bishop Martirii built the Chapel of the Deposition of the Robe and the Garter (belt) of Our Lady above the gatehouse ("the Virgin's Gate") leading to the bridge over the Volkhov. In 1233, the Chapel of St. Theodore was built over the gatehouse leading north to the Nerev End. In 1296, Archbishop Kliment built the Chapel of the Resurrection over the gatehouse leading west into the Zagorodskii *konets*. The following year, Hegumen Kirill of the Iur'ev Monastery built the Chapel of the Transfiguration over the south gatehouse leading to the Ludin *konets*. In 1305, the boiar Simeon (Semen') Klimovich built the Chapel of the Intercession over the gatehouse leading west to Prusskaia Street in the Zagorodskii *konets*; Posadnik Grigorii Iakunovich rebuilt it in 1389. In 1311, Archbishop David built the Chapel of St. Vladimir over the other gatehouse leading northeast to the Nerev *konets*. In 1461, Archbishop Ioann rebuilt the chapel over the Virgin's Gate. NPL, 41-42, 234; 72, 282; 328; 92, 332; 93, 334; 383; Muscovite masters built the current fortress walls between 1484 and 1490; a third of which was paid for by Archbishop Gennadii and the grand prince paying the rest. Paul, "The Military Revolution," 34n122; idem, "Continuity and Change," 308.

109   NPL, 396; N4, 390; Karger, 64.

110   NPL, 401; Makarii (1857), 13.

111   NPL, 416; Karger, 123-124.

112   NPL, 423, N3, 239; Makarii (1857), 13, 33-34. The clock tower collapsed in 1671 and was rebuilt by Metropolitan Ioakim in 1673. Karger, 126-128; Makarii (1857), 33. The current tower is still referred to as Evfimii's (sounding) clock tower (*zvonitsa*).

113   NPL, 420. The granary may have been in the Detinets and may have been used by church personnel, or for storing grain used to make the Eucharistic bread. Thus, it was probably ecclesiastical in nature, although it could have served the entire House of Holy Wisdom as well as the boiars living in the Detinets.

114   NPL, 423.

115   Houses are shown inside the Detinets south of *Piskpulskaia Ulitsa* (Bishop's Street, named for the bishops and running east and west

across the fortress) in several depictions of Novgorod, such as the Mikhailovskaia or Znamenskaia icon and the Flor-Lavrovskaia icon, dating to the seventeenth or eighteenth century, as well as in drawings by seventeenth century Western European visitors. See Gornostaev, 145-150; Gusev (1900), esp. 7, 10-11, 12; idem (1913); Ianin (1977), 97; Johansen, 147-152; Kushnir, 73, 83; Makarii (1860), 2:59.

116 "The Novgorod Judicial Charter," Article 26, in Ianin, ed., ZDR, 306; PRP, 2:223.
117 NPL, 24, 209; N4, 146-147; *Ipat.* (PSRL 2.1), 14; PskL, 2:76; *Sof. 1* (PSRL 5), 157; *Sof. 1* (PSRL 6), 222; Paul (2008), 85.
118 NPL, 51, 249; Paul (2008), 91.
119 NPL, 94, 335; *Sof. 1* (PSRL 6), col. 371; *Mosk.*, 160.
120 The Detinets also served as a central fortress during sieges, where soldiers and citizens could hold out against Lithuanians, Suzdalians, and other attackers; in 1268 siege engines were built in the archbishop's courtyard. NPL, 86, 316. The *Sofia First Chronicle* mentions the siege engines (*poroky*), but not where they were built. *Sof. 1* (PSRL 6), 343.
121 Paul (2007), 249.
122 St. Il'ia's (the Prophet Elijah) on the south side of the market in the Slavno *konets*, stands next to a Church of Peter and Paul. (When I visited Novgorod in 2007, it was a factory with its domes and drums removed, though the apses are still clearly visible.) It is not clear which St. Paul's is meant in the chronicles. It could be Vasilii fortified the area just around St. Il'ia and Sts. Peter and Paul in the Slavno *konets*. The Church of Sts. Peter and Paul of the Leatherworkers could also be meant, but that is across the river north of the Sofia Side and is not specifically mentioned until 1407 (although this could have been a reconstruction of an earlier church). It could be that the archbishop built a wall from the south side of the Slavno *konets* around the Market Side and ended across the Volkhov from the Church of Peter and Paul of the Leatherworkers. Another, no longer extant, Church of Peter and Paul could also be meant, as several are mentioned in the chronicles over the centuries. The remnants of stone-filled earthen embankments, which may be the walls mentioned in the chronicles, encircle both Sides of the old city today. On these embankments, see Kostochkin, 119-122, especially the map on page 121.
123 NPL, 346. The Older Redaction only notes that Archbishop Vasilii "built a fortress in stone in two years." NPL, 99-100.
124 Ibid., 349.

125 NPL, 379. The *Sofia First Chronicle* mentions the building of a small stone fortress on the Luga River but does not mention the wall or the archbishop. *Sof. 1* (PSRL 6), 484.
126 NPL, 100. Paul, "Vasilii Kalika," 257.
127 NPL, 339. The grand prince signed the Orekhov or Noteborg Treaty with the Swedes on the island on August 12 that year. A modern stone monument commemorates this first treaty between Russia and Sweden. For the treaty, see GVNP, Nos. 28 and 38, pp. 55-56, 67-68; Paul, "Vasilii Kalika," 255-256.
128 The fortress at Kopor'e was built initially by the Teutonic Knights in 1241 and destroyed by Aleksandr Iaroslavich. In 1279, his son, Dmitrii, obtained permission from Novgorod to rebuild the fortress. In 1333, Lithuanian Prince Narimont (Gleb) sent his son Aleksandr to the Novgorodian Land and Aleksandr was given the fortresses and towns of Ladoga, Orekhov, Korel town (Keksholm), and half of Kopor'e "for his patrimony and heritage and his children." Aleksandr returned to Lithuania in 1338 but left his *namestniki*. In 1383, Patriki Narimontovich arrived from Lithuania and was also given the fortresses and towns of Orekhov, Korel town (Keksholm), half of Kopor'e, and Lusko Village. NPL, 78, 295, 323, 345-346, 349, 379. Paul, "Vasilii Kalika," 256-257.
129 That is, unless you consider the fortress at Staraia Ladoga, which was said to be under the administration of an archiepiscopal namestnik. The fortress had been built by the local *posadnik*, Pavel, and the Ladogans, in 1116, and was thus not an archiepiscopal project. NPL, 20, 204.
130 Probably only architects and master builders went with him, not common workers. The remnants of Vasilii's walls can be seen just north of the Church of St. John in the courtyard of the fortress. The current fortress is from a much later date. See Paul, "Vasilii Kalika," 259-260.
131 Paul (2007), 249, 254, 257; Idem, "Vasilii Kalika," 265. Interestingly, this is one of the first times that the Novgorodians addressed their archbishop as "*gospodine*," ("lord, sir") rather than by the ecclesiastical title of *Vladyka*, literally "master," but used as a polite form of address for Russian bishops and in no way indicative of political power. The use of the term *gospodin* is also attested to in a number of birchbark and other documents. See Zalizniak, doc. 49, p. 651; doc. 55, p. 565; doc. 67, p. 534; doc. 84, p. 285; doc. 98, doc. 307, pp. 677-678; doc. 354, pp. 549-550; and doc. 358, p. 550. There is an excellent online database of the birchbarks set up by the INTAS-Project: "Birchbark Literacy from Medieval Rus: Con-

tents and Contexts," *"Derevnerusskie berestianie gramoty,"* April 2004, <http://gramoty.ru/birchbark> (April 2, 2024). Documents from after the Muscovite Conquest show that Novgorodian metropolitans were at times referred to as *"Velikii Gospodin"* as well as *"Gosudar'"*, while petitioners sometimes referred to themselves as the metropolitans' "slaves;" this in a period when the metropolitans were supposedly less powerful than their predecessors in independent Novgorod. These forms of address were probably copied from tsarist protocol with no intention of the titles having political significance. SPbII RAN, F. 171, *Fond Novgorodskogo Sofiiskogo arkhiereiskogo doma,* pereplet I, No. 11, fols. 21-25; No. 12, fols. 26-27; No. 13, fol. 28; No. 20/1, fol. 43; No. 21, fol. 46; No. 37, fol. 174.

132 *Avraamki,* 202.
133 Weickhardt, 421; Paul (2007), 246.
134 Weickhardt, 421.
135 Weickhardt, 421. Ianin (1970), 2:59-60. See also Khoroshev (1989), 121-139.
136 Weickhardt, 421.
137 "The Novgorod Judicial Charter," Article 26, ZDR, 306; PRP, 2:223.
138 Grekov, ed. (1940), Article 25, pp. 240; ZDR, 334; Kaiser, ed. (1992), 91; PRP, 2:306.
139 Grekov, ed. (1940), Articles 14, 50, 82, pp. 238-239, 244-245, 249; Ianin, ed., ZDR, 333, 336, 339; PRP, 2:304, 311-312, 317. See also Paul (2007), 247.
140 Sumnikova and Lopatev, eds., 66; Shchapov (1989), 70.
141 GVNP, doc. 1, pp. 9-10. See also Ianin (2003), 208, 249; Paul (2007), 250.
142 Often the preamble mentions the *stepennyi* ("incumbent" or sometimes translate as "high") *posadnik* and *tysiatskii,* the other *posadniki* and *tysiatskie,* and other offices and social groups, and sometimes the *veche*. See, for example, GVNP, docs. 1-3, pp. 9-13; docs. 6-9, pp. 15-20; doc. 14, pp. 26-28; doc. 36, pp. 64-65; doc. 43, pp. 76-79.
143 GVNP, doc. 11, p. 23.
144 Ibid., 24. "Feoktist's treaty" is believed to be GVNP, doc. 9, pp. 19-20, concluded in 1307 or 1308; Feoktist also sealed two *riady* with Grand Prince Mikhail in 1304 and 1305, thought to be two versions of the same *riad*; GVNP, doc. 6, pp. 15-16, and doc. 7, pp. 16-18. Ianin called these "project treaties," but it is not clear why a project or draft treaty would already be sealed. Ianin (1991), 152-161.

145	GVNP, doc. 77, pp. 130-132.
146	Ibid., p. 130.
147	Ibid., p. 132. See also, Paul (2007), 262. The text literally speaks of "our Greek Orthodox faiths," in the plural.
148	David (one document); Dalmat (one document), Feoktist (four documents), Vasilii Kalika (one document), Aleksei (one document), Simeon (two documents), Evfimii II (five documents), and Feofil (one document). See GVNP, doc. 29, pp. 56-57 (s.a. 1262-1263); doc. 6, pp. 15-16; doc. 7, pp. 16-18 (s.a. 1304-1305); doc. 36, pp. 64-65 (s.a. 1306-1307); doc. 9, pp. 19-20 (s.a. 1307-1308); doc. 11, pp. 22-24 (after February 10, 1316); doc. 41, pp. 73-74 (January 6, 1342); doc. 18, pp. 33-4 (s.a. 1375); doc. 90, p. 147 (s.a. 1415-1421; doc. 57, pp. 95 (1418-1421); doc. 70, pp. 115-116 (1440-1447); doc. 71, p. 117 (end of 1441); doc. 95, pp. 150-151 (1448-1454); doc. 72, pp. 117-119 (Feb. 27, 1448); doc. 96, pp. 151-153 (1459-1469); doc. 99, pp. 154-155 (1471-1482).
149	"If the prince will not affix his seal, then [obtain] the seal at [the Pskov archives at] the Holy Trinity Cathedral. And there is no irregularity in this [procedure]." It is assumed that the seal obtained at the Trinity Cathedral was the archbishop's, although this is not specified. Grekov, ed. (1940), Article 82, p. 249; ZDR, 339; *PRP* 2:296.
150	GVNP, doc. 29, pp. 56-57 (s.a. 1262-63). Ianin dates the treaty to between 1259 and 1263. Ianin (1991), 82.
151	NPL, 83, 311-312; Ianin (1991), 82-83; N. P. Likhachev, 1:37-40; RFA (1948), 1:259. Grand Prince Aleksandr died on November 14, 1263 while returning from the Horde.
152	Ianin (1991), 85. Prince Boris Alekseevich sat for his father in 1299, but the *Novgorodian First Chronicle* notes that Boris called a *veche* and, "with all the men of Novgorod," placed Feoktist in the archiepiscopal office. Boris was apparently absent from Novgorod in 1300. NPL, 90-91, 330-331.
153	Paul (2007), 250.
154	GVNP, doc. 6, pp. 15-16; doc. 7, pp. 16-18 (s.a. 1304-1305); doc. 9, pp. 19-20 (s.a. 1307-1308). Paul (2008), 99.
155	Archbishop Evfimii II's 1435 letter to Riga, asking that a bell-maker be sent to Novgorod, is the only document in which the archbishop alone is mentioned. Its non-political focus meant no consensus among the political elite was needed. GVNP, doc. 65, p. 108.
156	Paul (2007), 268-269.

Chapter Six

1. Martin (2007), 40.
2. Noonan (1986): 321-348; idem (1981), 47-117; Franklin and Shepard, 3-70.
3. *Lavrent.*, 8-9.
4. Ibid., 9-10.
5. *The Novgorodian First Chronicle* reports s.a. 1130 that seven boats sank sailing back from Gotland with loss of life and merchandise; In 1188, Novgorodian merchants were plundered by (other) Varangians on Gotland. NPL, 22, 206-207; 39, 229. "Byzantine" art has been found in the churches of Garda and other locales on Gotland and has been tied to artistic motifs found in and around Novgorod. Cutler, 257-266. This study, however, argues for a "byzantinizing" of worship, and not a presence of Russian merchants on the island. There was also a Novgorodian merchant colony (as well as other Rus' merchants) at Reval (Tallinn) in the thirteenth century. Slessarev, 179. Cf., Rybina, 26.
6. Martin (2007), 166-167. Peterhof, established in the twelfth century, was northeast of the market, on the opposite corner of Il'in and Slavnaia (modern Bolshaia Moskovskaia) Streets from the Church of the Dormition; a Swedish Courtyard was built in the seventeenth century south of that. The Gothic Courtyard was south of the market where the Hotel Russia now stands. See Rybina, esp. 22, 124-129.
7. Paul (2008), 81, 95-96.
8. NPL, 96, 338.
9. Ibid.
10. Ibid., 96; 338-339. Fennell calls them "guns." Fennell (1968), 96.
11. NPL, 96-97; 339. Fennell notes there is an Udroma River in the region of Iaroslavl' and a village of Udrom in the Rzheva district, west of Tver'; he presumes the latter is meant. Fennell (1968), 96.
12. NPL, 97, 339.
13. *Ipat.* (PSRL 2.2), 277, (s.a. 1114); Paul (2007), 258. Marco Polo, who was not above retelling legends from the East, did not recount this one, but did write of "great quantities of costly furs...such numbers of these furs that it is truly marvelous," and that Rus' "produces precious furs – sable, ermine, vair [from the Eurasian red squirrel – MP], ercolin, and foxes in abundance, the best and the most beautiful in the world." Polo, 331-332.
15. Ibid., 399.
16. Ibid., 29, 216. The chronicler, however, did not believe this accusation.

17	Długosz, 14:697-698. The treasure was returned to Novgorod when Archbishop Makarii arrived from Moscow in 1527. PskL, 1:103-104
18	"Povest' o Shchile Posadnike Novgorodskom," in Kushelev-Bezborodko and Kostomarov, eds., 4:21-26.
19	"Povest' o Mikhaile Klopskom," in PLDR, 5:334-349.
20	Khoroshev (1989), 86.
21	The city is said to have kept its treasury in the recesses that can still be seen in the choir gallery and tower walls. Karger cites the Pskov chronicles that in December, 1547, the Tsar discovered a treasure hidden in the walls of the great staircase from the time of Prince Vladimir Iaroslavich, but the Pskov chronicles report he was in Novgorod and Pskov on 28 December and the *Novgorodian Second Chronicle* reports that Ivan the Terrible arrived in Novgorod on November 14, 1547 and stayed 10 days. He also visited the city in the spring of 1547 and the winter of 1548, but there is no mention of him finding treasure in the cathedral during these visits. PskL. 1:112; 2:230; N2, 151-152, 185; Karger, 112; Grekov, *Izbrannye trudy*, 3:51; P. Tikhomirov (1891-1900), 2.1:157.
22	Khoroshev (1989), 73.
23	"Statute of Novgorod Prince Vsevolod [1135-37] on Church Courts, Church People and Trade Measures," Art. 17, in ZDR, 252; Art. 12 in PRP, 2:164.
24	NPL, 349; Paul, "Vasilii Kalika," 255-257.
25	NPL, 412-413; *Mosk.*, 244-245 (s.a. 1419-1421). In 1421, Konstantin concluded a treaty with the grand master of the Livonian Order on behalf of Novgorod.
26	*Mosk.*, 298.
27	Ypres was one of the most important of the Flemish cloth-producing centers. It is not clear if the Rus' sources used this as a general term for Flemish cloth irrespective of its place of origin, or if it specifically came from Ypres.
28	A *korablik* or *korablenik*, Russian for "little ship," was a gold coin with an image of a ship on it, hence its name. Tikhomirov identifies it as an English coin. P. Tikhomirov (1891-1900), 1:317. In the *Slovar' russkogo iazyka XI-XVII vv.*, it is identified as a Western European coin, but the country is not identified. Bogatova et al., eds. 7:303. The *Slovar' russkogo iazyka* identifies it as the English Noble. Slovar' russkogo iazyka 10:2033. The Noble was first coined under Edward III between 1344 and 1346 and was last minted under Edward IV in 1464, after which the New Noble or Rose Noble was coined. See Frey, 160.

29 *Mosk.*, 305.
30 Ibid., 307. The boiars gave similar gifts.
31 *Sorok*, or *sorochka*, meaning a bundle of forty (sorok) luxury furs (sables and martens); hence, 5 *sorochek* (five "forties" of fur) would be 200 sable furs. See Kovalev and Noonan, 653-682.
32 *Mosk.*, 305.
33 PRP 2:176; Martin (1985), 51. See below.
34 Grekov, *Izbrannye trudy*, 4:7-436; 3:40-191.
35 Grekov, *Izbrannye trudy*, 3:88. Ivan the Terrible's sack of Novgorod in 1570 probably explains the decline in the number of sof'iane, although there were other socio-economic problems throughout Muscovy after Ivan's death in 1584 leading up to the Time of Troubles. For a discussion of Ivan the Terrible and Novgorod, see Paul, "Continuity and Change," 300-305. See also Platonov (1923); idem (1924), 21.
36 Paul, "Continuity and Change," 292-293.
37 A *ved* (pl. *veda*) was a unit of measure used in carpentry, noted, but not defined, in the *Slovar' russkogo iazyka XI-XVII vv.* Bogatova, et al., eds.
38 *Vereteno* – spindle, shank (of an anchor).
39 Grekov, *Izbrannye trudy*, 3:79-85, esp. 82-85. Cf., 110-113 (for 1593).
40 NPL, 353; *Mosk.*, 172 (s.a. 1342).
41 NPL, 363; N4, 386.
42 NPL, 99, 343; *Mosk.*, 170. He went to Volynia again three years later.
43 "The Novgorod Judicial Charter," Art. 23, in ZDR, 306; PRP, 2:222.
44 *Polnyi pravoslavnyi bogoslosvkii entsyklopedicheskii slovar'*, 2:1848-1849. After the Muscovite Conquest, Sergei is said to have levied higher fees than his predecessors; Gennadii was deposed for charging fees for ordinations after the Moscow Council of 1503 outlawed the practice. Feodosii II was removed in 1551, in part, after Moscow received a letter denouncing him for charging high taxes on the clergy. Smirnov, 241.
45 For ransom, see NPL, 95, 337; N4, 257. For tribute, see NPL, 380. See also Chapter Five, above.
46 The charters are published in PRP, 3:465-470. For studies of the charters, see Grigor'ev; RFA (1951), 2:53-59; Zimin (1961): 28-40.
47 Nikitskii saw the *sof'iane* (sing. *sof'ianin*) as the entire collective of servitors of the archbishop whereas Kartashev saw them as the clergy attached to the Cathedral of Holy Wisdom, like the cathedral canons in Western Christendom. In the *Novgorod Judicial Charter*, the *sof'iane* are listed among the bailiffs. Nikitskii (1873),

	191-192; "The Novgorodian Judicial Charter," Art. 23, PRP, 2: 215; ZDR, 306; Kartashev, 1:188; Kaiser (1980), 236n75.
48	In the Roman Empire, the vicarius (pl. vicarii) was assistant to the prefect in a diocese under the Diocletian reforms. The church adopted the diocesan structure and vicarial office from the Roman civil administration. Berger, 764. The Russian Orthodox Church has an official called a *vikarii*, but it appears only under the patriarchate and is akin to a Catholic auxiliary bishop (or a *chorepiskopus* in the Greek Orthodox Church, mentioned in Chapter One), not a Catholic vicar. Novgorod did not have a *vikarii* until the metropolitanate of Varlaam (r. 1592-1601) when Silvestr was made vikarii of Karelia and Orekhov in 1595. Smirechanskii 1:20. Stroev, 379, 731; Zdravomislov, 36.
49	Grekov, "Pskovskaia sudnaia gramota," Arts. 2 and 109, pp. 237, 249; ZDR, 332, 341-42; PRP, 2: 322; "The Novgorod Judicial Charter," Arts. 5, 6, 8, 9, and 27, in ZDR, 30-307.
50	"The Novgorod Judicial Charter," Arts. 21, 23, and 26, ZDR, 306; Kaiser, ed. (1992), 81, 82; idem (1980), 102; PRP, 2:214, 215.
51	The chronicles and other documents mention other activities. We have already noted that Vasilii Kalika and his *namestnik*, Boris, brought peace between two factions in the city in 1342 and Lavrentii, *namestnik* of the Bishop of Smolensk, was witness to a commercial treaty.
52	Ianin (1970), 2:51-87, 179-196, 272-277; Ianin and Gaidukov, 3:79-86, 181-92, 286-92.
53	The seals of the *namestniki* of Ladoga date to the late thirteenth century, only during the tenure of Archbishop Kliment. Those from Torzhok date to the early fourteenth to the early fifteenth centuries, during the archiepiscopates of David, Moisei, Vasilii Kalika, Aleksei, Ioann, and Evfimii I.
54	"The Novgorod Judicial Charter," Art. 8, ZDR, 305; PRP, 2:213.
55	NPL, 414.
56	Ibid., 67, 273.
57	The office of *d'iak* was found in the secular administration in Novgorod and also elsewhere in Rus. The Novgorodian *veche* had a *d'iak* whose office (*izba* – hut) was near the *Iaroslavovo Dvorishche*, and the grand prince's Boiar Duma (council) in Moscow also had secretaries (*d'iaki*) attached to it. *D'iaki* were also attached to rural churches, and are noted in the *pistsovye knigi*. PKOP, 1, 17, 38, 48, 86, 177.
58	*Mosk.*, 320. Interestingly, Feofil affixed his seal himself to a charter recognizing the sovereignty of Grand Prince Ivan III. No *kliuchnik* is mentioned in that capacity. See Paul (2007), 268.

59 The *Novgorodian First Chronicle* relates that "on May 31 (1217), a bakery caught fire in the middle of the morning...and all who had fled into the stone churches *with their goods were all burnt there together with their goods*. And in the Varangian church *all the countless Varangian merchandise was burned*." See NPL, 57, 258; Emphasis added. The Varangian church, i.e., the Church of St. Olaf in the *Gotskii Dvor*, is called a *bozhnitsa*, rather than a *tserkov'* (church) or *khram* (temple), the terms used for Orthodox places of worship. The Scandinavians and Germans assigned their own watchmen for St. Olaf's and the Church of St. Peter and they were locked in every night by the merchant elder. See Slessarev, 178. On churches being used as warehouses, see also Cherepnin (1969), 305, 313, 315-316.

60 NPL, 90, 329.

61 NPL, 352. The *pistsovye knigi* also mention *storozhi* at rural churches, for example, at the Church of St. Nicholas the Great in The Nikol'skoi *Pogost* in Shung, north of Lake Onega, at the Church of the Prophet Elijah in Ilinskoi *Pogost* in Venitsy on the Oiat River, and at The Church of Michael the Archangel in Ozery in the Mikhailovskoi *Pogost*. PKOP, 1, 38, 53. See also, 177, 202, 212.

62 NPL, 411.

63 bid., p. 368 (s.a. 1362); p. 369 (s.a. 1364); p. 372 (s.a. 1374); p. 375 (s.a. 1377); p. 375 (s.a. 1378); p. 378 (s.a. 1382); p. 384 (s.a. 1390); p. 393 (s.a. 1398); p. 394 (s.a. 1399); p. 406 (s.a. 1416).

64 Ibid., 94, 335.

65 Ibid., 69-70, 277.

66 Ibid., 409. The chronicle says Simeon sent an entreaty (*moleniia*) "with a priest and his boiar," ("*s popom da s" svoim boiarom*"), rather than just with "a boiar."

67 Grekov, *Izbrannye trudy*, 3:59-62, 93-94, 96.

68 Paul (2007), 260.

69 In 1547, there were nine cooks and six bakers in the archiepiscopal kitchens (which had been rebuilt in stone by Evfimii II in 1442). Grekov, *Izbrannye trudy*, 3:62.

70 Ibid., 60-61.

71 Ibid., 96-98.

72 Ibid., 55-57.

73 Ibid., 64.

74 Stefanovich, 31-108.

75 RGB F. 304.I, No. 215, *Stoglav (Postanovlenie Moskovskogo sobora 1551 g.)*, Chapter 41, Question 14, fols. 129-129v; Kozhanchikov (1863), 134-135; Emchenko, 309.

76	Kollmann (1980), 74-76.
77	Franklin (2000), 203-205.
78	RGB F. 304.I, No. 215, Chapter 25, fol. 90v.; Kollmann (1980), 65-66.
79	Kollmann (1980), 66-67.
80	AI, 1.104:146-148. Seminaries were not established in each eparchy until the reign of Catherine the Great. Kollmann (1980), 68.
81	"The Novgorod Judicial Charter," Arts. 36 and 38, in ZDR, 307-308; Kaiser, ed. (1992), 84, 85; PRP, 2:217, 218. Article 38 mentions "a man who serves the archbishop, a boiar, a member of the *zhitye liudi*, a merchant, a monastery, a borough or street." That is, "the archbishop's man" is mentioned among the free men. The section allows these men to settle a dispute outside of court without having to kiss the cross (swear an oath), a right unlikely to have been granted to a slave. That said, there is no indication that the archbishops had manumitted their slaves between the eleventh century and the fifteenth when the *Judicial Charter* was issued.
82	"Statutory Privilege Charter of the Smolensk Prince Rostislav Mstislavich [1128-1160]," Art. 2, in ZDR, 213; PRP, 2:39; DAI, 1.4:5-8. Although relating to the bishop of Smolensk, the Novgorodian archbishops received similar grants. See below.
83	Budovnits, 47-48; Shchapov (1989), 87-88; 124-163.
84	*Lavrent.*, 124; NPL 165-166; Shchapov (1976), 18, 23; Zimin (1963), 68, 72, 74.
85	Shchapov (1989), 91, 103, 104; idem (1976), 39; Protas'eva, 1:96; ZDR, 134-208; Kaiser (1980), 50.
86	*Lavrent.*, 124; "Statute of Saint Prince Volodimir," Art. 3 of the Sinodal Redaction, in ZDR, 148; PRP, 1:237, 244; DAI, 1.1:1-2.
87	Shchapov (1989), 76-87, esp., 77-78.
88	Ibid., 90-94.
89	"The Statute of Saint Prince Volodimir," Art. 19, in ZDR, 149-150; Shchapov (1976), 63, cf., 24, 32, 40, 71; idem (1989), 91; Art. 6 of the Second Redaction and Art. 11 of the Third Redaction, in PRP, 1:242, 245-246. Parenthetical text from Kaiser, ed. (1992), 44.
90	"The Statute of Prince Iaroslav," Art. 1, in ZDR, 139-140, 148-150; Kaiser, ed. (1992), 45-50. The First Redaction, PRP, 1:237-238.
91	Paul (2008), 86, 110.
92	These may, in fact, have been the first such local charters issued, though the "Statutory Privilege Charter of the Smolensk Prince Rostislav Mstislavich," establishing the eparchy of Smolensk, states that the bishopric was approved by Metropolitan Mikhail (r. 1131-1145), suggesting it predates the Novgorodian charters

	by about five years. See Art. 16, in ZDR, 216; Art. 8 in PRP, 1: 42; Kaiser, ed. (1992), 51-55.
93	The Church of the Tithe is meant here, rather than the Cathedral of Holy Wisdom in Kyiv.
94	"Statute of the Novgorod Prince Vsevolod [1135-37] on Church Courts, [Church] People, and Trade Measures," Art. 4, in ZDR, 251; DAI, 1.3:3; PRP, 2:162-163. Parenthetical text from Kaiser, ed. (1992), 59-60. See also Martin (1985), 50; Nikitskii (1893), 19-20.
95	More than 500 tally-sticks have been excavated in Novgorod, used to measure the bundles to determine if they contained the standard 40 pelts. Kovalev (2002).
96	Martin (1985), 159. See also 240n20. Anna Khoroshkevich calculated 500,000 pelts were sold annually in Novgorod. Khoroshkevich, 52.
97	Lesnikov, 259-278; Martin (1985), 159-163.
98	"The Statutory Charter of the Novgorod Prince Sviatoslav Ol'govich," Art. 1, in ZDR, 224; PRP, 2:117. Parenthetical additions are from Kaiser, ed. (1992), 57-58.
99	Ibid., Art. 2, in ZDR, 225; PRP, 2:117.
100	Kaiser explains that the new or "fur" *kuna*, entering circulation sometime in the twelfth century, equaled one quarter of a *grivna*. Kaiser, ed. (1992), 57; see also ZDR, 228; PRP, 2:117.
101	Ibid., Art. 3, in ZDR, 225; PRP, 2:117.
102	Rybina; Kovalev (2003).
103	Martin (1985), 54-57.
104	Zarubin, 184; Martin (1985), 78-79.
105	Martin (1985), 80.
106	Ibid.
107	"Statutory Charter of the Novgorod Prince Sviatoslav Ol'govich," Art. 4, in ZDR, 225; PRP, 2:117.
108	Khlebnikov, 30-32; Rozhkov, 438-441; Blum, 179-80, 200-201.
109	Grekov, *Izbrannye trudy*, 3:64.
110	Ibid., 3:71.
111	Ibid., 3:61.
112	Ibid., 3:136.
113	Paul, "The Military Revolution," 21; Kotoshikhin, 172-173.
114	Grekov notes that the price of one *pud* of copper rose from 227 *dengi* in 1593 to 2,200 *dengi* in 1661. 100 candles cost 42 *dengi* in 1593 and 200 *dengi* in 1661. A ream of paper cost 66 *dengi* in 1593 and 120 *dengi* in 1661. Grekov, *Izbrannye trudy*, 3:136.
115	PRP, 2: 176; Martin (1985), 51.
116	*Mosk.*, 305. The equation of the St. John's association to a Western

	guild is unsatisfactory, since Rus' probably had no such institutionalized guilds, but this term is sometimes found in Western scholarship.
117	Paul (2008), 86-87.
118	Abramovich, ed. (1930), 39; *Lavrent.*, 159, 181; *Paterik Kievskogo Pecherskogo monastyria*, 7; Shchapov (1989), 134-136.
119	Shchapov (1989), 87-88, 124-163, esp. 147-149; Grekov (1953), 139-141, 142; Budovnits, 47-48. The bishop's land acquisition is probably what Budovnits had in mind when he wrote that the church did not acquire land until the thirteenth century since, as we have just said, the monasteries began receiving land as early as the eleventh century. That said, that Ioakim built his cathedral as well as the Perun Monastery in the 990s suggest that he owned the land on which they were built, though this, again, might be legendary. The princely charters, just discussed, only granted tribute from certain districts to the Novgorodian bishops, not ownership of them.
120	The Older Redaction of the *Novgorodian First Chronicle* names Vladimir alone as the patron, while the Younger Redaction attributes the building to both Vladimir and Luka. NPL, 16, 181.
121	NPL, 29, 216.
122	NPL, 29, 216.
123	Danilova, 46-47. Andrei Gnevushev lists only 5,257 obzha of land in the archbishops' possession, but his analysis did not include all the *pistsovye knigi*. Gnevushev, 348.
124	*Akty sotsial'no-ekonomicheskoi istorii Severo-vostochnoi Rusi*, 3.15:31, 3.17:33-34; Martin (1985), 83.
125	AAE, 1.94:73; Danilova, 147.
126	Shapiro.
127	Danilova, 159.
128	Ibid., 150.
129	NPL, 396; Danilova, 150.
130	Danilova, 154.
131	Paul (2007), 260. See above.
132	SPbII RAN, F. 171, perepl. I, No. 6, fols. 12-13 (1603); perepl. I, No. 19, fols. 36-42; perepl. II, No. 81, fols. 64-65 (1650).
133	Danilova, 159.
134	Ibid., 152-153.
135	Shapiro, 239.
136	Ibid., 154-155, 157.
137	Danilova, 159.
138	Ibid., 149-150.

139 Martin (1985), 79; Kopanev, 442-462.
140 NPK, 3:8-13.
141 On icon painting see Ouspensky and Lossky. Primary sources indicate the archbishops levied a "duty" or "fee" of eggs (*iachnaia poshlina*) on the priests, in the Novgorodian eparchy. It must be noted, however, that sources are from well after the period under study. SPbII RAN, F. 171, pereplet. II, No. 83, fols. 67-68 [from the metropolitanate of Nikon (r. 1649-1652)].
142 The grand prince's villages held by Iurkinskii Zakharov, the son of Fineev, in Vutrogoshch, owed 2 cheeses and 20 eggs, and the peasants on lands held by the *Pomeshchiki* Gribaka (Grigorii) Zhukov and Danil Vetrianii in the Kotorskaia *Pogost* also in the Shelonskaia Piatina owed 440 eggs and 60 eggs respectively.   Prince Ivan Andreevskii received 700 eggs from the peasants on his estates in the Shelonskaia *Piatina* and his *kliuchnik* received 315 eggs and 28 sheepskins according to the old receipts. According to the new receipts, Prince Ivan received 1,650 eggs from peasants on his estates there. NPK, 4:106-107.
143 Ibid., 4:8-10.
144 Ibid., 4:12.
145 "Statute of Iaroslav," Short Redaction, Arts. 28, 29; ZDR, 169-170; Shchapov (1987), 175-181; idem (1989), 117, 121; PRP, 1:261.
146 "Statute of Iaroslav," Short Redaction, in ZDR, 169-170, Shchapov (1976), Arts. 28, 29, 33, p. 113; idem (1972), 282-3; idem (1989), 121; Art. 26 and 27 in PRP, 1:261.
147 ZDR, 170; Shchapov (1976), Art. 32, p. 113; idem, (1989), 121; PRP, 1:261.
148 ZDR, 168; Shchapov (1976), Art. 7, p. 87; idem (1972), 186-7; idem (1989), 119; Art. 5 in PRP, 1:259-260.
149 "The Russkaia Pravda, the Expanded Redaction," Art. 107, in ZDR, 71-72; PRP, 1:135.
150 Ibid., Art. 109, in ZDR, 72; PRP, 1:135.
151 Ibid., Art. 8, in ZDR, 305; PRP, 2:213.
152 Ibid., Art. 23, in ZDR, 306; PRP, 2:215.
153 Ibid., Art. 33, in ZDR, 305; PRP, 1:216.
154 "Statutory Charter of Grand Prince Vasilii Dmitrievich to the Dvina Land 1397/98," Sections 7, 8, and 10, in Kaiser, ed. (1992), 112; PRP, 3:162-166.
155 PRP, 3:346-357.
156 See Chapter Two, above.
157 AAE, 1.382: 484-485. See also P. Tikhomirov (1891-1900), 2.1:62-64
158 *Nikon*. (PSRL 12), 258; *Sof.* 1 (PSRL 6), 49, 224. His resignation

charter is dated June 26, 1504. GIM, Sinod. No. 997, fol. 1551. Cf. RNB Q.XVII.50, fols. 227v.-230.

159 N2, 147, 184; N4, 611. Gennadii's retirement document said that he wanted to return to a monastery. AAE, vol. 1, doc. 384, pp. 488; see also P. Tikhomirov (1891-1900), 2.1:64. See also Paul, "Continuity and Change," 283-284.

160 Žužek, 149. On the Byzantine and Rus' practices of exacting fees at ordination, see RIB 6.6:92; Beneshevich, ed., (1915), 2:2-5, esp. 5; Kollmann (1978), 352-353; Golubinskii (1995), 2.1:69. On Justinian's Novella, see Justinian, Novella 123, p. 606. On the Novellae of Isaac Comnenus, see von Lingenthal, ed., 3:322.

161 Chapter 87 of the Stoglav forbade taking fees, while Chapter 88 set the ordination fees. RGB F. 304.I, No. 215, Chapters 87 and 88, fols. 274-277v.; Kozhanchikov (1863), 251-254; Emchenko, 393-394; Kollmann (1978), 352-354. Gennadii paid 2,000 rubles to the grand prince for his own consecration in 1485, so the Muscovite authorities were by no means beyond reproach in this matter. *Tipografskaia letopis'*, 235.

162 Kollmann (1978), 352.
163 Ibid., 469.
164 According to the Stoglav, Consecration to the priesthood in Novgorod cost 15 rubles, other offices cost 20 or 30 rubles. RGB F. 304.I, No. 215, Chapter 41, Question 15, fols. 130-130v.; Kozhanchikov (1863), 135-136; Emchenko, 309; Kollmann (1978), 457.

165 Makarii, *Istoriia*, 4.2:143; Paul, "Continuity and Change," 284.
166 RGB F. 304.I, No. 215, Chapter 5, Question 2, fols. 39-40v. and Chapters 44 and 45, fols. 152v.-158; Kozhanchikov (1863), 43; Emchenko, 254, 322-326; Kollmann (1978), 370.

167 On the fees, see also Tomilin, 38.
168 RNB, f. 728, No. 1553, Sof. 1548, *Kniga zapisei "sofiiskoi poshlina"* (1557).

169 Archbishop Feodosii II (r. 1542-1551) wrote a letter to the clergy of the Vodskaia *Piatina* calling on them to combat paganism there. He added that they had not been paying the *poshlina*. DAI, 1.43:57-60. Archbishop Leonid (r. 1571-1573) was disliked for the fees he charged, although the Stoglav Council had confirmed the right to raise them. N2, 174; AAE 1.229:221.

170 PskL, 2:63; Tikhomirov (1891-1900).1:8-9; Paul, "Continuity and Change," 278.

171 Kollmann (1978), 366.
172 *Mosk.*, 308.

Chapter Seven

1. Lazarev (1947), 91.
2. Popova (1980); idem (1984); Lazarev (1969), 19.
3. Brumfield (1993), 26.
4. Brumfield (1993), 26; idem (1983), 36-83, esp. 37.
5. Brumfield (1993), 26.
6. Ibid., 27.
7. Brumfield (1993), 35; idem (1983), 74.
8. Brumfield (1993), 38.
9. Ibid., 70.
10. Brumfield (1993), 70; idem (1983), 47.
11. Brumfield (1993), 70.
12. Paul, "Continuity and Change," 308.
13. Ibid., 294-295.
14. See Photius (Patriarch of Constantinople).
15. Zguta (1972), 297-313; idem (1978).
16. On the *byliny*, see Astakhova; Rybakov (1963); Smirnov and Smoltskii, eds.; Speranskii.
17. The authenticity of the Igor Tale has been much debated; for the various interpretations, see A. A. (Anton Anatol'evich) Gorskii. For the tale itself, see Dmitriev and Likhachev, eds. (1967). On *Zadonshchina*, see Dmitriev, Likhacheva, and Likhachev.
18. The church railed against the *skomorokhi* and other elements of popular culture as pagan holdovers. Feodosii of the Kyiv Caves Monastery called the *skomorokhi* "evils to be shunned by good Christians." Feodosii Pecherskii, 2.2:195; Zguta (1972), 297-298.
19. Rowell, 149-188.
20. Admittedly, the readership of the chronicles was extremely small.
21. *Lavrent.*, 1-9; N4, 1-3; Cf., RNB F.IV.165, *Khronograf*, which begins with biblical history and moves through Roman, Byzantine, and Bulgarian history before getting to Rus' history.
22. Khans Berke (r. 1258-1266) and Tuda-Mengu (r. 1282/3-1287) personally converted to Islam, but it became the state religion of the Golden Horde only under Khan Uzbek (r. 1313-1341). Halperin (1985), 29.
23. NPL, 69, 275-6; 75, 287; 83; 31, 218.
24. Ibid., 73, 284.
25. Ibid., 67, 273.
26. Ibid., 16, 18, 22, 397, 401, 408-409.
27. Ibid., 275-276.
28. Ibid., 79, 297.

29	Ibid., 420.
30	Ibid, 55, 255.
31	Ibid., 29, 215. The Younger Redaction adds that the monastery's construction "was a relief to Christians and a joy to the angels."
32	Ibid., 59, 259; 356.
33	Ibid., 58; 60, 261; 73, 284; 344.
34	Khoroshkevich, 141. Admittedly, all of these were written by churchmen.
35	NPL, 33, 221.
36	Ibid., 76, 289.
37	Iugrian was the medieval Russian term for the peoples known today as the Khantsy and Mansi.
38	NPL, 40-41; 232-233.
39	Ibid., 272-273.
40	Ibid.
41	Froianov and Dvornichenko, 157.
42	Novgorod is first mentioned in the *Novgorodian First Chronicle* under the year 854, in the *Sofia First Chronicle* under the year 859 and in the *Lavrentian Chronicle* under the years 862. *Sof.* 1 (PSRL 6.1) (2000 ed.), cols 13-14; *Lavrent.*, 6, 8, 10, 20; NPL, 107.
43	On the earliest cultural layers and dating the foundation of the city, see Ianin and Aleshkovskii, 32-61; Ianin (1977), 213-229.
44	Kolchin and Ianin, 3-137, esp., 108; Nosov, 5-17; Orlov (1964), 267; idem (1978), 194-200.
45	Ghillebert de Lannoy wrote there were 350 churches in the city when he visited in 1415. Potvin and Mouzeau, eds., 33.
46	Birnbaum (1996) 107.
47	*Nikon.* (PSRL 9), 69. None of the earlier chronicles mention Ioann's church patronage. His tenure is also uncertain, with some sources saying he took office in 1008 and others in 1019.
48	*Lavrent.*, 183.
49	*Lavrent.*, 283; *Ipat.* (PSRL 2.2), 260. The *Lavrentian Chronicle* gives Stefan's office as hegumen of the Kyiv Caves Monastery. The *Hypatian Chronicle* says he was hegumen prior to his episcopate and names his see sub anno 1091. *Ipat.* (PSRL 2.3), 200. See also his Life in Rostovskii, 2:228 (under April 27); *Kniga zhitii sviatykh*, vol. 8 (April), folios 121v.-124, esp. 123.
50	On the titular metropolitans of Pereislav and Chernihiv in the late eleventh century, see Poppe (1997), 350-352ff.
51	*Lavrent.*, 208; *Suzdal.*, 293 (s. a. 1123); *Ipat.* (PSRL 2.3), 197-198. Priselkov (2003), 310.
52	*Lavrent.* 208-209.

53	*Suzdal.*, 245 (s.a. 1222, noted when the church was rebuilt); Poppe (1997), 357; Priselkov (2003), 292.
54	*Ipat.* (PSRL 2.1), 286; Poppe (1997), 357-358.
55	*Suzdal.*, 406.
56	*Suzdal.*, 411. "German," again, is used here as a general term for Western European.
57	*Suzdal.*, 412 (s.a. 1196).
58	*Suzdal.*, 453.
59	Elements of the *Lavrentian Chronicle* suggest a chronicle, or at least annalistic notes, being kept or edited under the auspices of the bishops at Rostov in the thirteenth century, in Tver' or Vladimir-on-Kliazma (under the metropolitan) in the early fourteenth century, in Pereislav (Pereiaslavl-Russkii), and, of course, the compilation in 1377 by Lavrentii in Nizhnii Novgorod. Guimon, 38, 291-293.
60	Ibid., 218.
61	*Lavrent.*, 118; Cross, Morgilevski, and Conant, 480-481.
62	*Lavrent.*, 124; Cross, Morgilevski, and Conant, 481-482. Construction began in 991 and it was dedicated on May 11 or 12, 996. Vladimir also erected churches in the Kyivan suburbs, to the Transfiguration in Vasiliev, and the Church of the Mother of God in Vyshhorod. *Lavrent.*, 125 (s.a. 996), 129 (s.a. 1007), 153 (s.a. 1039); Cross, et al., "The Earliest Medieval Churches of Kiev," 488-489. Several chronicles also mention Vladimir's construction of the stone Church of St. George in Kyiv. *Ermolin.*, 15; *Ermitazh.*, 365.
63	*Lavrent.*, 151; NPL 18, 180; Cross, et al., "The Earliest Medieval Churches of Kiev," 490. The chronicle notes in the same passage that Iaroslav also built the Chapel of the Annunciation over the Golden Gate, the Monastery of St. George, and the Convent of St. Irene.
64	*Suzdal.*, 348.
65	*Mosk.*, 168, 324.
66	See Conant, 75-92.
67	*Suzdal.*, 437.
68	*Suzdal.*, 438. Konstantin became Prince of Vladimir in 1217, so while not really a minor prince, he was never as famous as other Princes of Vladimir, Moscow, or Kyiv.
69	N3, 208. In 995, Ioakim also built a monastery on the site of a shrine to Perun, south of the Iur'ev Monastery on Lake Il'men. It is known to this day as the Monastery "on Perun." N4, 346, 545. Conant attributes the cathedral to Prince Vladimir, not Bishop Ioakim. Conant, 77. Makarii notes it is uncertain when or where the first episcopal palace was built. Makarii (1857), 7.

70 For more recent scholarly doubt as to the existence of the oaken cathedral and the Church of Ioakim and Anne, if not of Ioakim himself, see Ianin (1977), 124-130; Sivak, 9-15.

71 Ioakim's death is mentioned in the *Sofia First* and the *Novgorodian Third Chronicles*, but not his place of burial. N3, 210. *Sof.* 1, 136. The Church of Ioakim and Anne was allegedly destroyed when the current Cathedral of Holy Wisdom was built in 1045-1050. Gordienko (1991), 55-56. Manuscript sources claim Ioakim's remains were moved to the *Martirievskaia Papert'* of the Cathedral of Holy Wisdom on October 12, 1699 under Metropolitan Iov. RNB Mikhailovskii Q. 348, fol. 2v.; N3, 275; P. Tikhomirov (1891-1900), 1:16-17; 2.2:331-332. It is worth noting that there is also a chapel of Ioakim and Anne in Holy Wisdom.

72 N2, 121. Conant calls it "the first truly Russian church of monumental character." Conant, 77, and Fig. 2, p. 79. He doubts that these "tops" were wooden domes like those found in later Russian church architecture, and in another article states that they could be "roofs, spires, pinnacles, or domes." Cross, et al., "The Earliest Medieval Churches of Kiev," 496.

73 Karger places the first Holy Wisdom immediately to the west of the current little church of St. Andrew Stratelates, where artifacts from a pre-Christian burial site have been uncovered; the remnants of the Church of Boris and Gleb, built by Sotko (Sadko) in the eleventh century, were uncovered just to the north of the Church of St. Andrew Stratelates in 1940-1941. Karger, 92-95.

74 On different dates for the destruction of the old cathedral and the likely oral tradition behind them, see Guimon, 270-272.

75 One manuscript says the cathedral stood 60 years and burned on March 14, 1049 (6557 AM). See RNB HCPK Q. 36, fol. 148. The current cathedral was consecrated by Bishop Luka Zhidiata on September 14, although what year is unclear. The *Sofiia First Chronicle* says it was 1050; another manuscript, along with the *Novgorodian Third Chronicle*, say 1052 (6560 AM). *Sof.* 1, 80; N3, 212; RNB HCPK Q. 36, fol. 148; Karger, 16-23, esp. 16; Tsarevskaia (2005), 3, 6.

76 Golubinskii (1995), 1.2: 109; Khoroshev (1989), 14.

77 On the Kyivan cathedral, see Poppe (1981), 15-65. Conant, 75-92; Logvin; Lazarev (1978); Komech, 147-150; Lazarev (1971), plates 175-178. On Hagia Sophia in Istanbul, see Mango (1972); idem (1962); Kähler; Mainstone. See also Bogoslovskii. 1:185-215; Durylin.

78 A cathedral dedicated to Holy Wisdom was also built in Trebizond during the reign of the Emperor Manuel I (r. 1238-1263), an

79 obvious link with Constantinople, then under Latin control (1204-1261). See Talbot, ed.

79 The fresco of the Emperor Constantine and his mother, Helena, just inside the south entrance (on the northern wall of the Martirievskaia *Papert'*) and dated to the late 11th century, and the fact that the cathedral was dedicated on the Feast of the Exaltation of the Cross, September 14/27, (it was Helena who discovered the True Cross in the fourth century), show a conscious effort to link the cathedral with Constantinople (and Jerusalem). Tsarevskaia (2005), 6, 18, 27 and 29; cf. Karger, 118-120. See also. Plate 86 in Faensen and Ivanov.

80 Kyiv, Constantinople, and Jerusalem all had churches dedicated to Holy Wisdom. In Jerusalem, it was built next to the Praetorium, patronized by Empress Eudocia (ca. 400-460) and first described by the German archdeacon Theodosius in about 530. See Theodosius, 20.

81 Kiprian, the first bishop of Tobol'sk (r. 1621-1624) – who grew up in Novgorod and was later metropolitan of Novgorod (r. 1626-1634) – named the cathedral in Tobol'sk, after the cathedral in Novgorod. P. Tikhomirov (1891-1900), 2.1:76. The cathedral in Vologda is also named after the one in Novgorod; Vologda being part of the Novgorodian Land until 1421. The current cathedral there was built between 1568 and 1570. Makarii, *Istoriia*, 4.2:15.

82 Prince Vseslav's campaigns, especially his pillaging of the Novgorodian cathedral in 1067, likely led the monks who wrote the chronicles, to blacken his name, contributing to the folklore surrounding him. The *Lavrentian Chronicle* portrayed him as being conceived by sorcery. *Lavrent.*, 155. He is depicted as a werewolf in the *Igor Tale* and the Volkh Vseslavich/Volga Sviatoslavich *byliny* cycle. *Iroicheskaia pesn' o pokhode*, 36. Cf., Farrell, 725–744; Haney, 7; Jakobson and Szeftel, 83; Oinas, 513–522; Rychka, 68-72.

83 The *Hypatian Chronicle* claims Vseslav stole a church tabernacle (*ierusalim*) and liturgical vessels and seized a *pogost*. Ipat. (PSRL 2.2), 608 (s.a. 1178).

84 On Vseslav and the cathedrals in Polatsk and Novgorod, see *Lavrent.*, 166; *Ipat.* (PSRL 2.2), 155; NPL, 17, 186; N3, 212; N4, 123; *Sof.* 1, 186-187. The current cathedral in Polatsk is an eighteenth-century edifice in the Vilnius Baroque style with only a few parts dating back to Vseslav's time. Duk, 63-67; Kyshnerevich, 76-80; Lavretskii, 74-75; Tarasov, 58-62. On the three eleventh-century cathedrals of Holy Wisdom, see Mokeev; Rappoport, 24.

85 NPL, 310. Cf. Grand Prince Aleksandr Mikhailovich's 1327 speech to Pskov. PskL, 2:90.

86	NPL, 82, 310. The Younger Redactions speaks of "the ecclesiastical houses." For other examples, see NPL 64, 268 (s.a. 1224); 73, 284 (s.a. 1234); 77-78, 290-294 (s.a. 1240); 78, 296 (s.a. 1242); 82, 310 (s.a. 1259); 95, 336 (s.a. 1316).
87	Sof. 1, 251; Golubinskii (1995), 1.2:109.
88	NPL, 54, 253.
89	NPL, 89, 320-321 (s.a. 1270). Paul, "Iaroslavichi," 53.
90	NPL, 51, 249 (s.a. 1210). His father was Mstislav Rostislavich the Bold (Khrabryi) of Smolensk, an earlier prince of Novgorod (Prince of Bilhorod, r. 1161; 1171-1173; Prince of Smolensk, r. 1175-1177; and Prince of Novgorod, r. 1179-1180). He died while prince of Novgorod and was buried in the cathedral. Cf., Paul (2008), 90-91.
91	NPL, 57 (s.a. 1218). The phrase could indicate the prince attended a Divine Liturgy in the cathedral.
92	NPL, 88, 320 (s. a. 1270). The prince's ambassadors, in fact, used this formula in addressing the city. Paul, "Iaroslavichi," 53.
93	NPL, 16, 181. Prince Vladimir and his mother, Anna, lie in sarcophagi on the south side of the cathedral overlooking the Martirievskaia *Papert'*. Both have modern, painted effigies and there is a nineteenth century fresco of Vladimir holding a model of Holy Wisdom in the archway over his sarcophagus. Tsarevskaia (2005), 3.
94	Karger, 102.
95	The chronicles mention Nikita's death in late January and then state that the cathedral was frescoed "in the spring." Thus, his money was used, but the extent of his oversight or patronage prior to his death, is not known. NPL, 19, 203; N3, 213. All that is left of these frescoes are the images of the prophets in the drum of the main dome. The Christ Pantocrator in the dome was heavily modified in the 1600s and destroyed during the Second World War although there are photographs of it from the nineteenth century. See Tsarevskaia (2005), 14, 19-22, 29. Cf. Faensen and Ivanov, pl. 85. The aforementioned fresco of Constantine and Helena just inside the south door indicates Nikita's icons are not the first to adorn the cathedral, but this was probably a case of princely rather than episcopal patronage.
96	NPL, 213; 29, 215; N3, 214. Remnants of those frescoes can be seen on the north side of the Martirievskaia *Papert'* below Prince Vladimir's sarcophagus. Tsarevskaia (2005), 24, 35. More mundane repairs of the cathedral were also undertaken at the behest of the archbishops: Nifont ordered the roof covered in lead in 1151 and

had the exterior of the cathedral plastered. Archbishop Dalmat had the roof re-leaded in 1261, as did Vasilii in 1333 and again in 1341 (following a fire), and Ioann in 1396 (after another fire), and again in 1408. See NPL, 29, 215; 83, 311, 345, 353, 388, 400; N3, 235.

97 An illuminated lectionary, GIM, Sobranie A. I. Khludova, No. 30, *Evangelie aprakos XIV v.*, composed in the archbishop's workshop and now in the State History Museum in Moscow, dates to the 1340s or early 1350s, that is, the second half of Vasilii's archiepiscopate and is stylistically very similar to the decorations on the "Vasilii Gates" ordered by Vasilii in 1336 and now in Aleksandrovo near Moscow (where they were taken by Ivan the Terrible). The Holy Gates of the Likhachev collection in the Russian Museum in St. Petersburg are also said to be of this style (both sets of gates are "fire gilt"), leading art historians to conclude that Archbishop Vasilii was probably the patron of all these works and that they illustrate his personal involvement in their creation and his personal artistic tastes. On the Vasilii Gates, see Loukomski, plate XVI; Makarii (2003), 111-119. See also Popova (1984), plate 22; Lazarev (1969), 19. On the Likhachev Gates, see Mann, ed., 90, 140-141, fig. 144.

98 NPL, 347, 353; Lazarev (1969), 19.

99 NPL, 354; N3, 225.

100 NPL, 400.

101 On the gates, see Daniec, 67-97; Krause and Schubert, 47; Tsapenko, 34-38; Poppe, "K istorii romanskikh dverei," 191-200; Raba (1977), 161-173: Goldschmidt; Mende, 74-83; Brumfield dates the gates to 1117. Brumfield (1983), 41. The other famous set of doors in the cathedral, the Korsun Doors, are thought to have been hung at the west entrance (where the Magdeburg Gates now hang) just after its construction. Those now hang at the entrance to the Chapel of the Nativity of the Virgin on the southeast side of the cathedral. See Tsarevskaia (2005), 36, 48, 51. Bishops continued to refurbish the cathedral. Archbishop Lev (now metropolitan), continued this tradition by reestablishing a library in the choir gallery in 1996 (as of 2018 it numbered some 7,400 volumes). See Savushkina. On the fate of the old library, see below.

102 There are forty-seven burials in the cathedral: the first was the cathedrals patron, Prince Vladimir Iaroslavich, in 1052. The pre-1478 bishops buried in the cathedral are: Ioakim (reinterned), Luka (the first prelate buried in the cathedral), Nikita, Ioann Pop'ian, Arkadii, Il'ia, Gavriil, Martirii, Mitrofan, Antonii, Spiridon, Dalmat, Kliment, David, Vasilii Kalika, Simeon, and Evfimii I. For the

burial places of the other fourteen bishops and archbishops from before 1478, see Chapter Three. Archbishop Gurii (r.1900-1910; d. 1912) was the last bishop (and last person) buried in the cathedral. Arsenii (Stadnitskii, Archbishop of Novgorod and Staraia Rus'), 457-459; Ianin (1988), 193.

The sarcophagi or grave of only three bishops are visible in the cathedral today. Bishop Nikita's sarcophagus is in the north niche of the Chapel of the Nativity of the Mother of God between it and the Chapel of Ioakim and Anne. His shrouded relics can be viewed under a glass lid. When I visited the cathedral on May 13, 2007, the feast of the uncovering of his relics (in 1558), the deacons opened the glass lid and allowed pilgrims to kiss Nikita's hand through the shroud. Archbishop Il'ia's sarcophagus is in the northwest corner of the cathedral between the west gallery and the *Papert'* of John the Forerunner (*Predtechenskaia Papert'*, now housing the Chapel of the Beheading of John the Baptist). Metropolitan Gavriil II is buried under a slab in the southwest corner of the *Papert'* of John the Forerunner. The others are buried below the *paperti*. In addition to these three bishops and Prince Vladimir and Princess Anna, Prince Fedor Iaroslavich is said to lie in a sarcophagus in a niche on the north side of the main church (although Valentin Ianin argues that this is actually Prince Dmitrii Shemiaka, whose remains have been misidentified as Fedor's since 1616. The real Fedor is apparently still in the Iur'ev Monastery, where he was buried in 1233. See Ianin (1988), 89-113). Prince Mstislav Rostislavich's tomb has already been mentioned. The *posadniki*, as well as Prince Vasilii Mstislavich, are buried below the floors in the *paperti*. Tsarevskaia (2005), 48, 57, 59.

103   The bishop-saints from before 1478 buried in the cathedral are Ioakim, Luka, Nikita, Arkadii, Il'ia (Ioann), Gavriil (Grigorii), Martirii, Antonii, Vasilii Kalika, and Simeon. St. Affonii (r. 1635-1649; d. 1652), is the only post-1478 bishop-saint buried in the cathedral. On Affonii, see *Rospis'*, *Pribavl.* N2, 189.

104   In addition to the aforementioned princes, Vasilii Mstislavich (grandson of Mstislav the Bold by his son Mstislav Mstislavich the Daring), and Fedor Iaroslavich (Prince of Novgorod, r. 1228-1229) (Mstislav the Daring's grandson and Vasilii Mstislavich's nephew were buried in the cathedral in 1218 and 1233 respectively. With Mstislav the Bold and his grandson and great grandson there are three generations of the Rostislavichi, all of them considered saints, buried in the cathedral. Mstislav Rostislavich Bezokii ("The Eyeless") Prince of Rostov (r. 1175-1176) and Novgorod (r.

1160-1161 and 1177-1178), died in 1178 and was also buried in the cathedral. Additionally, the *posadniki* Stepan Tverdislavich and Mikhail Fedorovich were buried in the cathedral in 1243 and 1268 respectively. Ianin (1988), 15, 59-61, 67-69, 192-95.

105 N3, 240.

106 One example is the Church of St. Simon in the Zverin Monastery, built in 1466 and consecrated by Iona, though none of the sources specifically mention him as sponsor. N2, 141; N4, 456, 609.

107 These figures include church construction, renovation, and decoration. They include the two projects bishops Arkadii and Martirii patronized while still hegumens as well as a few non-ecclesiastical constructions, such as the fortress at Orekhov and buildings in the archiepiscopal compound (like a bakery). There are a few churches the archbishops probably patronized, like the "*Vladyka's* Church" built by Martirii in 1192 while he was hegumen, and painted in 1199 while he was archbishop. The original construction is counted as an archiepiscopal construction, but as to the painting in 1199, it seems likely but is ultimately uncertain that Martirii patronized it or if it was the next hegumen. Some structures are left out, like Kopor'e, Korela, and the fortress at Staraia Ladoga. This is likely an incomplete list, as Ghillebert de Lannoy mentioned 350 churches in Novgorod alone in 1415, about a hundred more than I have counted. However, Lannoy is unlikely to have counted them all himself and may be passing on hearsay, so his figure should not to be taken as exact. See Potvin and Mouzeau, eds., 33, Mund, 49.

108 The monk Vasilii built the Church of St. Vasilii in 1262, and the chronicler noted that Boris Gavshchinich probably supported him. NPL, 83, 312.

109 Some projects were patronized by more than one of these groups or people. Thus, in 1345, Archbishop Vasilii, commissioned by Andrei, son of the *tysiatskii*, and Paul Petrovits, rebuilt the Church of St. Paraskeva-Piatnitsa (originally built in 1156) after it had burned down. NPL, 357; N3, 215.

110 Prince Iaroslav Vladimirovich (r. Prince of Novgorod 1182-1184, 1187-1196, 1197-1199) – son of Vladimir Mstislavich and grandson of Mstislav the Great – built the Church of the Transfiguration on the Nereditsa in 1198 (he is called "Grand Prince" in the *Novgorodian First Chronicle*); his wife built a monastery on Mikhailitsa Street the following year. These are the last princely projects built in Novgorod. NPL, 44, 237-238. Eight of the eleven projects date to between 1039 and 1135; thus, princely patronage really fell off

in the second quarter of the twelfth century. While few in number, these were, admittedly, some of the largest and most important churches in Novgorod, including the Cathedral of Holy Wisdom, the Church of St. George in the Iur'ev (St. George's) Monastery (built by Prince Vsevolod Mstislavich in 1119), the Church of St. Nicholas on the Market (built by Mstislav Vladimirovich and Vsevolod Mstislavich between 1113 and 1136), and The Church of St. John the Forerunner on the Opoki (built by Prince Vsevolod Mstislavich in 1127-30). On the Cathedral of Holy Wisdom, see above. On the Church of St. George in the Iur'ev Monastery, see NPL 21, 206; N3, 214. On the Church of St. Nicholas, see NPL 20, 205; N3, 213. On the Church of John the Forerunner, see RNB f. 550, F.IV.165, fol. 468v.; NPL 21, 206; N2, 123; N4, 144; *Stepennaia Kniga*, 1:195. The current church was rebuilt by Archbishop Evfimii II in 1453. N3, 240.

111   NPL, 210; N2, 124; N4, 146; PskL, 1:9; *Stepennaia Kniga*, 1:195. The church was rebuilt by Archbishop Evfimii in 1453. N3, 240.
112   NPL, 354.
113   *Kitov*, i.e., *kiot* – icon case.
114   NPL, 29, 216. The Church of the [Transfiguration of the] Savior is the main church of the Spaso-Mirozhskii Monastery and still stands at the confluence of the Mirozhska and Velikaia Rivers in Pskov. On the church, see Brumfield (1993), 35; idem (1983), 74; Spegal'skii, 20-221; Alferova, 5, 24. The Church of Saint Clement used to stand just outside the fortress in Staraia Ladoga.
115   Karger, 25-27.
116   N3, 214. The church was painted in 1125. It stands in what is left of the Antoniev Monastery just south of the Humanities Institute of the Iaroslav-the-Wise Novgorod State University. There are traces of medieval iconography, but many of the frescoes are seventeenth or eighteenth century.
117   N3, 214; N4 143. The church still stands in the Iur'ev Monastery; most of the extant icons are from the nineteenth century. Karger, 240-242, 246.
118   N2, 123; N3, 214, 240; N4, 144-145.
119   NPL, 23, 208; N2, 124; N4, 146; *Stepennaia Kniga*, 1:195.
120   Brumfield (1993), 35. For pictures of the frescoes, see Faensen and Ivanov, plates 122-127.
121   These were the Church of the Annunciation (1179), a stone church in the Annunciation Monastery (1180) (possibly a repetition in the entry for 1179), the church of the Epiphany over the Detinets' gates (1182), the church of the Holy Fathers (also 1182), and the

	Church of St. John (on the Opoki) in the Marketplace (a reconstruction) (1184). The church of St. Blaise was rebuilt in 1184 by an unknown patron; as this had been Il'ia's parish church, it is quite possible he and his brother were the patrons. NPL, 36, 37; 225, 227, 228; N4, 172.
122	These were the Church to Anam, Azari, and Misail and the Prophet Daniel in 1189, and the Church to the Purification of the Virgin in the archbishop's compound in 1191. NPL, 39, 230.
123	This was the Church (and Monastery) of the Transfiguration (on an island) in Staraia Russa in 1192. NPL, 40, 231.
124	NPL, 42.
125	Martirii also had the following churches built: the Church of the Deposition of the Robes of the Mother of God (over the city gates) (1195), the Church of the Resurrection in the monastery (1195), the Church of St. Nikifor (1197), and the Church of the Transfiguration (rebuilt in stone) in his monastery in Russa (1198), NPL 41-44, 234, 237.
126	Mitrofan's palace could perhaps be attributed to Mitrofan, but the chronicles are vague on the matter – in any event, it was not a church originally, and for these reasons, I do not include it in the total.
127	NPL, 52, 250.
128	Ibid., 57, 258.
129	Between 1218 and 1312, about twenty churches and chapels were built by other patrons, so the hiatus is not in church construction as a whole, but in archiepiscopal patronage.
130	It was apparently just outside the gate of the Detinets in the Nerev End. NPL, 94, 335.
131	Lazarev (1969), 19. The chronicles do not agree as to who patronized two projects in 1335, namely the Church of the Dormition in the Zverin Monastery and the Church of the Resurrection in the Derevianitskii Monastery. According to the Novgorodian First Chronicle, Vasilii patronized the former while Moisei (between his first and second episcopal tenures) sponsored the latter. Moisei then built another Church of the Resurrection in the Zverin (Zverinets). It seems that the chronicler may be confused and switched the Resurrection to the Zverin Monastery. NPL 346-347. According to the Novgorodian Third Chronicle, Moisei built both. N3, 225. The Novgorodian Fourth Chronicle mentions Vasilii as builder of the Church of the Resurrection, but the second church (or Moisei's patronage of it) is not mentioned. N4, 266. The Zverin Monastery is now a seminary.

132	NPL, 361; N3, 227. There are still churches by these names at the Derevianitskii Monastery (between the Market Side and the Khutyn Monastery), but the current edifices date to the eighteenth centuries. Archbishops Aleksei and Ioann II were buried in the papert' of the fourteenth century Church of the Resurrection in 1390 and 1417 respectively, but I do not know if their remains are still interred at the monastery. See Rospis', Pribavl. N2 (PSRL 3), 182.
133	Alpatov, 10-11.
134	Alpatov, plates 10, 14, and 15, and color plate 11 of paintings made by Tatiana Shcherbatova-Sheviakova in 1930. Though depicted with haloes, they were not canonized until the late fifteenth century. See also, Makarii, *Istoriia*, 3:124-125, 229.
135	The church has been rebuilt and stands in the cemetery in Volotovo east of Novgorod. The frescoes, however, have not been restored. The Church of the Transfiguration of the Savior at Kovalevo was also destroyed, as were the Church of the Transfiguration at Nereditsa, the cupolas of the Cathedral of Holy Wisdom, and other churches. Remnants of some of the frescoes in Holy Wisdom and the other churches have survived, and the exteriors of several have been rebuilt, but the interiors remain bare. See above and also Chapter Two of Brumfield (1983).
136	In addition to the frescoes of this church, a large stone bas-relief cross called the Aleksiev Cross stands just inside the north door of the Cathedral of Holy Wisdom with the inscription "In the year.... this cross was carved (pisan- literally "written", or perhaps "painted", though it is unpainted now) in Novgorod at the behest of the God-loving Right Reverend (presviashennogo) Oleksiia [Aleskei] and erected for the worship of faithful Christians. God grant to Archbishop Oleksiia many years and health and salvation and to his children and the whole world." The cross is said to commemorate Dmitrii Donskoi's victory over the Tatars at Kulikovo Field in 1380, from which the Novgorodians were conspicuously absent. See Tsarevskaia (2005), 44, 51, 55-56. Bas-relief is not unusual for Orthodox crosses, though sculpture in-the-round is, since the latter is seen as idolatry. Makarii, *Istoriia*, 3:154.
137	In 1411 "Vladyka Ioann erected a wonderworking church of stone to the Holy Confessors." NPL, 403. He also gilded the main dome of the cathedral in 1408.
138	The Monastery of the Resurrection on Red Hill east of the Plotnitskii *konets* was founded on the same day as Simeon's election

in 1415, suggesting he sponsored it to commemorate his election. NPL, 405. The Church of the Resurrection still stands in the Tikhvin Cemetery on the east side of Novgorod.
139 Cf. *Avraamki*, 193 (s.a. 1451).
140 Ibid., 192 (s.a. 1448).
141 The chronicles mention several times that Evfimii rebuilt churches on their old foundations ("na starinoi osnove"), but it is not clear if they were artistically or architecturally the same as the earlier structure. N3, 240; N4, 445. Iona also built a church on its old foundations in 1463. N4, 446. Only about fifty of more than three hundred medieval churches still stand in Novgorod. On Evfimii II's artistic tastes see Karger, 122-126; Lazarev (1947), 134; Bernadskii, 244.
142 Specifically, the stretch from Liudin Street to the Volkhov. *Avraamki*, 202.
143 The *Avraamki* Chronicle states that Prince Vasilii Vasil'evich went to strengthen the fortress "at the behest and with the blessing of Vladyka Iona." Ibid.
144 See N3, 241. Two other churches were built at the skete at the same time, but the sources do not indicate that Iona sponsored them.
145 *Avraamki*, 206.
146 Ibid., 220.
147 See Chapter Two in Antipov.
148 Mann, ed., 63.
149 Brumfield (1983), 46; Conant argues there were elements of "bulbous domes" in twelfth century manuscripts. Conant, 91.
150 Luka or Prince Vladimir Iaroslavich brought in Byzantine artists to build the Cathedral of Holy Wisdom, just as Iaroslav did in Kyiv, probably due to a lack of local skills; but in later centuries, it is clear that local artisans and masters built and decorated many of the churches. Polatsk was incorporated into the Grand Principality of Lithuania in 1307, which may explain why ties with that city ended. Smolensk was not incorporated into Lithuania until 1404. The Lithuanian takeover of both cities, however, does not necessarily explain the end of cultural interaction with Novgorod, since we know that the Lithuanian grand princes continued to patronize Rus' artisans as shown by frescoes by Pskovite artists painted in 1470 under the patronage of Casimir IV Jageillon in the Chapel of the Holy Cross in the Wawel Cathedral in Krakow. See Bogdanova and Shulakova, 148-164.
151 Popova (1984), 23. These ties apparently ended in the fourteenth century.

152 NPL, 42.
153 The church was heavily damaged during the Second World War and has since been rebuilt; it still stands in the marshland southeast of the city, across the river from the Iur'ev Monastery, and fragments of the medieval frescoes still survive. See Karger, 248-251; Etingof; Pivovarova.
154 Henrik Birnbaum gives the year as 1239, but there was no episcopal election that year. There is a Hegumen Sava, of the Antoniev Monastery who was a candidate in 1359, but that is much too late to be the same one. Birnbaum (1996), 110, 131. In 1229, the *Novgorodian First Chronicle* names Hegumen Spiridon of the Iur'ev Monastery, and Osaf, Bishop of Volodymyr-in-Volynia, as two of the archiepiscopal candidates: the third is merely called Grechin ("a Greek"). NPL, 275. Birnbaum argues that Grechin is, in fact, the surname of Olisei Petrovich Grechin, son of the Novgorodian boiar Petr Mikhailovich. Elsewhere in the chronicle, Grechin or Gr'chin (Greek), means a Greek, and is not a surname. For example, the term is used to refer to both Metropolitans Feognost and Isidor, who were "Greeks" or Byzantines sent by the Patriarch of Constantinople. See NPL 98, 342, 419. Thus, this argument is unconvincing.
155 Ianin, Kolchin, and Khoroshev, 149-151.
156 NPL, 348.
157 Popova (1984), 17.
158 N3, 231. Cf., Vzdornov (1983); idem (1976); Lazarev (1971), plates 175-178. Theophanes also painted icons in the Church of St. Michael the Archangel in Moscow in 1399. Mosk. (PSRL 25), 229. Grand Princes Ivan III and Vasilii III replaced the Archangel Church with the current edifice in 1505-1508. The Church of the Transfiguration in Novgorod dates to 1374 and some of the 1378 frescoes survive, including the Old Testament Trinity in the northern gallery and Christ Pantocrator in the dome.
159 Tsarevskaia (2001). The frescoes date to the 1360s or 1370s and, according to Karger, were thought by some scholars to be early works of Theophanes the Greek. Karger, 198, 210-212.
160 Popova (1984), 22. The church was destroyed during the war and has been rebuilt, but the frescoes have been lost. On a visit to the church on May 21, 2007, the guide pointed to a small section of frescoes along the wall (going up about two feet from the floor) that are all that remain of the medieval paintings.
161 Ibid., 22-3. The much earlier Ostromir Gospel (copied, according to the colophon, between October 21, 1056 and May 12, 1057 by

Deacon Grigorii and then stored in the Cathedral of Holy Wisdom), is a copy of a no-longer-extant South Slavic original, exemplifying the First South Slavic influence on Novgorod. Cooper, 119.

162   The dislike of Catholic clergy and the fear of them making inroads into the Novgorodian Land continued after independent Novgorod; Archbishop Gennadii received a letter in 1491 warning of Latin (Catholic) monks in Pskov who were telling the people that the churches had been united at Florence, which was true, but the Rus' Church had rejected the Union half a century before. AI, 1.286:522-523.

163   NPL, 416. The *Novgorodian Second Chronicle* says that "Evfimii built a great stone chamber (polatu)." N2 (PSRL 3), 141. Novgorod's Faceted Chamber or Palace (Granovaia Palata) - only part of Evfimii's overall ensemble, and the only part that survives – possibly influenced the Palace of Facets in the Moscow Kremlin built during the reign of Ivan the Great.

164   GVNP, doc. 65, p. 108.

165   Pachomius the Serb wrote of Evfimii that "All who came from strange or foreign lands were received with love and given rest." Florovskii, 15; Profiridov, 49. See also Iablonskii, 80-83.

166   The Sigtuna or Magdeburg Gates, created in Magdeburg in the 1150s and now serving as the west doors of the cathedral, were also apparently brought to Novgorod during Evfimii's tenure. Scholars long thought that they were taken in a twelfth or thirteenth-century raid on the Swedish town of Sigtuna, near Uppsala, though that myth has long been debunked. Mende, 74, 81; Poppe, "K istorii romanskikh dverei," 191-200; Trifonova, 230-242; Goldschmidt; Brumfield (1983), 41.

167   AfED, 309-315; 373-386, 468-73; Miller (2006), 1:348-349; Paul, "Continuity and Change," 280-283.

168   Other examples of cultural transfer include the thirteenth century Gospel covers from Limoges in France and a panagia from Spain from the fourteenth to sixteenth century, both formerly belonging to the Antoniev Monastery and now in the Palace of Facets. These were monastic property and do not necessarily tell us about the archbishops' role in cultural transfer. See Gormina, plates 14-16, (no pagination).

169   Noonan (1975), 316-339.

170   On the archbishop's role in compiling and drawing up the chronicles, see also Kloss and Lur'e, 80-81; Gippius (1998), 345-364; Lur'e, "Letopis' Lavrentevskaia," and B. M. Kloss, "Letopis' novgorodskaia pervaia," in SKKDR 1:241-247.

171	The library is said to have been instituted by Iaroslav the Wise and was later housed in the choir gallery in the upper level of the Cathedral of Holy Wisdom, accessible by a staircase in the southwestern tower. Much of it is said to have been lost during the Swedish occupation during the Time of Troubles. Tsarevskaia (2005), 59-60.
172	The last two volumes of the library are catalogs from the mid-nineteenth century. Grekov refers to the library as the "Manuscripts of the Sofiiskaia Library of the St. Petersburg Spiritual Academy" in his *Novgorodskii dom Sviatoi Sofii,* published in 1914 and reprinted in his collected works. Grekov, *Izbrannye trudy*, 4:60. The Library of Holy Wisdom (or Sofiiskaia Library) was moved to the Saltykov-Shedrin State Public Library (now the Russian National Library) in 1919. RNB F. 728 Biblioteka Novgorodskogo Sofiiskogo sobora, 5 vols. (Leningrad: Gosudarstvennaia publichnaia biblioteka imeni Saltykova-Sherdina otdel rukopiesei i redkykh knig, 1984), 1:1. The Ostromir Gospel, while housed in the cathedral according to its colophon, is not part of the Sofia Collection, as it was removed to Moscow, where it became part of the Tsar's library. It is numbered RNB F.p.1.5. The Biblioteka Novgorodskogo Sofiiskogo sobora collection at the Russian National Library consists of 323 books, of which only 29 are from before 1478.
173	The gospel aprakos was the oldest known East Slavic text until the discovery of the Novgorodian Codex in July 2000. The codex, a practice tablet of wax on boards containing Psalms 75 and 76, has been dated to the first quarter of the eleventh century, predating the Ostromir Gospel by a generation. See Ianin, and Zalizniak. "Novgorodskii kodeks," 3-25; idem, "Novgorodskii Psaltyr," 202-209.
174	The menaia are Orthodox liturgical books divided into monthly volumes.
175	For example, RNB f. 728 Fond Biblioteki Novgorodskogo Sofiiskogo sobraniia, Sof. 1441, No. 1446, Sbornik novgorodskikh gramot, is the source for 34 of the documents published in AAE, vols. 3 and 4. There are other archiepiscopal sborniki which are not part of the Collection of the Library of Holy Wisdom, such as the formuliarnik (logbook) of Archbishop Feodosii II (r. 1542-1551), which was part of the Library of Holy Wisdom, but which Feodosii took with him when he retired to the Iosifo-Volokolamsk Monastery in 1551. It was found there at the end of the eighteenth century and is now in the Russian National Library. It contains, among other things, copies of Archbishop Vasilii Kalika's letter

to the Bishop of Tver', Metropolitan Iona's letter to Archbishop Evfimii II regarding Prince Dmitrii Shemiaka, Archbishop Feofil's charter to Pskov, and several resignation documents of unnamed archbishops. RNB Q. XVII.50, fols. 198v.-200, 135v.-136. While the *Akty istoricheskie* and the *Dopolneniia k aktam istroicheskim* are poorly cited (they often cite "sbornik from the Imperial Public Library," or "see the Catalog of the Imperial Public Library," as sources when there are hundreds of sborniki and a number of catalogs and finding aids in the Russian National Library, the former Imperial Public Library), it is clear Q.XVII.50 and other sborniki from the House of Holy Wisdom are the sources of a number of documents published in AI, (e.g., 1.53:101-103; 1.284-285:520-521.) See also Abelentseva (2003), 122-158.

176 Novgorodian Metropolitan Gavriil II (r.1775-1800) ordered the gathering of monastic library collections in the Library of Holy Wisdom in 1775. Abramovich (1905-1910), 1:iv-v.

177 RNB F. 728, No. 2, Sof. 2, Evangelie aprakos of 1325-1359, fol. 269v.; No. 3, Sof. 3, Evangelie aprakos of 1362, 41v.-42. Abramovich (1905-1910), 1:9-18, 18-76; Grekov, *Izbrannye trudy*, 4:57; Kuprianov, 51-53; Granstrem, 33.

178 RNB f. 728, No. 3, Sof. 3, Evangelia aprakos of 1362, fols. 41v.-42.

179 RNB f. 728, No. 193, Sof. 191, Mineia noiabrskaia; No. 198, Sof. 196, Mineia fevral'skaia; No. 200, Sof. 198, Mineia martovskaia of 1369; No. 203, Sof. 201, Mineia aprel'skaia of 1464; No. 207, Sof. 205, Mineia maiskaia of 1463; No. 209, Sof. 207, Mineia iunskaia of 1439; No. 305. Sof. 303, Mineia fevral'skaia of 1475.

180 RNB f. 728, No. 413, Sof. 410, Sbornik sluzhb russkim sviatym XV v., fols. 1-4, 18-33.

181 N2, 179; Grekov, *Izbrannye trudy*, 4:57.

182 RNB f. 728, No. 3, Sof. 3, Evangelie aprakos of 1325-1359.

183 Golubinskii (1995), 1.1:837; paraphrased in Lenhoff (1977), 42.

184 Bel'skii, 12; Lenhoff (1977), 42.

185 Lenhoff (1977), 42.

186 Ibid., 50.

187 It was written in 1563, after Feodosii's episcopate. RNB Q.XVII.50, 277v. It is not surprising that no other documents personally written by an archbishop have been found since medieval writing culture depended on scribes or copyists.

188 The Older (or Synodal) and Younger Redactions and the Academic and Archeographic Commission manuscripts.

189 Among this group, the *Novgorodian Second Chronicle* comes down to us only in sixteenth and seventeenth century manuscripts. The

	earliest copy of the *Novgorodian Third Chronicle* dates to the late seventeenth century. Ziborov, "Letopis' Novgorodskaia II," in SKKDR 2.2:51.
190	Guimon, 198; Lur'e (1968): 1-22; Shambinago, 254-270; Tvorogov, "Ioakim," in SKKDR 1:204-205.
191	Shakhmatov (1908); idem (1938). For further discussion and dating of the chronicles, see Lur'e (1976); idem (1994).
192	Lavrent. (PSRL 1), 163.
193	Ibid., 166-167.
194	Guimon, 38
195	Ibid., 243-253.
196	Ibid., 42.
197	Guimon makes a distinction between keeping annual entries in a "living" chronicle and copying, editing, or writing up a chronicle "in one sitting." Ibid., 72
198	Gippius (2006), 114-251; Guimon, 213-214, 217.
199	Gippius (2006), 215; Guimon, 217.
200	Guimon, 217.
201	Piotrovskaia, "Kirik Novgorodets," in SKKDR 1: 215-217, esp. 215.
202	NPL, 24; Guimon, 188, 403.
203	The "Uchenie chislakh" is found in several manuscripts: RNB, Sobr. Pogodina, No. 76, fols. 342-346; SPbII RAN, Sobranie Arkheograficheskoi Komissii, No. 245 (b Sof. 475), fols. 45v-50v.; RGADA, Sobranie F. F. Mazurina, F. 196, No. 1069, XIII v. fols. 115v-116v; RGB, F. 256, Sobranie N. P. Rumiantseva, No. 35, fols. 1-4. See also Kirik Novgorodets, 174-191; cf., Evgenii (Bolkhovitinov, Metropolitan of Kyiv and Halych), 123-129; Golubinskii (1995), 1.1:792-793; Piotrovskaia, "Kirik Novgorodets," in SKKDR 1:216-217.
204	NPL, 27.
205	NPL, 28, 214. This probably explains how the chronicler knew what Nifont had said to the metropolitan. Cf. Ipat. (PSRL 2.2), 340-341 (s.a., 1147).
206	Shakhmatov (1908), 183.
207	NPL, 27. How scholars know that German rather than Kirik wrote this is unknown. Kirik would have been 34 years old in 1144 based on autobiographical information at the end of the Uchenie o chislakh (written in 1136, when he was 26). He, therefore, very easily could have written the entry for 1156 in defense of Nifont. On Kirik's age, see Zubov, 192-195.
208	NPL, 29, 216.

209	NPL, 27, 39. On German's authorship, see Likhachev, "Novgorodskaia letopis' XIII i XIV vv.," in Istoriia russkoi literatury, 2.1:114-115; idem (1947), 212-215; Prozorovskii, 1-28; Tvorogov, "German Voiata," in SKKDR 1: 105-106. The Church of St. James in the Nerev *konets* was built in 1172 by an unnamed patron. It was rebuilt in 1226, again by an unnamed patron. (There is another Church of St. James on Dobrynia Street, built in 1181, also by an unnamed patron).
210	NPL, 70; Likhachev, "Novgorodskaia letopis' XIII-XIV vv.," in Likhachev, ed., Istoriia russkoi literatury 2.1:115; Shakhmatov (1908), 184. Cf., Gippius (1992), 59-86; Gimon and Gippius, 18-47; Kloss, "Letopis' Novgorodskaia pervaia," in SKKDR 1:246.
211	Shakhmatov (1908), 193. Petr's chronicle survives in the *Moskovskii letopisnii svod* and parts of the *Lavrentevskii svod*.
212	Vasilii's rearrangement came down to the year 1329, the year before he was elected archbishop. Cf., Kloss, "Letopis' Novgorodskaia pervaia," in SKKDR 1: 245-247.
213	The Synodal Copy was also reworked at the Iur'ev Monastery. See Kloss, "Letopis' Novgorodskaia pervaia," in SKKDR 1:245-247.
214	Kloss (2000), xvi; Lur'e, "Matfei Mikhailov," in SKKDR 2.2:105.
215	N4, xvi-xvii; Bobrov, "Letopisi Novgorodskie," 105-106; Lur'e, "Letopis Novgorodskaia IV," in SKKDR 2.2:51-52.
216	Lur'e, "Letopis Novgorodskaia IV," in SKKDR 2.2:51-52. The much shorter *Novgorodian Fifth Chronicle* also dates to before 1446.
217	On Novgorodian art and its place in wider Russian art history, see Lazarev (1977); idem (1969); idem (1947); Likhachev, Laurina, and Pushkarev; Evseeva, and Sorokalyi, eds., 149-225; Filatov; Popova (1980); Gordienko (1984), 156-167; Gormin and Yarosh, et al.; Lazarev and Vzdornov.
218	Lazarev (1969), 17; idem (1983), 35.
219	Lazarev (1969), 16-17.
220	RGB F. 304.I, No. 215, fols. 151v.-152; Kollmann (1978), 282.
221	NPL, 42.
222	See Ianin, Kolchin, and Khoroshev.
223	See Zalizniak, doc. 549, pp. 406-407, in which a priest asks for two icons of cherubim – "Six-winged angels" – for a Deesis, and doc. 558, pp. 407-408, in which the priest Mina asks Grechin to deliver icons to him by St. Peter's Day.
224	Metropolitan Makarii, archbishop of Novgorod from 1526-1542, ordered Novgorodian iconographers to Moscow to make up for the loss of local icon workshops (and iconographers) following the fire of 1547, indicating how much control the church hierarchy

	could exercise if it chose too. This, however, is from a later period and not indicative of theological control over the content of icons. See Hamilton, 158.
225	Lazarev (1969), 18-19. The confusion as to who patronized the Church of the Dormition in the Zverin Monastery has already been discussed.
226	NPL, 347-348; Mann, ed., 82.
227	Gordienko (1991), 62. Vasilii is not the only iconographer among the archbishops. In the sixteenth century, Archbishop Makarii painted the icons in the small iconostasis now in the Chapel of the Nativity of the Mother of God. Tsarevskaia (2005), 47.
228	One artist he influenced was Andrei Rublev, considered the greatest Rus' iconographer.
229	Tsarevskaia (2005), 38.
230	Mann, ed., 91. The Puchezh Shroud, from 1441, was sent to a monastery in Puchezh by Novgorodian Metropolitan Iov in 1717 and was moved to the Kremlin in 1918. Putsko, "Iskusstvo Novgoroda i Pskova v 13-15 vekakh," in Veimarn, ed., 2.1:150-151; Volbach and Lafontaine-Dosogne, 313, figs. 335 and 336a.
231	Putsko.
232	Gippius, "Povelel Iurii," 30-37; Miasoedov. Kosta's crater is cataloged in Evans and Wixom, eds., 294-295.
233	Sokolof, 13. Henrik Birnbaum argues Petr Mikhailovich and Maria were Olesei Petrovich Grechin's parents. See above.
234	The sions in Novgorod are the oldest in Russia, and may have influenced others found in Pskov, Moscow, Smolensk, and elsewhere. On the Malyi Sion, whose two parts from two different periods were joined in the twelfth century, see Bocharov, 28-29 and pl. 13. Nicholas Oikonomides argues the upper portion is, in fact, Byzantine (not Rus') in origin, from the middle eleventh century and came to Novgorod at the time of the construction of Holy Wisdom. See Oikonomides, 239-249, esp. 243-244.
235	Mann, ed., 90, 94, fig. 60.
236	Lazarev (1977), 35-36, 44.
237	These include saints who lived before 1917 but were canonized afterwards, like Makarii, but not saints from the Soviet period. This list is based on Durnovo (1892-1898), 1:7-181, and other sources, including several archival manuscripts and modern published sources. Cf. Barsukov, 46-47, 56-57, 138, 186-189, 241, 247-251, 272-274, 332-333, 380-382, 389-391, 524-528, 608-609.
238	Vologda was third with 46 saints, Moscow was fourth with 36, followed by the Troitskii-Sergeev Monastery with 24, Vladimir with

20, Rostov with 19, and Pskov with 17. The total for all Rus' was 623 saints. A number of these are, however, from after 1478. See BAN Druzhin No. 83, fol. 41v.-42v. Another manuscript lists only 122 Kyivan saints, 57 Novgorodian saints, and 16 Pskovite saints. BAN Kalikin No. 29, fols. 1-2v., 8v.-14. These lists are not necessarily complete. The official journal of the Novgorodian eparchy gave the figure of 21 bishops among a total of 114 Novgorodian saints. See "O prazdnovanii vsekh sviatykh. Since the canonization process in the Orthodox Church has never been as institutionalized as in the Roman Catholic Church, there may not be a consensus on the exact number of saints.

239 Patriarch Nikon (Metropolitan of Novgorod, r. 1649-1652) was the subject of a saint's life written from 1681-1686 by Ioann Shusherin-Ripatov. Bubnov and Lavrent'ev, "Ioann Kornil'ev Shusherin-Ripatov," in SKKDR 3:2:69-71. An eighteenth-century recension without a beginning is housed in the Russian National Library in St. Petersburg (RGB F. 304.II, No. 189, Zhitie Patriarkha Nikona). Despite these efforts, Nikon was never canonized, though there have been renewed calls for it in recent years. Archbishop Feodosii II (r. 1542-1551) was also the subject of a life written up by one of his students, but he too has not been canonized. See Kuntsevich, ed.

240 This includes those who lived in Kyiv, Vladimir and Moscow up to 1448. The canonized metropolitans in Kyiv were Mikhail (whom some scholars say never really existed), Ilarion, Ioann II, Nikolai, Konstantin, Kirill III, and Maksim (who transferred the see to Vladimir in 1299). Canonized metropolitans in Moscow were Peter (who transferred the see to Moscow in 1325), Feognost, Aleksei, Kiprian, Dionisii, and Fotii.

241 That is, from autocephaly in 1448 to the establishment of the patriarchate in 1589, excluding Iona, the first autocephalous metropolitan. These are Filipp, murdered under Ivan the Terrible, and Iov, who became the first Russian patriarch. By "Muscovite metropolitan" is meant the metropolitans residing in Moscow, though technically they were titled "Metropolitan of All Rus'" until 1589. Occasionally the title "Mitropolit Moskovskii" appears, and Iona was "Metropolitan of Kyiv and All Rus'" until his death.

242 The See of Perm' was transferred to Vologda in 1589.

243 The See of Tobol'sk was created in 1620.

244 Five from after 1480 were also canonized: Gennadii, Serapion, Pimen, Makarii, and Affonii.

245 Colophons from three menaion readers for February, April, and

	June and now in the Russian National Library identify them as having been written under Evfimii II. RNB f. 728, Sof. 196, fol. 201; Sof. 200, No. 202, fol. 211v.; Sof. 207, No. 209, fol. 236.
246	"Povest' o pobede Novgorodtsev nad Suzdal'tsami," in Kushelev-Bezborodko and Kostomarov, eds., 1:241-242; "Skazanie o bitve Novgorodtsev s Suzdal'tsami," in Dmitriev and Likhachev, PLDR, 4:448-53; BLDR, 6:444-449. The story of the battle and the icon appears in a sixteenth century collection of Novgorodian saints' lives. RNB Titov 1084, Sbornik zhitii novgoroskikh chudotvortsev, fols. 19-22. The icon was housed in the Church of the Transfiguration on Il'ina Street until the Church of the Lady of the Sign was built across the street in the seventeenth century. The *Znamenie* icon is now in the Cathedral of Holy Wisdom, displayed to the right of the Royal Doors of the iconostasis. See Tsarevskaia (2005), 25, 32-33, 47-48.
247	Lazarev (1969), 35-36. This icon is in the Novgorod Museum and dates to the 1460s. The other, a sixteenth-century version, is now in the Russian Museum in St. Petersburg. Hamilton, 144-146.
248	Barsukov, 188, 382; Prokhorov, "Pakhomii Serb," in SKKDR 2.2:167, 175.
249	RNB f. 728, No. 413, Sof. 410, Sbornik sluzhb russkim sviatym, fols. 1-4 and 18-33; cf., Prokhorov, "Pakhomii Serb," in SKKDR, 2.2:167, 175; Rozhdestvenskaia, "Iona," in SKKDR 2.1:426-427.
250	RNB f. 728, No. 209, Sof. 207, Mineia iunskaia (1439); No. 196, Sof. 196, Mineia fevral'skaia (1439). No. 200, Sof. 198, Mineia martovaia (1369); Sof. 200, No. 202, Mineia aprel'skaia (1441).
251	N2, 183; N3, 228, 239. 275; N4, 491; L. Dmitriev (1973), 54; Filaret, 1:341-342; 3:13-14; Khoroshev (1986), 140-41. The Life of Evfimii claims this took place in 1449. Sluzhba i zhitie izhe vo sviatykh otsa nashego Evfimiia, 32-33; P. Tikhomirov (1891-1900), 1:98.
252	N2, 183.
253	Since the year began September 1, the discovery of Il'ia's grave would be the same year as Aaron's vision.
254	RNB Titov 1084, fols. 42-51; Filaret, 1:342; P. Tikhomirov (1891-1900), 1:32. In one manuscript, Il'ia's remains were found on October 4, 6944 AM (1436 AD). See RNB Mikhailovskii Q. 351, fols. 10-10v. A second one also gives 1436 but with no date. RNB Mikhailovskii Q. 348, fol. 3v. A third gives the year as 6946 AM, or 1438 AD. See BAN Kalikin No. 29, fol. 9. The Novgorodian First Chronicle mentions the discovery of Il'ia's remains but offers no details. NPL, 420. A Soviet era description gives the year as 1439. Alekseev, Porfiridov, and Semenov, 29.

255 Mineia (Moscow: Moscow Patriarchate, 1988), book for February, 335; Filaret, 1:173-207, 342. Two later Novgorodian bishops are also commemorated on February 10 (Den' sobora novgorodskikh sviatitelei): Archbishop Pimen (r. 1552-1570), and Metropolitan Affonii (r. 1635-1649). Il'ia is also commemorated on the day of his death, September 7. Simeon appears in a collection (actually a service book with musical notation) of the sixteenth century, with a feast day on June 15. He appears at the bottom of the page, outside of the chart. While he and several other Novgorodian archbishops appear in the chart, their services are not included in the book. See GIM Chudov. 61, fol. 375.

256 NPL, 420; N2, 183; N4, 491. Anna is traditionally said to be the same person as Ingegerd, Iaroslav's third wife. However, Soviet archaeologists who examined the remains found them to be of a woman much younger than Ingegerd was when she died. Thus, Anna is thought to have been Iaroslav's first wife who may have died in Novgorod prior to Iaroslav taking the Kyivan throne. Some sources said the remains were of Vladimir Iaroslavich's wife, and some modern scholars support this. Samsonov, 56-75.

257 NPL, 16, 181.

258 Thus, Evfimii's actions would be closer to beatification in the Catholic Church, though the comparison is imprecise.

259 Golubinskii (1871) 73, 82. As early as 1500, a Church of St. Evfimii was built at the Viazhishche Monastery where Evfimii was buried. See Makarii (1860), 1:599. Evfimii is also mentioned in a sixteenth century book of church statues (ustav, actually a collection of monastic rules and services of monastic and other saints) as "Evfimii the Great, Archbishop of Novgorod the Great and New Wonderworker." RGADA F. 201 Sobranie kniazia M. Obolenskogo, No. 126, Tserkovnyi Ustav, XVI veka, fols. 211-211v. He appears in several other manuscripts from the sixteenth and seventeenth century. See GIM, Chudovskoe sobranie No. 61(8), Sbornik XVI v., fol. 372; RGADA F. 181, Rukopisnyi fond MGAMID, No. 591, Sbornik dukhovnogo soderzhaniia, XVII v., fol. 823; No. 573, Ustav, XVI v., fol. 68v.-69v.

260 Golubinskii (1903), 142, 145.

261 Ibid., 157. The life of Serapion appears in a collection of saints' lives from the Troitse Sergiev Lavra dated to 1633. See RGB F. 304.I, No. 694, Zhitie russkikh sviatykh (1633), fols. 157-175v.

262 The second, Muscovite, edition was compiled after he became metropolitan of Moscow and All Rus' in 1542. The August volume, for example, is dated 1553, although a colophon from Kuzma Ind-

	ikoplov specifies that he finished on January 19, 1542, exactly two months before Makarii became metropolitan. GIM Sinod. 997, Minei Chet'i Mitropolita Makariia, avgust', fol. 1, 1319. Cf. Paul, "Continuity and Change," 294.
263	RNB f. 728, Sof. 1317, No. 1322, Velikie Minei Chet'i, sentiabr', fols. 103-105.
264	Makarii himself was officially canonized on June 6, 1988, as part of the celebration of the Millennium of the Baptism of Rus', thus continuing the veneration of Novgorodian prelates into the next millennium of Christianity. Makarii (2002), 326; Tysiacheletie kreshcheniia Rusi, 12. He, however, is listed among the saints of Moscow (as Makarii the Wonderworker) in several earlier lists of saints. See BAN Kalikin No. 29, 15v., (where his death is dated December 31, 1564); BAN Druzhina No. 83, fol. 18 (where his death is dated December 25, 1570 AD/7078 AM); RNB Mikhailovskii Q. 351, fol. 21; Tolstoi, 261-262. He is absent from several other manuscripts. See for example, RNB Mikhailovskii Q. 348; RNB HCPK Q. 36. His icon appears over the archway to the Russian State Archive of Ancient Documents, hence a former archbishop of Novgorod – and later Moscow-based metropolitan – watches over the ancient history of Rus', whereas his predecessors kept watch over history by patronizing the chronicles.
265	Golubinskii (1903), 100.
266	Ibid., 103, 105.
267	GIM Sinod. 962, Sinodal'nyii tom, fols. 525 v., 526, 526 v.; Sinodal'nyi tom (PSRL 13), 378-379. According to the legend, the cowl was given to Vasilii almost three hundred years after Il'ia (Ioann). N3, 225. That said, Il'ia and other Novgorodian prelates before Vasilii appear in icons wearing the white cowl.
268	During the early Soviet period, Nikita's remains were kept in a paper bag in the History Museum in Novgorod. They were then kept in the Church of St. Nicholas on the Marketplace in Novgorod. In 1957, they were moved to the Church of Sts. Philip the Apostle and Nicholas the Wonderworker on the Trade Side (the only church still opened for religious services in the later Soviet period). They were returned to the cathedral on May 13, 1993 (the feast of the recovery of the remains). See Elagin, 11-14; A. Rapoport, 48. Cf. Tsarevskaia (2005), 49.
269	The icons were later taken to Moscow for display. On the opening of Nikita's tomb, see RGB f. 304.I, No. 673, Mineia Chet'ia, Genvar' (1629), fols. 370-374v.; RNB f. 728, Sof. 1481, No. 1481, Sbornik nachala XVII veka, fol. 145; N2, 158-159; Filaret 1:144 (Filaret dates

	the opening to 1553); P. Tikhomirov (1891-1900), 1:43, 2.1:175-176; Murav'ev, 4:513-515. Nikita is also found in a seventeenth century book of church statutes. RGADA F. 181, No. 591, fols. 824-824v. He is absent from several others.
270	Paul, "Continuity and Change," 300-305.
271	N2, 187; N3, 263; P. Tikhomirov (1891-1900), 2.2:11-14
272	The feast of the Mother of God of the Sign is commemorated in a sixteenth century book of church statutes (ustav), but Il'ia is not mentioned. RGADA F. 201, No. 126, Tserkovnyi ustav, fols. 141-143v.
273	SPbII RAN, F. 171, perepl. I, No. 17, fol. 34.
274	SPbII RAN, F. 171, perepl. I, No. 18, fol. 35.
275	SPbII RAN, F. 171, perepl. I, No. 22, fol. 48.
276	Grekov, ed. (1927), 216. Archbishop Pimen (r. 1552-1572) is included in several lists of Novgorodian saints. RNB Mikhailovskii Q. 348, fol. 9; RNB Mikhailovskii Q. 351, fol. 12. In some, his death is dated to 7000 AM (1492AD): BAN Kalikin No. 29, fol. 9v.; BAN Druzhin No. 83, fol. 10.
277	There were two Novgorodian metropolitans of this name in addition to the Makarii who became Metropolitan of Moscow: one reigned from 1619 to 1626 and another from 1652 to 1662. The display at the Novgorod Museum in did not specify which one was meant.
278	The icon (Catalog number NGM KP 2972 DPZh-33) is in the Novgorod State Museum Reserve. Novgorod State Museum Reserve, Online Collection, Exhibits. (https://novgorodiss.kamiscloud.ru/entity/OBJECT/101872?query=%D0%B0%D0%BB%D1%84%D0%B0%D0%B-D%D0%BE%D0%B2%D1%8B&index=0) (accessed February 28, 2023).
279	Melnick, trans. and ed. (1997), 2:45 and Sketch 69.
280	Bishops Ioakim, Nikita, and Luka Zhidiata, and Archbishops Nifont, Il'ia, Gavriil, Feoktist, Moisei, Vasilii Kalika, Ioann, Evfimii II, and Serapion (r. 1506-1509). Neither Ioann Pop'ian nor Ioann II are saints. Interestingly, an Ioann also appears (in addition to Il'ia-Ioann) in a post-Soviet group icon in the Cathedral of Holy Wisdom, which may be based on these earlier patterns.
281	Melnick, trans. and ed. (1998), 1:21, 54 (September 18), and Sketch 76.
282	Ibid., 138 (April 8).
283	Ibid., 50 (September 7).
284	Ibid., 110 (January 25). Moisei is also depicted in a full-length icon now on display in the Novgorod Museum.

285 Ibid., 168 (June 17).
286 Ibid., 128 (March 11).
287 Ibid., 77 (November 5/November 18).
288 Orlova and Popov, 196-206. Ostrowski (2009), 278.
289 These were replaced by iconographic effigies in 1722. An embroidered effigial covering for Evfimii's tomb is now on display in the Novgorod Museum. Mann, ed., 178-179, figs. 176 and 177.
290 Zertsalov, ed. 1.1.2:1-2. Zertsalov does not cite his source, other than to say it is a document from "the Moscow Archive of the Ministry of Justice," p. iii. The original is RGADA, F. 210, Razriadnyi Prikaz. Prikaznyi Stol. (Stolby "dopolnitel'nogo" otdela "Bezglasnye,") Opis 17, No. 32, O nepravdakh i neprigozhikh rechakh novgorodskogo mitropolita Kipriana. A new effigy icon had been painted and lays atop Il'ia's sarcophagus. Nikita's relics are, again, covered in a shroud, but are visible under glass. So far, Metropolitan Lev has not been denounced to Moscow for covering the relics.
291 Il'ia also appears in several service books from the sixteenth and seventeenth centuries. See GIM Chudov. 61, fol. 378; RGADA F. 181, No. 591, fol. 818v.; RGB F. 304.1, No. 664, Mineia Chet'ia sent. XVII v., fols. 59v.-62.
292 NPL, 36, 226; "Povest' o postroennii blagoveshchenskogo monastyria v Novgorode," in Kushelev-Bezborodko and Kostomarov, eds., 1:255-256; "Povest' o Blagoveshchenskoi tserkvi," PLDR 4:464-467.
293 Ibid., 33, 221.
294 "Povest' o pobede Novgorodtsev nad Suzdal'tsami," in Kushelev-Bezborodko and Kostomarov, eds., 1:241-242; "Skazanie o bitve Novgorodtsev s Suzdal'tsami," in PLDR, 4:448-453. See also RNB F.IV.165. On the legend of the Mother of the Sign in the *Stepennaia Kniga*, see Lenhoff (2004), 178-186. While the tale was uniquely Novgorodian, veneration of the Mother of God of the Sign was not; her image was often found on episcopal seals in Rus' throughout the medieval period, including Novgorodian archiepiscopal seals as early as the incumbency of Nifont (i.e., a generation before Il'ia). The image is also found on the metropolitans' seals in Kyiv as early as the incumbency of Nikifor (r.1104-1121), as well as on episcopal seals from Smolensk, Polatsk, Halych, and other sees. The archbishops' namestniki also used the image on their seals. Ianin, (1970) 1:174-79, 253-54; 2:174-185, 195-196, 264-265, 267-271, 277; Ianin and Gaidukov, 3:27-29, 36-38, 67-68, 261-262, 284-289.

295	"Povest' o Shchile Posadnike Novgorodskom," in Kushelev-Bezborodko and Kostomarov, eds., 1:21-26; Eremin, 1:122-151. NPL, 333, 381-382; N4, 254, 601. Cf. RNB Osnovnoe Sobranie Rukopisnykh Knig (OSRK) No. 2574/Q1-1361, Povest' o novgorodskom posadnike Shchile. Il'ia is again referred to as Ioann, his name in the schema. Though there was a later Archbishop Ioann, his tenure was seventy-nine years after the consecration of the Shchilov Monastery. In a manuscript version in the Library of the Academy of Sciences in St. Petersburg, the archbishop is unnamed, referred to as merely "the archbishop of the city." BAN 1.2.24, Sbornik kontsa XVII-nachala XVIII vv., fols. 292-293. It is published in V. I. Sreznevskii (1904), 132-133.
296	"Povest' o puteshestvii Ioanna Novgorodskogo," in Kushelev-Bezborodko and Kostomarov, eds., 1:245-248; "Povest' o puteshestvii Ioanna Novgorodskogo na bese," in PLDR, 4:454-463; BLDR, 6:450-459; Gudzii, 207-209. There are a number of Byzantine and Rus' tales in which the capture of demons figures prominently. See Durnovo (1905); Fomichev, 141-149. A series of icons of the tale are discussed in Gusev (1903). The tale may also be very loosely based on the pilgrimages of Archbishops Antonii or Vasilii Kalika to Constantinople and the Holy Land in the thirteenth and fourteenth centuries.
297	Iablonskii, 109-114; Prokhorov, "Pakhomii Serb," in SKKDR 2.2:167, 175. Cf., Filaret, 3:312-314. The legend of Il'ia's journey is found in a fifteenth century compilation of saints' lives. See RNB, Solovetskoe Sobranie, No. 617/500. It is also included at the end of the service for Archbishop Il'ia (Ioann) in Makarii's Novgorodian edition of the Velikie Minei Chet'i. RNB f. 728, Fond Biblioteki Novgorodskogo Sofiiskogo sobraniia Sof. 1317, No. 1322, Velikie Minei Chet'i, sentiabr', fols. 101-106, esp. 103-105 and at the end of his life in RNB Titov 1084, fols. 27-34.
298	"Povest' o puteshestvii Ioanna Novgorodskogo," in PLDR, 4:456-457.
299	A bronze pot (rukomoinik) belonging to Archbishop Il'ia was kept in his cell in the Church of St. Il'ia, built in the Palace of Facets in Novgorod and consecrated in 1822. An inscription on an adjacent wooden door identified it as the water vessel referred to in the legend. See Gusev (1903), 48, pic. 26; Makarii (1857), 27-28, 32. Lev Dmitriev wrote that it still survived in the St. Nicholas Church on the Market. See Likhachev, ed., *Istoriia russkoi literatury*, 227n2.
300	"Povest' o puteshestvii Ioanna Novgorodskogo," in PLDR, 4:454-455.

301 Ibid., 4:456-457.
302 Ibid., 4:456-457. This aspect of the tale probably comes from the aforementioned account of Hegumen Daniil, who visited the site in 1106-1107 and witnessed candles spontaneously lighting on Holy Saturday. See Golubinskii (1995), 1.1:835. Even today, the Orthodox believe in the Miracle of the Holy Fire, which is said to occur every year just after noon on Holy Saturday in the Church of the Resurrection (the Church of the Holy Sepulcher) in Jerusalem. They claim that when the Orthodox patriarch of Jerusalem enters the Holy Sepulcher on Holy Saturday, the oil lamp he carries is miraculously lit by the Holy Spirit, while the Catholic patriarch has to light his candle by natural means. Auxentios (Bishop of Photiki); Klameth; Meinardus, 242-253; Runciman (1955), 88.
303 A. Alekseev (2005), 296; L. Dmitriev (1973), 153-158.
304 "Povest' o puteshestvii Ioanna Novgorodskogo," in PLDR, 4:458-459.
305 Ibid., 4:460-463.
306 According to Pakhomii's Life of Iona, the archbishop "did not spare great expense [in gold and sables] for the sake of the glorious memory of God's saints." "Povest' ob Ione," in PLDR, 5:369-371; Terras, 55.
307 "Povest' o Moisee, Arkhiepiskope Novgorodskom," in Kushelev-Bezborodko and Kostomarov, eds., 4:10-15; The tale mentions an incident in which Sergei, who is said to have gone mad while archbishop, arrived at the St. Michael Monastery at Skovorodka southeast of Novgorod and demanded that Moisei's grave be opened, but the priest there refused. It is unlikely that Sergei, or even his successor, Gennadii, would have patronized a tale that showed Sergei in such a bad light. If it was composed during their archiepiscopates, it was probably not done so under their auspices. See Iablonskii, 105-108, esp. 107; Prokhorov, "Pakhomii Serb," in SKKDR 2.2:168, 174.
308 "Povest' o Evfimie, Arkhiepiskope Novgorodskom," in Kushelev-Bezborodko and Kostomarov, 4:16-26; Iablonskii, 80-83; Prokhorov, "Pakhomii Serb," in SKKDR 2.2:167, 172.
309 A menaion reader for November composed in Novgorod in 1438 indicates that Pakhomii was there before that, working under the aegis of Evfimii. See RNB. f. 728, Fond Biblioteki Novgorodskogo Sofiiskogo sobraniia Sof. 191, Mineia noiabrskaia (dated 1436 in the catalog), fol. 307. Pachomius then went to the Troitse-Sergiev Lavra and was brought back to Novgorod by Archbishop Iona in 1459 after Evfimii II's death, at which time he wrote the Life of

Evfimii. He then went to Moscow, returning again to Novgorod where he reworked the Life of Ioann (Il'ia) and wrote the Life of Moisei some time before 1484. See Prokhorov, "Pakhomii Serb," in SKKDR 2.2:167-168.

310 Prokhorov, "Pakhomii Serb," in SKKDR 2.2:168. In addition to the lives of Novgorodian archbishops, he wrote lives for Sergei of Radonezh, Nikon of Radonezh, Metropolitan Aleksei, Kirill Belozerskii, Saava Vysherskii, and Prince Mikhail and Fedor of Chernihiv. He also wrote the "Laudable Words" (*pokhvalnoe slovo*) of the Eulogy to Varlaam of Khutyn, the Virgin of the Sign in Novgorod, Sergei of Radonezh, "on the Protection of the Virgin (Prokhov)" and tales of the finding of the relics of Metropolitan Aleksei, the miracles of Varlaam of Khutyn, Baty's Slaughter, and the transfer of the relics of Metropolitan Peter. He also wrote services for Varlaam of Khutyn, the Mother of God of the Sign, Sergei of Radonezh, Nikon of Radonezh, Metropolitan Aleksei, Antonii of the Kyiv Caves Monastery, Kirill Belozerskii, Saava Visherskii, Metropolitan Iona, Mikhail and Fedor of Chernihiv, Stefan of Perm', the transfer of the relics of Metropolitan Petr, and of Peter and Fevronii of Murom. See Iablonskii, 37-80, 84-105, 114-197.

311 "Povest' o Nifonte, Episkope Novgorodskom," in Kushelev-Bezborodko and Kostomarov, 4:1-9.

312 Dmitrieva, "Vasilii (v inokakh, Varlaam)," in SKKDR 2.1:114.

313 "Povest' ob Antonii Rimlianine," in Kushelev-Bezborodko and Kostomarov, eds., 1:263-270. The Antoniev Monastery was founded in 1117, during the tenure of Bishop Ioann Pop'ian, not Nikita, who died in 1108.

314 "Prorochestvo sv. Varlaama," in Kushelev-Bezborodko and Kostomarov, eds., 1:277-280; Iablonskii, 117. Antonii had been a monk at the Khutyn Monastery prior to becoming archbishop in 1211. The *Novgorodian First Chronicle* mentions no such inclement weather over Peter's Fast during Antonii's two tenures (1211-1219, 1225-1228), although it mentions other strange or noteworthy events, such as great fires in Novgorod in 1211 and 1217, the Lithuanians burning Pskov during Peter's Fast in 1213, the appearance of a flying serpent or dragon on Quinquagesima Sunday (February 1) in 1214, and a famine in 1215 that severely inflated food prices. NPL, 52-57, 250-58. Peter's Fast runs from the second Monday after Pentecost to St. Peter's Day, June 29.

315 GIM F. 450, E. V. Barsova, Op. 1, d. 681, Zhitie Prepodobnogo Lazaria Muromskogo chudotvortsa; Pashkov, 3-13; Likhacheva and Prokhorov, "Zhitie Lazaria Muromskogo," in SKKDR 2.1:288-290.

316	The mentally ill were thought touched by God, having sacrificed their sanity for spiritual understanding and gifts. Holy foolishness (iurodstvo in Russian, salo in Greek), was a popular idea in both the Byzantine Empire and Rus'. See Kobets, 367-388. This is similar to the belief in Ancient Greece and other cultures that epilepsy was a "sacred malady," although Hippocrates looked for natural causes for the ailment. See Edwards, ed. 5:381.
317	"Povest' o Mikhaile Klopskom," in PLDR, 5:334-349; L. Dmitriev (1958), 99-110; Kobets, 378-383. Mikhail is thought to have died between 1453 and 1458, although one manuscript says he died in 1452. RNB Mikhailovskii Q. 351, fol. 13 v.
318	"Povest' o Mikhaile Klopskom," in Kushelev-Bezborodko and Kostomarov, eds., 4:41. Feodosii was, of course, never consecrated.
319	"Povest' o Mikhaile Klopskom," in PLDR, 5:334-349; Kushelev-Bezborodko and Kostomarov, eds., 4:42; Khoroshev (1989), 86.
320	"Povest' o Mikhaile Klopskom," in Kushelev-Bezborodko and Kostomarov, eds., 4:42. Evfimii I served six years, not a long tenure, but three times as long as Feodosii, his immediate predecessor, and just as long as Simeon, who preceded Feodosii. These were short in comparison to Aleksei and Evfimii (29 years each) and Ioann II (17 years).
321	"Povest' o Mikhaile Klopskom," PLDR, 5:334-349; Kushelev-Bezborodko and Kostomarov, eds., 4:42-43.
322	The alleged desire to be consecrated in Moscow may have been an effort by Novgorod (written by an unknown monk of the Klopskii Monastery) to explain Evfimii II's consecration in Smolensk. It is portrayed as the fulfillment of a divine message revealed by St. Mikhail of Klopskii rather than an effort by Evfimii II or the Novgorodians to abandon Orthodoxy and "go Latin" or become part of the Lithuanian metropolis. That is, it was Euthymian propaganda to counter the archbishop's alleged anti-Muscovite behavior.
323	"Vospominanie o blagoslovennom Ione," also called the "Povest' ob Ione"; in Kushelev-Bezborodko and Kostomarov, eds., 4:27-35; PLDR, 5:334-349.
324	"Vospominanie" or "Poves't ob Ione," in Kushelev-Bezborodko and Kostomarov, eds., 4:29; PLDR, 5:354-356. Filaret relayed the account as a first-person recollection by Iona himself and gave a slightly different version of the prophesy: "not knowing me at all, [he] called me by name: 'Vaniusha, [another diminutive of Io-

	ann or Ivan] study your letters (uchis' gramate), (for) you will be archbishop of Novgorod.'" Filaret, 3:309; see also P. Tikhomirov (1891-1900), 1:272.
325	N3, 235.
326	The *Novgorodian Second Chronicle* claims the white cowl was given to Archbishop Vasilii Kalika in 1339. N2, 140 (s.a. 1424). The *Novgorodian Third Chronicle* mentions it sub anno 1335. N3, 225. The right of the Novgorodian archbishops to wear the white cowl (and use red wax seals – the latter a privilege usually reserved for the grand prince and the metropolitan) was confirmed by a church council in 1564. GIM, Sinod. 962, Sinodal'nyi Tom, fols. 526v.-528; Sinodal'nyi Tom (PSRL 13), 378-380; AI, 1.173:331-333; The documents in AI gives the date 7072 AM or 1564 AD; Pavel Tikhomirov dates the council to 1565. P. Tikhomirov (1891-1900), 1:179; 2.1:180.
327	"Povest' o Novgorodskom belom klobuke," in Kushelev-Bezborodko and Kostomarov, eds., 1:287-298; Labunka (1998), passim; Khoroshev (1989), 91-98.
328	Donald Ostrowski dates the tale to the middle to late sixteenth century in response to the Moscow Council of 1564 that confirmed the privilege to the Archbishop of Novgorod and the Metropolitan of Moscow and All Rus'. Ostrowski, (2002), 27-54, esp. 43-45; idem (2009), 274.
329	There is a somewhat similar tale on how the Patriarch of Alexandria came to wear a golden crown and have the title "ecumenical", although there are enough differences that is seems unlikely the two legends are related. According to one legend, the title was granted by the Roman pontiff, while the gold crown, called the lira, was given to Patriarch Theophilus II by Byzantine Emperor Basil II in 1026. RGADA F. 27 Tainyi prikaz, op. 1, No. 561, Skazanie o tom, pochemu Aleksandriiskii patriarkh nosit na glave zolotuiu liru (koronu) i nazyvaetsia sudeiu vselenskim, esp. 2vv.-3.
330	Khoroshev (1989), 268; Mongait, 92-104. As noted earlier, Iakunina argues the remains are those of Archbishop Simeon, not Vasilii Kalika. Iakunina, 105-107. Cf. Ianin (1988), 61-66; Ostrowski (2009), 276. The white cowl (with pearls in the outline of a cross) excavated in 1946 is now on display in the Palace of Facets in the Novgorod Detinets, catalog number NGM KP 3766 in the Novgorod State Museum Reserve. Novgorod State Museum Reserve, Online Collection, Exhibits. (https://novgorod-iss.kamiscloud.ru/entity/OBJECT/102777?exposition=3827568&index=12) (accessed September 24, 2022).

331	Markelov, 38. See also Plate 25 in Kivelson, Petrone, Kollmann, and Flier, eds., after p. 90.
332	"Povest' o Novgorodskom belom klobuke," in Kushelev-Bezborodko and Kostomarov, eds., 1:297.
333	Vasilii actually received the *polystaurion* from Metropolitan Feognost in 1346, not from the patriarch. MM, 1.156:348; NPL, 343-344; 358; Meyendorff (1981), 84, 246, 277; P. Tikhomirov (1891-1900), 1:177n5, 178-179.
334	The Greek phrase, transliterated in Cyrillic in the text, is the famous "Mnogo leta!" – literally "Many years to the lord," a phrase sung during the Divine Liturgy in praise of the bishop – Despota, again, being the term of respect for a Greek bishop, the source or origin of the title Vladyka in the Russian. "Povest' o Novgorodskom belom klobuke," in Kushelev-Bezborodko and Kostomarov, eds., 1:297. The Pantocrator was, again, destroyed in World War II and the dome remains unpainted.
335	"Povest' o Novgorodskom belom klobuke," in Kushelev-Bezborodko and Kostomarov, eds., 1:298.
336	On the theory of the Third Rome, see Lebedev, ed., 1:277-279; Malinin; Skrynnikov; On the *Velikie Minei Chet'i* and the *Stepennaia Kniga* see Miller (1979), 263-382.
337	The tale was condemned as "false and incorrect" (izhevoi i ne pravoi) by the Moscow Council of 1667. Ostrowski sees it as evidence of continued Novgorodian opposition to Moscow after 1478. See Ostrowski (2009), 271–284.

Works Cited

Archival Sources

Biblioteka [Rossiiskoi] Akademii Nauk (BAN), Manuscript Division, St. Petersburg
  BAN 1.2.24, Sbornik kontsa XVII-nachala XVIII vv.
  BAN Sobranie Druzhina
    Druzhin No. 83, Kniga glagoemaia poisanie o rossiiskikh sviatykh XVIII v.
  BAN Sobranie F. Kalikina
    Kalikin No. 29, Ukazatel= rossiiskikh sviatym s nachala Russkoi zemli po XVII veke
Gosudarstvennyi istoricheskii muzei (GIM), Division of Manuscripts and Old Printed Books, Moscow
  GIM Chudovskoe Sobranie
    Chudov. No. 61(8), Sbornik XVI v.
    Chudov. No. 270
  GIM F. 450, E. V. Barsova
    Op. 1, d. 681, Zhitie Prepodobnogo Lazaria Muromskogo chudotvortsa
  GIM Sinodal'noe Sobranie
    Sinod. No. 181, Minei-Chet'i, iiun'
    Sinod. No. 132, Novgorodskaia Kormchaia, 1282
    Sinod. No. 562, Sbornik mitropolich'ikh gramot
    Sinod. No. 915, Gennadievskaia Biblia, 1499
    Sinod. No. 962, Sinodal'nyii tom
    Sinod. No. 997, Minei Chet'i Mitropolita Makariia, Avgust', 1553
  GIM, Sobranie A. I. Khludova
    Khludov, No. 30, Evangelie aprakos XIV v.

Rossiiskaia gosudarstvennaia biblioteka (RGB) Scientific-Research Division of Manuscripts, Moscow
    RGB F. 256, Sobranie N. P. Rumiantseva
        No. 35 Vypiski iz rukopisnykh knig Novgorodskoi Sofiiskoi Biblioteki
        No. 204 Sbornik polemicheskii protivoereticheskii
    RGB F. 304.I, Glavnaia Biblioteka Troitse-Sergievoi Lavry
        No. 215, Stoglav (Postanovlenie Moskovskogo sobora 1551 g.)
        No. 664, Mineia Chet'ia, Sentiabr', XVII v.
        No. 673, Mineia Chet'ia, Genvar', 1629
        No. 694, Zhitie russkikh sviatykh, 1633
    RGB F. 304.II, Dopolnitel'noe Sobranie Rukopisei Biblioteki Troitse-Sergievoi Lavry
        No. 189, Zhitie Patriarkha Nikona, sostablennoe Ivanom Kornikovichem Shusherinym (bez nachala)

Rossiiskii gosudarstvenyi arkhiv drevnikh aktov (RGADA), Moscow
    F. 27, Tainyi prikaz
        Op. 1, No. 561, Skazanie o tom, pochemu Aleksandriiskii patriarkh nosit na glave zolotuiu liru (koronu) i nazyvaetsia sudeiu vselenskim (1026)
    F. 181, Rukopisnyi fond Moskovskogo Glavnogo arkhiva Ministerstva inostrannykh del
        No. 573, Ustav XVI v.
        No. 591, Sbornik dukhovnogo soderzhaniia XVII v.
    F. 196, Rukopisnoe Sobranie F. F. Mazurina
        No. 1069, XIII v.
    F. 201, Sobranie kniazia M. Obolenskogo
        Obolenskii No. 126, Ustav tserkovnyi XVI v.
    F. 210, Razriadnyi prikaz, Prikaznyi stol
        Stolby "dopolnitel'nogo" otdela "Bezglasnye"
        Opis 17, No. 32, O nepravdakh i neprigozhikh rechakh Novgorodskogo mitropolita Kipriana

Rossiiskaia natsional'naia biblioteka (RNB), Manuscript Division, St. Petersburg
  RNB F. 550 Osnovnoe sobranie rukopisnoi knigi (OCPK)
    OCPK F.IV.165, Khronograf
    OCRK Q. IV. 298, Sbornik
    OCPK Q.XVII.50, Formuliarnik novgorodskogo arkhiepiskopa Feodosiia (Evfimii Igumen. Sbornik istoricheskogo i bogoslovskogo soderzhaniia)
    OCPK Q.XVII.88 Sbornik smeshannogo soderzhaniia
  RNB Sobranie Mikhailovskogo
    Mikhailov. Q. 348, O sviatykh Velikonovgorodskikh episkopekh i arkhiepiskopekh prepodobnykh chudotvortsekh
    Mikhailov. Q. 351, Kniga ob derzhashchaia viede sobranie vsekh rossiiskikh sviatykh
  RNB Sobranie Pogodina
    Pogodin No. 76
  RNB Sobranie Sankt-Peterburskoi Dukhovnoi Akademii (SpbDA)
    SPbDA A. 11.30
    SPbDA 430
  RNB Sofiiskoe Sobranie
    F. 728, Biblioteka Novgorodskogo Sofiiskogo sobraniia
      Sof. 2, No. 2, Evangeliia Aprakos (1325-1359)
      Sof. 3, No. 3, Evangeliia Aprakos (1362)
      Sof. 191, No. 191, Mineia noiabrskaia (1436)
      Sof. 196, No. 196, Mineia fevral'naia (1439)
      Sof. 198, No. 200, Mineia martovaia (1369)
      Sof. 200, No. 202, Mineia aprel'skaia (1441)
      Sof. 201, No. 203, Mineia aprel'skaia (1464)
      Sof. 207, No. 209, Mineia iunskaia (1439)
      Sof. 303, No. 305, Mineia fevral'skaia (1475)
      Sof. 410, No. 413, Sbornik sluzhb russkim sviatym
      Sof. 1317, No. 1322, Velikie Minei Chet'i. Sentiabr'
      Sof. 1441, No. 1446, Sbornik novgorodskikh gramot
      Sof. 1464, No. 1469, Sbornik istoricheskii
      Sof. 1465, No. 1470, Sbornik istoricheskii
      Sof. 1548, No. 1553, Kniga zapisei sofiiskoi poshlina (1557)

RNB Solovetskoe Sobranie
Solov. No. 617/500, Spisok Zhitii
Solov. No. 858, Kormchaia, 1493g.
RNB F. 775 Sobranie A. A. (Andreia Aleksandrovicha) Titova
Titov 1084, Sbornik Zhitii novgorodskikh chudotvortsev
Titov 2727, O moshchakh sviatykh pochivaiushchikh v kievskikh Peshcherakh

Sankt-Peterburgskii Institut Istorii Rossiiskoi Akademii Nauk (SPbII RAN)
F. 11, Sobranie Arkheograficheskoi komissii
No. 240, Komissionyi spisok Novgorodskoi pervoi letopisi
F. 171, Fond novgorodskogo sofiiskogo arkhiereiskogo doma
Perepletok I (1504-1640)
K. 2, Kollektsiia aktovikh knig Imperatorskoi Arkheografiicheskoi komissii
No. 245, (b Sof. 475)

Published Sources

Primary Sources

Abramovich, D. I. (Dmitrii Ivanovich), ed. *Kievo-Pecherskii paterik*. Kyiv: Z drukarni Vseukraïns'koï akademiï nauk, 1930.

Adam of Bremen. *The History of the Archbishops of Hamburg-Bremen*. Francis J. Tschan, ed. and trans. New York: Columbia University Press, 1959.

Akty istoricheskie, sobrannye i izdannye Arkheograficheskaia komissieiu. 5 vols. St. Petersburg: Ekspeditsii zagotovleniia Gosudarstvennykh bumag, 1841-42.

Akty otnosiashchesiia k istorii zapadnoi Rossii, sobrannye i izdannye Arkeograficheskoi komissieiu. 5 vols. St. Petersburg: v Tipografii Edvard Pratsa, 1846-53. Reprinted The Hague: Mouton, 1970.

Akty, sobrannye v bibliotekakh i arkhivakh Rossiiskoi Imperii Arkheograficheskoiu ekspeditsieiu Imperatorskoi Akademii nauk. 4 vols. St. Petersburg: Tipografii II Otedeleniia Sobstvennoi E. I. V., Kantseliarii, 1836.

Akty sotsial'no-ekonomicheskoi istorii Severo-vostochnoi Rusi. 3 vols. Moscow: AN SSSR, 1952-1964.

Antonii (Dobrynia Iadreikovich [Andreikovich]; Archbishop of Novgorod). *Puteshestvie Novgorodskogo arkhiepiskopa Antoniia v Tsargrad v kontse 12-go stoletiia*, Pavel Savvaitov, ed. (St. Petersburg: Izdatel'stvo Arkheograficheskoi komissii, 1872; St. Petersburg: tipografiia Imperatorskoi Akademii nauk, 1877)

------. "Kniga Palomnik: Skazanie mest sviatikh vo Tsaregrade." Kh. M. (Khrisanf Mefodevich) Loparev, ed., *Pravoslavnii palestinskii sbornik.* Vol. 17, part 3. St. Petersburg: Izdanie Imperatorskogo Pravoslavnogo Palestinskogo Obshchestva, Tipografii V. Kirshbaum, 1899.

Aquinas, Thomas. *Summa Theologica.* 22 vols. London: Burns, Oates and Washbourne, 1913-1922.

Aristotle. *The Politics.* T. A. Sinclair, trans. Revised by Trevor J. Saunders. Harmondsworth, England and New York: Penguin Books, 1981.

Arsenii (Stadnitskii, Avksentii Georgevich; Archbishop of Novgorod and Staraia Rus'). "Rech Vysokopreosviashchennogo Arseniia, arkhiepiskopa Novgorodskogo pri pogrevenii arkhiepiskopa Guriia 4-go marta." *Pribavleniia k Tserkovnym vedomostiam* No. 11 (March 1912): 457-459.

Athanasius, *Historia Arianorum* and *Letters.* In Philip Schaff, ed. *Nicene and Post Nicene Fathers*, Series 2, vol. 4: *Athanasius: Selected Works and Letters.* New York: Christian Literature Publishing Co., 1892.

Baranov, K. V. (Konstantin Vladimirovich), ed. *Pistsovye knigi Novgorodskoi zemli.* Moscow: Drevlekhranilishche, Arkheograficheskii tsentr, 1999-.

Basil The Great, *Letters.* 2 vols. Sister Agnes Clare Way, trans. With notes by Roy J. Deferrari. *Fathers of the Church.* vols. 13, 28. Washington, D. C.: Catholic University of America Press, 1951, 1981.

Bekker, Immanuel, ed. *Theophanes continuatus: Ioannes Cameniata, Symeon Magister, Georgius monachus.* Bonn: E. Weber, 1838.

Beneshevich, V. N. (Vladimir Nikolaevich), ed. *Kanonicheskii Sbornik XIV titulov: so vtoroi chetverti VII veka do 883g.: k drevneishei istorii isochnikov prava greko-vostochnoi tserkvi.* St. Petersburg: F. Vaisberga i P. Gerishchnina, 1905.

------. *Drevne-slavianskaia kormchaia XIV titulov bez tolkovanii.* Vol. 1. St. Petersburg: Tipografii Imperatorskoi Akademicheskoi Nauk, 1906. Reprint Leipzig, Germany: Zentralantiquariat der DDR, 1974.

------. *Sbornik pamiatnikov po istorii tserkovnogo prava: preimushchestvenno russkoi tserkvi do epokhi Petra Velikogo.* Petrograd: Izdanie "Kult'ura i Znanie", 1914. [Tipografiia A. O. Tip. Dela, 1915.]

Bodianskii, O. (Osip), ed. "Napisanie vdovogo popa Georgiia Skripitsy iz Rostova grada o vdovstvuiushikh popakh." *ChIOID.* Book 6, Section 4 (1848): 45-50.

Bugoslavskii, S., ed. "Pouchenie ep. Luki Zhidiaty po rukopisiam XV-XVII vv." *Izvestiia Otdelenia russkogo iazika i slovesnosti Imperatorskoi Akademii nauk* 18, No. 2 (1913): 194-237.

Budge, E. A. (Ernest Alfred) Wallis, ed. and trans., *The Monks of Kûblâi Khân, Emperor of China or, The History of the Life and Travels of Rabban Sâwmâ, Envoy and Plenipotentiary of the Mongol Khâns to the Kings of Europe, and Markôs who as Mâr Yahbh-Allâhâ III became Patriarch of the Nestorian Church in Asia* (London: Religious Tract Society, 1928).

von Bunge, F. G. (Frederich Georg), ed. *Liv- Est- und Kurländische Urkundenbuch nebst Regesten.* 15 vols. Reval: in Commission bei Kluge und Ströhm, 1853-1914.

Bychkov, A. F. (Afanasii Fedorovich), ed. *Novgorodskie letopisi.* 2 vols. St. Petersburg: Izdatel'stvo Arkheograficheskoi kommissii, 1879. Reprinted A. I. (Aleksandr Ivanovich) Tsepkov, ed. Riazan: Aleksandria, 2002.

Catholic Church. *Code of Canon Law: Latin-English Edition.* Washington, DC: Canon Law Society of America, 1983.

Cicero, Marcus Tullius. *De Legibus Libri Tres. A Revised Text with English Notes.* W. D. Pearman, ed. Cambridge, MA: J. Hall and Sons, 1881.

Cherepnin, Lev Vladimirovich, ed. *Russkie feodal'nye arkhivy XIV-XV vekov.* 2 vols. Moscow: AN SSSR 1948-1951.

------. *Pamiatniki prava perioda obrazovaniia russkogo tsentralizovannogo gosudarstva, XIV-XV vv.* Vol. 3 of L. V. (Lev Vladimirovich) Cherepnin and S. V. (Serafim Vladimirovich) Iuskhkov, eds., *Pamiatniki russkogo prava* Moscow: Gosudarstvennoe izdatel'stvo iuridicheskoi literatury, 1955.

------. *Novgorodskie berestianye gramoty kak istoricheskii istochnik.* Moscow: Nauka, 1969.
Cherepnin, L. V. (Lev Vladimirovich), and S. V. (Serafim Vladimirovich) Iuskhkov, eds. *Pamiatniki russkogo prava.* 8 vols. Moscow: Gosudarstvennoe izdatel'stvo iuridicheskoi literatury, 1952-1961.
Chistiakov, O. I. (Oleg Ivanovich), ed. *Rossiiskoe zakonodatel'stvo X-XX vekov.* 9 vols. Moscow: Iuridicheskaia literature, 1984.
Comnena, Anna. *The Alexiad of Anna Comnena.* E. R. A. Sewter, trans. London and New York: Penguin Books, 1969.
Connolly, R. (Richard) Hugh. *Didascalia Apostolorum the Syriac Version Translated and Accompanied by the Verona Latin Fragments.* Oxford: Clarendon, 1929.
Constantine Porphyrogenitus. *De Administrando Imperio.* Gy. Moravcsik, ed. R. J. H. Jenkins, trans. Washington, DC: Dumbarton Oaks Center for Byzantine Studies, 1967.
Constantine of Preslav, "Proglas." In P. Dinenkov, K. Kuev, and D. Petkanova, eds. *Khristomatiia po staroblgarska literatura.* 2nd ed. Sofia: Nauka i izkustvo, 1967.
Cyprian of Carthage. *S. Thasci Caecili Cypriani Opera omnia.* Wilhelm August Ritter von Hartel, ed., 3 vols. Vienna: Apud C. Geroldi filium, 1868-1871; Reprinted as Vol. 3 of Corpus Scriptorum Ecclesiasticorum Latinorum in three parts, New York: Johnson Reprints, 1965.
------. *Letters.* In Alexander Roberts, James Donaldson, and A. (Arthur) Cleveland Coxe, eds. *Fathers of the Third Century: Hippolytus, Cyprian, Caius, Novatian, Appendix.* Volume 5 of *The Ante-Nicene Fathers: Translations of the Writings of the Fathers down to A.D. 325.* Grand Rapids, MI: W.B. Eerdmans, 1951.
Darrouzès, Jean. *Notitiae episcopatuum Ecclesiae Constantinopolitanae.* Paris: Institute Français d'Études Byzantines, 1981.
Dawson, Christopher, ed. *The Mongol Missions: Franciscan Missionaries in Mongolia and China in the Thirteenth and Fourteenth Centuries.* New York: Sheed and Ward, 1955.
Dinenkov, P. N. (Petur Nikolov), K. M. (Kiuo Markov) Kuev, and D. N. (Donka Nikolova) Petkanova, eds. *Khristomatiia po staroblgarska literatura.* 2nd ed. Sofia: Nauka i izkustvo, 1967.

Długosz, Jan. *Opera omnia*. 15 vols. Alexander Przezdiecki, Ignacy Polkowski, and Pauli Żegotaed, eds. Cracow: Tipographia Kirchmajeriana, 1863-1887.
Dmitriev, L. A. (Lev Aleksandrovich). *Povesti o zhitii Mikhaila Klopskogo*. Moscow and Leningrad: AN SSSR, 1958.
Dmitriev, L. A. (Lev Aleksandrovich) and D. S. (Dmitrii Sergeevich) Likhachev, eds. *Nachalo russkoi literatury: XI-nachalo XII v.* Moscow: Khudozhestvennaia literatura, 1978. Volume 1 of *Pamiatniki literatury drevnei Rusi*.
------. *Pamiatniki literatury drevnei Rusi XII veka*. Moscow: Khudozhestvennaia literatura, 1980. Volume 2 of *Pamiatniki literatury drevnei Rusi*.
------. *Pamiatniki literatury drevnei Rusi XIII veka*. Moscow: Khudozhestvennaia literatura, 1981. Volume 3 of *Pamiatniki literatury drevnei Rusi*.
------. *Pamiatniki literatury drevnei Rusi XIV-seredina XV veka*. Moscow: Khudozhestvennaia literatura, 1981. Volume 4 of *Pamiatniki literatury drevnei Rusi*.
------. *Pamiatniki literatury drevnei Rusi vtoraia polovina XVI veka*. Moscow: Khudozhestvennaia literatura, 1982. Volume 5 of *Pamiatniki literatury drevnei Rusi*.
------. *Pamiatniki literatury drevnei Rusi konets XV-pervaia polovina XVI veka*. Moscow: Khudozhestvennaia literatura, 1984. Volume 6 of *Pamiatniki literatury drevnei Rusi*.
------. *Pamiatniki literatury drevnei Rusi seredina XVI veka*. Moscow: Khudozhestvennaia literatura, 1985. Volume 7 of *Pamiatniki literatury drevnei Rusi*.
------. *Pamiatniki literatury drevnei Rusi vtoraia polovina XVI veka*. Moscow: Khudozhestvennaia literatura, 1986. Volume 8 of *Pamiatniki literatury drevnei Rusi*.
------. *Pamiatniki literatury drevnei Rusi konets XVI-nachalo XVII vekov*. Moscow: Khudozhestvennaia literatura, 1987. Volume 9 of *Pamiatniki literatury drevnei Rusi*.
------. *Pamiatniki literatury drevnei Rusi XVII veka*. Moscow: Khudozhestvennaia literatura, 1988-89. Volume 10 of *Pamiatniki literatury drevnei Rusi*.
Dopolneniia k Aktam istoricheskim sobrannye i izdannye Arkheograficheskoiu komissieiu. 12 vols. St. Petersburg: Ekspeditsii zagotovleniia Gosudarstvennykh bumag, 1846-1872.

Douglas, David C., gen. ed., Dorothy Whitelock, ed., *English Historical Documents c. 500-1042.* Volume 1 of 13 vols. London: Eyre and Spottiswoode, 1955.
Emchenko, E. B. (Elena) *Stoglav: Issledovanie i tekst.* Moscow: Indrik, 2000.
Eremin, I. P. (Igor' Petrovich). "Iz istorii starinnoi russkoi povesti: povest' o posadnike Shchile (issledovanie i teksty)." *Trudy Kommissii po drevne-russkoi literature.* Vol. 1 (1932): 122-151.
Eustratiades, S., ed. "Typikon tes en Konstantinoupolei mones tou hagiou megalomartyros Mamantos." *Hellenika: historikon periodikon demosieuma ekdidomenon kath'examenon,* (1928): 245-314.
Evgenii (Bolkhovitinov, Evfimii Alekseevich, Metropolitan of Kyiv and Halych). "Svedeniia o Kirike, predlagavshem voprosy Nifonty Novgorodskomy," *Trudy i letopisi Obshchestva istorii i drevnostei rossiiskikh,* pt. 4, book 1 (1828): 123-129.
Feodosii Pecherskii, *Sochinenia,* I. I. (Izmail Ivanovich) Sreznevksii, ed. In *Uchenye zapiski vtorogo otdelenie Imperatorskoi Akademii nauk,* vol. 2, No. 2. St. Petersburg: Tipografii Imperatorskoi Akademii nauk, 1856.
Franklin, Simon, trans. *Sermons and Rhetoric of Kievan Rus'.* Vol. 5 of *The Harvard Library of Early Ukrainian Literature.* Cambridge, MA: Harvard University Press, 1991.
Funk, F. X. (Francis Xavier). *Didascalia et Constitutiones apostolorum.* Turin: Bottega d'Erasmo, 1979.
Gregory of Tours. *History of the Franks.* Lewis Thorpe, trans. London: Penguin, 1974.
Grekov, B. D. (Boris Dmitrievich), ed. "Novye materialy o dvizhenii Stepana Razina," *Letopis' zaniatii Arkheograficheskoi komissii za 1926.* Vol. 34. Leningrad: AN SSSR, 1927: 203-238.
------. ed. "Pskovskaia sudnaia gramota." IZ 6 (1940): 237-254.
Gusev, P. L. (Pavel L'vovich), ed. *Pistsovaia kniga Velikogo Novgoroda, 1583-84 gg.* St. Peterburg: Tipografii Glav. upravleniia udielov, 1908.
Henricus Lettus (Heinrich von Lettland). *Chronicon Livoniae/Livländische Chronik.* A. Bauer and L. Arbusow, eds. Darmstadt: Wissenschaftliche Buchgesellschaft, 1959.
Ianin, V. L. (Valentin Lavrentevich), ed. *Zakonodatel'stvo Drevnei Rusi.* Vol. 1 of O. I. (Oleg Ivanovich), Chistiakov, ed. *Rossiiskoe zakonodatel'stvo X-XX vekov.* 9 vols. Moscow: Iuridicheskaia literature, 1984).

Ibn Battutah (Abu Abdullah Muhammad ibn Battutah) and Tim Mackintosh-Smith. *The Travels of Ibn Battutah*. London: Picador, 2002.
Il'ia (a.k.a., Ioann; Archbishop of Novgorod) "Pravila Chernoriztsem." In K. I. (Kapiton Ivanovich) Nevostruev, ed. *Materialy dlia istorii russkoi tserkvi*. 2 vols. Khar'kov: universitetskaia tipografiia, 1862-1863. Published serially in *Dukhovnyi vestnik* (1862-1863). No. 3 (March 1863): 31-36.
Iroicheskaia pesn' o pokhode na polovtsov udel'nogo kniaza Novgoroda-Severskogo Igoria Sviatoslavicha pisanna derevnim russkim iazykom v izkhode XII stoletia s perelozheniem" na upotrebliaemoe nyne narechie. Moscow: v Senatskoi tipografii, 1800.
Jaffe, Philipp, ed. *Bibliotheca rerum germanicarum*. 6 vols. Berlin: N.p. 1864-73.
Joachim, Erick and Walter Hubatsch. *Regesta historico-diplomatica Ordinis S. Mariae Theutonicorum, 1198-1525*. 2 vols. in 3 parts. Gottingen: Vanderhoeck and Ruprecht, 1948-1973.
Justinian. *Corpus iuris civilis*. Vol. 3 *Novellae*. Rudolph Schoell and Wilhelm Kroll, eds. Berlin: Apud Weidmannos, 1895.
Kaiser, Daniel H., trans. and ed. *The Laws of Rus', Tenth to Fifteenth Centuries*. Salt Lake City: Charles Schlacks, Jr., 1992.
Kalaidovich, K. F. (Konstantin Fedorovich), ed. *Pamiatniki rossiiskoi slovesnosti XII v.: izdannye s ob"iasneniem, variantami i obraztsami pocherkov*. Moscow: Tipografiia Semena Selivanovskogo, 1821.
Kantor M. (Marvin), and R. S. (Richard Stephen) White, trans. *The Vita of Constantine and the Vita of Methodius*. Ann Arbor: Michigan Slavic Publications, University of Michigan, 1976.
Kirik Novgorodets, "Uchenie im zha vedati cheloveku chisla vsekh let." *Istoriko-matematicheskie issledovannia* 4 (1953): 174-191.
------. "Voproshanie Kirika." In A. S. (Aleksandr Stepanovich) Pavlov, ed. *Russkaia istoricheskaia biblioteka*. St. Petersburg: Izdatel'stvo Arkhiograficheskoi kommissii,1908. Vol 6, doc. 2, cols. 21-62.
Klemming, G. E. (Gustav Edvard), ed. "Förbindelsedikt," also known as the "Sammanfogningen mellan Gamla och Nya Krönikan." Vol. 1 of *Svenska medeltidens rim-krönikor*, 3 vols. Stockholm: P.A. Norstedt & söner, kongl. boktryckare, 1865.

Kotoshikhin, Grigorii Karpovich. *O Rossii v tsarstvovanii Alekseia Mikhailovicha*. 4th ed. St. Petersburg: Izdatel'stvo Imperatorskoi Arkheograficheskoi komissii, 1906.

Kozhanchikov, D. E., ed. *Stoglav*. St. Petersburg: v tipografii Imperatorskoi Akademii nauk, 1863.

Kushelev-Bezborodko, Grigorii Aleksandrovich, graf, and N. I. (Nikolai Ivanovich) Kostomarov, eds. *Pamiatniki starinnoi russkoi literatury*. 4 vols. St. Petersburg: Tipografii P. A. Kulish, 1860-1862.

Kuntsevich, Georgii Zakharovich, ed. *Feodosii: Arkhiepiskop Novgorodskii (1491-1563) (Ego zhitie)*. St. Petersburg: Tipografiia R. Golke, 1898.

Lebedev, V. I. (Vladimir Ivanovich), ed. *Khrestomatiia po istorii SSSR, s drevneishikh vremen do kontsa XVII veka*, 3rd ed. Vol. 1. Moscow: Ministerstvo Obrazovaniia, 1949.

Leo Diaconus. *Leonis Diaconis Caloënsis Historiae liberi decem*. In *Corpus Scriptorum Historiae Byzantinae*. Bonn: Weber, 1828.

Likhachev, D. S. (Dmitrii Sergeevich). "Novgorodskaia letopis' XIII-XIV vv." In Institut russkoi literatury (Pushkinskii dom). *Istoriia russkoi literatury*. 10 vols. Moscow and Leningrad: AN SSSR, 1941-1956: 114-121.

Likhachev, D. S., (Dmitrii Sergeevich), L. A. (Lev Aleksandrovich) Dmitriev, A. A. (Anatolii A.) Alekseev, and I. V. Panyrko, eds. *Biblioteka literatury drevnei Rusi*. 20 vols. St. Petersburg: Rossisskaia Akademiia Nauk, 1999-.

Likhachev, D. S. (Dmitrii Sergeevich), and V. P. (Varvara Pavlovna) Adrianova-Peretts, eds. *Povest' Vremennykh Let*. 2 vols. Moscow and Leningrad: AN SSSR, 1950.

Marasinova, L. M. (Liudmilla Mikhailovna). *Novye Pskovskie Gramoty XIV-XV vekov*. Moscow: Izdatel'stvo Moskovskogo Universiteta, 1966.

Meyer, Leo, ed. *Livländische Reimchronik*. Paderborn: Ferdinand Schöningh, 1876.

Michell, Robert, and Nevill Forbes, eds. *The Chronicle of Novgorod 1016-1471*. New York: AMS Press, 1970.

Migne, J. P. (Jacques-Paul), ed. *Patrologiæ cursus completus: sive bibliotheca universalis, integra, uniformis, commoda, oeconomica, omnium SS. patrum, doctorum, scriptorumque ecclesiasticorum. Series latina*. 221 vols. Paris: Apud Garnieri Fratres, editores et J.-P. Migne successores, 1844-1891.

------. *Patrologiae cursus completus: seu bibliotheca universalis, integra, uniformis, commoda, oeconomica, omnium SS. Patrum, doctorum, scriptorumque ecclesiasticorum. Series graeca in qua prodeunt patres, doctores scriptoresque ecclesiae graecae A.S. Barnaba ad Photium.* 161 vols. Paris: J-P. Migne, 1855-1867.

von Miklosich, Franz, Ritter, and Joseph Müller, eds. *Acta et diplomata graeca medii aevi sacra et profana.* 6 vols. Vindobanea [Vienna]: Carolus Gerold, 1860-1890.

Monumenta Germaniae Historica. Scriptores rerum Germanicarum. Nova Series. Vol. 9. Berlin: Weidmann, 1955.

Murav'ev, Andrei Nikolaevich. *Zhitie sviatykh rossiiskoi tserkvi takzhe iverskikh i slavianskikh.* 12 vols. St. Petersburg: v Tipografii II Oteleniia Sobstvennioi E. I. V. Kantseliaria, 1865.

Napierskii, K. E. (Karl Eduard). *Gramoty kasiushchiesia do snoshenii sever-zapadnoi Rossii s Rigoi i Ganzeiskimi gorodami v XII, XIII, i XIV vv.* St. Petersburg: v Tipografii Imperatorskoi Akademii nauk, 1857.

------. *Russisch-Livländische Urkundenbüch.* St. Petersburg: Buchdr. der Kaiserlichen Akademie der Wissenschaften, 1868.

------. *Russko-Livonskie akty.* St. Petersburg: Buchdr. der Kaiserlichen Akademie der Wissenschaften, 1868.

Nasonov, A. N. (Arsenii Nikolaevich), ed. *Novgorodskaia pervaia letopis': starshego i mladshego izvodov.* Moscow and Leningrad: AN SSSR, 1950.

Nevostruev, K. I. (Kapiton Ivanovich). *Drevnerusskie poucheniia i poslaniia ob inocheskoi zhizni s pimecheniem K. I. Nevostureva.* Khar'kov: universitetskaia tipografiia, 1862.

------. *Materialy dlia istorii russkoi tserkvi.* 2 vols. Khar'kov: universitetskaia tipografiia, 1862-1863.

------. *Nekotorye drevne-russkie poucheniia ob inocheskoi zhizni.* Moscow: universiteskaia tipografiia, 1866.

Novgorodskii gosudarstvenyi obediinenyi muzei-zapovednik, Ekspozitsii g. Velikii Novgorod Palata arkhiepiskopa Evfimiia II na Vladychnom dvore Novgorodsko Kremlia, (https://novgorod-iss.kamiscloud.ru/entity/OBJECT?exposition=3827568). Accessed September 24, 2022.

Novikov, N. I. (Nikolai Ivanovich), ed. *Drevniaia rossiiskaia vivliofika ili Sobranie raznikh drevnykh sochinenii, iako-to: rossiiskie posolstsva v drugie gosudarstva, redkie gramoty opisaniia svadebnikh obriadov i drugikh istoricheskikh i geograficheskikh dostopamiatnostei i mnogie sochineniia drevnikh rossiskikh stikhotvortsev, izdavaemaia pomesiachno Nikolaem Novikovim.* Part 4, April-June. St. Petersburg: Tipografii Akademii Nauk, 1774.

Okhotina, N. A. (Natalia Aleksandrovna). "The Tale of the Valamo Monastery," *Ortodoksia* 42 (1993): 124-135.

Okhotina-Lind, N. A. (Natalia Aleksandrovna). *Skazanie o Valaamskom Monastyre.* St. Petersburg: Glagol, 1996.

Palladius, (Bishop of Aspuna). *Palladius, The Lausiac History.* Robert T. Meyer, ed. and trans. Westminster, MD: Newmann Press, 1965.

Pashuto, V. T. (Vladimir Terent'evich), and I. V. Shtal, eds. *Gedimino Laiskai.* Vilnius: Academy of Science of the Lithuanian SSR, 1966.

Paterik Kievskogo Pecherskogo monastyria. St. Petersburg: Izdatel'stvo Imperatorskoi arkheograficheskoi komissii, 1911.

Percival, Henry R. *The Seven Ecumenical Councils of the Undivided Church: Their Canons and Dogmatic Decrees.* New York: Edwin S. Gorham, 1901. Reprinted in Philip Schaff, ed. *Nicene and Post-Nicene Fathers.* 2nd Series. Vol. 14. Grand Rapids, MI: Wm. B. Eerdmans Publishing Company, 1979.

Peter Diaconus, *Chronica Monasterii Casinensis.* Vol. 7 (1846) of G. H. (Georg Heinrich) Pertz, ed. MGH *Scriptores.* 30 vols. Hannover: Hahn, 1826-1934.

Photius (Patriarch of Constantinople), *Photii bibliotheca.* Immanuel Bekker, ed., 2 vols. Berlin: G. Reimeri, 1824-1825.

Pistsovye knigi Obonezhskoi piatiny 1496 i 1563 gg. Leningrad: AN SSSR, 1930.

Pliguzov, Andrei I. ed., *Documentary Sources on the History of the Rus' Metropolitanate: The Fourteenth to the Early Sixteenth Centuries.* Cambridge: Harvard University Press, 2025.

Pliguzov, A. I. (Andrei Ivanovich) and A. V. Kuz'min, eds. *Russkii feodal'nyi arkhiv: XIV-pervoi treti XVI veka.* Moscow: Iazyki slavianskikh kul'tur, 2008.

Pliguzov, A. I. (Andrei Ivanovich), G. V. Semenchenko, L. F. Kuz'mina, and V. I. Buganov, eds. *Russkii feodal'nyi arkhiv XIV-pervoi treti XVI veka*. 5 vols. Moscow: AN SSSR, 1986-1992.
Polnoe sobranie russkikh letopisei:
- *Lavrent'evskaia letopis'*. PSRL 1. Leningrad: AN SSSR, 1926.
- *Suzdal'skaia letopis'*. PSRL 1. Leningrad: AN SSSR, 1927.
- *Ipat'evskaia letopis'*. PSRL 2, Pt. 1. St. Petersburg: Tipografiia Eduarda Pratsa, 1843. PSRL 2, Pt. 2. St. Petersburg: Tipografiia M. A. Aleksandrova, 1908. PSRL 2.3. Petrograd: Petrogradskaia Pervaia Trudovaia Artel Pechatnikov, 1923.
- *Novgorodskaia vtoraia letopis'*. PSRL 3. St. Petersburg: v Tipografii Eduarda Pratsa, 1841. Reprinted Dusseldorf: Brücken-Verlag and Vaduz: Europe Printing 1973.
- *Novgorodskaia tretiaia letopis'*. PSRL 3.
- *Novgorodskaia chetvertaia letopis'*. PSRL 4.1. Moscow: Iazyki russkoi kul'tury, 2000.
- *Pskovskaia pervaia letopis'*. PSRL 5.1. Moscow: Iazyki russkoi kul'tury, 2003.
- *Pskovskaia vtoraia letopis'*. PSRL 5.2. Moscow: AN SSSR, 1955.
- *Sofiiskaia pervaia letopis'*, *starshego izvoda*. PSRL 6, Pt. 1. Moscow: Iazyki russkoi kul'tury, 2000.
- *Sofiiskaia vtoraia letopis.'* PSRL 6, Pt. 2. Moscow: Iazyki russkoi kul'tury, 2001.
- *Letopis' po Voskresenskomu spisku*. PSRL 7. St. Petersburg: v Tipografii Eduarda Pratsa, 1856.
- *Prodolzhenie Letopisi po Voskresenskomu spisku*. PSRL 8. St. Petersburg: v Tipografii Eduarda Pratsa, 1859.
- *Letopisnyi sbornik imenuemyi Patriarsheiu ili Nikonovskoi letopis'iu*, PSRL 9. St. Petersburg: Tipografiia Eduarda Pratsa, 1862; PSRL 10 (St. Petersburg: v tipografii Ministerstva vnutrennykh del, 1885; PSRL 12. St. Petersburg: Tipografiia I. N. Skorokhodova, 1901; PSRL 13, 2 pts. St. Petersburg: Tipografiia I. N. Skorokhodova, 1904, 1906.
- *Letopisnyi sbornik imnuemyi letopis'iu Avraamki*. PSRL 16. St. Petersburg: Tipografiia F. Eleonskogo i ko., 1899.
- *Stepennaia kniga tsarskogo rodosloviia*, PSRL 21, 2 pts. St. Petersburg: Tipografiia M. A. Aleksandrova, 1908 and 1913.
- *Ermolinskaia letopis'*. PSRL 23. St. Petersburg: Tipografiia M. A. Aleksandrova, 1910.

- *Tipografskaia letopis'*. PSRL 24. Petrograd: Vtoraia gosudarstvennaia tipografiia, 1921.
- *Nachala Letopisi po Ermitazhnomu spisku*. PSRL 25. Moscow and Leningrad, AN SSSR, 1949.
- *Moskovskii letopisnyi svod kontsa XV veka*. PSRL 25.
- *Vologodsko-Permskaia letopis'*. PSRL 26. Moscow and Leningrad: AN SSSR, 1959.
- *Novgorodskaia vtoraia (arkhivskaia) letopis'*, PSRL 30. Moscow: AN SSSR 1965.
- *Gustynskaia letopis'*. PSRL 40. Moscow: Dmitrii Bulanin, 2003.
- *Novgorodskaia letopis' po spisku P. P. Dubrovskogo*. PSRL 43. Moscow: Iazyk Slavianskoi kul'tury, 2004.

Polo, Marco. *The Travels*. London: Penguin Classics, 1958.

Ponomarev, A. I. (Aleksandr Ivanovich), ed. *Pamiatniki drevnerusskoi tserkovno-uchitel'noi literatury*, 1st ed. St. Petersburg: S. Dobrodeev, Tipografiia, 1894.

Popov, A. N. (Andrei Nikolaevich). "Istoriko-literaturnyi obzor drevne-russkikh polemicheskikh sochinenyi protiv Latinian XI-XV vv." ChOIDR Book 2 (1878) and Book 2 (1879): 344-359.

Prosvetitel' ili oblichenie eresi zhidostvuiushchikh. Tvorenie Iosifa igumena. 4th ed. Kazan': Imperatorskii universitet, 1903.

Potvin, Charles and J. C. Mouzeau, eds. *Oeuvres de Ghillebert de Lannoy*. Louvain: Impr. de P. et J. Lefever, 1878.

Pravoslavnyi Sobesednik. Kazan': Kazanskia Dukhovnaia Akademiia, 1855-1917.

Prokhorov, G. M. ed. "Khozhdenie igumena Daniila," In L. A. (Lev Aleksandrovich) Dmitriev, and D. S. (Dmitrii Sergeevich) Likhachev, eds. *Pamiatniki literatury drevnei Rusi XII veka*. Moscow: Khudozhestvennaia literatura, 1980: 24-115, 627-645.

Regel, V. E. (Vasilii Eduardovich), ed. *Analecta byzantino-russica*. St. Petersburg: N.p., 1891. Reprint New York: Burt Franklin, 1963.

Roberts, Alexander, James Donaldson, and A. (Arthur) Cleveland Coxe, eds. *The Ante-Nicene Fathers: Translations of the Writings of the Fathers down to A.D. 325*. New York: The Christian Literature Company, 1888. Reprinted: Grand Rapids, MI: W.B. Eerdmans, 1951-.

------. "Teaching of the Twelve Apostles" (a.k.a., the Didache). In *Fathers of the Third and Fourth Centuries: Lactantius, Venantius, As-*

terius, Victorinus, Dionysius, Apostolic Teaching and Constitutions, Homily. Volume 7 of Ante Nicene Fathers Grand Rapids, MI: W.B. Eerdmans, 1951-.

Russkaia istoricheskaia biblioteka. 39 vols. St. Petersburg: Izdatel'stvo Arkhiograficheskoi kommissii, 1872-1927.

Russkaia Pravoslavnaia Tserkov'. "Mitropolit Leningradskii i Novgorodskii Aleksii." ZhMP (1989) No. 7:7.

Russkaia Pravoslavnaia Tserkov', Sviateishii pravitelstvuiushchii sinod. *Kniga zhitii sviatykh. Blagosloveniem zhe Sviateishogo pravitel'stvuiushchogo vserossiiskogo sinoda*. 12 vols. Moscow: n. p., 1837.

Ryan, W. F. (William Francis) and Moshe Taube, *The Secret of Secrets: The East Slavic Version: Introduction, Text, Annotated Translation, and Slavic Index*. London: The Warburg Institute, 2019.

Savvaitov, P. I. (Pavel Ivanovich), A. I. (Aleksandr Ilich) Timofeev, and S. K. Sergei Konstantinovich) Bogoiavlenskii, eds. *Novgorodskiia Pistsovyia Knigi*, 6 vols. St. Petersburg: Senatskaia Tipografiia, 1859-1910. Vols 1-3 reprinted The Hague: Mouton, 1969.

Sakharov, A. M. (Anatolii Mikhailovich), ed. *Sbornik dokumentov po istorii SSSR dlia seminaraskikh i prakticheskikh zaniatii*, pt. 2, XIV-XV vv. Moscow: Vyshaia shkola, 1971.

Shchapov, Ia. N. (Iaroslav Nikolaevich). *Drevnerusskie kniazheskie ustavy XI-XVI vv*. Moscow: Nauka, 1976.

Sluzhba i zhitie izhe vo sviatykh otsa nashego Evfimiia arkhiepiskopa novgorodskogo chudotvortsa. St. Petersburg: Izdatel'stvo redaktsia zhurnala "Kronshtadtskii Maiak." Otechestvennaia tipografiia, 1907.

Subbotin, N. I. (Nikolai Ivanovich) ed. *Deianie moskovskikh soborov 1666 i 1667 godov*. Published by the Brotherhood of St. Petr Metropolitan, 2nd ed. Moscow: Sinodalnaia tipografiia, 1893.

Sumnikova, T. A. (Tat'iana Alekseevna), and V. V. (Vladimir Vladimirovich) Lopatin, eds. *Smolenskie gramoty XIII-XIV vekov*. Moscow: AN SSSR, 1963.

Strehlke, Ernest, ed. *Tabulae Ordinis Theutonici: ex tabularii regii Berolinensis codice potissimum*. Berlin: Weidmann, 1869.

Tanner, Norman P., ed. *Decrees of the Ecumenical Councils*, 2 vols. London and New York: Sheed and Ward and Georgetown University Press, 1990.

Theiner, Augustino, ed. *Vetera monumenta Poloniae et Lithuaniae gentiumque finitimarum.* 3

Thietmar von Merseburg, (Bishop of Merseburg). *Die Chronik Des Bischofs Thietmar Von Merseburg Und Ihre Korveier Überarbeitung.* Robert Holtzmann, ed. 2. unveranderte Auflageed. of Monumenta Germaniae Historica ... Edidit Societas Aperiendis Fontibus Rerum Germanicarum Medii Aevi. Scriptores Rerum-Germanicarum, Nova Series, Tomuvs IX. Berlin: Weidmannsche Buchhandlung, 1955.

Theodosius. *De situ Terrae Sanctae im ächten Text.* Johann Gildemeister, ed. Bonn: Bei Adolph Marcus, 1882.

Thomas, John, and Angela Constantinides Hero, eds., with the assistance of Giles Constable. *Byzantine Monastic Foundation Documents: A Complete Translation of the Surviving Founders' Typika and Testaments.* 5 vols. Washington, DC: Dumbarton Oaks, 2000.

Tikhomirov, M. N. (Mikhail Nikolaevich), and L. V. (Leonid Vasilevich) Milov. *Zakon sudnyi liudem prostrannoi i svodnoi redaktsii.* Moscow: AN SSSR, 1961.

Tikhomirov, P. I. (Pavel Ilich), ed. *Zhitie izhe vo sviatykh otsa nashego Moiseia arkhiepiskopa Novgoroda pogibaiushchego v Skovorodskim monastyre.* Novgorod: Novgorodskii Gubernskii Pravlenii, 1890. Second edition published 1895.

------. *Zhitie prepodobnogo otsa nashego Arseniia arkhiepiskopa Novgorodskogo chudotvortsa s istorikami svedeniiami o postroenki Novgorodskogo Malo-Kirillova monastyra.* Novgorod: Novgorodskii Gubernskii Pravlenii, 1891.

Trudy Otdela drevnerusskoi literatury. 8 vols. Moscow and Leningrad: AN SSSR, Institut russkoi literatury (Pushkinskii dom), 1934-1951.

Valk, S. N. (Sigizmund Natanovich), ed. *Gramoty Velikogo Novgoroda i Pskova.* Moscow: AN SSSR, 1949.

Zachariä von Lingenthal, K. E. (Karl Edward) *Jus graeco-romanum.* 4 parts in 2 vols. Leipzig (Lipsiae): T. O. Weigel, 1856-1865.

Zalizniak, A. A. (Andrei Anatol'evich). *Drevnenovgorodskii dialekt.* 2nd ed. Moscow: Iazyki slavianskoi kul'tury, 2004.

Zertsalov, A. N. (Aleksandr Nikolaevich), ed. "O 'nepravdakh i neprigozhikh rechakh' novgorodskogo mitropolita Kipriana (1627-1633)," *Chteniia v Imperatorskom obshchestve istorii i drev-*

nostei rossiiskikh pri Moskovskom universitete (1896), bk. 1, pt. 1, No. 2:1-28.
Zhitie prepodobnogo otsa nashego Arseniia novgorodskogo chudotvortsa. Novgorod: Tipografiia M. Klasson, 1887.
Zhitie sviatitelia Iona arkhiepiskopa novgorodskogo. St. Petersburg: Izdanie Redaktsii zhurnal "Mirskoi Vestnik," 1868.
Zhitie sviatitelia Serapiona Arkhiepiskopa Novgorodskogo. Troitskaia Sergeeva Lavra: Sobstvennaia tipografiia, 1912.
Zimin, A. A. (Aleksandr Aleksandrovich) and S. A. Levina, eds. *Ioasafovskaia letopis'.* Moscow: AN SSSR, 1957.
Zimin, A. A. (Aleksandr Aleksandrovich) and Ia. S. (Iakov Solomonovich) Lur'e, ed. *Poslaniia Iosifa Volotskogo.* Moscow and Leningrad: AN SSSR, 1959.

Secondary Sources

XI Congrès International de Sciences Historiques. Résumés des Communicationes. 2 vols. Göteborg, Stockholm and Uppsala: Almqvist & Wiksell, 1960-1962.
Abelentseva, O. A. (Ol'ga Alekseevna). "Okhrannaia gramota papy Evgeniia IV poslu russkomu Fome (O Tverskom posolstve na Ferraro-Florentiiskii sobor." In A. P. Pavlov and A. G. Man'kov, eds. *Rossiiskoe gosudarstvo v. XIV-XVII vv.: sbornik statei, posviashchennyi 75-letiiu so dnia rozhdeniia Iu.G. Alekseeva.* St. Petersburg: Dmitrii Bulanin, 2002: 40-47.
------. "Formuliarnik novgorodskogo arkhiepiskopa Feodosiia (RNB Q. XVII.50) i ego rukopisnaia traditsiia," TODRL 53. St. Petersburg: Dmitrii Budanin, 2003: 122-158.
Abramovich, D. I. (Dmitrii Ivanovich) *Sofiiskaia biblioteka* 3 vols. St. Petersburg: Tip. Imperatorskoi Akademii nauk, 1905-1910.
Alef, Gustave. "Muscovy and the Council of Florence." SR 20 (1961): 389-401. Reprinted in *Rulers and Nobles in Fifteenth Century Muscovy.*
------. *Rulers and Nobles in Fifteenth Century Muscovy.* London: Variorum Reprints, 1983.
Alekseev, Aleksei I. (Alexey Alexseev). "A Few Notes on the Strigol'niki Heresy." CMR 46, Nos. 1-2 (January 2005): 285-296.
------. *Religioznye dvizheniia na Rusi poslednei treti XIV—nachala XVI v.: strigol'niki i zhidovstviushchie.* Moscow: "Indrik", 2012.

Alekseev, Iu. G. (Iurii Georgievich). "'Chernye liudi' Novgoroda i Pskova (k voprosu o sotsial'noi evoliutsii drevnerusskoi gorodskom obshchiny). IZ 103 (1979): 242-274.

Alekseev, V. N., N. G. Porfiridov, and A. I. (Aleksandr Ignat'evich) Semenov. *Moshchi Sofiiskogo sobora.* Novgorod: Novgorodskaia gosudarstvennaia tipografiia, 1931.

Aleksei II (Aleksei Mikhailovich Ridiger; Kirill (Vladimir Mikhailovich Gundyayev); Patriarch of Moscow and All Rus), eds. *Pravoslavnaia entsiklopediia.* 69 vols. Moscow: Pravoslavnaia entsiklopeidiia, 2000-2023.

Alferova, G. V. (Gali Vladimirovna) "Sobor Spaso-Mirozhskogo monastyria." *Arkhitekturnoe nasledstvo* 10 (1958): 3-32.

Alpatov, M. V. (Mikhail Vladimirovich) and L. A. (Leonid Antonovich) Matsulevich. *Freski tserkvi Uspeniia na Volotovom Pole.* Moscow: Iskusstvo, 1977.

Amvrosii (Ornatskii; Archbishop of Penza and Saratov), *Istoriia Rossiiskoi ierarkhii. Sobrannaia byvshim Novgorodskoi seminarii prefektom, filosofii uchitelem, sobornym ieromonakhom Amvrosiem.* 6 vols. Moscow: Sinodal'naia Tipografiia., 1807-1815.

Angold, Michael. *Church and Society in Byzantium Under the Comneni 1081-1261.* Cambridge: Cambridge University Press, 1995.

------. *The Byzantine Empire, 1025-1204: A Political History.* 2nd ed. London and New York: Longman, 1985, 1997.

Antipov, I. V. (Il'ia Vladimirovich). *Novgorodskaia arkhitektura vremeni arkhiepiskopov Evfimiia II i Iony Otenskogo.* Candidate dissertation, St. Petersburg State University, 2005.

Arendt, Hannah. *Between Past and Future: Eight Exercises in Political Thought.* New York: Penguin, 1993.

Aristov, Vadym. "'Uchenik Akima' Efrem, 'izhe ny uchashe'." *Paleoslavica* 30, 1-2 (2022): 49-60.

Astakhova, A. M. (Anna Mikhailovna). *Byliny severa.* 2 vols. Moscow and Leningrad: AN SSSR, 1938-1951.

Attwater, Donald. *The Christian Churches of the East.* 2 vols. Milwaukee: Bruce, 1961-1962.

Auxentios (Bishop of Photiki). *The Paschal Fire in Jerusalem: A Study of the Rite of the Holy Fire in the Church of the Holy Sepulchre.* 3rd ed. Berkeley CA: St John Chrysostom Press, 1999.

Avgustin (Nikitin; Archimandrite). "Pravoslavnaia missiia Velikogo Novgoroda," ZhMP No. 3 (1993): 51-60.

Baiov, Alekseĭ Konstantinovich. *Shelonskaia operatsiia Tsaria Ioanna III Vasilevich i Shelonskaia bitva v 1471 godu 14 iuliia. Voenno-Istoricheskoe Izsledovanie*. Petrograd: Tipografii Imperatorskoi Nikolaevskoi voennoi akademii, 1915.

Barsukov, N. P. (Nikolai Platonovich). *Istochniki russkoi agiografii*. St. Petersburg: Tipografii M. M. Stasulevich, 1882. Reprinted Leipzig: Zentralantiquariant DDR, 1970.

Baldi, Donato. *Enchiridion locorum sanctorum*. Jerusalem: Typis PP. Franciscanorum, 1955.

Balovnev, D. A. (Dmitrii Anatol'evich). "Prikhodskoe dukhovenstvo XV-nachala XVI veka po Novgorodskim pistsovym knigam (Chislennost' i osobennosti sostava)." *Otechestvennaia istoriia* 4 (Jul.-Aug. 2004): 131-139.

Barber, Malcolm. *The Two Cities: Europe from 1050-1320*. London and New York: Routledge, 1992.

Barker, Ernest. *Social and Political Thought in Byzantium from Justinian I to the Last Palaeologus*. Oxford: Clarendon Press, 1957.

Barley, M. W. (Maurice Willmore), ed. *European Towns: Their Archaeology and Early History*. London: Academic Press, 1977.

Barnes, Carl F., Jr. "Cathedral." In Joseph R. Strayer, ed., *Dictionary of the Middle Ages*, Vol. 3: 191-2.

Batalden, Stephen, ed. *Seeking God: The Recovery of Religious Identity in Orthodox Russia, Ukraine and Georgia*. Dekalb, IL: Northern Illinois University Press, 1993.

Begunov, Iu. K. (Iurii), and A. N. Kirpichnikov. *Kniaz' Aleksandr Nevskii i ego epokha: issledovaniia i materialy*. St. Petersburg: Dmitrii Bulianin, 1995.

Beliakova, E. V. (Elena Vladimirovna), L. V. (Liudmilla Vladimirovna) Moshkova, and T. A. (Tat'iana Anatol'evna) Oparina, *Kormchaia kniga: ot rukopisnoi traditsii k pervomu pechatnomy izdaniiu*. Moscow and St. Petersburg: Institut Istoriii RAN, Tsentr Gumanitarnykh initsiativ, 2017.

Beliav, I. D. (Ivan Dmitrievich). *Istoriia Novgoroda Velikogo ot drevnieishikh vremen do padeniia*. Vol. 2 of *Razskazy iz russkoi istorii*. Moscow: v Synodalnoi tipografii, 1866.

Bel'skii, L. P. (Leonid Petrovich). "Antonii arkhiepiskop novgorodskii i ego puteshestvie v Tsargrad." *Panteon literatury* 3, No. 3 (March 1890): 1-19.

Belobrova, O. A. (Ol'ga Andreevna). "O 'Knige Palomnike' Antoniia Novgorodskogo." *Vizantiiskie ocherki. Trudy sovetskikh uchenykh k XV mezdunarodnomu kongressu vizantinistov.* Moscow: Nauka, 1977: 225-235.

Belovinskii, L. V. (Leonid Vasil'evich) *K istorii russkoi pravoslavnoi tserkvi.* Moscow: Gosudarstvennii institut kul'tury, 1992.

Benson, Robert. *The Bishop-Elect.* Princeton, NJ: Princeton University Press, 1968.

Berger, Adolf. *Encyclopedic Dictionary of Roman Law.* Philadelphia: American Philosophical Society, 1953.

Bernadskii, V. N. (Viktor Nikolaevich). *Novgorod i Novgorodskaia Zemlia v XV veke.* Moscow and Leningrad: AN SSSR, 1961.

Bernstein, David J. *The Mystery of the Bayeux Tapestry.* London: Weidenfeld and Nicolson, 1986.

Billington, J. H. (James H.). *The Icon and the Ax: An Interpretive History of Russian Culture.* New York: Alfred A. Knopf, 1966.

Birnbaum, Henrik. *Lord Novgorod the Great: Essays on the History and Culture of a Medieval City.* Los Angeles: Slavica Publishers, 1981.

------. "Kiev, Novgorod and Moscow: Three Varieties of Urban Society in Early Slavic Territory" in Barisa Krekic, ed. *Urban Society of Eastern Europe in Premodern Times.* Berkeley and Los Angeles: University of California Press, 1987: 1-62.

-----. "When and How Was Novgorod Converted," HUS 12p13 (1988-1989). *Proceedings of the International Congress Commemorating the Millennium of Christianity in Rus-Ukraine:* 505-530.

------. *Novgorod in Focus.* Columbus, OH: Slavica Publishers, 1996.

Birnbaum, Henrik, and Michael S. Flier, eds. *Medieval Russian Culture.* Berkeley: University of California Press, 1984-1994.

Black, J. L. (Joseph Laurence). *Nicholas Karmazin and Russian Society in the Nineteenth Century: A Study in Russian Political and Historical Thought.* Toronto: University of Toronto Press, 1975.

Blomkvist, Nils, ed. *Culture Clash or Compromise: The Europeanization of the Baltic Sea Area, 1100-1409 AD* (Acta Visbyensia XI). Visby, 1998: 98-108.

Blum, Jerome. *Lord and Peasant in Russia: From the Ninth to Nineteenth Century.* New York: Atheneum Books, 1961, 1967.

Bobrov, A. G. (Aleksandr Grigorevich). "Letopisi Novgorodskie." In L. V. (Liudmilla Viktorovna) Sokolova and O. V. (Oleg Viktorovich) Tvorogov, *Literatura Drevnei Rusi. Bibiliograficheskii slovar'*. Moscow: Prosveshchenie, 1996: 105-106.

------. "Novgorodsko-pskovskie otnosheniia i Florentskaia Uniia." TODRL 50 (1996): 359-373.

------. *Novgorodskie letopisi XV veka*. St. Petersburg: Dmitrii Bulanin, 2001.

------. "Velikii kniaz Dmitrii Iur'evich Shemiaka v drevnerusskoi literature i knizhnosti." TODRL 63 (2014): 516-540.

Bocharov, G. N. (Genrikh Nikolaevich). *Prikladnoe iskusstvo Novgoroda Velikogo*. Moscow: Nauka, 1969.

Bogatova, G. A. (Galina Aleksandrovna), et al., eds. *Slovar' russkogo iazyka XI-XVII vv*. 31 vols. and supplements to date. Moscow: Nauka, 1975-2019.

Bogdanova A. D. (Anna Dmitrievna), and T. V. (Tamara Vasil'evna) Shulakova. "Pskovskie freski v starinnoi stolitse Pol'shi," in *Kirillo-Mefodievskie traditsii v Pskove: materialy chetvertykh chtenii 12 maia 2015 goda v Pskovskoi oblastnoi universal'noi nauchnoi biblioteke*. I. M. Andreeva, ed. Pskov: Pskovskaia oblastnaia universal'naia nauchnaia biblioteka, LOGOS Plius, 2015: 148-164.

Bogoslovskii, N. "Sviataia Sofiia v Velikom Novgorode." *Khristianskoe chtenie* (1877). pt. 1: 185-215.

Børtnes, Jostein. *Visions of Glory: Studies in Early Russian Hagiography*. Jostein Børtnes and Paul L. Nielsen, trans. Oslo: Solum Forlag, 1988.

Botvinnik, N. M., and E. I. Vaneeva, comps. *In memoriam: Sbornik pamiati Ia. S. Lur'e*. St. Petersburg: Antheneum-Feniks, 1997.

Brakke, David. *Athanasius and the Politics of Asceticism*. Oxford: Clarendon, 1995.

von Brandt, Ahasver, and Wilhelm Koppe. *Städtewesen und Bürgertum als geschichtliche Kräfte Gedächtnisschrift für Fritz Rörig*. Lübeck: M. Schmidt-Römhild, 1953.

Breck, J., et al., eds. *The Legacy of St. Vladimir: Byzantium, Russia, America*. Crestwood, NY: St. Vladimir's Seminary Press, 1990.

Brumfield, William Craft. *Gold in Azure: One Thousand Years of Russian Architecture*. Boston: David R. Goldine, 1983.

------. *A History of Russian Architecture*. Cambridge: Cambridge University Press, 1993.

Brundage, James A. *Medieval Canon Law*. London and New York: Longman, 1995.
Budovnits, I. U. (Isaak Urielevich). *Monastyri na Rusi i borba s nimi krest'ian v XIV – XVI vekakh: po "zhitiiam sviatykh."* Moscow: Izdatel'stvo Nauka, 1966.
Charanis, Peter. "The Monastic Properties and the State in the Byzantine Empire." DOP 4 (1948).
------. "The Monk as an Element of Byzantine Society." DOP 25 (1971): 61-84.
Cherniavsky, Michael. "The Reception of the Council of Florence in Moscow." CH 24 (1955): 347-59.
Christiansen, Eric. *The Northern Crusades: The Baltic and the Catholic Frontier 1100-1525*. Minneapolis: University of Minneapolis Press, 1980.
Conant, Kenneth John. "Novgorod, Constantinople, and Kiev in Old Russian Church Architecture." SEER 3, No. 2 (1944): 75-92.
Cooper, Henry R., Jr. *Slavic Scriptures: The Formation of the Church Slavonic Version of the Holy Bible*. Madison and Teaneck, NJ: Fairleigh Dickinson University Press; London: Associated University Presses, 2003.
Cracraft, James. *The Church Reforms of Peter the Great*. Stanford: Stanford University Press, 1971.
Cross, Samuel H., H. V. Morgilevski, and K. J. (Kenneth John) Conant. "The Earliest Medieval Churches of Kiev." Speculum 11, No. 4 (October 1936): 477-499.
Crummey, Robert O. *The Formation of Muscovy, 1304-1613*. London and New York: Longman, 1987.
Cunningham, Agnes. *The Bishop in the Church: Patristic Texts on the Role of the Episkopos* Wilmington, DE: Michael Glazier Inc., 1985.
Curta, Florin, and Paul Stephenson. *Southeastern Europe in the Middle Ages 500-1250*. Cambridge: Cambridge University Press, 2006.
Cutler, Anthony. "Garda, Källunge, and the Byzantine Tradition on Gotland." *The Art Bulletin* 51, No. 3 (Sep., 1969): 257-266.
Dal', Vladimir Ivanovich. *Poslovitsy russkogo naroda. Sbornik V. Dalia*. Moscow: Gosudarstvennoe Izdatel'stvo khudozhestvennoi literatury, 1957.
------. *Tolkovyi slovar' zhivogo velikorusskogo iazyka*. 4 vols. Moscow: Russkii Iazyk, 1978.

Daniec, Jadwiga Irena. *The Message of Faith and Symbol in European Medieval Bronze Church Doors.* Danbury, CT: Rutledge Books, 1999.

Danilova, L. V. (Liudmila Valerianovna). *Ocherki po istorii zemlevladeniia i khoziaistva v Novgorodskoi zemli v XV-XVI vv.* Moscow: AN SSSR, 1955.

Davidenko, D. G. "Moskovskii Simonovskii Monastyr'." *Pravoslavnaia entsiklopediia.* Moscow: Pravoslavnaia entsiklopediia, 2017. 47: 479.

Davies, R. W. "Revisions in Economic History: XVI. Russia in the Early Middle Ages," *The Economic History Review* 5, No. 1 (1952): 116-127.

Dejevsky, Nikolai. "The Churches of Novgorod: The Overall Pattern." in Henrik Birnbaum and Michael Flier, eds. *Medieval Russian Culture.* Berkeley and Los Angeles: University of California Press, 1984: 206-223.

------. "Novgorod: Origins of a Russian City." in M. W. Barley, ed. *European Towns: Their Archaeology and Early History.* London: Academic Press, 1977.

Delektorskii, F. I. (Fedor Ivanovich). "Kritiko-bibliograficheskii obzor drevne-russkikh skazanii o Florentiskoi unii." *Zhurnal ministerstva narodnogo proveshcheniia* 300 (July 1895): 131-184.

Dickinson, Anna. "A Marriage of Convenience? Domestic and Foreign Policy Reasons for the 1943 Soviet Church-State 'Concordat'." *Religion, State and Society* 28, No. 4, (2000): 337-346.

Dimitrii Rostovskii (Typtalo, Daniil Saavich; Metropolitan of Rostov and Iaroslavl'). *Zhitiia sviatykh po izlozheniiu sviatitelia Dimitriia Rostovskogo.* 12 vols. Barnaul: Izdatel'stvo Prp. Maksima Ispovednika, 2007.

Dimnik, Martin. *Mikhail, Prince of Chernigov and Grand Prince of Kiev, 1224-1246.* Toronto: Pontifical Institute of Medieval Studies, 1981.

Dmitriev, F. M. (Fedor Mikhailovich). *Istoriia sudebnykh instantsii v grazhdanskogo appelliatsionnogo sudoproizvodstva ot sudebnika do uchrezhdeniia o guberniiakh.* Moscow: Universitetskaia tipografiia, 1859.

Dmitriev, L. A. (Lev Aleksandrovich). *Zhitiinye povesti russkogo severa kak pamiatniki literatury XIII-XVII vv.: evoliutsiia zhanra legendarno-biograficheskikh skazanii.* Leningrad: Nauka, 1973.

Dmitriev, Lev Aleksandrovich and Dmitrii Sergeevich Likhachev, *Slovo o polku Igoreve*. Leningrad: Soviet pisatel'; Leningradskoe otdelenie, 1967.
Dmitriev, Lev Aleksandrovich, O. P. Likhacheva, and Dmitrii Sergeevich Likhachev. *Skazaniia i povesti Kulikovskoi Bitve*. Leningrad: Izdatel'stvo Nauka, Leningradskoe otdelenie, 1982.
Douglas, John A. "The Orthodox Principle of Economy and its Exercise." *Theology* 24, No. 139 (January 1932): 39-47.
Droblenkova, N. F. (Nadezhda Feoktistovna), and G. M. (Gelian Mikhailovich) Prokhorov. "Kiprian (ok. 1330-16.IX.1406) Mitropolit Kievskii i vseia Rusi." SKKDR 2.1: 464-475.
Duk, Denis Vladimirovich. "Sviataia Sofii o sedmi versek": khram v Polotske ot dereviannogo – k kamennomu." *Rodina*, No. 6 (June 2007): 63-67.
Durnovo, N. N. (Nikolai Nikolaevich). *Ierarkhiia vserossiiskoi tserkvi ot nachala khristianstva v Rossii i do nastoiashchego vremeni*. 3 vols. Moscow: E. Lissner and Iu. Romana, 1892-1898.
-----. *Legenda o zakliuchennom bese vizantiuskoi i starinnoi russkoi literature*. Moscow: Tipografiia G. Lissner i D. Sobko, 1905.
Durylin, S. N. (Sergei Nikolaevich). *Grad Sofii. Tsar'grad i Sviataia Sofiia v russkom narodnom religioznom soznanim*. Moscow: Tipografiia tovarishchestvo I.D. Sytina, 1915.
Edwards, I. E. S. (Iorwerth Eiddon Stephen), ed. *Cambridge Ancient History*. Cambridge and New York: Cambridge University Press, 1970-.
Eizo, Maiuki. "Izbranie i postavlenie Vasiliia Kaliki na Novgorodskoe vladichestvo v 1330-1331 gg." in A. A. Gippius, E. N. Nosov, and A. S. Khoroshev, eds. *Velikii Novgorod v istorii srednevekovoi Evropy; k 70-letiiu Valentina Lavrent'evicha Ianina*. Moscow: Russkie Slovari, 1999: 207-217.
Elagin, Mikhail. "Osviashchenie khrama Sviatitelia Nikolaia v Novgorode," ZhMP No. 4 (1979): 11-14.
Emeliakh, L. I. (Liubov' Isaakovna) ed. *Pravoslavie v Drevnei Rusi: sbornik nauchnykh trudov*. Leningrad: Ministerstvo Kul'tury RSFSR, Izdanie Gosudarstvennogo Muzeia Istorii Religii i Ateizma, 1989.
Etingof, O. E. (Ol'ga Evgen'evna), ed. *Tserkov' Spasa na Neredise: Ot Visantii k Rusi. K 800-letiiu pamiatnika*. Moscow. Indrik, 2005.

Evans, Helen, and William D. Wixom, eds. *The Glory of Byzantium. Art and Culture of the Middle Byzantine Era A. D. 843-1261.* New York: Metropolitan Museum of Art, Distributed by Harry N. Abrams, Inc., 1997.

Evseev, I. E. (Ivan Evseevich). "Pouchenie Luki Zhidiaty, arkhiepiskopa Novgorodskogo," in *Pamiatniki drevnerusskoi tserkovno-uchitel'noi literatury,* 1st ed. (St. Petersburg: S. Dobrodeev, Tipografiia, 1894): 7-24.

Evseeva, L. M. (Lillia Mikhailovna) and V. M. (Viktory Mikhailovich) Sorokatyi, eds. *Ikony Tveri, Novgoroda i Pskova XV-XVI vv.* Moscow: Indrik, 2000.

Fadeev, L. A. "Proiskhozhdenie i rol' sistemy gorodskikh kontsov v razbitii drevneishikh russkikh gorodov." In Valentin Lavrent'evich Ianin, ed. *Russkii gorod.* Moscow: Moskovskii Gosudarstvennyi Universitet, 1976: 17-31.

Faensen, Hubert, and Vladimir Ivanov. *Early Russian Architecture.* Mary Whittall, trans. London: Paul Elek, 1975.

Farrell, Dianne E. "Shamanic Elements in Some Early Eighteenth Century Russian Woodcuts," SR 52, No. 4 (Winter 1993): 725-744.

Fedotov, G. P. (Georgii Petrovich). *The Russian Religious Mind.* 2 vols. Cambridge, MA: Harvard University Press, 1966.

Fennell, John L. I. "The Attitude of the Josephians and the Trans-Volga Elders to the Heresy of the Judaisers." *Slavonic and East European Review* 29, No. 3 (1951): 486-509.

------. *Ivan the Great of Moscow.* London and New York: Macmillan and St. Martin's Press, 1961.

------. "The Campaign of King Magnus Eriksson Against Novgorod in 1348: An Examination of the Sources." JfGO 32 (1966): 1-9.

------. "The Tver' Uprising of 1327: A Study of the Sources." JfGO 15 (1967): 161-79.

------. *The Emergence of Moscow, 1304-1359.* London: Secker and Warburg, 1968.

-----. *The Crisis of Medieval Russia, 1200-1304.* London and New York: Longman, 1983.

------. *History of the Russian Church to 1448.* New York: Longman, 1995.

Fennell, John L. I., and Anthony Stokes. *Early Russian Literature.* Berkeley and Los Angeles: University of California Press, 1974.

Filaret (Gumilevskii, Dmitrii Grigor'evich). *Russkie sviatye, chtimye vseiu tserkov'iu ili mestno.* 12 vols. Chernihiv: v tipografiii Il'inskogo monastyria, 1861-1865.

Filatov, Viktor Vasil'evich. *Prazdnichnyi riad Sofii Novgorodskoi. Drevneishaia chast' glavnogo ikonostasa Sofiiskogo sobora.* Leningrad: Avrora, 1974.

Fine, John V. A., Jr. *The Early Medieval Balkans.* Ann Arbor: University of Michigan Press, 1983.

------. *The Late Medieval Balkans.* Ann Arbor: University of Michigan Press, 1987.

Fletcher, Roy. The Chronicle of Ireland: Then and Now." *Early Medieval Europe,* Vol. 21, No. 4 (November 2013): 422-454.

Flier, Michael S. "The Semiotics of Faith in Fifteenth Century Novgorod: An Analysis of the Quadripartite Icon." CASS 25 (1991): 121-58.

Flier, Michael S., and Daniel Rowland, eds. *Medieval Russian Culture,* Vol. 2. Berkeley: University of California Press, 1984.

Florovskii, Georgii. *Puti russkogo bogoslovia,* 3rd ed. Paris: YMCA Press, 1983.

Fomichev, S. A. (Sergei Aleksandrovich). "Poema Pushkina 'Monakh' i Povest' o puteshestvii Ioanna Novgorodskogo na bese." In Viacheslav Anatol'evich Koshalev, ed. *Novgorod v kul'ture Drevneĭ Rusi: materialy Chteniĭ po drevnerusskoĭ literature, Novgorod, 16-19 maia 1995* Novgorod: Novgorodskii Gosudarstvennii Universitet, 1995: 141-149.

Franklin, Simon. *Writing, Society, and Culture in Early Rus, 930-1300.* Cambridge: Cambridge University Press, 2000.

Franklin, Simon, and Jonathan Shepard. *The Emergence of Rus' 750-1200.* New York: Longman, 1996.

Frey, Alfred Romer. *A Dictionary of Numismatic Names: Their Official and Popular Designations.* New York: American Numismatic Society, 1917.

Froianov, I. Ia. (Igor' Iakovlevich). *Kievskaia Rus': Ocherki sotsial'no-ekonomicheskoi istorii.* Leningrad: Izdatel'stvo Leningradskogo Gosudarstvennogo Universiteta, 1974.

------. *Kievskaia Rus': Ocherki sotsial'no-politicheskoi istorii.* Leningrad: Izdatel'stvo Leningradskogo Gosudarstvennogo Universiteta, 1980.

Froianov, Igor' Iakovlevich and A. Iu. (Andrei Iur'evich) Dvornichenko. *Goroda-gosudarstva Drevnei Rusi*. Leningrad: Izdatel'stvo Leningradskogo Gosudarstvennogo Universiteta, 1988.
Fuhrman, Joseph T. "Metropolitan Cyril II (1242-1281) and the Politics of Accommodation." *JfGO* 24 (1976): 166-172.
Gabriel, Richard A. *The Mongols: The Battle of Sajo River*. Carlisle, PA: US Army War College, 1992.
Gadziatskii, S.S. (Sergei Sergeevich). "Vodskaia i Izhorskaia zemli Novgorodskogo gosudarstva." *IZ* 6 (1940) 100-148.
Gaidukov, P. G. (Petr Grigor'evich), ed., *Goroda i vesi srednevekovoi Rusi: Arkheologiia, istoriia kul'tura: K 60-letiiu Nikolaia Andreevicha Makarova*. Moscow and Vologda: Drevnosti Severa, 2015.
Germanos, Metropolitan of Il'ia. "Ē ʼEkklēsiologiko-istorikē, Kanonikē kai Nomikē schesis 'Episkopou kaí Monon,'" Holy Synod [of the Greek Church]. October 2001 (http://www.ecclesia.gr/greek/holysynod/eisigiseis/germanos.htm). Accessed February 1, 2022.
Gill, Joseph. *The Council of Florence*. Cambridge: Cambridge University Press, 1959.
Gippius, A. A. (Aleksei Alekseevich), E. N. (Evgenii Nikolaevich) Nosov, and A. S. (Aleksandr Stepanovich) Khoroshev, eds. *Velikii Novgorod v istorii srednevekovoi Evropy; k 70-letiiu Valentina Lavrent'evicha Ianina*. Moscow: Russkie Slovari, 1999.
Gippius, A. A. (Aleksei Alekseevich). "Novye dannye o ponomare Timofee-novgorodskom knizhnike serediny XIII veka." *Informatsionnyi biulleten' MAIRSK* 25 (1992): 59-86.
------. "K kharakteristike novgorodskogo vladychnogo letopisaniia XII-XIV vv." In *Velikii Novgorod v istorii srednevekovoi Evropy; k 70-letiiu Valentina Lavrent'evicha Ianina*. Moscow: Russkie Slovari, 1999: 345-364.
------. "Povelel Iurii synu svoemu Mstislavu zhenit'sia v Novgorode." *Znanie – Sila* 2-3 (1999): 30-37.
------. "Novorodskaia vladichnaia letopis' XII-XIV vv i ee avtory (Istoriia i strukturea teksta v linvisticheskom osveshchenii) I." *Lingvisticheskoe istochnikovedenie i istoriia russkogo iazyka 2004-2005* (2006): 114-251.
Giraudo, Gianfranco. "Voprošanie Kirikovo: remarques sur la vie d'une communauté paroissiale dans la rus' kiévienne du XIIe

siècle." In *Proceedings of the International Congress Commemorating the Millennium of Christianity in Rus'-Ukraine,* HUS 12-13 (1988-1989): 743-760.

Gnevushev, A. M. (Andrei Mikhailovich). *Ocherki ekonomicheskoi i sotsial'noi zhizni sel'skogo naseleniia Novgorodskoi oblasti posle prisoedineniia Novgoroda k Moskve.* Kyiv: Tipografiia Imperatorskogo universiteta sv. Vladimira, 1915.

Goehrke, C. (Carsten). "Einwohnerzahl und Bevölkerungsdichte altrussischer Städte Methodische Möglichkeiten und vorläufige Ergebnisse." FOG 18 (1973): 25-53.

------. "Gross-Novgorod und Pskov/Pleskau." In Manfred Hellmann, K. Zernack, and G. Schramm, eds. *Handbuch der Geschichte Russlands.* Vol. 1. Stuttgart: A. Hiersemann, 1981: 431-483.

Goldfrank, David M. "Burn, Baby, Burn: Popular Culture and Heresy in Late Medieval Russia." *Journal of Popular Culture* 34, No. 4 (1998): 17-32.

------. "The Judaic-Reasoning Novgorod Heretics and Some Echoes of Spain in Late Medieval Russia." RH 44, No. 4 (2017): 1-25.

------. "Satan's Playground? One Key to the Mindset of Prosvetitel'." CASS 57 (2023): 64-91.

Goldschmidt, Adolph. *Die Bronzeturen von Novgorod und Gnesen.* Magdeburg and Leningrad: Verlag des Kunstgeschichtlichen Seminars der Universität Marburg A. L., 1932.

Golubinskii, E. E. (Evgenii Evstigneevich). *Kratkii ocherk istorii pravoslavnykh tserkvei bolgarskoi, serbskoi, i rumyskoi ili moldo-valashskoi.* Moscow: v Universitetskoi tipografii Katkov, 1871.

------. "Istoriia kanonizatsii sviatykh v russkoi tserkvi." *Chteniia v [Imperatorskom] obshchestve istorii i drevnostei rossiiskikh pri Moskovskom Universitete* 1 (1903). Reprinted as *Istoriia kanonizatsii sviatykh v russkoi tserkvi.* Moscow: Universitetskaia tipografiii, 1903.

------. *Istoriia russkoi tserkvi,* 2 vols., 4 pts. Moscow: N.p. 1901-1917. Reprinted Moscow: Izdatel'stvo Spaso-Preobrazhenskogo Valaamskogo Monastyria, 1995.

Gordienko, Elissa Aleksandrovna. "Osnovnye napravleniia v khudozhestvennoi kul'ture Novgoroda XIV v." In O. I. (Ol'ga Il'inichna) Podobedova, *Drevnerusskoe iskusstvo: XIV-XV vv.* Moscow: Nauka, 1984: 156-167.

------. *Vladychnaia palata Novgorodskogo Kremlia*. Leningrad: Lenizdat, 1991.
Gormin, Vladimir, and Liudmila Yarosh, et al. *Novgorod. Art Treasures and Architectural Monuments, 11th –18th Century*. Leningrad: Avrora, 1984.
Gormina, N. V. (Natal'ia Vladimirovna). *Vladychnaia Palata: Iuvelirnoe iskusstvo XI-XIX vekov/Palais a Facette de Monseigneur: orfevrerie XI-XIX S*. Novgorod: Novgorodskii Gosudarstvennyi Ob'edinennyi Muzei-Zapovednik, GPP imeni Ivana Fedorova, 1993.
Gornostaev, A. M. (Aleksei Mikhailovich). "Plan Novgoroda na ikone Znameniia Bozhiei Materi v Novgorodskom Znamenskom Sobore." *Izvestiia Imperatorskogo Arkheologicheskogo obshchestva* (1865): 145-150.
Gorskii, A. A. (Anton Anatol'evich). *"Slovo o polku Igoreve" i "Zadonshchina": istochnikovedcheskie i istoriko-kul'turnye problemy*. Moscow: Rossiiskaia akademiia nauk, Institut rossiiskoi istorii, 1992.
Gosudarstvennaia biblioteka SSSR imeni V.I. Lenina. Otdel rukopisei. *Zapiski Otdela rukopisei Vsesoiuznaia biblioteka im. V.I. Lenina*. 51 vols. Moscow: Gosudarstvennoe sotsial'no-ekonomicheskoe izdatel'stvo, 1938-2000.
Grabar', I. E. (Igor' Emmanuilovich). *O russkoi arkhitekture. Issledovaniia. Okhrana pamiatnikov* Moscow: Nauka, 1969.
Grachev, A. Iu. (Artem Iur'evich). "K voprosu o roli i meste dukhovenstva v voennoi organizatsii drevnei Rusi." *Pskovskii voenno-istoricheskii vestnik* (2015) No. 1: 43-46.
Granberg, Jonas. "The Political and Administrative Structure of Novgorod." In Nils Blomkvist, ed. *Culture Clash or Compromise: The Europeanization of the Baltic Sea Area, 1100-1409 AD* (Acta Visbyensia XI). Visby, 1998: 98-108.
------. "The Sovet Gospod of Novgorod, in Russian and German Sources," JfGO 47 (1998): 396-401.
------. *Veche in the Chronicles of Medieval Rus: A Study of Functions and Terminology*. Göteborg: Fakulteit Gescheidenis Universitet von Göteborg, 2004. [Veche v drevnerusskikh pis'mennykh istochikakh: funktsiia i terminologia. In Timofei Guimon and E. A. Mel'nikova, *Politicheskie instituty Drevnei Rusi. Part of the Series*

Drevneishie gosudarstva Vostochnoi Evropy. Materialy i issledovaniia, 2004. Moscow: Vostochnaia Literatura, 2006.]

Granstrem, E. E. (Evgennia Eduardovna). *Opisanie russkikh i slavianskikh pergamennykh rukopisei: rukopisi russkie, bolgarskie, moldovlakhiivksii, serbskie.* Leningrad: Tip. Gosudarstvennaia publichnoi biblioteki, 1953.

Green, Vivian H. H., "Elections, Church." In Joseph R. Strayer, ed., *Dictionary of the Middle Ages.* Vol. 4: 421-425.

Grekov, B. D. (Boris Dmitrievich). *Novgorodskii dom sviatoi Sofii: opyt izucheniia organizatsii i vnutrennikh otnoshenii krupnoi tserkovnoi votchiny, chast' I.* St. Petersburg: M. Aleksandrova, 1914. Reprinted in *Izbrannye trudy*, vol. 4: 7-436.

------. *Kievskaia Rus'.* Moscow: Gosudarstvennoe Izdatel'stvo politicheskoi literatury, 1953.

------. "Ocherki po istorii khoziaistva Novgorodskogo Sofiiskogo Doma XVI-XVII vv." In *Izbrannye trudy*, vol. 3: 40-191.

------. *Izbrannye trudy.* 4 vols. Moscow: AN SSSR, 1957-1960.

Grekov, B. D. (Boris Dmitrievich), L. V. (Lev Vladimirovich) Cherepnin, and V. T. (Vladimir Terent'evich) Pashuto, eds. *Ocherki istorii SSSR. Period feodalizma, IX-XV vv.* Part I. Moscow: AN SSSR, 1953.

Grigor'ev, V. V. (Vasilii Vasil'evich). *O dostovernosti iarlykov, dannykh khanami Zolotoi ordy russkomu dukhovenstvu: istoriko-filologicheskoe issledovanie.* Moscow: Universitetskaya tipograpfiia, 1842.

Gudzii, N. K. (Nikolai Kallinikovich). *Khrestomatiia po drevnei russkoi literatury.* Moscow: AN SSSR, 1955.

Guimon (also spelled Gimon) T. V. (Timofei Valentinovich), and A. A. (Aleksei Alekseevich) Gippius. "Novye dannye po istorii teksta Novgorodskoi pervoi letopisi." *Novgorodskii istoriicheskii sbornik* 7 No. 17 (1999): 18-47.

Guimon (also spelled Gimon), Timofei, and E. A. Mel'nikova. *Politicheskie instituty Drevnei Rusi.* Part of the series *Drevneishie gosudarstva Vostochnoi Evropy. Materialy i issledovaniia. 2004.* Moscow: Vostochnaia literatura, 2006.

Guimon (also spelled Gimon), Timofei V. *Historical Writing of Early Rus (c. 1000-c. 1400) in a Comparative Perspective.* Leiden and Boston: Brill, 2021.

Gurevich, A. Ia. (Aron Iakovlevich). "Zapadnoevropeiskie videniia potustoronnego mira i 'realizm' srednikh vekov." In *Trudy po znakovym sistemam VIII k 70-letiiu akademika. Dmitriia Sergeevicha Likhacheva*. Tartu, Estonia: Tartuskii gosudarstvennyi universitet, 1977: 3-27.

Gusev, P. I. (Petr Ivanovich). *Novgorod XVI veka po izobrazhenie na khutynskoi ikone "Videnie ponomaria Tarasiia"*. St. Petersburg: Tipografiia A. P. Lopukhina, 1900.

------. *Novgorodskaia ikona sv. Ioanna (Ilii) arkhiepiskopa v deianiiakh i chudesakh*. St. Petersburg. A. P. Lopukhina, 1903.

------. *Novgorodskii Detinets po izobrazheniiu na ikone Mikhailovskoi tserkvi*. St. Petersburg: Sinodal'naia tipografiia, 1913.

Halecki, Oskar. *From Florence to Brest 1439-1596*. 1st ed. Rome: Sacrum Poloniae Millennium, 1958. Published by Fordham University Press. 2nd ed. Hamden, CT: Archon Books, 1968.

Halperin, Charles J. "Judaizers and the Image of the Jew in Medieval Russia: A Polemic Revisited and a Question Posed." *CASS* 9, No. 2 (1975): 141-155.

------. "The Ideology of Silence: Prejudice and Pragmatism on the Medieval Religious Frontier," *Comparative Studies in Society and History* 26, No. 3 (July 1984): 442-466.

------. *Russia and the Golden Horde: The Mongol Impact on Medieval Russian History*. Bloomington, IN: Indiana University Press, 1985.

------. "The East Slavic Response to the Mongol Conquest," *Archivum Eurasiae Medii Aevi* 10 (1998-1999): 98-117.

------. "Novgorod and the Novgorodian Land," *CMR*, 40, 3 (July-September 1999): 345-363.

Hamilton, George Heard. *The Art and Architecture of Russia*, 3rd Ed. New Haven: Yale University Press, 2002.

Hamm, Michael F., ed. *The City in Russian History*. Lexington, KY: University Press of Kentucky, 1976.

Haney, Jack V. *The Complete Russian Folktale*. Armonk, NY: M. E. Sharpe, 1999.

Hansen, Mogens Herman. *A Comparative Study of Thirty City-State Cultures: An Investigation*. Copenhagen: Konelige Danske Videnskabeunes Selskab, 2000.

Heintschel, Donald. *The Mediaeval Concept of an Ecclesiastical Office*. Washington, DC: Catholic University of America, 1956 *Canon Law Studies* 363.

Helle, Knut, E. I. Kouri, and Torkel Jansson. *The Cambridge History of Scandinavia*. Vol. 1. Cambridge University Press, 2003.
Hellie, Richard. E. "Rewriting Pre-Mongol Russian History Once Again," RH 16, No. 1 (1989): 67-76.
Hellmann, Manfred, K. Zernack, and G. Schramm, eds. *Handbuch der Geschichte Russlands*. Stuttgart: A. Hiersemann, 1976-1980.
Herman, Emil. "The Secular Clergy" Chapter 23. In Joan M. Hussey, ed. *The Cambridge Medieval History* Vol. 4. *The Byzantine Empire*, part 2: *Government, Church, and Civilization* Cambridge: Cambridge University Press, 1967.
Hirsch, Siegfried, Hermann Pabst, and Harry Bresslau, eds. *Jahrbücher des Deutschen Reichs unter Heinrich II*. 3 vols. Berlin: Duncker und Humblot, 1862-1875.
von Hurter, Friedrich. *Geschichte Papst Innocenz des Dritten und seiner Zeitgenossen*, 3rd ed., 4 vols. Hamburg: Friedrich Perthes, 1835-1844.
Hussey, Joan M. *The Orthodox Church in the Byzantine Empire*. Oxford: Clarendon Press, 1986.
-----. Ed. *The Cambridge Medieval History*, Vol. 4, *The Byzantine Empire*, part 2: *Government, Church, and Civilization*. Cambridge: Cambridge University Press, 1967.
Iablonskii, V. M. (Vasilii Mikhailovich). *Pakhomii Serb i ego agiograficheskie pisaniia. Biograficheskii i bibliograficheski-literaturnyi ocherk*. St. Petersburg: Sinodal'naia tipografiia, 1908.
Iakunina, L. I. (Lidiia Ivanovna). "Tkani iz raskopok v Sofiiskom novgorodskom sobore," *Kratkie soobshcheniia instituta istorii material'noi kul'tury* 24 (1949): 105-107.
Ianin, V. L. (Valentin Lavrentevich). "Iz istorii vysshikh gosudarstvennykh dolzhnostey v Novgorode," in V. I. (Viktor Ivanovich) Shunkov, ed. *Problemy obshchestvnno-politicheskoi istorii Rossii i slavianskikh stran: sbornik stateĭ k 70-letiiu akademika M.N. Tikhomirova* (Moscow: Izdatel'stvo vostochnoi literatury, 1963): 118-127.
------. "Problemy sotsial'noi organizatsii novgorodskoi respubliki," *Istoriia SSSR* 1 (1970): 44-54.
------. *Aktovye pechati drevnei Rusi X-XV vv.* vols. 1 and 2. Moscow: Nauka, 1970.
------, ed. *Russkii gorod*. Moscow: Izdatel'stvo Moskovskogo Gosudarstvennogo Universiteta, 1976.

------. *Ocherki kompleksnogo istochnikovedeniia: Srednevekovyi Novgorod*. Moscow: Vysshaia shkola, 1977.

------. "Pechat' novgorodskogo episkopa Ioanna Pop'iana." *Vospomagatel'nye istoricheskie distsipliny* 9 (1978): 47-56.

------. *Nekropol' Novgorodskogo Sofiiskogo sobora: tserkovnaia traditsiia i istoricheskaia kritika*. Moscow: Nauka, 1988.

------. "The Archaeology of Novgorod." *Scientific American* 262, No.3 (1990): 84-91.

------. *Novgorodskie akty XII-XV vv. Khronologicheskii komenmentarii*. Moscow: Nauka, 1991.

------. "'Bolotovskii' Dogovor: O vzaimootnosheniakh Novgoroda i Pskova v XII-XV vv." *Otechestvennaia istoriia* No. 6 (1992): 3-14.

------. *Novgorodskie posadniki*. 2nd ed. Moscow: Iazyki slavianskoi kul'tury, 2003.

------, ed. *Stolichnye i periferiinye goroda Rusi i Rossii v srednie veka i v rannee novoe vremia: doklady tretei nauchnoi konferentsii* (Murom, 17-20 maia 2000 g.) Moscow: Drevnekhranilishche, 2003.

------. "Medieval Novgorod." Chapter 8 in Maurine Perrie, ed. *From Early Rus' to 1689*, Volume 1 of *The Cambridge History of Russia* 3 vols. Cambridge and New York: Cambridge University Press, 2006.

Ianin, V. L. (Valentin Lavrent'evich), and P. G. (Petr Grigor'evich) Gaidukov, *Aktovye pechati drevnei Rusi X-XV vv*. Vol. 3. Moscow: Nauka, 1998.

------. "Drevnerusskie vislye pechati zaregistrirovannye v 1998-1999 gg." *Novgorod i Novgorodskaia zemlia* 14 (2000): 283-314.

Ianin, V. L. (Valentin Lavrent'evich), B. A. (Boris Aleksandrovich) Kolchin, and A. S. (Aleksandr Stepanovich) Khoroshev. *Usad'ba novgorodskogo khudozhnika XII v*. Moscow: Nauka, 1981.

Ianin, V. L. (Valentin Lavrent'evich), E. N. Nosov, et al. *The Archaeology of Novgorod, Russia: Recent Results from the Town and its Hinterland*. Mark A. Brisbane, ed. Katherine Judelson, trans. Lincoln, England: The Society for Medieval Archaeology Monograph Series, 13, 1992.

Ianin, V. L. (Valentin Lavrentevich), and A. A. (Andrei Anatol'evich) Zalizniak. "Novgorodskii kodeks pervoi chetverti XI v. – drevneishaia kniga Rusi." *Voprosy iazykoznaniia* No. 5, (2001): 3-25.

------. "Novgorodskii Psaltyr nachala XI veka – drevneishaia kniga Rusi," *Vestnik Rossiskoi akademii nauk* 71, No. 3 (2001): 202-209.
Institut russkoi literatury (Pushkinskii dom). *Istoriia russkoi literatury*. 10 vols. Moscow: AN SSSR, 1941-1956.
Iushkov, S. V. (Serafim Vladimirovich). *Ocherki po istorii feodalisma v Kievskoi Rusi*. Moscow and Leningrad: AN SSSR, 1939. Reprinted The Hague: Mouton, 1969.
------. *Obshchestvenno-politicheskii stroi i pravo Kievskogo gosudarstva*. Moscow: Izdatel'stvo iuridicheskoi literatury, 1949. Reprinted The Hague: Mouton, 1969.
Jackson, Tatiana N. "'Strana gorodov' i ee stolitsa: Novgorod v kartine mira srednevekovykh skandinavov"/"Garðaríki and Its Capital: Novgorod on the Mental Map of Medieval Scandinavians," *Slovene* 4 (1) (January 2015): 170-179.
Jakobson, Roman and Marc Szeftel, "The Vseslav Epos," in Roman Jakobson and Ernest J. Simmons, eds., *Russian Epic Studies*. *Memoirs of the American Folklore Society* 42 (Philadelphia: American Folklore Society, 1949): 13-86.
Johansen, Paul. "Novgorod und die Hanse." In Ahasver von Brandt and Wilhelm Koppe. *Städtewesen und Bürgertum als geschichtliche Kräfte Gedächtnisschrift für Fritz Rörig*. Lübeck: M. Schmidt-Römhild, 1953: 121-152.
Johnson, Edgar Nathaniel. *The Secular Activities of the German Episcopate 919-1024*. Chicago: the University of Chicago Libraries. Reprinted Lincoln, NE: The University of Nebraska Studies, vols. XXX-XXXI, 1930-1931.
Kähler, Heinz. *Hagia Sophia*. Ellyn Childs, trans. New York: Praeger, 1967.
Kaiser, Daniel H. *The Growth of the Law in Medieval Russia*. Princeton: Princeton University Press, 1980.
Kalinnikov, V. *Mitropolity i episkopy pri Sv. Vladimire*. Kyiv: Tipografiia G. T. Korchak-Novitskogo, 1888.
Karamzin, Nicholai Mikhailovich. *Zapiski o drevnei i novoi Rossii*. Richard Pipes, ed. Cambridge, MA: Harvard University Press, 1959.
------. *Istoriia gosudarstva rossiiskogo*. 12 vols. St. Petersburg: Izdanie Evg. Evdokimova, 1892. Reprinted The Hague and Paris: Mouton, 1969.

Karger, Mikhail. *Novgorod Velikii: Arkhitekturnye pamiatniki*. Leningrad and Moscow: Iskusstvo, 1966.
Kartashev, A. V. (Anton Vladimirovich). *Ocherki po istorii russkoi tserkvi*. 2 vols. Paris: YMCA Press, 1959. Reprinted Moscow: Nauka, 1991.
Kazakova, N. A. (Natalia Aleksandrovna), and Ia. S. (Iakov Solomonovich) Lur'e, *Antifeodal'nye ereticheskie dvizheniia na Rusi XIV-nachala XVI veka*. Moscow: AN SSSR, 1955.
Kazhdan, Alexander P., et al., eds. *The Oxford Dictionary of Byzantium*. 3 vols. New York and Oxford: Oxford University Press, 1991.
Kerner, Robert J. *The Urge to the Sea: The Course of Russian History - The Role of Rivers, Portages, Ostrogs, Monasteries, and Furs*. Berkeley and Los Angeles: University of California Press, 1946.
Khlebnikov, N. I. (Nikolai Ivanovich). *O vliianii obshchestva na organizatsiiu gosudarstva v tsarskii period russkoi istorii*. St. Petersburg: Tipografii A. M. Kotomina, 1869.
Khoroshev, A. S. (Aleksandr Stepanovich). *Politicheskaia istoriia russkoi kanonizatsii XI-XVI vv*. Moscow: Izdatel'stvo Moskovskogo universiteta 1986.
------. *Tserkov' v sotsial'no-politicheskoi sisteme Novgorodskoi feodal'noi respubliki*. Moscow: Izdatel'stvo Moskovskogo Gosudarstvennogo Universiteta, 1989.
Khoroshkevich, A. L. (Anna Leonidovna). *Torgovlia velikogo Novgoroda s Pribaltikoi i zapadnoi Evropoi v XIV –XV vekakh*. Moscow: AN SSSR, 1963.
Kiprian, Metropolitan of Kyiv and All Rus'. "Zhitie i zhizn' i malo ispovedanie ot chiudes izhe vo sviatykh otsa nashego Petra mitropolita arkhiepiskopa Kievskogo i vseia Rusi. Spisano Kiprianom mitropolitom smirenym Kiev'skym i vseia Rusi." *Velikie Minei Chet'i sobrannye Vserossiyskim mitropolitom Makariem*, fasc. 12. Moscow: Arkheograficheksaia kommissiia, 1909.
Kivelson, Valerie A., Karen Petrone, Nancy Kollmann, and Michael Flier, eds., *The New Muscovite Cultural History: A Collection in Honor of Daniel B. Rowland*. Bloomington, IN: Slavica, 2009.
Klameth, Gustav. *Das Karsamstagsfeuerwunder der heiligen Grabeskirche*. Wien: Mayer and Comp., 1913.
Kleimenov, V. I. (Vitalii Igorevich) and V. I. (Viacheslav) Tikhokin.

"'Boevye popy' Severo-Zapada Rusi v XIII-XIV vv kak fenomen pogranich'ia." Paper presented at the conference Usable Pasts. Sbornik materialov VII mezhdunarodnoi konferenctsii. Natsional'nyi Issledovatel'skii Universitet Vyshaia Shkola Ekonomiki, St. Petersburg, 15-16 April 2022.

Klibanov, A. I. (Aleksandr Il'ich). *Reformatsionye dvizhenii v Rossii v XIV – pervoi polovine XVI vv.* Moscow: Nauka, 1960.

Klibanov, A. I. (Aleksandr Il'ich), et al., eds. *Tserkov' obshchestvo i gosudardstvo v feodal'noi Rossii.* Moscow: Nauka, 1990.

Kliuchevskii, V. O. (Vasilii Osipovich). *Drevnerusskie zhitiia sviatykh kak istoricheskii istochnik.* Moscow: Izdatel'stvo K. Soldatenkova, 1871. Reprinted Paris and The Hague: Mouton, 1968.

------. *Sochineniia v vos'mi tomakh.* 8 vols. Moscow: Gosudarstvennoe izdatel'stvo politicheskoi literatury, 1956-1959).

------. *Boiarskaia Duma Drevnei Rusi. Dobrye liudi Drevnei Rusi.* Moscow: Ladomir, 1994.

------. *Russkaia Istoriia: polnyi kurs lektsii v trekh knigakh.* Rostov-na-Donu: Feniks, 2000.

Kloss, B. M. (Boris Mikhailovich) "Letopis' Novgorodskaia pervaia." SKKDR, 1:245-247.

------. *Izbrannye trudy.* Vol. 1. *Zhitie Sergiia Radonezhskogo.* Moscow: Iazyki russkoi kul'tury, 1998.

------. "Vtoroe predislovie k izdaniiu 2000 goda." *Novgorodskaia chetvertaia letopis'.* Moscow: Iazyki russkoi kul'tury, 2000.

Kloss, B. M. (Boris Mikhailovich) and Ia. S. (Iakov Solomonovich) Lur'e. "Russkie letopisi XI-XV vv." *Metodicheskie rekomendatsii po opisaniiu slaviano-russkikh rukopisei dlia Svodnogo kataloga rukopisei, khraiashchikhsia v SSSSR,* Vol. 2. (1976).

Kobets, Svitlana. "The Russian Paradigm of *Jurodstvo* and its Genesis in Novgorod," *Russian Literature* 48 (2000): 378-383.

Kochin, G. E. (Georgii Evgen'evich). *Pamiatniki istorii Velikogo Novgoroda i Pskova.* Leningrad and Moscow: Gosudarstvennoe Sotsial'no-ekonomicheskoe izdatel'stvo. Leningradskoe otdelenie, 1935.

Kochkurkina, S. I. (Svetlana Ivanovna), A. M. (Andrei Mikhailovich) Spiridonov, and T. N. (Tatiana Nikolaevna) Jackson, *Pis'mennye izvestiia o karelakh.* Petrozavodsk: "Karelia," 1990.

Kolchin, B. A. (Boris Aleksandrovich) and V. L. (Valentin Lavrent'evich) Ianin, "Arkheologii Novgorod 50 let," *Novgorodskii sbornik.* Moscow: Nauk, 1982: 3-137.

Kollmann, Jack E., Jr. *The Moscow Stoglav ("Hundred Chapters") Church Council of 1551.* Ph.D. Dissertation, University of Michigan, 1978.

------. "The Stoglav and Parish Priests." RH 7, Nos. 1-2 (1980): 65-91.

Komech, A. I. (Aleksei Il'ich). "Rol' predelov v formirovanie obshchei kompozitsii Sofiiskogo sobora v Novgorode," in G. K. Vagner, D. S. Likhachev, and P. A. Rappoport, *Srednevekovaia Rus'.* Moscow: Nauka, 1976: 147-150.

Kopanev, A. I. (Aleksandr Il'ich.). "K voprosu o structure zemlevladeniia na Dvine v XV-XVI vekakh." *Voprosy agrarnoi istorii* 1 (1968): 442-462.

Koshalev, Viacheslav Anatolevich, ed. *Novgorod v kul'ture Drevneĭ Rusi: materialy Chteniĭ po drevnerusskoĭ literature, Novgorod, 16-19 maia 1995.* Novgorod: Novgorodskii Gosudarstvennii Universitet, 1995.

Kostochkin, V. V. (Vladimir Vladimirovich). *Russkoe oboronnoe zodchestvo kontsa XIII-nachala XVI vekov.* Moscow: Nauka, 1962.

Kovalev, R. K. (Roman Konstantinovich). "Novgorodskie derevniannye birki: Obshchie nabliudeniia." *Rossiiskaia arkheologiia* 1 (2002): 38-50.

------. *The Infrastructure of the Novgorodian Fur Trade in the Pre-Mongol Era (CA. 900-CA. 1240).* Ph. D. dissertation. University of Minnesota, 2003.

Kovalev, R. K. (Roman Konstantinovich), and Thomas S. Noonan. "The 'Furry Forties:' Packaging Pelts in Medieval Northern Europe," *States, Societies, Cultures: East and West [Essays in Honor of Jaroslav Pelenski]* (New York, 2004), 653-682.

Krause, Hans Joakim, and Ernst Schubert. *Die Bronzetür der Sophienkathedrale in Nowgorod.* Leipzig: Insel-Verlag, 1968.

Krekic, Barisa, ed. *Urban Society of Eastern Europe in Premodern Times*: Berkeley and Los Angeles: University of California Press, 1987.

Krustalev, D. G. (Denis Grigor'evich). *Severnye krestonostsy Rus' v borb'e za sfery vlianiia v Vostochnoi Pribaltike XII-XIII vv.* 2 vols. St. Petersburg: Evrasia, 2009.

Kuchkin, V. A. (Vasilii Andreevich). "Skazanie o smerti mitropolita Petra." TODRL 18: 59-79.

Kul'pinova, T. N. (Tatiana Nikolaevna), N. N. (Nina Naumovna) Zherve, and Ia. A. Strakhova, eds. *Gde Sviataia Sofiia, tam i Novgorod*. St. Petersburg: Sofiia Publishers, 1997.
Kuprianov, I. K. (Ivan Kuprianovich). *Obozrenie pergamentnykh [pergamennykh] rukopisei Novgorodskoi Sofiiskoi Biblioteki*. St. Petersburg: Tip. Imperatorskogo Akademii Nauk, 1857.
Kuzmina, Olga Vladimirovna. *Respublika Sviatoi Sofii*. Moscow: Veche, 2008.
Kyshnerevich, Aleksandr. "Khram ili tsitadel'? Istoricheskie portrety Sofiiskogo sobora v Polotske: mif i real'nost'." *Rodina* 6 (2007): 76-80.
Kushnir, Il'ia Iosifovich. *Arkhitektura Novgoroda*. Leningrad: Lenizdat, 1982.
Labunka, Miroslav. "Religious Centers and Their Missions to Kievan Rus': From Olga to Volodimir." *Proceedings of the International Congress Commemorating the Millennium of Christianity in Rus'-Ukraine*, HUS 12-13 (1988-1989): 159-193.
------. *The Legend of the White Cowl: The Study of its "Prologue" and "Epilogue."* Munich: Ukrainische freie Universität, 1998.
Langer, Lawrence N. "The Posadnichestvo of Pskov: Some Aspects of Urban Administration in Medieval Russia." *SR* 43, No.1 (1984): 46-62.
Laurent. V. (Vitalien). *Le corpus de sceaux de l'Empire byzantin*. 5 vols. Paris: Editions du centre national de la recherche scientifique, 1963-1975.
Lavretskii, Gennadii. "Sofiia – Premudrost' Polotskaia." *Rodina* 6 (2007): 81-82.
Lazarev, V. N. (Viktor Nikitich). *Iskusstvo Novgoroda*. Moscow and Leningrad: Gosudarstvennoe Izdatel'stvo Iskusstvo, 1947.
------. *Novgorodskaia ikonopis'/ Novgorodian Icon-painting*. Moscow: Iskusstvo, 1969.
------. *Drevnerusskie mozaiki i freski*. Moscow: Iskusstvo, 1971.
------. *Stranitsy istorii novgorodskoi zhivopisi*. Moscow: Iskusstvo, 1977.
------. "Freski Sofii Kievskoi." In *Vizantiiskoe i drevnerusskoe iskusstvo*. Moscow: Iskusstvo, 1978.
------. *Stranitsy istorii novgorodskoi zhivopisi: dvustoronnie tabletki iz sobora sv. Sofii v Novgorode*. Moscow: Iskusstvo, 1983.

Lazarev, Viktor Nikitich, and Gerol'd Ivanovich Vzdornov. *The Russian Icon*. Nancy Darby, ed., Collette Joly Dees, trans. Collegeville, MN: Liturgical Press, 1997.
Leader-Temple, John and Giuseppe Marcotti. *Sir John Hawkwood (L'Acuto): the Story of a Condtierre*. London: T. F. Unwin, printed by G. Barbera, 1889.
Lenhoff, Gail. "Kniga Palomnik: A Study in Old Russian Rhetoric." *Scando-Slavica* 23 (1977): 39-61.
------. "Novgorod's Znamenie Legend in Moscow's Steppennaia Kniga." *Moskovskaia Rus': Spetsificheskie cherty razvitiia*. Budapest: Lorand Eotvos University Press, 2004: 178-186.
Lenhoff, Gail, and Janet Martin. "Marfa Boretskaia, Posadnitsa of Novgorod: A Reconsideration of Her Legend and Her Life." SR 59, No.2 (2000): 343-368.
Lermontov, M. Iu. (Mikhail Iur'evich). *Polnoe sobranie stikhotvorenii v dvukh tomakh*. 2 vols. Leningrad: Sovetskii pistatel, 1989.
Lesnikov, M. P. (Mikhail P.). "Torgovye snosheniia velikogo Novgoroda s tevtonskim ordenom v kontse XIV i nachale XV veka." IZ 39 (1952): 259-278.
Leuschner, Jörg. *Novgorod: Untersuchungen zu einigen Fragen seiner Verfassungs- und Bevölkerungsstruktur*. Berlin: Osteuropastudien der Hochschulen des Landes Hessen. Reihe I. Giessener Abhandlungen zur Agrar- und Wirtschaftforschung des Europäischen Ostens 117, 1980.
Levin, Eve. "Novgorod Birchbark Documents: The Evidence for Literacy in Medieval Russia," in Charles L. Redmand, ed. *Medieval Archaeology. Papers of the Seventeenth Annual conference of the Center for Medieval and Early Renaissance Studies*. Binghamton: State University of New York, 1989.
------. "Dvoeverie and Popular Religion." In Stephen Batalden, ed. *Seeking God: The Recovery of Religious Identity in Orthodox Russia, Ukraine, and Georgia*. Dekalb, IL: Northern Illinois University Press, 1993.
Likhachev, D. S. (Dmitrii Sergeevich). *Russkie letopisi i ikh kul'turno-istoricheskoe znachenie*. Moscow and Leningrad: AN SSSR, 1947.
------. "'Sofiiskii vremennik'... i novgorodskii politicheskii pereverot 1136 g." IZ 25 (1947): 240-265.

Likhachev, D. S. (Dmitrii Sergeevich), ed. *Istoriia russkoi literatury X-XVII vekov: uchebnoe posobie.* Moscow: Prosveschenie, 1980.

------. *Slovar' knizhnikov i knizhnosti drevnei Rusi.* 3 vols. in 5 Pts. Leningrad and St. Petersburg: Nauk, 1987-1993.

Likhachev, D. S. (Dmitrii Sergeevich), V. (Vera K.) Laurina, and V.A. (Vasilii Alekseevich) Pushkarev. *Novgorodskaia ikona XII-XVII vekov.* Leningrad: Avrora, 1983.

Likhachev, N. P. (Nikolai Petrovich). *Materialy dlia istorii vizantiiskoi i russkoi sfragistiki.* Leningrad: Nauka, 1928.

Lind, John H. "Sources and Pseudo Sources on the Founding of the Valamo Monastery," *Scandinavian Journal of History* 11 No. 2 (1986): 115-133.

------. "Fortaelling om Valamoklosteret. En nufunden kilde til klosterets aeldste historie," *Historisk Tidskrift för Finland* 1 (1992), 1-30.

------. "Consequences of the Baltic Crusades in Target Areas: The Case of Karelia." In Alan V. Murray, ed. *Crusade and Conversion on the Baltic Frontier, 1150 – 1500.* Aldershot, UK, and Burlington, VT: Ashgate, 2001.

Logachev, K. I. "Iubilei mitropolita Aleksiia." ZhMP No. 8 (1989): 11-13.

Logvin, G. N. (Grigorii Nikonovich). *Sofiia Kievskaia Gosudarstvennyi arkhitektornyi-istoricheskii zapovednik.* Kyiv: Mistetstvo, 1971.

Lot, Ferdinand. *L'art militaire et les armées au Moyen Age en Europe et dans le Proche Orient.* 2 vols. Paris: Payot, 1946.

Loukomski (Lukomskii), G. K. (Georgii Kreskentievich). *L'Architecture religieuse russe du XIe siècle au XVIIe siècle.* Paris: Librairie Ernest Leroux, 1929.

Lukin, Pavel V. "The Veche and the 'Council of Lords' in Medieval Novgorod: Hanseatic and Russian Data." RH 41, No. 4 (2014): 458-503.

------. "Urban Community and Consensus: Brotherhood and Communalism in Medieval Novgorod." *Imagined Communities in the Baltic Rim: From the Eleventh to the Fifteenth Centuries.* Wojtek Jezierski, Lars Hermanson, and Matti Peikola, eds. Amsterdam: Amsterdam Univrsity Press, 2016.

------. "German Merchants in Novgorod: Hospitality and Hostility, Twelfth–Fifteenth Centuries," Chapter 5 in Sari Nauman, Wojtek Jezierski, Christina Reimann, and Leif Runefelt, eds., *Baltic Hospitality from the Middle Ages to the Twentieth Century*. Cham, Switzerland: Palgrave Macmillan, 2022: 117-142.

Lupinin, Nickolas, Donald Ostrowski, and Jennifer B. Spock, eds., *Tapestry of Russian Christianity: Studies in History and Culture*. Columbus, OH: Department of Slavic and East European Languages and Cultures and the Resource Center for Medieval Slavic Studies, The Ohio State University, 2016.

Lur'e, Ia. S. (Iakov Solomonovich). *Ideologicheskaia bor'ba v russkoi publitsistike kontsa XV – nachala XVI veka*. Moscow and Leningrad: AN SSSR, 1960.

------. "The Problem of Source Criticism (With Reference to Medieval Russian Documents)," SR 27, No. 1. (Mar., 1968): 1-22.

------. *Obshcherusskie letopisi XIV-XV vv.* Leningrad: Nauka, 1976.

------. "Matfei Mikhailov." SKKDR 1:105.

------. Dve istorii Rusi XV veka: rannie i pozdnie, nezavisimye i ofitsial'nye letopisi ob obrazovanii Moskovskogo gosudarstva. St. Petersburg: D. Bulanin, 1994.

Macauley-Jackson, Samuel, and Lefferts Augustine Loetscher, eds. *The New Schaff-Herzog Encyclopedia of Religious Knowledge; Embracing Biblical, Historical, Doctrinal, and Practical Theology, and Biblical, Theological, and Ecclesiastical Biography from the Earliest Times to the Present Day*. 13 vols. Grand Rapids: Baker Book House, 1949-1951.

Mainstone, Rowland J. *Hagia Sophia: Architecture, Structure, and Liturgy of Justinian's Great Church*. New York: Thames and Hudson, 1988.

Majeska, George P. "Politics and Hierarchy in the Early Rus' Church: Antonii, A 13th-Century Archbishop of Novgorod." In Nickolas Lupinin, Donald Ostrowski, and Jennifer B. Spock, eds., *Tapestry of Russian Christianity: Studies in History and Culture*. Columbus, OH: Department of Slavic and East European Languages and Cultures and the Resource Center for Medieval Slavic Studies, The Ohio State University, 2016: 23-38.

Makarievskaia chteniia. Russkaia kul'tura XVI veka – epoka Mitropolita Makariia. Materialy X rossiiskoi nauchnoi konferentsii posviashchenoi pamiati sviatitelia Makariia. Vypusk 10. Mozhaisk: Terra, 2003.

Makarii (Bulgakov, Mikhail Petrovich; Metropolitan of Moscow and Kolomna). *Istoriia russkoi tserkvi.* 5 vols. St. Petersburg: Tipografiia R. Golike, 1877-1889 Reprint Moscow: Izdatel'stvo Spaso-Preobrezhenskogo Valaamskogo Monastyria, 1995-1997.

Makarii, (Mirolibov, Nikolai Kirillovich; Archbishop of the Don and Novocherkass). *Opisanie Novgorodskogo arkhiereiskogo doma.* St. Petersburg: Tipografiia Eduarda Veimara, 1857.

------. *Arkheologicheskoe opisanie tserkovnykh drevnostei v Novgorode i ego okrestnosti.* 2 vols. Moscow: Tipografiia V. Got'e, 1860.

Makarii (Veretennikov, Petr Ivanovich; Archimandrite). *Zhizn' i trudy Sviatitelia Makariia Mitropolita Moskovskogo i vseia Rusi.* Moscow: Izdatel'skii Sovet Russkoi Pravoslavnoi Tserkvi, 2002.

------. "Vasil'evskie Vrata." In *Makarievskaia chteniia. Russkaia kul'tura XVI veka – epoka Mitropolita Makariia. Materialy X rossiiskoi nauchnoi konferentsii posviashchenoi pamiati sviatitelia Makariia.* Vypusk 10. Mozhaisk: Terra, 2003: 111-119.

Maksimovich, M. A. (Mikhail Aleksandrovich). *Sobranie sochinenii.* 3 vols. Kyiv: Tipografiia M. P. Fritsa, 1876.

Malinin, V. N. (Vasilii Nikolaevich). *Starets Eleazarova Monastyriia Filofey i ego poslaniia.* Kyiv: Tipografiia Kievo-Pecherskoi Uspenskoi lavry, 1901.

Malyshevskii, I. I. "Russkie izvestiia o evreiakh v Kieve i iuzhnoi Rusi v X-XII vv." *ChIONL* (1888), book 2, pt. 1: 49-52.

Mango, Cyril. *Materials for the Study of the Mosaics of St. Sophia at Istanbul.* Washington, DC: Dumbarton Oaks Research Library and Collection, 1962.

------. *The Art of the Byzantine Empire,* 312-1453; Sources and Documents. Englewood Cliffs, NJ: Prentice Hall, 1972.

Mann, C. Griffith, ed. *Sacred Arts and City Life: The Glory of Medieval Novgorod.* Baltimore, St. Petersburg, and Novgorod: The Walters Museum, The State Russia Museum, the Novgorod State Museum Palace Editions, 2005.

Markelov, G. V. (Gleb Valentinovich). "Novgorodskie sviatye po ikonopisnym podlinnikam." In Viacheslav Anatol'evich Koshalev, ed. *Novgorod v kul'ture Drevneĭ Rusi: materialy Chteniĭ po drevnerusskoĭ literature, Novgorod, 16-19 maia 1995.* Novgorod: Novgorodskii Gosudarstvennii Universitet, 1995: 34-43.

Martin, Janet. "The Land of Darkness and the Golden Horde: The Fur Trade Under the Mongols XIII-XIV centuries." *CMRS* 19 (1978): 401-421.

------. *Treasure of the Land of Darkness: The Fur Trade and its Significance for Medieval Russia.* Cambridge: Cambridge University Press, 1985.

------. *Medieval Russia 980-1584.* Second Edition. Cambridge: Cambridge University Press, 2003.

Marx, Karl, and Friedrich Engels. *Marx & Engels Collected Works.* 50 volumes. London: Lawrence and Wishart, 2015.

McClintock, John, and James Strong, eds. *Cyclopedia of Biblical, Theological, and Ecclesiastical Literature.* New York: Harper Brothers, 1889.

Meinardus, Otto. "The Ceremony of the Holy Fire in the Middle Ages and to-day" *Bulletin de la Société d'Archéologie Copte* 16 (1961-2): 242-253.

Melnick, Gregory, trans. and ed. *An Icon Painter's Notebook: The Bolshakov Edition. An Anthology of Source Materials.* Torrance, CA: Oakwood Publications, 1995.

------. *The Postnikov Collection.* Vol. 1 of *An Iconographer's Sketchbook: Drawings and Patterns.* Torrance, CA: Oakwood Publications, 1997.

------. *The Tyulin Collection.* Vol. 2 of *An Iconographer's Sketchbook: Drawings and Patterns.* Torrance, CA: Oakwood Publications, 1998.

Menache, Sofia. *Clement V.* Cambridge: Cambridge University Press, 1998.

Mende, Ursula. *Die Bronzetüren des Mittelalters, 800-1200.* Munich: Hirmer, 1994.

Metz, René, "Clergy." In Joseph R. Strayer, ed. *Dictionary of the Middle Ages,* 13 vols., vol. 3: 440-446.

Meyendorff, John. *Byzantium and the Rise of Russia: A Study of Byzantino-Russian Relations in the Fourteenth Century.* Cambridge: Cambridge University Press, 1981.

------. "Clergy, Byzantine." In Joseph R. Strayer, ed., *Dictionary of the Middle Ages.* Vol. 3, 446-447.

Miasoedov, V. K. (Vladimir Konstantinovich). *Kratiry Sofiiskogo Sobora v Novgorode* (St. Petersburg: Tipografiia M. A. Aleksandrova, 1914).

Mikhailov, A. V. "Poslednii put' Vasiliia Kaliki." *Novgorod i Novgorodskaia Zemlia: istoriia i arkheologiia* 11 (1997): 315-320.

Miller, David B. "The Velikie Minei Chetii and the Stepennaia Kniga of Metropolitan Makarii and the Origins of Russian National Consciousness." FOG 26 (1979): 263-382.

-----. "The Kievan Principality in the Century before the Mongol Invasion: An Inquiry into Recent Research and Interpretation," HUS 10, No. 1/2 (June 1986): 215-240.

------. "Monumental Building as an Indicator of Economic Trends in Northern Rus' in the Late Kievan and Mongol Periods: 1138-1462." *American Historical Review* 94, No. 2 (1989): 360-90.

------. "Monumental Building and its Patrons as Indicators of Economic and Political Trends in Rus' 900-1262." JfGO 38 (1990): 321-355.

------. "The Orthodox Church." Chapter 15 in Maurine Perrie, ed. *From Early Rus' to 1689*, Volume 1 of *The Cambridge History of Russia* 3 vols. Cambridge and New York: Cambridge University Press, 2006.

Mitsik, Iu. A (Iurii) and L. D. Federova, "Kyivo-Pecherska lavra, Sviato-Uspen'ska Kyivo Pecherska lavra." In V. A. Smolii, ed. *Entsiklopediia istorii Ukraini*, 11 volumes in 12 parts. Kyiv: Institut Istorii Ukraini Natsional'na Akademia Nauk Ukraini, Naukova dumka, 2003-2019. 4:187-195.

Mokeev, Gennadii Iakovlovich. "Tri Sofii," *Novaia kniga Rossii* 5 (2001): 44-47.

Mongait, A. L. (Aleksandr L'vovich). "Raskopki v Martir'evksii paperti Sofiikogo sobora v Novgorode." *Kratkie soobshcheniia o dokladakh i polevykh issledovaniiakh Instituta istorii material'noi kul'tury* 24 (1949): 99-104.

Moskovich, Wolf, Shmuel Schwarzband, Z. Davydov, Anatolii Alekseev, and L. Finberg, eds. *Jews and Slavs*, 5 vols. Jerusalem: Israeli Academy of Sciences and Humanities, Hebrew University of Jerusalem, and Gesharim, 1993-1996.

Mund, Stéfane. "Opisanie Novgoroda i Pskova v memuarakh Voyages et Ambassades Rytsaria Gil'bera de Lannoa (1413)." *Drevniaia Rus'* 1 (7) (March 2002): 47-50.

Mundy, John H. *Europe in the High Middle Ages, 1150-1309*. London: Longman, 1973.

Murray, Alan V., ed. *Crusade and Conversion on the Baltic Frontier, 1150 – 1500*. Aldershot, UK, and Burlington, VT: Ashgate, 2001.

------. *Clash of Cultures on the Medieval Baltic Frontier 1100-1350.* Aldershot, UK, and Burlington, VT: Ashgate, 2009.
Musin, Aleksandr Evgen'evich. "1165g. Arkhiepiskop Il'ia-Ioann i kompleks tserkovnykh drevnostei s Fedorovskogo raskopa." *Novgorod i Novgorodskaia Zemlia: istoriia i arkheologiia* 10 (1996): 147-158.
------. *Khristianizatsiia Novgorodskoi zemli v IX – XIV vekax: pogrebal'nyi obriad i khristianskie drevnosti.* St. Petersburg: RAN IIMK, 2002.
------. *Milites Christi Drevnei Rusi: voinskaia kul'tura russkogo Srednevekov'ia v kontekste religioznogo mentaliteta.* St. Petersburg: Izdatel'stvo Peterburgskoe Vostokovedenie, 2005.
------. *Zagadki doma Sviatoi Sofii: Tserkov' Velikogo Novgoroda v. X-XVI vv.* St. Petersburg: Peterburgskoe vostokovedenie, 2016.
Nadson, A. "The Writings of St. Cyril of Turau." *The Journal of Byelorussian Studies* 1 (1965): 4-15.
Nauman, Sar, Wojtek Jezierski, Christina Reimann, and Leif Runefelt, eds., *Baltic Hospitality from the Middle Ages to the Twentieth Century.* Cham, Switzerland: Palgrave Macmillan, 2022.
Nazarenko, A. V. (Aleksandr Vasil'evich). "Russkaia tserkov' v XI - treti XV v." In *Pravoslavnaia entsiklopediia.* Moscow: Pravoslavnaia entsiklopediia, 2000. 1:38-60.
------. "Novgorodskii kholop Dudika i sobolia paderbornskogo episkopa Mainverka," in P. G. Gaidukov, ed., *Goroda i vesi srednevekovoi Rusi: Arkheologiia, istoriia kul'tura: K 60-letiiu Nikolaia Andreevicha Makarova.* Moscow and Vologda: Drevnosti Severa, 2015.
Nazarova, Evgenyia L. "The Crusades Against the Votians and Izhorians in the Thirteenth Century." In Alan V. Murray, ed. *Crusade and Conversion on the Baltic Frontier, 1150 – 1500.* Aldershot, UK, and Burlington, VT: Ashgate, 2001. 177-195.
Nesin, M. A. (Mikhail Aleksandrovich). "Arkhimandrity Vechevogo Novgoroda," *Novogardia* 4 (2019): 44-139.
Nicholas, David. *The Growth of the Medieval City: From Late Antiquity to the Early Fourteenth Century.* New York: Longman, 1997.
------. *The Later Medieval City: 1300-1500.* New York: Longman, 1997.
Nielsen, Torben K. "The Missionary Man: Archbishop Anders Sunesen and the Baltic Crusade, 1206-21." In Alan V. Murray, ed., *Crusade and Conversion on the Baltic Frontier, 1150-1500.* Aldershot, UK: Ashgate, 2001: 95-117.

Nikitin, A. L. (Andrei Leonidovich). *Osnovaniia russkoi istorii: mifologemy i fakty*. Moscow: Agraf, 2000.
Nikitskii, A. I. (Aleksandr Ivanovich). "Ocherki iz zhizny Velikogo Novgorod. I. Pravitelstvennyi Soviet," *Zhurnal ministerstva narodnogo proveshcheniia* 145 (1869): 294-309.
------. *Ocherk vnutrennei istorii Pskova*. St. Petersburg: Tip. K. Zamyslovskogo, 1873.
------. *Ocherk vnutrennei istorii tserkvi v Novgorode*. St. Petersburg: Tipografii V. S. Valasheva, 1879.
------. "Otnosheneniia novgorodskogo vladyki k nemetskomu kupechestvu po novym dannym." *Zhurnal ministerstva narodnogo proveshcheniia* (1883): 1-15.
------. *Istoriia ekonomicheskogo byta velikogo Novgoroda*. Moscow: Universitetskaia tipografiia, 1893.
Nikol'skii, Konstantin Timofeevich (archpriest). *Ob antiminsakh pravoslavnoi russkoi tserkvi*. St. Petersburg: V tip. Iakova Treia, 1872.
------. *Posobie k izucheniiu ustava bogosluzheniia pravoslavnoi tserkvi*, 7th ed. St. Petersburg: Sinodal'naia tip., 1907.
Noonan, Thomas S. "Medieval Russia, The Mongols, and the West: Novgorod's Relations with the Baltic 1100-1350." *Mediaeval Studies* 37 (1975): 316-339.
------. "Ninth Century Dirham Hordes from European Russia: A Preliminary Analysis." *Viking Age Coinage in the Northern Lands: The Sixth Oxford Symposium on Coinage and Monetary History*. M. A. S. Blackburn and D. M. Metcalf, eds. BAR international Series 122/1. Oxford: BAR, 1981: 47-117.
------. "Why the Vikings First Came to Russia." *JfGO* 34 (1986): 321-348.
Norwich, John Julius. *The Apogee*. Vol. 2 of *Byzantium*. New York: Alfred A. Knopf, 1992.
Nosov, E. N. (Evgenii Nikolaevich). "Novgorodskii detinets i gorodishche (k voprosy o rannykh ukrepleniiakh i stanovlennii goroda)." *Novgorodskii istoricheskii sbornik* 5, No.15 (1995): 5-17.
Obolensky, Dmitri. "Byzantium, Kiev, and Moscow: A Study in Ecclesiastical Relations." *DOP* 11 (1956): 23-78.
------. *Byzantium and the Slavs: Collected Studies*. London: Variorum Press, 1971.

------. "A Byzantine Grand Embassy to Russia in 1400." *Byzantine and Modern Greek Studies* 4 (1978): 123-32. Reprinted in *The Byzantine Inheritance of Eastern Europe*.

------. "A Late Fourteenth Century Byzantine Diplomat: Michael Archbishop of Bethlehem." *Byzance et les Slaves. Melanges Ivan Dujcev*. S. Dufrenne, ed. Paris: Association des Amis des Etudes Archeologique (1979): 299-315. Reprinted in *The Byzantine Inheritance of Eastern Europe*.

------. *The Byzantine Commonwealth: Eastern Europe, 500-1453*. London: Sphere Books, 1974. Reprinted Crestwood, NY: St. Vladimir's Seminary Press, 1982.

------. *The Byzantine Inheritance of Eastern Europe*. London: Variorum Press, 1982.

Oikonomides, Nicolas. "St. George of Mangana, Maria Skleraina, and the 'Malyj Sion' of Novgorod." DOP 34 (1980-1981): 239-246.

Oinas, Felix J. "The Problem of the Aristocratic Origin of Russian Byliny," SR 30, No. 3 (Sept. 1971): 513–522.

Okhotina, N. A. (Natal'ia Aleksandrovna). "Russkaia tserkov' i mongol'skoe zavoevanie XIII v." In A. I. (Aleksandr Il'ich) Klibanov, et al., eds. *Tserkov' obshchestvo i gosudardstvo v feodal'noi Rossii*. Moscow: Nauka, 1990: 67-84.

Oman, Charles. *The History of the Art of War in the Middle Ages*. 2 vols. New York: Burt Franklin, 1969.

Onasch, Konrad. *Gross-Nowgorod: Aufstieg und Niedergang einer russischen Stadtrepublik*. Vienna and Munich: Verlag Anton Schroll and Co., 1969.

"O prazdnovanii vsekh sviatykh Novgorodskikh." *Sofia*, No. 4 (1998).

Orlov, S. N. (Sergei Nikolaevich). "K Topografii Novgoroda X-XVI vv." In M. N. (Mikhail Nikolaevich) Tikhomirov, ed. *Novgorod: k 1100 letiiu goroda. Sbornik statei*. Moscow: Nauka, 1964: 264-285.

------. "Topografiia Novgoroda X-XII vekov." *Problemy arkheologii II. Sbornik statei v pamiat' professora M. I. Artamanova*. Leningrad, Izdatel'stvo Leningradskogo Gosudarstvennogo Universiteta, 1978: 194-200.

Orlova, M. A. (Maria Alekseevna) and G. V. (Gennadii Viktorovich)

Popov. *Naruzhnye rospisi srednevekovykh pamiatnikov arkhitektury. Vizantiia, Balkany. Drevniaia Rus'*. Moscow: Nauka, 1990.

Ostrowski, Donald. "Ironies of the Tale of the White Cowl." *Palaeoslavica* (Χρισαι πύλαι/Златая врата [Golden Gate]: Essays Presented to Ihor Ševčenko on His Eightieth Birthday by His Colleagues and Students, edited by Peter Schreiner and Olga Strakhov, Cambridge, MA) 10, No. 2 (2002): 27-54.

------. "Image of the White Cowl." In Valerie Kivelson, Karen Petrone, Nancy Kollmann, and Michael Flier, eds., *The New Muscovite Cultural History: A Collection in Honor of Daniel B. Rowland*. Bloomington, IN: Slavica, 2009: 271-284.

------. "Unsolved Evidentiary Issues concerning Rus' Heretics of the Late Fifteenth-Early Sixteenth Centuries", in *Seeing Muscovy Anew: Politics—Institutions—Culture. Essays in Honor of Nancy Shields Kollmann*. Michael S. Flier, Valerie Kivelson, Erika Monahan, and Daniel Rowland, eds. Bloomington, IN: Slavic, 2017: 123-139.

------. *Europe, Byzantium, and the "Intellectual Silence" of Rus' Culture*. Leeds: Arc Humanities Press, 2018.

Ouspensky (Uspenskii), L. (Leonid), and V. Lossky. *The Meaning of Icons*. Crestwood, NY: St. Vladimir's Seminary Press, 1982.

Panchenko, A. M. (Aleksandr Mikhailovich). "Vasilii Kalika," in L. V. (Liudmilla Viktorovna) Sokolova and O. V. (Oleg Viktorovich) Tvorogov, eds., *Literatura Drevnei Rusi. Bibliograficheskii slovar'*. Moscow: Prosveshchenie, 1996: 24-26.

Panova, T. D. (Tatiana Dmitrievna). *Nekropoli Moskovskogo Kremlia*. 2nd ed. Moscow: Gosudarstvennyi Istoriko-Kultyrnyi Muzei-Zapovednik "Moskovksii Kreml', 2003.

Papadakis, Aristeides. "Byzantine Monasticism Reconsidered." *Byzantinoslavica* 43 (1986): 34-46.

Pares, Bernard. *A History of Russia*. New York: Alfred A Knopf, 1953.

Parsons, Anscar John. *Canonical Elections: An Historical Synopsis and Commentary*. Washington, DC: Catholic University of America, 1939. *Canon Law Studies* 118.

Pashkov, A. M. (Aleksandr Mikhailovich). "'Zhitie Lazaria Muromskogo,' v istorii kul'tury Karelii XVIII-XX vv.", *Kizhskii Vestnik. Sbornik statei* 8, I. V. Mel'nikov, ed., (Petrozavodsk: Gosudarstvennyi istoriko-arkhitekturnyi i etnograficheskii muzei-zapovednik "Kizhi", 2003): 3-13.

Paul, Michael C. "Episcopal Election in Novgorod, Russia 1156-1478." CH 72, No. 2 (June 2003): 251-275.
------. "The Military Revolution in Russia, 1550-1682." *The Journal of Military History* 68, No. 1 (January 2004): 9-45.
------. "The Iaroslavichi and the Novgorodian Veche 1230-1270: A Case Study on Princely Relations with the Veche," RH 31, No. 1-2 (Spring-Summer 2004): 39-59.
------. "Secular Power and the Archbishops of Novgorod Before the Muscovite Conquest." *Kritika: Explorations in Russian and Eurasian History* 8, No. 2 (Spring 2007): 231-270.
------. "Was the Prince of Novgorod a 'Third-rate Bureaucrat' after 1136?" *Jahrbücher für Geschichte Osteuropas* 56, Heft 1(2008): 72-113.
------. "Archbishop Vasilii Kalika of Novgorod, the Fortress of Orekhov, and the Defense of Orthodoxy." Chapter Twelve in Alan V. Murray, ed. *Clash of Cultures on the Medieval Baltic Frontier 1100-1350.* Farnham, UK, and Burlington, VT: Ashgate, 2009: 253-271.
------. "Continuity and Change in the Novgorodian Archiepiscopal Office, 1478-1591," *Orientalia Christiana Periodica.* Vol. 75, Fasicle 2 (2009): 273-317.
-----, "L'organisation sociale," in Olga Sevastyanova and Philippe Frison, eds., *Novgorod ou la Russie oubliée: Une république commerçante (XIIe-XVe siècles)* (Charenton-le-Pont: Le Ver à soie, Virginie Symaniec éditrice, 2015): 229-242.
Pavlov, A. P., and A. G. Man'kov, eds. *Rossiskoe gosudarstvo v. XIV-XVII vv.: sbornik statei, posviashchennyi 75-letiiu so dnia rozhdeniia Iu. G. Alekseeva.* St. Petersburg: Dmitrii Bulanin, 2002.
Pechnikov, M. V. "Spornye voprosy istorii strigol'nichestva v Novgorode vo vtoroi polovine XIV veke." in V. L. (Valentin Lavrent'evich) Ianin, ed. *Stolichnye i periferiinye goroda Rusi i Rossii v srednie veka i v rannee novoe vremia: doklady tretei nauchnoi konferentsii (Murom, 17-20 maia 2000 g.)* Moscow: Drevnekhranilishche, 2003.
Perrie, Maurine, ed. *From Early Rus' to 1689,* Volume 1 of *The Cambridge History of Russia* 3 vols. Cambridge and New York: Cambridge University Press, 2006.
Pimen, (Izvekov, Sergei Mikhailovich; Patriarch of Moscow and All Rus'). "Mitropolity Leningradskomu i Novgorodskomu Alek-

siiu – 60 let. Privetstvennoe poslanie Sviateishego Patriarkha Pimena Mitropolity Leningradskomu i Novgorodskomu Alekseiu." ZhMP No. 8 (1989): 10.

Piotrovskaia, E. K. "Kirik Novgorodets." SKKDR 1:215-217.

Pivovarova, N. V. (Nadezhda Valer'evna). *Freski tserkvi Spasa na Nereditse v Novgorode: ikonograficheskaia programma rospisi*. St. Petersburg: APC, Dmitii Bulanin, 2002.

Platonov, S. F. (Sergei Fedorovich). *Veche v Velikom Novgorode*. Novgorod: Novgorodskoe obshschestvo liubitelei drevnostei, 1916.

------. *Ivan Groznyi*. Petrograd: Brokgauz-Efron, 1923.

------. *Smutnoe Vremia*. Prague: Legiografiia, 1924. Reprinted: The Hague: Europe Printing, 1965.

------. *Polnyi kurs lektsii po russkoi istorii*. St. Petersburg: Krystall, 1997.

Pliguzov, A. I. (Andrei Ivanovich). "On the Title 'Metropolitan of Kiev and All Rus'," HUS 15, Nos. 3/4 (December 1991): 340-353.

------. "Archbishop Gennadii and the Heresy of the Judaizers." HUS 16 (1992): 269-281.

Pliguzov, A. I. (Andrei Ivanovich), and A. L. (Anna Leonidovna) Khoroshkevich. "Russkaia Tserkov' i antiordynskaia bor'ba v XIII-XV vv. po materialam kratkogo sobraniia khanskikh iarlykov russkim mitropolitam." In A. I. (Aleksandr Il'ich) Klibanov, et al., eds. *Tserkov' obshchestvo i gosudardstvo v feodal'noi Rossii*. Moscow: Nauka, 1990: 84-102.

Pliguzov, A. I. (Andrei Ivanovich) and G. V. Semenchenko, "Novgorodsko-Pskovskie otnosheniia vo vtoroi polovine 1430-kh godakh i formuliarnik mitropolita Isidora," *Problemy istorii Novgoroda i Novgorodskoi zemli XV v. Tezisi dokladov i soobshenii nauchnogo simpoziuma* (Novgorod: N. p., 1986): 11-14.

Podobedova, O. I. (Ol'ga Il'inichna). *Drevnerusskoe iskusstvo: XIV-XV vv*. Moscow: Nauka, 1984.

Podskalsky, Gerhard. *Christentum und theologische Literatur in der Kiever Rus' 988-1237*. Munich: Beck, 1982.

Podvigina, N. L. (Nata'lia L'vovna). *Ocherki sotsial'no-ekonomicheskoi i politicheskoi istorii Novgoroda Velikogo v XII-XIII vv*. Moscow: Vysshaia shkola, 1976.

Pokrovskii, I. M. (Ivan Mikhailovich). *Russkie eparkhii v XVI-XIX vv. ikh otkrytie sostav i predely*. 2 vols. Kazan': Tsentral'naia tipografiia, 1913.

Polnyi pravoslavnyi bogoslovskii entsyklopedicheskii slovar', 2 vols. St. Petersburg: Izd. P. P. Soikina [1913].
Ponomarev, A. I. (Aleksandr Ivanovich). "Sv. Kirill, episkop Turovskii i ego poucheniia." *Pamiatniki drevnerusskoi tserkovno-uchitel'noi literatury.* 1st ed. St. Petersburg: S. Dobrodeev, Tipografiia, 1894.
Popova, O. S. (Ol'ga Sigismundovna). *Iskusstvo Novgoroda i Moskvy pervoi poloviny chetyrnadtsatogo veka: ego sviazi s Vizantiei.* Moscow: Iskusstvo, 1980.
------. *Russian Illuminated Manuscripts.* Kathleen Cook, Vladimir Ivanov and Lenina Sorokina, trans. New York: Thames & Hudson, 1984.
Poppe, Andrzej. "Eshche raz o nazvanii novgorodsko-pskovskikh eretikov 'strigol'nikami'." *Kul'tura Drevnei Rusi.* Moscow: Institut arkheologii, AN SSSR, 1966: 204-208.
------. *Panstwo i kościół na Rusi w XI wieku.* Warsaw: Państwowe Wydawn. Naukowe, 1968.
------. "Russko-vizantiinskie tserkovno-politicheskie otnosheniia v seredine XI veka." *Istoriia SSSR* (1970) No. 3: 108-124.
------. "K istorii romanskikh dverei Sofii Novgorodskoi." In G. K. Vagner, D. S. Likhachev, and P. A. Rappoport. *Srednevekovaia Rus'.* Moscow: Nauka, 1976: 191-200.
------. "The Political Background of the Baptism of Rus'. Byzanto-Russian Relations between 986-989," DOP 30 (1976): 195-244.
------. "The Original Status of the Old-Russian Church." *Acta Poloniae historica* 39 (1979): 4-45. Reprinted in *The Rise of Christian Russia.*
------. "The Building of the Church of St. Sophia in Kiev." *The Journal of Medieval History* 7 (1981): 15-65. Reprinted in *The Rise of Christian Russia.*
------. *The Rise of Christian Russia.* London: Variorum Reprints, 1992.
------. "The Christianization and Ecclesiastical Structure of Kyivan Rus' to 1300," HUS 21 No. 3-4 (1997): 311-392.
Porfiridov, N. G. (Nikolai Grigor'evich). "Imennye vladychnye pechati Novgoroda." *Sovetskaia arkheologiia* 3 (1958): 222-225.
Postan, Michael, "The Trade in Medieval Europe: The North." In *Trade and Industry in the Middle Ages.* Vol. 2 of *Cambridge Economic History of Europe.* M. Postan and E. E. Rich, ed. Cambridge: Cambridge University Press, 1952: 119-256.

Presniakov, A. E. (Aleksandr Evgen'evich). *Obrazovanie Velikorusskogo gosudarstva*. Moscow: Bogorodskii Pechatnik, 1998.
Priselkov, M. D. (Mikhail Dmitrievich). "Mitrololit Ilarion, v skime Nikon, kak borets za nezavisimuiu russkuiu tserkov'. Epizod iz nachal'noi istorii Kievo-Pecherskogo monastyria." In *Sergeiu Fedorovichu Platonovu ucheniki, druz'ia i pochitateli*. St. Petersburg: Tipografiia glavnogo upravleniia udelov, 1911: 188-201.
------. *Ocherki po tserkovno-politicheskoi istorii Kievskoi Rusi X-XII vv*. St. Petersburg: Nauka, 2003.
Profiridov, N. G. (Nikolai Grigor'evich). *Drevnii Novgorod. Ocherki iz istorii russkoi kul'tury XI-XV vv*. Moscow and Leningrad: AN SSSR, 1947.
Prokhorov, G. M. (Gelian Mikhailovich). *Povest' o Mitiae: Rus i Vizantiya v epokhu Kulikovskoi bitvy*. Leningrad: Nauka, 1978.
------. "Kiprian," TODRL 39 (1985): 53-71.
------. "Pakhomii Serb." SKKDR 2:167-177.
Pronshtein, Aleksandr Pavlovich. *Velikii Novgorod v XVI veke: ocherk sotsial'no-ekonomichekskoi i politicheskoi istorii russkogo goroda*. Kharkiv: Izdatel'stvo Kharkivskogo gosudarstvennogo Universiteta im. Gorkogo, 1957.
Protas'eva, T. N. (Tatiana). *Opisanie rukopisei Sinodal'nogo sobraniia*. 2 vols. Moscow: Glavnoe arkhivnoe upravlenie, Arckheograficheskaia komissiia, Gosudarstvennyi istoricheskii muzei, 1970-1973.
Prozorovskii, Dmitrii Ivanovich. "Kto byl pervym pisatelem pervoi novgorodskoi letopisi," *Zhurnal ministerstva narodnogo prosveshcheniia* 75, No. 9 (July1852): 1-28.
Putsko, V. G. (Vasilii Grigor'evich). "Shityi deisus Novgorodskogo Arkhiepiskopa Evfimiia," *Sofia* 3 (2002).
Raba, Joel. "Evfimii II Erzbischof von Gross-Nowgorod und Pskov: Ein Kirchenfürst als Leiter einer weltlichen Republic." JfGO 25 (1977): 161-173.
------. "Church and Foreign Policy in the Fifteenth Century Novgorodian State." CASS 13, No.1-2 (1979): 52-58.
Rácz, Endre and György Ruzsa. *Nowgorod, Pleskau, und der russische Norden*. Hanau: W. Dausien, 1981.
Radishchev, A. N. *Puteshestvie iz Peterburga v Moskvu*. Moscow and Leningrad: Gosudarstvennoe izdatel'stvo khudozhesvennoi literatury, 1961.

Raffensperger, Christian "Revisiting the Idea of the Byzantine Commonwealth," *Byzantinische Forschungen* 28 (2004): 159-174.
Rapoport, A. *Velikii Novgorod i ego okrestnosti: putevoditel'*. 2nd ed. Moscow: Aiaks Press, 2005.
Rappoport, P. A. (Pavel Aleksandrovich). *Zodchestvo drevnei Rusi*. Leningrad: Nauka, 1986.
Rapov, O. M. (Oleg Mikhailovich), and N. G. Tkachenko. "Russkie izvestiia Titmara Merseburgskogo." In *Vestnik Moskovskogo gosudarstvenogo universiteta* 8, No. 3 (1980): 65-66.
Rasmussen, K. (Knud). "Velikij Novgorod i moderne sovjetisk historiografi." *Svantevit* 2, No.2 (1977): 65-70.
------. "'300 zolotykh poiasov' drevnego Novgoroda." *Scando-Slavica* 35 1979, 93-103.
Razin, E. A. (Evgenii Andreevich). *Istoriia voennogo iskusstva*. 3 vols. St. Petersburg: Izdatel'stvo "Poligon," 1999.
Redmand, Charles L., ed. *Medieval Archaeology. Papers of the Seventeenth Annual Conference of the Center for Medieval and Early Renaissance Studies*. Binghamton: State University of New York, 1989.
Reynolds, Susan, *Kingdoms and Communities*. Oxford: Clarendon Press, 1984.
Riabinin, Evgenii A. "Ot iazychestva k dvoeveriiu po arkheologicheskim materialam Severnoi Rusi," in L. I. (Liubov' Issakovna) Emeliakh ed., *Pravoslavie v Drevnei Rusi: sbornik nauchnykh trudov*. Leningrad: Izd. GMIRiA, 1989.
Riasanovsky, Nicholas V. *A History of Russia*. 3rd ed. Oxford and New York: Oxford University Press, 1977.
Rock, Stella. "What's in a Word: A Historical Study of the Concept Dvoeverie." CASS 35, No.1 (2001): 19-28.
Rowell, S. C. (Stephen Christopher). *Lithuania Ascending, A Pagan Empire within East-Central Europe, 1295-1345*. Cambridge: Cambridge University Press, 1994.
Rozhdestvenskaia, M. V. "Iona." SKKDR 1:426-427.
Rozhkov, N. A. (Nikolai Aleksandrovich). *Sel'skoe khoziastvo Moskovskoi Rusi v XVI veke*. Moscow: Universitetskaia tipografiia, 1899.
Runciman, Steven. *A History of the First Bulgarian Empire*. London: G. Bell and Sons, Ltd., 1930.

------. *The Eastern Schism, A Study of the Papacy and the Eastern Churches During the XIth and XIIth Centuries.* Oxford: Oxford University Press, 1955.

------. *The Byzantine Theocracy.* Cambridge and New York: Cambridge University Press, 1977.

Rybakov, Boris A. *Drevnaia Rus': skazaniia, byliny, letopisi.* Moscow: AN SSSR, 1963.

------. *Strigol'niki: russkie gumanisty XIV stoletiia.* Moscow: Nauka, 1993.

Rybakov, Boris A., et al., eds. *Istoriia SSSR,* Vol. 2. Moscow: Nauka, 1966.

Rybina, E. A. (Elena Aleksandrovna). *Inozemnye dvory v Novgorode XII-XVII vv.* Moscow: Izdatel'stvo Moskovskogo Gosudarstvennogo Universiteta, 1986.

Rybnikov, P. N. (Pavel Nikolaevich) and Aleksei Evgen'evich Gruzinskii. *Pesni sobrannye P. N. Rybnikovym.* Moscow: Sotrudnik shkol, 1909-1910. Reprinted The Hague: Europe Printing, 1968.

Rychka, Vladimir. "Krest Charodeia: tri Sofii Vseslava Polotskogo: vzgliad iz Kieva." *Rodina* 6 (2007): 68-72.

Samsonov, I. "Supruga Iaroslava Mudrogo – blagovernaia kniginia Irina i ee rol' v otnosheniiak Rusi so Skandinaviei." *Zhurnal Moskovskoi patriarkhii,* No. 12, (2004): 56-75.

Saunders, J. J. (John Joseph). *The History of the Mongol Conquests.* London and Boston: Routledge and Keegan Paul, 1971.

Schaff, David S. *The Middle Ages from Gregory VII, 1049 to Boniface VIII, 1294,* Volume 5, Part 1 of Philip Schaff. *History of the Christian Church.* New York: Charles Schribner and Sons, 1907.

Schaff, Philip. *History of the Christian Church.* 8 vols. New York: Charles Schribner and Sons, 1907.

Savushkina, N. "Biblioteka Sofiiskogo Sobora." *Sofia,* No. 1 (2004).

Sels, Lara, Jürgen Fuchsbauer, V. S Tomelleri, and Ilse de Vos, eds. *Editing Mediaeval Texts from a Different Angle: Slavonic and Multilingual Traditions: Together with Francis J. Thomson's Bibliography and Checklist of Slavonic Translations: To Honour Francis J. Thomson on the Occasion of His 80th Birthday: Together with Proceedings of the Attemt Workshop Held at King's College London, 19-20 December 2013 and the Attest Workshop Held at the University of Regensburg, 11-12 December 2015.* Orientalia Lovaniensia Analecta, 276. Leuven: Peeters, 2018.

Sergeevich, V. I. (Vasilii Ivanovich). *Veche i kniaz'*. Moscow: A. M. Mamontov, 1867.
Sevastyanova, Olga. "In Quest of the Key Democratic Institution of Medieval Rus': Was the 'Veche' an Institution that Represented Novgorod as a City and a Republic?" JfGO Neue Folge, Bd. 58, H. 1 (2010): 1-23.
Sevastyanova, Olga, and Philippe Frison, eds. *Novgorod ou la Russie oubliée: Une république commerçante (XIIe-XVe siècles)*. Charenton-le-Pont: Le Ver à soie, Virginie Symaniec éditrice, 2015.
Shakhmatov, A. A. (Aleksei Aleksandrovich). *Razyskaniia o drevneishikh letopisnikh svodakh*. St. Petersburg: M. A. Aleksandrova, 1908.
------. *Obozrenie russkikh letopisnysk svodov XIV-XVI vv*. Moscow and Leningrad. AN SSSR, 1938.
Shambinago, S. K. (Sergei Konstantinovich). "Ioakimovskaia letopis'." IZ 21 (1947): 254-270.
Shapiro, A. L. (Aleksandr L'vovich). *Agrarnaia istoriia Severo-Zapada Rossii, vtoraia polovina XV-XVI v*. Leningrad: Nauka, 1971.
Shaw, Christine. *Julius II: The Warrior Pope*. Oxford: Basil Blackwell, 1993.
Shchapov, Ia. N. (Iaroslav Nikolaevich). *Kniazheskie Ustavy i Tserkov' V Drevnei Rusi, XI-XIV vv*. Moscow: Nauka, I972.
------. "Vasilii Kalika." In Joseph L. Wieczynski, ed., *Modern Encyclopedia of Russian and Soviet History* Gulf Breeze, FL: Academic International Press, 1979. Vol. 41: 224-225.
------. "O sisteme prava na Rusi v XI-XIII vv.," *Istoriia SSSR* 5 (1987), 175-181.
------. *Gosudarstvo i tserkov' drevnei Rusi X-XIII vv*. Moscow: Nauka, 1989.
Shevyrev, S. P. (Stepan Petrovich). *Istoriia russkoi slovesnosti*. 4 vols. Moscow: Tipografiia Barmeteva, Imperatorskaia Akademiia Nauk, 1857-1887.
Shunkov, V. I. (Viktor Ivanovich). ed. *Problemy obshchestvnno-politicheskoi istorii Rossii i slavianskikh stran: sbornik stateĭ k 70-letiiu akademika M.N. Tikhomirova* (Moscow: Izdatel'stvo vostochnoi literatury, 1963).
Shtykhov, Georgii. "Sofiia Ivana Khozerova." *Rodina* 6 (2007): 74-75.

de Sismondi, J.C. L. S. (Jean-Charles Leonard Semonde) *Histoire des républiques italiennes du moyen age.* 10 vols. Paris: Furne, 1840.
Sivak, Svetlana I. "O dereviannoi Sofii v Novgorode," *Russia medievalis* 7, No.1 (1992): 9-15.
Skrynnikov, R. G. (Ruslan Grigorevich). *Tretii Rim.* St. Petersburg: Izdatel'stvo Dmitrii Bulanin, 1994.
Slovar' russkogo iazyka. St. Petersburg: Tipografiia Imperatorskoi Akademii nauk and Leningrad: AN SSSR, 1891-1927. Reprinted London: Flegon Press, 1984.
Smirechanskii, V. D. *Istoriko-statisticheskii sbornik svedenii o Pskovskoi eparkii.* 2 vols. Pskov: Gubernatorskaia statisticheskaia komissiia, 1875-1895.
Slessarev, Vsevolod. "Ecclesiae Mercatorum and the Rise of Merchant Colonies." *The Business History Review* 41, No. 2 (Summer 1967): 177-197.
Smirnov, I. I. (Ivan Ivanovich). *Ocherki politicheskoi istorii Russkogo gosudarstva 30-50-x godov XVI veka.* Moscow and Leningrad: AN SSSR, 1958.
Smirnov, Iu. I. (Iurii Ivanovich), and V. G. (Viktor Gershonovich) Smoltskii, eds. *Novgorodskie byliny.* Moscow: Nauka, 1978.
Smith, R. "Some Recent Discoveries in Novgorod." *Past and Present* 5 (1954):1-10.
Smolii, V. A. ed. *Entsiklopediia istorii Ukraini,* 11 volumes in 12 parts, Kyiv: Institut Istorii Ukraini Natsional'na Akademia Nauk Ukraini, Naukova dumka, 2003-2019.
Sobolevskii, A. I. (Aleksei Ivanovich). "Zametki o sobstvennykh imenakh. 4. Zhidiata." In A. I. Sobolevskii, *Materialy i issledovaniia v oblasti slavianskoi filologii i arkheologii.* Published serially in SORIaS 88, No.3 (1910): 255-256.
Sokol Edward. "Veche." In Joseph L. Wieczynski, ed., *Modern Encyclopedia of Russian and Soviet History.* 60 vols. Gulf Breeze, FL: Academic International Press, 1979. Vol. 41: 238-242.
Sokolof, Dmitrii Pavlovich (Archpriest). *A Manual of the Orthodox Church's Divine Services.* New York and Albany: Wynkoop, Hallenbeck, and Crawford, 1899.
Sokolova, L. V. (Liudmilla Viktorovna) and O. V. (Oleg Viktorovich) Tvorogov. *Literatura Drevnei Rusi. Bibliograficheskii slovar'.* Moscow: Prosveshchenie, 1996.

Sokolov, Platon Petrovich. *Russkii arkhierei iz Vizantii i pravo ego naznacheniia do nachala XV veka.* Kyiv: I. I. Chokolov, 1913.
Solov'ev, Petr Ivanovich. *Opisanie Novgorodskogo Sofiiskogo Sobora sostavnennoe protoiereem Petrom Solov'evym, kliucharem Novgorodskogo kafedral'nogo Sofiiskogo sobora.* St. Petersburg: Arkheograficheskoe obshchestvo, 1858.
Solov'ev, S. M. (Sergei Mikhailovich). *Istoriia Rossii s drevneishikh vremen.* 29 books in 15 vols. Moscow: Izdatel'stvo sotsial'no-ekonomicheskoi literatury, 1959-1966.
Spegal'skii, Iu. P. (Iurii Pavlovich). *Pskov: Khudozhestvennye pamiatniki.* Leningrad: Lenizdat, 1972.
Speranskii, M. N. (Mikhail Nestorovich). *Byliny.* 2 vols. Moscow: M. and S. Sabashnikov, 1919.
Sreznevskii, I. I. (Ismail Ivanovich). *Drevnie pamiatniki russkogo pis'ma i iazyka (X-XIV vekov): obshchee povremennoe obozrenie.* 2nd ed. St. Petersburg: Tipografii Akademii Nauk, 1882.
-----. *Obozrenie drevnikh russkikh spiskov Kormchei knigi.* St. Petersburg: Tipgrafiia Imp. Akademii Nauk, 1897.
Sreznevskii, V. I. (Vsevolod Ismailovich). *Svedeniia o rukopisiakh pechatnikh, izdaniakh i drugikh predtetakh postupivshikh v rukopisnoe otdelenie Biblioteky Imperatorskoi Akademii nauk v 1903g.* St. Petersburg: Tipografii Imperatorskoi Akademii nauk, 1904.
Strayer, Joseph R., ed. *Dictionary of the Middle Ages.* 13 vols. New York: Scribner, 1982-1989.
Stefanovich, P. S. (Petr Sergeevich). *Prikhod i prikhodskoe dukhovenstvo v Rossii v XVI-XVII vekakh.* Moscow: Indrik, 2002.
Steindorff, Ludwig. "Empire Building and Ecclesiastical Emancipation," in David Goldfrank and Kevin M. Kain, eds. *Russia's Early Modern Patriarchate: Foundations and Mitred Royalty, 1589-1647.* Washington-London: Academia Press, 2021: 7-24.
Sterk, Andrea. *Renouncing the World Yet Leading the Church: The Monk-Bishop in Late Antiquity.* Cambridge, MA: Harvard University Press, 2004.
Stevenson, Francis Seymour. *A History of Montenegro.* New York: Arno Books, 1977.
Stroev, P. M. (Pavel Mikhailovich). *Spiski ierarkhov i nastoiatelei monastyrei rossiiskiia tserkvi.* St. Petersburg: Kalasheva, 1877.
Talbot, David Rice, ed. *The Church of Haghia Sofia at Trebizond.* Edinburgh: Edinburgh University Press, 1968.

Tarasov, Sergei. "Ot Okhridskogo Ozera do beregov Dviny. Polotskaia Sofiia dukhovnoe nachalo i istoricheskoe otobrazhenie." *Rodina* 6 (2007): 58-62.

Tatishchev, Vasilii Nikitich. *Istoriia Rossiiskaia.* 7 vols. A. I. Andreev, et al., eds. Moscow and Leningrad: AN SSSR, 1962.

Taube, Moshe. "The Kievan Jew Zacharia and the Astronomical Works of the Judaizers." In Wolf Moskovich, Shmuel Schwarzband, Z. Davydov, Anatolii Alekseev, and L. Finberg, eds. *Jews and Slavs,* 5 vols. Jerusalem: Israeli Academy of Sciences and Humanities, Hebrew University of Jerusalem, and Gesharim, 1993-1996: 3:168-198.

------. *The Cultural Legacy of the Pre-Ashkenazic Jews in Eastern Europe.* Berkeley: University of California Press, 2003.

------. *The Logika of the Judaizers. A Fifteenth Century Translation from Hebrew.* Critical edition of the Slavic texts presented alongside their Hebrew sources with Introduction, English translation, and commentary. Jerusalem: Israel Academy of Sciences and Humanities, 2016.

Tel'pis, G. "Mitropolit Leningradskii i Novgorodskii Antonii – pochetnyi chlen LDA," ZhMP No. 9 (1979): 15.

Terras, Victor. *History of Russian Literature.* New Haven: Yale University Press, 1991.

Thomson, Francis J. "On Translating Slavonic Texts into a Modern Language: Some Critical Remarks on a New English Translation of Early East Slav Sermons, Together with a Translation of Luke of Novgorod's Homily to the Brethren." *Slavica gandensia* 19 (1992): 205-217.

-----, "Checklist of Slavonic Translations," in *Editing Mediaeval Texts from a Different Angle: Slavonic and Multilingual Traditions: Together with Francis J. Thomson's Bibliography and Checklist of Slavonic Translations: To Honour Francis J. Thomson on the Occasion of His 80th Birthday: Together with Proceedings of the Attemt Workshop Held at King's College London, 19-20 December 2013 and the Attest Workshop Held at the University of Regensburg, 11-12 December 2015.* Edited by Lara Sels, Jürgen Fuchsbauer, V. S Tomelleri, and Ilse de Vos. Orientalia Lovaniensia Analecta, 276. Leuven: Peeters, 2018.

Thompson, M. W. (Michael Welman). *Novgorod the Great: Excava-*

tions at the Medieval City by A. V. Artsikhovskii and B. A. Kolchin. London: Evelyn, Adams, and McKay, 1967.

Tikhomirov, M. N. (Mikhail Nikolaevich). *Drevnerusskie goroda.* 2nd ed. Moscow: Gosudarstvennoe izdatel'stvo politicheskoi literatury, 1956.

Tikhomirov, M. N. (Mikhail Nikolaevich), ed. *Novgorod: k 1100 letiiu goroda. Sbornik statei.* Moscow: Nauka, 1964.

Tikhomirov, P. I. (Pavel Il'ich). *Biografii pervikh deviati Novgorodskikh episkopov.* Novgorod: Novgorodskii Gubernskii Pravlenii, 1862.

------. *Kafedra novgorodskikh sviatitelei so vremeni pokoreniia Novgoroda Moskovskoi derzhavie v 1478 godu do konchiny poslednego mitropolita Novgorodskogo Iova v 1716 godu.* 2 vols. in 3 books. Novgorod: Gubernskii Pravlenii, Tip. I. I. Ignatovskogo, 1891-1900.

Tolochko, P. P. (Petr Petrovich). *Kiev i Kievskaia zemlia v epokhu feodal'noĭ razdroblennosti XII-XIII vekov.* Kyiv: Naukova Dumka, 1980.

Tolstoi, M. V. (Mikhail Vladimirovich). *Kniga glagolemaia opisanie o rossiiskikh sviatykh.* Moscow: v universitetskoi tipografii, 1887.

Tomilin, A. S. (Aleksandr Sergeevich). *Velikonovgorodskaia sviatitel'skaia kafedra v istoricheksom znachenii.* St. Petersburg: Tipografiia Departamenta vneshnei torgovlii, 1851.

Trifonova, A. N. (Anna Nikolaevna). "Bronzovye dveri Sofiiskogo Sobora v Novgorode." *Novgorod i Novgorodskaia Zemlia: istoriia i arkheologiia* 9 (1995): 230-242.

Troianovskii, S. V. (Sergei Viktorovich). "O nekotorikh rezul'tatakh raskopok v Novgorodskom kremle v 1992-1996 gg." *Novgorod i novgorodskaia zemlia, istoriia i arkheologiia*, no. 12, (1998): 58-70.

-----. "The Great Bridge of Novgorod: Republican History through Material Evidence" in: Dominique Colas and Oleg Kharkhordin, eds. *The Materiality of Res Publica: How to Do Things with Publics.* Newcastle upon Tyne: Cambridge Scholars Publishing, 2009: 51–114.

Tsapenko, Mikhail, ed. *Early Russian Architecture.* Moscow: Progress Publisher, 1969.

Tsarevskaia, T. Iu. (Tatiana Iur'evna). *Tserkov' Fedora Stratilata na ruch'iu.* Velikii Novgorod and Moscow: Severnyi Palomnik, 2001.

------. *Sofiiskii sobor v Novgorode.* 2nd ed. Moscow: Severnyi palomnik, 2005.

Tysiacheletie Kreshcheniia Rusi. Pomestnyi Sobor Russkoi Pravoslavnoi tserkvi. Troitse Sergieva Lavra 6-9 iunia, 1988. Moscow: Izdatel'stvo Moskovskoi Patriarkhii, 1990.

Tvorogov, O. V., "Daniil." SKKDR 1:109-112.

------. "German Voiata." SKKDR 1:105-106.

------. "Ioakim." SKKDR 1:204-205.

------. "Ioann (v miru Il'ia)" SKKDR 1:209.

------. "Luka Zhidiata, episkop novgorodskii," SKKDR 1:251.

Urban, William. *The Baltic Crusade*. Dekalb: Northern Illinois University Press, 1975.

------. *The Prussian Crusade*. 2nd ed. Chicago, Illinois: Lithuanian Research and Studies Center, 2000.

Vagner, G. K. (Georgi Karlovich), D. S. (Dmitrii Sergeevich) Likhachev, and P. A. (Pavel Aleksandrovich) Rappoport. *Srednevekovaia Rus'*. Moscow: Nauka, 1976.

Vasil'evskii, V. (Vasilii Grigorevich). "Zapiski o postavlenii russkikh episkopov pri mitropolite Feognoste v Vatikanskom grecheskom sbornike." *Zhurnal ministerstva narodnogo proveshcheniia* pt. 255, No. 2 (February, 1888): 445-463.

Vaughn, Sally M. "St. Anselm: Reluctant Archbishop?" *Albion: A Quarterly Journal Concerned with British Studies* 6, No. 3 (Autumn 1974): 240-250.

Veimarn, Boris Vladimirovich, ed. *Vseobshchaia Istoriia Iskusstv*. 6 vols. in 8 books. Moscow: Iskusstvo, 1956-1966. vol. 2, book 1 (Iskusstvo srednykh vekov).

Venevitinov, M. A. (Mikhail Alekseevich). "Khozdenie igumena Daniila v sviatuiu zemliu v nachalie XII st.," LZAK 7 (1884): 1-138.

Vernadsky, George. "The Heresy of the Judaizers and the Policies of Ivan III of Moscow." *Speculum* 8 (1933): 436-454.

------. *Ancient Russia*. Vol. 1 of *A History of Russia*. New Haven, CT: Yale University Press, 1947.

------. *Kievan Russia*. Vol. 2 of *A History of Russia*. New Haven, CT: Yale University Press, 1948, copyright renewed 1976.

------. *The Mongols and Russia*. Vol. 3 of *A History of Russia*. New Haven, CT: Yale University Press, 1953.

------. *Russia at the Dawn of the Modern Age*. Vol. 4 of *A History of Russia*. New Haven, CT: Yale University Press, 1959.

------. *Medieval Russian Laws.* New York: Octagon Books, 1965.
Veselovskii, A. N. "Razyskanie v oblasti russkogo dukhovnogo stikha XIX. Epizod o rae i ade v poslanii novgorodskogo arkhiepiskopa Vasiliia." SORIaS 53 (1891), No. 6: 91-104.
Vodov, V. (Vladimir) "Gerasim – Mitropolit Litovskii ili 'vseia Rusi'? O belom piatne v istorii Rusi XV veka." In N. M. Botvinnik and E. I. Vaneeva, comps., *In memoriam: Sbornik pamiati Ia. S. Lur'e.* St. Peterburg: Antheneum-Feniks, 1997: 236-238.
Volbach, Wolfgang Fritz, and Jacqueline Lafontaine-Dosogne. *Byzanz und der christliche Osten.* Berlin: Propyläen Verlag, 1968.
Voyce, Arthur. *Russian Architecture: Trends in Nationalism and Modernism.* New York: Philosophical Library, 1948.
Vzdornov, G. I. (Gerol'd Ivanovich). *Freski Feofana Greka v tserkvi Spasa Preobrazheniia v Novgoroda: k 600-letiu sushchestvovaniia fresok 1378-1978.* Moscow: Iskusstvo 1976.
------. *Feofan Grek.* Moscow: Iskusstvo, 1983.
Ware, Timothy (Father Kallistos). *The Orthodox Church.* Baltimore, MD: Penguin Books, 1963, 1964.
Warren, Ann K. "Cathedral Chapter." In Joseph R. Strayer, ed. *Dictionary of the Middle Ages.* Vol. 3: 265-266.
Weickhardt, George G. "The Canon Law of Rus', 1100-1551." RH 28, nos. 1-4 (2001): 411-446.
Wieczynski, Joseph L. "Archbishop Gennadius and the West: The Impact of Catholic Ideas on the Church of Novgorod." *Canadian-American Slavic Studies* 6 (1972): 374-389.
Wieczynski, Joseph L., ed. *Modern Encyclopedia of Russian and Soviet History.* 60 vols. Gulf Breeze, FL: Academic International Press, 1976-2001.
Zagraevskii, S.V. (Sergei Vol'fgangovich). "Vopros podlinnosti antiminsa XII veka iz Nikololo-Dvorishchenko sobora." *Materialy XVIII mezhdunarodnoi kraevedcheskoi konferentsii* (19 aprelia 2013 goda). (Vladimir, 2014): 179-189.
Zarubin, L. A. "Vazhskaia Zemlia v XIV-XV vv." *Istoriia SSSR* No. 1 (1970): 180-187.
Zdravomislov, Konstantin Iakovlevich. *Ierarkhi Novgorodskoi eparkhii ot drevneshikh vremeni do nastoiashchego vremeni.* Novgorod: Parovaia tipografiia I. I. Ignatovskogo, 1897.
Zernack, K. (Klaus). *Die burgstädtlischen Volksversammlungen bei den*

Ost-und Westslawen zur verfassungsgeschichtlichen Bedeutung der Veče. Wiesbaden: Harrassowitz, 1967.
------. "Fürst und Volk in der ostslavischen Fruhzeit." FOG 18 (1973): 9-23.
Zguta, Russell. "Skomorokhi: The Russian Minstrel-Entertainers." SR 31, No. 2 (June, 1972): 297-313.
------. "Witchcraft Trials in Seventeenth Century Russia." *American Historical Review* 82, No. 5 (Dec. 1977): 1187-1207.
------. *Russian Minstrels: A History of the Skomorokhi.* Philadelphia. University of Pennsylvania Press, 1978.
Ziborov, V. K. "Letopis' Novgorodskaia II." SKKDR 2.2:51.
Zimin, A. A. (Aleksandr Aleksandrovich). "O khronologii dogovornykh gramot Velikogo Novgoroda s kniazami XII-XIV vv." *Problemy istochnikovedeniia* 5 (1956): 318-320.
-----. "Kratkoe i prostrannoe sobraniia khanskikh iarlykov, vydannykh russkim mitropolitam." *Arkheograficheskii ezhegodnik za 1961*, No. 1: 28-40.
------. "Pamiat' i pokhvala Iakova mnikha i Zhitie kniazia Vladimira po drevneishemu spisku." *Kratkie soobshcheniia Instituta slavianovedeniia* 37 (1963): 66-75.
-------. "Iz istorii sobraniia rukopisnykh knig Iosifo-Volokolamskogo Monastyria." *Zapiski Otdela rukopisei Vsesoiuznaia biblioteka im. V. I. Lenina.* Moscow: Gosudarstvennoe sotsial'no-ekonomicheskoe izdatel'stvo. Vol 38 (1977): 15-29.
------. *Vitiaz na Rasput'e: Feodal'naia voina v Rossii XV v.* Moscow: Mysl', 1991.
Zubov, V. P. "Premechaniia k 'Nastavleniiu, kak cheloveku poznat' schislenie let' Kirika Novgorodtsa." *Istoriko-matematicheskie issledovaniia* 4 (1953): 192-195.
Zuckerman, Constantine. "The 'Psalter' of Feodor and the Heresy of the Judaisers in the Last Quarter of the Fifteenth Century." HUS 11, Nos. 1-2 (1987): 72-99.
Žužek, P. Ivan. *Kormčaja Kniga: Studies on the Chief Code of Russian Canon Law.* Rome: Pont. Institutum Orientalium Studiorum, 1964.

Index

Acts of the Apostles, bishops or "overseers" found in, 35, 295n16; and election of Matthias by lot, 149, 294n15, consecration by laying on of hands, 297n65

Aleksandr Iaroslavich Nevskii (grand prince of Vladimir), arrives in Novgorod with metropolitan, 57; Battle of the Neva, 86, 167; builds fortress of Kopor'e, 359n128; Christians among Finno-Ugrian tribes in his *zhitie* (saint's life), 84; at funeral of Varlaam of Khutyn, 121; treaty with Dalmat and Novgorod, 190

Aleksandr Mikhailovich (prince of Novgorod, prince of Tver', grand prince of Vladimir), Pskov excommunicated for harboring, 58, 101, 176; supports candidate for bbp. of Pskov, 105, 138; 196

Aleksei (Novgorodian abp.), 264, 317n79; as builder, 184, 186, 240, 356n107; and cultural patronage, 127, 159, 245-246, 252-253, 255; election and consecration, 280, 338n10, 338n20, 347n135, 356n99; and heresy, 61, 87-88, 316n61; fresco of, 246, 265, 270; as peacekeeper, 177, 179; and *polystaurion* privilege, 60; and Pskov, 100, 317n76; relations with metropolitans, 60-62, 69, 308n88; resignation and return, 34, 60; retirement, 335n307; from white clergy, 203, 341n62

Aleksei (Kyivan metropolitan), 60-62, continued use of the Kyivan title, 229; sainthood, 263-264, 392n240, 400n310; Kiprian as his successor, 308n93, 400n310

Alexius I Comnenus (Komnenos) (Byzantine emperor), use of lots to make a decision, 150-151

Andrei Bogoliubskii (Andrei Iureevich) (grand prince of Vladimir), siege of Novgorod, 98; and cathedral in Vladimir, 235

Andrei Rublev, 226; influenced by Feofan Grek, 391n228

Angold, Michael, on bishop's right to bless new monasteries, 333n293

Anna (Novgorodian princess), buried in Novgorod cathedral, 262, 377n93, 379n102; identity as wife of Iaroslav the Wise, 394n256

Anna Comnena (Byzantine

princess), on father's use of lots, 150; views of Western warrior-clergy, 167, 353n33
Anthony IV (patriarch of Constantinople), Novgorodian letter to, 71, on the church and the emperor, 170
Antioch (AD 341) (church council), 41, 44, 135, 298n90, canons included in *Kormchaia kniga*, 300n113
Antoniev Monastery (Novgorod), Abp. placed hegumen of, 121, 331n263; Archimandrite Sava buried in, 118-119; foundation allegedly blessed by Bp. Nikita, 334n296, 400n313; hegumen as unsuccessful candidate for Abp., 141
Antonii (Dobrynia Iadreikovich) (Novgorodian abp.), burial, 378n102, 379n103; and chronicle, 244; competition with Abps. Mitrofan and Arsenii over office, 34, 56-57, 100-101, 143, 154, 175, 232, 244; accused of bribing the prince, 139; converts Mitrofan's palace into Church of St. Antonii, 244; *Kniga Palomnika*, 19, 129, 253, 398n296; monk at Khutyn Monastery, 141, 232, 335n307, 400n314; named Arsenii hegumen of Khutyn, 120; sainthood, 262-263; and *Prophesy of St. Varlaam*, 268

Antonii Rimlianin, named hegumen by Abp. Niftont, 120, 121; *zhitie*, 268, 334n296
Apostolical Canons, authorship and dating of, 38, 39, 296n50; candidates for the episcopate in, 38-39; and episcopal elections, 133, 135; forbidding clergy from secular office, 169, 293n1; knowledge of in Rus' church, 441; in Novgorodian *Kormchaia Kniga*, 296n51; similarities to Church Fathers and church councils, 40-41
Archimandrite of Novgorod, as abp. candidates, 137, 143, 157; as builders, 240, 332n287; appointed by Abp. or elected by *veche*, 129, 331n263; at Iur'ev Monastery, 60, 121, 331n263; at Khutyn Monastery, 3, 331n263, 332n284, 333n288; list of, 332n283; as peacemakers, 178-179; question of authority over all Novgorodian monasteries, 118-119; traditional view of, 332n285, 333n289
Arkadii (Novgorodian bp.), builder and founder of monastery 143, 331n262, 380n107; and chronicle 255; election and consecration, 130-131, 138, 144, 156, 339n20; possible mention in Questions of Kirik, 94; sainthood, 262, 263,

Index   469

265, 379n103
Arkazhskii (Arkadii) Monastery (Novgorod), Abp. Mitrofan stays at 57; founded by Abp. Arkadii, 331n262, landownership by 143, Abp. Gavriil consecrates church in, 335n298
Arsenii (Novgorodian abp.), election, 139; removal from office before consecration, 43, 121, 156, 203, 347n135; dispute with Abps. Antonii and Mitrofan over office, 100, 143, 154, 232, 244, 299n102; placed as hegumen of Khutyn by Abp. Antonii, 120; placed as archimandrite in Iur'ev Monastery by Abp. Spiridon, 331n263; sainthood and *zhitie*, 292n81
Arsenii (candidate for bp. of Pskov and abp. of Novgorod), 105, 137, 138
Arsenii (*kliuchnik* at Lisitsa Hill Monastery, candidate for abp.) 141, 142, 203
Athanasius of Alexandria, and episcopal candidacy of Dractonius, 33-34, 294n7, 294nn7-8
Athanasius I (patriarch of Constantinople), forbid lay interference in episcopal election, 134
Auctoritas vs. *Potestas* (influence vs. power), 32, 162, 353n45
Augustine of Hippo, reluctant to be bp., 147; monastic rule, 120
Avraam (Novgorodian *tysiatskii*), sent envoy to Pskov, 176
Avraamki (chronicle), and archiepiscopal construction projects 240, 384nn142-143; on Abp. Iona placing as archimandrite of Khutyn Monastery, 331n263

Balovnev, Dmitrii, on parish churches and personnel in the *Pistsovye knigi,* 102, 284, 325n178, 325n180
Baptism of Rus', and beginning of Novgorod as a city, 232-233; chronicle account of, 47, 338n17; historical confusion surrounding, 301n4, 301n7, 312n5; incomplete conversion even after, 79, 82, 84; one of five "conversions" of Rus', 300n1
Basil the Great, letters to chorepiscopi, 40-41; inclusion in Novgorodian *Kormchaia kniga*, 298n81
Basil II Bulgaroktonos (Byzantine emperor), and Baptism of Rus', 47, 301n4; complains of too many monasteries, 336n320; gives gold crown to Patriarch of Alexandria, 402n329; and Bulgarian church, 73
Battle of the Novgorodians with

the Suzdalians, and Il'ia, 231, 250, 261-262, 265-266; icons of, 1, 265, 267; tale of, 267
Bernadskii, Viktor, on Novgorod's importance to Russian art, 6
Bilhorod (Belgorod), bps. of as metropolitan vicar, 52; Il'ia's letter to bp. of, 18, 75, 95, 319n123, one of first bishoprics in Rus' 338n17
Birnbaum, Henrik, on abps. as metropolitan's *protothronos*, 303n28; on class make-up of white and black clergy 323n158; on Olisei Petrovits Grechin as archiepiscopal candidate, 385n154, 391n233; on number of churches in Novgorod, 233; and traditional view of abps., 24, 26; on Novgorod's population, 287-288n9
Birchbark documents, 20, 151, 359-360n131; and Olisei Petrovits Grechin, 258
Bobrov, Aleksandr, on Metropolitan Isidor and Novgorod, 310n131, 310n132, 310n134
Boris (archiepiscopal *namestnik*), 178, 355n95, 365n51
Boris Alekseevich (prince of Novgorod), placed Feoktist as abp. with *veche*, 361n152
Brumfield, William, on importance of Novgorod to Russian architecture, 227; on Nifont's "Greek church", 243, 381n114
Budovnits, Isaak, dating of church landownership, 207
Byliny (epic tale), as secular culture in Rus', 229, 372n16; Vseslav of Polatsk in, 376n82

Caesaropapism, 164-165, 350n7
Carthage (AD 419) (church council), as basis for episcopal theory, 34; episcopal prerogatives, 42, 45
Casimir IV (Kazimierz) (king of Poland and Lithuanian grand duke), negotiations to be prince of Novgorod, 86, 188-190; patron of Pskovite artists, 384n150
Cassian, John (Desert father), and view of episcopal office, 33, 119, 294n4
Cathedral of the Dormition (Moscow), and consecration of bps., 156, 347n133; frescoes of Il'ia and Nikita over south portal, 265; charter requiring Feofil's consecration in, 310n128,
Cathedral of the Dormition (Vladimir), as princely construction, 235
Cathedral of Holy Wisdom (Hagia Sophia) (Constantinople), as great church of Eastern Christendom, 236; links to other Holy Wisdoms, 375-376nn78-80

Cathedral of Holy Wisdom (Kyiv), links to other Holy Wisdoms, 236, 376nn79-80
Cathedral of Holy Wisdom (Novgorod), art and architecture of, 20, 47, 77, 159, 205, 213. 227, 235-238, 258, 260, 357n107, 376n79; 377n95, 378n101, 383nn135-136, 384n150, 385-386n161, 386n166, 393n246, 396n280; built over pagan site, 48, 302n10; burials in, 49, 262, 266, 270, 306n75, 323n155, 349n138, 375n71, 377n90, 377n93, 378-380n102-104, 395n268; ceremonies and liturgies in, 57, 68, 81, 98, 157; choir of, 100, 204; city treasury and archive held in, 159, 187, 197, 363n21; and archiepiscopal elections, 129-131, 146-147, 343n84; land-ownership by, 26, 211; library of, 16, 91, 222, 226, 252-253, 262, 378n101, 387nn171-172, 387-388n175, 388n176; location of *veche* meetings, 9, 178; patrons of, 181, 213, 227, 249, 374n69; place of sanctuary, 180, 232; as symbol of city, 173, 231, 237, 270-271, 280; Vseslav of Polatsk and, 356n103, 376n82; wooden cathedral, 48, 181, 227, 235, 301n9, 369n119, 375n70, 375n72, 375nn74-75

Cathedral of Holy Wisdom (Polatsk), 236, 376n84
Cetinje, Montenegro, prince-bishop of, 350n1
Chalcedon (AD 451) (church council), 41, 56, 95, 115, 169, 255; canons included in Novgorodian *Kormchaia kniga*, 298nn83-84, 299n98
Chernihiv (Chernigov), bp. of, 71, 311n149, 338n17; titular metropolitan of, 373n50; Prince Mikhail of, 400n310; Nifont's peace embassy between Kyiv and, 174; Nifont and marriage of Prince Sviatoslav Ol'govich of, 94
Chernye liudi, 62, 178, 185
Christiansen, Eric, and Novgorod's location along "the Catholic frontier," 171
Chud (Finnic tribe), Orthodox missions to, 82, Abp. Mitrofan's failure to convert, 305n56; Novgorodian campaign against 323n155
Chudov Monastery (Moscow), Abp. Feofil imprisoned in, 121, 157, 347n136, 348n138
Church courts, 26-27; archiepiscopal immunity charters and, 117; cases given to, 109; church people under jurisdiction of, 198; charter exempting Novgorod from metropolitan's, 63; princely statutes and, 112-113, 329n218

Church-State Symphony, 164
Church of Boris and Gleb (Novgorod), as location of Abp. Feoktist's *narechenie*, 57, 157, fees for writing sales documents shared with priest of, 209; and Sadko (Satko), 375n73
Church of Constantine and Helena, Olisei Grechin as priest of, 249-250, 331n263
Church of the Dormition (Novgorod), consecrated by Abp. Gavriil in Arkadii Monastery, 335n298; build by archimandrite in Kolomtsy, 332n287; built by prince and abp. in the Marketplace, 227, 240, 243; in Volotovo Field, fresco of abps. in, 127, 245-246, 270; in Zverin Monastery, foundations possibly laid by Abp. Vasilii, 245, 382n131, 391n225; icons in, 258
Church of Entry into Jerusalem (Novgorod), Abp. Vasilii hires Isaia the Greek to fresco, 250, 259
Church of Holy Wisdom (Jerusalem), symbolic ties between Novgorod cathedral and, 236, 376nn79-80
Church of the Mother of God (Novgorod), 244; by the town gate, 204, 249
Church of the Mother of God of the Sign (Novgorod), 264
Church of the Nativity of the Mother of God (Antoniev Monastery, Novgorod), 242
Church of Paraskeva-Piatnitsa (Novgorod), rebuilt by Abp. Vasilii, 380n109
Church of the Resurrection (Holy Sepulcher) (Jerusalem), basis for Novgorod's Great and Little Sions, 260, tale of Abp. Il'ia and, 267-268, 321n137; and the Miracle of the Holy Fire, 399n302
Church of St. Clement (Kliment) (Staraia Ladoga), first stone church built entirely under archiepiscopal patronage, 213, 242, 243, Abp. Nifont's consecration of, 323n159
Church of St. George in the Marketplace (Novgorod), Abp. Nifont's antimension, 325-326n182
Church of Sts. Ioakim and Anne (Novgorod), first stone church in 235; scholarly doubt on Bp. Ioakim's church, 48, 227, 375nn70-71
Church of St. James (Novgorod), in Nerev End; Novgorodian chronicler German Voiata and, 255-256, 390n209
Church of St. John Chrysostom (Novgorod), Evfimii II and 240, 247; legend surrounding collapse of, 271-272

Church of St. John the Forerunner on the Opoki (Novgorod), built by Prince Vsevolod Mstislavich and Abp. Nifont, 227, 242, 381n110; center of wax merchants' association, 199; held city's weights and measures, 193; rebuilt "on old foundations" by Abp. Evfimii, 227, 247, 381-382n121

Church of St. Lazarus (Novgorod), Abp. Iona's patronage of, 249

Church of St. Michael (Moscow), Abp. Simeon consecrated in, 156, 347n133; painted by Theophanes the Greek, 385n158

Church of St. Nicholas (Novgorod), in the Marketplace, Abp. Nifont's antimension found in, 325-326n182 built by Princes Mstislav and Vsevolod, 242, 381n110; Bp. Nikita's relics kept in, 395n268; *veche* meetings near, 9

Church of St. Nicholas (Novgorod), in the Nerev End; built by Abp. David, 245; *posadnik* buried in, 356n96

Church of St. Nicholas (Novgorod), in Otenskii Skete, built by Abp. Iona, 249

Church of Sts. Peter and Paul (Novgorod), consecrated by Abp. Aleksei, 100, several churches by that name, 239, 358n122

Church of Sts. Philip and Nicholas (Novgorod), only church still open in Soviet period; held Bp. Nikita's relics, 395n268

Church of St. Sergei of Radonezh (Novgorod), painted on Abp. Iona's orders, 249

Church of St. Simon (Zverin Monastery) (Novgorod), perhaps built by Abp. Iona, 249, 380n106

Church of St. Theodore Stratelates (Novgorod), painted by Serbian artists, 250, ties to Abp. Evfimii II, 337n3

Church of the Tithe (Kyiv), built by Vladimir the Saint, 207, 235

Church of the Transfiguration on Il'ina Street (Novgorod), and Abp. Il'ia, 267, and Icon of the Mother of God of the Sign, 393n246; painted by Theophanes the Greek, 250, 259, 385n158

Church of the Transfiguration (Kizhi), as example of early wooden church architecture, 301n9

Church of The Transfiguration at Kovalevo (Church of the Savior) (Novgorod), frescoed by Serbian masters, 250, 383n135

Church of the Transfiguration

in Mirozhskii Monastery (Pskov), built by Abp. Nifont, 227; as "Greek Church" based on architecture and icons, 243, 259

Church of the Transfiguration on Nereditsa Hill (Church of the Savior) (Novgorod), Abp. Antonii stays at, 57; built by Iaroslav Vladimirovich, 380n110; frescoed by Olisei Grechin, 249; loss of frescoes, 383n135

Church of the Transfiguration (Orekhov), built by Abp. Iona, 249

Church of the Transfiguration (Staraia Russa), built by Bp. Martirii, 324n159, 331n262, 382n125; frescoed by Olisei Grechin,244 324n159,

Church of the Twelve Apostles (Novgorod), 225, 228, 235, 247

Clement I (pope), letters of, 39, 40, 41, 43, 297nn72-73

Conant, Kenneth, on Novgorodian cathedral's patron, 374n69; on first, wooden cathedral in Novgorod, 301n9, 375n72; on onion domes in Rus', 384n149

Constantine VII Porphyrogenitus (Byzantine emperor), claims Patriarch Ignatius converted Rus' rather than Photius, 301n4

Constantine VIII (Byzantine emperor), co-emperor at time of Baptism of Rus' 301n4

Constantinople, and Bulgarian church, 73, 312n160; Abp. Antonii's travel book on, 19, 129, 253, 398n296; early Rus' church from Bulgaria rather than, 48; cathedral of, 236, and links to Novgorodian cathedral, 376n80; churchmen came to Novgorod seeking charity, 196; election by lots taken from, 150-154; First Council of (AD 381) (church council), 41, 300n115; iconographers from, 250, 259; monastic *typika* from, 333n292; Moscow, 170; Rus' trade with, 7, 194, 210; saintly cults from, 226

Council of Lords (*sovet gospod*), in Novgorod, 10, 24-27, 159, 279; abp. presiding over, 26, 159; executive organ of *veche*, 27; met in Palace of Facets, 182; scholarly doubt of existence of, 27, 289-290n27

Crater (krater) (church vessel), 222, 260

Cyprian of Carthage, views on episcopate, 40, 78; similarity to church councils and other Church Fathers, 41, 42, 43

Cyril (a.k.a. Constantine) and Methodius, 90-91, Constantine of Preslav mistaken for Cyril, 317n85

Cyril of Jerusalem, Luka's sermon similar to address to catechumens by, 93

Dalmat (Novgorodian abp.), consecrated in Novgorod, 57, 157; first abp. builder since Mongol Conquest, 245; placed, not elected, 138; nominated Kliment as possible successor, 146; procession to welcome visiting dignitaries, 188; treaties, 190, 361n148

Dan' (tribute paid to Golden Horde), and Muscovite grand princes, 288-289n16; Novgorodian fur and silver important part of, 6, 162, 195, abps. and 177-178, 202

Daniil (Chernihiv hegumen), pilgrimage to Jerusalem, 320n135, and Miracle of the Holy Fire, 399n302

Daniil Romanovich (grand prince of Halych), nominated Metropolitan Kiril II, 305-306n61

Danilova, Liudmila, and archiepiscopal landownership, 214, 215, 216; archiepiscopal control of honey and flax production, 217

David (King of Israel), a Christian should strive to forgive as God forgave, 116, use of lots by 149, 150

David (Novgorodian abp.), attached monks to monastery in Nerev End, 204, 205; as builder, 245, 357n108; burial 378n102; and chronicle, 255; election and consecration, 339n20, 347n135; and Shchilov Monastery 334n296; sent to ransom Novgorodians seized by Grand Prince Mikhail, 177; treaty with Grand Prince Mikhail, 188

Denha (Nestorian patriarch), use of lots, 151

Derevianitskii Monastery (Novgorod), Abp. Evfimii I from, 141; Abps. Moisei or Vasilii as patrons of church in, 382n131; Abp. Vasilii orders frescoing of church in 245; founded by Abp. Moisei, 333n296; Abps. Aleksei and Ioann II retired to and buried in, 122, 335n307, 383n132

Detinets (Novgorod), archbishops' civil construction in, 180-184, 236, 247, 357n113; archaeological layers in, 232-233; boiars living in 357-358n115; and great bridge, 8, 267; *posadnik* of Prusskaia Street in, 355n94; role as fortress during siege, 358n120

Didache, 36, 38

Didascalia Apostolorum, 36-38

Dimnik, Martin, on archiepiscopal candidates, 343n87

Dionisii (abp. of Suzdal'), emis-

sary from patriarch and metropolitan, 52, 87, 88, 298n83, 299n97; his archiepiscopal title, 302nn15-16
Dmitrii Aleksandrovich (grand prince of Vladimir), patron of *Novgorodian Synodal Kormchaia*, 295n26; patron of *Pravila Chernoriztem*, 319n124; military actions on behalf of Novgorod, 190, 359n128
Dmitrii Ivanovich Donskoi (Muscovite grand prince), and Aleksiev Cross 159, 383n136; encroachment on Novgorodian fur-bearing regions, 162-163; peace with Novgorod, 177; names Dionisii metropolitan, 302n16; names Pimen metropolitan and is excommunicated by Metropolitan Kiprian, 62-63, patriarch reprimands Abp. Moisei for disobedience to, 60
Dmitrii Mikhailovich (prince of Tver', grand prince of Vladimir), rivalry with Iurii of Moscow for *iarlyk*, 195-196
Dmitrii Miroshkinits (Novgorodian *posadnik*), Abp. Mitrofan and burial of, 180
Dmitrii Shemiaka (prince) 70, actually buried in Novgorod cathedral, 379n102; Abp. Evfimii II and, 388n175
Dobrynia (Novgorodian *posadnik*), and conversion of Novgorod, 80, 313n8
Dormition Monastery (Novgorod); tale of founding and Abps. Il'ia and Gavriil, 266
Dorpat (Derpt, Tartu, Iur'ev), Novgorodian loss of trade to 6; bp. marches on Izborsk 166-167; campaign against, 190; envoys and treaties with, 172, 173, 353n54
Dracontius, and monastic opposition to the episcopate, 33, 294n8
Dudika (slave), his slander of Bp. Luka, 53-54, 206
Dvina Land (along Northern Dvina River), Abp. landholdings in, 214, 218; Novgorodian fur-bearing regions along 6, 218; war with Moscow over, 63-66, 69. 178, 179, 276; Novgorodian loss of, 214
Dvina Judicial Charter, 214, 220, 370n154
Dvornichenko, Andrei, on importance of Novgorod, 232

Economy (*oikonomia*) (Orthodox principle), 133
Elijah (Old Testament prophet), in Abp. Vasilii's letter on the earthly paradise, 96, 322n143
Enoch (Old Testament patriarch), in Abp. Vasilii's letter on the earthly paradise, 96, 322n143

Ephod (Breastplate of Destiny), 149; *Urim* and *Thummim* (lots kept in Ephod), 149, 344n95
Efrem (acting bp. of Novgorod), 49, 80; as teacher, 91; mistaken for Ephrem the Syrian, 80, 91, never consecrated bp., 49, 156, 347n135
Efrem (Kyivan metropolitan), 53, 54; possibly same as Novgorodian acting bp., 304n34
Efrem (titular metropolitan of Pereislav), as builder, 234
Eizo, Maiuki, and archiepiscopal elections 131, 137; and Pskovite candidate for bp., 138
Ephrosinius (Evrosim), and Abp. Vasilii's letter on the earthly paradise, 96, 320n140
Euthimius II (patriarch of Constantinople), opposition to Metropolitan Grigorii Tsamlak, 70
Evfimii I (Emelian Bradatii) (Novgorodian abp.), election and consecration of, 67, 338n10, 338n20, 345-346n118; from Derevianitskii Monastery, 141; made peace with grand prince, 177; and *First Sofiia Chronicle*, 257; issued charter to Pskov, 326n185; in *Tale of Mikhail Klopskii*, 197, 269; 401n320
Evfimii II (Ioann Viazhitskii) (Novgorodian abp.), 24; as builder and cultural patron, 90, 156, 181, 182, 183, 186, 193, 205, 225, 227, 237-238, 240, 241, 243, 247, 248, 253, 257, 259, 260, 271, 324n159, 357n112, 366n69, 381nn110-111, 384n141, 386n163, 386n166, 399n309; effigy, 397n289; burial in Viazhitskii Monastery, 122; 336n316; from Lisitsa Hill Monastery, 141, and Prince Dmitrii Shemiaka, 311n140; election of, 338n10, 338n20; and Metropolitan Isidor, 68; and alleged opposition to Union of Florence, 310-311nn135-136; and Pskov, 68, 104, 176-177, 355n85; promotion of Novgorodian saints, 261-263, 267, 394n258; in *Tale of Mikhail Klopskii*, 269, 270; wait for consecration, 67, 138-140, 155-156, 347n135; Visitation to Zavoloch'e region, 83, 100, 313n27, 342n63; and Western culture, 205, 251, 361n155; from white clergy, 323n158; *zhitie* and sainthood 19, 128, 262-265, 268, 393n251, 394n259, 396n280, 399-400n309, 401n322

Fedor Danilovich (Novgorodian *posadnik*), 178, 184, 355n94, 356n96
Fedor Iaroslavich (prince

of Novgorod), burial in Novgorod cathedral, 379n102, 379n104

Fedotov, Georgii, on *veche*, 26, 129

Fennell, John, on unsatisfactory brevity of chronicle descriptions, 12, 22; on Luka's homily, 92-93; on devastation of Mongol Conques, 324n161; on Rus' losses at Battle of Kalka River, 341nn55-56; and siege engines built in Detinets, 362nn10-11

Feodor (Novgorodian bp.), 49; and pagan uprising, 81; "fictitious soul", 302n14

Feodor (Tver' bp.), letter from Abp. Vasilii Kalika on earthly paradise, 19, 91, 95-97

Feodosii I (Novgorodian abp.), never consecrated, 67, 121, 156, 347n135, 401n318; was hegumen of Klopskii Monastery, 139, 141, 142; never took part in embassies, 175, 354n74; never patronized construction projects, 241; 247; elected by lot, 338n10, 338n20; in *Tale of Mikhail Klopskii*, 269, 401n320

Feodosii II (Novgorodian abp.), letter to Votskaia clergy to fight paganism, 83, 371n169; on Christian forgiveness, 116; colophon in his own hand, 253, 388n187; deposed for overtaxing clergy, 364n44; his logbook (*formuliarnik*), 387n175; *zhitie* of, 392n239

Feodosii III (Novgorodian abp.), and Novgorodian bishop-saints, 266; deposed for opposing Empress Catherine I, 287n4

Feodosii (Moscow metropolitan), absence of Novgorod abps. from consecration of, 69; warns Abp. Iona about Lithuanian metropolitan, 71; refusal to establish Pskov eparchy, 326n188; last to use title "Metropolitan of Kyiv," 327n198

Feodosii (hegumen of Kyiv Caves Monastery), 234; sermons of, 318n93; attack on *skomorkhi*, 372n18

Feofan Grek (Theophanes the Greek), 250, 259

Feofan (Prokopovich) (Novgorodian abp.), and Petrine church reforms, 2; on Millennium of Russia monument, 272

Feofil (Novgorodian abp.), charter to Pskov, 326n185; deposed after Muscovite Conquest, 4, 121; diplomacy with grand prince, 176, 177, 199, 212; draft treaty with king of Poland, 189; elected by lot, 338n10, 338n20, 343n84; as "archbishop-elect," 156, 310n128;

hands over power to grand prince, 192, 203, 277, 365n58; in Abp. Iona's administration, 141, 306n74, 342n68; allegedly ignored Judaizers, 87, 88; legend of his treasure, 197; Muscovite fear he would abandon Orthodoxy 71; in *Novgorodian Judicial Charter*, 113; sources disagree on his fate, 122, 157, 335n312, 347-349nn136-138; withheld cavalry at Battle of Shelon' River, 167, 216

Feofilakt (Kyivan metropolitan), presumed first Kyivan metropolitan, 301n7

Feognost (Kyivan metropolitan), from Byzantium, 385n154; Abp. Moisei's complaint to patriarch about, 59; death of plague, 323n152; excommunicates Grand Prince Aleksandr Mikhailovich and Pskov, 58-59; and Pskovite candidate for bp., 105, 138; and election and consecration of Abp. Vasilii, 58, 136-138, 156; awards *polystaurion* to Abp. Vasilii, 58-59, 307n79, 403n333; his registry of episcopal consecrations, 342n74, 346n131; visit to Novgorod, 58, 201

Feognost (bp. of Sarai), on priests in the army, 169

Feoktist (Novgorodian abp.), and Annunciation Monastery, 141, in tale of founding, 334n296, retired to, 335n307; And chronicles, 255; election and consecration in Novgorod, 43, 57, 157, 339n20, 361n152; first Novgorodian abp. to bless a treaty, 188-191, 360n144; no embassies by, 354n74; patronized no churches, 241; sainthood, 263, 396n280

Fifths (*Piatiny*) (divisions of the Novgorodian land), 284; Bezhetskaia, 284; Derevskaia, 216, 284; Obonezhksaia, 284; Shelonskaia, 217, 218, 284; Vodskaia, 82, 83, 218, 284

Filaret (Moscow patriarch), and Novgorodian bishop-saints, 264, 266

Filaret (Gumilevskii), on Abp. Iona's background, 337nn4-5; 401-402n324; on Abp. Iona's election by the Novgorodians, 345n114; on Abp. Nifont's archiepiscopal title, 305n49; and Feofil's burial 348n138

Filipp I (Moscow metropolitan), fear of Novgorodian betraying Orthodoxy, 71, 311n154

Flemish wool cloth (Ypres cloth), 195, 363n27

Florence (Basel-Florence-Ferarra) (church council) (1431-1445), Isidor's visit to Novgorod on way to, 68, 310nn134-135; tale of,

310n131; Union of Eastern and Western churches (1439), 386n162; Novgorodian abps. silent on union, 66

Fotii (Photius) (Kyivan metropolitan), combatting *Strigol'niki* heretics, 44-45, 52, 87, 104; "encyclical" against Metropolitan Grigorii Tsamblak, 70, 311n146; Abp. Ioann II's visit to, 66; misnumbers canon of First Constantinople, 300n115; never consecrated Abps. Feodosii or Evfimii II, 66-67, 139; confirmed that widowed priests must retire, 342n6

Franklin, Simon, on burial practices as evidence of Christianization, 314n32

Froianov, Igor, on importance of Novgorod, 232, on election of bps. in all Kyivan Rus' cities, 337-338n9

Furs and fur trade, 194, 209; 364n31, 368n96; and Dvina Land, 6, 214; Marco Polo on quality of furs from Rus', 362n13; Novgorod wars with Moscow over, 63-64, 69, 163, 179, 196; importance to Novgorod, 6-7, 194-196, 209-211; Abps. participating in, 211, 218, 223, 285; fur tithe or tribute, 210, 214

Gangra (church council), 45, 300n113

Gavriil (Grigorii) (Novgorodian abp.), as builder with Abp. Il'ia, 240-244, 266, 317n79; burial, 378n102; 379n103; and chronicle, 255; consecrates Khutyn Monastery, 335n298; monastic founder, 334n296; sainthood, 262, 263, 396n280; visit to Pskov, 99, 344n159; from white clergy, 323n158

Gavriil II (Novgorodian metropolitan), burial in Novgorod cathedral, 379n102; ordered monastic libraries to be gathered into cathedral library, 388n176

Gedymin (Gediminas) (Lithuanian grand prince), attempt to establish eparchy in Pskov, 105, 138

Gelasi, (archimandrite in Pskov), oversaw church in city instead of Novgorodian abp., 68, 326n184

Gelasius I (pope), on church and state, 164; on *auctoritas* and *potestas*, 353n45

Gennadii (Novgorodian abp.), appointment by grand prince, 131, 158; and calculations for Easter, 2; and Catholic monks in Pskov, 386n162; and Detinets walls, 357n108; and impression of Inquisition, 172; and Judaizer heresy, 87-88; and first East Slavonic Bible, 2, 228; from

Chudov Monastery, 157, patronized *zhitia* of several abps., 268; removal for simony, 221, 337n327, 347n137, 354n44, 371n159, 371n161; sainthood, 263, 392n241; and tales, 270, 399n307

Gerasim (Lithuanian metropolitan), consecrates Abp. Evfimii II, 269; execution, 67, 309n125; Metropolitan Fotii's possible successor, 67, 309n127;

German (Novgorodian bp.), death allegedly by "Byzantine methods, 54; "fictitious soul", 302n14, 304n40; from Kyiv Caves Monastery, 342n67; sainthood, 49, 262, 263; listed among Kyivan saint, 349n138

German Court (trading enclave) (Peterhof), 6; 252; Novgorod abp. interaction with, 86; Church of St. Peter in, 195; location in Novgorod, 362n6

German Voiata (chronicler), 255-256, 33n327, 389n207

Ghillebert de Lannoy (Flemish traveler), views of Novgorodian abp., 173-174; on size of Novgorodian army, 288n9; on number of churches in Novgorod, 373n45, 380n107

Gippius, Aleksei, on "boundaries" in *Novgorodian First Chronicle*, 254-255, 257

Gnevushev, Andrei, on economics of archiepiscopal administration, 200, 215, 369n123

Golubinskii, Evgenii, on his church history, 20,22; on Abp. Antonii's *Kniga Palomnik*, 253; on Abp. Iona's consecration, 345n114, 399n302; on Abp. Nifont's title, 305n49; on autocephalous status of Novgorodian abps., 50; on election of bps. in canon law, 132; on Metropolitan Gerasim's title, 309n127; study of canonizations, 263

Gordienko, Elissa, on Abp. Vasilii as iconographer, 259; and Abp. Moisei's *polystaurion*, 307n81

Gotland, treaty with Novgorod, 190; Novgorodian trading community on, 194, 362n5

Gotland Court (trading enclave) (Gothic Court), Novgorod abps. interacting with, 86; Western merchants confined to, 252, Church of St. Olaf in, 194-195; location in Novgorod, 362n6

Granberg, Jonas, skepticism as to existence of *sovet gospod*, 290n27

Gregory of Tours, on warrior bps., 165

Grekov, Boris, study of abp. administration, 200, 204-205; on prices in sixteenth century, 368n114; use of archiepisco-

482   Index

pal library, 387n172
Grigorii (Lithuanian metropolitan), 71, 311n153
Grigorii Tsamblak (Lithuanian metropolitan), 70-71, 311n146
Grivna (monetary unit), fee of seven for ordination, 41, 221; gold or silver, 199, 298n86, 368n100
Guimon, Timofei, on laconic nature of chroniclers, 12; on "boundaries" in *Novgorodian First Chronicle* after 1330, 255

Halecki, Oskar, on Metropolitan Isidor and Pskov, 104
Halperin, Charles, discounts grand princes embezzling *dan'*, 289n16
Halych (Galich, Galicia), metropolitanate of, 230, 347n131, 389n203
Hanseatic League, trade and political relations with Novgorod, 6, 7, 18, 173, 185, 188, 195, 210, envoys to Pskov, 290n27
Herman, Emil, on Orthodox abps. being autocephalous, 50; on episcopal control of his diocese, 77
Hilarion (Ilarion, Larion) (Kyivan metropolitan), appointed by Iaroslav the Wise, 53, 304n31; and Luka, 54-55, appointment canonical, 304n32, fate of, 304n34; his sermon

"On the Law and Grace," 91
Hussey, Joan, episcopal office incompatible with secular office in canon law, 169

Iamburg (Iam, Kingisepp), 185, Abp. Evfimii II rebuilt, 247
Iarlyk (Mongol charter), (immunity charter to church), 86, 175, 202, 315n47; (patent of princely office), 195
Iaroslav Iaroslavich (grand prince of Vladimir), 190, 237; quarrels with Novgorod, 270
Iaroslav the Wise (Iaroslav Vladimirovich) (Kyivan prince), Rus' church possibly founded under, 48; appoints Hilarion metropolitan, 53, 304n31; built Kyivan cathedral, 235, 236, 384n150; and Kyiv's golden age, 226, 374n63; church statute of, 27, 81, 110, 112, 113, 115, 207, 208, 209, 219, 313n15, 329n218; and building of Novgorod cathedral, 227; founded library in Novgorod, 387n171, wives, 394n256
Iaroslav Vladimirovich (prince of Novgorod), and election of Bp. Martirii, 144-145; sponsor of church at Nereditsa, 249, 380n110
Iaroslavovo Dvorischche (princely compound in Novgorod), as meeting place for the *veche*,

9, 62, 178, four sorcerers burned at the stake near, 82
Ignatius of Antioch, view of the episcopate, 40, 295-296n28, 296n48
Ignatius (patriarch of Constantinople), Rus' possibly converted under, 301n4
Il'ia (Ioann) (Novgorodian abp.), burial 378n102, 379n103; as builder and cultural patron, 241, 335n298; with brother, 243-244; and chronicle, 255-256; placed by metropolitan, 138, 294n3; and Suzdalian siege of Novgorod, 98, 231, 250; icon of, 265; possible mention in "Questions of Kirik," 94, 319n124; tales of, 261, 264, 266-268, 334n296, 398n299; in other tales, 395n267, 398n295; from white clergy, 33; rules (including the *Pravila Chernoriztsem*), 18, 75, 95; sainthood and *zhitie*, 262-263, 265, 394n255, 396n272, 397n291, 398n295
Ioakim (Novgorodian metropolitan, later Moscow patriarch), rebuilt Abp. Evfimii II's clocktower, 357n112; and *Ioakimovskaia letopis'*, 254
Ioakim Korsunianin (Novgorodian bp.), arrival in Novgorod, 48, 301n8, 338n17; possibly founded city of Novgorod, 232; founded first monastery in Novgorod eparchy, 122, 369n119, 374n69; and first Novgorod cathedral, 181, 227, 235; "fictious soul," 302n14; possibly legendary, 48-49, 80, 81, 91, 93, 194, 375nn70-71; and *Ioakimovskaia letopis'*, 254, 312n5; sainthood, 262-263, 379n103, 396n280

Ioann I (Kyivan metropolitan), church construction by, 233-234; 373n47

Ioann I Pop'ian (Novgorodian bp.), alleged autocephalous status, 50; retired to monastery, 121; Antoniev monastery founded during his episcopate, 400n313

Ioann II (Kyivan metropolitan), raised Novgorod to archiepiscopate, 49

Ioann II (Novgorodian abp.), burial, 122, 378n102, 383n132,; and chronicle, 255; conflict with Metropolitan Kirprian, 62-66; as builder, 181-182, 186, 237, 240, 241, 247, 378n96, 383n137; and war against Karelians, 84, 85; election by lot and consecration, 156, 338n10, 338n20, 347n135; election by lot approved by Metropolitan Pimen, approval of election by lots, 62, 136; 340n43; from Khutyn Monastery,

141; retired to Derevianitskii Monastery, 335n307 and Pskov, 104-106, 326n185

Iona (Novgorodian abp.), 70; appointed or elected, 154, 345n114; appoints archimandrite, 331n263; as builder, 186, 241, 246, 247, 249, 384n141, 384nn143-144; cultural patronage, 253, 262, 310n135; 380n106, 399n306, 399n309; burial, 122; grand prince's letter warning against Lithuanian metropolitan, 311n153; from Otenskii Skete, 141; and Pskov, 104, added Pskov to title, 106; privileges granted to monasteries, 117; in *Tale of Mikhail Klopskii*, 269; sainthood and *zhitie*, 19, 128-129, 262, 263-265, 268, 269, 323n158, 337n4, 401n324

Iona (Moscow metropolitan), first autocephalous head of Rus' church, 69, 392n241; letter to Evfimii II re: Dmitrii Shemiaka, 70, 311n140, 388n175; letters warning about Grigorii Tsamblak, 71; sainthood, 263; 337n4, 345n114, 400n310

Isaac Comnenus (Byzantine emperor), and payment for ordination, 44, 221, 371n160

Isidor (Kyivan metropolitan, Catholic cardinal), Byzantine background, 385n154; journey to and from Council of Florence, 67-68, 310n131-132, 310n134; removal of Pskov from Novgorod abp, jurisdiction, 68, 104, 326n185

Iur'ev Monastery (Novgorod), Abp. Arsenii as later hegumen of, 121, 139; 299n102; abp. candidates from, 141, 143, 146; Church of St. George in, 242, 381n110, 381n117; and Dmitrii Shemiaka, 379n102; hegumen elected by *veche* or appointed by abp., 331n263; *Novgorodian First Chronicle* and, 254, 256, 390n213; and Novgorodian archimandrite, 118, 119, 331n253, 332n285, 332n288; wealth of, 143

Iur'ev (on-Dniepr) (Bila Tserkva), bp. as Kyivan metropolitan's vicar, 52, 276

Iurii Danilovich (prince of Moscow, grand prince of Vladimir), competition with princes of Tver' for *iarlyk*, 195-196, and fortress of Orekhov, 185

Iurii Dolgorukii, (grand prince of Kyiv), and Abp. Nifont's release from Kyiv, 55; and Nifont's title, 305n49

Ivan I Kalita (grand prince of Moscow), 161, Abp. David's attempted bribe of, 177; 288n16; and campaign against Pskov, 101

Ivan III The Great (grand prince

of Moscow), and conquest of Novgorod, 11, 130, 167, 177, 192, 196, 197, 199, 269, 277, 365n58; and charter with Abp. Feofil, 310n128; and *Dvina Judicial Charter*, 214; and election of Abp. Sergei, 157; and fear of Novgorod going "Latin," 71, 311n153; land confiscations in Novgorod, 214, 278; and Moscow Kremlin, 235, 385n158, 386m163; and removal of Abp. Feofil, 121

Ivan IV The Terrible (tsar of Russia), 264, 271, 298n91, 363n21 392n241; and sack of Novgorod, 6, 197, 364n35; and Vasilii Gates, 378n97

Iziaslav II Mstislavich (grand prince of Kyiv), and appointment of Metropolitan Klim, 55-56

Izborsk (Pskov fortress), 167, 169

Izhorians (Finnic tribe, also Ingrians or Ingermans), conversion efforts by Catholics and Orthodox and Christianity among them, 82-84, 313n20

John Chrysostom (patriarch of Constantinople), Abp. Vasilii's use of in his letter on the earthly paradise, 96, 321-322n141

John Tzimiskes (Byzantine emperor), and abolition of See of Preslav, 75, 312n161

Jonah (Old Testament prophet), and use of lots, 149

Judaizers (heretics), debate on actual Jewish influence in, 317n74; alleged negligence of Novgorodian abps. in dealing with, 87-88; from Lithuania, 353-354n55; and Prince Mikhail of Kyiv, 316n70

Justinian (Byzantine emperor), Corpus Iuris Civilis, 147-148, 221, 343-344n92

Kaiser, Daniel, on archiepiscopal seal in place of prince's, 190; on archbishop's slave, 206; on dating of Prince Vsevolod's charter, 208; on Council of Lords in Pskov, 289-290n27

Kalinnikov, V., date of establishment of Novgorod eparchy, 301n8

Karamzin, Nikolai, influence on Russian historiography, 4; on democratic nature of Novgorod's government, 290n37

Karger, Mikhail, on Ivan the Terrible and Novgorod's cathedral treasure, 363n21; location of first Novgorodian cathedral, 375n73; on Novgorod's abps. and their cathedral, 237; on upper-class origins of

Novgorod's abps., 99
Kartashev, Anton, on Metropolitan Isidor's return from Florence, 310n134; on the *sof'iane*, 364-365n47
Kazakova, Natalia, on Abp. Vasilii and the *Strigol'niki*, 87
Keksholm (Korela, Korel town, Priozersk), Novgorodian archbishop's *namestnik* and, 202; missionary work and Christianity among Finnic tribes near, 82, 84; as land grant to Novgorodian service princes, 359n128; Swedish crusaders attack, 195
Khirotoniia (*cheirotonia*, laying on of hands, ordination, consecration), in Bible, 35, 295n17; and episcopal consecration, 57, 136, 137, 156, 157
Khoroshev, Aleksandr, on Abp. Aleksei and execution of heretics, 316n61; and class background of Novgorod abps., 99; on Abp. Evfimii I, 197; on Abp. Ioann II and Pskov, 325n175; and Bp. Luka's alleged autocephalous tendencies, 53-54; on metropolitans and election of Novgorod's abps., 132; on identity of Metropolitan Efrem, 304n34; on Abp. Nifont's autocephalous tendencies, 55-56; Marxist viewpoint, 24, 25
Kiprian (Cyprian) (Kyivan metropolitan), views of bps., 43-44, 135; conflict with Novgorod, 61-66, 170-171; rejection by Moscow, 61-63; eventual acceptance in Moscow, 63
Kirik of Novgorod (chronicler), and Abp. Il'ia's *Pravila Chernoriztsem*, 94-95, 319n124; as chronicler, 255, 389n207; *Uchenie o chislakh*, 255-256; "Questions of Kirik" (*Voproshanie Kirika*) 94
Kirill (Kiur'iak) (first Novgorodian archimandrite), 332n283; building projects, 333n288, 357n108
Kirill I (Kyivan metropolitan, ca. 1040s), questionable existence of, 303n20
Kirill II (Kyivan metropolitan, ca. 1230), appointed by Grand Prince Daniil of Halych, 305n61; on lay interference in episcopal elections, 134; and Abp. Arsenii's consecration,139; 341n58;
Kirill III (Kyivan metropolitan, ca. 1260), his authority over Novgorod, 52; consecration of Abp. Dalmat, 157; visits to Novgorod, 57; his canons in *Novgorodian Synodal Kormchaia of 1282*, 75; sainthood, 392n240
Kirill (bp. of Turau), his sermons compared to those of Novgorodian abps., 92
Khutyn Monastery (Novgorod),

Abp. Antonii and, 335n307, 400n314; Abp. Arsenii and, 139, 232, 299n102, 331n263; abp. candidates from, 141; Abp. Gavriil consecrates, 335n298, hegumen placed by abp. or elected by *veche*, 120-121; and archimandrite, 3, 332n284, 332-333n288; landownership by, 142-143

Klim Smoliatich (Kliment) (Kyivan metropolitan), attempted return to office, 305n48; canonicity of his appointment, 304n32; conflict with Abp. Nifont's opposition to, 55, 243, 256, 276

Kliment (Novgorodian abp.), nominated by Abp. Dalmat, 146; as builder, 245, 357n108; and chronicles, 255; election and consecration, 339n20, 347n135; gives sanctuary to former *posadnik*, 180; his *namestnik* in Ladoga, 365n53; and *Novgorodian Syndoal Kormchaia of 1282*, 295n26; *Pravila Chernoriztsem* written under, 319n124

Klopskii Monastery (Novgorod), Abp. Feodosii from, 139, 141; landownership, 142

Kliuchevskii, Vasilii, on democratic nature of Novgorodian government, 12; abp. as president of Council of Lords, 25

Kollmann, Jack, on parishes appointing and paying priests, 206; priests and marriage fee, 221

Kolomtsy Monastery (Novgorod), Abp. Moisei and, 121, 179

Kolyvan (Revel, Tallinn), 6, Novgorod's silence on Catholic bps. of, 172; Novgorodian merchant enclave in 362n5

Konets (end) (borough of Novgorod), 9, Abps. political ties to Nerev *konets*, 179, 245; referral court members from each, 187; *posadnik* for each, 355n93, 356n97; *veche* from each, 9

Konstantin (Muscovite prince), as Novgorodian service prince, 199, 363n25

Kopor'e, Christianity among Finnic tribes near, 82, 84, and Novgorodian princes, 359n128, 380n107

Kormchaia Kniga ("Pilot's Book," Eastern canon law, Nomocanon), documents found in, 39, 41, 169, 298n85; importance as a source, 17-18; Novgorodian archbishops' knowledge of, 94-95 no single accepted text, 298n82

Kusov, Matvei Mikhailov (chronicler), 257

Kyiv (Kiev), Novgorodian bps. consecrated in, 347n135; Novgorod second in impor-

tance to, 10; saints of 261, 392n240
Kyiv Caves Monastery (Kievo-Pecherskii), Novgorodian bps. buried in, 121, 122, 348-349n138; *Paterik* of, 268; sermons of Hegumen Feodosii of, 318n93

Lavrentian Chronicle (*Rus' Primary Chronicle, Povest' vremennykh let*), importance as a source, 17; portrayal of Prince Vseslav of Polatsk in, 376n82
Lazar of Murmansk (tale), appearance of Abp. Vasilii in, 268
Lazarev, Viktor, on Abp. Evfimii II's influence on iconography, 260; on Abp. Vasilii's art patronage, 227, 258; archiepiscopal oversight of iconography workshop, 257
Lermontov, Mikhail, on democratic Novgorod, 12-13, 290n38
Lenhoff, Gail, on candidates for abp. thrice rejecting office, 34; on rhetorical devices in Abp. Antonii's *Kniga Palomnik*, 253
Leonid (Novgorodian abp.), executed by Ivan the Terrible, 264; disliked for his high fees, 371n169
Leontii (Kyivan metropolitan), sent bps. out to Rus' eparchies, 48; possibly legendary, 301n7
Leontius (abp. and patriarch of Preslav), not recognized by Constantinople, 73
Likhachev Gates, and Abp. Vasilii's "Byzantine current," 258; similarity to the Vasilii Gates, 378n97
Lind, John, 84, on dating monastic founding and manuscript, 314nn34-35
Lithuania, grand princes patronizing Rus' art, 384n150; metropolitanate of, 43, 61-62, 66, 67, 70-71, 134, 179, 230, 309n127, 401n322; Novgorodian service princes from, 186, 359n128; vying with Moscow for control of Novgorod, 5, 22; wars with, 72, 86, 352n37, 400n314
Livonia, Novgorodian silence on bps. of 166, 172; *Livonian Rhymed Chronicle*, 291n64; Rus' campaign in, 305n56
Luka Zhidiata (Novgorodian bp.), burial, 49, 378n102. 379n103; and Cathedral of Holy Wisdom, 81, 213, 227, 249, 369n120, 375n75, 378n102, 384n150; and his slave, Dudika, 53-54, 206; Homily or Sermon to the Brethren, 18, 91-93, 97, 114, 318n111; possibly first Novgorodian bp., 48-49,

80-81, 301n8; sainthood, 262-263, 396n280; surname, 302n11

Lur'e, Iakov, on Abp. Vasilii and the *Strigol'niki*, 87; on Jewish influence on Judaizers, 317n74

Magnus Eriksson (king of Sweden and Norway), crusade against Novgorod, 83, 85-86, 176, 185-186, 196

Makarii (Bilhorod bp.), possible recipient of Il'ia's letter, 75, 319n123,

Makarii (Novgorodian abp., Moscow metropolitan), importance in Ivan the Terrible's court, 2; missionary activity in Novgorodian Land, 82-83; orders Novgorodian iconographers to Moscow, 390n224; as iconographer, 391n227; and *Velikie Minei Chet'i* and *Stepennaia Kniga*, 228, 263, 271, 395n262, 398n297; promotion of Novgorodian saints, 263-264-265, 268, 272; returns with treasury, 215, 363n17; sainthood, 261, 391n237, 392n244, 395n264

Makarii II (Novgorodian metropolitan), promotion of Novgorod's bishop-saints, 264-265,

Manuel II (patriarch of Constantinople), and Serbian church, 74

Maksim (Kyivan metropolitan), transferred see to Vladimir, 392n240; consecrates Abp. Dalmat in Novgorod, 157

Mark (Nestorian metropolitan of Cathay), elected by lots, 151

Martin, Janet, on candidates for abp. thrice rejecting office, 34; importance of Novgorod to Rus' foreign trade, 194; on Novgorodian fur trade, 209; role of abps. in fur trade, 211, 216; differences in land-usage by abps., 218

Martirii Rushanin (Novgorodian bp.), burial, 378n102; and the chronicle, 255;
election by lots, 145, first to be elected by lot, 154, 338n20; as builder, 240-241, 244, 249, 317n78, 324n159, 335n298, 357n108, 380n107, 382n125; Names new hegumenia, 120, 331n263; never held archiepiscopal title, 302n15; sainthood, 262, 263, 379n103; visitation to Staraia Russa, 99

Mary (mother of Jesus), her assumption as evidence of the earthly paradise, 96, 322n143

Matthias (apostle), elected by lot 149, 294n15

Matvei Mikhailov Kusov (chronicler), 257

Meyendorff, John, on *polystaurion* privilege, 58, on Abp. Vasilii's election and consecration, 137-138, 347n131;

on episcopal election, 343-344n92; on the term "chosen by God," 338-339n20
Michael of Bethlehem (abp.), patriarch's ambassador to Novgorod, 170
Mikhail (bp. of Iur'ev), built church in Kyiv Caves Monastery, 234
Mikhail the Syrian (Kyivan metropolitan), and Baptism of Rus', 48; possibly legendary, 301n7, 392n240
Mikhail Aleksandrovich (Lithuanian prince), and Judaizers, 88, 251, 316nn69-70
Mikhail Aleksandrovich (prince of Tver', grand prince of Vladimir); baptized by Abp. Vasilii, 58, 98, 105, 306n69; Abp. Vasilii taught him reading and writing in Novgorod, 58, 91
Mikhail Daniilovich (Novgorodian *posadnik*), placed seal on lots during abp. election, 147, 345n115
Mikhail Fedorovich (Novgorodian *posadnik*), buried in Novgorod cathedral, 380n104
Mikhail Fedorovich (tsar of Russia), and veneration of Novgorodian bishop-saints, 264, 266
Mikhail Iaroslavich (prince of Tver', grand prince of Vladimir), 188, 177; *riady* with Novgorod, 188, 191, 360n144
Mikhail Klopskii (Novgorod *iurodivyi*), 401n317; tale of, 197, prophesy about Abp. Evfimii I, 269; prophesy about Abp. Evfimii II, 269, 270, 401n322; prophesy of Abps. Iona's archiepiscopate, 128, 269
Mikhail Vsevolodovich (prince of Chernihiv, prince of Novgorod, Kyivan grand prince), and election of Abp. Spiridon, 145-146, 343n87; as prince of Novgorod, 343n79
Miller, David, on economic impact of Mongol Conquest, 324n161
Mitrofan (Novgorodian abp.), burial, 378n102; candidate for abp. in 1193, 145; competition with Abps. Antonii and Arsenii for office, 34, 56-57, 100-101, 143, 154, 244, 382n126; and the chronicle, 255; driven out of office, 57, 101, 305n56; election, 339n20; nominated by Grand Prince Vsevolod "Big Nest, 305n57
Mirozhskii Monastery (Pskov); frescoes of, 259, Abp. Nifont and, 213, 227, 243, 268, 324n159
Moisei (Novgorodian abp.), and books, 16, 253; as builder, 181, 240-241, 245, 317n79, 333n296, 382n131; burial, 399n307; and chronicle, 255;

complaint against Metropolitan Feognost and embassy to Constantinople, 58-60, 201, 308n82; election and consecration, 57, 339n20, 346n118, 347n135; fresco of, 246, 265, 270; from Iur'ev Monastery, 141; and Pskov, 101, 176; *polystaurion*, 59, 222, 307n79, 307n81; retirements, 34, 121, 142, 280; sainthood, and *zhitie*, 128, 262-265, 268, 396n280, 396n284, 400n309; and *Strigol'niki*, 87, 315n59, 316n60

Moscow (church councils); council of 1503, and ordination fee, 41, 221, 364n44; council of 1547, 263; council of 1549, 263; council of 1551 (Stoglav), 97, 205, 221-222, 258, 334n297, 371n169; council of 1564, 263-264, 334n297, 402n326, 402n328; council of 1667, 334n297, 342n64, 403n337

Mother of God of the Sign (*Znamenie*), church service, 268, 307n77, 400n310; feast day, 264, 396n272, 397n294; icon of, 250, 261, 264; and Il'ia, 231, 261, 267

Mongol Conquest, impact on Novgorodian archiepiscopal office, 52 ,100

Mstislav Iur'evich (prince of Novgorod), and election of Abp. Arkadii, 144

Mstislav Mstislavich Udaloi (prince of Novgorod), 57, 183, 237; and removal of Abp. Mitrofan, 305n56; escape from Mongols, 341n55, 393n246

Mstislav Rostislavich (Bezokii) (prince of Rostov, prince of Novgorod), burial in Novgorod cathedral, 379-380n104

Mstislav Rostislavich (Khrabryi) (prince of Smolensk, prince of Novgorod), Apb. Il'ia officiates at funeral, 98; buried in Novgorod cathedral, 323n155, 377n90, 379n102, 379-380n104

Mstislav Vladimirovich (The Great) (Kyivan grand prince, prince of Novgorod), 174; enlarged Novgorod, 181; and Church of St. Nicholas, 242, 380-381n110

Muscovite Conquest of Novgorod, decline in Moscow-Novgorod relations in century before, 64, 70, 75, 163; fundamentally changed archiepiscopal office, 4; and land confiscations, 214-217; Novgorod "going Latin" as pretext for, 71, 86;

Musin, Aleksandr, on Christianization of Finnic tribes, 84; on episcopal elections, 339n34, 340n47; on Abp. Nifont's *antimension*, 325-

326n182; on Novgorodian warrior-priests, 168-169, 353n41

Narimont (Lithuanian prince), baptized by Abp. Vasilii, 98-99, 105; Novgorodian service prince, 359n128

Neva River, key Novgorodian trade route, 7, 185; conversion efforts along, 82-83; crusades along, 83, 86. 167; Novgorodian defenses along, 101, 185

Nicaea (church councils), First, 41, 133, 135, 298n83, 300n115; Second, 133-134, 135

Nicholas IV Mouzalon (patriarch of Constantinople), elevates Nifont to abp., 55

Nifont (Novgorodian abp.); artistic style of, 237, 242, 243, 259; as builder and patron, 213, 227, 235, 240-241, 323-324n159; and knowledge of nomocanon, 298n82, and Catholicism, 72, 86, 251; confrontation with Metropolitan Klim, 55, 276, 305n44, 305n49; alleged corruption, 196, 241-242, 244; chronicles and, 255-257; embassies of, 174-175; first Novgorodian abp., 55-56, 243, 305n49, 302n15, 325-326n182; and "Questions of Kirik," 18, 72, 81, 94; sainthood and *zhitie*, 263, 265, 268, 349n138, 396n280

Nikita (Novgorodian bp.) frescoed Novgorod cathedral, 237; sainthood and *zhitie*, 263-265, 268, 323n155, 349n138, 378n102, 379n103, 396n269, 396n280; tales, 334n296,

Nikitskii, Aleksandr, his works on Novgorod and Pskov church, 22; on size of Rus' monasteries, 123; abp. activity confined to Novgorod and Pskov, 124; on Novgorodian abp. personnel, 364n47; on abp. election by *veche*, 129

Nilus (patriarch of Constantinople), letter against simony and the *Strigol'niki*, 44, 87-88

Novgorod Judicial Charter, legal powers of abp. in, 112-113; confirmation of earlier laws, 113; Feofil referred to as "archbishop-elect," 156; referral hearings in archbishop's chamber, 182, 187; fees for abp. officials in, 201; abp. officials mentioned in, 203, 206, 364-365n47, 367n81; court fees mentioned in, 220

Novgorodian First Chronicle, abps. as teachers in, 91; "boundaries" showing abp. role in its writing, 255; chroniclers of, 255-256; compilation in abp. scriptorium and redactions, 105, 252, 254-256; church consecrations mentioned in, 90; defends Abp. Nifont from claims of

corruption, 196, 241; importance as source on abps., 16
Novgorod the Great, constitution of, 9-11, 360n142; abp. as part of, 159-163, 173; democratic or oligarchic nature of, 13-14; *posadniki* and *tysiatskii* in, 13, 161, 278; see also Council of Lords and *veche*
Novgorodian Synodal Kormchaia of 1282, contents of, 36, 38, 75, 295n23, 296n51, 298n81, 298nn83-85, 299n101, 298n112, 299n93, 300n113; and Abp. Kliment, 295n26, and other Rus' *Kormchie knigi*, 298n82

Obolensky, Dmitry, on wealth of Novgorodian archeparchy, 293n104; on patriarchal approval for Hilarion's nomination, 304n31; on patriarchate in Serbia, 312n164
Olgerd (Algirdas) (Lithuanian grand prince), nominates candidate for metropolitan, 134; 1346 campaign along Shelon' River, 325n173
Olisei Petrovits (Aleksei Petrovich) Grechin (icon painter), as alleged candidate for arbp., 249-250, 385n154, excavation of his workshop, 258; hired by Bp. Martirii to paint church, 249; elected archimandrite 331n263
Ontsifor Lukich (Novgorodian *posadnik*), and city unrest in 1342, 178; reforms of 1354, 10, 146, 343n82; tied to election by lots, 154; and fragmentation of *posadnichestvo's* power, 162, 171, 280
Ostromir Gospels, gift to abp. library, 222, 252, 385-386n161; as oldest East Slavic codex, 387n173
Ostrowski, Donald, on why Orthodox would not debate the faith, 315n52; on date of *Tale of the White Cowl*, 402n328; on tale as opposition to Muscovite rule, 403n337

Pachomius the Serb, as author of Novgorodian tales and *zhitie*, 267, 386n165, 399n309
Palace of Facets (Novgorod), and influence on Palace of Facets in Moscow; built by Western masters, 172, 205, 251; Council of Lords meeting in, 26, 28; Abp. Evfimii II and, 182-184, 247; as museum, 307nn77-78, 307n81, 386n168, 398n299, 402n330; referral cases heard in, 187, 330n257
Panteleimon Monastery (Novgorod), land granted to by Abp. Nifont, 117
Papadakis, Aristeides, on Orthodox monasticism, 119
Paul (Apostle), attribution of some of letters, 295n19; and

early bps., 294-295nn16-18, 295n20; on ideal attributes of bps., 35, 43; view of bps. in First Letters to Timothy and Titus, 35-36, 317n83; sent to preach, 90

Patriarch of Constantinople, and Baptism of Rus' 301n4; letters addressing *Strigol'niki* heresy in Novgorod, 87, 103; Abp. Moisei's complaint to, 59, 201; and Serbian church, 74; theory that patriarchate established Rus' church only in 1030s, 48; metropolitan-candidates travel to, 134; Abp. Nifont granted archiepiscopal title for supporting, 55-56, 385n154; right of patriarch and bishops' council to choose Kyiv metropolitan, 51, 55-56; considered Tsamblak as illegitimate metropolitan, 70; theory that Novgorod was directly answerable to, 50-51; theory that Novgorod was autocephalous of, 303n20

Peremyshl (Przemysl), Abp. Antonii sent to be bp. of, 57

Perm', bishopric carved out of Novgorod archeparchy, 325n176

Peter the Deacon, on Eastern views of popes and Western episcopate, 168

Petr (Kyivan metropolitan), use of Kyivan title, 229, 303n26; *zhitie* written by Metropolitan Kiprian, 134; rule on widowed priests, 342n64

Philotheus Kokkinos (patriarch of Constantinople) and *polystaurion* privilege, 59

Pimen (Kyivan metropolitan), approval of Novgorod's practice of election by lots, 62, 136; rival of Kiprian, 62, 306n73

Pimen (Novgorodian abp.), on veneration of Bp. Nikita, 264; killed by Tsar Ivan IV, 266; sainthood, 392n244, 394n255; 396n276

Pistsovye knigi (land cadasters), on archiepiscopal landownership, 17, 214-216, 369n123; church personnel mentioned in, 102, 365n57, 366n61; differences in land usage in, 218; shortcomings of, 214

Pitirim (Novgorodian metropolitan), promotion of earlier bishop-saints, 264-265

Pius II (pope), placed Uniate metropolitan in Lithuania, 71

Platonov, Sergei, on Novgorodian government, 24; on Novgorod's importance, 7

Poezdki (pastoral visits, visitations), 99-101

Polatsk (Polotsk), cathedral of, 236-237, 376n84; icon school, 249, 259; incorporation into Lithuania, 384n150; see also Vseslav Briacheslavich

Polystaurion; as a personal privilege, 59, 306n74; as sign of patriarchal favor, 58-59; Abp. Mosei's, 22, 59, 307n81; Abp. Vasilii's 22, 58, 270-271, 306-307n75; Abp. Aleksei's use without permission, 60

Poppe, Andrzej, on canonicity of Metropolitan Klim's appointment, 304n32; on early metropolitans, 301n7; on titular metropolitans in Pereislav and Chernihiv, 373n50

Pravosudie mitropolich'e, and episcopal control over monasteries, 115

Priselkov, Mikhail, on "Korsun Legend" and later establishment of Rus' church, 48; claims Hilariion became chronicler Nikon, 304n34

Protothronos, Novgorodian abp. as metropolitan's, 52, 303-304n28,

Pskov; attempt to have own bp., 138; "the lords" in, 290n27

Pskov Caves Monastery (Pskov-Pecherskii), Abp. Feodosii II's letter to, 116

Pskov Judicial Charter, reference to "the lords", 27; confirms archiepiscopal authority in Pskov, 106-107; on joint hearings for cases involving church people and others, 110; confirmation of earlier laws, 113; secular roles of abp. in Pskov, 187; archbishop's seal equivalent to princes, 190

Quinisext (Trullo, church council) (AD 692), on duties of a bp., 42, 90

Raba, Joel, studies on Novgorod abps., especially Evfimii II, 24; and election by lot, 154-155, 345n115

Resurrection Monastery on Red Hill (Novgorod), as commemoration of Abp' Simeon's election, 383n138

Riga, Novgorod's silence on abps. of, 171-172; Novgorod's treaties with, 173, 353n54, Abp. Evfimii II asks for a bellmaker from, 361n155; Bp. of Smolensk and, 187

Riurik (Rus' founder), first ruled in Novgorod, 194

Rostislav Iurievich (prince of Novgorod), 175

Rostislav Mikhailovich (son of Mikhail of Chernihiv), drew lots in 1229, 147, 343n87

Rostislav Mstislavich (Smolensk prince); statutory charter, 112, 113

Rowell, S. C., on Novgorod's commercial importance, 7; on election of Novgorod abps., 130, 138

Rublev, Andrei (icon painter),

influenced by Feofan Grek, 391n228
Rus' Primary Chronicle, see Lavrentian Chronicle
Rybakov, Boris, on Novgorod abps. and *Strigol'niki*, 87, 316nn60-61
Russkaia Pravda, in *Novgorodian Synodal Kormchaia*, 75; and princely support for church, 108; and court fines, 219,

St. Mamas Monastery (Constantinople), on hegumen's election by lots, 152
St. Michael Monastery at Skovorodka (Novgorod), Abp. Moisei founds, 333-334n296; and Abp. Sergei, 399n307
Sadko (Sotko Sytinits), and Church of Boris and Gleb, 375n73; and use of lots, 345n115
Sardica (church council), on ideal attributes of bps., 42; in *Novgorodian Synodal Kormchaia*, 298n91
Sava of Serbia, appointed abp. by patriarch of Constantinople, 74
Serapion (Novgorodian abp.), removed from office, 116; sainthood, 265, 392n244, 394n261, 396n280
Sergei (Novgorodian abp.), background, 349n141; death, 350n142; election and consecration, 131, 151, 158; and fees on clergy, 222, 364n44; and Judaizers, 87; madness of, 399n307
Shapiro, Aleksandr, and confiscation of archbishops' land, 214-215; Abp. utilized lands differently, 217; Novgorod's population, 288n9
Shchapov, Iaroslav, on eastern abps., 50; on bps. as ambassadors, 175-176; and church landownership, 212; and church statutes, 219; and abp. election in Novgorod, 130, 338n12; on early Kyivan metropolitans, 301n7; on political power of Novgorod's abp., 290n32
Shchil (Novgorodian *posadnik*), Novgorod abps. in tale of, 197, 267, 333-334n296
Shelon' River, Battle of, 71, Abp. Feofil and cavalry at, 205, 216
Shepard, Jonathan, see Franklin, Simon
Sides (*Storona*) (divisions of Novgorod), 8-9; linked by great bridge, 184
Simeon (Samson) (Novgorodian abp.), burial, 306-307n75, 378n102, 379n103, 402n330; on church courts in Pskov, 114, 116; and chronicle, 255-256; decline in archiepiscopal activity under, 247, 354n74; election and consecration, 67, 156, 338n10, 338n20, 345-346n118, 347n133; from

Khutyn Monastery, 141; and the plague, 322-323n152; and Resurrection Monastery on Red Hill, 383n138; visitations to Karelia, 83, 100; sainthood, 262-263, 394n255

Sion (tabernacle), Great and Little Sions of Novgorod, 260, 391n234

Skhariya (Zechariah ben Aharaon ha-Kohen) (Judaizer heresiarch), 88, 251, fate, 316n69

Smen Mikhailovich (Novgorodian *posadnik*), Abp. Kliment gives sanctuary to, 180

Smolensk, Novgorod and princes of, 11; Abp. Evfimii II consecrated in, 67, 269, 346n122. 347n135, 401n322; iconography school of, 249, 259

Sof'iane (cathedral officials in Novgorod), definition, 364n47; fees to, 201; listed among court personnel, 202; number of, 200; as possible electors of abp., 144-145; and Pskov, 177

Sokol, Edward, on *veche* electing the abp., 23, 130

Sortition (election by lot), 131, 142, 154; evolution of in Novgorod, 144-146, 154; biblical and Byzantine origins of, 149-150, 155

South Slavic Influence (First and Second), and Novgorod, 250, 259, 298n83; 385-386n161

Spiridon (Novgorodian abp.), appoints Arsenii as archimandrite, 331n263; blesses Aleksandr Nevskii, 86; burial, 378n102; and chronicle, 255; election and consecration, 145-146, 154, 347n135; from Iur'ev Monastery, 141; and Mongol Invasion, 98. 231

Staraia Ladoga (town), missionary work near, 82, 84; visitation of abps., 99, 323n159; and archbishop's *namestnik*, 101, 160, 202, 203, 278, 325n175, 359n129, 365n53; and Novaia Ladoga, 323n159

Staraia Russa (Russa), visitations by abps., 99; Bp. Martirii and, 145, 324n159, 331n262, 382n125,

Stefan (Novgorodian bp.), "fictitious soul", 302n14; murdered by his slaves, 206

Stepan Tverdislavich (Novgorodian *posadnik*), buried in Novgorod cathedral, 380n104

Stefanovich, Petr, on rights of church or monastic patrons (*ktitor*), 205

Stepennaia Kniga, begun by Abp. Makarii in Novgorod, 2, 228; and Rus' and Muscovite national consciousness, 271; legend of the Mother of the Sign in, 392n294

Stoglav (church council of 1551), see Moscow (church councils)

Strigol'niki (heretics), beliefs of, 197; executions, 61; and Novgorodian abps., 87

Stroev, Pavel, lists of Rus' churchmen, 332n283, 332-333n287; list of Rus' monasteries, 336n324, 342n66, 344n113

Studion Monastery (Constantinople), *typikon* as basis of other Eastern Christian monastic *typika*, 333n292

Sviatoslav Olgovich (prince of Chernihiv, prince of Novgorod), church statute of, 208, 210; Abp. Nifont forbids priests from officiating at wedding of, 94, 319n120

Svidrigailo (Lithuanian grand prince), and Metropolitan Gerasim, 309n125

Tatishchev, Vasilii, and conversion of Novgorod, 80, 301n8, 313n8; on Abp Nifont and Prince Sviatoslav, 319n120; on *Ioakimovskaia Letopis'*, 254

Teutonic Order, Brothers of the Sword (or Livonian Order, branch of), 166, 351n26, 363n25; war against Novgorod, 166-167

Tikhomirov, Mikhail, importance of Novgorod in Rus' culture, 6; on Novgorod's size and commercial importance, 289n20; on Novgorod's wooden cathedral, 301n9; on death of *Strigol'niki*, 316n61; on Abp Nifont and Prince Sviatoslav, 319n120

Tikhomirov, Pavel, biographies of Novgorodian Abps., 20, 127-128; on Abp. Il'ia's rules, 94-95; on Abp. Sergei's madness, 350n142

Timofei the Sexton (chronicler), 255, 256

Tobol'sk, cathedral named after Novgorod cathedral, 376n81

Torzhok (Novyi Torg), Abp. Antonii in, 101; abp. *namestnik* in, 160, 202-203, 365n53

Tribute, see Dan'

Trinity Monastery (Klopskii, Novgorod), Abp. Feodosii retires to, 121; Abp. Feodosii from, 141, 142, 269

Tver', Abp. Moisei and excommunication of, 58, 176; Abp. Vasilii's letter to Bp. Feodor of, 91, 95; competition with Moscow for *iarlyk*, 195

Typikon (monastic rule), 119-120, 333n292; and election of hegumens, 151-154; liturgical vs. disciplinary, 344n113

Uchilishcha (schools), in Novgorod, 205

Ustiug, fought over by Novgorod and Moscow, 64, 196

Uzbek (khan of the Golden Horde), converted Mongols

to Islam, 230, 372n22; forged immunity charter of, 315n47; granted *iarlyk* to Iurii of Moscow, 195

Valaamskii Monastery (Lake Ladoga), tale of, 84, and violence against pagans, 84
Varlaam (founder of Khutyn Monastery), Prophesy of St. Varlaam (tale), Abp. Antonii's portrayal in, 268; Abp. Spiridon officiating at funeral of, 121
Vasilii I (prince of Moscow), statutory charter to Dvina Land, 220; and war with Novgorod over Metropolitan Kiprian and Dvina Land, 64-66, 69; and Patriarch Anthony IV of Constantinople, 170
Vasilii II (prince of Moscow), and Novgorod's harboring of Prince Dmitrii Shemiaka, 70; Abp. Evfimii II's embassy to, 177
Vasilii Kalika (Grigorii) (Novgorodian abp.); as builder, 181, 184-185; 359n130; burial, 270, 307n78, 378nn102-103; cultural patronage of, 205, 227, 237, 245, 250, 258-259, 378n97; baptizes prince Mikhail Aleksandrovich, 58, 98; election and consecration, 105, 136-138, 156; and fortress of Orekhov, 185-186, 198; letter to Bp. Feodor of Tver', 19, 91, 95-97, 318n90, 320n136, 321n137, 321n141; nephew Matvei, 85, 176; officiated at *posadnik*'s funeral, 99, 178-179; as peacemaker, 178; and the plague, 98, 100, 322n152; awarded *polystaurion*, 58-59, 307n79; rearrangement of chronicle, 256, 390n212; his revival of the archiepiscopal office, 100, 162. 280; sainthood, 262-263; and *Strigol'niki* heresy, 87, 316n60; in tales, 268; and treaty with Sweden, 83, 85-86, 251; and white cowl, 270-271, 306n75, 402n326; from white clergy, 33, 141, 294n3, 323n158; 341-342n63

Vasilii Mstislavich (prince of Novgorod), buried in Novgorod cathedral, 379n102, 379n104

Veche (public assembly in Novgorod), traditional view of, 9-10, 12-13, 23-27, 159-160; patriarchal letter addressed to, 353n51, 365n57; and election of Novgorodian officials, 129-130; locations of, 179

Velikie Minei Chetii, first edition from Novgorod, 2, 228; Novgorod abps. included in, 263

Vernadsky, George, on episcopal appointments, 132;

on different types of abps., 303n18; and monastic *typika*, 333n 292

Vladimir Iaroslavich (prince of Novgorod), and Antoniev Monastery, 242; buried in Novgorod cathedral, 262, 377n93; sponsor of Novgorod cathedral, 181, 213, 227; laid out Novgorod, 181, 227, 235, 384n150

Vladimir the Saint (Vladimir Sviatoslavich) (Kyivan prince); and Baptism of Rus', 47-48, 80, 130, 313n6, 338n17; Church of the Tithe, 207; church statute of, 27, 81, 108-110, 113, 207-208, 329n218

Vladimir-on-Kliazma; church council (1274), 41, 75, 221; decrees included in *Novgorodian Synodal Kormchaia*, 298n85

Volodymyr (Vladimir-in-Volynia); Abp. Vasilii consecrated in, 58, 136-138, 156; bp. of as candidate for Novgorodian abp., 145

Vologda, cathedral named after Novgorod cathedral, 376n81

Volokolamsk Monastery, and Abp. Feodosii II, 116, 387n175

Voproshanie Kirika ("The Questions of Kirik"), 18; and Abp. Nifont's view of Catholicism, 72, 86; and evidence of earlier *Kormchaia kniga* in Novgorod, 94, 298n82; Abp. Arkadii possible mentioned in, 94; Abp. Il'ia perhaps a questioner in, 81, 94; included in *Novgorodian Synodal Kormchaia*, 318n112

Vseslav Briacheslavich, (prince of Polatsk, prince of Novgorod, Kyivan grand prince), looting of Novgorod cathedral, 236, 376n82; portrayed as sorcerer and werewolf, 376n82

Vsevolod Mstislavich (prince of Novgorod), as builder in Novgorod, 213, 227, 240, 242, 381n110; his dismissal as prince in Novgorod, 183, 277; statutory charter of, 112, 113, 208, 212, 363n23, 368n94,

Vytautas (Vitold) (Lithuanian grand prince), met Abp. Evfimii I, 177; nominated Grigorii Tsamblak as metropolitan, 70

Ware, Timothy (Metropolitan Kallistos), on metropolitans and abps. in the East, 51

Warrior-clerics; canon law opposed to, 169; Novgorodian priests as, 168-169; Western bps. as, 165-167; condemned in West, 165; condemned in East, 167-171

Weickhardt, George, on episcopal courts, 114, 187, 309n111

White cowl (Novgorodian

archiepiscopal regalia), in art and literature, 246, 269-271, 395n267; found in archaeological excavations, 306n75, 307n78, 402n330; Novgorodian abp. right to wear, 263, 402n326

Zadonshchina, warrior-monks appearing in, 352n39

Zavoloch'e (Novgorodian territory), Abp. Evfimii II's visitation to, 83, 100; overseen by all-city *veche*, 160

Zdravomislov, Konstantin, biographies of Novgorod abps., 21, 128; on Abp. Sergei, 350n142

Zhitie (saint's life), Abp. Evfimii II and writing of, 262; composed by Pakomii the Serb, 268; unreliability as sources, 127-128; still useful as cultural documents, 16, 19

Znamenanie (*narechenie*, nomination of a bp.), 57, 156-157; see also *khirotoniia*

Žužek, P. Ivan, on Abp. Nifont's knowledge of the *Kormchaia kniga*, 298n82

Zverin Monastery (Novgorod), Abps. Vasilii. Moisei, and Iona's patronage of, 245-246, 249, 258, 380n106, 382n131

www.ingramcontent.com/pod-product-compliance
Lightning Source LLC
Chambersburg PA
CBHW071134300426
44113CB00009B/967